Novels
for Students

National Advisory Board

Novels
for Students

**Presenting Analysis, Context, and Criticism on
Commonly Studied Novels**

Volume 15

David Galens, Project Editor

Foreword by Anne Devereaux Jordan

THOMSON
GALE

Detroit • New York • San Diego • San Francisco • Cleveland • New Haven, Conn. • Waterville, Maine • London • Munich

Novels for Students

Project Editor
David Galens

Editorial
Sara Constantakis, Anne Marie Hacht, Michael L. LaBlanc, Ira Mark Milne, Pam Revitzer, Jennifer Smith, Daniel Toronto, Carol Ullman

Permissions
Debra Freitas, Shalice Shah-Caldwell

Manufacturing
Stacy Melson

Imaging and Multimedia
Lezlie Light, Kelly A. Quin, Luke Rademacher

Product Design
Michelle DiMercurio, Pamela A. E. Galbreath, Michael Logusz

ISBN 0-7876-4898-1
ISSN 1094-3552

Printed in the United States of America
10 9 8 7 6 5 4 3 2 1

Table of Contents

The Informed Dialogue: Interacting with Literature

When we pick up a book, we usually do so with the anticipation of pleasure. We hope that by entering the time and place of the novel and sharing the thoughts and actions of the characters, we will find enjoyment. Unfortunately, this is often not the case; we are disappointed. But we should ask, has the author failed us, or have we failed the author?

We establish a dialogue with the author, the book, and with ourselves when we read. Consciously and unconsciously, we ask questions: "Why did the author write this book?" "Why did the author choose that time, place, or character?" "How did the author achieve that effect?" "Why did the character act that way?" "Would I act in the same way?" The answers we receive depend upon how much information about literature in general and about that book specifically we ourselves bring to our reading.

Young children have limited life and literary experiences. Being young, children frequently do not know how to go about exploring a book, nor sometimes, even know the questions to ask of a book. The books they read help them answer questions, the author often coming right out and *telling* young readers the things they are learning or are expected to learn. The perennial classic, *The Little Engine That Could, tells* its readers that, among other things, it is good to help others and brings happiness:

"Hurray, hurray," cried the funny little clown and all the dolls and toys. "The good little boys and girls in the city will be happy because you helped us, kind, Little Blue Engine."

In picture books, messages are often blatant and simple, the dialogue between the author and reader one-sided. Young children are concerned with the end result of a book—the enjoyment gained, the lesson learned—rather than with how that result was obtained. As we grow older and read further, however, we question more. We come to expect that the world within the book will closely mirror the concerns of our world, and that the author will *show* these through the events, descriptions, and conversations within the story, rather than *telling* of them. We are now expected to do the interpreting, carry on our share of the dialogue with the book and author, and glean not only the author's message, but comprehend how that message and the overall affect of the book were achieved. Sometimes, however, we need help to do these things. *Novels for Students* provides that help.

A novel is made up of many parts interacting to create a coherent whole. In reading a novel, the more obvious features can be easily spotted—theme, characters, plot—but we may overlook the more subtle elements that greatly influence how the novel is perceived by the reader: viewpoint, mood and tone, symbolism, or the use of humor. By focusing on both the obvious and more subtle literary elements within a novel, *Novels for Students* aids readers in both analyzing for message and in determining how and why that message is communicated. In the discussion on Harper Lee's *To Kill a Mockingbird* (Vol. 2), for example, the mockingbird as a symbol of innocence is dealt with, among other things, as is the importance of Lee's use of humor which "enlivens a serious plot, adds depth to the characterization, and creates a sense of familiarity and universality." The reader comes to understand the internal elements of each novel discussed—as well as the external influences that help shape it.

"The desire to write greatly," Harold Bloom of Yale University says, "is the desire to be elsewhere, in a time and place of one's own, in an originality that must compound with inheritance, with an anxiety of influence." A writer seeks to create a unique world within a story, but although it is unique, it is not disconnected from our own world. It speaks to us *because* of what the writer brings to the writing from our world: how he or she was raised and educated; his or her likes and dislikes; the events occurring in the real world at the time of the writing, and while the author was growing up. When we know what an author has brought to his or her work, we gain a greater insight into both the "originality" (the world of the book), and the things that "compound" it. This insight enables us to question that created world and find answers more readily. By informing ourselves, we are able to establish a more effective dialogue with both book and author.

Novels for Students, in addition to providing a plot summary and descriptive list of characters— to remind readers of what they have read—also explores the external influences that shaped each book. Each entry includes a discussion of the author's background, and the historical context in which the novel was written. It is vital to know, for instance, that when Ray Bradbury was writing *Fahrenheit 451* (Vol. 1), the threat of Nazi domination had recently ended in Europe, and the McCarthy hearings were taking place in Washington, D.C. This information goes far in answering the question, "Why did he write a story of oppressive government control and book burning?" Similarly,

it is important to know that Harper Lee, author of *To Kill a Mockingbird,* was born and raised in Monroeville, Alabama, and that her father was a lawyer. Readers can now see why she chose the south as a setting for her novel—it is the place with which she was most familiar—and start to comprehend her characters and their actions.

Novels for Students helps readers find the answers they seek when they establish a dialogue with a particular novel. It also aids in the posing of questions by providing the opinions and interpretations of various critics and reviewers, broadening that dialogue. Some reviewers of *To Kill A Mockingbird,* for example, "faulted the novel's climax as melodramatic." This statement leads readers to ask, "Is it, indeed, melodramatic?" "If not, why did some reviewers see it as such?" "If it is, why did Lee choose to make it melodramatic?" "Is melodrama ever justified?" By being spurred to ask these questions, readers not only learn more about the book and its writer, but about the nature of writing itself.

The literature included for discussion in *Novels for Students* has been chosen because it has something vital to say to us. *Of Mice and Men, Catch-22, The Joy Luck Club, My Antonia, A Separate Peace* and the other novels here speak of life and modern sensibility. In addition to their individual, specific messages of prejudice, power, love or hate, living and dying, however, they and all great literature also share a common intent. They force us to *think*—about life, literature, and about others, not just about ourselves. They pry us from the narrow confines of our minds and thrust us outward to confront the world of books and the larger, real world we all share. *Novels for Students* helps us in this confrontation by providing the means of enriching our conversation with literature and the world, by creating an *informed* dialogue, one that brings true pleasure to the personal act of reading.

Sources

Harold Bloom, *The Western Canon, The Books and School of the Ages,* Riverhead Books, 1994.
Watty Piper, *The Little Engine That Could,* Platt & Munk, 1930.

Anne Devereaux Jordan
Senior Editor, TALL
(Teaching and Learning Literature)

Introduction

Purpose of the Book

The purpose of *Novels for Students (NfS)* is to provide readers with a guide to understanding, enjoying, and studying novels by giving them easy access to information about the work. Part of Gale's "For Students" Literature line, *NfS* is specifically designed to meet the curricular needs of high school and undergraduate college students and their teachers, as well as the interests of general readers and researchers considering specific novels. While each volume contains entries on "classic" novels frequently studied in classrooms, there are also entries containing hard-to-find information on contemporary novels, including works by multicultural, international, and women novelists.

The information covered in each entry includes an introduction to the novel and the novel's author; a plot summary, to help readers unravel and understand the events in a novel; descriptions of important characters, including explanation of a given character's role in the novel as well as discussion about that character's relationship to other characters in the novel; analysis of important themes in the novel; and an explanation of important literary techniques and movements as they are demonstrated in the novel.

In addition to this material, which helps the readers analyze the novel itself, students are also provided with important information on the literary and historical background informing each work. This includes a historical context essay, a box comparing the time or place the novel was written to modern Western culture, a critical essay, and excerpts from critical essays on the novel. A unique feature of *NfS* is a specially commissioned critical essay on each novel, targeted toward the student reader.

To further aid the student in studying and enjoying each novel, information on media adaptations is provided, as well as reading suggestions for works of fiction and nonfiction on similar themes and topics. Classroom aids include ideas for research papers and lists of critical sources that provide additional material on the novel.

Selection Criteria

The titles for each volume of *NfS* were selected by surveying numerous sources on teaching literature and analyzing course curricula for various school districts. Some of the sources surveyed included: literature anthologies; *Reading Lists for College-Bound Students: The Books Most Recommended by America's Top Colleges;* textbooks on teaching the novel; a College Board survey of novels commonly studied in high schools; a National Council of Teachers of English (NCTE) survey of novels commonly studied in high schools; the NCTE's *Teaching Literature in High School: The Novel;* and the Young Adult Library Services Association (YALSA) list of best books for young adults of the past twenty-five years.

Input was also solicited from our advisory board, as well as educators from various areas.

From these discussions, it was determined that each volume should have a mix of "classic" novels (those works commonly taught in literature classes) and contemporary novels for which information is often hard to find. Because of the interest in expanding the canon of literature, an emphasis was also placed on including works by international, multicultural, and women authors. Our advisory board members—educational professionals—helped pare down the list for each volume. If a work was not selected for the present volume, it was often noted as a possibility for a future volume. As always, the editor welcomes suggestions for titles to be included in future volumes.

How Each Entry Is Organized

Each entry, or chapter, in *NfS* focuses on one novel. Each entry heading lists the full name of the novel, the author's name, and the date of the novel's publication. The following elements are contained in each entry:

- **Introduction:** a brief overview of the novel which provides information about its first appearance, its literary standing, any controversies surrounding the work, and major conflicts or themes within the work.

- **Author Biography:** this section includes basic facts about the author's life, and focuses on events and times in the author's life that inspired the novel in question.

- **Plot Summary:** a factual description of the major events in the novel. Lengthy summaries are broken down with subheads.

- **Characters:** an alphabetical listing of major characters in the novel. Each character name is followed by a brief to an extensive description of the character's role in the novel, as well as discussion of the character's actions, relationships, and possible motivation.

  Characters are listed alphabetically by last name. If a character is unnamed—for instance, the narrator in *Invisible Man*–the character is listed as "The Narrator" and alphabetized as "Narrator." If a character's first name is the only one given, the name will appear alphabetically by that name.

  Variant names are also included for each character. Thus, the full name "Jean Louise Finch" would head the listing for the narrator of *To Kill a Mockingbird,* but listed in a separate cross-reference would be the nickname "Scout Finch."

- **Themes:** a thorough overview of how the major topics, themes, and issues are addressed within the novel. Each theme discussed appears in a separate subhead, and is easily accessed through the boldface entries in the Subject/Theme Index.

- **Style:** this section addresses important style elements of the novel, such as setting, point of view, and narration; important literary devices used, such as imagery, foreshadowing, symbolism; and, if applicable, genres to which the work might have belonged, such as Gothicism or Romanticism. Literary terms are explained within the entry, but can also be found in the Glossary.

- **Historical Context:** This section outlines the social, political, and cultural climate *in which the author lived and the novel was created.* This section may include descriptions of related historical events, pertinent aspects of daily life in the culture, and the artistic and literary sensibilities of the time in which the work was written. If the novel is a historical work, information regarding the time in which the novel is set is also included. Each section is broken down with helpful subheads.

- **Critical Overview:** this section provides background on the critical reputation of the novel, including bannings or any other public controversies surrounding the work. For older works, this section includes a history of how the novel was first received and how perceptions of it may have changed over the years; for more recent novels, direct quotes from early reviews may also be included.

- **Criticism:** an essay commissioned by *NfS* which specifically deals with the novel and is written specifically for the student audience, as well as excerpts from previously published criticism on the work (if available).

- **Sources:** an alphabetical list of critical material used in compiling the entry, with full bibliographical information.

- **Further Reading:** an alphabetical list of other critical sources which may prove useful for the student. It includes full bibliographical information and a brief annotation.

In addition, each entry contains the following highlighted sections, set apart from the main text as sidebars:

- **Media Adaptations:** a list of important film and television adaptations of the novel, including source information. The list also includes stage adaptations, audio recordings, musical adaptations, etc.

- **Topics for Further Study:** a list of potential study questions or research topics dealing with the novel. This section includes questions related to other disciplines the student may be studying, such as American history, world history, science, math, government, business, geography, economics, psychology, etc.

- **Compare and Contrast Box:** an "at-a-glance" comparison of the cultural and historical differences between the author's time and culture and late twentieth century/early twenty-first century Western culture. This box includes pertinent parallels between the major scientific, political, and cultural movements of the time or place the novel was written, the time or place the novel was set (if a historical work), and modern Western culture. Works written after 1990 may not have this box.

- **What Do I Read Next?:** a list of works that might complement the featured novel or serve as a contrast to it. This includes works by the same author and others, works of fiction and nonfiction, and works from various genres, cultures, and eras.

Other Features

NfS includes "The Informed Dialogue: Interacting with Literature," a foreword by Anne Devereaux Jordan, Senior Editor for *Teaching and Learning Literature* (*TALL*), and a founder of the Children's Literature Association. This essay provides an enlightening look at how readers interact with literature and how *Novels for Students* can help teachers show students how to enrich their own reading experiences.

A Cumulative Author/Title Index lists the authors and titles covered in each volume of the *NfS* series.

A Cumulative Nationality/Ethnicity Index breaks down the authors and titles covered in each volume of the *NfS* series by nationality and ethnicity.

A Subject/Theme Index, specific to each volume, provides easy reference for users who may be studying a particular subject or theme rather than a single work. Significant subjects from events to broad themes are included, and the entries pointing to the specific theme discussions in each entry are indicated in **boldface.**

Each entry may have several illustrations, including photos of the author, stills from film adaptations, maps, and/or photos of key historical events, if available.

Citing Novels for Students

When writing papers, students who quote directly from any volume of *Novels for Students* may use the following general forms. These examples are based on MLA style; teachers may request that students adhere to a different style, so the following examples may be adapted as needed.

When citing text from *NfS* that is not attributed to a particular author (i.e., the Themes, Style, Historical Context sections, etc.), the following format should be used in the bibliography section:

> "Night." *Novels for Students.* Ed. Marie Rose Napierkowski. Vol. 4. Detroit: Gale, 1998. 234–35.

When quoting the specially commissioned essay from *NfS* (usually the first piece under the "Criticism" subhead), the following format should be used:

> Miller, Tyrus. Critical Essay on "Winesburg, Ohio." *Novels for Students.* Ed. Marie Rose Napierkowski. Vol. 4. Detroit: Gale, 1998. 335–39.

When quoting a journal or newspaper essay that is reprinted in a volume of *NfS*, the following form may be used:

> Malak, Amin. "Margaret Atwood's *The Handmaid's Tale* and the Dystopian Tradition," *Canadian Literature* No. 112 (Spring, 1987), 9–16; excerpted and reprinted in *Novels for Students,* Vol. 4, ed. Marie Rose Napierkowski (Detroit: Gale, 1998), pp. 133–36.

When quoting material reprinted from a book that appears in a volume of *NfS*, the following form may be used:

> Adams, Timothy Dow. "Richard Wright: Wearing the Mask," in *Telling Lies in Modern American Autobiography* (University of North Carolina Press, 1990), 69–83; excerpted and reprinted in *Novels for Students,* Vol. 1, ed. Diane Telgen (Detroit: Gale, 1997), pp. 59–61.

We Welcome Your Suggestions

The editor of *Novels for Students* welcomes your comments and ideas. Readers who wish to suggest novels to appear in future volumes, or who have other suggestions, are cordially invited to contact the editor. You may contact the editor via e-mail at: **ForStudentsEditors@gale.com.** Or write to the editor at:

Editor, *Novels for Students*
Gale Group
27500 Drake Road
Farmington Hills, MI 48331–3535

Literary Chronology

1840: Thomas Hardy is born on June 2 in a village near Dorchester in the southwestern region of England.

1849: Sarah Orne Jewett is born on September 3 in South Berwick, a shipbuilding town inland from the Maine coast.

1850: Edward Bellamy is born on March 26 in Chicopee Falls, Massachusetts.

1862: Edith Wharton (born Edith Newbold Jones) is born on January 24 to a wealthy and well-connected New York family.

1877: Hermann Hesse is born on July 2 in Calw, Württemberg, Germany.

1885: Sinclair Lewis is born in Sauk Centre, Minnesota, a small town on the Central Plains of the United States.

1886: Thomas Hardy's *The Mayor of Casterbridge* is published.

1888: Edward Bellamy's *Looking Backward: 2000–1887* is published.

1896: Sarah Orne Jewett's *The Country of the Pointed Firs* is published.

1898: Edward Bellamy dies on May 22 from complications from tuberculosis and digestive disorders.

1905: Edith Wharton's *The House of Mirth* is published.

1909: Eudora Welty is born on April 13 in Jackson, Mississippi.

1909: Sarah Orne Jewett dies on June 24 from a brain hemorrhage that followed a stroke.

1917: Anthony Burgess (born John Anthony Burgess Wilson) is born in Manchester, England.

1919: Hermann Hesse's *Demian* is published.

1920: Sinclair Lewis's *Main Street* is published.

1921: Edith Wharton is awarded the Pulitzer Prize for *The Age of Innocence*.

1927: George Lamming is born on June 8 in Carrington Village, a small settlement about two miles from Barbados's capital, Bridgetown.

1928: Thomas Hardy dies on January 11 in Dorchester after a brief illness. His ashes are interred in Poets' Corner in Westminster Abbey.

1930: Sinclair Lewis is awarded the Nobel Prize in literarture.

1935: William Patrick (W. P.) Kinsella is born on May 25 on a farm near Edmonton in northern Alberta, Canada.

1937: Edith Wharton dies on August 11 of a heart attack in St. Brice-sous-Foret, France.

1946: Hermann Hesse is awarded the Nobel Prize in literature.

1950: S.E. Hinton (born Susan Eloise Hinton) is born in Tulsa, Oklahoma. Some sources give her birth year as 1948.

1951: Sinclair Lewis dies in Rome.

1953: George Lamming's *In the Castle of My Skin* is published.

1957: Kyoko Mori is born in Kobe, Japan.

1962: Anthony Burgess's *A Clockwork Orange* is published.

1962: Hermann Hesse dies from a brain hemorrhage.

1967: Giles Foden is born to farmers in Warwickshire, England.

1970: Eudora Welty's *Losing Battles* is published.

1973: Eudora Welty is awarded the Pulitzer Prize for *The Optimist's Daughter*.

1975: S.E. Hinton's *Rumble Fish* is published.

1982: W. P. Kinsella's *Shoeless Joe* is published.

1993: Anthony Burgess dies from cancer in London, England.

1993: Kyoko Mori's *Shizuko's Daughter* is published.

1998: Giles Foden's *The Last King of Scotland* is published.

2001: Eudora Welty dies on July 23 from complications from pneumonia.

Acknowledgments

The editors wish to thank the copyright holders of the excerpted criticism included in this volume and the permissions managers of many book and magazine publishing companies for assisting us in securing reproduction rights. We are also grateful to the staffs of the Detroit Public Library, the Library of Congress, the University of Detroit Mercy Library, Wayne State University Purdy/Kresge Library Complex, and the University of Michigan Libraries for making their resources available to us. Following is a list of the copyright holders who have granted us permission to reproduce material in this volume of *Novels for Students* *(NfS)*. Every effort has been made to trace copyright, but if omissions have been made, please let us know.

COPYRIGHTED MATERIALS IN *NfS,* **VOLUME 15, WERE REPRODUCED FROM THE FOLLOWING PERIODICALS:**

American Literature, v. xliv, March, 1972. Copyright © 1972 Duke University Press. Reproduced by permission.—*The American Scholar*, Spring, 1995. Copyright © 1995 by the United Chapters of the Phi Beta Kappa Society. Reproduced by permission of the publishers.—*Callaloo*, v. 11, Spring, 1988. Copyright © 1988 by Charles H. Rowell. Reproduced by permission of The Johns Hopkins University Press.—*Canadian Review of American Studies*, v. 24, Winter, 1994. © Canadian Review of American Studies 1994. Reprinted by permission of the publisher.—*Extrapolation*, v. 30, Fall, 1989. Copyright © 1989 by The Kent State University Press. Reproduced by permission.—*Journal of American Studies*, v. 26, April, 1992 for "Reconstructing American Law: The Politics of Narrative and Eudora Welty's Empathic Vision" by Eve Kornfeld. Reproduced by permission of Cambridge University Press and the author.—*Modern Fiction Studies*, v. 24, Winter, 1978–1979; v. 33, Spring, 1987. Copyright © 1979 by Purdue Research Foundation, West Lafayette, IN 47907. All rights reserved. Reproduced by permission of The Johns Hopkins University.—*Southern Literary Journal*, v. 29, Spring, 1997. Copyright 1997 by the Department of English, University of North Carolina at Chapel Hill. Reproduced by permission.—*Studies in American Fiction*, v. 16, Autumn, 1988. Copyright © 1988 Northeastern University. Reproduced by permission.—*Studies in Short Fiction*, v. 32, Winter, 1995. Copyright 1995 by Newberry College. Reproduced by permission.—*Studies in the Novel*, v. 11, Spring, 1979. Copyright 1979 by North Texas State University. Reproduced by permission.—*World Literature Today*, v. 57, Winter, 1983. Copyright 1983 by the University of Oklahoma Press. Reprinted by permission of the publisher.

COPYRIGHTED MATERIALS IN *NfS,* **VOLUME 15, WERE REPRODUCED FROM THE FOLLOWING BOOKS:**

Daly, Jay. From *Presenting S. E. Hinton*. Twayne Publishers, 1987. Reproduced by permission.—Light, Martin. From *The Quixotic Vision of Sinclair Lewis*. Purdue University Press, 1975. ©

1975 by the Purdue Research Foundation.—Rose, Ernst. From *Faith from the Abyss: Hermann Hesse's Way from Romanticism to Modernity*. New York University Press, 1965. © 1965 by New York University. Reproduced by permission.—Stelzig, Eugene L. From *Hermann Hesse's Fictions of the Self: Autobiography and the Confessional Imagination*. Princeton University Press, 1988. Copyright © 1988 by Princeton University Press. Reproduced by permission.

PHOTOGRAPHS AND ILLUSTRATIONS APPEARING IN *NfS*, VOLUME 15, WERE RECEIVED FROM THE FOLLOWING SOURCES:

Amin, Major General Idi, addressing the people of Kampala, photograph. AP/Wide World Photos. Reproduced by permission.—Anderson, Gillian, as Lily Barth, Eric Stoltz as Lawrence Selden in a scene from Edith Wharton's novel "The House of Mirth," directed by Terence Davies. The Kobal Collection. Reproduced by permission.—An arch extends over a road in Bridgetown, Barbados, photograph by Bob Krist. CORBIS. Reproduced by permission.—Bellamy, Edward, photograph. The Library of Congress.—Burgess, Anthony, photograph. AP/Wide World Photos. Reproduced by permission.—Dillon, Matt, Mickey Rourke, and William Smith, in the film "Rumble Fish," 1983, photograph. The Kobal Collection. Reproduced by permission.—Fictional map of Wessex, created by Thomas Hardy, photograph. Source unknown.—Foden, Giles, photograph. © Jerry Bauer. Reproduced by permission.—Hardy, Thomas, photograph. Archive Photos, Inc. Reproduced by permission.—Hesse, Hermann, photograph. The Library of Congress.—Hinton, S.E., photograph by Thomas Victor. Reproduced by permission of the Estate of Thomas Victor.—Jackson, Joseph "Shoeless Joe," photograph. AP/Wide World. Reproduced by permission.—Japanese woman, photograph. Archive Photos, Inc. Reproduced by permission.—Jewett, Sarah, photograph. Source unknown—Jung, Carl, photograph. The Library of Congress.—Kinsella, W.P., photograph. AP/Wide World. Reproduced by permission.—Lamming, George, photograph by Tony Arruza. CORBIS. Reproduced by permission.—Lancaster, Burt, Kevin Costner, in the film "Field of Dreams," 1989, photograph. The Kobal Collection. Reproduced by permission.—Lewis, Sinclair boyhood home in Sauk Centre, Minnesota, photograph. Harry Ransom Humainties Research Center. Reproduced by permission.—Lewis, Sinclair, photograph. The Library of Congress.—McDowell, Malcolm, and others, in the film "A Clockwork Orange," 1972, photograph. The Kobal Collection. Reproduced by permission.—Mori, Kyoko, photograph by Katherine McCabe. Reproduced by permission of Kyoko Mori.—Old fishing docks in Portland, Maine, photograph. Courtesy of The Library of Congress.—Pedestrians walking on Theatre Street, photograph. © Hulton/Archive Photos, Inc. Reproduced by permission.—Suffragist, (holding sign "Help us to win the vote"), photograph. The Granger Collection, New York. Reproduced by permission.—Title page from "Looking Backward: 2000–1887" by Edward Bellamy, illustration. The University of Michigan Library. Special Collections Library, University of Michigan. Reproduced by permission.—Welty, Eudora, 1962, photograph. NYWTS/The Library of Congress.—Wharton, Edith, 1905, photograph. The Library of Congress.—Women preparing food in Kampala, Uganda, photograph by Liba Taylor. CORBIS. Reproduced by permission.

Contributors

Bryan Aubrey: Aubrey holds a Ph.D. in English and has published many articles on twentieth-century literature. Entry on *Shoeless Joe*. Original essay on *Shoeless Joe*.

Greg Barnhisel: Barnhisel teaches writing and directs the Writing Center at the University of Southern California. Entry on *In the Castle of My Skin*. Original essay on *In the Castle of My Skin*.

Liz Brent: Brent has a Ph.D. in American culture, specializing in film studies, from the University of Michigan. She is a freelance writer and teaches courses on the history of American cinema. Entries on *The Country of the Pointed Firs* and *Demian*. Original essays on *The Country of the Pointed Firs* and *Demian*.

Douglas Dupler: Dupler has published numerous essays and has taught college English. Original essays on *The Last King of Scotland* and *Shizuko's Daughter*.

Joyce Hart: Hart has degrees in English literature and creative writing and is a published writer of literary themes. Entry on *Shizuko's Daughter*. Original essay on *Shizuko's Daughter*.

David Kelly: Kelly is an adjunct professor of English at College of Lake County and Oakton Community College in Illinois. Entry on *Main Street*. Original essay on *Main Street*.

Lois Kerschen: Kerschen is a writer and public school district administrator. Entry on *Looking Backward: 2000–1887*. Original essay on *Looking Backward: 2000–1887*.

Rena Korb: Korb has a master's degree in English literature and creative writing and has written for a wide variety of educational publishers. Entry on *The House of Mirth*. Original essay on *The House of Mirth*.

Candyce Norvell: Norvell is an independent educational writer who specializes in English and literature. She holds degrees in linguistics and journalism. Entries on *Losing Battles* and *The Mayor of Casterbridge*. Original essays on *Losing Battles* and *The Mayor of Casterbridge*.

Susan Sanderson: Sanderson holds a Master of Fine Arts degree in fiction writing and is an independent writer who has lived in Africa. Entry on *The Last King of Scotland*. Original essay on *The Last King of Scotland*.

Chris Semansky: Semansky teaches literature and composition online. His essays, stories, and poems appear regularly in magazines and journals. Entry on *A Clockwork Orange*. Original essay on *A Clockwork Orange*.

Kelly Winters: Winters is a freelance writer. Entry on *Rumble Fish*. Original essay on *Rumble Fish*.

A Clockwork Orange

Anthony Burgess
1962

Published in 1962, Anthony Burgess's *A Clockwork Orange* is set in the future and narrated by fifteen-year-old Alex in Nadsat—a language invented by Burgess and comprised of bits of Russian, English, and American slang, rhyming words, and "gypsy talk". The British edition of the novel contains three sections divided into seven chapters, for a total of twenty-one chapters, the number symbolizing adulthood. The original American edition, however, contains only twenty chapters, as the publisher cut the last chapter because he felt it was too sentimental. A new American edition came out in 1987 with the expunged chapter restored. Although Burgess claimed that the book is neither his favorite nor his best, *A Clockwork Orange* helped to establish his international reputation, owing largely to Stanley Kubrick's film adaptation of it in 1971. The novel's title alludes to the Cockney saying, "as queer as a clockwork orange," which means that something can appear to be natural, but on the inside it is actually artificial. Burgess's novel explores issues such as the relation between evil and free will, and the state's role in human affairs.

Burgess, a self-avowed anarchist, visited Leningrad (in what was then the Soviet Union) in 1961 and was appalled at the degree to which the communist state controlled people's lives. He based the character of Alex and his band of thugs ("droogs" in Nadsat) on Russian and British gangs of the 1950s and 1960s. The Russian *stilyaqi*, or style-boys, reminded Burgess of the teddyboys, a macho British youth subculture. "Inspiration" for a

Anthony Burgess

In 1959, while an education officer in Brunei, Borneo, doctors diagnosed Burgess with a cerebral tumor, giving him a year to live. It was then he began writing in earnest, steadily turning out novels, columns, and reviews. He dropped his first and last names because he felt it was inappropriate for a member of the British Colonial Service to publish under his own name. Burgess did not die within the year, and continued writing at a torrid pace, churning out eleven novels between 1960 and 1964 alone.

In 1962 Burgess's novel *A Clockwork Orange* was published, a satirical work detailing the violent exploits of a futuristic teenage gang and its Beethoven-loving leader, Alex. The novel satirizes psychologist B. F. Skinner's theories of human behavior and the welfare state. Stanley Kubrick's adaptation of the novel into a feature film in 1971 won Burgess numerous new readers and secured the novel's reputation as one of the most controversial in English literature. Unfortunately for Burgess, because he was financially strapped, he had sold the film rights to *A Clockwork Orange* for just $500 (U.S.) and received less than $3,000 (U.S.) in payments after the film's release.

Burgess edited and published numerous books after *A Clockwork Orange* including novels, screenplays, autobiographies, critical studies, documentaries, and an opera. None of them ever achieved the degree of notoriety that *A Clockwork Orange* received. These works include *The Novel Today* (1963); *The Eve of Saint Venus* (1964); *Language Made Plain* (1964); *Here Comes Everybody: A Study of James Joyce's Fiction* (1965); *Tremor of Intent* (1966); *The Novel Now* (1967); *Earthly Powers* (1980), winner of the Prix du Meilleur Livre Etranger in 1981; *Enderby's Dark Lady* (1984); and his autobiography *Little Wilson and Big God* (1986). Burgess's last novel, *Byrne: A Novel*, written in ottava rima (a stanza of eight lines of heroic verse with a rhyme scheme of *abababcc*), was published posthumously in 1995.

violent scene in the novel stems from an incident in 1943 when a group of AWOL (absent without leave) American soldiers attacked and raped Burgess's then-pregnant wife, Llewela Isherwood Jones, in London, killing their unborn child. Though his wife died more than two decades later, Burgess attributed her subsequent alcoholism and death from cirrhosis of the liver to that incident.

Author Biography

John Anthony Burgess Wilson was born in 1917 in Manchester, England, to Joseph, a cashier and pub pianist, and Elizabeth (Burgess) Wilson. His mother and sister died of the flu in 1919, and Burgess was raised by a maternal aunt, and later by his stepmother. He studied in England at Xaverian College and Manchester University, from where he graduated in 1940 with a degree in English language and literature, though his chief passion was music. After serving in the Royal Army Medical Corps during World War II, Burgess pursued a career in education, teaching at Birmingham University and Banbury Grammar School and working for the Ministry of Education.

Almost all of Burgess's novels explore the conflicts between good and evil, the spirit and the flesh. Born a Catholic in Protestant England, Burgess believed that although people are born depraved, they retain the capacity to choose, and it is this capacity that makes human beings human. A fellow of the Royal Society of Literature, Burgess died of cancer in London, England, in 1993.

Plot Summary

First Section

A Clockwork Orange opens with Alex, the main character of the novel, and his droogs, Dim, Pete, and Georgie, drinking drug-laced milk at the Korova Milkbar. After leaving the Milkbar, the four commit what is to be the first in a string of "ultraviolent" acts, savagely beating up an old man carrying library books and destroying his books. Next, the group comes across a rival gang in a warehouse. Billyboy, the leader, and his five droogs are raping a young devotchka (girl), and Alex's crew attacks them, beating them back until the millicents (police) arrive.

Alex and his gang next come to a house with the word "HOME" on the front gate. This marks a turn in the novel towards the fabular (fantastical), and away from the realistic. After telling the woman answering the door that his friend is sick and he needs to use her phone, Alex breaks into the house with his gang, now wearing masks. They viciously beat the woman's husband and pillage the house, then gang rape the woman. The man, F. Alexander, is a writer working on a book called *A Clockwork Orange*, which Alex calls a "gloopy" title. The book critiques the welfare state and government oppression of civil liberties. The droogs destroy the book. (This scene echoes an event from 1943 in Burgess's own life, when his wife was raped and brutalized by a gang of American soldiers.)

After returning to the Milkbar, Alex hits Dim for ridiculing a woman singing opera at the bar. Georgie and Pete side with Dim, Pete remarking, "If the truth is known, Alex, you shouldn't have given old Dim that uncalled-for tolchock [blow].... if it had been me you'd given it to you'd have to answer." Alex returns to his parents' flat and falls asleep masturbating while listening to Beethoven. In the morning, his Post-Corrective Advisor, P. R. Deltoid, visits him, warning Alex that one day the police will catch him if he continues with his antics. After Deltoid leaves, Alex visits a music store, where he picks up two ten-year-old girls, brings them back to his apartment, plies them with liquor, and rapes them.

At the Milkbar, Pete, Georgie, and Dim convince Alex that they need to rob a larger house. Alex goes along with the plan, to show he is a good "brother" and leader. That night, they break into the house of an elderly wealthy woman who is feeding her cats. She fights with Alex, and he knocks

her out with one of her statues. When Alex tries to escape after hearing the police sirens, Dim hits him with his chain, knocking him out. The police arrive and arrest Alex, as Georgie, Pete, and Dim abandon him. The police take him to a cell, where he is visited by Deltoid, who spits in his face. Alex later learns that the old woman he fought with has died of a heart attack. "That was everything," Alex says. "I'd done the lot, now. And me still only fifteen."

Second Section

The second section, chapters eight through fourteen, describes Alex's life in the "staja" (state penitentiary), after he is sentenced to fourteen years there. A model prisoner—despite killing a fellow prisoner who had been making sexual advances towards him—Alex makes fast friends with the chaplain, who allows him to listen to classical music on the chapel stereo. Prison officials and the Minister of the Interior offer Alex the opportunity to undergo Ludovico's Technique, an experimental treatment that guarantees his release from prison and ensures he will never return, and Alex agrees. Burgess models the idea of Ludovico's Technique on the work of B. F. Skinner. Skinner, a mid-twentieth-century behavioral psychologist, wanted to build a society based on a system of rewards and punishments. He believed that human behavior could be conditioned, once people learned to associate "good" behavior with the pleasure of the reward they received for it, and associate "bad" behavior with the pain of punishment. These methods were used for a time on juvenile delinquents and retarded children. Skinner outlines his ideas in his book *Beyond Freedom and Dignity.*

For two weeks, Alex is given injections of a drug that makes him physically ill whenever he witnesses violent acts. His eyelids clamped open, Alex is forced to watch films packed with scenes of torture, rape, and beating. After being shown a film detailing Nazi atrocities from World War II, with Beethoven's Fifth Symphony as its sound track, Alex develops an aversion to both violence and Beethoven, whose music he loves. At the conclusion of the treatment, Alex is paraded before a panel of prison and state officials, during which time he grovels in front of a tormentor taunting him to fight and is sickened by his own lustful response to a beautiful woman. Alex has been stripped of free will to choose his actions, and Dr. Brodsky pronounces him fit for release from prison.

Third Section

In the third section, Alex becomes a victim. In his absence, Alex's parents have taken a boarder, Joe, so Alex is forced to the streets, where he encounters the people he victimized in the first section. He is being beaten by a group of old men in the Public Biblio (library), one of whom Alex and his gang had beaten before. Alex is then "rescued" by three policemen, two of whom turn out to be Billyboy and Dim. The government had recruited the two in its efforts to use society's criminal elements for its own repressive purposes. Billyboy and Dim take Alex out to the country, beat him, and leave him for dead. Alex then wanders through a village and comes upon the house with "HOME" written on the gate. F. Alexander, the writer beaten by Alex earlier, recognizes Alex from the newspaper and takes him in, planning to use him in a campaign to "dislodge this overbearing government."

While Alexander and his liberal friends brainstorm how to use Alex as an example of government repression, the writer recognizes Alex as the person who beat him up and raped his wife a few years ago. With his friends' help, Alexander locks Alex in an apartment and plays classical music, Otto Skadelig's Symphony Number Three, driving Alex into a suicidal frenzy because of the sickness and pain he feels listening to the music. Alex jumps out the window, but does not die. He awakens in the hospital, his love for violence restored. Meanwhile, the Minister of the Interior visits Alex, telling him that Alexander and his friends have been imprisoned, and offering Alex a well-paying job in exchange for his support of the government.

In the last chapter, Alex is back at the Korova Milkbar, this time with a new group of droogs, who resemble the old group. Although they engage in ultraviolent acts, Alex says that he mostly gives orders and watches. He is "old" now, eighteen. He meets one of his former gang members, Pete, who is married and works for an insurance company, and Alex begins to fantasize about also being married and having children. "Youth must go, ah yes," he says. "But youth is only being in a way like it might be an animal."

Characters

Alex

Alex is the fifteen-year-old narrator and protagonist of the novel. Like his "droogs," Dim, Georgie, and Pete, he speaks in Nadsat. He is witty, charming, intelligent, violent, sadistic, and totally without remorse for his actions. He leads his gang on crime sprees, raping, beating, and pillaging, and becomes upset when his gang does not engage in their crimes with style. Alex's love of music, particularly Beethoven, marks him as an aesthete, and this attitude carries over to the way he "performs" his violent acts, often dancing. His attitude towards others is primarily ironic; he calls his victims "brother" and speaks as if with a perpetual smirk. The extent of Alex's evil nature is evident in his fantasies. For example, he dreams about nailing Jesus to the cross. Authorities are perplexed as to how Alex became the way he is. His guidance counselor, P. R. Deltoid, asks him, "You've got a good home here, good loving parents, you've got not too bad of a brain. Is it some devil that crawls inside you?" Alex remains his evil self, even after two years in prison and Ludovico's Technique, though he behaves differently. In the last chapter, however, Alex matures and begins to weary of his violent ways, fantasizing about having a wife and children. Burgess notes that among other things, Alex's name suggests nobleness, Alexander meaning "leader of men."

F. Alexander

F. Alexander—whom Alex describes as "youngish" and with horn-rimmed glasses the first time he sees him, and "a shortish veck in middle age, thirty, forty, fifty" the second time he sees him—is a liberal and a writer, outraged at the government's repression of individual liberties. Ironically, he is writing a book called *A Clockwork Or-*

ange, which addresses "[t]he attempt to impose upon man, a creature of growth and capable of sweetness . . . laws and conditions appropriate to a mechanical creation." In the novel's first section, Alex breaks into Alexander's house, where he and his gang beat him and viciously rape his wife. Beaten almost to death by Billyboy and Georgie in the third section, Alex winds up back at Alexander's house. At first, Alexander wants to use Alex as an example of the government's repressive policies, and he befriends Alex, who considers him "kind protecting and like motherly." However, when Alexander realizes that Alex is the person responsible for beating him and raping his wife a few years past, he plots revenge. Along with his liberal friends, Alexander locks Alex up in an apartment, and plays classical music loudly on the stereo. Alex, who has been conditioned by Ludovico's Technique to become violently ill when hearing the music, attempts suicide by jumping out a window. He wakes up in the hospital badly injured. The suicide attempt leads government scientists to remove Ludovico's clockwork from Alex's brain. In an ironic reversal, F. Alexander is himself imprisoned for his actions and Alex is made a hero.

Alex's Parents

Alex's parents, whom Alex sometimes refers to as "pee and em," are passive though decent people. They behave in loving, if stereotypical, ways. His mother, for example, prepares meals for him to have when he returns from his adventures. They are afraid of Alex, though, and show no interest in knowing what he really does when he goes out with his friends. Although they do not take him back when he is released from prison, their interest in Alex returns after his suicide attempt and after the newspapers run stories about how he is a victim of government repression.

Billyboy

Billyboy leads a rival gang with whom Alex and his droogs battle. In the first section, when Alex, Dim, Georgie, and Pete come across Billyboy and his thugs attempting to rape a young girl in a warehouse, Alex's gang routs them. Billyboy's ugliness upsets Alex's aesthetic sensibility. Alex says of him: "Billyboy was something that made me want to sick just to viddy [see] his fat grinning litso [face]." In their new capacity as police, Billyboy and Georgie beat up Alex after he is released from prison and leave him for dead.

Dr. Branom

Dr. Branom works with Dr. Brodsky to rid Alex of his free will and humanity through Ludovico's Technique. He is friendly but insincere.

Dr. Brodsky

Dr. Brodsky is the psychologist in charge of administering Ludovico's Technique on Alex. He is a hypocrite and in many ways morally worse than Alex. He is a philistine of sorts, knowing nothing about music, which is, for Burgess, a "figure of celestial bliss." Materialist and scientist that he is, Brodsky considers music merely an "emotional heightener." He plainly takes pleasure in Alex's misery, laughing at the pain he experiences during the treatment. Before Alex is released from prison, Brodsky demonstrates to state and prison officials how Ludovico's Technique has turned Alex into a "true Christian."

D. B. daSilva

DaSilva is one of F. Alexander's liberal friends who helps him with Alex in the book's third section. Alex describes him as having effeminate behavior and a strong scent (aftershave or body odor).

P. R. Deltoid

Deltoid is Alex's state-appointed "Post-Corrective Advisor." He visits Alex after his night of ultraviolence in the novel's first section. Alex describes him as overworked and wearing a "filthy raincoat." Deltoid cannot understand why Alex, with a good home and parents, has turned out to be a juvenile delinquent. He visits Alex in jail and contemptuously spits in his face.

Dim

Dim is one of Alex's droogs. He is loud, brutish, stupid, and irritates Alex with his crassness and vulgarity. When Dim insults a woman singing opera at the Korova Milkbar, Alex punches him in the mouth, triggering the gang's resentment against Alex's tyrannical leadership. Alex also fights Dim the next day, cutting his wrist with a knife to show the gang that he is still the leader. By the novel's third section, Dim has joined the police force, along with Billyboy. The two of them rescue Alex, who is being attacked by a gang of old men, and take Alex to the country, where they beat him up and leave him for dead. As Burgess's characters are composites of Anglo and Russian youth culture, Dim could be read as an abbreviation for the Russian name, Dimitri.

Z. Dolin

Z. Dolin is one of F. Alexander's liberal friends who helps him with Alex in the novel's third section. Alex describes him as "a very wheezy smoky kind of veck" who is fat and sloppy, wears thick glasses, and chain smokes.

Georgie

Georgie is one of Alex's droogs, and second-in-charge. He attempts to take over the gang after Dim rebels against Alex at the Korova Milkbar, and leads the mutiny resulting in Alex's arrest at the end of the book's first section. More interested in money than violence per se, Georgie dies after being hit on the head by a man he and his droogs terrorize while Alex is in prison.

Joe

Joe is the boarder Alex's parents take in when Alex is sent to jail. Alex describes him as "a working-man type veck, very ugly, about thirty or forty." Joe has become a kind of surrogate son to Alex's parents, and he almost comes to blows with Alex when Alex comes home to see him eating eggs and toast with his parents.

Marty

Marty is one of the two ten-year-old girls that Alex picks up at the music store, plies with liquor, and rapes. He calls them "sophistos," meaning they are pretentious and try to act like adults. When the girls come to their senses and discover what Alex has done to them, they call him a "[b]east and hateful animal."

Minister of the Interior

The Minister of the Interior is a manipulative politician who symbolizes governmental repression and mindless bureaucracy. He chooses Alex—who refers to him as the "Minister of the Interior Inferior"—as a guinea pig for Ludovico's Technique, believing the treatment has the possibility to rid the country of undesirable elements. He turns Alex's attempted suicide to his favor by imprisoning F. Alexander, whom he describes as a "writer of subversive literature," and tricking Alex into a photo opportunity with him while Alex is still in the hospital. He wins Alex's favor by offering him a government job, a new stereo, and by playing Beethoven's Ninth Symphony for him.

Pete

Pete is the quietest of Alex's droogs, and the least questioning of his authority. In the last chapter, Alex runs into Pete and his wife. Pete now works for an insurance company and goes to harmless wine and scrabble parties at night, having given up his criminal ways. He represents maturity, and after seeing him, Alex begins thinking of marrying and settling down.

Prison Chaplain

The chaplain, a careerist and an alcoholic, befriends Alex in prison, permitting him to pick the music for services and listen to the stereo in chapel while reading the Bible. The chaplain finally speaks out against Ludovico's Technique when Alex is about to be released, arguing that human beings should be able to choose their actions. He is the character perhaps closest to Burgess's own philosophical position in the novel, and demonstrates this when he asks Alex, "What does God want? Does God want goodness or the choice of goodness? Is a man who chooses the bad perhaps in some way better than a man who has the good imposed upon him?" Alex, however, is clueless, and wants nothing more than to be released from prison. When the chaplain speaks out against the treatment in front of prison and state officials, he jeopardizes his own career.

Rex

Rex is a policeman and the driver who waits in the car, smoking and reading, while Billyboy and Dim beat Alex in the novel's third section.

Rubinstein

Rubinstein is one of F. Alexander's liberal friends who helps him with Alex in the third section of the novel. Alex describes him as "very tall and polite," and with an "eggy beard" (blonde).

Sonietta

Sonietta is one of the two ten-year-old girls that Alex rapes.

Themes

Free Will

A Clockwork Orange explores the ideas of good and evil by asking what it means to be human. Burgess asks and answers the question, "Is a man who has been forced to be good better than a man who chooses evil?" Alex chooses evil because it is in his nature to do so. His impulse towards good is artificial because it comes from outside of him, instilled by a government bent on controlling the populace by controlling their desires. By eliminating all of the bad in Alex through the Ludovico Technique, the government also eliminates that very thing that constitutes his humanity: his freedom to choose. They treat the symptom, not the cause of Alex's evil, oblivious of their own complicity in his behavior. For Burgess, an evil Alex is a human Alex and, hence, preferable to an Alex who has been programmed to deny his own nature. F. Alexander, the writer Alex and his droogs beat up, is one of the mouthpieces for this idea. At one point he says to Alex, "They have turned you into something other than a human being. You have no power of choice any longer. You are committed to socially acceptable acts, a little machine capable only of good." Later, he adds, "The essential intention [of the Ludovico Technique] is the real sin. A man who cannot choose ceases to be a man." The repetition of Alex's phrase "What's it going to be then, eh?" throughout the novel also underscores the theme of free will and individual choice.

Power

A Clockwork Orange pits the intrusive powers of the state against the liberties of the individual. Burgess looks at the relationship between the state and the individual in a society that has deteriorated and is on the brink of anarchy. Left to its own devices, the state will attempt to control the individual through regulation, law, and brute force. This is evident in the manner in which Alex is used by the state as an example of its power to "rehabilitate" criminals. Rather than rehabilitate them, they reprogram them, brainwashing them. The cynical power-mongering of the state is embodied in the character of the Minister of the Interior, who manipulates Alex first into "volunteering" for the Ludovico Technique, and then into siding with the government after Alex's suicide attempt and return to his evil nature. A society in which the state has so much power, Burgess suggests, is one in which individual liberties such as freedom of speech and expression are crushed.

Selfhood

To fully grasp the human condition, Burgess implies in *A Clockwork Orange*, individuals must both recognize and accept their evil nature and recognize how society attempts to stifle it. Although Alex does not seem to understand the implications of the Ludovico Technique when it is initially explained to him, he does have an understanding of his own nature and how society has helped to form

Topics for Further Study

- The setting for Burgess's novel is a dystopian society. What are some of its dystopic elements? Does the United States share any of these elements? Are there ways in which the United States can be described as a dystopia? Provide examples.

- Burgess claimed that *A Clockwork Orange* emphasizes the idea that free will is a central ingredient of what it means to be human. Write an essay agreeing or disagreeing with this notion and provide support for your argument from the novel.

- With your classmates, make a list of all the crimes that Alex and his droogs commit, then assign appropriate punishment for each crime. Be as specific as possible. On which items do you disagree with others in your group? What does this say about your own ideas of justice and the role of society in punishing criminals?

- With members of your class, draw up a list of slang terms or other words you use that older generations would not recognize. To what degree does using these words define your interaction with friends?

- Research the punishment for first-degree murder in your state. If possible, would you recommend that convicted murderers be given the opportunity to undergo the Ludovico Technique in lieu of the state sentence for murder? Why or why not? Explain if there are certain conditions you would attach.

- Research cases of political scandal in your own city or state and describe how that scandal is represented in newspaper or television accounts. How did the accused characterize their situation or their attackers? What does this tell you about the role of media in shaping public opinion?

- The Korova Milkbar symbolizes the decadence of Burgess's society in the novel. Name an analogous institution that symbolizes twenty-first-century American values and support your claim.

it. At one point he waxes philosophical, expressing an understanding of his "essential" self:

> More, badness is of the self, the one, the you or me on our oddy knockies [lonesome], and that self is made by old Bog or God and is his great pride and radosty [joy]. But the not-self cannot have the bad, meaning they of the government and the judges and the schools cannot allow the bad because they allow the self.

Alex knows he is evil, telling readers, "What I do I do because I like to do." The novel implies his degree of insight is greater than most people's insight. He accepts himself for who he is, rather than hiding behind illusions of what he should be according to others and the government. He experiences no guilt for his actions but embraces and revels in his evil side.

Morality

Burgess's moral universe in *A Clockwork Orange*, as in his other novels, can be described as a conflict between Augustinianism and Pelagianism. Augustinianism is derived from St. Augustine (354–430), who believed in humankind's innate depravity. Pelagianism is derived from Pelagius (c. 355–c. 425), whose doctrine held roughly that human beings were perfectible, and that evil was the result of superstition, social forces, the environment, and the like. In Burgess's novel, the government adhered to Pelagius-like thinking in that it tried to change human beings, to turn them away from their evil behavior through whatever means necessary. In Alex's case, it is the Ludovico Technique. Alex, who embraces his evil nature as if it were a second skin, chooses to be that way, but shows promise of choosing a different way in the book's final chapter, demonstrating that Burgess is not the consummate Augustinian that some critics have made him out to be. The tug between Augustinianism and Pelagianism creates the moral tension that sustains Alex's story, but it is a tension that remains largely unresolved.

Dystopia and Dystopian Ideas

A Clockwork Orange describes a dystopian society. The opposite of utopias, or ideal societies, dystopias are severely malfunctioning societies. Dystopian novels such as George Orwell's *1984* portray bleak landscapes, corrupt social institutions, and characters among whom trust or authentic communication is impossible. The Korova Milkbar, where fifteen-year-olds can drink drug-laced milk, symbolizes the decadence of the novel's setting, as does the fact that Alex—a charming rapist, killer, and thief—is the most appealing character in the story. Dystopian novels have a rich history and include works such as Jonathan Swift's eighteenth-century classic, *Gulliver's Travels*. However, they became especially prevalent and popular after World War II, as people increasingly took a dim view of human nature and the possibility for social change. Twentieth-century dystopian works include Aldous Huxley's *Brave New World*, Ayn Rand's *Atlas Shrugged*, and Ray Bradbury's *Fahrenheit 451*.

Style

Language

Nadsat, which means "teen" in Russian, is the language spoken in *A Clockwork Orange*. It is a mixture of Russian, English, and American slang, and rhyming words and phrases, with a touch of Shakespearean English. The singsong rhythm of the speech underscores the heavily stylized world of the novel and of Alex's own mind. Although many readers often initially struggle with understanding this slang of futuristic teenagers, they quickly pick up the speech patterns and the few hundred new words through the context in which they are used. By mirroring the violent acts the characters commit, Nadsat has a kind of onomatopoeic quality. That is, the words sound like the actions they describe. For example, "collocoll" means bell, and it also sounds like a bell ringing. Nadsat is also often highly metaphoric and ironic. The word "rabbit," for example, means to work, and the word "horrorshow" means beautiful. The former is metaphoric because working, for Alex, means engaging in meaningless and frenetic activity, which he associates with a rabbit's behavior. The latter is ironic because "horrorshow" suggests the opposite of what it means. Some of the words are just plain silly rhymes, reflecting a child's playful constructions. For example, "eggiwegg" for egg and "skolliwoll" for school.

Structure

The novel is divided into three sections of seven chapters each. In his introduction to the 1987 American edition of the novel, Burgess notes that "Novelists of my stamp are interested in what is called arithmology, meaning that [a] number has to mean something in human terms when they handle it." At twenty-one, citizens in Great Britain, the United States, and Russia can vote; the age sym-

Compare
&
Contrast

- **1960s:** Following years of heated protests and demonstrations, the United States passes the Civil Rights Act. The Act enforces the constitutional right to vote, guarantees relief against discrimination in public accommodations, and authorizes the Attorney General to initiate suits to protect constitutional rights in public facilities and public education.

  Today: Some states have enacted hate crime legislation, which penalizes criminals for committing crimes based on a person's race, sexuality, religion, gender, ancestry, or national origin.

- **1960s:** The space race between the Soviet Union and the United States gathers momentum, as the Soviets send the first man into space to circle the earth, and the Americans land a man on the moon.

  Today: The space race of the 1960s has given way to international cooperation to explore the

heavens. Led by the United States, the International Space Station draws upon the scientific and technological resources of sixteen nations: Canada, Japan, Russia, eleven nations of the European Space Agency, and Brazil. Launch of the space station is set for 2004.

- **1960s:** The "Cold War" between the United States and the Soviet Union causes each country to be deeply suspicious of the other.

  Today: After the Soviet Union's dissolution, relations between Russia and the United States become warmer and more productive.

- **1960s:** The Beatles and the Rolling Stones gain international popularity and help shape the desires and tastes of youth culture.

  Today: The influence of rock and roll on contemporary youth is still strong, but other kinds of music such as techno, heavy metal, and world pop also exert strong influence.

---

bolizes a mature human being. The novel is the story of one human being's growth into an adult, among other things.

Historical Context

1960s

In 1961, the year after Burgess had written his first draft of *A Clockwork Orange*, he and his wife took a trip to Leningrad (now St. Petersburg) in what was then the Soviet Union. During that trip, Burgess was appalled and intrigued by the roaming gangs of hoodlums he saw, called *stilyaqi*. Burgess noted how the police, preoccupied with ideological crimes against the state, had a difficult time controlling these unruly youths. He also noted the similarities of the Russian and British youth subcultures and was inspired to fashion a hooligan

character who was a composite of the ways in which youth spoke, acted, and dressed in Russia and England.

Hence, Alex and his droogs—"droog" derived from the Russian word "drugi," which means "friends in violence." The stilyaqi, or style-boys, sprung up in Russia during the 1940s and were roughly contemporaneous with American beats. The stilyaqi listened to jazz and later to American rock and roll. The Soviet government considered them troublesome juveniles.

The London youth subculture included groups known as teddyboys, mods, and rockers. Teddyboys emerged in the 1950s, as England was economically recovering from World War II and at the beginning of a consumer boom. Like many youth subcultures, they dressed to shock the status quo, wearing Edwardian-style drape jackets, suede Gibson shoes with thick crepe soles, narrow trousers, and loud ties. Like the greasers in movies such as

A scene from the 1971 film version of the novel

American Graffitti, the teddyboys listened to rock and roll, fought rival gangs (often with razors and knives), and engaged in random vandalism. With the British pop-music boom of the 1960s, many teddyboys became rockers, wearing leather jackets, hanging out in working-class pubs, and riding motorcycles.

The mods, short for modernists, also emerged during the late 1950s in England. A more elitist group than the teddyboys, they wore their hair short; rode scooters; donned army anoraks; danced to groups such as the Creation, the Jam, and the Small Faces; and took amphetamines. The mods were sometimes referred to as "rude boys," and evolved into the "punks" and "skinheads" of the 1970s and later. For Burgess, however, being a mod, a stilyaqi, or a teddyboy, did not mean one practiced individual freedom. The trendy consumerism in which these group members engaged signaled a mindlessly slavish conformity.

Burgess also hated the control the state had over the individual, believing this control curtailed individual freedom. This state control was nowhere more evident than in the Soviet Union in the early 1960s, where Burgess saw firsthand the extent to which the communist government regulated the individual's life. Burgess especially detested the way in which communism shifted moral responsibility from the individual to the state. Though Britain was and is a democratic government, by the 1950s the Labour Party had nationalized many industries including coal (1946), electricity (1947), and the railways (1948). Also, in 1946, the National Health Service was founded to take care of British citizens' medical needs. This welfare state was odious to Burgess, who believed that it put the needs of society over the freedom of the individual.

Critical Overview

When *A Clockwork Orange* was published in 1962, it had twenty-one chapters. Its American edition, however, was published with only twenty chapters a year later, the publisher W. W. Norton having removed the last chapter because they thought it was too sentimental. It was not until 1987 that American editions were published with the last chapter included. Of the controversy, Burgess writes in his essay "*A Clockwork Orange* Resucked," found in the 1987 edition: "My book was Kennedyan and accepted the notion of moral progress. What was really wanted was a Nixonian book with no shred of optimism in it."

The reviews the novel received were generally favorable and emphasized both its thematic elements and its style. An anonymous reviewer for the *New York Times* calls the book "brilliant," and writes, "*A Clockwork Orange* is a tour-de-force in nastiness, an inventive primer in total violence, a savage satire on the distortions of the single and collective minds." The 1987 American edition carries a blurb from *Time* magazine which states, "Anthony Burgess has written what looks like a nasty little shocker, but is really that rare thing in English letters—a philosophical novel."

The novel has received its share of attention from academic critics as well. John W. Tilton, writing in *Cosmic Satire in the Contemporary Novel*, praises Burgess's use of Nadsat, saying that Burgess used it "[t]o assure the survival of the novel by creating a slang idiom for Alex that would not grow stale or outmoded as real slang does." In his study of Burgess's novels entitled *The Clockwork Universe of Anthony Burgess*, critic Richard Mathews writes that "*A Clockwork Orange* is a masterpiece as both a novel and a film."

Comparing the kind of government in the novel to "a rotten mechanical fruit," Mathews argues that Alex's "disturbed spirit may somewhere awaken our sleeping moral sensibilities." Robert O. Evans, in his essay on Burgess in *British Novelists since 1900*, considers the work "an expression of disgust and revulsion about what has happened to society in our lifetimes." In her essay, "Linguistics, Mechanics, and Metaphysics: Anthony Burgess's *A Clockwork Orange*," Esther Petix writes, "The reader is as much a flailing victim of the author as he is a victim of time's finite presence." Petix notes that, like Alex, the reader also comes of age in reading the book, and "is charged with advancement and growth."

Criticism

Chris Semansky

Semansky teaches literature and composition online. His essays, stories, and poems appear regularly in magazines and journals. In this essay, Semansky examines Burgess's narrative technique.

When we tell stories or listen to them, there is always a teller, someone describing the situation and relating the action, often commenting on it. When the person telling the story is also involved in the story, the teller is called a first-person nar-

> Even Jesus Christ can be seen as a kind of antihero, as he was an outsider who was beaten down and persecuted for beliefs he would not surrender."

rator. When novelists use such narrators, they must choose between a first-person central narrator and a first-person peripheral narrator. Both use the first-person pronoun "I," but the latter involves a narrator who, although telling the story from his or her point of view, is a minor player in the events described, often an observer of things happening to others. A first-person central narrator, on the other hand, also involves a narrator who tells the story from his or her point of view, but who is a major player in them—that is, the narrator describes events directly related to him or her. In *A Clockwork Orange*, Burgess uses a first-person central narrator, Alex, who details his violent antisocial crimes in an often humorous and intimate manner. In so doing, Burgess creates sympathy for a character who in most ways is abominable.

Alex refers to himself as "your humble narrator" or "handsome young narrator," calling attention to the reader's role, as well as his own. Often Alex addresses readers, "Oh brother," or "Oh, my brothers," asking them to share in his own reaction to events as he recalls them. This technique draws readers into the story, lessening the emotional distance between themselves and Alex. In "*A Clockwork Orange* Resucked," Burgess's introduction to the 1987 American edition of the novel, Burgess writes that he wanted to "titillate the nastier propensities of my readers." He certainly succeeds, as readers are positioned as voyeurs to the lurid and violent acts detailed. In this way, they are both shocked and intrigued by Alex's brutality. This is the same kind of fascination that readers have when reading confessions of a serial killer, or other first-person true crime stories. But Alex's story is no confession; he does not seek forgiveness. Rather, he revels in his exploits and celebrates them, and if anything, is nostalgic at the end of the novel for his violent past and diminishing violent desires. He wants readers to share this sense of loss with him, hence his appeal to them throughout the book. Readers are "brothers" because Alex assumes that at some level they share his fascination with evil and their dark side, just as he does his own. Alex's apparent scrupulous honesty in relating his tale also appeals to readers, especially in comparison to other characters such as the Minister of the Interior and P. R. Deltoid, both of whom Alex represents as manipulative, deceitful, and oppressive. Alex appears to be honest because he relates things about himself that most people would feel uncomfortable or embarrassed doing.

Readers also sympathize with Alex when he returns home from prison only to be rejected by his parents, and when he is beaten by Dim and Billyboy and cannot defend himself because of his conditioned aversion to violence. Alex's honesty, his willingness to share the details of his crimes and his thinking surrounding those crimes, his emotional vulnerability, and his role as a victim of governmental oppression, however, do not make him a hero. Rather, he is a kind of antihero. In contrast to heroes—who, according to Aristotle, are of noble birth and intentions but have a tragic flaw— antiheroes are defined by their status as outsiders who often exist in an absurd or incomprehensible universe and feel defeated and trapped in their lives. Antiheroes live on the fringes of society and often come from poor or working-class backgrounds. Readers typically feel superior towards them. Oddly, the cartoon character Charlie Brown is a kind of antihero, as he is unloved and unwanted by his "friends," and dogged by bad luck. Arthur Miller's character Willy Loman, of *Death of a Salesman,* is another antihero, in that he lives an absurd existence and can find no meaning in his life. Even Jesus Christ can be seen as a kind of antihero, as he was an outsider who was beaten down and persecuted for beliefs he would not surrender. In his study of Burgess entitled *Anthony Burgess,* critic A. A. DeVitis notes that other characteristics of antiheroes can include the character's knowledge of his or her lack of opportunity, the character's self-pity, the presence of a large ego, and a will to dominate others. Often, the antihero cannot comprehend the nature of his rebellion and struggles.

Alex makes a compelling antihero. His will to dominate is evident in his control of his droogs, especially Dim and Georgie, and in his sexual domination of women such as F. Alexander's wife and the two ten-year-old girls he meets at the record store and rapes. His parents work in a factory, and he is sufficiently "bad" enough to warrant a post-

corrective advisor provided by the state. DeVitis notes that Burgess said of Alex, he "asks little from life . . . but society has so organized things that he cannot have even this little." This is what makes Alex appealing to readers. It is almost irrelevant that the little he does ask entails beating, raping, killing, and maiming others, because he proves himself human and vulnerable at the same time. Readers pity Alex, just as he pities himself, for his inability to fully be his evil, violent self after undergoing the Ludovico Technique. Burgess scholar John J. Stinson offers another view for readers' reaction to Alex: his language. In *Anthony Burgess Revisited,* Stinson observes that because of Burgess's "linguistic inventiveness" with Nadsat, "Readers come to have ambivalent feelings only when their moral reactions, linguistically stupefied into unwatchfulness, suddenly rouse themselves and come up panting indignantly." Stinson claims that the language acts as a kind of distancing device by which readers can shield themselves from the impact of so much violence. In a *New York Times* article titled "On the Hopelessness of Turning Good Books into Films," Burgess himself said, "It is as if we were trying to read about violence in a foreign language and finding its near-incomprehensibility getting in the way of a clear image."

In *Anthony Burgess,* Samuel Coale notes another way that Burgess has made Alex a sympathetic character: by giving him an artistic consciousness. Alex not only dresses sharply and describes his fights as if they were choreographed, but he also loves classical music, especially Beethoven. For many readers, this suggests that he cannot be all bad. Coale observes:

> There are, then, at least two Alexes confronting the reader. Is he merely a clockwork automaton, a creature of his mechanized society, whose violence is merely an extension of his own boredom and sense of worthlessness? Or is he, in fact, better than his clockwork society, an artistic and intelligent person? His appreciation of music emphasizes this dichotomy.

Coale's quotation, however, tells us more about his own assumptions as to what makes a person "worthy" than it does about Alex's own actual worth. Alex is, in fact, both an effect of a "mechanized society" *and* "an artistic and intelligent person." But being artistic and intelligent does not in and of itself give a person worth. The flaw in Burgess's Manichean universe, and in Coale's reading of the apparent choice of Alexes the novel offers readers, is that a developed intellect and aesthetic sensibility are somehow valuable in themselves, without any relation to their use. There can be no real criticism of the welfare state when there are no realistic people representing its values and ideals. In the end, Alex serves as an index of sorts for readers' own ideological leanings. Their responses to him will differ according to their politics, and to their own capacity to recognize the potential for evil in themselves.

Source: Chris Semansky, Critical Essay on *A Clockwork Orange*, in *Novels for Students*, The Gale Group, 2002.

Rubin Rabinovitz

In the following essay, Rabinovitz examines ethical values in Burgess's Clockwork Orange.

In Anthony Burgess's most famous novel, *A Clockwork Orange*, the most obvious clash of values is between the lawless hero and a society that hopes to control him. This struggle obscures another conflict which is nevertheless very important: the opposing views of libertarians and authoritarians on how best to provide social controls. The theme of libertarian-authoritarian opposition recurs throughout Burgess's novels, often as a conflict between points of view Burgess has called Pelagian and Augustinian. The best exposition of this idea is given by Tristram Foxe, the protagonist of Burgess's novel *The Wanting Seed*.

Foxe (who is a history teacher) explains that Pelagianism is named for Pelagius, a monk whose teachings were condemned by the church. Pelagius argued against the doctrine of original sin and advocated the idea of human perfectibility; hence he is the patron of libertarian societies. St. Augustine, a contemporary of Pelagius, reaffirmed the doctrine of original sin; human perfectibility, he said, was possible only with God's grace. Because grace is not universally granted, there must always be sin, war, crime, and hence the need for social controls. Augustine therefore emerges as patron of the authoritarians.

Burgess often presents social history as a cyclical alternation of Pelagian and Augustinian parties which oppose one another like yin and yang. With the Augustinians in power there is a period of social stability which comes as the result of a rigidly enforced authoritarian moral code. Such controls make it appear that the populace is inherently ethical and encourage a growing faith in human perfectibility; eventually the strictness of the Augustinians seems superfluous. The populace begins to demand more freedom, libertarian arguments gain credibility, and finally there is a transition to a Pelagian form of government.

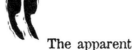 **The apparent inconsistencies in Burgess's dualistic moral views are sometimes seen as the result of his utilization of the Eastern yin-yang principles."**

The Pelagians fare no better. Their libertarianism gives way to permissiveness and then to an anarchic period of crime, strikes, and deteriorating public services. After a transitional phase, the popular outcry for more law and order heralds the rise of a new Augustinian party and the beginning of another cycle.

This issue comes up in *The Clockwork Testament*, one of Burgess's more recent novels. Enderby, the hero, is obsessed with Augustine and Pelagius and decides to write about them. He finishes a dozen pages of a film script (included in Burgess's novel) which culminate in a debate between the two, Augustine arguing in favor of the doctrine of original sin and Pelagius disagreeing. The script is never completed and, fittingly, the dispute is never settled.

In *A Clockwork Orange*, the anarchic quality of the society portrayed early in the novel indicates that Pelagian liberals are in power. Upon Alex's release from prison he finds that a broken elevator has been repaired and that the police force has been enlarged; these are signs that a more authoritarian party has taken over. But the new regime is not as strong in its authoritarianism as, for example, the Augustinian society in *The Wanting Seed*. It avoids the extremes of Augustinianism—wars and religious fanaticism—because Burgess in portraying libertarian and authoritarian parties in a society committed to an underlying Pelagian dogma is satirizing the Labor and Conservative Parties of the English Welfare State.

The new government in *A Clockwork Orange* therefore is only in a subdued way Augustinian. Its leaders, however, do indicate their lack of faith in human perfectibility by utilizing the Ludovico technique and by getting their jails ready for great numbers of political offenders. The characters in the novel who most oppose this government are naturally those who are extreme libertarians.

A principal spokesman for the libertarians is the writer F. Alexander. His book proclaims his belief in human perfectibility and free will but Alexander's histrionic prose style makes his Pelagian sentiments somewhat suspect. When a friend ascertains that it was young Alex who raped his wife, Alexander gives up his liberalism and agrees to collaborate in a plan to drive Alex to suicide. Another Pelagian character is P. R. Deltoid, Alex's rehabilitation officer. He epitomizes the libertarian belief that criminals should be reeducated and not punished; but despite Deltoid's efforts Alex remains incorrigible. "Is it some devil that crawls inside you?" Deltoid asks hardly the sort of question one would expect from a Pelagian. After learning that Alex has killed an old woman, Deltoid spits in his face: like F. Alexander, he has been reduced to a betrayal of his principles.

These failures of Pelagianism make it appear that Burgess, as some critics have maintained, favors an Augustinian point of view. But in *The Wanting Seed*, where he gives his most vivid portrayal of each type of society, Burgess seems to take the side of the Pelagians. In that novel the Pelagians undermine family life and encourage homosexuality as a form of population control; the Augustinians solve the population problem by staging pseudowars in which the participants are decimated and their flesh canned for human consumption. Even at their moral nadir, the Pelagians seem restrained when compared to the cannibalistic Augustinians.

In *Tremor of Intent* Burgess again seems to favor the Augustinian side when the views of a Pelagian scientist are satirized. Burgess's unsympathetic presentation of the scientist's views may, however, have another explanation. In *The Novel Now* he is critical of writers like H. G. Wells whose enthusiasm for technology leads them to rhapsodize over scientifically organized utopian societies. For Burgess, science deals only with external factors: it may improve living conditions, but it cannot alter the human condition. In *Tremor of Intent*, the shallowness of the scientist's arguments may be as much related to his profession as to his Pelagian beliefs.

It seems imprecise, then, to assume that Burgess consistently favors either an Augustinian or a Pelagian point of view. Similarly, those of Burgess's characters who are strongly committed to a single side in the Pelagian-Augustinian cycle fare badly. During one phase they are frustrated because they are out of power; during the next they are disappointed when their social theory fails to live up to its promise. Many of Burgess's heroes learn to change; like Alex, they begin to see how their old unilateral views fit into a cycle of interacting polar opposites. In *Tremor of Intent*, for example, the hero achieves this kind of understanding when he says, "Knowing God means also knowing his opposite. You can't get away from the great opposition."

An interaction of polar opposites in *A Clockwork Orange* emerges from Burgess's juxtaposition of the Augustinian views of Alex and the Pelagian views of F. Alexander. Many of Alex's characteristics are Augustinian: his dictatorial domination of his friends, his brutality, and his belief that criminals deserve punishment and not rehabilitation. Alex thinks that the world is wicked and does not believe in human perfectibility; F. Alexander, on the other hand, writes that man is "a creature of growth and capable of sweetness." Alexander's arguments in favor of free will indicate his Pelagianism; the connection Alex makes between evil and determined behavior recalls St. Augustine's concept of predestinarian grace. Like St. Augustine himself, Alex is redeemed after a sinful youth and, as an author, favors the confessional mode.

Many of the characteristics of Alex and F. Alexander may be resolved into examples of extremes that follow the pattern of polar antitheses: predator and victim; uncontrolled libido (rapist) and controlled libido (husband); youth and adult; man of action and man of ideas; destroyer and creator; conservative and liberal; alienated man and integrated man. The similarity of the names Alex and Alexander indicates an underlying kinship between the two which emerges if their opposing values are seen as the polar extremes of the same cycles. Alex (who comments on the similarity of the names) refers to his antagonist as "the great F. Alexander"; he himself is often called "little Alex."

The relativism resulting from this evenhanded treatment of contrasting values, however, sometimes leaves Burgess open to a charge of moral ambiguity. Burgess seems to be aware of this possibility, and in *Tremor of Intent* he tries to show that a belief in his cyclical system need not lead to a weakened moral stance. Here, an important ethical criterion is the degree of commitment to the cyclical system itself. Life and reality are expressed in polar oppositions which alternate cyclically; a commitment to the cyclical system, then, is tantamount to a commitment to life and reality. For Hillier, the hero of *Tremor of Intent*, an involvement with the cyclical system is the beginning of moral behavior. Those who ignore the cyclical system or attempt to disengage themselves from it—Hillier calls them "neutrals"—are guilty of immoral behavior which may be extremely destructive because, deceptively, it seems innocuous.

Hillier concludes that the neutrals are morally inferior to evildoers: the wicked are at least morally committed, albeit to a polar extreme which Hillier (recently ordained a priest) opposes. "If we're going to save the world," he says, "we shall have to use unorthodox methods. Don't you think we'd all rather see devil-worship than bland neutrality?"

The superiority of evildoers to neutrals is perhaps a reason for Alex's redemption in the original version of *A Clockwork Orange*. Alex is firmly committed to evil: he enjoys a sadistic fantasy in which he helps to crucify Christ, and, in a discussion of goodness, calls himself a patron of "the other shop." The neutrals are the scientists who destroy Alex's freedom of choice by administering the Ludovico technique. Dr. Brodsky, for example, cares little about the ethical questions raised by the treatment: "We are not concerned with motive, with the higher ethics. We are concerned only with cutting down crime." Alex—one would think he had little right to throw stones—calls Brodsky and his fellow scientists "an evil lot of bastards," and complains that their use of Beethoven's music in the treatment is "a filthy unforgivable sin." Burgess apparently feels that science lends itself easily to the neutrality he detests; though Alex is often beaten in the novel and once driven to attempt suicide, this is the only place where he moralizes about his oppressors.

There are a number of reasons why Burgess considers the scientists who rob a man of his capacity for ethical choice morally inferior to the criminals they treat. In Christian terms, Alex as a sinner must be permitted to enhance the possibilities for his salvation by choosing good over evil. A man rendered incapable of moral choice can never attain salvation; but a sinner may choose to repent and win redemption.

In terms of Burgess's cyclical system, Alex in his youth may be predestined to do evil; but with maturity comes freedom, when his determined phase is transformed into its polar opposite. The Ludovico treatment, invented by ethical neutrals, forces its victims to become neutral; it removes

What Do I Read Next?

- Like *A Clockwork Orange*, Aldous Huxley's *Brave New World* (1939) and George Orwell's *1984* (1949) explore what a future dystopian society might look like.

- Burgess's novel, *The Wanting Seed* (1962), published the same year as *A Clockwork Orange*, looks at a dystopian society dealing with overpopulation and food shortages. Critics often compare the novel to Orwell's *1984*.

- B. F. Skinner's novel *Walden 2* (1948) attempts to show how it is possible to build a good community based on positive reinforcement of good behavior. Burgess's novel can be seen as a critique of Skinner's ideas.

- In 1971, Thomas Churchill interviewed Burgess for the *Malahat Review* (Vol. 17). In this interview, Burgess discusses a range of subjects including his novels *A Clockwork Orange*, *Enderby*, and *Nothing Like the Sun*.

- In a 1972 issue of *Transatlantic Review* (Vol. 42–43), Carol Dix interviews Burgess about the film version of *A Clockwork Orange*, and Burgess discusses a range of subjects including his plans for future novels.

them from the cyclical process and prevents their transition into a mature phase. The neutralizing treatment turns Alex into a perpetual victim whose weakness provokes violence in those who encounter him. But when Alex's ability to choose is restored he finally grows tired of violence, and reforms.

Burgess's moral point of view, however, still seems ambiguous. The neutrals, both in *Tremor of Intent* and in *A Clockwork Orange*, are given rather small roles; and in his zeal to condemn the neutrals Burgess seems to be condoning criminal behavior. It was perhaps with this problem in mind that Burgess made the following comment in an article entitled, appropriately enough, "The Manicheans":

The novelist's need to be adventurous, to pose problems, to shock into attention, is bound to lead him to ground perilous for the faithful. And there is something in the novelist's vocation which predisposes him to a kind of a Manicheeism. What the religious novelist often seems to be saying is that evil is a kind of good, since it is an aspect of Ultimate Reality; though what he is really saying is that evil is more interesting to write about than good.

It may be that Burgess is speaking of himself; like Milton writing *Paradise Lost*, Burgess may occasionally be distracted by aesthetically interesting wickedness. But this hardly explains Hillier's enthusiasm for devil-worship, an endorsement which perhaps makes him unique among even the most liberal of modern clergymen.

The apparent inconsistencies in Burgess's dualistic moral views are sometimes seen as the result of his utilization of the Eastern yin-yang principles. Yin and yang may be expressed in morally relevant categories like good and evil, or in categories like hot and cold which have no moral connotations: such a view can lead to moral relativism. The Christian idea of an omnipotent, benevolent God, on the other hand, implies a belief in the superiority of good over evil and leads to moral absolutism.

In an attempt to make use of the Eastern yin-yang idea as well as elements of Christian belief from his background, Burgess has turned to Manichaeism, an eclectic religion which flourished both in the Orient and in the West. Manichaeism incorporates a number of Christian doctrines; moreover, one of its central ideas is a dualistic opposition both in nature (light and darkness) and in ethics (good and evil) which in some ways resembles the opposition of yin and yang. Very often, Burgess's use of Manichean dualism does work to reconcile differences in Eastern and Western thought; but problems arise when a choice must be made between relativism and absolutism. In Eastern terms, where a thing may be seen as both itself and its opposite, such a choice may not be necessary; but to a Westerner, part-time absolutism is self-contradictory. Absolutism seems to demand absolute fidelity, and in this sense Burgess's moral point of view appears ambiguous or inconsistent.

In places Burgess seems to be an absolutist; in others, a relativist. *A Clockwork Orange*, for example, seems to be dominated by moral relativism when one examines the values of Alex and F. Alexander in the light of the yin-yang principles. But this apparent inconsistency is at times explained by another conflict, a struggle between the individual and the state. Here Burgess makes no attempt to maintain the balance of the yin-yang principles: he is vehemently on the side of the individual.

An emphasis on individualism becomes apparent after a series of symmetrical events in which many of the characters who have been abused by Alex find him helpless and avenge themselves. The revenge is no harsher than the act which provoked it, but an important difference does emerge: though the state condemns Alex's brutal crimes, it sanctions and encourages the avengers' brutality—even though it has already exacted its own vengeance in the form of a prison term. For Burgess, society's brutality is more threatening than the individual's; its power is inhuman, enormous, and unrestrained. Burgess, commenting on *A Clockwork Orange*, has indicated that he meant to encourage a comparison between Alex's brutality and society's: "The violence in the book is really more to show what the State can do with it."

Alex is an enemy of the state and, as he predicts early on, the state will attempt to destroy not only what is evil in him but also his individuality: "The not-self cannot have the bad, meaning they of the government and the judges and the schools cannot allow the bad because they cannot allow the self. And is not our modern history, my brothers, the story of brave malenky selves fighting these big machines?" Unlike Alex, whose violence is subdued when he outgrows the role of clockwork man, the state remains a machine, always inhuman and conscienceless in its violence.

The hero of *The Wanting Seed*, like Alex, learns that it is unwise to trust the state: "he that saw whatever government was in power he would always be against it." And Burgess himself takes the same stand: "My political views are mainly negative: I lean towards anarchy: I hate the State. I loathe and abominate that costly, crass, intolerant, inefficient, eventually tyrannical machine which seeks more and more to supplant the individual." Like Alex, Burgess sees the state as an evil mechanism against which individual humans must defend themselves.

It becomes clear, then, that Burgess's moral values are far less ambiguous than they first appear. When he is speaking in his own voice, Burgess reacts to youthful violence with a conventional sense of dismay. If this tone had been introduced in *A Clockwork Orange*, the novel could easily have become polemical. Without redeeming qualities, the morally repulsive Alex would be a cardboard villain; and similarly the ethically attractive qualities of F. Alexander must be balanced by a personality which is, like his prose style, devoid of grace. Nor is the effect of these characterizations unrealistic; a charming psychopath usually makes a better impression than a righteous neurotic. In this fashion Burgess's system leads to the creation of characters who are round in E. M. Forster's sense.

Burgess's cyclical system works best when it is applied to the subject which concerns him the most, human individuality. Here it becomes a useful metaphor for portraying psychological complexity, for delineating the unpredictability of human beings responding to conflicting urges.

Burgess has indicated that he feels these conflicts within himself just as he observes them in others. One might make a comparison between Burgess the young composer and Alex the music-lover, or between Burgess the middle-aged novelist and the writer F. Alexander. Like Anthony Burgess, F. Alexander has written a book called *A Clockwork Orange*; and Alex, who tells his own story, is in a sense also the author of a book with the same title. Burgess is hinting that he detects within his own personality elements of both characters, that they form a yin-yang opposition which he sees within himself. But if he indicts himself, Burgess also invites the reader to examine his own capacity for playing the roles of both Alex and F. Alexander.

Source: Rubin Rabinovitz, "Ethical Values in Burgess's *A Clockwork Orange*," in *Studies in the Novel*, Vol. 11, No. 1, Spring 1979, pp. 43–50.

Rubin Rabinovitz

In the following essay, Rabinovitz explores the dichotomies that coexist within the protagonist in Burgess's Clockwork Orange.

In his most famous novel, *A Clockwork Orange*, Anthony Burgess explores a number of interesting issues such as free will, the meaning of violence, and a cyclical theory of history. Resolving these issues, however, is complicated by an extraneous factor: the American editions of the novel lack Burgess' original conclusion and end with what is the penultimate chapter of the first English edition.

A good summary of the deleted section is provided by Burgess himself:

> In the final chapter of the British edition, Alex is already growing up. He has a new gang, but he's tired of leading it; what he really wants is to have a son of his own—the libido is being tamed and turned

> For Alex, life has aspects both of determinism and free will, line and circle, clockwork and orange."

social—and the first thing he now has to do is to find a mate, which means sexual love, not the old in and out.

The hero's abrupt decision to turn away from his old pattern of violence has caused some unrest among Burgess' critics. Shirley Chew, writing in *Encounter* feels that with Alex's fantasy of domestic life "the novel loses its integrity and falls into the sentimental." The ending, Chew says, makes it appear that Burgess condones and even shares the hero's taste for violence. And A. A. DeVitis, author of a recent study of Burgess' fiction, says that the last chapter was "wisely omitted from the American edition."

The American publisher, like Shirley Chew, felt that the last chapter was too sentimental; but Burgess has defended the original conclusion:

> When they were going to publish it in America, they said "we're tougher over here" and thought the ending too soft for their readers. If it was me now, faced with the decision I'd say no. I still believe in my ending.

On the face of it, publisher and critics seem right: the novel did enjoy better sales in America than in England, and Stanley Kubrick chose to use the shortened American edition for his film version of the book. But the original ending is not as sentimental as it first appears; there is truth, even poetic justice, in the idea of yesterday's reprobate changing diapers for his own neophyte reprobate.

If Alex remains violent, as he does in the American version, the reader's attitude towards him is mainly one of condemnation; but Burgess' inquiry into the origins of violence requires a hero who cannot be so easily condemned and dismissed. The original version in a sense provides the less sentimental ending if Alex is transformed from a monster into an ordinary human being with whom the reader can identify. Obdurate Alex is a threat to safety; Alex reformed threatens moral complacency, by suggesting that a love of violence is universal.

Regardless of which ending one prefers, Burgess wrote his novel assuming that it would appear intact, and it deserves to be considered in the complete version. As it turns out, many of his ideas are clarified when the last chapter is restored. An example is Burgess' treatment of the theme of freedom and determinism. Burgess appears in *A Clockwork Orange* to disapprove of the Ludovico technique (a scientific process for forcing criminals to reform); the loss of free will seems to be too great a price to pay. But if this is true, and if Burgess shares the point of view of the Chaplain and F. Alexander who oppose the Ludovico technique for similar reasons, it is unclear why Burgess portrays these characters in a sardonic fashion.

The novel's final statement about free will comes in the deleted chapter, when Alex says that in his youth he had not been free but determined. In his violent phase, he says, he had been

> one of these malenky toys you viddy being sold in the streets, like little chellovecks made out of tin and with a spring inside and then a winding handle on the outside and you wind it up grrr grrr grrr and off it itties, like walking, O my brothers. But it itties in a straight line and bangs straight into things bang bang and it cannot help what it is doing. Being young is like being like one of these malenky machines.

The young are like clockwork men; their proclivity towards violence is built into them. His son, Alex says, will also go through a violent phase, and Alex "would not be able to really stop him. And nor would he be able to stop his own son, brothers."

Alex concludes that there is a cycle of recurring phases in which each young man undergoes a period of existence as a violent, mechanical man; then he matures, gets greater freedom of choice, and his violence subsides. The cycle, says Alex, will go on forever: "and so it would itty on to like the end of the world, round and round and round . . . " The circularity of the repeating pattern leads Alex to compare the progress of generations to an image of God turning a dirty, smelly orange in his hands, "old Bog Himself (by courtesy of Korova Milkbar) turning and turning and turning a vonny grahzny orange in his gigantic rookers." The determined progress of the clockwork man, who must move in a straight line, is thus contrasted with the circular shape and movement of God's orange, symbol of life and organic growth. The "vonny grahzny" orange is also like the world, which on the same page is called "grahzny vonny." For Alex, life has aspects both of determinism and free will, line and circle, clockwork and orange.

Burgess used similar line-circle imagery in *The Wanting Seed*, which was published in the same year as *A Clockwork Orange*. In both novels, determinism and mechanical progress are associated with lines, while freedom and organic growth are associated with circles. Reality for Burgess often emerges from the interaction of contrary principles like these; in *A Clockwork Orange* Alex's linear, determined youth is contrasted with his freedom in maturity when he decides to marry, have a child, and give up his violence. But the cycle continues, and paradoxically Alex's freedom will lead him to have a child who once more will be subjected to the deterministic phase of the process.

By the end of the novel, Alex is mature enough to deal with this paradox. Troubled as he is by the idea that his son will be violent, he remains resolute in his desire to have children. The growth of Burgess' heroes is often indicated by their willingness to accept life and the mixed bag of contradictory values it offers.

The sense that Alex has accepted life is enforced when he finally answers the question which introduces each part of the novel and which is repeated eleven times: "What's it going to be then, eh?" Initially the question seems only to be about what sort of drink to order, but as it recurs it acquires existential overtones. The answer finally comes towards the end of the deleted chapter:

> But first of all, brothers there was this vesch of finding some devotchka or other who would be a mother to this son. I would have to start on that tomorrow, I kept thinking. That was something like new to do. That was something I would have to get started on, a new like chapter beginning. That's what it's going to be then, brothers . . .

The question is answered just after Alex sees himself as a participant in the historical cycle and his life as a microcosmic version of the cycle. He has understood that history grows out of the struggle of opposing forces and has accepted a similar clash of contradictory urges in his own personality.

Alex's ideas suggest that Burgess has been influenced by Hegel's theory of history; and some of the characters in his other novels (like the history teacher who is the protagonist of *The Long Day Wanes*) actually discuss Hegel's theory Burgess' system, however, differs in a number of respects from Hegel's. In the Hegelian dialectic, the opposition of thesis and antithesis produces a synthesis which resembles the stages that preceded it, but which is also different in some ways from these stages. The new element in the synthesis leads to the idea—very important in Hegelian thought—that progress comes with the dialectical historical cycle.

Burgess' theory denies this idea of progress. His system posits two antithetical, alternating stages; the third stage is actually only a repetition of the first. In this system, innovations are never permanent; the changes in one era are undone by a regressive process in the next, so there can be no true historical progress.

The idea that history repeats itself and the pessimistic outlook which it engenders may come from Toynbee or Spengler, whose cyclical theories of history were in vogue when Burgess was a student. Vico, whom Burgess mentions in his Joyce criticism, may also be a source. Burgess calls himself a Manichean, and he often takes a dualistic Manichean view of contending moral forces.

Another important source of Burgess' theory is the opposition of yin and yang principles in Chinese philosophy. Burgess refers to the yin-yang in his autobiographical first novel, *A Vision of Battlements*, and in a number of essays. According to Robert Morris, the yin-yang principles help to explain the historical dilemma of Crabbe, the hero of *The Long Day Wanes*:

> The East, as Burgess sees it, is both active and passive, containing the principles of yin-yang, humming at both poles of the dialectic at once. It is a phenomenon alien to the West, which, nurtured on Hegelian propositions, submits to the certainty of either cyclical or lineal progression.

Morris' comment is useful for understanding how yin and yang are related to dichotomies in *A Clockwork Orange* such as line and circle, organism and mechanism, and determinism and free will.

Burgess feels that it is his work as an artist to portray conflicting elements which eventually blend into a single confluent entity. In *Urgent Copy*, a collection of reviews and essays, he gives an example: impressed by the juxtaposition of Spanish and British cultures in Gibraltar, he composed a symphony in which disparate themes relating to these cultures clash initially but ultimately harmonize. The symphony was written before any of his novels, and this process of juxtaposing conflicting values provided him with a method he later used in his writing. A good discussion of how this principle works elsewhere in Burgess' *oeuvre* may be found in Thomas LeClair's study of his fiction.

Burgess, then, follows the yin-yang principles in understanding change as a clash and interaction of opposed values which can lead either to chaos or to harmony. In the concluding essay of *Urgent Copy*, he explains that, though one would like to live by a single set of values, reality is most often apprehended in sets of opposing values like good and evil, white and black, rich and poor. Politicians and theologians, who claim they can find unity in merging these values, actually offer either promises (a classless society, for example) or intangibles (God, metaphysical ideas). Only a work of art, says Burgess, can achieve a synthesis of opposites which presents an immediate vision of unity, Obviously, *A Clockwork Orange* is meant to serve as an example of the sort of work that can truly reconcile opposing values.

Source: Rubin Rabinovitz, "Mechanism vs. Organism: Anthony Burgess's *A Clockwork Orange*," in *Modern Fiction Studies*, Vol. 24, No. 4, Winter 1978–1979, pp. 538–41.

Sources

"Books of the Times," in *New York Times*, March 19, 1963.

Burgess, Anthony, *A Clockwork Orange*, Ballantine Books, 1988.

———, *A Clockwork Orange*, W. W. Norton, 1987.

———, "Introduction: *A Clockwork Orange* Resucked," in *A Clockwork Orange*, W. W. Norton, 1987.

———, "On the Hopelessness of Turning Good Books into Films," in *New York Times*, April 20, 1975, pp. 14–15.

Coale, Samuel, *Anthony Burgess*, Frederick Ungar Publishing Co., 1981.

DeVitis, A. A., *Anthony Burgess*, Twayne Publishers, Inc., 1972.

Evans, Robert O., "The Nouveau Roman, Russian Dystopias, and Anthony Burgess," in *British Novelists Since 1900*, edited by Jack I. Biles, AMS Press, 1987, pp. 253–66.

Mathews, Richard, *The Clockwork Universe of Anthony Burgess*, The Borgo Press, 1978.

Petix, Esther, "Linguistics, Mechanics, and Metaphysics: Anthony Burgess's *A Clockwork Orange*," in *Critical Essays on Anthony Burgess*, edited by Geoffrey Aggeler, G. K. Hall, 1986, pp. 121–31.

Rabinovitz, Rubin, "Ethical Values in Burgess's *A Clockwork Orange*," in *Studies in the Novel*, Vol. 11, No. 1, Spring, 1979, pp. 43–50.

———, "Mechanism vs. Organism: Anthony Burgess' *A Clockwork Orange*," in *Modern Fiction Studies*, Vol. 24, No. 4, Winter 1978, pp. 538–41.

Stinson, John J., *Anthony Burgess Revisited*, Twayne Publishers, 1991.

Tilton, John, *Cosmic Satire in the Contemporary Novel*, Bucknell University Press, 1977.

Further Reading

Aggeler, Geoffrey, *Anthony Burgess: The Artist as Novelist*, University of Alabama Press, 1979.

> Aggeler examines Burgess's books thematically. Burgess read and commented on Aggeler's book as it was being written.

Burgess, Anthony, *Little Wilson and Big God*, Weidenfeld & Nicolson, 1987.

> Burgess's autobiography is entertaining and illuminating, and well worth reading. He discusses his attitudes towards the reception both of his novel, *A Clockwork Orange*, and its film adaptation.

Hammer, Stephanie Barbe, "Conclusion: Resistance, Metaphysics, and the Aesthetics of Failure in Modern Criminal Literature," in *The Sublime Crime: Fascination, Failure and Form in Literature of the Enlightenment*, Southern Illinois University Press, 1994, pp. 154–74.

> Hammer discusses *A Clockwork Orange* as an example of criminal literature.

Pritchard, William H., "The Novels of Anthony Burgess," in *Massachusetts Review*, Vol. 7, No. 3. Summer 1996.

> Pritchard explores the reader's feelings towards Alex and notes the novel's ability to almost make the reader feel relieved when Alex returns to his violent self.

Tilton, John, *Cosmic Satire in the Contemporary Novel*, Bucknell University Press, 1977.

> Tilton's chapter on *A Clockwork Orange* explores the novel's main theme of free choice and suggests that Alex illustrates the belief that moral oppression violates individual civil rights as well as spiritual existence.

The Country of the Pointed Firs

Sarah Orne Jewett

1896

The Country of the Pointed Firs (1896) is considered by many critics to be the masterpiece of Sarah Orne Jewett, one of the greatest "local color" writers of the nineteenth century. Jewett wrote stories and novels set in coastal fishing and shipbuilding towns of her native Maine. As in many of Jewett's stories, *The Country of the Pointed Firs* addresses themes of nostalgia, memory, and storytelling, as well as community, family, and friendship. Her character sketches of the aging population of seamen and the widows of seamen are inflected with the local Maine dialect, which she captured with accuracy and liveliness. In recent years, Jewett's works have been praised for their strong, independent, elderly female characters, of which her greatest creation is Mrs. Todd in *The Country of the Pointed Firs*.

In *The Country of the Pointed Firs*, the unnamed narrator is a writer from Boston who has rented a room for the summer in the home of Mrs. Todd in the fictional town of Dunnet Landing, Maine. Throughout the summer, the narrator is captivated by the quaint community of Dunnet Landing, populated by the elderly men and women of the declining shipping industry. Most of the people she meets are between the ages of sixty and ninety, and they all have stories to tell about the town, the sea, and the families who inhabit their tiny community.

Sarah Orne Jewett

Author Biography

Theodora Sarah Orne Jewett was born September 3, 1849, in South Berwick, a shipbuilding town inland from the Maine coast. Jewett suffered from arthritis as a girl and attended school only sporadically because of her ill health. Her real education came from her father, a doctor who often brought the young Jewett along with him on medical visits throughout the countryside. From these experiences, Jewett learned the art of detailed character observation. Her father also encouraged her to read the great works of American and European literature. At the age of sixteen she graduated from Berwick Academy.

Jewett's first story was published in a magazine when she was nineteen. Her real success began in 1869 when she was twenty, with the publication of one of her stories in the *Atlantic Monthly*. Her early stories were published under the pseudonyms Alice Eliot, A. D. Eliot, and Sarah C. Sweet. The *Atlantic Monthly* did not accept another of her stories until a few years later, when her work caught the attention of *Atlantic Monthly* editor and novelist William Dean Howells, who subsequently published many of her works. Howells encouraged Jewett to collect her published stories in her first

book *Deephaven* (1877), named after the fictional town in which her tales were set.

In 1878, Jewett's father, her closest companion, died. The deep friendship Jewett had enjoyed with her father was replaced in 1880 by what became a lifelong companionship with Annie Fields. For the next twenty-nine years, Jewett and Fields enjoyed a relationship, which at the time was termed a "Boston marriage"—the two women lived, traveled, and entertained together. Jewett divided her time between living in Boston with Fields and staying in her childhood home in South Berwick, where she wrote prolifically. Jewett and Fields traveled throughout Europe on four different occasions. They developed a wide circle of friends, including many of the notable American and European literary figures of the day, such as Henry James, Rudyard Kipling, Christina Rossetti, and Mark Twain.

Throughout her life, Jewett published many stories in *Harper's*, *Century*, and the *Atlantic Monthly*. Her short story collections include *Old Friends and New* (1879), *Country By-Ways* (1881), *A White Heron and Other Stories* (1886), and *A Native of Winby and Other Tales* (1893). Her novel *The Country of the Pointed Firs* (1896), indisputably Jewett's masterpiece, was hailed at the time as a mature work demonstrating the culmination of the author's literary development over nearly thirty years of publication. Jewett wrote three other novels: *A Country Doctor* (1884), *A Marsh Island* (1885), and *The Tory Lover* (1901).

In 1902, Jewett's life was forever changed when, on her fifty-third birthday, she fell from a carriage, suffering head and spinal injuries. Jewett never fully recovered, mentally or physically, from these injuries. Although she continued to entertain visitors and write personal letters, Jewett ceased writing professionally at this point. Jewett died on June 24, 1909, from a brain hemorrhage that followed a stroke.

Plot Summary

Mrs. Todd

The narrator of *The Country of the Pointed Firs* is a writer from the city who has decided to spend her summer in the small coastal town of Dunnet Landing, Maine. She has rented a room in the home of Mrs. Todd, a woman in her sixties who serves as the local herbalist, offering herbal remedies to help heal the physical and emotional ailments of the local community. Mrs. Todd, however, is on friendly terms with the local doctor, as they both understand the importance of each other's role in the community. Mrs. Todd spends most of her days out gathering various herbs and plants to create the concoctions that she sells from her home.

The narrator has come to Dunnet Landing because she has a long piece of writing to complete by the end of the summer, but she is soon distracted by the goings-on in Mrs. Todd's house. She is expected to act as store clerk, selling Mrs. Todd's remedies from her doorstep while Mrs. Todd is out gathering herbs. The narrator soon realizes that she is not getting any writing done because of this activity, and rents out an old abandoned schoolhouse nearby as a place she can go to write.

Captain Littlepage

One day while the narrator is writing at the schoolhouse, Captain Littlepage, an old seaman in his eighties, stops in and proceeds to tell her a long story. He explains that he was retired from the sea sooner than he had wanted because of the wreck of a ship he was commanding. He describes the circumstance of the wreck, which left the few survivors stranded in a remote location near the North Pole. While waiting for a supply ship to carry him home, Captain Littlepage stayed in the cabin of an old Scottish seaman named Gaffett. Captain Littlepage tells the narrator the story told him by Gaffett.

Gaffett told Captain Littlepage of a shipwreck off the Greenland coast that happened many years earlier, and which only he and two other men survived. In a small boat they took from the wrecked ship, Gaffett and the men sailed further north into uncharted regions. There they discovered what appeared to be a town inhabited by people, but when Gaffett and the men stepped ashore, the town seemed to disappear, and the inhabitants appeared as ghosts. Captain Littlepage explains that Gaffett believed these creatures to be ghosts, or in a "kind of waiting-place" between life and death. Littlepage tells the narrator that he is the only person alive who still knows this story, as Gaffett has probably died.

Green Island

One day, Mrs. Todd takes the narrator out in a boat to Green Island, an outer island where Mrs. Todd's eighty-six-year-old mother lives with Mrs. Todd's brother, William. The narrator finds Mrs. Todd's mother, Mrs. Blackett, delightful, and ob-

Media Adaptations

- *The Country of the Pointed Firs* was recorded on audiotape in 1982 by Jimcin Recordings, read by Cindy Hardin, and distributed by Books on Tape.

serves that mother and daughter are very fond of one another. Mrs. Blackett invites them in for tea. William, who is about sixty, is very shy of meeting people and stays away from the house at first, but eventually comes in and is introduced to the narrator. The narrator takes a walk with William. Later, she takes a walk with Mrs. Todd, who tells the narrator that the man she married, Nathan Todd, now deceased, was not the man she loved. After a pleasant meal with Mrs. Blackett, the narrator and Mrs. Todd sail back to the coast.

Poor Joanna

One day, Mrs. Fosdick, an old friend of Mrs. Todd, comes from out of town to visit. The narrator finds Mrs. Fosdick to be enchanting company and the three women sit together for hours, discussing local gossip from decades earlier. Mrs. Fosdick and Mrs. Todd tell the narrator the story of a woman they refer to as "poor Joanna," long since dead. As a young woman, Joanna was treated badly by a man who used her and then ran off, never to be seen or heard of again. In shame, Joanna chose to move out to a small, uninhabited island off the coast, where she lived alone and never left for the remainder of her life. Various members of the local community stopped by her island occasionally to bring her food and supplies as gifts, but she remained reclusive throughout the many years she lived there.

Mrs. Todd explains that she sailed one day to the island with a pastor to visit Joanna and bring her a gift. The pastor was insensitive to Joanna's situation, but after the two women sent him out to walk around the island, Joanna confessed to Mrs. Todd that she had "committed the ultimate sin." (Exactly what she meant by this is not specifically indicated.) Later, the narrator asks a local seaman to take her in his boat to Joanna's long-since-deserted island.

The Bowden Family Reunion

Late in the summer, the narrator travels by carriage with Mrs. Todd and Mrs. Blackett to a large reunion of the Bowden family, to whom they are related. The narrator is very pleased by the people she meets at the reunion, and is happy to see that both Mrs. Todd and Mrs. Blackett enjoy themselves immensely. The narrator notes that there are many close ties among people at the reunion, although they see each other only once or twice a year. Mrs. Blackett, in particular, is clearly well-loved by everyone.

Elija Tilley

Walking along the shore near the end of summer, the narrator comes upon Elijah Tilley, an old seaman, who invites her to his cabin for a visit. Tilley talks with great sadness about the loss of his beloved wife, Sarah, who died eight years earlier. He explains that he never wants to remarry, and that he is content living by himself with the memory of his wife.

Goodbyes

At summer's end, the narrator leaves Dunnet Landing to return to her home in the city. Mrs. Todd dispenses with emotional partings and simply tells the narrator she is going out for a walk and will not be on shore to see her off.

Characters

Mrs. Blackett

Eighty-six-year-old Mrs. Blackett is Mrs. Todd's mother. She lives on Green Island with her son William. Mrs. Blackett is very lively, as well as extremely healthy and active for her age. The narrator meets Mrs. Blackett for the first time on Green Island, where the elderly lady shows a warm, comfortable hospitality that quickly dispenses with formality, and she treats her new acquaintance like an old friend. Mrs. Blackett enjoys teasing her sixty-seven-year-old daughter by treating Mrs. Todd as if she were the frailer of the two. Mrs. Blackett comes to shore toward the end of the novel to attend the Bowden family reunion. She is clearly a great favorite among many people and the narra-

tor refers to her as a "queen" because of her much favored status in the community.

William Blackett

William Blackett, who is about sixty years old, is Mrs. Todd's younger brother. He lives on Green Island with his mother, Mrs. Blackett. William is very shy of people, especially women, and stays away when the narrator first lands on the island. Eventually, however, he comes in to meet the narrator. Later, William takes the narrator for a walk on the island, showing her a lookout point that he describes as the most beautiful view in the world. The narrator is quite certain the island is the only place in the world he has ever been. At the Blackett home, the narrator learns that William loves to sing. On the day of the Bowden family reunion, William does not show up because of his extreme shyness, even with his own extended family.

Mrs. Susan Fosdick

Susan Fosdick is an old friend of Mrs. Todd, who visits her from out of town. The narrator is apprehensive at first that Mrs. Fosdick, an unknown guest, will be joining the household for a time, but, upon meeting Mrs. Fosdick, she immediately likes her. Mrs. Fosdick talks of old gossip with Mrs. Todd, while the narrator listens. She brings up the story of "poor Joanna," which the narrator finds very sad and intriguing.

Captain Littlepage

Captain Littlepage is an old retired sea captain who stops by the schoolhouse to talk with the narrator one afternoon. At first, she finds his talk dull, but eventually becomes engrossed in the story he tells of a shipwreck he experienced, which left him stranded at a remote missionary station near the North Pole. There he met an old seaman named Gaffett, who told him a mysterious story of his own shipwreck years earlier. Captain Littlepage tells Gaffett's story of discovering a mysterious village in uncharted territory in the North Pole region, in which the inhabitants seemed to be ghosts, or creatures in a waiting-place between life and death. Captain Littlepage tells the narrator that he believes he is now the only living person who knows of Gaffett's discovery.

The Narrator

The unnamed narrator of *The Country of the Pointed Firs* is a writer from the city, perhaps Boston, who has decided to stay the summer in the small coastal town of Dunnet Landing, Maine, to complete a long writing task. She is frequently distracted from her writing, however, by the local inhabitants who seek her out and tell her their stories. While in Dunnet Landing, she rents a room in the home of Mrs. Todd, the local herbalist. Mrs. Todd includes her in a variety of excursions and visits that acquaint the narrator with the aging inhabitants of the town and the tales they have to tell about themselves and other members of the community. Mrs. Todd takes the narrator to visit her mother and brother on Green Island, introduces her to Mrs. Fosdick, and brings her along to a large family reunion. At the end of the summer the narrator leaves Dunnet Landing, taking with her a sense of the nostalgia, loss, and loneliness that characterizes the aging population of this shipping village. She also, however, has enjoyed the vitality, strong sense of community, and storytelling skills of these people, who she probably will never see again.

Elijah Tilley

Elijah Tilley is an old seaman whom the narrator encounters one day near the end of her stay in Dunnet Landing. He invites the narrator to visit him in his small cabin, where he tells her about his deceased wife, Sarah, who died eight years earlier. Tilley's life still revolves around his happy memories of his wife, almost as if she were still alive.

Mrs. Almira Todd

Mrs. Almira Todd is the local herbalist of Dunnet Landing. She spends her days gathering plants, flowers, and herbs, from which she brews various remedies for the emotional and physical ailments of the local population. Mrs. Todd and the local medical doctor, however, are amicable with one another, as they both understand the importance of each other's role in the community. The narrator rents a room in Mrs. Todd's house for the summer and spends much of her time with Mrs. Todd over the course of the summer. Mrs. Todd is the narrator's entry into the local community; she introduces her to various people, tells her about the local inhabitants, and takes her on various excursions. On a walk one day, Mrs. Todd tells the narrator that the man she married, Nathan Todd, was not the man she really loved. Although she never reveals who this true love was, she explains that he, too, married someone else. Another time, Mrs. Todd takes the narrator in a sailboat to meet her mother and brother, who live on an island. When Mrs. Todd's old friend Mrs. Fosdick visits, the narrator is again made privy to important stories about people who

once lived in Dunnet Landing. Toward the end of the narrator's stay, Mrs. Todd takes her to the Bowden family reunion.

Themes

Community

Community is one of the central themes of *The Country of the Pointed Firs*. The entire novel focuses on the narrator's description of the tiny community of Dunnet Landing. As the central character, Mrs. Todd functions as a touchstone by which the narrator is able to perceive the lines that interconnect the individual members of the community. The narrator meets or hears of many members of the community through Mrs. Todd, and learns of their relationships to one another. Although most of the people she meets—all of them over the age of sixty and either widowed or widowers—seem to lead generally solitary lives, the strong community ties that hold Dunnet Landing together are clearly indicated.

The Bowden family reunion demonstrates most powerfully the strong communal ties among the town's citizens. The lines between family and community are in fact blurred, as a wide network of people turn out to be related to each other through ties of both blood and marriage. Thus, the Bowden family reunion is more like a town gathering. The narrator also observes that, although the various members of the family and town live on remote farms or islands and may only see each other once a year, the bonds of affection and shared memory maintain a sense of interconnection that transcends geographical distance. Mrs. Blackett, for instance, who lives on a remote island and rarely comes ashore, turns out to be the "queen" of the reunion, sharing strong affections with everyone at the gathering. There is a poignancy to the narrator's portrayal of this community because it represents a disappearing segment of Maine culture.

Storytelling

The narrative of *The Country of the Pointed Firs* consists of a series of encounters the narrator has with various town members who proceed to disclose to her long stories of their pasts. It becomes clear that the stories these characters tell are stories they have told many times before to many people. As the narrator returns from her encounters with each of these characters and relates the stories to Mrs. Todd, Mrs. Todd nods knowingly,

Topics For Further Study

- Jewett is considered one of the best American regional writers of the nineteenth century. Other important American regional, or local color, writers include Harriet Beecher Stowe, Bret Harte, Mark Twain, and Willa Cather. Research and write an essay about one of these writers and her or his major works. How would you describe this author's literary style? What major themes are treated in the author's works?

- Jewett was known for her accurate and endearing portrayals of the Maine coast and its inhabitants. Several notable painters from Maine have depicted their own visions of the landscape and inhabitants of Maine, including Winslow Homer, Edward Hopper, and Andrew Wyeth. Write an essay about one of these artists and his major works. How would you describe his style of painting? What does he convey about the landscape and people of Maine through this visual medium? Pick one of this artist's paintings to discuss in detail.

- In *The Country of the Pointed Firs*, Jewett describes a large community event, skillfully por-

traying the general sense of the event while paying attention to the details of character interaction. Write a description of a large community or family event that you have attended, such as a wedding, family reunion, or holiday celebration. What were the important events of the day? What were some of the significant interactions between various members at this event? What was your own experience of the event?

- The stories told by the local inhabitants in *The Country of the Pointed Firs* may be categorized as oral history—tales passed down from one generation to the next through oral, rather than written, storytelling. It is often valuable to record in written form the oral histories of elderly people in their community or family. Think of a story that has been told within your own family or community and write it down the way you recall it having been told. You may want to ask someone to tell the story again, or ask about stories you have not yet heard. Why do you think it is important to preserve this story in written form?

---

indicating that she herself has heard all of these stories before. Jewett thus explores the theme of storytelling as it relates to community, friendship, and personal identity. That is, *The Country of the Pointed Firs* is in part a tale about the role played by storytelling in the lives of individuals, in their relationships to others, and in their sense of community as a group of people who share a common set of stories. Each character appears to define him or herself by the stories that they repeatedly tell to anyone who will listen, and the community of Dunnet Landing is largely defined by the sense of a common history as passed down through storytelling. The story of "poor Joanna," for example, is told to the narrator by both Mrs. Todd and Mrs. Fosdick, and concerns a woman whose personal history now belongs to the history of the community. Through this novel, Jewett celebrates the hu-

man urge to narrate stories, as indicated by the narrator's need to repeat to the reader all of the stories she was told during her summer at Dunnet Landing.

Memories and Nostalgia

Memories and nostalgia are important themes in *The Country of the Pointed Firs*. All of the people the narrator meets are between the ages of sixty and ninety, with the bulk of their lives behind them. Hence, many of these characters live primarily in the past, nursing their memories, both bitter and pleasant. The town has changed because of the decline in the shipping industry, and there are many aging sailors and sea captains who once led lives of adventure, travel, and physical challenge. They express a strong sense of nostalgia for both their own personal past and for what the town was like during their youth. Captain Littlepage, for instance, describes with nostalgia days long past when the town thrived on the shipping industry, and all the men spent much of their time at sea. Elijah Tilley, another aging sailor, also lives in a world of memory and nostalgia. His life revolves around the memory of his now deceased wife, and he is overcome with nostalgia for the happiness he enjoyed in days long gone. Throughout *The Country of the Pointed Firs*, Jewett portrays an aging community in a period of economic decline, the members of which live nostalgically in the past in a world of personal and communal memories.

Style

Narrative Voice

The Country of the Pointed Firs is narrated in the first-person, meaning that the narrator is a character in the story and that the perspective she presents to the reader is limited to her own personal observations. The narrator is not named at any point in the book, and little direct information about her is provided. She indicates that she is middle-aged, is a writer, and has come to Dunnet Landing from the city to spend the summer working on a long writing piece. Critics have often praised Jewett for the skill with which she creates the narrative voice in this novel; the narrator is not simply an objective observer of the events she records, nor is she overly intrusive in imposing her own opinions on the reader.

Embedded Narrative

Throughout the narrative of *The Country of the Pointed Firs*, Jewett employs a literary device known as an embedded narrative or story-within-the-story. In other words, in telling the story of *The Country of the Pointed Firs*, the narrator includes long quotations from other characters as they relate their own stories to her. With one character, Jewett creates an even more complex embedded narrative when the narrator quotes Captain Littlepage as he tells her the story of a shipwreck told to him many year earlier by Gaffett, another aging seaman. Thus, there are three layers of narrative embedded within the overarching narrative.

Local Dialect

The use of local dialect is characteristic of the fiction of "local color" writers of the nineteenth century, and Jewett has often been praised for her use of local Maine dialect in her stories and novels. In *The Country of the Pointed Firs*, she quotes many different characters in Dunnet Landing whose speech is inflected with the local phrasing and idioms of coastal Maine. Mary Ellen Chase observed in a 1968 introduction to *The Country of the Pointed Firs and Other Stories*:

> Even fifty years ago Mrs. Todd's speech would be easily understood anywhere along the coast of Maine; yet she and her language are bound to become anachronistic, unconscious contributors to the social history of a region.

Critics often note the accuracy and naturalness of Jewett's use of local Maine dialect in the dialogue of her characters. In 1962, Richard Cary observed, "The natives [in Jewett's fiction] speak a language which has the color and texture of the soil they walk upon." Cary continues:

> The felicity of her style is most manifest in her management of native idiom. She extracts the peculiarities of speech from the earth of their origin, turns up their roots with some of the soil still clinging, yet preserves unharmed their vibrant connection with life.

Plot

Critics often point out that *The Country of the Pointed Firs* does not have a complex plot or strong dramatic development. The plot in this novel has been described as episodic, meaning that it is structured as a series of relatively isolated events or incidents, each of which individually does not develop along a clearly indicated line of narrative movement. However, this is not seen as a weakness in the story. Rather, the episodic plot structure conveys to the reader the atmosphere of the sleepy, rural town of Dunnet Landing, in which the biggest event of the year is a family reunion, and most of the characters are elderly people who spend their time reflecting backward on their past, rather than looking forward to any particular goals or hopes or dreams for their futures.

Character Sketch

The Country of the Pointed Firs is to some extent made up of a series of character sketches. The narrator moves the story along by describing her series of encounters with a number of the local inhabitants of Dunnet Landing. A character sketch is a brief description of a particular person, real or fictional, that provides the reader with a strong sense of who the person is in a short piece capturing the essential elements of that person. Jewett offers a series of character sketches of Captain Littlepage, Mrs. Blackett, William Blackett, and Elijah

Tilley, among others. The importance of each character to the narrative is indicated by many of the chapter titles, which simply name the character to be sketched within that chapter. The portrayal of the character Mrs. Todd, whom critics generally agree is Jewett's greatest character in all of her fiction, provides the overarching character sketch of the book.

Historical Context

Decline of the Shipping Industry

The Country of the Pointed Firs takes place some time in the last quarter of the nineteenth century. This time in U.S. history is significant to Jewett's setting in a shipping and fishing village of coastal Maine.

The heyday of Maine's economy were the years 1830 to 1860, when fishing and shipbuilding were the dominant industries, and coastal towns were centers of economic and cultural prosperity. As a result of developments in industry and changes in the economy, however, the merchant shipping industry in Maine suffered a severe decline in the years following the Civil War. Industrialization developed roughly over the course of the second half of the nineteenth century in the United States. Industry, employing masses of laborers in urban settings to perform factory work, drew from the rural areas to the cities many young people in search of work.

The fictional town of Dunnet Landing portrayed in *The Country of the Pointed Firs* is thus a realistic depiction of the conditions of Maine coastal towns from which most of the young people had fled. They left behind an aging population who recalled the great days of the shipping industry when a majority of the male population were sailors, fishermen, or shipbuilders.

The Status of Women

Jewett's stories, such as *The Country of the Pointed Firs*, focus on strong-willed, financially-independent women, often widows whose lives do not revolve around men. Jewett herself never married, choosing instead to focus her personal life on a close female companion. Although she and her female characters enjoyed personal and financial independence, Jewett did not live to see the granting of the right to vote to women in the United States.

During the second half of the nineteenth century, when Jewett lived and wrote, women in the United States struggled to obtain the right to vote. The U.S. women's suffrage movement—the struggle for the right for women to vote in local, state, and national elections—can be dated from the Seneca Falls Convention of 1848, held in Seneca Falls, New York. The first national convention of the newly formed women's movement was held in 1850. In 1869, the National Woman Suffrage Association was founded with the intended strategy of calling for an amendment to the United States Constitution granting women the right to vote. Also in 1869, the American Woman Suffrage Association was founded to push for amendments to state constitutions allowing women the right to vote. In 1890, these two organizations merged to form the National American Woman Suffrage Association. Prominent women in the suffrage movement included Lucretia Mott, Elizabeth Cady Stanton, Lucy Stone, and Susan B. Anthony.

In 1890, Wyoming became the first state that allowed women to vote. Over the next thirty years, fourteen more states granted women the right to vote. In 1920, the Nineteenth Amendment to the United States Constitution guaranteed women the right to vote on an equal basis with men—ten years after Jewett's death.

Local Color, Regionalism, and Realism in American Literature

Jewett is widely considered to be one of the greatest "local color" writers of the nineteenth century. Local color writing emerged in the United States in the period after the Civil War, and remained popular throughout the remainder of the nineteenth century. Local color writing focuses on the specific features of character, dialect, folklore, and customs of a particular region of the country, often a small community in a rural area. Bret Harte, an early local color writer, portrayed the culture of gold mining towns in the West. Mark Twain drew from his childhood growing up along the Mississippi River to write his stories and novels. Harriet Beecher Stowe and Mary E. Wilkins Freemen, as well as Jewett, depicted the quaint community life of small towns on the East Coast. Local color stories often have a tone of nostalgia for the disappearing communities and ways of life affected by industrialization.

Originating in the Midwest in the 1880s and 1890s was the development of regionalism in American literature, which shared similarities with local color writing. The most representative Mid-

Compare & Contrast

- **1890s:** In the women's suffrage movement, American women struggle to obtain the right to vote in local, state, and national elections. The only nation in the world that allows women the right to vote at the national level is New Zealand, beginning in 1893.

- **Today:** Women in the United States and more than one hundred other countries have full voting rights. Some nations continue to deny women the right to vote. Many women in the United States now hold political office at the local, state, and national levels. However, no woman has ever been elected president or vice president of the United States.

- **1890s:** In the aftermath of the Civil War, Maine's once-thriving shipbuilding and fishing industries are in decline, causing economic de-

pression in the coastal towns. The homes of many inhabitants in the coastal towns of Maine are filled with relics from around the world, brought home by the sailors of days past.

- **Today:** Maine remains one of the most economically depressed states in the eastern United States. With the lowest income per capita in New England, Maine's rural populations along the coastline suffer the greatest poverty. Maine's primary industries are the manufacturing of timber into paper products and the tourist industry. Although the lobster industry remains important, the fishing industry is no longer a significant portion of the Maine economy. Many relics of the heyday of Maine's shipping industry, once kept in private homes of seamen and their descendents, are collected in the Maine Maritime Museum.

---

western regionalist writer was Hamlin Garland, whose stories of the hardship endured by pioneers on the Great Plains are represented in his collection *Main-Traveled Roads* (1891).

Local color writing is seen as a transitional style that led to realism in American literature. The focus of local color writers on accurately portraying the characteristics of a specific region lent their works a strong element of realism. However, local color stories are often tinged with romanticism, nostalgia, and a tendency to overlook the darker elements of any character or community. Jewett's fiction, particularly *The Country of the Pointed Firs*, is considered a transitional work that bridges the gap between local color writing and realism.

William Dean Howells, novelist and *Atlantic Monthly* editor, ushered in a new realism in American literature that allowed for critique of and commentary on contemporary social, political, and economic issues. Howells was a strong influence on Jewett and helped to launch her literary career. Jewett, in turn, exerted a strong influence on the novelist Willa Cather, who turned for inspiration to her

childhood in the pioneer town of Red Cloud, Nebraska, in her major works of regional, local color fiction.

Critical Overview

Jewett is widely regarded as one of the best American local color authors of the nineteenth century, and *The Country of the Pointed Firs* is indisputably her masterpiece. At the time of its initial publication in 1896, Jewett was firmly established as one of the leading writers of her day and a master of the "local color" tale, vividly portrayed through her Maine coast characters in previous stories. Paula Blanchard observes that, by 1891, Jewett "was one of America's best-loved and most admired authors."

The Country of the Pointed Firs was warmly received by British and American critics of the day, who saw in Jewett's narrator a mature version of her earlier narrators. The book was praised for its

Old fishing docks in Portland, Maine, similiar to the novel's setting

avoidance of the sentimentality and quaintness that could be detected in her earlier works, as well as the more skillful degree of involvement on the part of the narrator with the events and characters she describes.

In an 1897 review of *The Country of the Pointed Firs*, Alice Brown opined, "*The Country of the Pointed Firs* is the flower of a sweet, sane knowledge of life, and an art so elusive that it smiles up at you while you pull aside the petals, vainly probing its heart." Brown concluded, "No such beautiful and perfect work has been done for many years; perhaps no such beautiful work has ever been done in America."

In her preface to a 1925 edition of *The Country of the Pointed Firs*, Willa Cather ranked Jewett's novel along with *The Scarlet Letter* (1850) by Nathaniel Hawthorne, and *Huckleberry Finn* (1884) by Mark Twain, as the three most enduring works of nineteenth-century American fiction. From the mid-1920s through the 1950s, however, Jewett's works fell out of popularity and her once prominent literary name receded into the background of American letters. The label of "local color" writer contributed to a general regard for Jewett's work as beneath the standards of the literary cannon. Further, many critics regarded her work as minor in its scope and significance, pri-

marily due to the focus of her stories on seemingly insignificant details of the lives of older women. Barbara H. Solomon, writing in 1979, explained the neglect of *The Country of the Pointed Firs* throughout the mid-twentieth century was due to the fact that "it is so thoroughly a woman's book about the world of women—old women at that." Solomon continues:

> The women of Dunnet Landing, capable, busy, and sensible, are Jewett's subject, and as long as the topic of women's activities and their relationships with one another seemed unfashionable, the novel was invariably thought of as a "minor" masterpiece or "quaint" classic.

In the latter half of the twentieth century, critics took up her works with renewed interest. Since the early 1960s, Jewett's works, particularly *The Country of the Pointed Firs*, have been given a broader scope of interpretation and critical analysis. Feminist critics in particular saw her fictions as the work of a proto-feminist. Such critics praised her portrayal of strong female characters, her attention to the details of domestic life, and her focus on women as the central figures within a small community.

In a 2000 edition of *The Country of the Pointed Firs*, the biographical note observes that the continuing power and significance of this more than one-hundred-year-old novel is due to the fact that "[t]he artistry of Jewett's creation . . . remains as alive and fresh and accessible as the day Jewett wrote the first chapter."

Criticism

Liz Brent

Brent has a Ph.D. in American culture, specializing in film studies, from the University of Michigan. She is a freelance writer and teaches courses on the history of American cinema. In the following essay, Brent discusses the theme of death in Jewett's novel.

On first reading, Jewett's *The Country of the Pointed Firs* may strike the reader as lighthearted and quaint, depicting a series of quirky elderly characters in a quiet, sleepy town where not much happens. However, there is an atmosphere of darkness and death that permeates the novel, constituting a central focus of the narrative.

The inhabitants of Dunnet Landing encountered by the narrator are all between the ages of sixty and ninety years old. Because of their advanced age, they carry with them an awareness of their own approaching death. The awareness of their own mortality fills these characters with a sense of nostalgia, as they often seem to inhabit memories long past as much as they do the present. These characters are all facing their own impending deaths and whatever afterlife awaits them. It seems as if the narrator herself, gazing out from the shores of Dunnet Landing, gets a glimpse into the afterlife toward which her acquaintances gaze. One morning, looking out at an island offshore with Mrs. Todd, the narrator notes, "The sunburst upon that outermost island made it seem like a sudden revelation of the world beyond this which some believe to be so near."

Captain Littlepage describes to the narrator the story he was told by an aging seaman years earlier about a mysterious town near the North Pole. Captain Littlepage describes this town as a "waiting-place between this world and the next," in which the inhabitants all seem to be ghosts. Captain Littlepage's obsession with this town full of ghosts suggests his preoccupation with his own impending death, as if he himself were occupying a waiting-place between life and death. Dunnet Landing, likewise, seems to be a sort of waiting-place between life and death, in which the inhab-

> **Funerals are, in fact, community events central to the life of the town, serving in part to bring the community together, as most every-one seems to know everyone else."**

itants, with one foot in the grave, look back on a long life and gaze into the distance at the afterlife which awaits them. At one point, the narrator describes Mrs. Todd as if she were one of the ghosts inhabiting the "waiting-place between this world and the next" described by Captain Littlepage; the narrator momentarily feels as if Mrs. Todd "would now begin to look like the cobweb shapes of the arctic town."

Nonetheless, the inhabitants of Dunnet Landing, though approaching the age at which death lurks just around the corner, seem astoundingly hale and hearty, as if they could almost overcome death with their vitality. The narrator says of the old fishermen who continue to live and work around the port, that the sea

> affected the old fishermen's hard complexions, until one fancied that when Death claimed them it could only be with the aid, not of any slender modern dart, but the good serviceable harpoon of a seventeenth-century woodcut.

In addition to nearing their own deaths, the inhabitants of Dunnet Landing have all experienced the deaths of loved ones. In part because it is a seaport, the town is inhabited largely by the widows of sailors, most of whom were lost at sea. When Mrs. Todd shows the narrator the Bowden family graveyard, she observes that it contains the remains of few men, because most of them were drowned in shipwrecks or buried at sea. There are, however, several old men encountered by the narrator who are widowers. The narrator, in fact, does not meet any married couples during her summer at Dunnet Landing. The widows she becomes acquainted with include Mrs. Todd, Mrs. Blackett, and Mrs. Fosdick. Mrs. Begg, whose funeral the narrator attends, is said to have survived three husbands, all lost at sea. The widowers include Captain Littlepage and Elijah Tilley.

Elijah Tilley, whom the narrator meets toward the end of her stay in Dunnet Landing, is a widower whose entire life is consumed with the memory of his wife, who died eight years earlier. He tells the narrator, "I can't git over losin' of her no way nor no how." His entire home is devoted to keeping the memory of his wife alive, as he maintains it in the exact same manner she had. Thus, although he has been living alone for eight years, his home looks more like that of a fastidious housewife than of an aged seafaring man. The narrator describes his living room as a "clear bright room which had once enshrined his wife, and now enshrined her memory."

In addition to the deaths of their husbands and wives, the aging population of Dunnet Landing has survived the deaths of many other loved ones. Mrs. Fosdick, for example, "had been the mother of a large family of sons and daughters,—sailors and sailors' wives,—and most of them had died before her." While visiting Mrs. Todd, Mrs. Fosdick informs her host of the recent death of her sister Louisa.

Although the aging inhabitants of Dunnet Landing are constantly reminded of death, this does not lessen the pain caused by the loss of even one beloved individual. As Elijah Tilley says of his deceased wife, "There ain't one o' her old friends can ever make up her loss." Likewise, the narrator notes that the loss of Mrs. Begg, a lifelong friend of Mrs. Todd, is a source of great sadness. Watching the funeral from afar, the narrator observes that Mrs. Todd "held a handkerchief to her eyes, and I knew, with a pang of sympathy, that hers was not affected grief." Thus, while Dunnet Landing seems to be a town characterized by death, this does not mean the citizens are immune to the sense of loss and sadness that accompanies the death of a loved one.

In addition to contemplating their own impending deaths, and the deaths of loved ones long since gone, the inhabitants of Dunnet Landing often attend funerals of the newly dead. Funerals are, in fact, community events central to the life of the town, serving in part to bring the community together, as most everyone seems to know everyone else. The narrator comments that, because friends and relatives live so far apart on isolated islands and remote farms, "Even funerals in this country of the pointed firs were not without their social advantages and satisfactions."

Early in the story, the narrator attends the funeral of Mrs. Begg, and later watches the funeral procession from a window. The narrator explains that "Mrs. Begg had been very much respected, and there was a large company of friends following her to her grave." Attendance at the funeral procession and funeral service affirms a person's membership in the community, as indicated by the narrator's sense of regret at not joining the procession. She realizes, "I had now made myself and my friends remember that I did not really belong to Dunnet Landing."

Even the funeral of "poor Joanna," who had lived in self-isolation on Shell-heap Island for many years, was attended by the entire community. Mrs. Fosdick explains that the day of Joanna's funeral, which was held on Shell-heap Island, "there wa'n't hardly a boat on the coast within twenty miles that didn't head for Shell-heap cram-full o' folks an' all real respectful, same's if she'd always stayed ashore and held her friends." Mrs. Fosdick notes that those who attended the funeral "had real feelin', and went purpose to show it." Thus, even the most lonely and isolated member of the community becomes the focus of communal mourning upon her death.

The narrator experiences the end of her summer's stay in Dunnet Landing as a loss akin to that of death. As the book opens, she compares her feeling for the remote town to the feeling of love at first sight, which only deepens with time. She explains:

> When one really knows a village like this and its surroundings, it is like becoming acquainted with a single person. The process of falling in love at first sight is as final as it is swift in such a case, but the growth of true friendship may be a lifelong affair.

Because her attachment to the town is akin to one person's love for another human being, leaving the town is likewise experienced as the loss of a loved one. Sailing away from the coastal town to return to the city, the narrator observes, "Dunnet Landing and all its coasts were lost to sight." By the same token, the narrator feels as if taking her leave from the town is akin to experiencing her own death. Describing her empty room in Mrs. Todd's house after she has packed to leave, the narrator observes:

> When I went in again the little house had suddenly grown lonely, and my room looked empty as it had the day I came. I and all my belongings had died out of it, and I knew how it would seem when Mrs. Todd came back and found her lodger gone. So we die before our own eyes; so we see some chapters of our lives come to their natural end.

The overall effect of Jewett's treatment of the theme of death in *The Country of the Pointed Firs* is to address the universal human concern with mortality. Seeing the aged of Dunnet Landing, the narrator, a middle-aged woman, is reminded of her own approaching old age and death. She looks to Mrs. Blackett, in her eighties, and Mrs. Todd, in her sixties, as role models of old age, and thinks, "I hoped in my heart that I might be like them as I lived on into age, and then smiled to think that I too was no longer very young." She goes on, "So we always keep the same hearts, though our outer framework fails and shows the touch of time."

We all must die. Yet the narrator takes comfort in the immortality of nature and the human spirit, in spite of the death which inevitably awaits each individual. Commenting on the funeral of Mrs. Begg, the narrator notes that the funeral procession looks "futile and helpless"—an indication of the feeling of futility and helplessness, that is, powerlessness, of human beings over the forces of death. Yet the narrator goes on to observe, "The song sparrows sang and sang, as if with joyous knowledge of immortality, and contempt for those who could so pettily concern themselves with death." Of course, the birds themselves are not immortal, but Jewett suggests in this passage that nature is immortal, as is the human soul.

Source: Liz Brent, Critical Essay on *The Country of the Pointed Firs*, in *Novels for Students*, The Gale Group, 2002.

Margaret Baker Graham

In the following excerpt, Graham discusses the representations of time in Jewett's The Country of the Pointed Firs.

Feminist theory has recently offered new perspectives on Sarah Orne Jewett's *The Country of the Pointed Firs*. Much of this recent scholarship is based on the work of Nancy Chodorow and Carol Gilligan, who argue that females and males, because of socially constructed experiences, may espouse different values and speak in different voices. Briefly stated, the feminine perspective is cyclical, inductive, and communal; the masculine perspective linear, deductive, and hierarchical. Elizabeth Ammons argues that the narrative structure of *The Country of the Pointed Firs* is structured in opposition to masculine narrative: "Instead of being linear, it [*The Country of the Pointed Firs*] is nuclear: the narrative moves out from one base to a given point and back again, and so forth, like arteries on a spider's web." Josephine Donovan, like Ammons, finds Jewett's preference for non-linear plots "an essentially feminine literary mode expressing a contextual, inductive sensitivity, one that 'gives in'

> The sparrow is one symbol of immortality; the sea is a larger symbol of not only immortality but also infinity."

to the events in question, rather than imposing upon them an artificial, prefabricated 'plot.'" Karen Oakes comments on the "feminine fluidity" in *The Country of the Pointed Firs*; and Ann Romines perceives the structure of the book, with its gentle ebb and flow, as replicating "the domestic rhythms" that women know.

One feminist perspective that has not been fully addressed in discussions of *The Country of the Pointed Firs* is time, a concept that elucidates both structure and theme in Jewett's work. The feminist theory of time as articulated by the French poststructuralist Julia Kristeva suggests that Jewett offers a vision of life that includes the masculine, linear time and the feminine, cyclical time, yet ultimately transcends both to achieve monumental time.

In "Women's Time," Kristeva perceives linear time as an effort to define patterns when none may exist, to distort the relationship between synchronic events by forcing them into an orderly sequence of cause and effect. Because linear time suggests and repeats the hierarchical power relationships dominating Western civilization—one event or person controlling others—Kristeva criticizes linear time for being "at once both civilizational and obsessional." She identifies linear time as masculine. Juxtaposed to linear time is cyclical time, which Kristeva identifies as feminine because it is validated by "gestation, the eternal recurrence of a biological rhythm which conforms to that of nature . . ." Natural processes, such as the menstrual cycle and seasonal cycle, symbolize and reinforce the notion of time and events recurring without cessation and without agency. Monumental time is realized through mythology, what Kristeva calls "the archaic (mythical) memory." Kristeva is especially interested in resurrection myths as a revelation of monumental time. Although patriarchy has largely erased or rewritten resurrection myths, Kristeva believes that monumental time is essentially feminine

What Do I Read Next?

- *A Country Doctor* (1884) is Jewett's novel based on her father's experiences as a doctor serving inhabitants of rural Maine.

- *The Best Stories of Sarah Orne Jewett* (1925), edited and with an introduction by Willa Cather, includes Jewett's major short stories from throughout her career.

- *Uncle Tom's Cabin* (1852), by Harriet Beecher Stowe, is the masterpiece novel of one of the leading "local color" writers of the nineteenth century and a major influence on Jewett. *Uncle Tom's Cabin* was an extremely influential anti-slavery novel published before the Civil War.

- *The Adventures of Huckleberry Finn* (1884), by Mark Twain, is one of the greatest American novels of the nineteenth century and a major work of "local color" writing. It concerns the experiences of a white boy, Huck Finn, after he runs away from home in the company of Jim, an escaped slave. Twain was a personal acquaintance of Jewett.

- *The Complete Poems of Emily Dickinson* (1960) is a definitive collection of Dickinson's poems. Dickinson, a New England poet contemporary to Jewett, is considered one of the greatest American poets of the nineteenth century.

- *My Antonia* (1918) is considered the masterpiece of Willa Cather, a regionalist author of Nebraska pioneer life. Cather was a personal acquaintance of Jewett and was strongly influenced by her "local color" fiction.

---

because it extends the concept of cyclical time beyond the natural, temporal world: cyclical time is "*repetition*," while monumental time is "*eternity*." Kristeva wants to reclaim the feminine impulse behind mythic accounts of immortality, and she writes "of the various myths of resurrection which, in all religious beliefs, perpetuate the vestige of an anterior or concomitant maternal cult . . ."

Although the concept of time as feminine and masculine has been addressed only recently as part of the postmodern conversation, Sarah Orne Jewett, almost a hundred years ago, depicted the three visions of time—linear, cyclical, and monumental—in *The Country of the Pointed Firs*.

Captain Littlepage, Joanna Todd, and Elijah Tilley . . . living in linear time, are stunted; Almira Todd, by embracing cyclical time, flourishes, although her vision is limited in time and space. Woven through each section is the vision of the narrator, a woman visiting Dunnet Landing. It is her vision that fully integrates life's experiences and reaches beyond the temporal for the mythic and eternal, thus typifying the monumental concept of time.

Although linear time can be dynamic if it is conceived as a progression moving ceaselessly into the future, the linear characters—because they have suffered a loss from which they cannot recover—freeze time at different points on the continuum of past, present, and future. Captain Littlepage's loss is the decline of the shipping industry. Unable to recognize the recurring processes of life that remain, Littlepage is obsessed with the future. He wonders about an afterlife he once heard about: a town at the end of the world where people are shadows, "a kind of waiting place between this world an' the next." Dismayed that his former life has become a shadow and obsessed with the shadowy life that may await him, Littlepage becomes the story he cannot forget: His life is a waiting place between the temporal and the eternal.

While the Captain has an uneasy hope for the future, Joanna Todd, dead 22 years before the narrator comes to Dunnet Landing, abandoned hope because she assumed that her Calvinist God would not forgive the awful thoughts she had when she was jilted: "I have committed the unpardonable sin; you don't understand. . . . my thoughts was so wicked towards God that I can't expect ever to be forgiven. I have come to know what it is to have patience, but I have lost my hope." Without hope, she deliberately arrested her life, neither mourning for her lost relationship nor hoping for future joy. Significantly, there was no clock on Shellheap Island where Joanna Todd lived in cold isolation in a frozen present. Although one might expect only male characters to embody masculine time, the characterization of Joanna Todd shows that Jewett assumes a non-essentialist position. Margaret Roman notes that "Dunnet Landing is a place wherein the allocation of gender roles is called into question."

The last section about characters who live in linear time concerns Elijah Tilley, a fisherman who cannot move forward from the death of his wife eight years before. He tells the narrator, "Folks all kep' repeatin' that time would ease me, but I can't find it does. No, I miss her just the same every day." In his grief, he makes their house a shrine to his wife, refusing to change anything from the way it was eight years before.

The obsessions of Captain Littlepage, Joanna Todd, and Elijah Tilley are civilizational, as Kristeva suggests linear frameworks are, because their disappointments derive from patriarchal institutions, institutions moribund or repressive. Sailing, Captain Littlepage's occupation, had virtually died out by the late nineteenth century, the publication date of *The Country of the Pointed Firs*, as steam-driven ships replaced clipper ships. Sailing is an appropriate industry to represent not only New England society, but also the patriarchal nature of American capitalism since sailing was an exclusively male industry. It is the repressive nature of Calvinism, another moribund patriarchal institution in Jewett's New England, that (mis)leads Joanna Todd into a life of self-imposed isolation. Mrs. Fosdick, Almira Todd's friend, comments that New Englanders no longer talk about unpardonable sins as they used to. Calvinism was losing its vigor even when Joanna Todd was still alive as indicated by the ineffectual Parson Dimmick, who could not comprehend her pain. Almira Todd laments that "he seemed to know no remedies, but he had a great use of words."

The story of Sarah Tilley represents a third institution often spiritually and emotionally destructive to its participants: marriage. Although Elijah deludes himself into remembering his marriage as idyllic, the memories he recounts suggest that his wife suffered from the destructive effects of a patriarchal society that placed women in a subservient role. Elijah Tilley's wife was a timid woman afraid of bad weather, afraid to tell her husband she had broken a cup, afraid to sail to Green Island. Rather than understanding or helping his wife overcome her fears, Elijah Tilley worsened her fears by staying out late and laughing at her timidity. Elijah Tilley speaks fondly of his wife; however, it is Almira Todd, valuing Sarah Tilley as an individual, who provides the wife's first name, while Elijah, by referring to his wife only as "poor dear," strips Sarah of her individuality. To Almira Todd,

Sarah was one of the finest people she knew: "There's some folks you miss, and some folks you don't, when they're gone, but there ain't hardly a day I don't think o' dear Sarah Tilley." To Elijah, Sarah is an endearment, an object of sympathy and mild ridicule, and finally a symbol of the past wherein he traps himself.

Juxtaposed to Captain Littlepage, Joanna Todd, and Elijah Tilley, who suspend growth by refusing to accept process, Almira Todd embraces life. John Hirsch writes about Almira Todd: "She stands in counterpoint to Captain Littlepage with his Miltonic invocation and narrative, to the saintly poor Joanna, and to the Carlyle-like remorse of Mr. Tilley." Almira Todd's acceptance of recurring process is evident immediately in *The Country of the Pointed Firs* when she reveals she has been jilted. She fondly remembers her love for the man, but, unlike Joanna Todd, she does not lose hope; later she marries someone else. When Mr. Todd dies, she is not like Elijah Tilley, defining her being in terms of the patriarchal institution of marriage. Instead, she finds joy in her medicinal herbs. Almira Todd enjoys reminiscing about the past, but she is never trapped there. Appropriately, Almira Todd is a naturalist, a vocation that allows her to embrace cyclical time. The herb plot Almira Todd values symbolizes her character just as setting symbolizes the character of the stunted people. The waiting place represents Captain Littlepage's own life of waiting. Shellheap Island does not make Joanna the way she is; instead, its cold isolation reflects her nature. By making his home a shrine, Elijah has entombed himself with his wife's memory. The life-giving, health-restoring herbs, in turn, symbolize Almira Todd's own full and productive life.

The first and last sections of *The Country of the Pointed Firs* are a repetition of Almira Todd's communion with nature. The title of the first chapter is "The Return" and the last chapter "The Backward View," so that the book folds back into itself, emphasizing the cyclical nature of life. In the first section, the narrator describes the timeless repetition Almira Todd enjoys when she tends her herb plot:

> There were some strange and pungent odors that roused a dim sense and remembrance of something in the forgotten past. Some of these might once have belonged to sacred and mystic rites, and have had some occult knowledge handed with them down the centuries....

In the last section, the narrator again observes Almira Todd's participation in the ceaseless process of nature: "Now and then she stooped to pick something,—it might have been her favorite pennyroyal,—and at last I lost sight of her as she slowly crossed an open space on one of the higher points of land, and disappeared again behind a dark clump of juniper and the pointed firs." The first section and the last section, thus, encircle the entire book in a recurring vision of life as typified by Almira Todd's communion with nature.

In the Green Island and Bowden reunion chapters, sections 3 and 5, Jewett emphasizes the value of companionship and draws a striking contrast to the solitary lives of Captain Littlepage, Joanna Todd, and Elijah Tilley. The companionship in section 3 is the intimate, non-obsessive relationship of Mrs. Blackett and her children William and Almira. Mrs. Blackett and William live on an island as Joanna does, but their lives are not constricted. Life blooms there as the name "Green Island" implies, while Joanna's Shellheap Island is a fearful place associated with cannibalism. Joanna lived alone, not wanting visitors and never leaving the island. Mrs. Blackett and William, though, have each other for company, enjoy visitors, and travel to the mainland. William has an eccentric shyness that keeps him from most people, but it apparently does not stunt his life as Joanna's self-imposed, bitterly sought isolation did. While Joanna had no hope for herself, Mrs. Blackett, even in old age, "promised a great future, and was beginning, not ending, her summers, and their happy toils." Although Almira Todd no longer lives on Green Island, she shares in its heritage—what Melissa McFarland Pennell calls "the network of community."

Elizabeth Ammons identifies the center of the book as the Green Island section: "Instead of building to an asymmetric height, it [the book] collects weight at the middle: the most highly charged experience of the book, the visit to Green Island, comes at the center of the book . . ., not toward the end." However, section 5, the Bowden reunion, is equally central to the heart of the book by showing the value of this primal need for companionship, which reaches from the present to the far distant past. It is section 5, in which the narrator witnesses the rejuvenation of Almira Todd, that best explains the value of companionship:

> The excitement of an unexpectedly great occasion was a subtle stimulant to her disposition, and I could see that sometimes when Mrs. Todd had seemed limited and heavily domestic, she had simply grown sluggish for lack of proper surroundings. She was not so much reminiscent now as expectant, and as alert and gay as a girl.

Solitude, of course, is not without value. The first and last sections attest to Almira Todd's nec-essary solitude as a naturalist, and the narrator herself rents the schoolhouse because she needs a solitary place to write. The book suggests, however, that companionship provides the energy an individual needs to use solitude creatively rather than obsessively. Both the Green Island section and the Bowden reunion section stand as the nucleus of the book.

Sarah Orne Jewett, in a letter to Horace Scudder, admitted that she could not do as William Dean Howells suggested and write plot-driven works: "I have no dramatic talent. The story would have no plot. . . . It seems to me I can furnish the theatre, and show you the actors, and the scenery, and the audience, but there is never any play!" Jewett may have had no talent for masculine narrative structure, but this so-called weakness creates a strength of a different sort. The structure of *The Country of the Pointed Firs* can be conceived as one circle inside another, with the timeline represented by Captain Littlepage, Joanna Todd, and Elijah Tilley intersecting both. . . .

Although Almira Todd leads a successful life, her vision is limited. When she and Mrs. Fosdick discuss Joanna Todd, Almira Todd agrees with her friend that "Everybody's just like everybody else, now; nobody to laugh about, and nobody to cry about." The narrator thinks about eccentrics like Captain Littlepage and William, but says nothing. As a naturalist, Almira Todd has a concept of life that is limited to the temporal; she does not transcend space and time as the narrator does. Michael Vella writes, "the narrator learns to perceive within the flux of nature and history something transcendental and permanent within mortal man, something which serves for her as an intimation of immortality."

By accepting and transcending process, the narrator embraces monumental time. Just as nature and its processes affirm cyclical time, collective memory and recurring myths affirm monumental time. On the one hand, the narrator is delighted by the singularity she perceives in the people in Maine; on the other hand, she constantly searches beyond the familiar and limiting boundaries of the here and now for monumental time. One representation of monumental time is myth. Priscilla Leder writes, "Jewett frequently evokes mythology, especially that of the Greeks, who seem to signify an origin, a kind of prototype of western culture." Using Greek myth, the narrator compares Almira Todd to Antigone: "There was something lonely and solitary about her great determined shape. She might have been Antigone alone on the Theban plain. . . . An absolute, archaic grief possessed this country-woman; she seemed like a renewal of some historic soul. . . . " The mythic connection becomes historical when the narrator compares the Bowdens to the Greeks who created those myths:

> . . . we might have been a company of ancient Greeks going to celebrate a victory, or to worship the god of harvests in the grove above. . . . we were no more a New England family celebrating its own existence and simple progress; we carried the tokens and inheritance of all such households from which this had descended, and were only the latest of our line.

Again using history to erase temporal differences, the narrator finds a connection between Joanna Todd and others that the solitary woman could not perceive. Although Joanna Todd chose to isolate herself, the narrator believes she, like Almira Todd, was linked to others by a need for both solitude and companionship. On the one hand, all people are like Joanna in that some part of them is "remote and islanded." This need for seclusion helps people to "understand our fellows of the hermitic cells to whatever age of history they may belong." On the other hand, even isolated people can find joy in human contact. The narrator, as she stands on Shellheap Island and hears the laughter of children from a nearby boat, is sure that Joanna too must have enjoyed hearing such sounds on a summer afternoon. Joanna Todd, thus, is connected to events before her birth since her isolation imitates the hermitic life of the medieval age; she is also connected to events after her death since the narrator experiences feelings of kinship to the long dead woman.

In addition to using a mythic concept of history to reveal monumental time, the narrator embraces, as Kristeva does, the idea of immortality. Elizabeth Ammons writes that *The Country of the Pointed Firs* "anticipates . . . the feminist task of reconstructing, or if need be invention, a resolutely female spiritual context that can reclaim the energy of degraded symbols and images. . . . " This immortality is not grounded in Calvinism or other civilizational theology, which the narrator call one of the "contrivances of man." Rather than being sectarian, her immortality is a universal belief in resurrection. When the narrator watches a funeral procession, she hears the sparrows singing "as if with joyous knowledge of immortality, and contempt for those who could so pettily concern themselves with death." Occurring as it does in the Littlepage section, this attitude meliorates the Captain's unhappiness with the end of sailing and of life itself. Michael

Hobbs notes that the narrator can identify with the Captain's isolation "since she herself is an outsider" to Dunnet Landing; however, unlike Littlepage, she can comprehend timelessness and immortality in the world around her. The immortality of Joanna Todd is also affirmed when Almira Todd describes how a sparrow graced her funeral: "She'd got most o' the wild sparrows as tame as could be, livin' out there so long among 'em, and one flew right in and lit on the coffin an' begun to sing. . . . " Joanna, believing in her unforgiving god, had no hope for an eternal life, but the presence of the sparrow suggests she found it in spite of herself.

The sparrow is one symbol of immortality; the sea is a larger symbol of not only immortality but also infinity. In the Green Island section, the narrator, standing on the edge of the island and looking out at the sea, experiences a "sense of liberty in space and time." She achieves this freedom more fully in the conclusion of the book when she experiences the limitless feeling that comes from being at sea with all land invisible: "Presently the wind began to blow, and we struck out seaward to double the long sheltering headland of the cape, and when I looked back again, the islands and the headland had run together and Dunnet Landing and all its coasts were lost to sight." Kristeva writes that embracing a feminist perspective allows one to achieve a "fluidity" that opposes "the threats of death which are unavoidable whenever an inside and an outside, a self and an other, one group and another, are constituted." In *The Country of the Pointed Firs*, the sea symbolizes this kind of fluidity, allowing the narrator to transcend the ending of her experiences in Dunnet Landing and to escape the finality of death. Captain Littlepage, Joanna Todd, and Elijah Tilley cannot achieve this kind of fluidity because they set themselves apart from others. Embracing monumental time, however, the narrator transcends superficial change to see that one part of the world and another, the mythical and the historical, the immortal and the temporal are the same.

Source: Margaret Baker Graham, "Visions of Time in *The Country of the Pointed Firs*," in *Studies in Short Fiction*, Vol. 32, No. 1, Winter 1995, pp. 29–38.

Sources

"Biographical Note: Sarah Orne Jewett," in *"The Country of the Pointed Firs" and Other Stories* by Sarah Orne Jewett, Modern Library, Random House, Inc., 2000, p. x.

Blanchard, Paula, *Sarah Orne Jewett: Her World and Her Work*, Addison-Wesley Publishing, 1994, p. 2.

Brown, Alice, "Profitable Tales," in *Short Fiction of Sarah Orne Jewett and Mary Wilkins Freeman*, edited by Barbara H. Solomon, New American Library, 1979, pp. 251–53, originally published in *The Book Buyer*, October, 1897.

Cary, Richard, *Sarah Orne Jewett*, Twayne Publishers, 1962, p. 40, 52.

Cather, Willa, "Preface," in *"The Country of the Pointed Firs" and Other Stories* by Sarah Orne Jewett, Doubleday, 1956, pp. 6–11.

Chase, Mary Ellen, "Introduction," in *"The Country of the Pointed Firs" and Other Stories* by Sarah Orne Jewett, Norton, 1968, p. xi.

Graham, Margaret Baker, "Visions of Time in *The Country of the Pointed Firs*," in *Studies in Short Fiction*, Vol. 32, No. 1, Winter, 1995, pp. 29–38.

Solomon, Barbara H., ed., *Short Fiction of Sarah Orne Jewett and Mary Wilkins Freeman*, New American Library, 1979, p. 5, 6.

Further Reading

Church, Joseph, *Transcendent Daughters in Jewett's "Country of the Pointed Firs,"* Associated University Press, 1994.

> Church explores mother-daughter relationships in *The Country of the Pointed Firs*.

Howard, June, ed., *New Essays on "The Country of the Pointed Firs,"* Cambridge University Press, 1994.

> Howard offers a collection of recent critical essays on *The Country of the Pointed Firs*, covering such topics as community, gender, realism, regionalism, and nationalism, by a variety of literary critics.

Roman, Margaret, *Sarah Orne Jewett: Reconstructing Gender*, University of Alabama Press, 1992.

> Roman explores issues of the representation of women in Jewett's *The Country of the Pointed Firs*.

Silverthorne, Elizabeth, *Sarah Orne Jewett: A Writer's Life*, Overlook Press, 1993.

> Silverthorne provides a biography of Jewett.

Demian

Hermann Hesse

1919

Demian: The Story of Emil Sinclair's Youth (1919) is a semi-autobiographical novel by German writer Hermann Hesse. *Demian* was published in the aftermath of World War I and grew out of Hesse's experience of psychoanalysis with Carl Jung and J. B. Lang.

The novel is set in Germany in the decade preceding World War I, roughly 1904 to 1914. Narrated by Emil Sinclair, *Demian* describes Sinclair's personal inward journey to a genuine understanding of his deep inner self. The character Max Demian, Sinclair's schoolmate, helps to open Sinclair's mind to unconventional ways of thinking that ultimately lead to self-discovery. Through his years of grade school, high school, and university education, Sinclair encounters several personal teachers who lead him toward a revelation of true self-knowledge. The novel ends during World War I, when both young men have been wounded in battle.

Demian applies concepts of Jungian psychoanalysis in a strongly symbolic narrative drawing from Christian theology, Nietzschean philosophy, and Eastern mysticism. *Demian* struck a chord with Germany's postwar youth, who felt it expressed a common search for personal identity. Hesse's novel also resonated with a generation of youth in the United States during the 1960s and 1970s.

Hermann Hesse

Author Biography

Hermann Hesse was born July 2, 1877, in Calw, Württemberg, Germany. Both of his parents had been missionaries in the East Indies, and the young Hesse grew up in a Protestant family characterized by piety and religious devotion based on biblical study. Hesse was also freely exposed to Eastern philosophy and religion, as his maternal grandfather studied Indian culture. Hesse attended the Protestant Theological Seminary in Maulbronn, Germany, but found it unbearable and ran away. He then attended the Gymnasium in Cannstadt, Germany, from which he was later expelled. He eventually found steady employment in a bookshop. His first novel, *Peter Camenzind* (1904) is about a failed writer. The book was such a popular success that Hesse could afford to leave his job and become a full-time writer. His struggles with artistic aspiration are further expressed in the novels *Gertrud* (1910) and *Rosshalde* (1914).

When Germany engaged in the conflict that became World War I (1914–1918), Hesse moved to Switzerland, from where he openly opposed the war and German nationalism. Nonetheless, he aided German soldiers by serving as editor of a journal for German prisoners of war. Between the

years 1916 and 1917, Hesse went through a personal crisis as a result of illness and death in his family. His personal distress lead him to seek psychoanalysis with both Carl Jung and his disciple, J. B. Lang. The novel *Demian* (1919) is based on his process of self-discovery through analysis. Hesse subtitled *Demian* "The Story of Emil Sinclair's Youth," and published it under the pseudonym Emil Sinclair. However, when the novel was granted a prize for first-time novelists, Hesse admitted to being the author and returned the prize, since this was not his first novel.

In 1919 Hesse became a permanent resident of Switzerland, obtaining Swiss citizenship in 1924. His novel *Siddhartha* (1922) is based on the early life of Buddha, inspired by Hesse's travels in India before World War I. *Der Steppenwolf* (1927; translated as *Steppenwolf*) is about a middle-aged man struggling with spiritual yearnings and the desire to pursue artistic creation. *Das Glasperlenspiel* (1943; translated as *Magister Ludi: The Glass Bead Game*) is set in the future and takes place in an elite community of highly gifted intellectuals. In 1946 Hesse was honored with the Nobel Prize in Literature.

Hesse was married three times, the first two marriages ending in divorce. He had three children from his first marriage. Hesse died of a brain hemorrhage in 1962, at the age of eighty-five.

Plot Summary

Grammar School

The story of Emil Sinclair's youth, as narrated in *Demian*, begins when Sinclair is ten years old and attending a grammar school in the small German town where he lives with his parents and two sisters. Sinclair describes a formative childhood experience when he lied to another child, Franz Kromer, bragging he had stolen apples from a local farmer. Although Sinclair is innocent of any crime, Kromer blackmails him by threatening to report to the police or to the farmer that Sinclair has stolen the apples. For weeks afterwards, Kromer threatens Sinclair into providing him with whatever money he can pilfer from his house, as well as other items. Sinclair's life becomes dominated by his fear of Kromer and his fear of being found guilty by his parents or other authorities. Sinclair comes to feel that he has committed a sin, and that he now belongs to the evil, or "dark," realm of the world, rather than the good, "light" realm in which he was brought up.

In the second chapter, Max Demian, a new boy in Sinclair's school who is a few years older than he, begins to take an interest in Sinclair. Demian exposes Sinclair to unconventional interpretations of their religious studies. Eventually, Sinclair indicates to Demian that Kromer has been troubling him, and Demian manages to scare Kromer into leaving Sinclair alone. Although Sinclair is relieved to be rid of Kromer, he does not thank Demian or attempt to befriend him because he is ashamed that he did not solve the problem on his own.

In the third chapter, several years have passed and Sinclair and Demian develop a friendship. Though Demian is rumored to be atheist or Jewish, he decides to attend religious confirmation classes in the same year as Sinclair. Sinclair begins to feel a bond with Demian, who sits near Sinclair in confirmation class and frequently offers unconventional interpretations of the biblical stories they are being taught. Although he is disturbed by Demian's unconventional ideas, Sinclair feels that his mind is being opened by Demian's influence, and he begins to question his religious faith. However, both boys complete their confirmation.

Boarding School

In the fourth chapter, Sinclair is sent away to a boarding school, and does not see Demian for a long time. At boarding school Sinclair is not well-liked by the other boys. He becomes depressed and filled with self-hatred. One night, when Sinclair is out walking alone, Alfons Beck, the oldest boy in the school, runs into him on the street and invites him to go for a drink. At the bar Sinclair gets drunk for the first time in his life. The next morning he is filled with self-disgust and depression, feeling that he is a complete degenerate. After this event Sinclair enters a phase of debauchery and earns a reputation at school for drunkenness and unruliness. During this time he feels that he belongs completely to the dark world of sin, and feels terrible about himself. He becomes a poor student and is on the verge of expulsion from school for his bad behavior. Although he is a "ringleader" among the rebellious students, Sinclair feels lonely and friendless. He also feels resentful toward Demian, to whom he has written twice from school, but from whom he has received no reply.

Sinclair's life changes after he encounters a young woman in a park, whom he admires from afar but never approaches. He becomes infatuated with the young woman, whom he thinks of as Beatrice, as he does not know her real name. Sinclair's feeling of worship for Beatrice has a profound affect on his life. He stops drinking and almost overnight ceases his unruly and rebellious behavior. He becomes contemplative and studious, feeling he has entered the world of light and good once again. During this period Sinclair begins to paint images from his dreams. He paints a face that appeared to him in a dream, which looks to him like both Beatrice and Demian. He later paints an image from a dream of a bird emerging from a shell, and sends the painting to Demian.

In the fifth chapter, Sinclair, still in boarding school, continues to have many symbolic dreams and to paint. He understands his desire to "try to live in accord with the promptings which came from my true self," but is unsure how to achieve this end. He begins to sit outside of a particular church to listen to the music of the organist within. One day the organist, whose name is Pistorius, invites Sinclair to come inside the church and listen. Pistorius then invites Sinclair back to his room, where they discuss religious and philosophical ideas. Pistorius explains that he believes in the god called Abraxas, who represents both the light and the dark elements of the world.

Sinclair spends many evenings with Pistorius, during which time he is exposed to a broad range of ideas and beliefs drawn from many different religions and philosophies throughout the world. Pistorius becomes Sinclair's role model and encourages him to find his true self through discussing his dreams and ideas. One of the younger boys in school, Knauer, seeks out Sinclair for guidance in his own path of self-development. Sinclair explains to Knauer that he must come to terms with himself on his own in order to discover his own heart. Sinclair completes another painting of a face he saw in a dream. He comes to realize that the face is an image of his own "daemon," an "ideal and intensification" of his inner self. Shortly before graduating from school Sinclair finds himself criticizing Pistorius for the first time. This conflict ends their friendship, but Sinclair realizes that the break with his "guide" is a positive step in the direction of taking his own path in life.

University

In the sixth chapter, Sinclair realizes that his painting representing his inner self resembles the face of Demian's mother. He becomes filled with the desire to find her, but has no idea where she lives. He enrolls in the University of H., where he is disappointed by his courses. One day he runs into Demian, whom he has not seen in years, on the street in the town where he is attending university. Demian can see that Sinclair has become more advanced in the discovery of his inner self, and the two young men discuss religion, philosophy, and the politics and society of Europe. Demian invites Sinclair home to meet his mother, Frau Eva, whom Sinclair has only seen from a distance in the past. As soon as Sinclair sees Demian's mother, he realizes that she is certainly the face from his dream. She and Demian show Sinclair that they have hung his painting of the bird emerging from its egg in their home. Sinclair spends much of his time at their house discussing his ideas with their circle of friends, who engage in a variety of open-minded ideas about philosophy, religion, and society. Sinclair develops a special relationship with Frau Eva, and they often discuss his dreams and his desire to discover his inner self.

War

By the final chapter, Sinclair has achieved a sense of inner peace and harmony with himself. Soon, however, World War I breaks out, and both Sinclair and Demian fight in the army. When Sinclair is injured in the war, he awakens in a hospital bed to discover that Demian, also injured, is lying in the bed next to him. The next morning Sinclair discovers that Demian has died. Sinclair realizes that Demian has always been the key to his "daemon," his true inner self.

Characters

Beatrice

While in boarding school, Sinclair sees a young woman from a distance, walking in the park. He becomes infatuated with the woman, to whom he never speaks. He thinks of her as Beatrice, a reference to Dante, based on a painting he has seen of the fictional Beatrice. Sinclair describes Beatrice as "tall and slender, elegantly dressed," with "a touch of exuberance and boyishness in her face." Sinclair first sees her during his period of debauchery, when he is often drunk, failing in school, and in financial debt. The sight of Beatrice, however, sparks his imagination, inspiring him to reform his drunken, rebellious ways. He states that his thoughts of Beatrice have a "profound influence" on his life, inspiring him to turn away from the "dark," sinful side of life and strive for "purity

and nobility." He becomes self-reflective, and starts painting images of Beatrice. To Sinclair, the figure of Beatrice is an object of worship; he says that her image "gave me access to a holy shrine," and "transformed me into a worshiper in a temple." Eventually the image of Beatrice fades, but Sinclair continues to live out the transformation he underwent as a result of her place in his imagination.

Alfons Beck

Alfons Beck in an older boy at Sinclair's boarding school who encounters Sinclair on the street one evening and takes him to a bar, where Sinclair gets drunk for the first time in his life. After this night Sinclair enters a period of debauchery, during which time he gains a reputation for excessive drinking and raucous, rebellious behavior.

Max Demian

Max Demian is the central influence in Sinclair's personal development. Sinclair first meets Demian in grade school, when Demian encourages him to question traditional interpretations of biblical stories. Demian saves Sinclair from being tormented by Franz Kromer through means which are never revealed, although it seems as if he threatened Kromer with physical harm. When Demian enrolls in the same confirmation course with Sinclair a few years later, the two boys become friends. Demian continues to express unconventional ideas about religion, which Sinclair finds intriguing yet disturbing. After leaving his home town to attend a boarding school, Sinclair loses touch with Demian. He encounters Demian only once during his high school years, while in his drunken phase, and is embarrassed by his own behavior, which is rude and a turnoff to his childhood friend.

When Sinclair experiences a personal transformation, the image of Demian continues to haunt him, although he has completely lost touch with him. Sinclair next encounters Demian while he is attending university. The two young men immediately revive their friendship, and Demian takes Sinclair home to meet his mother.

Demian is a formative influence on Sinclair's life because he is the first person to open Sinclair's mind to a questioning of traditional values and ideas. Demian also has a strong symbolic significance, as he represents the true, deep inner self which Sinclair strives to discover. As the novel ends, Demian has died in an army hospital after being injured in combat during World War I. Sinclair, however, understands that Demian has become one with his own deep self, and now represents his "daemon," or true inner self.

Frau Eva

Frau Eva is Demian's mother. As a schoolboy, Sinclair never meets Demian's mother, although the two boys are friends. While on vacation from his boarding school, Sinclair comes across a picture of Demian's mother, and recognizes hers as a face from one of his dreams. He becomes overwhelmed with the desire to meet her, but has no idea where she and Demian are living. When he moves to a new town and enters university, Sinclair encounters Demian walking down the street, and Demian brings Sinclair home to meet his mother. Sinclair immediately recognizes Frau Eva as the image from his dream. He subsequently has many conversations with Frau Eva which help him further along the path of discovering his inner self. Frau Eva symbolizes many elements of Sinclair's search for himself, representing a mother, a lover, and a figure of the feminine element of his own psyche. Critics have interpreted the symbolic significance of Frau Eva in a variety of ways, psychoanalytically, religiously, and philosophically. Frau Eva is one of the most important elements of Sinclair's search to find his inner heart.

Dr. Follens

Dr. Follens is a young assistant professor in one of Sinclair's courses while at boarding school. In the course of one lecture, Dr. Follens mentions the ancient concept of the god Abraxas, who represents both the dark and light elements of the world. Although the professor mentions Abraxas only as an aside to his lecture, the idea sparks Sinclair's imagination, and becomes a central element of his personal belief system.

Knauer

Knauer is a younger boy at Sinclair's boarding school who seeks out Sinclair in search of greater wisdom and insight. Knauer is a sort of young disciple of Sinclair, in the same manner in which Sinclair himself was a sort of disciple of Demian during his school days. Knauer expresses to Sinclair his suicidal despair, his desire for insight, and his urge to discuss deep religious and philosophical concerns. Sinclair tells Knauer that he cannot show the younger boy the way to his true inner self, that each person must discover on his own his "innermost heart" and purpose in life. Knauer clings to Sinclair, always asking questions and seeking spiritual guidance, which Sinclair insists he cannot provide. Sinclair later realizes that he had learned important lessons of his own from the questions and ideas brought to him by Knauer. Toward the end of Sinclair's stay at the boarding school, Knauer slips out of his life.

Franz Kromer

Franz Kromer is a boy in Sinclair's home town who has a significant impact on Sinclair's life when Sinclair is ten years old. Franz Kromer is a tough kid, the type with whom the sheltered Sinclair rarely played as a child. However, one day, Sinclair tries to impress Kromer by making up a story that he had stolen some apples from a local farmer. Kromer claims he knows the farmer whose apples were stolen, and threatens to hand Sinclair over to the police for his crime unless Sinclair pays him a sum of money. Over the next few weeks Kromer bullies Sinclair into stealing change from his own parents and offering other gifts to the older boy in fear of being reported for the fictional crime he had supposedly committed. Sinclair's life becomes completely dominated by Kromer's threats and demands. When Demian learns that Kromer is the source of Sinclair's troubles, he engages in an unspecified confrontation with Kromer, after which Kromer leaves Sinclair alone and never bothers him again.

Pistorius

Pistorius is one of the important influences on Sinclair's development. He is an organist at a church but does not himself conform to any conventional religion. Sinclair hears Pistorius's organ music while out walking, and often sits outside the church on the steps to listen to the music. Eventually Pistorius invites him into the church to listen. One evening he invites Sinclair home with him, up to his attic room, where they lie on the floor staring into the fire. Pistorius is an unconventional thinker, and exposes Sinclair to a wide range of religious and philosophical ideas. He teaches Sinclair about the god known as Abraxas, who represents both the dark and the light elements of the world. Sinclair spends many nights in discussion with Pistorius throughout the remainder of his boarding school days. Shortly before leaving school, Sinclair learns that he has outgrown his teacher; he finds himself criticizing Pistorius for the first time, an event which brings an end to their friendship.

Emil Sinclair

Emil Sinclair is the protagonist and narrator of *Demian*, which is subtitled, "The Story of Emil

Sinclair's Youth." Emil is a semi-autobiographical figure based on the youth of Hermann Hesse, and is the result of Hesse's own experience of self-exploration through psychoanalysis. Sinclair tells the story of his personal development from age ten to approximately age twenty. He is influenced in his personal journey of self-discovery by a number of people he meets during this period, most significantly Max Demian, a fellow schoolboy. Sinclair describes his major formative experiences and friendships that aid in his inward journey. Demian opens Sinclair's mind by inviting him to question traditional interpretations of biblical stories. Sinclair is discomfited but intrigued by the unconventional ideas expressed by Demian.

Sinclair attends a boarding school in his high school years, during which he goes through several distinct phases of development. In his drunken, rebellious phase he becomes an unruly and undisciplined student, with a reputation for drinking and carousing. This phase of self-loathing ends abruptly when he sees a young woman from afar, to whom he never speaks, but who he thinks of as Beatrice. She represents an image of almost religious perfection which inspires him to transform himself overnight into a sober, self-reflective, conscientious person. During this period, he begins to paint faces and images from his dreams. Sinclair's other major influence is Pistorius, a freethinker who spends many evenings with Sinclair discussing a broad range of religious and philosophical ideas.

While attending university, Sinclair encounters Demian, with whom he had lost touch, and Demian introduces him to his mother, Frau Eva. Sinclair regards Frau Eva as a dream-image representing a spiritual, psychological, and emotional ideal. He becomes part of a larger circle of open-minded, freethinking people who congregate at the home of Frau Eva and Demian. Sinclair develops a clearer sense of his inner self and his own personal identity. When World War I breaks out, Sinclair becomes a soldier. The final step in his personal development comes when he finds that Demian himself has died. He then realizes that Demian represents his own inner "daemon," or true self, and resides within his own soul.

Sinclair's Father

Sinclair's father represents the good, "light," pious world of his family. After Sinclair feels he has entered the "dark" world associated with Franz Kromer, he feels not just distant, but actually superior to his father, as if he possesses knowledge his Father does not have. When Sinclair mentions to his father Demian's alternative interpretation of the biblical story of Cain and Abel, his father immediately dismisses it as incorrect. While Sinclair is at boarding school, his father writes him many times to express disapproval of the rebellious, drunken life he is leading. At one point, his father even comes to the school to threaten Sinclair with expulsion if he does not reform his unruly ways. After Sinclair makes the transformation from his period of unruliness to his period of striving for purity, his father's letters to him at school become more congenial. Sinclair's father is a symbol of the traditional way of thinking, from which Sinclair breaks away in order to develop his own ideas and personal identity.

Sinclair's Mother

Sinclair's mother represents the good, "light," pious world of his childhood family life. After Sinclair becomes involved with the "dark" world of Franz Kromer, he feels distanced from his mother. By the end of the novel, Demian's mother, Frau Eva, comes to represent Sinclair's true spiritual mother. While Frau Eva is extremely open-minded in her ideas about religion and philosophy, Sinclair's own mother is very traditional in her beliefs.

Sinclair's Sisters

Sinclair mentions his two sisters, but makes no distinction between them and does not name them. His sisters represent the good, "light," pious world of his childhood home. After his experience with Kromer, Sinclair feels distanced from his sisters because he no longer feels a part of their world of "light" and good.

Themes

Discovering the Inner Self & Formulating a Personal Identity

The central theme of *Demian* is the process of discovering a deep, true, inner self. The novel opens with a statement set off from the rest of the text: "I wanted only to try to live in accord with the promptings which came from my true self. Why was that so very difficult?" The novel then traces the difficult task of finding this true self in the face of societal pressures to conform. Sinclair encounters many obstacles in his quest for personal identity, including family, religion, and school. Demian is a significant early influence on Sinclair because

Topics For Further Study

- *Demian* takes place during two distinct eras of German history, and was published in a third era. Research and write about the history of Germany during *one* of these eras: the German Empire (1871–1914); World War I (1914–1918); or the Weimar Republic (1919–1933). What was the political system in Germany during the era? What was the status of Germany's relations with other European and world nations? What major political and social issues and conflicts faced the German people during the era?

- Hesse was strongly influenced by several authors roughly contemporary to his own life, including Thomas Mann, André Gide, and Franz Kafka. Write an essay about one of these authors. What are his major works of fiction? What central themes are addressed in his novels and stories? What similarities do you see between the fiction of this author and that of Hesse?

- *Demian* was written by Hesse soon after his experience of psychoanalysis, and is based on the influence of psychoanalytic theorists Sigmund Freud and Carl Jung. Hesse makes much use of the symbolism and imagery of dreams in *Demian*. Both Freud and Jung wrote extensively on the psychology of dreams and dream interpretation. Research and write about the dream theories of either Freud or Jung. What are his basic theories about the psychology of dreams? To what extent do you agree or disagree with this theory?

- Hesse's fiction is often characterized as impressionist. German impressionism was an aesthetic movement that influenced many artistic mediums in addition to literature, including painting, film, and music. Research the major works of German impressionism in *one* of these three media. What are the major impressionist artists and works in this medium? How is impressionism developed in this particular medium?

- *Demian* is the narrative of one young man's journey from childhood to adulthood, describing the development of his personal identity during the difficult years of adolescence. Write your own autobiographical narrative of your personal development up to this point in your life. What people or ideas have contributed to the formation of your ideas and personal identity? What struggles have you encountered in the process of becoming the person you are today? Describe the type of person you would like to be in the future. What obstacles might you encounter on the way to becoming that person?

---

he is the first person in Sinclair's life to invite a questioning attitude toward generally accepted ideas, such as the interpretation of certain biblical stories. When Sinclair is sent to boarding school, he loses touch with Demian, and, symbolically, with his inner self. He enters a phase of drunkenness in which any tendencies toward self-reflection are squelched. Only the sight of Beatrice, an idealized image of a woman he does not know, inspires Sinclair to continue on the path toward self-knowledge. By the time he has entered university Sinclair is well on his way toward a full realization of his personal identity and a full understanding of his inner self. When he meets Demian again after several years without contact, Sinclair is fully open to what Demian and Frau Eva, as well as their circle of friends, have to offer him in the way of defining his personal identity.

Dreams

The importance of dreams in achieving self-knowledge is a central theme throughout *Demian*. It is widely understood that *Demian* was written by Hesse to express his experience of personal insight gained through psychoanalysis. Hesse was analyzed by Lang, a disciple of Jung, who wrote extensively on the psychology of dreams. Hesse was also influenced by the writings of Sigmund Freud, and Freud's theory of dream psychology. Sinclair describes powerful and recurring dreams which help him gain insight into his true inner being. In particular, his dream of a bird emerging from a shell allows him to visualize his own inner urge to break away from societal norms in order to develop a sense of personal identity.

The Artistic Impulse

An important step in Sinclair's search for personal identity is the development of his artistic temperament. Inspired by the sight of Beatrice, Sinclair begins to express images from his dreams through painting. He at first tries painting Beatrice, and later paints the image of a face he saw in a dream. Painting becomes a process of expressing his inner being through the exploration of his dream images. His paintings thus ultimately symbolize his striving for a sense of wholeness through integrating all the elements of his true inner self. Hesse often wrote about young men struggling with an artistic temperament in a society that threatened to stifle individuality and thwart creative impulses. Thus, an important element of Sinclair's personal identity is his desire to unleash his impulse toward artistic creation.

Style

Narrative Voice

Demian is written in the first-person narrative voice. Emil Sinclair is both the narrator and the protagonist of the story. Hesse's choice of first-person narration is central to *Demian*, because Sinclair is describing his own inward journey toward self-knowledge and the formulation of his personal identity. Critics have noted that *Demian* does not have a strong or complex plot, because the novel is concerned with a process of self-reflection rather than a series of external events. It has also been noted that Sinclair's recollection of significant childhood events, powerful dreams, and internal struggles resembles the process by which a patient expresses himself to a psychoanalyst.

Setting

Demian is set in Germany during the decade preceding World War I, the early years of the twentieth century. It is interesting to note that Hesse's own youth did not coincide with these events, as he grew up during the final decades of the nineteenth century and was some forty years old at the point in history when his protagonist is about twenty years old. The setting of *Demian* is significant because Hesse drew a parallel between the historical transformation of Europe and the personal transformation of a youth coming of age. Toward the end of the novel Sinclair discusses the fate of Europe with Demian and his circle of free-thinking friends. He comes to feel that the impending war represents the birth pangs of a new Europe. Although Hesse was opposed to war, he felt that the war was necessary for Germany and all of Europe to be redefined. When the war begins, Demian and Sinclair are swept up in the atmosphere of excitement with which Germans first entered the war. They both become soldiers and are wounded in battle, although Demian dies and Sinclair lives. The setting of the war is significant to the novel in part because the generation of German readers—who felt that Hesse's novel spoke to their own experiences of war and their struggle for personal identity—had experienced combat directly.

Symbolism

Hesse makes strong use of symbolism in *Demian*. Sinclair describes many vivid and powerful dreams which are symbolic of his own personal struggles. A recurring symbol, which appears in his dreams and is then depicted in his painting, is that of a bird emerging from a giant egg, struggling to free itself from the shell in which it has been contained. This image symbolizes Sinclair's struggle to free himself from the emotional, religious, intellectual, and social restrictions of his family and conventional society. Sinclair sends his painting of the bird to Demian, and is moved when, years later, he finds that it hangs prominently in the house of Demian and his mother, Frau Eva. The personal freedom and self-determination symbolized by the bird's escape from the egg are realized by Sinclair in the company and the home of these two influences. Another recurring symbol is the face he sees in dreams and then paints. Sinclair recognizes the face, but his sense of who it resembles changes. At various points he sees the face as Beatrice, as Demian, and as Frau Eva. Ultimately the face symbolizes Sinclair himself, whose identity incorporates elements of the important people in his life.

Compare & Contrast

- **1871–1918:** This period of German history is known as the era of the German Empire. In 1871, the German Empire is formed, and under a newly created constitution, the empire is governed by an Emperor and two houses.

  1918–1933: This period of German history is known as the Weimar Republic. In the aftermath of World War I, Emperor William II is forced to abdicate. In 1918 a newly formed democratic German Republic is proclaimed, under a new constitution calling for a popularly elected president.

  1933–1945: This period of German history is known as the era of Nazi Germany or the Third Reich. Hitler rises to power in Germany when he is named chancellor in 1933. During the years of World War II (1939–1945) Hitler oversees the murder of some six million Jews (and others) in his Nazi death camps.

  1945–1949: In 1945, Germany is defeated in World War II by Allied forces and Hitler commits suicide. From 1945–1949, a defeated Germany is occupied by Allied forces.

  1949–1989: This period of German history is known as the era of partition. In 1949, Germany is divided into two nations: The German Democratic Republic (East Germany), under Soviet influence, and The Federal Republic of Germany (West Germany), under Allied influence. In 1961, Soviet forces construct a wall, known as the Berlin Wall, sealing East Germany off from West Germany and the Western World.

  Today: With the collapse of the Soviet Union in 1989, the Berlin Wall is brought down. East and West Germany are reunified after some forty years of partition. The reunified nation is named the Federal Republic of Germany.

- **1890–1914:** During the late 1890s and early 1900s, Germany's economy becomes rapidly industrialized, urbanized, and successful. Germany becomes one of the major industrial nations of the world.

- **1914–1918:** During the latter years of World War I, the German economy suffers. Severe food shortages result in malnutrition and starvation of many citizens. At the war's end, returning soldiers are left jobless and without adequate food supplies.

  1918–1923: During the years following World War I, the German economy faces severe setbacks, with massive unemployment and astronomical inflation.

  Today: The reunification of East and West Germany results in economic difficulties for the nation during the 1990s. Before reunification, West Germany had enjoyed prosperity and the most favorable wage rates and labor benefits in the world; however, merging with the economically stagnant former East Germany puts a severe strain on the economy. Other costs associated with reunification continue to weigh down the German economy, although the late 1990s see some economic recovery.

- **1914–1918:** In World War I, Germany is part of the Central Powers, which include Austria-Hungary and Turkey, is at war with the six nations of the Allies, including Britain, France, and the United States. Germany is defeated by the Allies in World War I.

  1939–1945: In World War II, Germany, part of the Axis Powers, is at war with the Allies, which include Britain and the United States. Germany, the initial aggressor in World War II, is defeated by the Allies.

  Today: Germany is a member of the European Union, an organization comprised of most of the nations of Western Europe to facilitate international trade and maintain peaceful international relations throughout Europe. A single European currency is implemented to further create economic cooperation among the nations of the European Community. Germany also belongs to the North Atlantic Treaty Organization (NATO).

Historical Context

Germany: 1871–1918

Demian is set in Germany, beginning approximately ten years before the start of World War I. The period of German history from 1871 to 1918 is known as the era of the German Empire. The German Empire was formed in 1871 from the combination of Prussia and three other German states. The government was ruled by an emperor, but also had a constitution and an elected legislative body. In *Demian*, Sinclair's school years are set during the reign of the emperor (also called the Kaiser) William II, which lasted from 1888 (when Hesse was ten or eleven years old) until the end of World War I (1918). William II also served as king of Prussia (the largest of Germany's five states).

Germany in World War I

World War I (also known as the Great War, or the First World War) began in 1914, when a Serbian nationalist assassinated the Archduke Franz Ferdinand, heir to the throne of the Austro-Hungarian Empire. The war that grew out of this conflict pitted the Central Powers (Germany, Austria-Hungary, Bulgaria and Turkey) against the Allies (France, Great Britain, Russia, Italy, Japan, and the United States). The war was initially popular among German citizens, who rallied together in a rush of nationalist pride. However, as the war progressed, German citizens on the home-front suffered the consequences of severe food shortages which led to massive malnutrition as well as starvation.

The War ended in 1918 when the Central Powers suffered defeat at the hands of the Allies. The Armistice of 1918 was followed by the Paris Peace Conference of 1919–1920, during which the Treaty of Versailles was drafted and signed. The Treaty of Versailles outlined specific principles for the restructuring of relations between the nations involved in the conflict. This included the call for a restructuring of Europe to create several independent nation states from the former empires of Austria-Hungary, Germany, Russia, and Turkey. The Treaty of Versailles also required extensive war reparations to be paid by Germany.

Germany in the Post-War Years

German soldiers returning from a war in which they were defeated came home to find widespread hunger, high unemployment rates, and outrageous rates of inflation. Over 11 million German men, about 18 percent of the population, had fought in the war effort, which resulted in some 2 million casualties. To make matters worse, a flu epidemic spread throughout Germany in the aftermath of the war. Civil discontent resulted in revolution, and in 1918 the emperor William II was forced to abdicate from the throne, making room for the formation of a new democratic German republic, unofficially known as the Weimar Republic. The Weimar Republic included a newly written constitution that called for a popularly elected president and provided women the right to vote for the first time. The Weimar Republic lasted until Adolph Hitler rose to power in 1933.

In the 1920s, during the early years of the new Weimar Republic, the German economy suffered. The Treaty of Versailles, ending World War I after German defeat, required Germany to pay enormous war reparations. In addition, Germany had gone into massive debt from wartime expenditures. The consequences of these conditions, and Germany's response to them, resulted in massive inflation in the early 1920s, reaching its peak in 1923. In that year the German mark fell rapidly by the minute, rendering the amount of a life savings almost worthless. After this point the German government initiated reforms and policy changes which allowed the economy to recover.

Critical Overview

The reception of Hesse's work by critics, both in Germany and abroad, changed over the course of several distinct phases in his life, as well as after his death. His first novel, *Peter Camenzind*, was popularly received by German critics and readers. However, during World War I, Hesse's move to neutral Switzerland and his public denouncement of war and German nationalism caused the German public to regard him as a traitor to his nation, resulting in the denouncement of his writing by most Germany readers and critics.

Demian was first published in 1919, within a year after the end of World War I. In an attempt to evade his declining reputation in Germany, Hesse submitted *Demian* under the pseudonym Sinclair (the same name as the novel's protagonist and narrator). The novel immediately struck a chord in German readers, particularly the generation of young men who fought in the war. In a 1947 introduction to *Demian*, German émigré novelist Thomas Mann described the impact of *Demian* on German readers at the time of its initial publication:

The electrifying influence exercised on a whole generation just after the First World War by *Demian*, from the pen of a certain mysterious Sinclair, is unforgettable. With uncanny accuracy this poetic work struck the nerve of the times and called forth grateful rapture from a whole youthful generation.

By the time Hesse publicly claimed authorship of *Demian*, a year after its initial publication, the groundwork was laid for a revival of his popularity as a German writer.

During the era of Nazi Germany (1933–1945), however, Hesse was again denounced as a traitor to the German people because he criticized nationalism and praised a number of prominent German-Jewish authors. However, Hesse's outstanding contribution to world literature was given international recognition when he was awarded the Nobel Prize in Literature in 1946. In the wake of World War II, with the fall of Nazi Germany and the award of the 1946 Nobel Prize in Literature, Hesse enjoyed another period of renewed interest and serious critical attention on the part of German critics.

Hesse's fiction enjoyed a popular revival during the 1960s and 1970s, when his impressionistic novels stressing self-reflection and the desire to turn away from conventional religion and thought in order to achieve a sense of deep personal identity resonated with the questioning ethos of the American youth counterculture. Anna Otten explains the phenomenon of three distinct generations that raised Hesse's status to that of a "cult" figure, explaining that, for German youth after World Wars I and II, as well as for American youth during the 1960s and 1970s, "In each instance it would seem that the cults were formed of young people who, profoundly dissatisfied with the world created by their elders, set out to seek new values."

In *Hermann Hesse* (1978), Joseph Mileck described the universal mythical elements of *Demian* which account for the novel's popularity among several generations of youth in different nations at different points in history:

> Sinclair's inner story emerges clear and his simple tale becomes mythic: a story of youth's timeless quest for the self, mirroring man's typological course from childhood innocence through doubt, sin, agony, and despair, to a hoped-for ultimate second innocence, his humanization . . . as Hesse would call it.

Discussion of *Demian* by literary critics often focuses on the element of Jungian psychoanalytic theory in the symbolic elements of the story. It is frequently pointed out that the characters of Demian and Frau Eva symbolize elements of Sinclair's inner psyche. Mileck, in the *Dictionary of*

Swiss psychiatrist Carl Jung, who treated Hesse

Literary Biography, describes the Jungian symbolism embodied by these two characters:

> Demian and Frau Eva are multidimensional symbols, concepts thinly actualized. Demian is Sinclair's Socratic *daimon*, his admonishing inner self, but he is also a Jungian imago, Sinclair's mental image of the ideal self, and is also the reflective, culturally unconditioned alter ego Sinclair must become before he can begin to "live himself." Frau Eva is Sinclair's Jungian anima, the soul, the unconscious with which his conscious mind must establish rapport in the process of individuation, and also life in all its fullness, heaven and earth, an actualized Magna Mater, mankind's origin and destiny.

In addition to the teachings of Jung and Sigmund Freud, the influence of the philosopher Frederich Nietszche in *Demian* has also been discussed, as have the many biblical references, from Cain and Abel to the Prodigal Son to Jacob.

Criticism

Liz Brent

Brent has a Ph.D. in American culture, specializing in film studies, from the University of Michigan. She is a freelance writer and teaches courses on the history of American cinema. In the

> Hesse's attitude toward religion as expressed in *Demian* thus calls for the importance of religious questioning on the part of the individual, while also acknowledging the value of some form of under-standing of oneself and the world in terms of religious ideas."

following essay, Brent discusses the theme of religion in Demian.

Sinclair's struggles with religion, particularly Christianity, throughout *Demian*, are central to the development of his personal identity and individualized belief system. This process of development occurs in two distinct stages. First, Sinclair begins to question the precepts of devout Christian faith in which he was raised. Secondly, Sinclair learns to consider the spiritual wisdom of other religions and belief systems from throughout the world and throughout history. By the end of the novel, Sinclair does not completely renounce Christianity, but picks and chooses elements of various religions and philosophies—including Christianity—by which to make sense of his true nature and his experience of the world around him.

In the first phase of his journey, Sinclair learns to question traditional interpretations of Christian doctrine. He does not, however, completely renounce Christianity, as ideas, beliefs, and stories drawn from the Christian tradition continue to play a key role in his journey toward his true inner self. He does, however, learn to interpret Christian doctrine in unconventional ways.

As the novel opens, Sinclair is ten years old and his understanding of the world is firmly rooted in the Christian precepts of good and evil. The young Sinclair perceives the world as consisting of two realms: the good, light world of religious piety; and the evil, dark world of sin. The first time Sinclair experiences an inkling of reli-

gious doubt is after he tells a lie, the consequences of which result in his feeling that he has entered the dark world of evil and sin. Because he is keeping a secret from his parents, the feeling that he possesses knowledge unknown to his father results in a perception that the "holy image" he had of his father as all-powerful has been diminished. Sinclair's feelings toward his father represent his feelings about God—thus, his perception of the "holy image" of God is likewise diminished by his personal experience of the "dark" realm of sin.

Sinclair's path toward the realization of his personal identity is aided by the influence of key people who open his mind to independent thought. Demian is the first such influence, encouraging Sinclair to question traditional interpretations of biblical stories, such as Cain and Abel, the Prodigal Son, and Jacob. For example, Demian interprets the biblical story of Cain and Abel, in which Cain is a murderer of his own brother, in such a way that Cain is considered the hero of the story. Demian also provides a nontraditional interpretation of the mark that God is said to have put on Cain's forehead. Rather than being a mark of sin, Demian interprets the "mark" as a metaphor for an air of "distinction" others perceived in Cain. Demian explains that it is likely Cain had "a little more intellect and boldness in his look than people were used to." This point is significant later in the story, because Demian and his mother, Frau Eva, describe various people (and eventually Sinclair) as having "the mark"—by which they mean such people have a quality of distinction about them which suggests a desire to strive for independent thought and true self-knowledge.

Demian goes on to explain to Sinclair that he is not claiming the biblical story of Cain to be inauthentic; rather, that "Such age-old stories are always true but they aren't always properly recorded and aren't always given correct interpretations." This explanation captures the attitude toward Christianity expressed by Hesse throughout *Demian*: Christianity contains some age-old wisdom, valuable lessons, and meaningful iconography, but each person must look beyond conventional interpretations of religion to find his or her own personal truths.

During confirmation classes, Demian's influence on the development of Sinclair's capacity for independent thought increases through the regular questioning of the teacher's traditional approach to biblical stories. Sinclair notes that, as a result of Demian's influence, "cracks had begun to appear in my religious faith." However, Sinclair asserts that these new ideas did not cause him to question the significance of a spiritual life, but, "On the contrary, I still stood in the deepest awe of the religious." Sinclair's strong feeling for the importance of some form of spirituality, although not necessarily a conventional Christian faith, remains constant throughout the novel.

Hesse's attitude toward religion as expressed in *Demian* thus calls for the importance of religious questioning on the part of the individual, while also acknowledging the value of some form of understanding of oneself and the world in terms of religious ideas. Sinclair explains that Demian "had accustomed me to regard and interpret religious stories and dogma more freely, more individually, even playfully, with more imagination." This freer, individualized interpretation of the Christian doctrine in which he was raised is the first step in Sinclair's journey toward his true inner self and the formulation of his personal identity.

In the second phase of his journey toward self-knowledge and self-actualization, Sinclair learns to draw from the wisdom of many religions, cultures, thinkers, and historical eras in order to formulate his own personal belief system. By the end of the novel, Sinclair's conception of himself and the world is no longer divided into "two realms" of light and dark, but includes a perception that both elements are part of a larger whole. Sinclair's concept of a god who encompasses both realms is referred to as Abraxas.

While in a class at boarding school, Sinclair finds a note stuck in his textbook that refers to a god called "Abraxas." Although he hasn't seen Demian in years, and has no idea where to find him, Sinclair is certain that the note has come from Demian by some mysterious means. The next day, his professor, Dr. Follens, lectures to the class about the ancient concept of Abraxas as expressing a "profound philosophy." He explains that the name Abraxas "occurs in connection with Greek magical formulas and is frequently considered the name of some magician's helper such as certain uncivilized tribes believe in even at present." Dr. Follens continues, "But it appears that Abraxas has a much deeper significance." He concludes, "We may conceive of the name as that of a godhead whose symbolic task is the uniting of godly and devilish elements." Sinclair understands from the lecture that Abraxas combines both good and evil, light and dark, into one realm, and is thus "the god who was both god and devil."

Although Demian does not name the god Abraxas until years later, the ideas he expressed to

Sinclair while they were still in grade school put forth a similar ideal of uniting both the "light" and "dark" elements of the world into one god, rather than separating the world of good from the world of evil. Demian argues that, in relegating part of the world to the realm of evil, "this entire slice of the world, this entire half is suppressed and hushed up." He asserts, "we ought to consider everything sacred, the entire world, not merely this artificially separated half!" Demian uses as an example the suppression of sexuality exerted through Christian teachings. His point is that the realm of life that includes sexuality should also be regarded as an element of the divine. (However, this does not mean that Demian advocates hedonism or debauchery; when Sinclair runs into Demian while on vacation during his period of drunkenness, Demian points out that excessive drinking seems to hold little spiritual or mystical value.)

The development of Sinclair's personal belief system is furthered by his exposure to a broad range of unconventional ideas as presented to him by key people in his life. Sinclair's friendship with Pistorius during his final year at boarding school further opens his mind to a wide range of religious and philosophical ideas. Rather than conforming to traditional Christian beliefs, Pistorius teaches Sinclair to consider Eastern religious beliefs, as well as philosophical ideas such as that of Frederich Nietzsche, and even scientific theories. Pistorius also exposes Sinclair to further exploration of the concept of Abraxas. Like Sinclair, Pistorius was raised in a deeply religious household, and yet has chosen not to follow the traditional practice of Christianity. Instead, he draws from a variety of sources of wisdom and mystical enlightenment to formulate his own understanding of the spiritual element of the world. Sinclair is further exposed to a broad range of unconventional religious and philosophical ideas toward the end of the novel, when he becomes part of the social circle of freethinkers who gather at the home of Demian and Frau Eva.

In *Demian*, Hesse ultimately does not renounce Christianity, but suggests the possibility of combining the beliefs and ideas of many different cultures, religions, and thinkers in order to formulate a personal understanding of oneself and the world. At one point in the novel, Pistorius comments that, although he is no longer faithful to the Christian church, "I'm still interested to see what kinds of gods people have devised for themselves." Hesse's message about religion in *Demian* may be summed up as the following: each individual must "devise" his or her own set of religious or spiritual ideas;

What
Do I Read
Next?

- *The Interpretation of Dreams* (1900) is the seminal text on dream theory by Sigmund Freud, the father of psychoanalysis. Hesse was familiar with the theories of Freud and considered him a strong influence.

- *Dreams* (1974) is a selection of writings about dreams by Carl Jung, one of the fathers of psychoanalytic theory. Hesse was a psychoanalytic patient of Jung, and *Demian* was written in part as an expression of the effect Jung had on him.

- *The Magic Mountain* (1924) is one of the best-known novels by Thomas Mann, a friend and fellow German writer to Hesse. *The Magic Mountain* is about a young man's experiences in a tuberculosis sanitarium in the mountains.

- *All Quiet on the Western Front* (1929), by Erich Maria Remarque, is a now-classic narrative based on the experiences of a German soldier in World War I.

- The *Complete Stories* (1983) of Franz Kafka includes many masterpieces by an author whom Hesse regarded as one of his major influences.

- Some of Kafka's most celebrated stories include "Metamorphosis" and "The Hunger Artist."

- *Siddhartha* (1922) is one of Hesse's most celebrated novels. It tells the story of the early life of Buddha.

- *Magister Ludi: The Glass Bead Game* (1943) is one of Hesse's most celebrated novels. It takes place in the future in an elite community of intellectuals and scholars.

- In *The Fairy Tales of Hermann Hesse* (1995), the author combines elements of Eastern religion and European folktales to create original stories relevant to the modern world.

- *German Expressionism* (1997), edited by Stephanie Barron and Wolf-Dieter Dube, provides images of German expressionist paintings as well as discussion of German expressionism in drama, music, film, and architecture.

- *The German Empire, 1870–1918* (2000), by Michael Stürmer, offers a social and political history of Germany during the era of the German Empire.

---

this should come about a result of much self-reflection, or soul-searching, as well as contemplation of many forms of spiritual wisdom from throughout history and culture; and no one set of beliefs is necessarily meaningful to any given individual. Hesse seems to be calling for a sort of religion of the individual, which draws freely from the wisdom of the ages throughout the world and is constructed by each person in accordance with "the promptings of [his] true self."

Source: Liz Brent, Critical Essay on *Demian*, in *Novels for Students*, The Gale Group, 2002.

Eugene L. Stelzig

In the following excerpt, Stelzig considers the Jungian context of Hesse's Demian.

. . . Hesse's novel emerged in a burst of confession. Written between September and October 1917, in the last stage of Hesse's treatment by Dr. Lang, it was not published until after the war. It appeared in spring 1919 under the name of the narrator, Emil Sinclair, and became for several years one of the most popular and influential books among German youth. Hesse's choice of a pseudonym (which he was forced to abandon in 1920 when his authorship was guessed by the critics) reflects his belief that through the crisis of the war he had emerged as a different writer, and it was also his way of resisting "the stupid role" of "the beloved writer of entertaining literature" that no longer suited him and that might put off a new generation "with the well-known name of an old uncle."

Though Hesse (like most Germans) seems never to have heard of Blake, *Demian* is his autobiographical marriage of heaven and hell in a late-Romantic, early modernist *Bildungsroman* strongly marked by the impact of Jungian analysis. As he wrote about the book a decade later, creative writing (*Dichtung*) is not a mere transcription of life, but a poeticizing of it (*ein Verdichten*), and in *Demian* as in the psychoanalytic *Märchen*, Hesse's metaphorizing of his experience turns on the exploration of the unconscious through a pervasive mother myth. As a modern romance of the inner self and a fictional reworking of carefully selected aspects of Hesse's childhood and youth, *Demian* incorporates some basic features and tendencies of Jungian thought: the assumption that the individual is the primary reality, the portentous-prophetic language about the challenges and hazards of individuation, the amoral or neutral attitude to the "dark" suggestions of the self, the sense of the mysterious connections between the inner and the outer worlds (compare Jung's concept of "synchronicity"), the endorsement of creative activity as an instrument of self-realization (for example, the "positive function" of expressing "for example, in writing, painting, sculpture, musical composition" the suggestions sent by the anima), the preoccupation with myth and religion transposed into psychic categories, the associative style of thinking and writing, and finally, some more bizarre aspects, like psychobiology (compare Pistorius's yoking, at the end of Chapter 5, of the vestigial air-bladder in fish with the "flying bladder" of dreams). Jung himself was not shy about seizing on the Jungian element of *Demian*, as a 1919 letter to Hesse shows, in which he first compliments him ("your book hit me like the beam of a lighthouse on a stormy night"), then proceeds to an interpretation of the ending that doesn't seem to fit the plot: "the Great Mother is impregnated by the loneliness of him that seeks her. In the shell-burst she bears the 'old' man into death, and implants in the new the everlasting monad, the mystery of individuality. And when the renewed man reappears, the mother reappears too—in a woman of this earth." Jung concludes with the enigmatic suggestion that *Demian* is indebted to him for more than Hesse is willing to admit:

> I could tell you a little secret about Demian of which you became the witness, but whose meaning you have concealed from the reader and perhaps also from yourself. I could give you some very satisfying information about this, since I have long been a good friend of Demian's and he has recently initiated me into his private affairs—under the seal of deepest secrecy. But time will bear out these hints in a singular way.

> I hope you will not think I am trying to make myself interesting by mystery-mongering; my *amor fati* is

> **The basic conception of *Demian* is a prophetic and highly didactic late Romantic version of the providential pattern of the Christian fall and redemption internalized in the life of the narrator."**

too sacred for that. I only wanted, out of gratitude, to send you a small token of my great respect for your fidelity and veracity, without which no man can have such apt intuitions. You may even be able to guess what passage in your book I mean.

The editor of Jung's letters suggests that the veiled reference is to Jung's "*Septem Sermones*, where the Gnostic figure of Abraxas plays a key role," and mentions that "the winged egg and Abraxas appear in a Gnostic mandala painted by Jung in 1916."

In any event, the tone of this letter is of a piece with what Mileck has characterized as Jung's "presumptuousness" about his influence on Hesse, which is evident in Jung's answer to an inquiry about their relationships: after noting that he met him in 1916, Jung mentions that Hesse had the benefit of the "considerable amount of knowledge concerning Gnosticism" that Jung had shared with Dr. Lang and that the latter "transmitted to Hesse. From this material he wrote *Demian*." Jung further claims that "the origins of *Siddhartha* and *Steppenwolf* . . . are—to a certain extent—the direct or indirect results of certain talks I had with Hesse. I'm unfortunately unable to say how much he was conscious of the hints and implications which I let him have." The co-optive and condescending tone of this communication seems to justify Hesse's tart conclusion that "for analysts, a genuine relationship to art is unattainable: they lack the organ for it."

Granted that *Demian* is significantly influenced by Hesse's protracted encounter with Jungian analysis, it is nevertheless true that the book resists any simple or consistent Jungian schematization of its basic ideas and symbols. Its leading characters, especially Demian and his mother, have obvious Jungian overtones, but not exclusively or unambiguously so: they are not paradigmatic fictional instances of psychological concepts, for *Demian* is not primarily a Jungian allegory, but a revised version, under the pressure of analysis, of Hesse's ongoing personal myth and fiction of the self. While the Jungian note is clearly the dominant one in the composition of *Demian*, the book is in fact a composite of various influences, or rather, confluences: of the conceptual world of the German Romantics and of the tradition of dialectical thinking culminating in Hegel; of Nietzschean ideas, of Christian as well as Gnostic motifs and of assorted other strands from Socrates to Dostoevsky, Bachofen and Freud. Some of these "influences" make for strange bedfellows—Ziolkowski has noted, for instance, how "Hesse creates a conscious stylistic tension by pitting Christian phraseology against Nietzschean thought"—and this matter is further complicated by the fact that Hesse and some of his "influences" may share a common source or tradition. In the case of Jung and Hesse, there is a shared literary and cultural heritage that can be readily invoked to explain similar symbols and ideas without getting into the quagmire (or infinite regress) of particular and demonstrable "influences."

Above and beyond the vexing question of Hesse's influences and borrowings, the autobiographical message of *Demian* is as direct as its symbolism is obscure: it is the creed of self-will proclaimed in a prophetic voice that gathers into itself echoes from Socrates and Jesus down to Nietzsche and Jung, and that also has strong affinities with the "inner light" tradition of Protestantism that in English literature finds its greatest expression in the late eighteenth century in Blake's prophetic books:

> An enlightened man has but one duty—to seek the way to himself, to reach inner certainty ... The realization that shook me profoundly ... was ... that I did not exist to write poems, to preach or to paint ... All of that was incidental. Each man had only one genuine vocation—to find the way to himself. He might end up as a poet or a madman, as prophet or criminal—that was not his affair, ultimately it was of no concern. His task was to discover his own destiny ... and live it out wholly and resolutely within himself.

With its uncompromising gospel of the inner self forged in the crucible of psychoanalysis, *Demian* represents an autobiographical revolution in Hesse's career, and one that, for understandable reasons (and especially in the U.S. in the wake of the Hesse wave of the 1960s), has received an extraordinary amount of attention from his critics. As

a writer, however, the "new" author of *Demian* is well below the level of formal and stylistic mastery Hesse had achieved in his best work before the war, *Rosshalde*. *Demian* is a remarkable and courageous book that breaks new ground as a consequence of probably the greatest crisis of Hesse's adult life, but it is also a "demonic" book whose author is as much controlled by as in control of his materials: too often its densely metaphoric and shrill confession comes across as a confused and confusing version of Hesse's disturbed state of mind during World War I.

Of its three major figures, only the narrator is a flesh-and-blood character, though from the perspective of the permissive late twentieth century, the summary of his student days as "a notorious and daring bar-crawler" is very tame stuff. Next to it the proletarian masculinity of Kromer, even if largely undeveloped, offers a breath of vitality. The two other major figures of this triptych of Hesse's inner self, Demian and Frau Eva, are more symbols than characters. The former, a composite of Socratic *daimon*, Christian conscience, Jungian Shadow, and Nietzschean *Übermensch*, and the latter, the most revealing projection of Hesse's mother myth, exist on the magical threshold of the inner and outer worlds, whose fundamental convergence had become an article of faith to the Hesse drawing on his Romantic heritage as reinforced by Jung. This esoteric coincidence or identity is also the subject of his story "Inside and Outside", which turns on the (Goethean) slogan, "nothing is outside, nothing is inside, for that which is outside is inside," that Hesse also used as the epigraph of the 1919 essay, "The Brothers Karamazov, or the Decline of Europe."

The basic conception of *Demian* is a prophetic and highly didactic late Romantic version of the providential pattern of the Christian fall and redemption internalized in the life of the narrator. In the opening chapter we witness Sinclair's fall from the paradise of childhood and innocence as a consequence of his lie (to impress a group of boys) about stealing apples from a garden. This symbolic episode, which is probably Hesse's conscious equivalent of the adolescent Augustine's robbing of the pear tree, shows how Sinclair's imagination is instrumental in his "fall" by driving a wedge of guilt, shame, and sin between him and his family as he succumbs to the blackmail of his "evil" Shadow, Kromer. Conversely, toward the end of the book this "Prodigal Son" beholds an apocalyptic vision of World War I as the beginning of the rebirth of a corrupt humanity. Seven of the eight chapter headings are references to the Bible, and the single non-Biblical one, "Beatrice," shows young Sinclair's attempt to turn *eros* into *agape*. Like Blake in his prophetic books, Hesse in *Demian* wields elements of the Biblical tradition to subvert Christian orthodoxies from a radical Protestant perspective. In his bold revaluation of scriptural figures—Cain, the Prodigal Son, the Unrepentant Thief at Golgotha—Hesse is at once drawing on and liberating himself from the Pietist teachings of his childhood, just as a much earlier and more famous autobiographer, Augustine, wielded the elements of his early education—the classical rhetoric of which he was such a brilliant student—in order to subvert the classical viewpoint for the sake of celebrating the Christian.

With *Demian* Hesse seeks to present the stages of individuation in almost exclusively symbolic terms as a progressive integration of the "light" and "dark" realms of Sinclair's divided self (thus the punning appropriateness of his name: sin/clair) as a Blakean marriage of heaven and hell under the Gnostic sign of Abraxas (and his totem, the sparrow-hawk), whose esoteric function is "the uniting of godly and devilish elements." In this figural autobiography the revaluation of values beyond the standard middle-class conceptions of good and evil takes the form of a confusing double movement through which external reality is internalized, and internal reality is externalized: that is, images appropriated from the outer world (Beatrice) become psychic stuff and metaphors of self, and inner images are transposed into the external world to function as figures in the plot (Demian and Frau Eva). While this double pattern includes a good deal of authorial sleight-of-hand, there is also an experimental daring in the manner in which Hesse deploys his symbols. The World War I years were, after all, those of a burgeoning *avant garde* and assorted modernisms, one of whose centers was Zürich, and their impact on *Demian* is clearly discernible in the book's more surreal dream sequences. In this connection it is also helpful to keep in mind the Romantic distinction between symbol and allegory, as updated by Jung in *Symbol of Transformation*, which Hesse had read, and which might well stand as the subtitle of *Demian*: "A symbol is an indefinite expression with many meanings, pointing to something not easily defined and therefore not fully known. But the sign always has a fixed meaning, because it is a conventional abbreviation for, or a commonly accepted indication of, something known." *Demian*'s signature of the

self is symbolic in this way, invested with a numinous aura, pointing enigmatically to the unknown.

The imagery of this prophetic book is also fluid and dynamic, with constantly shifting boundaries and domains. Hesse's ambitious experiment with such kinematic and transformational sequences is a not always successful attempt to express the metamorphic processes of the self. Though the proliferating imagery of *Demian* defies schematization, some of the patterns are carefully developed through an experimental combination of musical and pictorial elements. Unlike the ironically voiced despair of T. S. Eliot's roughly contemporaneous *The Waste Land* (which also explores through obscure symbols the terms of a personal and a cultural crisis) the affirmative (and sometimes even manic) creed of *Demian* seems to be, "I can connect everything with everything." Caught up in its visionary momentum, Hesse seems to have believed that the book was not only a totalizing trope of his, but also of humanity's—or at least Europe's—psyche.

Three leading symbol sequences are those of the sparrow-hawk, Beatrice, and Frau Eva. The first, already adumbrated in the Prologue's assertion that "each man carries the vestiges of his birth—the slime and the eggshell of his primeval past", is reintroduced in Chapter 2 when Demian points out the coat of arms (the sparrow-hawk) above the entrance of the Sinclair house, and is reinforced by his subsequent drawing of it in Chapter 3. The bird-egg leitmotif is later internalized when Sinclair dreams that Demian has forced him to eat the coat of arms: "When I had swallowed it, I felt to my horror that the heraldic bird was coming to life inside me, had begun to swell up and devour me from within." Thus the process of individuation and the onset of *Eigensinn* is experienced by the narrator as a symbolic pregnancy leading to the birth of a new self. When Sinclair re-externalizes this image by painting it, we have a fuller development of the central avian metaphor: "Now it represented a bird of prey with a proud aquiline sparrow-hawk's head, half its body stuck in some dark globe out of which it was struggling to free itself as though from a giant shell—all of this against a sky-blue background." After mailing his "painted dream bird" to Demian, Sinclair receives the dramatic reply that relates the sparrow-hawk to the Gnostic deity who presides over this stage of Sinclair's development: "The bird fights its way out of the egg. The egg is the world. Who would be born must first destroy a world. The bird flies to God. That God's name is Abraxas." The spiritual midwife of this difficult birth is Pistorius (a version of Hesse's analyst) who liberates Sinclair-Hesse from his old self by helping to deliver the new. As Sinclair puts it, their conversations (read psychoanalytic sessions) "helped me to form myself . . . to peel off layers of skin, to break eggshells, and after each blow I lifted up my head a little higher, a little more freely, until my yellow bird pushed its beautiful raptor's head out of the shattered shell of the terrestrial globe."

If the greater sparrow-hawk pattern points to the future, the compact Beatrice sequence shows the adolescent Sinclair's futile attempt to escape the mounting pressures of individuation. His etherealized worship of the young woman whom he saw at a distance in a park is his second attempt to return (the first was after Demian had freed him from the clutches of Kromer) to the childhood world of purity and light. Yet the very name Sinclair chooses for this young woman is ambiguous, for it points as much to the "sin" as to the "clair" of his self, since she is clearly the raptly sensuous and highly eroticized devotee of Rossetti's famous painting, Beata Beatrix: "I gave her the name Beatrice, for even though I had not read Dante, I knew about Beatrice from an English painting of which I owned a reproduction. It showed a young pre-Raphaelite woman, long-limbed and slender, with long head and etherealized hands and features." Far from checking his budding sex drive, Sinclair's Beatrice worship is a form of autoerotic fantasy that leads him right back to the "dark" self he had struggled to escape: the androgynous portrait he paints of her turns into a "mask, half male, half female," which he first recognizes as "Demian's face" and then as his "inner self," his "fate or . . . *daemon*." Sinclair's attempted flight has gone full circle to another self-encounter, which Hesse describes, with iconic references to Novalis and Nietzsche, as fated.

The Frau Eva sequence that dominates the latter part of the book is introduced under the sign of Abraxas and explicitly related to the "sexual drive" that Sinclair had sought to sublimate through his cult of Beatrice. More and more preoccupied by his inner world, Sinclair experiences a recurrent "fantasy" and "the most important and enduringly significant dream of [his] life," in which, returning to his father's house, he embraces under the aegis of the "heraldic bird" above the entrance a figure who is at once his mother and Max Demian:

> This form drew me to itself and enveloped me in a deep, tremulous embrace: I felt a mixture of ecstasy and horror—the embrace was at once an act of divine worship and a crime. Too many associations with my mother and friend commingled with this fig-

ure embracing me. Its embrace violated all sense of reverence, yet it was bliss.

This "dark dream of love" with its double violation of ancient sexual taboos that Sinclair is unable to "confess" even to his friend and guide Pistorius is *Demian*'s metaphorized burden of confession that Hesse shares with his readers. His critics have been reluctant to face the transparent Freudian suggestions of this mother myth, preferring instead the "safe" Jungian interpretation of mother-son incest as a symbol of rebirth. Thus Ziolkowski, while acknowledging the "erotic-incestuous implications" and "the remarkable language of double-entendre" of Frau Eva's exchanges with Sinclair, interprets these, with the help of a long quotation from Jung, as the desire, "by visionary paths to reenter the mother in order to be reborn again." Such a view is defensible, given the metaphoric density and ambiguities of the text, but when a more recent critic rejects out of hand a Freudian interpretation because Frau Eva "is not a libido object but remains an . . . image of the divine," he can only do so by positively ignoring the ample evidence in Hesse's narrative that Frau Eva is indeed—like Rousseau's beloved "Maman," Mrs. Warens—very much a libido object: "There were moments when I sat beside her and burned with sensual desire and kissed objects she had touched." Even if Sinclair's Oedipal desires are never fulfilled in fact, they are consummated in his imagination: "I had dreams, too, in which my union with her was consummated in new symbolic acts. She was an ocean into which I streamed. She was a star and I another on my way to her, circling round each other." The transfer of Sinclair's incestuous wishes from his own mother (whom he embraces in his recurrent dream) to Frau Eva, Demian's mother and the Magna Mater, is a masking myth that does not change the basic situation.

Before ever meeting Frau Eva, Sinclair has already painted the "half male, half female dream image of [his] *daemon*" and heaped it with lurid imprecations: "I questioned the painting, berated it, made love to it, prayed to it; I called it mother, called it whore and slut, called it beloved, called it Abraxas." When Sinclair is shown a photograph of Demian's mother, he has an ecstatic recognition in which again the internal and the external merge: "it was my dream image! That was she, the tall, almost masculine woman who resembled her son, with maternal traits . . . *daemon* and mother, fate and beloved." When the university student Sinclair meets up again with Demian after a long interval, his introduction to Frau Eva has all the earmarks

of a homecoming to the Eternal Mother (the setting, a house in "a garden by the river," is Edenic,
and the promise of an incestuous consummation.
Under the symbolic aegis of the sparrow-hawk
painting that he had earlier sent Demian, Sinclair
perceives Frau Eva as the (Hessean) trinity of
mother, goddess, and lover. The mythic aspect is
heavily stressed ("Frau Eva! The name fits her perfectly. She *is* like a universal mother!", as she
obligingly invokes the book's symbol of the "new"
self: "It is always difficult to be born. You know
the chick does not find it easy to break his way out
of the shell."

The last part of *Demian* moves toward a sexual union between Frau Eva and Sinclair, something she seems positively to encourage:

> At times I was dissatisfied with myself and tortured
> with desire: I believed I could no longer bear to have
> her near me without taking her into my arms. She
> sensed this ... Once, when I had stayed away for sev-
> eral days and returned bewildered she took me aside
> and said: "You must not give way to desires which
> you don't believe in. I know what you desire. You
> should, however, either be capable of renouncing
> these desires or feel wholly justified in having them.
> Once you are able to make your request in such a
> way that you will be quite certain of its fulfillment,
> then the fulfillment will come.

However, Sinclair—like Hesse—vacillates between the sense of Frau Eva as libido object and,
as he puts it, "only a metaphor of my inner self ...
whose purpose was to lead me more deeply into
myself." Because the erotic fulfillment to which
Sinclair aspires never occurs, the apocalyptic ending of *Demian* is actually anticlimactic. In a concluding episode that finally merges the Frau Eva
and the sparrow-hawk patterns, the momentum of
incestuous wishes is diverted by the outbreak of
World War I. Sinclair's sudden vision of a cloud
formation as a "gigantic bird that tore itself free
from the steel-blue chaos of the stormy skies and
flew off into the sky with a great beating of wings"
projects against the screen of the heavens the death
and rebirth symbolism of the self; and Sinclair's
prophetic perception of Frau Eva as the muse of
history is Hesse's portentous myth of Europe in the
throes of World War I:

> A huge city could be seen in the clouds out of which
> millions of people streamed in a host over a land-
> scape. Into their midst stepped a mighty godlike fig-
> ure, as huge as a mountain range, with sparkling stars
> in her hair, bearing the features of Frau Eva. The
> ranks of the people were swallowed up into her as
> into a giant cave and vanished from sight. The god-
> dess cowered on the ground, the mark [of Cain, which
> is Demian's and now Sinclair's sign] luminous on

her forehead. A dream seemed to hold sway over her:
she closed her eyes and her countenance became
twisted with pain.

In short, Hesse has generalized his personal
mother myth into an archetypal vision of cosmic
import.

Demian closes, as it opened, with only the reflecting figure of the narrator who, himself injured
in the war, receives in a field hospital Frau Eva's
farewell kiss from the lips of the dying Demian—
an odd consummation, that. The Narcissus motif
that Boulby has identified in the closing sentence
is appropriate because in a sense all the symbolic
permutations of character and episode in the book
are confessional self-projections on Hesse's part
that are now reabsorbed, like the figure of Demian,
into Sinclair-Hesse's consciousness: "But sometimes when I find the key and climb deep into myself where the images of fate lie aslumber in the
dark mirror, I need only bend over that dark mirror to behold my image, now completely resembling him, my brother, my master."

The confessional imagination of *Demian* is a
highly selective one, excluding elements of Hesse's
past treated in earlier works or dealing with them
in very different context, and incorporating aspects
of inner and outer biography not hitherto explored.
Thus the Maulbronn crisis treated in *Beneath the
Wheel* is not revisited, and the trauma of adolescent sexuality, so mawkishly mishandled in the
Hans-Emma relationship, is now paradigmatically
framed through the "light" and "dark" worlds of
Demian. If the biographical material taken up in
Beneath the Wheel is largely excluded, the period
at a *Gymnasium* subsequent to the Maulbronn crisis is touched on with the student "lowlife" scenes
of the Beatrice chapter. Conversely, the issue of
Hesse's unhappy marriage and the problems of the
mature artist, the autobiographical substance, as we
have seen, of *Gertrude* and *Rosshalde*, are absent
in *Demian*'s seriated psychoanalytic review of
Hesse's early life. Nature too, the lyrical synec-
doche of the mother world in Hesse's early fiction,
all but disappears, to be replaced by the mythic
presence of Frau Eva. And the animus to the father
so marked in the brief caricatures of *Camenzind*
and *Beneath the Wheel* surfaces now in Sinclair's
"recurring nightmare" of a "murderous assault" on
his father, but with the shocking suggestion of
Oedipal violence shifted to Sinclair's evil and tor-
turing Shadow: "Kromer whetted a knife, put it in
my hand; we stood behind some trees in the avenue and lay in wait for someone, I did not know
whom. Yet when this someone approached and

Kromer pinched my arm to let me know that this was the person I was to stab—it was my father." In contrast, the figure of the mother who is frequently absent or whose autobiographical significance is disguised or elided in much of Hesse's earlier fiction is now elevated into a looming *magna mater* symbol with explicit incestuous suggestions. It is only fitting that Hesse's autobiographical reinscription of the Christian story of the fall should change Eve's role from that of the weak female who succumbs to temptation into that of a wise and powerful Frau Eva, a blissful homecoming to whom constitutes Hesse's vision of paradise regained in *Demian*.

Source: Eugene L. Stelzig, "Chapter VI: Hesse's Marriage of Heaven and Hell," in *Herman Hesse's Fictions of the Self*, Princeton University Press, 1988, pp. 130–58.

Ernst Rose

In the following excerpt, Rose examines the protagonist's search for his integrated self in Hesse's Demian.

The events and characters in *Demian* are symbolic experiences of the soldier Emil Sinclair who is searching for his integrated self. Sinclair, unlike his artistic predecessors, no longer wants to escape, but strives to accept life. He tries "to give life to that which wanted to come out of me by its own force." In his quest for his self he first returns to his childhood. Soon its protecting warmth is destroyed by the discovery of an outside world of violence and danger under the influence of Franz Kromer, a boy from the other side of the tracks. Sinclair himself for a while shares in Kromer's values and becomes a petty thief.

From this situation Sinclair is rescued by Demian, an older and more mature schoolmate. (The name is a distortion of the Greek *Daimon*, "demon," also "fate" and "conscience," and was found by Hesse in a dream.) While Kromer is actually introduced as Sinclair's base "shadow", Demian is his psychopompos and can set the negative forces into their proper perspective. He frees Sinclair from his shadow and becomes his intimate friend. Sinclair learns to appreciate the strong mentality of Demian, who is capable of thought transference and whose own thoughts go far beyond the platitudes of his teachers and his pastor. After a confirmation class Demian submits a spirited plea in favor of Cain. According to him, Cain did not commit murder but was blackballed because of his independent mind. This suggests a study of the

Gnostic sects who worshipped the creative force, which they named Abraxas.

Demian uses this concept of Abraxas to instill in Sinclair an awareness of evil as a constituent part of the world and not as a mere outside force. We are all marked men like Cain, claims Demian, and Sinclair should therefore accept evil and no longer indulge in self-righteousness. He should no longer be afraid of the invisible divinity beyond bourgeois good and evil.

Sinclair first had to give up childlike innocence. Then he passed through a period where he could hope to become saved by a fixed system of moral values. He had to learn that there is no such salvation, as the good in man is inextricably intertwined with the evil. Now he must reach the third stage where he accepts God who is sending both good and evil and yet is meaningful in his own, inscrutable way.

The path to such an acceptance is beset with pitfalls. Sinclair revolts against Demian and for a while becomes a wastrel. But then he confronts his deeper and purer self in the figure of a lovely girl whom he never meets in person. This "Beatrice," as he calls her, saves him from the loss of his artistic abilities. He turns from his wasteful habits and begins to sketch her. As he draws, he recognizes himself in her and is able to design a better image of his self.

Another of Sinclair's pictures is that of a sparrow hawk breaking out of its shell. (At this point it should be remembered that Jungian practice encourages the patient to draw pictures in order to make him face his subconscious images.) Sinclair has reproduced this particular picture from memory, and it copies an escutcheon over the door of his parents' home to which Demian has once called his attention. In an unexplained manner Demian had inserted a note into Sinclair's notebook: "The bird is fighting to break the egg. The egg is the world. He who wants to be born, must destroy a world. The bird is flying to God. The God's name is Abraxas."

In his "flight" toward Abraxas, Sinclair meets a second guide in the person of the organist Pistorius, whose acquaintance he has made in a tavern where Pistorius is drinking to forget his sorrow at being an outcast and a seer. Pistorius encourages Sinclair in his restless pursuit of his true self, and the latter learns his lesson well. He now draws a picture of a woman he has seen in his dreams. The painting assumes the features of Sinclair's mother, but again, she actually represents his deepest unconscious, with which Sinclair must identify himself. Significantly, after Sinclair's evocation of his dream image Pistorius can no longer help his charge and drops out of the picture. He has represented the psychoanalytic physician whom the patient must finally reject, in order to become independent and be cured.

The cure is symbolized by Sinclair's meeting with Demian's mother. In a university town he again comes across Demian, who takes his friend home to his mother. Gossip has her living in incest with her son—a poetic transcription of her true character as a part of a mandala. The trio is united in the vision of a new Europe, a future world in which people who have forged their true personalities will emerge as leaders of a new humanity. Sinclair regrets only that he cannot win Frau Eva for himself. She tells him that she will come to him when his want of her is strong enough to draw her to him.

One night Sinclair marshals all his strength to call her. But instead, Demian enters with the news that the first world war has broken out. The two young men become soldiers, because as such they can help to sweep away the insincere bourgeois world and put the dynamic civilization of the future in its place. Since they move under the sign of Abraxas, the new world will of course not be traditionally humanistic.

The two friends are separated by the war and for the last time find each other again side by side in a hospital. Demian dies from his wounds, but before his death gives Sinclair a last kiss from Mother Eve, i.e., Sinclair becomes united with his real self. The latter looks into his soul and sees his "own image that now is entirely the likeness of him, my friend and mentor."

The basic theme of the book is the emergence of Sinclair's integrated self from his earlier schizoid separation into Demian and the conventional Sinclair. To be sure, the ultimate integration—the union with Demian's mother—is never attained. But it is at least visualized.

Source: Ernst Rose, "Chapter 5: The End of an Era," in *Faith from the Abyss: Herman Hesse's Way from Romanticism to Modernity*, New York University Press, 1965, pp. 45–56.

Sources

Mann, Thomas, "Introduction," in *Demian*, by Hermann Hesse, Harper & Row Publishers, 1965, pp. ix–x.

Mileck, Joseph, "Hermann Hesse," in *Dictionary of Literary Biography*, Vol. 66: *German Fiction Writers, 1885–1913*, edited by James Hardin, Gale Research, 1988, pp. 180–224.

———, *Hermann Hesse: Life and Art*, University of California Press, 1978, p. 99.

Otten, Anna, ed., *Hesse Companion*, University of New Mexico Press, 1977, p. xii.

Further Reading

Berghahn, V. R., *Imperial Germany, 1871–1914*, Berghahn Books, 1994.
Berghahn provides a history of the German empire, from its formation in 1871 until the beginning of World War I.

Hesse, Hermann, *Soul of the Age: Selected Letters of Hermann Hesse, 1891–1962*, Farrar, Straus and Giroux, 1991.
Soul of the Age is an edited selection of the letters of Hesse, including his correspondence with such notables as the writers Thomas Mann and André Gide, and modern Jewish philosopher Martin Buber.

Marrer-Tising, Carlee, *The Reception of Hermann Hesse by the Youth in the United States: A Thematic Analysis*, P. Lang, 1982.
Marrer-Tising offers discussion of the popularity of Hesse's novels among American youth during the 1960s and 1970s. Marrer-Tising explores thematic elements of Hesse's fiction which addressed ideas and concerns of the youth counterculture during this era of U.S. history.

Michels, Volker, ed., *Hermann Hesse: A Pictorial Biography*, Farrar, Straus and Giroux, 1975.
Michels provides photographs and other visual materials in conjunction with biographical discussion of Hesse's life and career.

Moyer, Laurence, *Victory Must Be Ours: Germany in the Great War, 1914–1918*, Hippocrene Books, 1995.
Moyer provides a history of Germany during World War I.

Richards, David G., *The Hero's Quest for the Self: An Archetypal Approach to Hesse's "Demian" and Other Novels*, University Press of America, 1987.
Richards discusses Hesse's fiction in terms of its mythological elements.

Serrano, Miguel, *C. G. Jung and Hermann Hesse: A Record of Two Friendships*, Daimon Verlag, 1997.
Serrano offers discussion of the ongoing friendship between Hesse and the great psychoanalytic theorist Carl Jung.

Tusken, Lewis W., *Understanding Hermann Hesse: The Man, His Myth, His Metaphor*, University of South Carolina Press, 1998.
Tusken provides analysis of the works of Hesse in terms of recurring thematic, symbolic, and psychological elements.

The House of Mirth

Edith Wharton

1905

While *The House of Mirth* was only Edith Wharton's second novel, Cynthia Griffin Wolff points out in the *Dictionary of Literary Biography*, with it Wharton "emerged as a professionally serious, masterful novelist." Published in 1905 it had the fastest sales of any of its publishing house's books at the time. The novel, as well as many of Wharton's other works, continues to enjoy great success to the present day.

In *The House of Mirth*, Wharton explores the status of women at the turn of the nineteenth to the twentieth century; indeed, Wolff believes that the novel "echo[es] the many dissatisfactions Wharton felt at this time." Heroine Lily Bart is a beautiful woman who has been brought up to achieve one goal: marry a wealthy, well-placed man. Although Lily, twenty-nine when the novel opens, has had opportunities to do so, her spirit has always recoiled from taking the step of marrying for money. However, the fate dealt to Lily in life is not spinsterhood but a fall from grace, that is New York's social circle, which comprises the only world Lily has ever known.

Over the past century, scholars and readers alike have applied numerous interpretations to this complex novel. Upon its initial publication, many readers saw it as a critique of the so-called marriage market. Contemporary scholars, however, have tended to read the novel, and Lily's actions, with a feminist slant. As Linda Wagner-Martin writes in her study *The House of Mirth*, "[It] is a key example of a woman's voice exploring signif-

icant women's themes in a covert manner: fiction as disguise."

Author Biography

Edith Wharton (born Edith Newbold Jones) was born on January 24, 1862, to a wealthy and well-connected New York family. After the Civil War ended, however, Wharton's parents were hit hard by inflation. To save money the family lived and traveled throughout Europe until Wharton was about ten years old, by which time she spoke five languages. After the family returned to the United States, Wharton embarked on a program of self-education, primarily fostered by her extensive reading. Just before her fifteenth birthday, Wharton finished her first creative work, a novella entitled *Fast and Loose*, which did not see publication until 1977. She also had a poem published in the *Atlantic Monthly* and two published in the New York *World* before her eighteenth birthday.

After her first engagement was broken, Wharton married Theodore Wharton in 1885. Soon thereafter she began to write stories, which she sold to popular magazines. Her first short story appeared in 1891, when she was twenty-nine years old. Wharton, independently wealthy, did not depend on writing for a living. Only after her first collection of stories, *The Greater Inclination*, was published in 1899 did Wharton wholeheartedly throw herself into her work and recognize herself as a professional writer. Around this time Wharton also developed a lasting friendship with the writer Henry James. He served as her mentor, and critics have often compared the works of these two writers. Between 1900 and 1914 Wharton produced almost fifty short stories as well as some of her finest novels, including *The House of Mirth* and *Ethan Frome*. A later work, *The Age of Innocence*, won the Pulitzer Prize in 1921.

In 1909 Wharton returned to France, where she had spent several winters. The next year, she made France her permanent residence, and in 1913 she divorced her husband. Throughout the next two decades, with the exception of the war years, Wharton traveled extensively throughout Europe, returning to American only once, in 1923, to be the first woman awarded the Doctor of Letters degree at Yale University.

In 1934, three years before her death, Wharton published her memoirs, *A Backward Glance*, which gracefully evoked old New York and its in-

Edith Wharton

habitants. Wharton was at work on *The Buccaneers* when she died of a heart attack on August 11, 1937, in St. Brice-sous-Foret, France. Her biographer, R. W. B. Lewis, believed this novel to be her finest piece of work from the 1920s onward. The novel was completed by Marion Mainwaring and published posthumously.

Plot Summary

Lily in the United States

The House of Mirth opens in New York City as Lily Bart misses the train that was to take her to a house party hosted by her friends Judy and Gus Trenor. She runs into longtime acquaintance Laurence Selden and, despite the impropriety of such actions at the time, accompanies him back to his apartment for a cup of tea. When she finally gets on the train, Lily sees Percy Gryce, who is an imminently marriageable, but dull, man. She pays him a great deal of attention both on the train and at the Trenors. However, just as Percy is on the verge of proposing marriage to her, Lily neglects to keep an engagement with him. Instead, she chooses to take a walk with Selden, who has come down to Bellomont specifically to see her. Selden and Lily are

Media Adaptations

- *The House of Mirth* was adapted as a film in 2000. It stars Gillian Anderson, Eric Stoltz, Dan Ackroyd, and Laura Linney, and was directed by Terence Davies. It is available from Sony Pictures Classics on VHS and DVD.

- *The House of Mirth* has been made available as an audiotape by several publishers in an unabridged edition.

attracted to one another, and Selden makes her feel that her intentions to marry Gryce—indeed, her intentions to marry wealthy—are "hateful." Lily returns to New York after asking Gus Trenor to help her invest her small income.

Trenor's financial help pays off immediately for Lily. She earns $10,000 in a short period of time. However, along with Trenor's financial help come his unwanted attentions, and after he lures Lily back to his house under the pretense of seeing Judy, Lily unhappily discovers that he has been giving her his own money with the expectation that she will have an affair with him. Lily vows to return Trenor's money, though she does not know where she will get it, as she recognizes the danger of compromising her reputation.

Meanwhile, Lily and Selden have been growing fonder of each other, despite the fact that Lily has come into possession of love letters that Bertha Dorset previously sent Selden. However, the night before Selden's engagement to see Lily, and perhaps ask her to marry him, he spies Lily fleeing the Trenors' home. He immediately assumes the worst, that Lily is having an affair with Trenor. Instead of keeping his appointment with Lily, Selden sails for Europe, which Lily later reads in the newspaper. Simon Rosedale pays her a visit to ask her to marry him, but Lily refuses. After Rosedale leaves, Lily receives a phone call from Bertha, inviting her on a trip to the Mediterranean.

Lily in Monte Carlo

Lily accompanies Bertha and George Dorset on a tour of the Mediterranean. Lily has been asked along primarily to keep George busy while Bertha carries on an affair. In Monte Carlo, Lily encounters Selden, who begs her to leave the Dorset's yacht, but Lily declares she cannot leave her friend. One night Bertha does not return to the yacht until the morning hours. George finally realizes what is going on, and he decides to see Selden (a lawyer) to begin divorce proceedings. However, Bertha shifts the blame to Lily, claiming that she compromised herself and George by not waiting for Bertha at the quay that would take them out to the boat. By that evening, George has decided not to go through with the divorce and he follows his wife's lead in chastising Lily. At a dinner, Bertha humiliates Lily in front of everyone by announcing that Lily will not return to the yacht with them, implying that Lily tried to seduce George.

Lily in New York

Lily returns to New York upon the death of Aunt Julia. Although everyone, including Lily, expected her to inherit Aunt Julia's estate, Lily is only bequeathed $10,000, which must be used to repay Gus Trenor. The bulk of the estate goes to Lily's cousin Grace Stepney. Meanwhile, Bertha, who returned to New York ahead of Lily, has been spreading rumors about Lily, and Lily's former friends roundly snub her. Carry Fisher comes to Lily's aid, procuring her work as a companion to nouveau riche families (families who have recently acquired fortunes, as opposed to those with "old money"). Carry also encourages Lily to marry George Dorset; she believes that if George had proof of his wife Bertha's infidelity, he would divorce her. In fact, George asks Lily to help him prove Bertha's infidelity, but Lily refuses. Somewhat desperate, Lily acquiesces to marry Rosedale when he pays her a visit, but he no longer wants to do so. Lily understands that he has changed his mind because she is no longer valuable to him since she has lost her reputation. He urges her to give Bertha's love letters to Selden to fight Bertha and rehabilitate herself in New York society, and says if Lily uses these letters to implicate Bertha, he will marry her. Again, Lily refuses.

Lily obtains a position as a personal secretary to Mrs. Hatch. While in Mrs. Hatch's employment, Selden begs Lily to leave as he finds Mrs. Hatch to be an unsavory character, but Lily says she will not leave and the two part angrily. However, shortly thereafter, Lily quits Mrs. Hatch's employ and goes to work in a hatmaker's shop. She is ill equipped for such a job and is fired. Later that day Lily runs into Rosedale, who takes her to tea and then accompanies her home. Rosedale is appalled by the circumstances in which Lily now lives. He offers to lend her the money to repay Trenor, purely as a business arrangement, but she tells him she is unable to accept his offer. She does not wish to compromise herself again.

Lily makes up her mind to use the letters to blackmail Bertha. On her way to the Dorset's home, however, she decides to visit Selden. The two speak of their past affection for each other, and Lily implicitly asks him for help and love, but Selden refuses to acknowledge her entreaties. Lily secretly burns Bertha's letters in his fireplace. That night Lily receives her legacy from Aunt Julia and immediately writes Gus Trenor a check in the amount of $10,000. Lily then takes an overdose of sleeping medication. The next morning Selden rushes to Lily's boarding house. He has finally "found the word he meant to say to her." It is, however, too late; Lily is dead.

Characters

Lily Bart

As *The House of Mirth* opens, its heroine, Lily Bart, is an unmarried woman in her late twenties. Though Lily was born into New York society, the financial ruin of her father brought to an end her world of ease, luxury, and social stability. While she enjoys the comforts of home afforded by her wealthy Aunt Julia, Lily lacks the means to keep up with her circle of friends, who enjoy the finest objects and entertainment their wealth can bring them. As Lily scrambles to keep up with her mounting bills, she knows that her only hope to maintain her social position is to marry and marry well.

The House of Mirth traces Lily's course as she unsuccessfully attempts to fulfill this goal. She is unable to marry any of the men who offer their hand because of her own ambivalence. Every time Lily comes close to winning a husband, such as Percy Gryce, she finds herself unable to follow through on her plan. Her attraction to Laurence Selden is partly responsible for her changes of mind, but so is her own recognition of the coarseness, dullness, and pettiness that inhabit many of her acquaintances. In marrying for money, Lily would join their ranks, and a stubborn core prevents her from doing so. Lily continues to main-

tain hold of her finer spirit by refusing to use Bertha Dorset's love letters to Selden to blackmail her way back into society, and by denying herself a means to live by using her inheritance to repay Gus Trenor.

Although the book opens with Lily at the peak of New York society, by its end she has descended into its depths. She has been ill-used by her so-called friends and cast out of their society. Her attempts to earn a living fail miserably, for as she tells Selden in her final days, "I have tried hard—but life is difficult, and I am a very useless person." Alone and penniless, Lily turns to Selden, who once loved her and who she once loved, but when he fails her, she takes an overdose of a sleeping draught. She dies the victim of a society that does not value a woman who plays by a more noble set of rules.

Bertha Dorset

Once Lily's friend, Bertha becomes her worst enemy. Bertha is a married woman, who in the course of the two years the novel takes place, has several affairs, including one with Selden. In the midst of an affair and needing to keep her husband George occupied, Bertha invites Lily to accompany the couple on a trip to Europe. When her husband discovers the affair, Bertha sacrifices Lily to save herself by implying publicly that Lily has attempted to seduce George. Not content with destroying Lily's reputation in Europe, Bertha also spreads rumors and gossip in New York, to the extent that Lily is completely cast aside by her former friends. Unbeknownst to Bertha, Lily holds power over her in the form of love letters that Bertha sent Selden. Lily refuses to capitalize on these letters, and when she burns the letters and dies, Bertha's secret is destroyed at the same time.

George Dorset

Cuckolded husband George Dorset is married to a woman who disrespects him and is unfaithful to him. After he finds out about his wife Bertha's affair in Monte Carlo, he turns to Lily for help. He asks her to help him prove Bertha's unfaithfulness, and says if she does so, he will marry her, but Lily refuses his request.

Gerty Farish

Considered to be drab and colorless, Gerty Farish is a social worker. She represents the "new woman" of the early twentieth century with her economic independence and career. Although she enjoys an enriching career, Gerty is unable to find romantic fulfillment. She devotes herself to Lily as she would devote herself to any of the other poor people to whom she ministers. As society abandons Lily, Gerty tries to help her. She obtains a job for Lily at the millinery shop and begs Lily to turn her back on her former way of life.

Carry Fischer

Carry Fischer, a divorcée, is a professional companion to wealthy society women. She befriends Lily after Lily's trip to Monte Carlo and tries to set Lily up in a profession similar to her own back in America. She also urges Lily to marry either George Dorset or Simon Rosedale.

Mattie Gormer

Mattie Gormer is a nouveau riche woman (meaning her fortune was recently acquired, as opposed to being "old money") who Lily meets through Carry Fisher. Lily travels as a companion to Mattie after her return from Monte Carlo, but once Mattie becomes friendly with Bertha Dorset, Lily's presence is no longer welcome.

Percy Gryce

The shy, dull Percy Gryce is one of Lily's suitors. Ignored by Lily, he marries a wealthy young woman instead.

Norma Hatch

Lily obtains employment as secretary to Norma Hatch, a rich woman from out West who has no place in New York society. Mrs. Hatch and her friends are conniving to get a young wealthy New Yorker to marry an older woman, and Selden, aware of Mrs. Hatch's unsavouriness, begs Lily to leave her employ. However, Lily does not leave until she is already implicated in the unsuccessful plan.

Aunt Julia Penniston

Aunt Julia, with whom Lily lives, helps out her niece with some bills like the dressmaker's, but does not provide any regular allowance. She is dismayed by some of Lily's behavior, such as her gambling, about which cousin Grace informs Aunt Julia. When Aunt Julia learns of Lily's adventures in Monte Carlo, she disinherits her. Aunt Julia dies before Lily returns to the United States, having left Lily only $10,000.

Simon Rosedale

Simon Rosedale is an interloper in New York society. Not only is he nouveau riche, he is Jewish. He speaks coarsely and uncouthly, yet at the same time he is one of the few people who show sensitivity to Lily's plight. For instance, he recognizes the difficulties foisted upon her by lower-class life. At one time Rosedale wanted to marry Lily, believing she would win him entry into New York aristocratic society. Later, when Lily wants to marry him, he refuses since her social banishment has stripped her of value.

Laurence Selden

Laurence Selden is a lawyer who inhabits the same circles as Lily. Like Lily, he is not wealthy but because he is a man, he is able to work at a profession that allows him economic and social independence. Selden and Lily have been acquaintances for close to a decade. The two are attracted to each other, yet Selden does not have the financial means to marry Lily, nor is he convinced that he would like to do so. However, it is Selden's voice and opinions that continually prevent Lily from following through on her plans to marry a wealthy man. In a sense, Selden acts as Lily's moral arbiter. For example, he implores her to leave the Dorset's yacht and Mrs. Hatch's employ. At the same time, Selden is unable to offer Lily any support other than words, and, more importantly, fails Lily by believing the worst about her, such as that she had an affair with Gus Trenor. Before she takes the fatal overdose, Lily turns to Selden, looking for the love he felt for her in the past. Selden allows Lily to leave that night, but he goes to visit her the next day, for "he had found the word he meant to say to her." It is too late, however; Lily is dead.

Grace Stepney

Cousin Grace Stepney makes sure that Aunt Julia knows of Lily's "bad" habits, like playing cards for money, along with the rumors society is spreading about Lily and Gus Trenor. After Lily is disinherited, Grace becomes the inheritor of Aunt Julia's estate. When Lily approaches Grace, desperately seeking money, she turns her down.

Nettie Struther

Nettie Struther is a former prostitute to whom Lily once gave money. She reemerges at the end of the novel, married to a man who accepts Nettie's past and the child she bore out of wedlock. Nettie runs a slum kitchen.

Gus Trenor

Judy's husband Gus develops an infatuation with Lily. Asked by Lily to help with her investments, he deceives her by giving her his own money. However, Lily does not learn of this deceit until much later. Gus attempts to use his financial power over Lily to make her his mistress. She refuses, but feels that she must pay him back the $10,000 he has already given her.

Judy Trenor

Judy Trenor is a force in New York society. As Lily notes, "Where Judy Trenor led, all the world would follow." After Lily's return from Monte Carlo, and after Judy learns that her husband has given Lily money, she cuts her former friend out of her life.

Themes

Women's Roles

As seen in *The House of Mirth*, women in early twentieth-century society had little chance to play any role other than wife and mother. The female leaders of society, Judy Trenor and Bertha Dorset, derive their power and social standing from their marriages. The women who work as companions, such as Carry Fisher, have been married in the past. Lily's only goal in life, the only "profession" for which she has been trained, has been to make a good marriage. When she fails to reach this achievement, she has no skills or even inner resources upon which to draw. Though she attempts to work, first as a professional companion and then as a milliner's assistant, her attempts are woefully inadequate, and Lily sinks deeper and deeper into poverty.

Only a few women in the novel choose alternate paths. Nettie Struther, a working-class woman, works out of her home and cares for her baby and husband. The unmarried Gerty Farish finds professional fulfillment as a social worker. Notably, Gerty is one of the few characters in the novel who truly cares for Lily. Even though she is neither a mother nor a wife, she is best at fulfilling the typically female role of nurturer.

Betrayal

Betrayal is at the heart of *The House of Mirth*. At almost every turn, Lily's friends and acquaintances betray her. Grace Stepney makes sure that Aunt Julia knows of Lily's bad habits, such as playing cards for money, and informs Aunt Julia that rumors are flying about Lily and Gus Trenor. Other times, the novel presents chains of betrayal. For example, Lily accepts money from Gus Trenor, thinking he is investing her own money, when in reality he is giving her his money in hopes of making

Topics for Further Study

- Read another work by Wharton that takes place within old New York society, such as *The Custom of the Country* or *The Age of Innocence*, and write an essay comparing and contrasting it to *The House of Mirth*.

- Research which professional opportunities were available to married and unmarried women at the turn of the nineteenth to the twentieth century. How do these opportunities compare to the opportunities women have today?

- Do you think Lily should have used her knowledge of Bertha's affairs to regain her place in New York society? Write an alternative ending to the book assuming Lily did use the letters in this manner.

- People like the Trenors and the Dorsets spent exorbitant amounts of money on luxuries. Conduct research to find out about the disparity of wealth at the turn of the century. How did the lives of the upper class compare to those of the middle and lower classes?

- Write an opening speech for a debate entitled "RESOLVED—Lily Bart's death was a suicide." Use details from the text to support or oppose this statement.

- Wharton writes of Selden in the final chapter, "He only knew that he must see Lily Bart at once—he had found the word he meant to say to her, and it could not wait another moment to be said," and later, "He knelt by the bed and bent over her, draining their last moment to its lees; in the silence there passed between them the word which made all clear." What do you think this word is and why?

her his mistress. When Judy Trenor finds out about Lily's acceptance of her husband's money, she casts Lily aside. The most damaging act of betrayal is played out by Bertha Dorset, who deliberately and falsely accuses Lily of trying to seduce her husband. In addition, Bertha actively sets out to ruin Lily's reputation and new acquaintanceships, to the extent of seeking out a friendship with Mattie Gormer, even though she occupies a lower rung on the social ladder, simply because she has employed Lily as a companion.

Ironically, Lily has at her disposal tools to betray her former friend in turn. She possesses Bertha's love letters to Selden. The public revelation of these love letters could bring about many different outcomes. She could give them to George Dorset, who would use them to get his much-wanted divorce, and then Lily could marry him. She could use them to force Bertha to befriend her again, and then reenter society as Simon Rosedale's wife. Lily, however, refuses to betray Bertha, even though her betrayal would be based in reality, not a lie. If she betrayed Bertha, Lily feels she would be betraying herself.

Appearances

Much is made of Lily's beauty throughout the novel, and this fixation on the physical body implicitly points to one of the novel's themes: the mutability of appearances. Lily's physical beauty leads men to desire her, but none of these men, including Percy Gryce and Gus Trenor, actually have any interest in knowing the "real" Lily Bart. They only want to possess her beauty. Selden, on the other hand, gets to know Lily better than almost anybody else. He learns that she feels conflicted both about marrying for money and the whole social milieu in which they move. However, when he sees things that look suspect, such as Lily leaving Gus Trenor's home, he immediately believes the worst of her, never troubling himself to look into the circumstances and discover the truth.

The appearance of impropriety is also key to Lily's situation and eventual downfall. From the opening chapter, when she is seen by Simon Rosedale leaving the lobby of Selden's apartment building, to the final chapter, when Selden views the letter she wrote to Trenor, she is constantly putting herself in positions where, without careful investigation, she could be judged harshly. At these times she is usually found wanting in propriety, even though in each case she has done nothing wrong. For example, she is accused of attempting to seduce George Dorset, an accusation that can be

upheld because she was on the Dorsets' yacht alone with George. New York society also believes that Lily connived to marry one of their wealthy young men to an arriviste (a person who has recently attained high social status without merit) divorcée, a belief that can be upheld because Lily was in this divorceé's employ. In both of these instances, Selden begs Lily to leave her situations prior to the implications of her wrongdoing, but Lily, lacking the capacity to understand how deeply people can ill use others, refuses to do so.

Style

Symbolism

Lily is the most potent symbol of *The House of Mirth*. Like the flower, her name signifies her to be a beautiful, delicate breed. Indeed, Lily's uniqueness and exquisiteness is often noted by people around her. For instance, at the tableau party: "It was as though she had stepped, not out of, but into Reynolds's canvas, banishing the phantom of his dead beauty by the beams of her living grace." The guests at the party note as well the "noble buoyancy of her attitude, its suggestion of soaring grace, ... [and] the touch of poetry in her beauty."

Lily has a finer sensibility than those around her. While Lily often acts in accordance with the social mores of her class, her actions demonstrate a more stringent moral calling than any of the other people who populate her world. She refuses to give Bertha's love letters to Selden to make her way back into the social scene, even though Bertha's deceit is what leads to her ultimate ostracism. She insists on paying back Gus even though he deceived her as to what the "investments" were, and despite the fact that he gave her money so she would sleep with him—in essence, attempting to turn her into a prostitute.

Metaphor and Imagery

The metaphor of the sea and water is crucial to *The House of Mirth*. Lily uses a seal that reads "Beyond! beneath a flying ship" to close her letters. As Katherine Joslin writes in *Edith Wharton*, this seal "symbolizes an impossible quest, the romantic flight to another world." Joslin points out how Wharton uses sea metaphors and imagery to depict Lily's plight as well as the environment of old New York. The world that Lily inhabits is one where the "new people" in society "rose to the surface with each recurring tide, and were either submerged beneath its rush or landed triumphantly beyond the reach of envious breakers." When Selden envisions rescuing Lily from marrying for money, he sees himself as dragging her back to land from a dangerous ship. He must carry her, not through "a clear rush of waves," but through "a clogging morass of old associations and habits." In many instances, Lily takes action that has a serious effect on her future, as when she neglects Percy Gryce at Bellomont. That day, the authorial voice notes, "She was like a water-plant in the flux of the tides, and today the whole current of her mood was carrying her toward Lawrence Selden." At other times, without money or a husband, Lily feels herself to be in the "dark seas," but when she feels safe again, it is as if she had "enough buoyancy to rise once more above her doubts."

Notably, the trip that Lily takes on the literal seas aboard the Dorset's yacht is what brings about her eventual downfall. After her return to New York, Lily continually perceives her position through water imagery. Unable to repay her debt to Trenor, she thinks about confiding her troubles in Selden, a thought that "became as seductive as the river's flow to the suicide. The first plunge would be terrible—but afterward, what blessedness might come!" After she is snubbed by Judy Trenor, she "had the doomed sense of the castaway who has signaled in vain the fleeing sails." Water imagery is not used in Lily's final moments, but when Selden finds out that she is dead, and how wrongly he judged her, the "bitter waters of his life surged high about him, their sterile taste was on his lips."

Pacing

The first half of *The House of Mirth* details Lily's travails at a leisurely pace. The reader follows Lily in her attempts to make a good marriage within the New York social milieu and her overall dealings with society members. Life seems at Lily's fingertips; she can marry Percy Gryce if she so desires, she is making money from investments, and she is growing closer to Selden. Despite her "advanced" age of twenty-nine, she is still the belle of New York.

The second half of the book moves at a much quicker pace as it chronicles Lily's ejection from society because of rumors spread by her "friend" Bertha Dorset. After this treachery, Lily's downfall is swift. She is disinherited, forced to sell her services as a companion to the nouveau riche, and even fired from her apprenticeship as a milliner. The end of the novel finds Lily in far distant circumstances from where she was as its beginning.

She occupies a dingy little room that she cannot even afford and finds herself cast out of her former circle. Alone and friendless, she dies, perhaps committing suicide. The pace of the writing in this half of the book fairly jumps from one terrible event to the next, an apt stylistic decision as it reflects the feelings of being unable to escape that which engulfs Lily. As the writing demonstrates, Lily is quickly drawn from one bad situation to a worse one. The pace of the book is perhaps nowhere as tellingly demonstrated as when Lily works for Mrs. Hatch: within the space of one chapter, Lily is exposed to an immoral circle that hopes to marry off a wealthy young bachelor to a much-older divorcée, is implicated by her role in this affair, and is accordingly ill judged by society.

Historical Context

New York City

The New York upper-class society of which Wharton writes in *The House of Mirth* could be characterized as one of affluence and relative ease. At the height of the social ladder were the aristocrats, such historical families as the Astors and the Vanderbilts. They came from old names and old money, and members of such families set the standards for other members of their social class. Arrivistes or the nouveau riche, people who had more recently earned their fortunes, also made up an important part of old New York society. Though they did not have a lustrous family history, they often held even greater wealth than the aristocratic families. The upper-class entertained themselves by attending the theater and opera; paying and receiving social calls; attending lunch, dinner, and house parties; traveling abroad; and summering in such fashionable spots as Newport, Rhode Island.

By contrast, New York was also associated with immigrants and poverty. Beginning in the mid-1800s, streams of immigrants, mostly from Europe, made New York their home. They sought opportunities for a better life, both economically and religiously, but many existed in miserable conditions. They lived in unhealthy, unsanitary, overcrowded tenement buildings. To earn enough money to survive, many families had to send their children to work as well. By the turn of the century, the percentage of the population living in poverty was swelling. In response to such problems, reformers worked to clean up the city. For example, a law passed in New York in 1901

Compare & Contrast

- **1900:** Forty-five percent of Americans live in urban centers. New York City's population rises above 1 million. Department stores, skyscrapers, public parks, and museums are all part of the new landscape of the city.

  Today: In 1990, 187 million Americans, representing about 75 percent of the population, live in urban areas. Conveniences and entertainment of all sorts can be found in modern cities, from shopping malls to IMAX movie theaters to countless museums.

- **1900:** Members of America's upper-class make up less than one-tenth of the country's population, yet they control over two-thirds of the country's wealth. The upper-class is essentially divided into two groups: old money and the nouveau riche. Members of the nouveau riche are known for their extravagance. For example, in 1897 one New York family spent close to $400,000 on a dance party. Some wealthy people, however, use their money to support social causes, giving money to art galleries, libraries, museums, universities, and cultural groups.

  Today: In 1998, just over 145,000 American families comprise the top 5 percent of wealthiest families in terms of income. This 5 percent

earns 20.7 percent of the country's overall income. As at the beginning of the century, some families are from old money and some are self-made. For example, the 1990s saw a rise in the number of people who became extremely wealthy through Internet companies. Some of these people practice philanthropy, but in 1998 households with an income of $100,000 and greater only gave 2.2 percent of their income to charities, averaging $2,550 per family.

- **1900:** By 1900 more than 90 percent of all American women are married. By the mid-1900s, about one in ten marriages end in divorce. Women initiate the great majority of divorces.

  Today: In 1990 there were 1,182,000 divorces among the American population—4.7 per 1,000. If this trend continues, younger Americans marrying for the first time have a 40 to 50 percent chance of divorcing in their lifetime. Still, Americans continue to wholeheartedly support the idea of marriage. Ninety-six percent of Americans express a personal desire to marry, and only 8 percent of American women would prefer to remain single rather than marry.

---

required that all new tenement buildings have an open courtyard to let in light and air.

The End of the Victorian Age

At the turn of the nineteenth to the twentieth century, "the cult of true womanhood" or "the cult of domesticity," still dictated the roles that women played in society. It was widely believed that a woman should devote herself to her family and the home. Women had almost no external personal identity; their social positions were primarily determined by their husbands' achievements and social status. A woman's role in life was to be a homemaker, and her single-minded purpose was to make a good marriage.

With the death of Britain's Queen Victoria in 1901, the Victorian era came to an end in Britain and the United States. Gradually women took on greater roles outside of the home. Wealthy women traveled, attended plays and concerts, became patrons of the arts, and joined service clubs that were a driving force behind the reform movements of the day. Women began to take up activities, such as smoking or gambling, which had previously been forbidden to them.

Working Women

By the close of the nineteenth century, increasing numbers of women, primarily members of the working class, were taking jobs outside of the

Gillian Anderson as Lily Bart and Eric Stoltz as Lawrence Selden in the 2000 film version of the novel

home. Single women began to flood the workplace, often taking jobs as nurses, teachers, or childcare workers. Married women might also be employed as clerical workers or as sales clerks in department stores. However, many married women had difficulty obtaining employment. Some people refused to hire them at all, while others forced female workers to resign upon marriage. Women also worked in factories and sweatshops, often under dangerous conditions. They labored long hours for little money. In response, some reformers fought for laws that would limit work hours for women and increase their wages. In the first few decades of the 1900s, many individual states passed such laws.

Critical Overview

The House of Mirth, Wharton's second novel, was published in 1905 to immediate critical and popular acclaim. Her editor at Scribners noted that it enjoyed the publishing house's quickest sales of the time. In comparing the novel to Wharton's earlier works, many critics found its complexity, characterization, and emotional resonance to show her im-

portant advances as a writer. The *New York Times Book Review* praises Wharton as the "most scholarly and distinctive writer of fiction of the day," while the *Saturday Review* notes that it is "one of the few novels which can claim rank as literature." *Review of Reviews* has extremely high praise, announcing that *The House of Mirth* is "worked out in a manner to stamp the writer a genius, and give her name a place in the history of American literature." Writers as celebrated as F. Scott Fitzgerald, William Dean Howells, Sinclair Lewis, and Joseph Conrad all valued *The House of Mirth*, which was recognized even in its day as Wharton's breakthrough novel.

The *Times Literary Supplement* commends Wharton's "trenchant knowledge of the human spirit and its curious workings," which is perhaps seen most clearly in Wharton's depiction of Lily Bart. As Henry James astutely comments, Lily was "very big and true—and very difficult to have *kept* big and true." One reviewer, Alice Meynell of London's *Bookman*, focuses her attention on Lawrence Selden, finding him the spokesman for a "better" world and thus the novel's important character.

At its publication, there were a few naysayers who responded to the moral purpose of Wharton's novel. As summed up by Linda Wagner-Martin in her book-length study *The House of Mirth*, these critics "claimed that unpleasantness was not the province of fiction, that by stressing the 'sordid,' Wharton did not only her work but her reader a grave disservice."

The House of Mirth has remained an important piece of literature through the years since its initial publication. In the 1960s, Irving Howe wrote in his introduction to *Edith Wharton: A Collection of Critical Essays* that with this novel, "Mrs. Wharton composed one of the few American novels that approaches the finality of the tragedy." In the 1970s, feminist scholars found interest in *The House of Mirth*, along with Wharton's other novels. Some scholars examined characters such as Lily Bart in light of the male-dominated society in which they lived. In *Edith Wharton's Argument with America*, Elizabeth Ammons writes of American culture as Wharton saw it:

> [It] offers them [young women] no means of realizing their dreams. Lily Bart, [and others] . . . all end up in bondage to the past not because Edith Wharton was cruel but because the liberation, the 'progress,' that America boasted of for women was, in her view, a mirage.

Since the 1970s, interest in Wharton's work has grown tremendously, as testified by the numerous books, essays, and studies published on her writing. As long ago as the 1920s, Arthur Hobson Quinn wrote in a pamphlet, "Which of *us* are truly alive as Lily Bart [and other Wharton characters]? And which of us will live as long?" The ongoing popularity of *The House of Mirth* bears out Quinn's prophecy.

Criticism

Rena Korb

Korb has a master's degree in English literature and creative writing and has written for a wide variety of educational publishers. In the following essay, Korb explores the types of power that Lily Bart holds and does not hold.

In the first scene of Wharton's masterpiece *The House of Mirth*, Laurence Selden queries Lily Bart, "Isn't marriage your vocation? Isn't it what you're all brought up for?" Lily replies with a sigh, "I suppose so. What else is there?" This brief, simple exchange underscores one of the most crucial truths to the tragedy of Lily Bart. As the characters who populate Lily's world accurately understand, a young woman's sole calling at the turn of the century was to marry, and in Lily's case, to marry well. In this era the country was firmly entrenched in "the cult of true womanhood," which called for a woman to devote herself to her family and her home. On the whole, Americans had little use for an unmarried woman nor did they see reason why she should enjoy any measure of that which is so important to Laurence Selden (Lily's male counterpart): "personal freedom." Note that the only major female character who deviates from this pattern is Gerty Farish, for whom Lily feels pity.

In Lily Bart, however, Wharton creates a woman with sensibilities far more modern than those of her environment. Lily refuses to wholly submit to society's gender roles, and is unable to marry a man who is beneath her simply to fulfill her expected purpose. Such incendiary behavior does not go unpunished, and Lily is ejected from society. However, she has been trained for no other direction in life than to ensnare a husband, and Lily comes to believe she has no options. She frankly tells Selden on the last day of her life, "I am a very useless person. . . . I was just a screw or cog in the great machine I called life, and when I dropped out of it I found I was of no use anywhere else." Rather than model herself after other women she knows, perhaps Gerty Farish or even Nettie Struther, Lily chooses to give herself up to a deep sleep—which notably is the only place where she allows herself to give in to the "the soft approach of passiveness"—that becomes her final sleep.

Unlike traditional protagonists, Lily lacks the power to create her own life. She is not unusual in this respect, for Wharton clearly shows the reader a society in which women only hold power through the men they marry. Judy Trenor and Bertha Dorset are both paradigms in society, but their power derives from their husbands' wealth, not through any intrinsic value of their own. As the authorial voice notes, "Bertha Dorset's social credit was based on an impregnable bank-account." In addition to grasping power through financial prowess, power for women may be obtained through personal connection. This method is epitomized through the character of Mattie Gormer, an arriviste to old New York who nevertheless is able to ascend the social ladder through her friendship with Bertha.

For Lily, an orphan with little money of her own, marriage remains the sole means to obtain a firm place in New York society and become powerful in her own right. The only tool at her disposal is her uncommon beauty, whose value was exalted by her mother Mrs. Bart, a woman who, after her husband's financial ruin, regarded Lily's beauty as "the last asset in their fortunes, the nucleus around which their life was to be rebuilt. She watched it jealously as though it were her own property and Lily its mere custodian." Thus, while still in her formative years, Lily became a prisoner of her own body. Further, when Mrs. Bart looked at Lily's beauty she also saw a force of destruction, "some weapon she had slowly fashioned for her vengeance" against the society that did not accord her enough respect because of her lack of great wealth. Although Lily also recognized her unique physical attraction, she "liked to think of her beauty as a power for good, as giving her the opportunity to attain a position where she should make her influence felt in the vague diffusion of refinement and good taste." Unfortunately, Mrs. Bart's belief system reflected that of the world around her; since her debut at the age of eighteen, Lily had several chances to wed wealth, but as she reveals to Selden, a marriage such as her mother envisioned is, at its very core, "disagreeable."

The novel introduces Lily to a series of men whom she might marry, none of whom are Lily's moral equal but all of whom carry far more weight in society. Lily, however, cannot bring herself to make such a marriage. Lily recognizes the inadequacies of the men: the dull Percy Gryce, who wants to collect a beautiful wife the same way he collects Americana; the frank-talking Simon Rose-dale, who wants a wife with social standing who will move him up the New York social ladder; and the pathetic George Dorset, who allows himself to be bullied and cuckolded by his wife. Even Laurence Selden, as summarized by Linda Wagner-Martin in her study *The House of Mirth*, has "a history of affairs with married women, a love of rhetorical games and flirtations, a tendency to make pronouncements and give orders, and a history of running away from confrontation." Indeed, Selden, whom Lily believes to be her one chance at love matched with happiness, shows little true regard for her happiness or even fundamental welfare.

Lily cannot marry any of these men, or such types of men—which is all society offers her—because she holds a power that is rendered useless by her shallow society: the power to make superior moral judgments. She is unable to ignore this quiet, ever-present inner voice, which alerts her to the banality, tedium, or downright distastefulness of these men and all that they offer. At Bellomont, after

> **"Lily cannot marry any of these men, or such types of men—which is all society offers her—because she holds a power that is rendered useless by her shallow society: the power to make superior moral judgments."**

practically guaranteeing herself a wedding proposal from Percy Gryce, Lily suddenly looks at these people who would forever populate her world in a different light: "That very afternoon they had seemed full of brilliant qualities; . . . [now] Under the glitter of their opportunities she saw the poverty of their achievement." Lily blames Selden for forcing her to acknowledge the ugliness of her marital intentions. "Why do you make the things I have chosen seem hateful to me?" she asks him at Bellomont. In truth, she functions as her own moral arbiter, for it is only Selden who is confident that wealth and social standing are the only things Lily cares for. Lily's actions—or her inaction when it comes to men—show that for all her talk, she cannot simply marry to reach those goals.

Because Lily aspires to a higher value, even though she fails to acknowledge it consciously, she sacrifices her other form of power: the power over other's reputations. Despite her lack of wealth or social standing, Lily holds power over Bertha Dorset in two ways, through Bertha's love letters to Laurence Selden and through knowledge of the affair that Bertha engaged in aboard the Dorset's yacht. These love letters are key to Lily's ability to dethrone Bertha and take her place in society by marrying George Dorset, or at the least, force her former "friend" to stop the malicious slander that has caused everyone in their circle to forsake Lily. Yet, Lily refuses to use either of these tools to unmask Bertha.

Many people encourage Lily to stoop to Bertha's level of blackmail and malicious talk. George Dorset pleads with Lily to save him from his loveless, miserable marriage: "'you're the only person'—his voice dropped to a whisper—'the only person who knows. . . . I want to be free, and you can free me.'" Carry Fisher, who becomes one of Lily's closest friends by the end of the novel, urges Lily to take up George's plan, provide the proof that Bertha was unfaithful so he can divorce and then become his wife. "He wouldn't stay with her ten minutes if he *knew*," Carry says. Lily lies to both George and Carry, claiming she knows nothing, thus preserving Bertha's reputation and extending the opportunity for Bertha to cause more damage to Lily's reputation. Simon Rosedale also knows that Lily has Bertha's letters. His words to Lily, "I know how completely she's in your power," emphasize that by taking up the devious tactics employed by others in their New York circle, Lily will assure herself a place within it. He proposes that Lily use the letters to force Bertha to let her back in society, and then he will marry her.

Such encounters make Lily comprehend that she actually holds power. George's pathetic demeanor and his obvious desire to divorce Bertha make it clear to Lily that it is within her power to marry him. Such ability, however, is hardly very far removed from the power that her beauty afforded her in the days before she was ousted from society, when she could have married Percy Gryce. Much more importantly, Lily's knowledge gives her the power to enact "revenge" against Bertha and attain "rehabilitation" into society. Although "there was something dazzling in the completeness of the opportunity," Lily refuses to follow such a course of action, even though holding on to such high standards holds no value in New York. Indeed, as Lily acknowledges in thinking over Rosedale's offer of marriage, "What debt did she owe to a social order which had condemned and banished her without trial?" It is no coincidence that Lily dies the night she burns Bertha's love letters. She deprives herself of the last material representation of power and her primary means to regain a place in society. That evening, she takes a few extra drops of her sleeping draught, and as it takes effect, as "gradually the sense of complete subjugation came over her," she gives up her will to live and sinks into her final sleep.

Source: Rena Korb, Critical Essay on *The House of Mirth*, in *Novels for Students*, The Gale Group, 2002.

Julie Olin-Ammentorp

In the following essay, Olin-Ammentorp challenges traditional feminist interpretations of Wharton's The House of Mirth.

In the past decade, feminist critics have done much to restore Edith Wharton to her proper rank among American novelists and to shed light on many aspects of her work previous critics had overlooked. Scholars such as Cynthia Griffin Wolff, Elizabeth Ammons, Judith Fetterley, and recently Wai-Chee Dimock have changed the understanding of Wharton's work through their perceptive analyses, focusing particularly on Wharton's insights into the social structures of the early part of this century and the ways in which these structures influenced and limited women's lives.

Yet the work of these feminist critics also raises issues of the limitations, or perhaps blindspots, of current feminist literary criticism, issues which go beyond their application to Wharton and her work. For instance, most feminist critics seem to imply that Wharton, though never one to ally herself with the feminist movements of her day, was a kind of inherent feminist, someone who both fought for and attained her rightful place as a novelist in a period when the novel was dominated by male authors and when upper-class women were taught, as Wharton was, to be more ornamental than intellectual. Moreover, these critics point out, Wharton protested the treatment of women through her portrayals of women caught in the inescapable bonds of social constructs. These points are fundamentally correct; Wharton was and did all these things. Yet in focusing only on these aspects of her life and career feminist critics overlook the Edith Wharton who, despite her mature anger over the random education her parents gave her, wrote that

> I have lingered over these details [describing the cooking she enjoyed as a child and young woman] because they formed a part—a most important and honourable part—of that ancient curriculum of house-keeping which . . . was so soon to be swept aside by the "monstrous regiment" of the emancipated: young women taught by their elders to despise the kitchen and the linen room, and to substitute the acquiring of University degrees for the more complex art of civilized living . . . I mourn more than ever the extinction of the household arts. Cold storage, deplorable as it is, has done less harm to the home than the Higher Education.

One point where feminist criticism seems particularly weak is in its treatment of the men in Wharton's fiction. This is particularly true in criticism of *The House of Mirth*, probably the best-known as well as the most astutely criticized of Wharton's novels. Judith Fetterley has claimed that in Wharton's novels, social waste is female; when one uses this as the guiding principle in reading *The House of Mirth*, the novel becomes the story of a young woman's destruction by a social system that maintains that upper-class women are meant to be ornamental, even while it forces them to prostitute themselves on the marriage market. A woman like Lily, Fetterley argues, has to accept her status as "a piece of property available for purchase by the highest bidder." Elizabeth Ammons joins Fetterley in arguing that power in the novel is patriarchal, pointing out that men are the makers of money in the novel and, thus, as the novel focuses on the economics of marriage, the source of all power. These points are important and undeniably true and help to explain the social structure in which Lily moves.

But a re-examination of Wharton's fiction in general, and of *The House of Mirth*, in particular, demonstrates that the social structures of Wharton's fictional world cause male waste as much as female. As Dimock has noted, "the actual wielders of power in the book are often not men but women," indeed, women like Bertha Dorset and Judy Trenor are hardly subservient to their husbands, despite their economic dependence on them; both of these women seem to have more freedom and power than their spouses. At no point does Wharton suggest that they warrant pity nor that they are victims of the system in the way Lily is. Lily herself is eager to grasp the money that could make her as great a social force as either of her friends, as is implied by her successive evaluations of the personal and economic attractions of men as different as Percy Gryce, Sim Rosedale, and Lawrence Selden. Women in this novel spend at least as much time assessing men as men do evaluating women. Despite the weakness of Wharton's males—a weakness that has become almost proverbial among Wharton critics—Wharton presents her male characters as meriting as much (or perhaps almost as much) sympathy as her female characters.

Three of the men most important to this novel, Gus Trenor, George Dorset, and Lawrence Selden, have been pretty much dismissed as a brute, a spineless coward, and a coward who should have known better, who should, in fact, have come to Lily's "rescue." Yet to re-examine these characters within the social context that Wharton so carefully establishes is to see that they cannot be judged quite so simply. Gus Trenor, despite his attempt to rape Lily as a way of making her "pay up" for the money he has given her, verges on the pathetic at moments. Not only is he ugly in a society which, as Wharton says in her autobiography, had "an almost pagan worship of physical beauty," but he is aware that his wife uses him as a pawn in the socio-economic

> **Wharton's point is not that Lily is victim, Selden victimizer, but that in spite of their different standings within the system, both are pitiable in their entrapment."**

system. Indeed, Judy Trenor values him only for his wealth while simultaneously refusing to acknowledge the costs of running a household or building a ballroom. Although Gus' violence in demanding that Lily "pay up" is in no way excusable, it is perhaps understandable in the context of a social system that views him primarily as a workhorse.

George Dorset may be Wharton's most pointed example of a man diminished by the social system. Early in the novel Judy Trenor remarks to Lily that the dyspeptic George "is not as dismal as you think. If Bertha [his wife] didn't worry him he would be quite different." As the novel develops Wharton reveals the uneven nature of the Dorsets' marriage: Bertha, "out of a job" when her affair with Selden ends, takes up with Ned Silverton, while George becomes increasingly dismayed. Rather than accusing Bertha of unfaithfulness and demanding her fidelity or, alternately, divorcing her, George allows Bertha to blackmail him into silence. At the same time he begs Lily to help him, telling her that she is the only one who can "save" him. When Lily refuses even to acknowledge that she could help George, he sinks into apathy. That Lily feels she cannot help George makes a double point: that the system of marriage wastes male potential as it does female, and that the Dorset marriage, although it continues, is a failure from every point of view except that of Bertha, who happily goes on spending George's income. Moreover, Lily's inability to "save" Dorset also has important implications for Lily's own need to be "saved."

While George Dorset and Gus Trenor have received their share of critical scorn, Lawrence Selden has received the brunt of critical wrath. Claiming that Lily is solely "victim" within the system, many critics have argued that Lawrence Selden, despite his relative moral attractions, is to be condemned for his failure to "save" Lily. Though not necessarily someone who would identify himself as a feminist, R. W. B. Lewis established the normative view of Selden in his biography of Wharton. Selden, Lewis argues, "is the one human being who might have supplied" a "viable alternative life for Lily." Lewis continues, "Selden himself, as she [Wharton] told Sara Norton, was 'a negative hero,' a sterile and subtly fraudulent figure whose ideas were not much to be trusted." Cynthia Griffin Wolff claims that "far from being Wharton's spokesman, Selden is the final object of her sweeping social satire." Similarly, Wai-chee Dimock believes that Selden "remains, to the end, a closet speculator . . . The 'republic of the spirit' turns out to be less a republic than a refined replica of the social marketplace, of which Selden is a full participating member." Three fundamentally faulty assumptions about Wharton's novel underlie such judgments of Selden. First, readers assume that Selden *could* have "saved" Lily and thus is culpable for not having done so; second, they judge Selden by a standard far harsher than that they use to judge Lily; and third, their expectations that Selden "save" Lily at all are problematic in terms of the novel as a whole.

First of all, readers and critics alike cannot assume fairly that Selden could have saved Lily. Whatever the limitations of Selden's heroism, Lily herself hardly makes the path to complete rescue an easy one. Selden, after all, proposes to her repeatedly in the novel, but she is as imbued with the idea of marriage for money and power as Selden is with the notion of romantic love. In addition, her inability to govern her own life stems from a fundamental indecisiveness, the result of the values inculcated in her by her culture, that prevents her from developing either a firm friendship or a love relationship with Selden. Finally, Wharton stresses repeatedly the social indoctrination that has made it almost impossible for either Lily or Selden to break through their carefully-cultivated emotional reserves. It is extremely problematic to fault Selden for not "saving" Lily; she will not permit herself to be saved.

Second, it is important not to set up a reverse double standard for judging Selden. While feminist critics see Lily generally, and correctly, as a product and a victim of society, they conveniently ignore Wharton's hint that "in a different way, [Selden] was, as much as Lily, the victim of his environment." They somehow expect Selden to transcend the codes of his class and place. It is gener-

ally understood that Lily's reluctance to wed is an expression of her "repugnance toward a relationship in which a woman is powerless" and a result of her examination of the hatred and hypocrisy in the marriages of her friends; yet the same considerations and observations are somehow supposed not to concern Selden. There may, indeed, be some grounds for judging Selden by standards different from those used for Lily: the stakes are different for the two of them. Because of her extreme specialization, Lily must "go into partnership"—that is, marry—in order not to "drop"; by comparison Selden's implied return to books and his law practice looks fairly comfortable. Nevertheless, these disparities do not justify condemning Selden for the same responses that are respected in Lily.

The novel as a whole reveals that such condemnations are in themselves wanting. Despite their efforts to live independent of the standards of their class, both Selden and Lily are limited by these standards: Lily cannot teach herself an independent existence, and Selden, although he is somewhat independent of others, cannot see the system in which both live as wholly as readers can. Readers, after all, have the advantage of Wharton's narration and of extended exposure to Lily's consciousness; by comparison, Selden's knowledge is extremely limited. Moreover, moral cowardice—of which both Selden and Lily have their share—is hardly a disgrace in Wharton's novel. It would take an almost superhuman effort to break out of a system so rigid and yet so flexible that it can, for instance, maintain with perfect equanimity that marriage is a romantic connection while demonstrating over and over that it is an economic relation. Irving Howe's relatively early (pre-feminist, one might say) remark on Wharton's work may still stand among the most perceptive summaries of her stance toward such characters as Lily and Selden:

> Mrs. Wharton understands how large is the price, how endless the nagging pain, that must be paid for a personal assertion against the familiar ways of the world, and she believes, simply, that most of us lack the strength to pay.

Lily finally manages to "pay up" her debt to Trenor, but this payment robs her of any further strength. In spite of his relative independence of social standards, Selden as well "lack[s] the strength to pay" for his release from the social system. Wharton's point is not that Lily is victim, Selden victimizer, but that in spite of their different standings within the system, both are pitiable in their entrapment.

In planning her novel, Wharton wrote that the most difficult obstacle to overcome was determining how to give "a society of irresponsible pleasure-seekers" the "typical human significance which is the story-teller's reason for telling one story rather than another." The solution, she discovered,

> was that a frivolous society can acquire dramatic significance only through what its frivolity destroys. Its tragic implication lies in its power of debasing people and ideals. The answer, in short, was my heroine, Lily Bart.

It is with such remarks in mind that feminist critics have claimed, as Fetterley has, that "social waste is female" in *The House of Mirth*. But in context, Wharton's remark is almost synecdochic: Lily Bart represents not just herself, not even her sex, but the whole group of women *and* men destroyed by a grappling and vicious social system which they are intelligent enough to understand but too weak to change.

In this way, Lily herself—along with Ned Silverton, who once aspired to writing epics, and Lawrence Selden, with his passion for the beautiful—can be seen as failed Edith Whartons: all fail to find a channel into which they can direct their creative energies productively. Wharton's portrayal of Lily's defeat and death suggests not only Wharton's appreciation of the binding force of social norms, but perhaps as well—and more disturbingly—a certain acceptance of these norms.

Indeed, if one accepts the notion that Selden as well as Lily may be a sympathetic character, one faces once again the problem of interpreting the novel's conclusion. It is entirely possible that Wharton intended the conclusion to be read as it is written—that, in fact, "in the silence there passed between them the word which made all clear." As much as Wharton regrets the waste implied in Lily's life and death, she may reconcile herself to it as well. For Wharton constructs her novel to imply the impossibility of one individual saving, or even helping, another; this is clearest in Selden's failure to help Lily but is reinforced as well by Lily's refusal to save George Dorset by supplying him with the information he needs to divorce Bertha.

Wharton may in fact have accepted her status as what Adrienne Rich has described as a "token" or "special" woman. Speaking to a group of women at the Modern Language Association, Rich noted that she, like Virginia Woolf addressing a women's college, was

> aware of the women who are not with us here because they are washing the dishes and looking after the children ... We seem to be special women here, we have liked to think of ourselves as special, and we have known that men would tolerate, even romanticize us as special, as long as our words and actions didn't threaten their privilege of tolerating or rejecting us and our work according to *their* ideas of what a special woman ought to be.

Surrounded by Henry James and a host of other admiring men, Wharton was clearly in the situation that Rich describes, that of the special woman who accepts her own success as something due to her, something she has earned. Wharton saw herself as someone who had made it on her own, through hard work and will power, and who—despite her compassion for those like Lily Bart—seems fundamentally to accept the failure of others as the natural result of social Darwinism. Other women, she implies, should not bother to educate themselves, much less write; they should instead learn the arts of household management. Despite her gratitude to those (all men) who helped her develop her intellect and her skill as a writer, Wharton prefers to ignore the possibility that women could benefit from systematic education or the cultivation of their potential as artists, as full human beings. Her attitude toward others seems, in short, to be a version of the "pull yourself up by your bootstraps" approach, one which most feminists now find somewhat wanting, given that society may leave some individuals with bootstraps that are very short, or even non-existent.

Yet this view of Wharton, too, is limited. Like both Woolf and Rich, Wharton was aware of the women who were in fact "washing the dishes and looking after the children." In *The House of Mirth*, Wharton portrays not only the Olympian heights of social glitter but also the wrong side of the "social tapestry", the lives of the numerous women who suffer that a few might be wealthy: charwomen, girls working long hours at an overheated and underlit milliner's shop. Wharton herself is something of an enigma when it comes to issues both of class and of self-perception. The professional writer every morning, she emerged meticulously, fashionably coiffed and clad, every noon to take over the role of the perfect hostess. Nor, apparently, did she see any contradiction between these roles, nor between the little girl who early experienced a love of fine clothing and admiration and the society that so long kept that girl from attaining her potential as a thinker and a writer. Similarly, Wharton was reputed to be unusually kind to her servants—a trait she passes on to Lily Bart—and she worked long hours to help relocate refugees from Belgium during World War I.

What Do I Read Next?

- Wharton's novel *The Custom of the Country* (1913) can be considered a companion piece to *The House of Mirth*. The novel chronicles the rise of Undine Spragg, a ruthless Midwesterner, up New York's social ladder. Unlike Lily Bart, Undine cares nothing about the people she harms as she attempts to achieve wealth and social standing.

- Wharton's autobiography *A Backward Glance* was published in 1934, three years before the author's death.

- According to scholar Linda Wagner-Martin, Wharton took as a literary model the titular heroine of Henry James's novella *Daisy Miller* (1878). Daisy, an American ingenue traveling in Europe with her mother, becomes compromised by her friendship with an Italian man. Her behavior alienates the American man who is courting her and alienates the other Americans living abroad.

- *Lost New York* (1971), by Nathan Silver, describes old New York society and environs.

- Kate Chopin's novel *The Awakening* (1899) tells the story of a woman, Edna Pontellier, determined to choose the terms and conditions of her own marriage. Despite the morals of her Louisiana society, Edna escapes a dreary marriage through an adulterous affair.

- In 1898 feminist author Charlotte Perkins Gilman published her nonfiction work *Women and Economics: A Study of the Economic Relation between Men and Women as a Factor in Social Evolution*. In this influential book Gilman states that women's dependence on men is neither natural nor beneficial. She claims that wives, like prostitutes, trade sex for economic stability.

Yet it appears that she never questioned her right to ask a dozen individuals to run her household. She was, perhaps, aristocratic ("special" in Rich's terms) in the way that Woolf was as well: She saw no problem in preventing others from developing their potential so that she might develop her own. At the bottom of this is a certain classism that is, or so one would hope, inimical to feminism in the 1980s.

Edith Wharton's challenge to feminist criticism is the challenge created by historical distance and by shifting definitions of feminism itself. Many feminist critics seem to have expected Wharton to be fifty years ahead of her time; further, they have shaped a Wharton who conforms to such expectations. In doing so they have oversimplified the complexities of Wharton's personality and times; they have brilliantly represented and respected a part of her genius, but they have detached it from the woman as a whole.

Source: Julie Olin-Ammentorp, "Edith Wharton's Challenge to Feminist Criticism," in *Studies in American Fiction*, Vol. 16, No. 2, Autumn 1988, pp. 237–44.

James W. Gargano

In the following essay, Gargano considers faith and social futility in Wharton's The House of Mirth.

Almost inevitably, critics of Edith Wharton's *The House of Mirth* focus their comments on the "moral" vitality of its social criticisms. Clearly, the novel's scenic art and the author's pointed intrusions into her narrative justify this critical emphasis. It is true, as Irving Howe asserts, that "the meanings of the book emerge through a series of contrasts between a fixed scale of social place and an evolving measure of moral value." In one of the most original essays on the novel that I have encountered, Diana Trilling ends up by seeing the heroine's fate in socio-moral terms: "Like the old Bolshevik who confesses to uncommitted crimes in attestation of the superior moral authority of the state, Lily affirms the absolute power of society over the life of the individual by her demonstration that she is finally incapable of effective action on her own behalf." Though he dwells primarily on the "naturalistic" aspects of the novel, Blake Nevius describes its theme as "the victimizing effect of a particular environment on one of its more helplessly characteristic products." Even Richard Poirier, whose brilliant analysis of *The House of Mirth* is almost a last word, finally traces Lily's doom to the absence in her society of "an ordering principle for her good impulses."

I believe that in the curiously didactic last chapters of the novel, Mrs. Wharton reached beyond her immediate social concerns toward a larger, perhaps ultimately philosophical vision. She permits her two sympathetic characters, Lily Bart and Lawrence Selden, to come into triumphant possession of a secret that reconciles Lily to death and Selden to life. This secret, contained in a "word" never divulged by the author, endows the seeming *absurdity of* existence with sanctity and ultimate grace. It affirms that a force of mysterious origin and sanction is to be found at the center of all life. Because Lily and Selden hear and finally respond to this word, their lost opportunities result in discovery rather than in waste and futility. Lily makes her clarifying discovery of the word on her deathbed. What might appear to be the tragic consequence of a misguided life is suddenly transformed into self-fulfillment. Her last struggle begins as a crisis of hope:

> As she lay there she said to herself that there was something she must tell Selden, some word she had found that should make life clear between them. She tried to repeat the word, which lingered vague and luminous on the far edge of thought—she was afraid of not remembering it when she woke; and if she could only remember it and say it to him, she felt that everything would be well.

For a moment, the thought of the word fades and she relapses into terror and loneliness. Then, the word becomes flesh as she feels a baby lying in her arms. Once again, she suffers misery and shock as she loses "her hold of the child." In her dying seconds, however, "the recovered warmth flowed through her once more, she yielded to it, sank into it, and slept."

In the last chapter of the novel, the word that consoles Lily is almost mystically transmitted to Selden. In a setting romantically appropriate to his mood, he acts with a kind of morning vigor and a spontaneous disregard for social ritual. Hurrying to see Lily at an unconventionally early hour, he is liberated and excited because "he had found the word he meant to say to her, and it could not wait another moment to be said." Amazed that he has not spoken it sooner, he now regards it as proclaiming a new day, as establishing a new order. Joyfully, he treats the word as if it were revelatory and revitalizing: "It was not a word for twilight, but for the morning." Although his commitment to the word is checked by Lily's death and by a brief resurgence of cynicism, he struggles past doubts into an enduring faith in it. The novel concludes, not with the naturalistic or moral harshness usually imputed to it, but with the serenity of a religious

The 'word' that reverberates through the last two chapters of *The House of Mirth* cannot be anything but faith."

affirmation: "He knelt by the bed and bent over her, draining their last moment to its lees; and in the silence there passed between them the word which made all clear."

None of the critics I have mentioned appear to take the ending of *The House of Mirth* seriously. None of them ask what the redemptive word is, and, finally, none of them try to determine the extent to which it attenuates Lily's tragedy. It seems advisable, then, to begin a critical quest for the meaning of Mrs. Wharton's novel with a search for the word and its implications.

The quest can appropriately begin with a look at the society in which Lily Bart schemes for success. Uninspired by the "word," the social circle derisively pictured in *The House of Mirth* rarely rises above elegance and comfort and often descends into sordid conniving and petty Grundyism. Money assures privilege, but privilege, too cheaply construed, dissipates into an expense of spirit and a waste of shame. Mrs. Wharton's smart set and its wealthy hangerson are curiously mindless and soulless, and those seeking entrance into the charmed circle wish to be assimilated into an expensive but not very expansive culture. The few old families not drawn into luxurious frivolities and vices derive their immunity from narrow imaginations and pinched spirits.

Mrs. Wharton exhibits her world in all its negative indifference to thought and idealism. She shows Lily's nascent hope blighted and Selden's life in the "republic of the spirit" reduced to a sterile posture. The calculating Bertha Dorset holds on to her fortune and her cowed husband, and the Brys and Rosedale are ready to pump their new-made millions into the perpetuation of a system that cruelly snubbed them. Goodness and the freedom to achieve it are commodities too fragile to survive in such a civilized social state; indeed, if one disregards the crucial last chapter of *The House of Mirth*, one may feel that the author is attempting to expose the existence of a social conspiracy against creative and moral impulses.

Nevertheless, despite her lively perception of human stupidity and weakness, Mrs. Wharton does not intend her novel to be misanthropic or merely satirical. Her theme, instead, insists that personal integrity represents an act of faith in a spiritual order beyond the of the world of appearance. In other words, Lily's worldly mistakes are disguised blessings: her final inability to marry Percy Gryce, after all her preparations have been seductively made, stems from an innate trust in something less musty than a moneyed imbecile. In addition, in refusing to be self-serving by helping herself to Bertha Dorset's husband or Rosedale's fortune, she actually serves a higher concept of self. In spite of her banalities and excesses, Lily finds it impossible to commit a final act of self-desecration. She renounces the prizes she was trained to seek and hearkens to Selden's timid confidences about the republic of the spirit. She knows that she cannot be saved by a society which in one way or another, can only destroy as it gratifies: to be a Judy Trenor is to be a comfortable lost soul, to be a Bertha Dorset is to be a desperate one. To initiate the newly-rich into society's inner sphere as Carrie Fisher does, is to live as a parasite in a well-furnished vacuum. Though Lily shares the vices and follies of all these women, she differs from them in possessing a vision, at first disquieting but ultimately consoling. Her apparent social descent is—besides being the frightful thing that haunts the critics of the book—largely a subconscious search for meanings fixed beyond the flux of wealth and social status.

What permanent truth embodied in what "word," it might be asked, does Lily discover? I cannot agree with Mrs. Trilling that Edith Wharton intends her heroine to acknowledge the tyrannous primacy of the "state." Indeed, Mrs. Wharton seems to be saying *that from a spiritual perspective, society, considered as the supreme* lawgiver, is an illusion or a downright fiction. It is an arena of distraction, a kind of Vanity Fair. What *The House of Mirth* asserts is that no life possesses spiritual vitality until it is motivated by belief in its own significance. Obviously, the enigmatic and revelatory word that Lily does not achieve until the end of her life is "faith". Only with it can a successful quest be pursued against all the equivocating counter-claims and inducements of society, against the ostensible absurdity of life itself. Lily's persistent problem is that she lacks conscious faith

even while she evades evil: of course, she resists grossness, but she is on good terms with the spiritual compromises that grow into horrors. In short, she will not allow her spiritual possibilities to be more than a polite conversation piece between herself and Selden. The shock of Gus Trenor's abortive sexual assault awakens her to the ugly possibilities of life: "Yes, the Furies might sometimes sleep, but they were there, always in the dark corner, and now they were awake and the iron dang of their wings was in her brain." Even the visitation of the Furies and her loss of Selden, however, do not significantly change her life: she soon invites disaster by slipping all too easily into an arrangement to distract George Dorset's attention from one of his wife's infidelities. Lily's major weakness, then, is the weakness of Denis Peyton in *Sanctuary*, of Glennard in *The Touchstone*, and of so many other characters in Mrs. Wharton's novels—a lack of faith in the "reality" and fundamental necessity of the spiritual life.

Faith, as Edith Wharton defines it, is no generalized and temperamental optimism; it is, instead, an almost mystical assurance that only moral action can save the ever-threatened continuity of human existence. Beset by dangers inherent in social arrangements, man clings to survival by the thread of his moral instincts; he is, at his best motivated by what Mrs. Wharton calls, in *Sanctuary*, "this passion of charity for the race." In other words, goodness is useful, and men and women must, under pain of extinction, bequeath it to their children. At one of her "grandest" moments, for example, Kate Orme in *Sanctury* is overwhelmed by "mysterious primal influences" and by a "passion of spiritual motherhood that made her long to fling herself between the unborn child and its fate." Although Lily never worries about future generations, her casual generosity to Nettie Struther saves the "poor working girl" and enables her to marry and have a child which—almost as an unmerited reward or rather a visitation of grace—teaches Lily "the central truth of existence." After holding the baby in her arms, Lily sees the courage and primal trust in Nettie's precarious new life: "It was a meagre enough life, on the grim edge of poverty, with scant margin for possibilities of sickness or mischance, but it had the frail audacious permanence of a bird's nest built on the edge of a cliff—a mere wisp of leaves and straw, yet so put together that the lives entrusted to it may hang safely over the abyss."

For Edith Wharton, the abyss is an everlasting peril, and the "frail audacious permanence" at times seems merely frail and futile. The "noble" act, in

Lily's case a renunciation of personal advantage, does not conspicuously alter the way of the world: the Trenors, Dorsets, and Brys—with the addition of Rosedale, the Gormers, and "Mrs. Norma Hatch, Emporium Hotel"—will continue their anarchic existence in an atmosphere of gold dust. Yet, Nettie Struther's and Lily's affirmations make a difference because they spring from depths of "faith," the first and most important of all words. After everything else has been said, Mrs. Wharton declares, it is necessary to believe in the meaning and utility of spiritual action. In *Sanctuary*, Kate Orme attains the vision of the continuity of life in a "mystic climax of effacement"; engulfed by an anguish which is also joy, she experiences a "surge of liberating faith in life, the old *credo quia absurdum* which is the secret cry of all supreme endeavour." Lily, too, stares into the absurdity and the abyss, and she is forced to acknowledge that she had not risen to the occasions when "Selden had twice been ready to stake his faith on Lily Bart." She has not attained the faith of Nettie's husband, who knowing of the girl's premarital freedoms, had nevertheless believed in her essential goodness. As Lily recalls Nettie's happiness, she struggles toward her own credo: "Her husband's faith in her had made her renewal possible."

The "word" that reverberates through the last two chapters of *The House of Mirth* cannot be anything but faith. It is the word that keeps Lily from the abyss; it is the word Selden must discover and treasure. In spite of her comparatively favorable portrait of Selden, Mrs. Wharton does not minimize his lack of faith, his timidity and subjection to appearances. All too ready to accuse Lily of self-interest, he suffers from a sort of moral snobbishness and aloofness that turn his republic of the spirit into an exclusive island for dilettantes. Even after he prides himself on having found out the "essential" Lily, he mistakenly assumes that she has made a clandestine visit to Gus Trenor's house. During her last conversation with him she tells him, "I needed the help of your belief in me"; yet, he cannot act because his "faculties seemed tranced, and he was still groping for the word to break the spell." For all his intelligence and discrimination, Selden cannot be simple enough to surrender to faith; he cannot rely on naive trust (which, for Mrs. Wharton, may be the highest perception) to clear the debris of suspicion and fear from his mind. The word itself evaporates as, in Lily's death chamber, he finds her compromising check made out to Gus Trenor. Only with an effort, perhaps like that of Kate Orme, can he reject the ambiguous appear-

ances that induce cynicism. When faith returns to him, however, he sees that "though all the conditions of life had conspired to keep them apart," he can rejoice that he had come to her "willing to stake his future on his faith in her."

The House of Mirth, it should be added, does not conclude with sentimental *éclat* , Lily's search for the knowledge contained in the word is built into the structure of the novel. All of her disappointments lead, however painfully, to a clarification of her baffling inconsistencies, her aversions, and her tortured waverings. It takes her a whole ambivalent life to evolve and possess a belief that dissolves the omnipresent and clamorous absurdity of her own, and the human, condition. But she does finally arrive at the *credo quia absurdum* that, for Mrs. Wharton, inspires all supreme endeavor.

Source: James W. Gargano, "*The House of Mirth*: Social Futility and Faith," in *American Literature*, Vol. 44, No. 1, March 1972, pp. 137–43.

Sources

Ammons, Elizabeth, *Edith Wharton's Argument with America*, in *Edith Wharton*, by Katherine Joslin, St. Martin's Press, 1991, p. 137.

Howe, Irving, "Introduction: The Achievement of Edith Wharton," in *Edith Wharton: A Collection of Critical Essays*, edited by Irving Howe, Prentice Hall, Inc., 1962, pp. 1–18.

James, Henry, "Letters," in *"The House of Mirth": A Novel of Admonition*, by Linda Martin-Wagner, Twayne Publishers, 1990, p. 9.

Joslin, Katherine, *Edith Wharton*, St. Martin's Press, 1991.

Meynell, Alice, in *"The House of Mirth": A Novel of Admonition*, by Linda Martin-Wagner, Twayne Publishers, 1990, p. 9, originally published in *Bookman* (London), Vol. 29, December 1905, pp. 130–31.

New York Times Book Review, in *Edith Wharton: The Contemporary Reviews*, edited by James W. Tuttleton, Kristin O. Lauer, and Margaret P. Murray, Cambridge University Press, 1992, p. 117.

Quinn, Arthur Hobson, "Edith Wharton," in *"The House of Mirth": A Novel of Admonition*, by Linda Martin-Wagner, Twayne Publishers, 1990, p. 11.

Review of Reviews, in *Edith Wharton*, by Katherine Joslin, St. Martin's Press, 1991, pp. 130–31.

Saturday Review, in *Edith Wharton*, by Katherine Joslin, St. Martin's Press, 1991, p. 131.

Times Literary Supplement (London), in *Edith Wharton: The Contemporary Reviews*, edited by James W. Tuttleton, Kristin O. Lauer, and Margaret P. Murray, Cambridge University Press, 1992, p. 117.

Wagner-Martin, Linda, *"The House of Mirth": A Novel of Admonition*, Twayne Publishers, 1990.

Wolff, Cynthia Griffin, "Edith Wharton," in *Dictionary of Literary Biography*, Vol. 9: *American Novelists, 1910–1945*, edited by James J. Martine, Gale Research, 1981, pp. 126–42.

Further Reading

Dwight, Eleanor, *Edith Wharton, An Extraordinary Life*, Harry N. Abrams, 1994.
    This work is an overview of the life and times of Wharton. It includes personal correspondence and photographs.

Bloom, Harold, ed., *Edith Wharton*, Chelsea House, 1986.
    Bloom offers a collection of critical essays on the works of Wharton.

Lewis, R. W. B., *Edith Wharton, A Biography*, Harper & Row, 1975.
    Lewis provides a comprehensive work about the life and literature of Wharton.

Lewis, R. W. B., and Nancy Lewis, eds., *Collected Letters of Edith Wharton*, Scribner's, 1989.
    This important collection of annotated letters provides four hundred of Wharton's letters.

McDowell, Margaret B., *Edith Wharton*, Twayne Publishers, 1991.
    McDowell's text is a critical overview of Wharton's writing.

Nevius, Blake, *Edith Wharton: A Study of Her Fiction*, University of California Press, 1953.
    Nevius discounts prevailing critical thought and presents insightful criticism of Wharton's work.

Wolff, Cynthia Griffin, *A Feast of Words: The Triumph of Edith Wharton*, Oxford University Press, 1977.
    Wolff's book presents a psychological biography of Wharton, as well as criticism.

In the Castle of My Skin

George Lamming
1953

In the Castle of My Skin, the first novel by Barbadian writer George Lamming, tells the story of the mundane events in a young boy's life that take place amid dramatic changes in the village and society in which he lives. First published in London in 1953, the novel uses such characteristic devices of modernist fiction as shifting perspectives and unreliable narration to recount the boyhood of a fairly traditional fictional protagonist: a sensitive, unusually intelligent young boy, with a protective mother, who grows up among his peers but, because of his intelligence, takes a different path.

The novel's main concern, however, is not the individual consciousness of the protagonist. Rather, Lamming uses the growth and education of G. (his hero) as a device through which to view the legacy of colonialism and slavery in Caribbean village society in the middle of the twentieth century, and to document the changes that time brings to this sleepy hamlet. The novel's primary concerns are larger than the experience of G. as an individual. Through his eyes, we see the effects of race, feudalism, capitalism, education, the labor movement, violent riots, and emigration on his small town and, by extension, on Caribbean society as a whole. In later books, Lamming continued to examine the Caribbean experience, as his protagonists migrated to London and the United States, returned to their homes in the Caribbean, and helped their home countries obtain independence. But in *In the Castle of My Skin*, as befits his choice of protagonist, the scope of perception is limited to the personal,

George Lamming

domestic, and village spheres. Through this restricted view, the reader receives a comprehensive image of significant sociocultural changes in a tradition-bound part of the world.

Author Biography

Along with the novelist V. S. Naipaul and the poet Derek Walcott, the Barbadian novelist George Lamming is one of the most important figures in Caribbean Anglophone (English-speaking) literature. Lamming was born June 8, 1927, in Carrington Village, a small settlement about two miles from Barbados's capital, Bridgetown. Carrington Village was much like Creighton Village in the novel *In the Castle of My Skin*, in that it retained the basic structure of a plantation settlement. Lamming was raised by his unmarried mother and by Papa Grandison, his mother's devoted godfather.

Lamming attended the Roebuck Boys School in Carrington Village and was awarded a scholarship to attend Combermere High School, where a teacher encouraged his writing. When he was nineteen, Lamming left Barbados for the nearby island of Trinidad, where he obtained a teaching position

at El Colegio de Venezuela. While in Trinidad, Lamming continued his involvement with the Anglo-Caribbean literary journal *Bim* and came to know a number of other writers like himself.

In 1950, feeling that Caribbean society was stifling his artistic ambitions, Lamming sailed for London. His literary output, previously limited to poetry, expanded. By 1960, Lamming had published four lauded novels and his study of cultural identity, *The Pleasures of Exile*. During this decade, he worked for the overseas division of the British Broadcasting Service and, as a result, traveled extensively, including a trip to the United States in 1955. During these travels, Lamming began to interest himself in political independence movements in the Caribbean islands.

In the 1960s, Lamming published no new book-length fiction, although he served as the editor of two special issues of *New World Quarterly*, one dedicated to the independence of Barbados and the other to the independence of Guyana. During this decade he was extremely active in the promotion of Caribbean literature, receiving fellowships, writing television scripts, serving on literary prize juries, and occupying the chair of Writer in Residence at the University of the West Indies.

In 1971, Lamming returned to fiction with the publication of his novel *Water with Berries*, a novel about anti-West Indian bigotry in England. Another novel, *Natives of My Person*, followed in 1972. In the last thirty years, Lamming has published no new novels, but in the 1990s he published three books of criticism, focusing on his enduring concerns: political self-determination, racism, and the legacy of the fraught relationships between the European powers and the peoples they colonized and enslaved.

Plot Summary

Chapter 1

In the Castle of My Skin opens with an image of what becomes the main motif of the book: flooding waters. The as-yet-unnamed protagonist, on his ninth birthday, is looking out the window of his house and talking with his mother about the unusual rains in the village. His mother tells him about his relatives. The chapter is narrated by the boy, who also uses the opportunity to describe the village.

Chapter 2

In the second chapter, the scope of the boy's vision widens to include others outside of his household. His mother bathes him in the yard outside his house while the neighbor boy, Bob, climbs up the fence to watch and laugh and call to the other boys. G.'s mother calls them "vagabonds" and curses at them when they tear down the pumpkin vine by playing on it. As she scolds Bob, Bob's mother emerges and hits Bob very hard on the ear and G.'s mother drags him away. A number of boys and girls come to gawk. As G. stands there naked, his overwrought mother tries to whip him with a branch for being so stupid.

The mothers of the village start talking among themselves about the "botheration" that their children bring them. Miss Foster tells a story about how Gordon's fowlcock befouled a white man's suit. As the children and mothers disperse, Bob and G. talk. Following these conversations, the narration subtly changes tone, as if G. is no longer narrating and has been replaced by an older, more experienced voice. This voice tells us about the history and social milieu of the village, focusing on the role of the landlord's overseers and describing how the power in the village reinforced the sense that black people and their language were inferior.

The narration returns to G.'s perspective and the setting changes to the village showers. The boys play around in the showers and are ejected by the supervisor for "fooling around," then they go to the railroad tracks to place pins and nails on the rails. As they walk back to the village, they stop and get food from a vendor. The chapter closes with Miss Foster, Bob's mother, and G.'s mother talking about the effects of the flood. Miss Foster talks with awe about how the landlord treated her well, giving her tea and sixty cents.

Chapter 3

Chapter 3 expands the scope of G.'s experience even more: we have gone from his immediate household to his neighborhood and, now, to his school. The narration also moves once more beyond G.'s immediate consciousness. The chapter begins with a description of the schoolyard and moves quickly to a description of the boys' assembly for Empire Day. The inspector gives them a speech about the special relationship between Barbados and England before inspecting the classes. A boy misbehaves and is flogged. The narration is then transcribed as lines spoken between a number of boys, like a play. Their conversation

concerns their feelings about their parents, until the play-style narration ends with a long story about the relationship between the teacher and his wife which is told by the flogged boy, whose mother is the teacher's servant.

The boys, back in class, inquire about the process of making coins with the King's face on them. They are curious about slavery, but their school tells them little or nothing about it. The head teacher receives an envelope containing a letter regarding his wife and a picture of her with another man. As the teacher, in a state of shock, ponders what to do about this letter and whether or not the students understand what is going on, the narration shifts to his perspective. He thinks about his responsibilities to the village, his obligation to be an example to the whole community. He contemplates possible reactions to this discovery of infidelity, how he should balance his personal feelings with his role as a teacher and his position as an icon of English reserve and propriety. Looking at his class, he demands silence.

The narration then returns to the boys' consciousness. One of the boys attempts to explain the roots of slavery by citing examples from the Bible. After a brief time in the boys' heads, we return to the mind of the head teacher, and the chapter closes as the boys examine the pennies given to them by the inspector for Empire Day.

Chapter 4

The narration shifts dramatically in the fourth chapter, where two entirely new characters are introduced, an "Old Man" and an "Old Woman." The two, who represent the old ways of the village, discuss the events in the village in the year since the floods with which the book opened. Mr. Slime has opened a "Penny Bank and Friendly Society" in which all of the inhabitants of Creighton Village put their money. They compare Mr. Slime to Moses. They foresee conflict between Slime and Creighton. Going to bed, they talk about Barbadians who have left the island, formerly for Panama and presently for America.

Chapter 5

The fifth chapter opens with the image of Savory, the fried-food vendor, arriving to sell cakes to the village. The villagers gather to buy food and discuss the events at the school and with Slime. Slime, now a village leader, has been involved with a strike at the docks in the capital city and has explained the situation to the villagers, some of whom work at the docks. The villagers discuss whether they would be willing to strike and lose their livelihoods. They talk about how Creighton is part owner of the shipping company and about how any outlay of money causes him great pain. The villagers discuss the writings of J. B. Priestly, which address the dangers of colonial administrators sympathizing too much with the inhabitants of the colonies, and talk about the growing civil disturbances in neighboring Trinidad.

The topic then turns to cricket because Barbados is soon to play a match against its neighbor. The villagers change the discussion from cricket to exchanging memories of the revolutionary Marcus Garvey as they talk about the inevitable end of the British empire. The chapter ends back at Savory's cart, where two women fight over accusations of an illegitimate pregnancy.

Chapter 6

The chapter begins, like the first chapter, with images of dripping water—this time, it is the dew dripping from the "hedges and high grass" of Belleville, the white neighborhood that G. and Bob cross to get to the beach. The neighborhood contrasts strongly with G.'s own neighborhood: the houses are "bungalows high and wide with open galleries and porticoes" and servants can be seen through the windows. The boys observe the changing shape of the clouds as they approach the shore. Arriving at the shore, G. notices that a tension is present between the boys and G. wonders about its cause. G. decides that it is a result of events earlier in the week involving his mother.

G. joins a group of boys—Trumper, Boy Blue, and Bob—as they joke with each other on the beach. Bob leaves, and Trumper muses philosophically about the passing of time before telling a long story about Jon and Brother Bannister. The boys try to catch crabs while they discuss marriage, fidelity, and polygamy in reference to the story of Bots and Bambina that Boy Blue tells. They watch a fisherman maneuver his net. Boy Blue, trying to catch crabs, gets caught in the undertow and the fisherman comes out to rescue him but tells him, "I should have let you drown." The boys walk back down the beach to get their clothes and return to the village.

Chapter 7

The boys, walking back to the villagers, pass a gathering of worshippers seated around a table who speak in tongues and dance. The worshippers try to get them to stay but Trumper encourages them to move on. As they do, Boy Blue presciently observes that in the village "there be only two great men round here, Mr. Slime and the landlord." They discuss Mr. Slime's plans to sell the land to the villagers. From there, the conversation turns to a discussion of American automats; the boys decide they like the traditional ways of food preparation better. They pass near the landlord's house and are clearly intimidated by the large wall outside. Sneaking around the fence, they observe an elegant party going on at the house in honor of the newly arrived ship, *Goliath*, and compare the behavior of the sailors they know with the manners of these officers.

As they sit under a tree watching and talking about the party, they hear a noise by the trash heap. Creeping over to where they heard the noise, they discover a man and a young woman making love in the shadows; the young woman appears to be Mr. Creighton's daughter. Realizing they are crouching on an anthill, they yelp, alerting the two lovers to their presence, and flee. The overseer and sailors chase them, looking for "native boys," but they disappear into the crowd of worshippers.

Chapter 8

With this chapter, we return to the narration featuring the transcribed "lines" of Pa and Ma. The old woman had gone up to the landlord's house to pay the rent and he, apparently disturbed by the changes in the village, talks with her about them. He is especially concerned about the violation of his daughter, which he and the old woman blame on "vagabonds" from the island, thus absolving the sailor whom she was really with of his responsibility. The old woman describes to her husband the "responsibility" Creighton feels for the village, but adds that he is thinking of selling the land and leaving.

Chapter 9

Again, as in the first chapter, it is morning, but this morning "broke foul" in the village. Men have not gone to work and the disturbances of the city have begun to affect Creighton Village. The head teacher tells a student that there is fighting in the city, but nobody seems to know exactly what is happening. The police are absent, the school and shops are closed. The old man persistently tries to find out what is happening, but nobody knows. Trumper comes running down the road back to the village, asking if Bob has returned yet and saying that the police might be looking for him. He says that the two of them had walked to the city, and that when they got there they saw that cars were badly damaged and that fighting had taken place. They got caught up in a battle between police and workers. Bob has returned by then and tells of getting involved in the rioting. He says that the strike had begun the previous night, spurred by a mass meeting at which Slime was a featured speaker. An old drunk woman staggers into town and relates that her son, Po King, has been shot to death. The village, agitated, waits for the fighting to reach it. With the help of the old woman, they reconstruct the events that led to the riot.

The villagers nervously wait for something to happen. Miss Foster says that she saw some men come into town with weapons and hide. They seem to be waiting to ambush the overseer. Soon after this, the village sees Mr. Creighton, with dirty clothes and a terrified face, walk through the town. Some men wait to attack him and follow him as he walks down the road. Mr. Slime appears, and without his approval the men are reluctant to actually set upon Mr. Creighton, and the landlord walks out of sight and escapes.

Chapter 10

After the passing of some years, "nothing" changes and the landlord stays. The old man has a dream and, as his wife listens, he utters a reverie of deep memories of slavery and the Middle Passage.

Chapter 11

Again the narration changes, this time back to first person in the voice of G., who talks about hiding a pebble. He tells of Trumper's departure for America and his own scholarship to the high school. He describes the differences between the village school and the high school, and talks of his alienation from his village friends. History continues to impinge upon his consciousness from afar; at the school they hear of the war in Europe (World War II), but it does not affect him in any immediate way until he hears that France has fallen to the Germans. A number of students leave to enlist; later that year, a large merchant ship is torpedoed in the harbor.

Life continues in the village as G. finishes high school. Boy Blue and Bob join the police force and Trumper has already emigrated. G. forms a friendship with an assistant at the school who encourages his intellectual development. Trumper writes G. telling him of America, and G. is given a job teaching English at a boarding school in Trinidad.

Chapter 12

For the first time, the old man and G. speak to each other. They talk of the changes in the village, especially of the growth of Slime's Penny Bank and Friendly Society and of the departure of Mr. Creighton's daughter. The old man is certain that Mr. Creighton himself, however, will never leave. As the chapter ends, the overseer surveys parcels of land.

Chapter 13

Chapter 13, like many of the previous chapters, opens as dawn breaks in the village. Savory arrives to sell his cakes, but the village's attention is taken by a fierce argument between the shoemaker and a man who claims ownership of his land. The village has not been officially notified of the sale of Creighton's estate to smaller landholders, but these landholders are already notifying the inhabitants that they will have to leave. The arguments that the residents make, based on length of tenure, are invalid against the claims of ownership. At noon the scene shifts to the house of Mr. Foster, who is also being evicted. He is furious, and the new landlord is afraid of getting the police involved because of the new "will" of the poor, as demonstrated in the riots. The overseer posts a bill officially notifying the village that Mr. Creighton has sold the land.

The head teacher goes to the house of the old man (whose wife is now dead) and informs him that his land has been sold as well. Since he is too old to find his own place, he will relocate to the Alms House. Resigned, the old man asks the teacher how Mr. Slime managed to acquire the whole village for resale.

Chapter 14

The final chapter returns to G.'s narrative voice. He comes back to the village from his high school and goes to his mother's house. She and G. quarrel about how he is not doing as well in school as he should, and about their differing visions of his upcoming life in Trinidad. As much as he wants to rebel against his mother, he realizes he will miss her cooking and he thinks about how to make cuckoo.

Trumper arrives at the house, having just returned from America, noticeably changed. He is more self-confident, speaks more quickly, and has adopted a black nationalist outlook that does not exist in Barbados. In America, he was confronted both by the vast economic opportunities (he impresses G. and his mother with his tales of telephones and electric fans) and by the United States' naked racism and discrimination. Trumper and G. go out and have a beer at Kirton's and talk politics. Trumper pulls out a small tape player and plays a recording of Paul Robeson. As the young men return to G.'s house, they hear men attempting to move the shoemaker's house, which collapses. Trumper and G. part ways. G. runs into Pa, on his way to the Alms House, who tells him that the changes in the village date from the floods that occurred on G.'s ninth birthday. As the book closes and G. prepares to leave for Trinidad, the thought occurs to him that he is saying farewell to this land.

Characters

Bob

Bob is one of G.'s friends from the village. As the book starts, he watches G. being bathed by his mother, climbs up the fence, and knocks it over. Bob's mother attempts to beat him for this but he runs away. During the riots, Bob and Trumper sneak into town to watch the events and are caught up in the fighting. Bob has to run back to the village, fearing being caught by the police. At the end of the book, he and Boy Blue become policemen.

Bob's Mother

Bob's mother is G.'s next-door neighbor. Bob is one of her two children. She is fed up with Bob's mischief and loses her temper with him after he knocks the fence down, but later apologizes. When G.'s mother laughs at the children's antics, Bob's mother complains about the "botheration" the children bring her.

Boy Blue

Boy Blue is one of G.'s friends. He takes part in almost all of their activities, and when they go to the beach he tells the long story about Bots and Bambina. He also almost drowns and has to be saved by the fisherman. At the end of the book, he becomes a policeman.

Mr. Creighton

Mr. Creighton (also known as the landlord) is the white man who owns the village. He is descended from the original English plantation owners who settled the island, set up sugar plantations, and imported slaves to work the plantations. After the abolition of slavery and the decline of the sugar plantations, many of the plantation-owning families (such as the Creightons) stayed on in the West Indies, living off of the rents paid to them by the descendants of the slaves who lived on their land. The plantations became villages, named after the former plantation owner.

Mr. Creighton is one such landlord. His relationship to the village is almost that of a feudal lord. The rent he charges on the land is his primary source of income, but he also has the responsibility for the upkeep of the village. The floods at the beginning of the novel cause a great deal of damage to the village's roads, and Mr. Creighton greatly resents having to pay for repairs. Other changes in the village (especially a greater degree of freedom among the black residents that results in a rape attempt upon his daughter, whom he sends back to England) make him feel dissatisfied with his situation. He also is part-owner of the shipping company against which the union strikes. In an action that serves as his farewell to his quasi-feudal role, he calls the Old Woman to the house to talk to her, then sells his land to the Penny Bank and Friendly Society headed by Mr. Slime. The sale of his land and the subsequent eviction of many of the residents mark the violent transition of the village into the modern, capitalist world.

Miss Foster

Miss Foster is one of G.'s mother's friends from the village. She has six children: "three by a butcher, two by a baker and one whose father had never been mentioned." After the flood, she goes to Mr. Creighton, who gives her tea and half a crown.

Mr. Foster

Mr. Foster works at the docks before the strike in the capital city. On the day of the riot, he does not go to work. When Mr. Creighton sells his land and the new owner comes to claim it, Mr. Foster attempts to treat him politely and respectfully but ends up losing his temper

G.

G. is the main character of the novel, and in much of the book he is the narrator as well. The book opens on his ninth birthday as he is being bathed by his mother. The book recounts his activities: he goes to school, spends time trading stories with his friends, gets into trouble, grows up. He ends up receiving a scholarship to the high school and, although he does not do particularly well in the upper school, he obtains a teaching job in Trinidad. Returning home before leaving Barbados, he finds that his relationship with his mother has changed. At the end of the book, much like James Joyce's Stephen Dedalus, he finds himself ready to fly away from the nets of his home island.

As a main character, G. is strangely unsatisfying; his psychological depths are not explored by the author in any great detail. It is not by coincidence that he is almost never named in the text (just about the only instance of his name appearing is in the second chapter, when Bob says "G. mother bathing him"). At times, G. seems to be a mirror, reflecting the events of the village, rather than living an independent life. Sandra Pouchet Paquet writes that G. "emerges as a figure whose personal experience crystallizes the experience of the entire community. In a sense, he is the village; the history of his dislocation echoes the dislocation of the village. He is a collective character."

G.'s mother

In Lamming's own words (from the introduction to the 1983 reissue of his novel),

> the mother of the novel is given no name. She is simply G.'s mother, a woman of little or no importance in her neighborhood until the tropical season rains a calamity on every household; and she emerges, without warning, as a voice of nature itself.

She is stern with G., beating him at times, but her strictness is motivated by a desire for G. to improve himself. When he goes off to the high school in the city, she keeps on G. to do well, even though his grades are never particularly good and he never is a brilliant student. Near the end of the book, when G. returns home before going to Trinidad, he and his mother bicker with each other until G. begins to feel nostalgic for his mother's cooking.

The three women who figure prominently in G.'s life (his mother, Miss Foster, and Bob's mother) are not given much characterization. They are "three pieces in a pattern which remained constant," the narrator says. "The flow of history was undisturbed by any difference in the pieces, nor was its evenness affected by any likeness." Where the younger generation, with their energy and mischief and "botheration," represents the changes that are imminent, the women represent the way that things have always been, the way that history seems to have passed Barbados by.

The Landlord

See Mr. Creighton

Ma

See Old Woman

Old Man

The Old Man (also called Pa), the character from whose perspective some of the book is narrated, represents history—not just the village's history but the whole history of Africans in the Caribbean. Most of his appearances in the book take place in the company of his wife, but after she dies the author provides us with a scene between he and G. (for whom he has been a surrogate father-figure) and the scene of his eviction from his house to the Alms House.

Old Woman

The Old Woman (also called Ma) is the Old Man's wife. The two of them, together, represent the entirety of the history of black people in the islands. Mr. Creighton pays her the honor of talking to her as an equal when he decides to sell the land. She dies a number of years before he actually sells the land, however.

Pa

See Old Man

The Shoemaker

The Shoemaker is a self-educated villager, suspicious of the colonial ideology. When he is evicted from his land, he puts up a fight. The new landlord tells him he can keep the house but must leave the land, but when they try to move the house it falls apart.

Mr. Slime

Mr. Slime starts out as the fifth grade teacher at the boys' school but, by the end of the novel, plays a much greater part. His first appearance is not in person; he is the person photographed with the head teacher's wife. We learn about him indirectly throughout the book: people talk about Slime but he never actually appears as Slime until the end, when Trumper and G. see him at the bar.

Slime represents the amorality and complexity of the new world that is coming to Barbados. He is a teacher, a politician, a union leader, a financier, and bank owner, and the villagers, set in their one-role lives, cannot understand Slime's mobility. Slime rises from his controversial post at the school to lead the union that strikes against Creighton's shipping company. He founds the Penny Bank and Friendly Society, ostensibly to improve the lot of the villagers but most likely as a route to self-aggrandizement. The Bank then buys the land from Creighton and sells it to speculators and investors. He is capitalism personified, shifting roles quickly and taking advantage of every situation. The villagers and Creighton are at his mercy.

Trumper

Trumper is G.'s boyhood friend from the village. When they are children, Trumper is an adventurous, daring boy. He was sent to a reformatory when he was nine, and during the riots he and Bob sneak off to the city to watch and have to flee back to the village. Eventually he emigrates from Barbados to America to seek his fortune. Returning to the village, he tells G. and his mother about the riches available in America but is strangely ambivalent about the U.S. He is unimpressed by the materialism of the nation, but his experiences with blatant Jim Crow-style racism taught him about black consciousness and nationalism.

Themes

Colonialism

The relationship between colonial powers and their colonies, and the effects that this relationship has on the inhabitants of the colonies, is the enduring concern of George Lamming. All of his works address these issues. As the first of his novels, *In the Castle of My Skin* appropriately anatomizes this dynamic as it bears upon a nine-year-old boy in one of Barbados' small rural villages.

The colonizing nation does not exert its power on the colonized people solely by using raw force such as that at the disposal of governmental or military bodies. Colonizing powers, especially those of European and Islamic origin, also felt themselves driven by the need to "spread the light" of their own civilization or religion, or at least many of their propagandists argued this. (The famous poem "The White Man's Burden" by Rudyard Kipling is perhaps the best known example of this idea.) More cynical observers have argued that these programs of education in colonized places serve, instead, as a type of psychological policing of the subject people. Colonizing powers often set up extensive structures of education in the values and objectives of the colonizing power and rewards for inhabitants who "play by the rules." In the schools, the colonized people are taught the colonizer's language (often having been forbidden to use their own) and instructed in the subject matter that the colonizing

power feels to be the basis of a "real education." Students who follow the rules and show promise are given scholarships to continue their studies, with the eventual prospect of a secure government job. Less promising students are often offered the opportunity to join the colonizer's military or police forces. At all levels, though, the colonizing power attempts to steer people away from the possibility of resistance, whether physical or intellectual.

Compounding the colonizer's ability to reward those who follow the rules and punish those who don't are the almost inevitable differences between subjects and colonizers. In England's first colony, Ireland, the difference was religion. In Barbados, the difference is racial. In his introduction, Lamming writes that

> Plantation Slave Society conspired to smash ancestral African culture ... the result was a fractured consciousness, a deep split in its sensibility which now raised difficult problems of language and values; the whole issue of cultural allegiance between the imposed norms of White Power and the fragmented memory of the African masses: between White instruction and Black imagination.

Throughout the novel, in the boys' school or in the relationships between villagers and the landlord, Lamming shows how the colonizing powers devalue everything associated with Africans and exalt everything associated with white English culture.

Lamming's entire book dissects various ways in which the colonizer's values are instilled within a native populace, but in Chapter 3 he describes one of its most basic incarnations: Empire Day at the elementary school. At this holiday celebration, commemorating and exalting the ties between England and its colonies, the boys sing "God Save the King," learn about Barbados's ("Little England's") "steadfast and constant" relationship to Big England. No hint of dissent or irony is heard from these children until one of the boys explains to them his theory of the "shadow king." "The English," this boy tells them, "are fond of shadows. They never do anything in the open." Without realizing it, this boy opens the door to the possibility of resistance.

Language

One of the first acts of a colonizing power, almost inevitably, is the imposition of language on the subject people. Fearing the possibility of plotting against them, the colonizers will generally forbid use of any language but their own in public discourse, and in some cases (such as among

American slaves or with the Kurdish people of Turkey) will punish anyone who uses the unofficial language. Colonial schools will teach the colonizer's language, and students who use it particularly well will be rewarded—certainly Lamming himself, given scholarships and teaching jobs, is an example of this. Language can be power, as Trumper observes:

> If you were really educated, and you could command the language like the captain on a ship, if you could make the language do what you wanted it to do, say what you wanted it to say, then you wouldn't have to feel at all. You could do away with feeling. That's why everybody wanted to be educated.

Race

Closely linked to colonialism in Lamming's novel is the issue of race. European colonists felt that darker-skinned people were primitive, inferior, and dangerous. For many years, slavery was the cornerstone on which the West Indian economy was built. A debate rages among scholars as to whether European racism caused African slavery or whether European racism was constructed to explain the necessity of slavery, but what is indisputable is that, by the twentieth century, the islands of the British West Indies had two very distinct primary social classes: white landowners and professionals of English descent and black manual laborers whose ancestors came from Africa.

The lessons of racism and black inferiority were taught everywhere, though usually cloaked in the ideology of the "white man's burden," the notion of benevolent white settlers improving the lives of benighted savages in Africa and the Americas. In places such as Barbados, where more than eighty percent of the population is considered to be of African descent, people are encouraged to join the white society by means of hard work and education. Successful people become metaphorically more "white," whereas those who remain low on the social ladder retain their "blackness." In the second chapter, Lamming describes the process of socially separating the black overseers from the villagers:

> Low-down nigger people was a special phrase the overseers had coined . . . The image of the enemy, and the enemy was My People. My people are low-down nigger people. My people don't like to see their people get on. The language of the overseer. The language of the civil servant.

Because it is freighted with social and political meanings, the category of race becomes the dividing line between everything positive and nega-

Topics for Further Study

- Lamming mentions, in passing, the names of a number of men who became heroes to West Indians of African descent: Marcus Garvey, Paul Robeson, even Patrice Lumumba. Research the lives of these men and of other important or inspirational figures such as Franz Fanon or Bob Marley. What qualities did they embody that addressed the desires of the West Indian population?

- When were the West Indies "discovered" by Europeans? Who settled them first? What different colonizing nations have been represented there, and which nations continue to maintain their presence? What role did slavery and plantation agriculture have in their colonization?

- In the novel, the character of Trumper leaves Barbados and emigrates to the United States. In this, he is like millions of other natives of the West Indies who came to the United States in the twentieth century and continue to come today. Where are the main communities of West Indians in the United States? What are some of the challenges they face? What tensions have arisen between West Indian communities and other immigrant or native communities in the United States?

- Like many other writers throughout history, George Lamming became an "exile"; he had to leave the country of his birth to find his artistic voice. Research the lives and careers of some other famous exiles of modern or ancient literature (Ovid, Boethius, Dante, Lord Byron, or James Joyce, for example). Why were they exiled? How did their exile figure in their work?

- Barbadians are proud to consider themselves citizens of "Little England," a place with a special relationship to the mother country. In the eighteenth and nineteenth centuries, England built one of the largest empires the world had ever known. What were some of the other important colonies? How did England try to instill its culture and values in the colonies?

tive in the community. Later on in the book, when the boys stumble upon the landlord's daughter and a sailor in a compromising position, the sailor screams for the overseer to catch the "native boys" and, later, the landlord's daughter claims that black "vagabonds," not the white officer, claimed her virtue. The idea of their own racial inferiority is so ingrained in the villagers that even the Old Woman curses these fictional "vagabonds," not being able to imagine that the landlord's daughter would lie.

Style

Narration

In *In the Castle of My Skin*, George Lamming makes use of many of the developments in narrative that took place in the first half of the twentieth century. The novel has always been a form that has permitted writers to experiment with points of view. Early novels were narrated by know-it-alls, as exchanges of letters, or, as in the case of Lawrence Sterne, by potentially pathological liars. Nineteenth-century novels continued these developments of narrative, but many of the most popular novels of that century relied either on omniscient third-person narrators with an ironic distance from the characters (such as Jane Austen's, Charles Dickens's, or George Eliot's) or first-person narrators who were characters in the story (such as Melville's Ishmael or Dickens's David Copperfield). Later in the century, writers such as the Frenchman Gustave Flaubert or the American Stephen Crane experimented with third-person narrators who, amorally, refused to pass judgments on the behavior of the characters.

Dramatic advances in psychology at the turn of the twentieth century brought writers' attention to the very roots of consciousness. Building on the theories of Freud, writers such as Virginia Woolf and James Joyce developed "stream-of-consciousness" narration, a technique that attempted to transcribe exactly the thoughts in a person's head. Lamming employs this and other techniques in his novel. Initially, the novel resembles an interior monologue, but although the language is not as carefully constructed as one would expect from a writer, the vocabulary is certainly above the level one would expect from a nine-year-old. The sentences remind one of how a nine-year-old would speak, however. Lamming suspends his narration between two poles. The literary scholar Sandra Pouchet Paquet explains this as the desire of the boys to be adults in their command of language; "their vocabulary and style of delivery," she argues

> strain toward that of the adult community . . . they struggle for a language that will express and clarify their thoughts and feelings about subjects as varied as language, history, politics and law.

Later in the book Lamming changes techniques numerous times. Leaving G.'s consciousness, the narrator becomes an omniscient third-person narrator, entering the consciousness of G.'s mother or the overseer or even the old man. In some chapters the characters' voices are transcribed as if they were speaking dialogue in a play. After G. goes to high school and returns to the village to talk to Trumper, the voice is much more confident, sophisticated, and worldly—just as a teenager sure of his new maturity would be. In order to achieve his goals of melding the personal and the political, Lamming chose to use all of the narrative tools at his disposal.

Imagery

As befits a novel set on an island only 166 square miles in area, *In the Castle of My Skin* is dominated by images of water. The first chapter opens with a hard rain, one that eventually causes devastating floods in the village. The second chapter, as well, depicts G. with water falling on him, this time from a skillet with which is mother bathes him. Throughout the book water is something that brings inconvenience (as with G.'s shower) or severe danger (as when Boy Blue almost drowns at the shore, or at the docks where the riot begins). Rain opens the chapter where the village learns about the riots, and Lamming uses the image of taps being opened to describe the village waking up in Chapter 13, the chapter in which the evictions are narrated.

Symbolically, Lamming equates the inexorable and irresistible motion of waters to what is often metaphorically called "the tide of history." The novel, although set in the life of a young boy turned young man, is really about the profound changes both in the village and in Barbadian society as a whole. The forces of history, of capitalism and colonialism and labor unrest and awakening racial consciousness, lap at the village like the tide, and there is nothing the village can do to stop them. All of the inhabitants of the village, from Creighton to G. to Mr. Foster, are caught up in these tides.

Compare & Contrast

- **1930s:** Barbados, a colony so closely linked to Britain that it is called "Little England" by colonial administrators, enjoys economic stability and a form of government that gives it more self-determination than many other British colonies. A growing labor movement (led partially by the Trinidadian Clement Payne, later deported, and Grantley Adams) attempts to organize sugar plantation workers and longshoremen.

  1950s: Because of labor unrest, persistent racial divisions, and the weakening of Britain after the Second World War, Barbadians strive for independence. The Crown grants the West Indian colonies the right to federate, which they do in 1958.

  Today: Barbados, after having achieved its independence in 1966, maintains ties to England as a member of the Commonwealth of Nations. In 1997, a commission is convened to discuss the possibility of cutting all ties with Great Britain.

- **1930s:** In the United States, racial discrimination is common. Many West Indians move to New York where they establish communities in Brooklyn, the Bronx, and Harlem. Once in the United States, they encounter growing ideas of black nationalism and pride, led by important figures such as Black Muslim founder Elijah Muhammad and West Indian Marcus Garvey.

- **1950s:** In the middle of this decade, spurred on by the landmark *Brown v. Board of Education of Topeka, Kansas* Supreme Court decision, African Americans begin to use the law to challenge segregation. In Birmingham, Alabama, Rosa Parks is arrested after refusing to give up her seat to a white person and a bus boycott begins—an event generally considered to be the beginning of the civil rights movement.

  Today: Legal (*de jure*) segregation is against the law in all states, but social (*de facto*) segregation endures all over America. In New York, thousands of people of African descent from the Caribbean community join with huge numbers of Puerto Ricans to form a significant Caribbean minority in the city. Tensions between Caribbean communities and others, including African Americans, continue.

- **1930s:** Motivated by economic depression, a dramatically lowering standard of living worldwide, and scarcity of jobs, labor unions gain ground throughout the United States and in many other nations.

  1950s: The labor movement continues to grow, but many unions in the United States are infected by organized crime and corruption. Compounding their difficulties, conservative business-oriented politicians seek to thwart the labor movement, investigating it for "Communist influence."

  Today: As the U.S. economy moves from an industrial base to a service base, the labor movement finds itself at a crossroads. Unions in such industries as steel, manufacturing, and transportation remain strong, but new unions spring up to organize such nontraditional constituencies as illegal immigrants, graduate students, and temporary workers.

- **1930s:** Technology among the ordinary people of the Caribbean islands is essentially at a nineteenth-century level. Electricity has yet to reach most communities.

  1950s: Access to electricity and telecommunications gradually reach the interior of many of the Caribbean islands.

  Today: Telecommunications technology allows anyone with access to a telephone line and a computer to communicate with anyone anywhere in the world. Caribbean culture reaches the Western world: Jamaican music (exemplified by Bob Marley, Peter Tosh, and Jimmy Cliff) is heard all over the world, and Derek Walcott and V. S. Naipul each win a Nobel Prize for literature.

Historical Context

British Colonization

British explorers, led by a Captain Gordon, first landed on Barbados in 1620, but it was not until seven years later that the British established a colonial presence on the island. Realizing that on the Atlantic, or east, coast of the island there were no safe natural harbors or landing places, the British explorers and colonizers set up settlements on the "leeward" (Caribbean or west coast) shore of the island. Bridgetown, the eventual capital of the island and the city in which, in Lamming's novel, the riots take place, was an early settlement. But the island's population has always lived largely in the rural areas, as befits an island with an almost entirely agricultural economy.

The "father" of Barbadian settlement by the English was Captain John Powell, who stopped on the island in 1625 in a journey homeward from Brazil. Financed by himself and four other merchants, a party of eighty settlers arrived on Barbados on February 17, 1627. These settlers were looking not to spread Christianity or to find a "New Jerusalem" but solely to enrich themselves. Clearing land for plantations, they planted tobacco and imported slaves—eight months after the colony was founded, one of the settlers wrote home that of 100 inhabitants forty were slaves. Soon indentured servants outnumbered slaves; by 1638, out of a total population of 6000, there were 200 slaves and 2,000 indentured servants.

This quickly changed, however, when the planters began growing sugar instead of tobacco, in response to low prices and growing duties on tobacco. Sugar needed a larger initial capital investment, brought greater profits, required more labor, and encouraged consolidation of small estates into large plantations. With less available land to give out at the end of an indenture and longer, harder work the norm, slave labor became preferable to servant labor. Slaves were imported by the thousands—by 1652, the population of the island was estimated at 18,000 whites (freemen and indentured servants) and 20,000 Africans. The "peculiar institution" of slavery established the complicated and often oppressive relationships between the white and black inhabitants of Barbados. As Lamming's novel demonstrates, the effects of slavery were still being felt 300 years after its institution and more than a century after its abolition.

Labor Unrest

At the dawn of the twentieth century, the industrial revolution had enriched tens of thousands of people, made England the world's greatest economic and military power, and "opened up" much of the world to trade and development. But workers, for the most part, did not live much better than they had in the 1820s, and in fact many of the industrial workers who had flocked to the cities for jobs were demonstrably worse off than they had been in the impoverished countryside. In the United States, England, France, and Germany, organizations that attempted to organize workers had existed for decades, but it was not until laws changed at the turn of the century that unions found themselves with any legal rights. Organizers were often the targets of violence perpetrated by "security forces" in the employ of industrialists, and strikes were brutal, chaotic affairs.

The first few decades of the twentieth century saw the unions make great advances in organizing in numerous industries, and unions began to associate themselves with political causes outside of their immediate purview of labor issues. Because of this, politicians everywhere in the industrial world began painting the unions as meddlers, as Communist agitators, and as potential traitors to the nation. A "Red Scare" in the United States during the 1920s and 1930s provided a serious obstacle to unionization. In this period, unions found fertile ground outside of the industrialized nations. In many South and Central American nations, labor unions began organizing the vast masses of poor people working in factories, railyards, and docks in the cities. As happened everywhere, industrialists fought against unionization, often with violence— and they were met with similar violence. The industrialists were often backed by the governments of their own nation or, if the companies were foreign-owned, by the governments of the nations in which the companies were headquartered. In the Caribbean, American sugar and fruit companies were among the firms that used military and governmental power to thwart unionization.

Critical Overview

In the Castle of My Skin, George Lamming's first novel, was an immediate success in the Anglophone West Indian literary communities of London (where many writers lived) and the Caribbean. As one of the first important statements of the links

A city in Barbados, Lamming's native country and the setting for the novel

between individual lived experience and the structures of racism and British colonialism, the novel (published with an introduction by the American Richard Wright, author of *Native Son*) was hailed as an important statement of the growing anticolonial movement in France and England. However, many also noted its skillful technique and elegant use of language.

Contemporary literary critics, as well, were positive for the most part. Graham Cotter of the *Canadian Forum* remarked that "if Mr. Lamming is at all representative of Barbadians, the colony has a more interesting 'personality' than any other West Indian Island. Certainly I have read no other West Indian literature which displays the keen perception and insight of this book." Cotter did feel, though, that the "sprawling structure" of the novel made it difficult to read. In the *Chicago Sunday Tribune*, M. S. Douglas effused that "one little Barbadian, grown up, has written in the most beautiful singing English a complex and brilliant novel of his boyhood and his people which miraculously has lost nothing of that dazzled wonder . . . probably very close to genius." H. C. Webster wrote in the *Saturday Review* that the novel was "highly rewarding both as a social and as a personal document." "Something strange, emotional and com-

passionate, something between garrulous realism and popular poetry . . . quite delightful," noted V. S. Pritchett in the *New Statesman and Nation*. And R. D. Charques praised the novel in the *Spectator* for being "a striking piece of work, a rich and memorable feat of imaginative interpretation."

Other critics, while still admiring the book, pointed out what they saw as faults, and most of these noted the loose structure of the novel. "The effect is one of a series of sharp and brilliant sketches rather than of a unit," Anthony West wrote in the *New Yorker*, and in Webster's largely positive review of the book (quoted above) in the *Saturday Review*, he added that it was "occasionally verbose [and] sometimes tedious." The most negative major review of the book appeared in the London *Times Literary Supplement*, which argued that

> Mr. Lamming appears to have been unable to make up his mind whether to explore the world of adolescent consciousness or the world of social history . . . It is an artistic flaw which is so glaring that after a time it ceases to matter; the eye is less irritated by a beam than by a series of motes.

This very aspect of the book—its combination of the personal and the political—criticized by the *TLS* has been the source of much of its enduring praise. More importantly, though, this was Lamming's attempt to contribute to the theory of the oppressed that Frantz Fanon was developing at the same time. Fanon, in his books *Black Skin, White Masks* and *The Wretched of the Earth*, argued that the colonial system has deep and unacknowledged psychological effects upon colonized peoples. His theories explain these effects, while Lamming's novels illustrate them. In most of Lamming's later writings, he expanded upon these themes. Because of this political content, moreover, the French leftist philosopher Jean-Paul Sartre bought the rights to translate the book into French and publish it in France in his journal *Les Temps Modernes*. The book won the Somerset Maugham Award for Literature in 1957.

Recent attention paid to Caribbean literature has paid off for Lamming's novel. The great success of such West Indian writers as V. S. Naipaul and Derek Walcott brought the eyes of the world to the English-language writers of the Caribbean, and to respond to this Schocken Books reissued the novel in 1983 (it was republished again in the 1990s by the University of Michigan Press). Lamming continues to write but has not published a novel since 1971. *In the Castle of My Skin* and the three books that followed continued the saga of a young Caribbean writer much like Lamming who went to London then returned to the Caribbean to involve himself in the independence struggle; they remain perhaps the definitive statement of the Caribbean colonial experience.

Criticism

Greg Barnhisel

Barnhisel teaches writing and directs the Writing Center at the University of Southern California. In this essay, Barnhisel describes how Lamming's novel provides a model for a Marxist analysis of the advance of market capitalism in a small rural community.

In the years following the collapse of the Soviet Union, the credibility of Marxism as a legitimate political program almost disappeared in the West. However, especially in the developing world, the ideas of Marxism have survived as a very compelling and powerful explanatory mechanism for answering the questions of why poverty and oppression and political corruption are so persistent in "Third World" societies. To many thinkers of the developing world, and many Western scholars sym-

pathetic to their struggles, the "triumph of the Free World" is a misnomer, a euphemism constructed to put the best face on the real winner of the Cold War: large-scale corporate capitalism. What is termed "democracy" and "freedom," in the eyes of many Marxist scholars, is "the illusion of a popular democracy," the Caribbean writer George Lamming said in a recent interview; what is called our "freedom," Lamming argues, is simply our "expand[ed] access to an infinite range of commodities."

The Caribbean has been an especially fertile ground for Marxist ideas about oppression, colonization, and the harmful effects of capitalism. After all, while the United States and Spain and Britain reaped the profits of the sugar and fruit and coffee industries, these island countries provided the land, labor, and protection for First World owners. And when, as in the Dominican Republic, Haiti, or especially Cuba, liberation movements arose on behalf of workers and peasants and slaves, the First World powers attempted to put those movements down with military force.

George Lamming grew up in one of these countries, the British colony (later the nation) of Barbados. His 1953 novel *In the Castle of My Skin* is a vivid portrait of a small village in Barbados in the late 1930s. Written using shifting perspectives, stream-of-consciousness narration, and typically modernist explorations of a young boy's understanding of the world, the book has generally been analyzed in terms of its technique or in terms of its psychological insight. However, the novel's content and Lamming's own enduring concerns with political and economic justice demonstrates that readers view this novel politically, as an analysis of and commentary on the development of modern commodity capitalism in a rural, agricultural, quasi-feudal society.

The interrelationships between race, class, and colonialism are always Lamming's concern, and he has adopted a Marxist analysis of their combination. Colonial powers, he argues, used race and class to divide people from each other and, ultimately, to reinforce their economic system (in this case, the almost feudal system of post-slavery plantation labor). Race was "the device which the old plantocracy used to segregate the forces of labor [and to] maintain control over those divisions," Lamming wrote recently. As Lamming wrote in his introduction to the 1983 reissue of his novel,

The world of men and women from down below is not simply poor. This world is black, and it has a long history at once vital and complex. It is vital because it constitutes the base of labor on which the entire Caribbean society has rested; and it is complex because Plantation Slave Society ... conspired to smash the ancestral African culture, and to bring about a total alienation of man the source of labor from man the human person.

Race, although its importance in maintaining the social order should not be undervalued, is not the primary vector of power in *In the Castle of My Skin*. In the novel, it is the capitalist drive for enrichment—both among individual "capitalists" and as a free-floating force of history—that drives the events of the novel. For Lamming, the original source of the injustice in the Caribbean was the colonial endeavor, which in turn was simply the result of the endless demand for "economic development." Although he does not bear him any particular enmity except as the embodiment of colonialism, Lamming identifies Columbus as the infecting agent who brought the forces of "economic development" to the New World. In his recent essay "Labor, Culture, and Identity," Lamming writes that Columbus

> was the carrier of a virus to which the people of the Caribbean would have no adequate response ... Materialism, linked to human progress, allowed the Western world to accept that even the enslavement of a people was morally justifiable if it contributed to the march toward economic development.

The term "economic development" is a crucial one here. In the United States and in the Western world generally, we have been taught by politicians and the media to regard this term positively: It means the material betterment of peoples' lives. However, Marxists view this term in a much different light. For them, "economic development" indicates the drive to obtain material value (or "capital") out of natural resources or human labor. "Economic development," for Marxists, is inherently exploitative. Lamming disagrees with those who see the "Age of Exploration" as being motivated simply by the desire to see and understand the world. For Lamming, the "Age of Exploration" was really an "Age of Exploitation," when the European powers (especially the Spanish, English, Portuguese, and Dutch) scattered exploration parties all over the world, looking for colonies with cheap labor that could produce such commodities as gold, sugar, spices, or textiles. The West Indies, with their brutal system of slavery and sugar plantations, are a perfect example of what "exploration" was really all about.

In *In the Castle of My Skin*, though, Lamming does not spend his time dissecting the plantation system or the immediate legacies of slavery.

> " For [Marxists], 'economic development' indicates the drive to obtain material value (or 'capital') out of natural resources or human labor. 'Economic development,' for Marxists, is inherently exploitative."

Rather, he sets the novel in the 1930s, at a time when the last vestiges of the plantation system were starting to disintegrate in the face of the immense power and energy of free-market capitalism. At the beginning of the novel, the town resembles a feudal estate of the middle ages. The "landlord," Mr. Creighton, owns the village and extracts rents from his tenants, who nonetheless go about their business largely on their own terms. Feudal society assumed that peasants essentially "belonged" to the land and to the lord of the manor and that the landlord could charge whatever rent he liked; in exchange, the church and other institutions of authority strongly encouraged lords to be fair and responsible for their tenants. Mr. Creighton follows this model: He provides a school and genuinely wants contact with his tenants. It is a paternalistic relationship that he wants, of course, but nonetheless it is a personal relationship.

Marxists point out that capitalism attempts to turn everything into a commodity that can be assigned a market value, bought, and sold. Slavery took this to its logical extreme when the Middle Passage took Africans from their homes, turned them into objects to be bought and sold, and brought them to American colonies. The Old Man, in his dream-reverie in Chapter 10, accesses what Jung might call his "racial memory," saying that "the silver of exchange sail cross the sea and my people scatter like cloud . . . Each sell his own."

But if slavery and the plantation system showed the truly brutal extent of capitalism, the aftermath of the plantation system succeeded, in a small and temporary way, in reversing history. Briefly, the plantations returned to feudalism. In a

What Do I Read Next?

- *In the Castle of My Skin* was Lamming's first novel. In the same decade that this novel appeared, he also published three other important works of fiction: *The Emigrants* (1955), *Of Age and Innocence* (1958), and *A Season of Adventure* (1960). Each of these novels explores dimensions of the life experiences of Caribbean people interacting with colonial powers.

- *The Pleasures of Exile* (1960), Lamming's "seminal work of self-inquiry and cultural assessment in the context of Caribbean cultural life," as described by Sandra Pouchet Paquet in *The Routledge Reader in Caribbean Literature*, may be Lamming's most influential and most-read book.

- Born on Martinique and of the same generation as Lamming, Frantz Fanon is a writer whose works of cultural criticism and theory formed the intellectual structure for many of the anti-colonial independence movements of the 1960s and 1970s. His most famous works, *Black Skin, White Masks* (1954) and *The Wretched of the Earth* (1961), analyze the psychological effects of colonization on the colonized people.

- In 1992, the Caribbean poet Derek Walcott was awarded the Nobel Prize for literature. His career as a poet and playwright spanned half of the twentieth century, but perhaps his greatest work is the epic poem *Omeros* (1989), a retelling of the Odysseus myth in a Caribbean, postcolonial context. Walcott, along with the novelist V. S. Naipaul, continues to be one of the most important and influential Caribbean writers in the world today.

---

quasi-feudal society such as Creighton Village, selling the land is inconceivable, for the land is metaphorically part of the Creighton family. The intrusions of capitalism undermine this certainty. As he explains to the Old Woman, changes in Barbadian society—specifically, the "rape" of his daughter by local "vagabonds"—show him that the world is changing. The violent changes in the island's class structure, epitomized by the strike and riots, affect his family when people start to cross the previously unquestioned borders separating white landowner from black laborer. (The irony, of course, is that his daughter was "violated" not by a local but by a white officer attending Mr. Creighton's party.) He decides that he will sell his land, turning what had not been a commodity into something that can be bought and sold.

Mr. Slime is the most interesting character in the novel precisely because he embodies the contradictory, complicated nature of capitalism. He is the inaccessible mind of the marketplace; this aspect of his character is underscored by how he is much more often talked about than actually present in the novel. Certainly it is in the best interests of the inhabitants of Creighton Village to be freed from their feudal dependence on Mr. Creighton, and by representing their interests as laborers and providing them with a "Penny Bank and Friendly Society" Mr. Slime does exactly this. He yanks the villagers from feudalism into the new capitalist world. In this world, their freedom of activity is enhanced as the old strictures disappear—but the social support network they previously relied upon (i.e., the charity and goodwill of their landlord) also disappear. Mr. Slime's bank buys the village's land, driven partially by the idea that this will allow the bank to then sell the land to the villagers who have lived there for generations. But a bank is an organization that must make a profit or die, and in order to make a profit the bank has to sell this land to people who can pay for its "fair market value." Selling the land on the open market allows for land speculators and investors to buy the land and do with it what they wish, for the villagers do not have enough money to buy the land.

The reappearance of G.'s boyhood friend Trumper at the end of the novel underscores the changes that have taken place in village life since his departure for America years before. Trumper has been living in the very heart of capitalism, and his descriptions of America focus on those aspects of the country: "the United States is a place where a man can make pots of money." Trumper has new clothes, a silver chain, fans and telephones; he has benefited from capitalism in the most basic, material sense. Yet he does not seem to like it. "There be people there in the hundreds o' thousands who would have give anything not to get out their mother's guts," he tells G. and his mother. He is angered by the changes engendered in the village by the breaking-up of Creighton's estate and counsels resistance. More than anything, his experience in America has taught him not to trust the Mr. Slimes of the world.

G., the main character, has a different relationship to capitalism than do the villagers or Trumper. Unlike his friends, he is destined to have the advantages of talent and intelligence help him through life. He views his mother's imminent difficulties of where to go with a degree of detachment, knowing that he will be going to Trinidad. At no time in the book are his emotions fully engaged. He is an observer and a listener, someone destined to be a writer, it seems. But the people who surround him—his mother, Mr. Foster, Trumper, Bob—do feel the powerful emotions and have the traumatic experiences that stamp upon G.'s consciousness what effects this fundamental change in Creighton Village society has brought. In this, the book ends on a strange note, seemingly asking whether or not a writer can be truly engaged in the struggles of the world or if, in order to be a good writer, one must stand aside and hone the skills of watching and listening. If the theme of the book says no, its events tell us yes.

Source: Greg Barnhisel, Critical Essay on *In the Castle of My Skin*, in *Novels for Students*, The Gale Group, 2002.

Joyce E. Jonas

In the following excerpt, Jonas examines the idea of boundaries in Lamming's In the Castle of My Skin.

West Indian novelist George Lamming's *In The Castle of My Skin* takes its title from a couplet in Derek Walcott's juvenilia:

> You in the castle of your skin
> I the swineherd.

Walcott here invokes a conventional romance situation—unattainable mistress and infatuated, self-denigrating admirer—with the added pungency of racial overtones suggested by "skin." Lamming, however, changes the possessive pronoun, thus reversing the entire situation and seizing the castle for himself. By this sleight of hand, the naked (black) skin, with its connotations of exposure, shame, and deprivation, is transformed into an image of impregnability, strength, and self-sufficiency. By changing the joke, Lamming slips the yoke.

Indeed, the technique of turning deprivation into plenitude is the strategy of the entire novel. Lamming's fiction stands on the threshold between two worlds facing both ways at once. For while one

> **At an existential level the floodwaters provide an image for the novel's exploration of ways to build defining walls around the self."**

view of *Castle* shows a tragic mask of deprivation, failure, and exile, the other reveals a triumphant comic grin. Tragedy requires a scapegoat, but comedy, though it may permit the victim to be bound to the very horns of the altar, always allows him to evade the sacrificial role and escape to the sound of echoing laughter. It is on this very margin between tragic sacrifice and comic reversal that Lamming's first novel is situated.

Universally, cultures have recognized the power and danger of the margin or threshold by identifying a trickster-deity who shall preside over the rites of passage. In the West Indies, as in Afro-America, folk-tales are told of the Trickster Anancy—half spider, half man—who, though perennially in tight situations, is singularly adept at turning the tables on his oppressor and emerging more or less unscathed. His ability to extricate himself lies in his gift for "spinning yarns." In African mythology, Anancy is a god, responsible for creation itself, though his kindness to humans has brought about his fall from the favor of Nyame, the supreme Sky God. Rejected from the heavens, he finds himself positioned *between* earth and sky. Trader par excellence, Anancy enters the world to make things happen, to recreate boundaries, to break and re-establish relationships, to reawaken consciousness of the presence and the creative power of both the sacred Center and the formless Outside. Then he returns to that hidden threshold which he embodies and makes available as a passage to 'save the people from ruin.'"

Not surprisingly, given his capacity to hide in rafters and weave his web in any nook or cranny, Anancy survived the Middle Passage, and still spins his yarns throughout the Caribbean. His survival in folk imagination surely has to do with his capacity to transform disruption, discontinuity, brokenness, and defeat into triumphant new configurations of possibility. His perennial rebellion, and his use of comic trickery and deceit to expose the inadequacies of authority figures must surely have endeared him to the imagination of an oppressed folk. For it is the triumph of the Trickster to so deconstruct and invert the given "text" of authority that the destined scapegoat of tragedy turns the tables and emerges laughing in a comedy of ironic reversal—the castle of MY skin!

As symbol for the "limbo dance" of the West Indian novelist, Anancy is without peer. Poetry may well find its inspiration in jazz, blues, and calypso, but West Indian narrative, I contend, owes its beings to another Muse—Anancy. For, as Wilson Harris has argued, the West Indian artist is working in a limbo—a void *between* two worlds. Surrounded by and exiled from the structures of an alien world view, he must create his own world in this absence, or else be forever a negative, an exiled scapegoat. The very form of his art must be redefined. It is precisely here, in the interstices of structure, that the Anancy artist creates a world that describes its own center, thus marginalizing the oppressive structures of the Great House. Anacy re-creates the world—weaving a universe of relationships from the very substance of his being as he narrates his story in his way. For it is by way of his verbal ingenuity, his "yarn," that he can escape nonentity and strategically relocate the center of the cosmos.

Lamming, as an Anancy artist, confronts the world view of "Mr Hate-To-Be-Contradicted," exposing the arbitrary nature of its premises and denying it the fixity and permanence it wishes to claim. He draws our eyes away from the structures of European domination to the folk themselves, to the spider weaving in the unswept corners of the house as it were. His strategy posits the possibility of a multiplicity of centers, and insists on relationships, connectedness, and pluralism as a necessary corrective to the inside/outside, above/below polarized hierarchies implicit in the Eurocentric expression of Great House/exploited tenantry.

Boundaries, thresholds, crossroads, and the marketplace of symbolic commercial intercourse are omnipresent in the rigidly structured Eurocentric landscape of *Castle*. They express a tragic world view in which hierarchies are inevitable, and principles of inclusion and exclusion are final and ultimate. High on the hill are the landlord's house and garden surrounded by a brick wall topped with broken glass, while below in the valley is the "tenantry"—the folk defined in terms of their relationship to the landlord:

> To the east where the land rose gently to a hill there was a large brick building surrounded by a wood and a high stone wall that bore bits of bottle along the top.

> At night the light poured down through the wood, and the house looking down from the hill seemed to hold a quality of benevolent protection. It was a castle around which the land like a shabby back garden stretched.

Yet another wall encloses the school yard:

> In one corner a palm-tree, and in the others three shrines of enlightenment that looked over the wall and across a benighted wooden tenantry.

The three "shrines" are the church with "dark stained hooded windows that never opened" and an interior that is "dark and heavy and strange"; the head-teacher's house; and the school itself "with windows all around that opened like a yawning mouth". It is not without significance that a language of sacredness is used for this structured landscape in which the folk stand *pro fana*, feeding their children as human sacrifices to the yawning mouth of the system.

The landscaped village with its lighted Great House on the hill overseeing the tenantry in the valley, and the sacred middle ground between them of religion and education, is a microcosm of the novel's broader landscape in which Big England and Little England co-exist in the parent-child relationship typical of colonialism. "Landlords" of authority—England, the Great House, the School, the Church—all "look down" disdainfully across their boundary walls at the folk of the tenantry.

The Great protect their interests by means of a system of overseers, supervisors, and inspectors, but the folk, by contrast, are without protection; they experience invasion of their fragile defining boundaries at every point. The frail walls of the village suggest a corresponding frailty of the walls of personhood for those who live there:

> The village was a marvel of small, heaped houses raised jauntily on groundsels of limestone, and arranged in rows on either side of the multiplying marl roads. Sometimes the roads disintegrated, the limestone slid back and the houses advanced across their boundaries in an embrace of board and shingle and cactus fence.

The villagers lack a clearly marked "road" of purpose. Defined by others, they are yet to define themselves. Their lack of identity, their constant experience of being "overseen," is symbolized in the incident of G's bathtime. As the neighbor's son Bob balances on the paling to watch, his weight causes a fence to crash: "the two yards merged. The barricade which had once protected our private secrecies had surrendered" (18). A crowd is attracted to the scene:

> On all sides the fences had been weighed down with people, boys and girls and grown-ups. The girls were laughing and looking across to where I stood on the pool of pebbles, naked, waiting. They looked at Bob's mother and the broken fence and me. The sun had dried me thoroughly, and now it seemed that I had not been bathed, but brought out in open condemnation and placed in the middle of the yard waiting like one crucified to be jeered at.

The scene recurs in different forms throughout the novel: shame and degradation consequent on the breaking down of defining boundaries, ritual beatings, ritual purifications. Mocking eyes rejoice over the trembling naked figure of another's embarrassment, glad to find a scapegoat for the shame they fear to confront within themselves. G's naked *skin* is his sole protection—his frail counterpart to the landlord's "castle" on the hill.

Boundary walls define the Great, then, but merely marginalize the folk, categorizing them as expiatory scapegoats for the Great. G and his friends transgress sacred boundaries when they secretly enter the grounds of the landlord's house to see what goes on at a party, and they witness the seduction of the landlord's daughter by a British sailor. Later, the story given out by the landlord is that his daughter was raped by the village boys. Here the "penetration" of sacred domains—the rape of class interests by the military—is projected onto the folk. Similarly, moral corruption within the ranks of those bonded together by a common "skin" is denied. Moral and economic problems are univocally displaced into simple racial hatred. Villagers conversing in the shoemaker's shop sum up the landlord's relationship with the folk with more acuity than they realize when one of them says; "He couldn't feel as happy anywhere else in this God's world than he feel on that said same hill lookin' down at us".

Ritual projection of guilt and shame onto an innocent victim is the recurring motif of the novel. Wilson Harris has already pointed to the number of ritual beatings and washing ceremonies in *Castle*. Repeatedly a scapegoat is singled out to bear the burden of another's disgrace. At the school's celebrations marking the Queen's birthday, the Headmaster, anxious to impress the inspector, is enraged when the ceremony is interrupted by a loud giggle. His response is dramatic. On the departure of the inspector he addresses the school in a voice "choked with a kind of terror". Punishment falls on the first available victim in ritualistic sadism: the innocent lad becomes a "human symbol of the blackest sin," is bound hand and foot, and a leather strap brought down repeatedly on his buttocks until his clothing is ripped and the "filth slithered down his legs." Like a sacrificial victim, the boy makes "a brief howl like an animal that had had its throat cut". Asked why he didn't run, the boy replies, "He had to beat somebody, and he made sure with me". Like the men in Foster's shop, the boy understands the human need for a sacrificial scapegoat. As his schoolfriends bathe away the filth and blood, the victim relates information about the Head teacher that fully explains the man's insecurities and his need to protect his image at all cost.

The pattern is repeated at a wayside revival service. Once again an authority figure humiliates and denigrates a victim while worshippers and onlookers alike exult in projecting their own shame onto the chosen scapegoat. Watching the preacher's tactics with a reluctant convert, G comments, "I was sure they were going to sacrifice him, and I wanted to see how it was done". The words "born again" disturb him: "There was something very frightening about them, and particularly the context in which they were placed. The hymn had been started in order to control the tittering of the spectators… The preacher was a kind of spiritual bailiff who offered salvation as a generous exchange for the other's suffering". Experience eventually teaches the lad that the circle of worshippers with the preacher at its center is a structured world akin to that of the landlord's walled houses on the hill; to enter it is to accept castration and assume the eternal role of child before the controlling authority of the Great.

When her pumpkin vine is trampled, G's mother has a sense of loss and futility that is wider-reaching than the immediate waste of the plant. Her voice "spoke as if from an inner void beyond which deeper within herself were incalculable layers of feeling". Her deprivation vents itself on G. The boy, completely innocent, stands naked in the center of a circle of spectators who rock with laughter as his mother engages in a ritualistic beating. A scapegoat is needed, and the naked boy serves the role. The innocent boy in the school, G in his mother's yard, the youth at the wayside service— all naked, all innocent, all chosen victims. The vulnerability of the naked self is evident.

Lamming's key metaphor for the invasion of boundaries and absence of defining walls of selfhood is the flood with which the novel opens.

Water seeps through ceiling and floor into the house where G lives with his mother. Outside, a lily is uprooted from the soil by the force of the rain. Invading floodwaters anticipate the later "flood" of worker riots that will invade the boundaries of privilege but leave in their wake a muddy residue of bourgeois profiteering personified in Mr Slime, founder of the Penny Bank—an organization that, despite its promise, yields no benefits to the village. At an existential level the floodwaters provide an image for the novel's exploration of ways to build defining walls around the self. For repeatedly the self experiences invasion by the Other: "Deep down he felt uneasy. He had been seen by another. He had become part of the other's world, and therefore no longer in complete control of his own. The eye of another was a kind of cage".

Release and freedom are found only in the darkness—in the darkened cinema, in the school lavatory. To embrace the light is to lose one's freedom. Light from the landlord's house dictates the lifestyle of the villagers; light at the wayside revival service calls the people to forsake their manhood and be "born again" into submissiveness; and Ma calls Pa away from his dreams of silver, pork, and weddings, away from his ruminations on existence, away from his gaze through the open doorway into the freeing darkness and back to the circle of light thrown by the lamp in their home—a lamp that obediently takes its cue in unquestioning piety from the light on the hill. Lamming consistently inverts the Judeo-Christian metaphors of European tradition and associates light with exploitative control, darkness with freedom. The lad at the open-air meeting confesses his fear of the candles his aunt burns to "keep away the spirits"! In Lamming's revision of the European text, it is only when one has the courage to step out of the light—beyond the narrow circle of the known into the unknown, undreamed-of realm of darkness that a new order of things is made possible. The alternative is to be "a prisoner in the light, condemned to be saved".

Subtly Lamming inverts the conventional hierarchy of images. To be born again now appears as acquiescent auto-castration, and what Eurocentric authority calls enlightenment is discovered to be confinement within the denigrating oversight of an alien world view. By the end of his novel, Lamming brings us to the final inversion when the *black* skin itself, far from being a mark of shame and frailty, is revealed as a stronghold—a mask behind which the self is safe from invasion; "The likenesses will meet and make merry, but they won't know you, the you that's hidden somewhere in the castle of your skin", G exults. To be held in "le regard" of the other is to be misdefined. One moves into Being when the defining process is from within. G's drama is an existential taking-possession of the boundaries of the self; he converts the cage of the already-defined into the fortress of the ever-signifying.

Source: Joyce E. Jonas, "Carnival Strategies in Lamming's *In the Castle of My Skin*," in *Callaloo*, Vol. 11, No. 2, Spring 1988, pp. 346–60.

Carolyn T. Brown

In the following excerpt, Brown looks at the myth of the Fall as a metaphor for maturation in Lamming's In the Castle of My Skin.

In 1958 George Lamming wrote that the modern black writer's endeavor is like that of "every other writer whose work is a form of self enquiry, a clarification of his relations with other men, and a report on his own highly subjective conception of the possible meaning of man's life." A writer's self-inquiry constitutes his first world—"the world of the private and hidden self, the world hidden within the castle of each man's skin." And if he is honest, he will bear witness to the impact that a second world, the social, has made on his consciousness. Finally, because a man cannot escape "the essential need to find meaning for his destiny," the writer must confront his third world, his "definition of himself as man in the world of men." When he looks fully into these three worlds of his self, he finds a "very concrete example of ... the human condition ... a condition which is essentially ... originally tragic." The contemporary human condition, writes Lamming, involves a "universal sense of separation and abandonment, frustration and loss, and above all, of man's direct inner experience of something missing."

All over the world and in different periods, that sense of absence has given rise to a myth of a past time of perfection from which man has fallen, a myth of a golden age or an Eden. In coming to terms with that archetypal sense of absence through the medium of the autobiographical fiction *In the Castle of My Skin* George Lamming revivifies the archetype of the Fall, now in Barbadian garb, as it touches each of his worlds. Not only is much of his personal life projected into the fictional character G, but the novel articulates the history of an entire village, as the protagonist individually and the villagers collectively come into historical consciousness and in so doing lose their innocence. "Archetypes come to life only when one patiently tries to discover why and in what fashion they are meaningful to a living individual," wrote Carl Jung. A fascinating example is the particular manner in which the myth of the Fall as a metaphor for maturation infuses Lamming's narrative, dignifying with eternal human significance the life of a poor, black child struggling to adulthood in Barbados.

Calling the biblical Fall "one of the most essential symbolic teachings of the Christian religion." Jung argued that the myth expresses the psychic fact that man experiences "the dawn of consciousness as a curse." Adam—the primitive man, responding to instinct, innocent without self-consciousness of his impulses and actions—rested secure in his trust of nature. That things were the way they were was not problematic. But in turning away from instinct and opposing himself to it, modern man, recognizing his nakedness, creates consciousness and with it the inevitability of choice, doubt, fear. Eating the apple from the tree of knowledge marks the sacrifice of the natural man, of the unconscious, of the capacity to live in the world through simple response without judgments of good and evil. And modern man, fallen, in an "orphaned and isolated state where [he is] abandoned by nature and driven to consciousness," aware of the insecurity implied by freedom to choose, said Jung, wishes he could avoid the problems thus engendered and may wonder whether the childlike, preconscious state were not preferable, He experiences loss and absence. Jung further argued that each individual reenacts the psychic history of the race in his emergence from preconsciousness and movement into the dualistic stage, characteristic of "youth" from puberty to mid-life, in which he experiences himself both as "I," the innermost psychic self, and as "also I," the self adjusting to making its way in the physical and social world.

In the early chapters of *In the Castle of My Skin* Lamming frankly acknowledges his use Old Testament metaphor, but only to mock its simplistic nature. Humorously he compares the flood which opens the novel to the biblical Flood. Only once does he overtly contemplate the Garden of Eden story, which he merges with Lucifer's rebellion against God. In chapter three the schoolboys, having been denied knowledge of Barbadian history by the colonialist school system, speculate as to how Queen Victoria could have freed them from slavery. They arrive at a composite explanation which, though naïve, articulates the assumptions underlying British rationalizations for colonialist rule. Though in origin different, the Garden of Eden

> *In this novel chronological time belongs to the adult observer re-flecting on how the village and he have changed. For the villager and the child, time does not exist."*

or heaven and the empire are identified with one another. Because both are products of God's will and under His dominion, to rebel against either is to become a moral outlaw, a Lucifer, a rebel against God. Rebellion, while offering the exhilaration of new possibility, produces loneliness so terrible that the rebels repent, preferring bondage to freedom. And bondage to the empire will facilitate their return to the true garden in heaven. Thus in his only overt consideration of the myth of the Fall, Lamming blasts the colonialists' exploitation of Christian theology in the interests of perpetuating economic and psychological enslavement. Lamming's analogy affirms that colonial Barbados was no paradise, except perhaps for the British.

Yet on a subtler level the myth does pervade the novel, and metaphorically Barbados is indeed a garden. A matured G, looking back, describes the house of the landlord Creighton as "a castle around which the land like a shabby back garden stretched." While the shabbiness under the colonial regime is never in doubt, neither—it turns out—is its gardenlike quality. In considering how the regime impinges on his second world, Lamming never retreats from resistance; still, when that rule is replaced by the native bourgeoisie. bringing about the sale of the land and destruction of a way of life, then the loss of that simple, harmonious community—poignantly symbolized by Pa's removal to the almshouse—is felt severely enough that village life seems in retrospect like an innocent paradise. The verdure of the land is known only after the trees are downed, and the land's value becomes evident only when it is sold. G's mother voices this truth in an aphorism: "You never miss the water till the well run dry; / You never miss a mother till she close her eye" Just as the child's lack of consciousness of being a person separate from the mother gives way before the evidence that he is himself not her, so man—the villagers—no longer in a monistic relationship with the source of sustenance, the natural world, becomes forcefully conscious of his separateness with profound regret.

While the villagers experience the social and political changes as disastrous, the novel's judgment of these changes is more complex. For although throughout most of the novel G's experience of the world is like that of the villagers, their fall is single. His is double. The sociopolitical narrative of social change in a Barbadian village deals with the single fall, which is, it appears, a fall only in part. Even desirable change involves loss: "Whether you were glad or sorry to be rid of [things,] you couldn't bear the thought of seeing them for the last time". The narrator's fall, on the other hand, has a second part and a different quality, for he also becomes alienated from the village community. In gaining access to the narrator's double fall, we enter the writer's first world, the world of the innermost self, and perhaps not surprisingly find ourselves involved with issues of autobiography as a genre.

Of course Lamming, like G, was once a boy growing up in Barbados. But *In the Castle of My Skin* resembles autobiography more than superficially. First, its mode is self-reflective and so has a natural tendency toward irony. In autobiography the narrator is both the observer and the observed, and as such the genre can only be written after the writer has separated himself enough from living experience to objectify it. If the writer, now matured, tries to re-create experiences as he lived them (this Lamming does), his double vision characteristically produces irony. In Lamming's novel the double vision accounts for the humor in the early part of the novel, for he recounts events as the child and the villagers experienced them, but with the hindsight of the matured observer. Naturally by the end, as the ages and perspectives of the observer and the observed converge, the humor disappears, and the ironic distance diminishes.

The novel shares with autobiography a second feature: the use of Edenic imagery to depict childhood. In "The Myth of the Fall: A Description of Autobiography" Martha Lifson explores the curious fact that many autobiographies—those of Augustine, Rousseau. Wordsworth and Thoreau, among others—invoke garden-of-paradise imagery in describing childhood: "The light, the peace, the friendly insect, the stillness, and particularly the timelessness, are all images that recur frequently in autobiographical scenes of childhood." Later she

adds to this list a "sense of order" and "abundance of nature."

Although "light" is not a prominent metaphor in his novel. Lamming sometimes uses light-dark imagery in crucial ways, as will be seen. "Peace" and "stillness," while indeed appropriate to the chapters at the beach, would not seem to describe the raucous, often quarreling interchanges of village life unless we understand them as commotion which occurs within the context of the steady rhythms of that life, commotion which signals no disruption. The theme of Edenic harmony emerges strikingly in depictions of the land, the sky, the sea, the sand of the beach with its wondrous crabs appearing and disappearing. The crabs, vibrating with luminous significance, are the Barbadian equivalent of Lifson's "friendly insects," emblematic of the eternal wonder of the universe, with which the child feels at one. It emerges in the fisherman, masterful and at ease in his element, who personifies man's harmony with the natural world and capacity for securing abundance from its unspoiled state. Though the village is poor and ragged, no one appears to be in real want. The rootedness of the village order and the unconscious assumption that the village will remain unspoiled are Edenic qualities too. G's friend Trumper alone voices what others only vaguely intuit.

> When you up here [at the landlord's house] … you see how it is nothin' could change in the village. Everything's sort of in order. Big life one side an' small life a next side, an you get a kin' o' feelin' of you in your small corner an' I in mine. Everything's kind of correct.

Still, as Lifson noted, it is the child's sense of timelessness which most emphatically evokes paradise.

In this novel chronological time belongs to the adult observer reflecting on how the village and he have changed. For the villager and the child, time does not exist. G is aware of time as sequence but not as progression. The villagers similarly cannot imagine the radical changes set in motion by Mr. Slime's formation of the Penny Bank and the Friendly Society. Thus the consequences, unexpected, shock them not just because of specific effects, but because they had not conceived that real change was possible. "This land ain't the sort of land that can be for buy or sell … 'Twas always an' 'twill always be land for we people to live on," protests a bewildered woman.

Thus a maturer Lamming joins in choosing Edenic imagery to transcribe his childhood. For G and the villagers, conflicts occur within the unexpected, natural rhythms of life and create neither alienation nor self-division. The paradise Lamming evokes is one of naïve inner harmony, based on the assumption that the world is what it is and everyone has a secure place in it, not on the judgment of it as good in itself. So also affirms the book of Genesis: knowledge of good and evil arises only after the apple is eaten.

Although Lamming's evocation of Eden is powerful, equally if not more forceful are the images of disappearance and destruction, of the Fall, which resonate throughout the novel. Sudden, mysterious, unexpected disappearances of objects, emblems of the more catastrophic loss of psychic grounding, punctuate the text. The humorous story of the drunk man's penny and cent—one rolled into the gutter in full view under a full moon, the other was carefully secured under a stone, and both vanished—echoes through the narrator's later, nearly frantic search for the special pebble which, having seized the narrator's attention, vanishes contrary to all logical causality through some strange, indecipherable intervention, in the midst of security, in the Garden of Eden, without source or explanation, without preparation, cataclysmically enters the serpent.

The novel tells of two falls: the simple sale of Eden itself (the village land) through the agency of the serpent Mr. Slime, and the more complex disinheritance of G, who loses his identity. Repeatedly, Lamming projects the predicament precipitating the fall as closed. Only two alternatives (they appear either as opposites or as identical—it makes no difference) are postulated, and the protagonist must choose between them. Although in the predifferentiated state G embraced both alternatives without conflict, yet with the coming of an unforeseen, intervening force he is compelled to choose between illusory alternatives. The refusal to choose places him in limbo; choosing leads him into exile or destroys him. Always he loses the harmony of his prelapsarian state.

The tales told by the boys at the beach rehearse G's later experience of this psychological predicament. Boy Blue tells the story of Bots, Bambi and Bambina, of a village man living contentedly with two common-law wives. Under external pressure he arbitrarily marries one of them. All continues the same until, without warning, the formerly warm and sociable man becomes silently morose, takes to drink and dies. The boys explain his enigmatic behavior thus: "Something go off pop in yuh head' an you ain't the same man you think you was". The story is preceded by Trumper's tale of Jon, who,

similarly coerced into choosing between two women, Sue and Jen, attempts to watch his wedding from a tree, waiting to discover what will happen as, simultaneously in facing churches, his two brides-to-be vainly await his arrival at the altar. Images of a duality which is no duality repeat elsewhere—two moods of the ocean on either side of the lighthouse, the oppositions of life and death, Creighton and Slime, god and dog in Pa's dream. Always frustration and loss follow choice.

Such predicaments are emblematic of the narrator's situation near the end of the novel, when he finds himself separated from the village by his education and from his intellectual peers by his ties to village life.

> I remained in the village living, it seemed, on the circumference of two worlds. It was as though my roots had been snapped from the centre of what I knew best, while I remained impotent to wrest what my fortunes had forced me into.

Repeatedly as situations necessitate choice between false, arbitrary or meaningless alternatives, the individual remembers that it had formerly been possible to have wholeness, to appropriate all alternatives and so avoid loss. Trumper explains Jon's perspective: able imaginatively to marry both women as well as observe from the tree, he accepts the psychic reality as primary and fails even to consider as problematic the failure of the three events to proceed simultaneously in actuality. Instead he waits patiently for the groom, himself or another, to arrive for the weddings. Trumper comments, "P'raps it ain't [logical] … but that don't make it not so." When Boy Blue objects that living a contradiction makes wholeness impossible, Trumper responds, "I don't know. … P'raps you can if you feel you can". In dream, in memory, in imagination, the mind contemplates and realizes multiple, incompatible alternatives. Since all perceptions ultimately must be subjective, the subjective projection can become more actual than the objective manipulation of physical matter. Eden is not just a folk village, a childhood mentality, but also, as in Jung, a psychic position.

Lamming contrasts archetypally the atemporal, paradisiacal Barbadian life and Slime's modern, analytical approach to it. In introducing the novel, Richard Wright, speaking of the clash of the folk and the modern worlds, focuses on its sociopolitical dimensions, highlighting the Third World cultures versus modern industrialism. Wright further argues that the clash occurs in the mind of every man who grows up in the one culture to find himself an adult in the other. For the atemporal, dream-fantasy mode which accounts for the label "poetic" so frequently bestowed on the novel arises from the child's preconscious mode of mental activity, and the temporal perspective of the matured observer is generated from the analytic, linear mode of mental life.

Lamming has embodied the opposed modes, the "atemporal folk" and the "linear modern," within the novel's narrative strategy. The adult observer perceives the causality of events, analytically and linearly, revealing the dynamics of social change. But the villagers' and child's perspective is atemporal. Several narrative strategies create the impression of timelessness. First, the time lapses between chapters vary radically and indefinitely. Rarely does the reader know how old G has become. Second, the narrative voice ranges from primarily first person, to primarily third person, to—in the chapters which are dialogues between Ma and Pa—primarily dramatic. The voices narrate a whole unified by harmony rather than by logic. Third, images felt to be similar to one another in essence, though different in form, emerge at unforeseen points to create a narrative of mood subliminally felt to dominate the linear narrative of events. As in a dream where the insights of the psyche are disguised in symbols and meaning emerges from decoding the emotional reverberations (not from simply remembering the narrative of the dream), so the emotional content of the novel is structured by a process of freely associating images and symbols which resonate against one another, allowing the correspondences to surface.

When he juxtaposes atemporal and analytical narrative modes. Lamming gives concrete form to Jung's concept of the self in youth experiencing its own duality, itself as "I" and "also I." Pa's enigmatic dream in chapter ten exemplifies this. The dream, voice of the unconscious function of the psyche and a balancing corrective to conscious thought, is here presented as the voice of the slave ancestors. It would seem to be a dream emerging from a kind of racial collective unconscious within the individual psyche. That voice describes the origins of Barbados through slavery as a terrible mistake, as the formation of an illusory duality between oppressed and oppressors which never should have been, one begun symbolically here by the sailor Christopher Columbus.

> The only certainty these islands inherit was that sailor's mistake, and it's gone on and on from father to son 'mongst the rich and the poor: in Slime and Creighton, landlord and politician, those who play at ruling and those at being ruled, and those who are neither one nor the other... The fate of these islands I do not know, but man must live like a god or a dog, or be a stone that is neither dead nor alive, a pool no wind will ever wrinkle. For there's always two worlds to one man if you're a man, two darknesses to one light...

The very concept of duality, of alternatives at once opposite and the same, is illusory. The necessity of choosing between Jen and Sue, folk and modern, unconscious and conscious, is an illusion. Here especially images of light, typical of Eden, become relevant. In Pa's dream, darkness represents the fallen state of the present; and light at the end of the dream—Pa's vision for the future—seems to signify a yearning for a final reintegration and return to what long ago, before the fall, had been whole. The hope of reintegration is what prevents Lamming's novel from representing life as in essence tragic, his later comments notwithstanding.

Source: Carolyn T. Brown, "The Myth of the Fall and the Drawing of Consciousness in George Lamming's *In the Castle of My Skin*," in *World Literature Today*, Vol. 57, No. 1, Winter 1983, pp. 38–43.

Sources

Charques, R. D., Review of *In the Castle of My Skin*, in *Spectator*, March 20, 1953, p. 354.

Cotter, Graham, Review of *In the Castle of My Skin*, in *Canadian Forum*, September 1953, p. 141.

Coulthard, G. R., *Race and Colour in Caribbean Literature*, Oxford University Press, 1962.

Douglas, M. S., Review of *In the Castle of My Skin*, in *Chicago Sunday Tribune*, November 22, 1953, p. 20.

Lamming, George, "Labor, Culture, and Identity," in *Caribbean Cultural Identities*, edited by Glyne Griffith, Bucknell University Press, 2001.

———, "The Occasion for Speaking," in *The Routledge Reader in Caribbean Literature*, edited by Alison Donnell and Sarah Lawson Welsh, Routledge, 1996.

Moses, Knolly, Interview with George Lamming for Panmedia Features, www.panmedia.com.jm/features/lamming.htm (September 20, 2001).

Pouchet Paquet, Sandra, "George Lamming," in *The Routledge Reader in Caribbean Literature*, edited by Alison Donnell and Sarah Lawson Welsh, Routledge, 1996.

———, *The Novels of George Lamming*, Heinemann, 1982.

Pritchett, V. S., Review of *In the Castle of My Skin*, in *New Statesman and Nation*, April 15, 1953, p. 460.

Review of *In the Castle of My Skin*, in *Times Literary Supplement*, March 27, 1953, p. 206.

Webster, H. C., Review of *In the Castle of My Skin*, in *Saturday Review of Literature*, December 5, 1953, p. 36.

West, Anthony, Review of *In the Castle of My Skin*, in *New Yorker*, December 6, 1953, p. 222.

Further Reading

Cudjoe, Selwyn, *Resistance and Caribbean Literature*, Ohio University Press, 1980.

Although this critical study does not write specifically about *In the Castle of My Skin*, it discusses the themes of political and cultural resistance to oppression and racism in a number of Caribbean novels, including Lamming's later works *Of Age and Innocence* and *Water with Berries*.

Parry, J. H., and P. M. Sherlock, *A Short History of the West Indies*, Macmillan, 1968.

Written in the mid-1960s, this book is certainly out of date, but as a brief history of all of the islands of the Caribbean up to approximately 1962, the book is more than sufficient. It is especially good at addressing the changing political relationships between the colonies and their colonial powers.

Taylor, Patrick, *The Narrative of Liberation*, Cornell University Press, 1989.

Taylor's book examines a number of topics such as Frantz Fanon, voodoo, and the trickster figure to come to an understanding of important strains in Afro-Caribbean life and thought. The final chapter, on Lamming and Derek Walcott, discusses how Afro-Caribbean people have used Western forms of literature to illustrate and comment on the social conditions of the West Indies. Taylor, surprisingly, finds Walcott and Lamming not radical enough in their analyses.

The Last King of Scotland

Giles Foden

1998

Giles Foden's *The Last King of Scotland*, published in 1998 to high praise from critics, is a novel encompassing both historical fact and fiction. In the novel, Scotsman Nicholas Garrigan tells the tale of how he came to be Idi Amin's personal physician and of his subsequent adventures. One of the novel's major concerns is Garrigan's relationship with Amin, a brutal dictator, and why Garrigan is so fascinated by the leader that he does not leave, even when faced with the certain knowledge of Amin's atrocities.

Garrigan is a fictional character who participates in historical events and interacts with real people, including Amin, the brutal president of Uganda between 1971 and 1979. Amin has been accused of cannibalism and of issuing orders that resulted in the brutal deaths of hundreds of thousands of his countrymen. Some historians believe that Amin's erratic and violent behavior stemmed from an acute case of syphilis, but others (including the fictional Garrigan), refute this.

Using his twenty years in Africa and his background as a journalist, Foden researched the events surrounding Amin's rise to power and downfall, interviewing many of those who watched and participated in the Ugandan ruler's eight-year reign. Foden makes the book feel like the memoir of an actual person by inserting fictional newspaper articles, journal entries, and authentic events.

During a 1998 interview with the online magazine *Boldtype*, Foden mentioned that he used conversations with Bob Astles, widely perceived to

Giles Foden

have been Amin's closest advisor, to construct Garrigan's character. As a British soldier who worked his way into Amin's favor, Astles was much more "proactive than Garrigan," according to Foden, but paid the price by spending ten years in a Ugandan jail after Amin's fall.

Author Biography

Born to farmers in Warwickshire, England, in 1967, Giles Foden moved to Africa when he was five years old. The family lived in various African countries for about twenty years. One of the countries they lived in was Uganda, the setting for Foden's first novel, *The Last King of Scotland*. Foden told the on-line literary magazine *Boldtype* that he relied upon the "vivid experiences" he gained while traveling with his father to rural African outposts when writing the novel.

For about three years, Foden worked as an assistant editor for the British publication the *Times Literary Supplement*, and he continues to write for a number of newspapers and magazines, including the *Guardian*. Upon its publication in 1998, critics hailed *The Last King of Scotland* as the work of a

bright new literary talent. The novel won several awards, including the 1998 Whitbread First Novel Award, the Somerset Maugham Award, a Betty Trask Prize, and the Winifred Holtby Prize. Foden's second novel, *Ladysmith*, is set in nineteenth-century South Africa.

Plot Summary

Part One

The Last King of Scotland opens with Nicholas Garrigan describing how he happened to become the personal physician to Idi Amin, president of Uganda in the 1970s. While Garrigan is serving as a physician at a "bush surgery" in the western Ugandan provinces, he is called to the scene of an automobile accident. Lying on the ground next to his wrecked Maserati is President Amin, who needs his wrist bandaged. A few months later, Garrigan is asked to come to the capital as Amin's personal physician. He complies because "you couldn't say no" to Amin.

Garrigan writes this account of his experiences, he says, "to provide a genuine eyewitness account" of the strange things that happened to him and to others during Amin's rule in Uganda. He explains how he decided to go to medical school and how his childhood love for adventure and interest in foreign lands put him on the road to practicing medicine in Africa. He is writing this story from his cottage in Scotland long after the events in Uganda have taken place.

Garrigan arrives in Kampala, Uganda, on January 24, 1971, to begin his job as a doctor with the Ugandan Ministry of Health. During his first night in Kampala, he hears shouting and tanks moving on the streets under his hotel window. The next morning, he hears a radio broadcast stating that, "our fellow soldier Major-General Idi Amin Dada" has taken power from President Apollo Obote. Frightened, Garrigan searches the town for some guidance on how to get to Mbarara, where he is due the next day. At the British Embassy, Nigel Stone suggests that he take a bus to Mbarara and asks him to "keep a weather out for anything untoward."

The bus trip to Mbarara is extremely uncomfortable and cramped. On the way, two events occur. Garrigan meets a young resident of Mbarara, Boniface Malumba, also known as Bonney, who invites him to visit his family's house. In the second incident, soldiers board the bus and demand money from the passengers. The scene is calm as everyone cooperates with the soldiers, until one man refuses to pay. The soldiers beat him, but when Garrigan tries to help the man with his injuries he chastises Garrigan for not coming to his assistance earlier. He angrily yells at Garrigan, "What good are you to me now? You said nothing when you should have come forward."

In Mbarara, Garrigan meets Dr. Alan Merrit, head of the clinic; his wife, Joyce; and the clinic staff, including Sara Zach, an Israeli physician. Garrigan falls into the clinic's routine, treating patients and learning more about tropical diseases than he ever thought possible. William Waziri, a Ugandan physician, takes Garrigan on a field trip during which they travel the countryside and conduct vaccination clinics. Garrigan realizes that he is falling in love with Sara. He spends a pleasant evening dining with Boniface Malumba's family.

Amin arrives in Mbarara and holds a huge rally at the town's stadium. Sara and Garrigan go together to listen, and he notices that she takes notes. A number of days later, he is in Sara's bungalow and notices a shortwave radio, one like everyone else owns, except that hers has both sending and receiving capabilities.

Time passes quickly, and Garrigan is now in his second year in Mbarara. He and Sara have become lovers. Meanwhile, a number of unsettling events occur. The sounds of gunfire and explosions come from the local army barracks one evening. Two Americans are reported missing and suspected murdered by Major Mabuse, a local military leader. While Garrigan and Sara are picnicking, a contingent of Ugandans dressed "in full Scottish paraphernalia" emerges from the jungle and marches past the couple, playing bagpipes.

Garrigan takes another vaccination field trip and returns to Mbarara to discover that rebels sympathetic to former President Obote have staged a raid on the town. There are numerous civilian casualties, including his friend Boniface and the Malumba family. Gugu, Boniface's brother, is the only survivor. Garrigan and Sara take in the traumatized child and create a sort of temporary family until Gugu's relatives from the countryside come to claim him.

After Gugu leaves, Sara and Garrigan's relationship deteriorates. Garrigan notices that she spends time with the nearby Israeli road-building crew. Waziri never returns from his vacation, and part of the clinic burns down. Sara leaves the clinic

without telling anyone, probably because Amin demands that all Asians and Israelis leave the country immediately. Garrigan hears a radio broadcast in which Amin claims to be "the last rightful King of Scotland." The incident in which Amin wrecks his Maserati occurs, and Garrigan is soon on his way to Kampala to be the president's personal physician.

Part Two

Even though Garrigan is now Amin's personal physician, he rarely gets to see his patient. He spends most of his time working at the Mulago Hospital and getting to know Kampala. Garrigan explains part of Amin's history, including how Amin's past military training with the Scots explains his obsessive interest in the nation. One afternoon while Garrigan is relaxing by a pool, Amin appears suddenly, rising up through the pool on a mechanized fountain of water. Later, Amin calls Garrigan to his house to treat his son who, as it ends up, simply has a small toy lodged in his nose. Amin is so happy with Garrigan that he gives him a van to drive around town. With increasing frequency, Amin behaves oddly and against the interests of the Western embassies in Kampala.

Stone, a member of the British Embassy in Kampala, calls Garrigan to a meeting where he asks him to help them control Amin's behavior via the use of drugs. Garrigan is stunned and rejects the idea.

Amin expels a number of British citizens from the country and forces others to "carry him in a litter through the streets as a sign of their devotion." Garrigan is attracted to the British ambassador's wife, Marina, and the two go on a boat ride and picnic together. Garrigan kisses her but she reacts angrily and demands to be taken home. A week later, Garrigan gets a call that Amin is terribly ill. He arrives to discover that Amin only has a bad case of gas. Garrigan figures out a way to burp Amin like a baby, despite the ruler's huge size. This creates a closer bond between Amin and Garrigan. An assassination attempt is made against Amin, and his reprisals are random and violent.

Though he is currently married to three other women, Amin, outfitted in full Scottish regalia, marries his fourth wife in a Christian ceremony. Garrigan remembers that during this period "life went on as normal with these little bizarre interventions butting up between." For example, Amin begins to send telegrams to different world leaders, such as Margaret Thatcher and the Queen of England. Amin marries again, bringing his total number of wives to five. One of Garrigan's medical colleagues begs him to perform an abortion on his lover, who also happens to be Amin's second wife, but Garrigan refuses. Later Garrigan learns that Amin's second wife has died from blood loss and that his medical colleague has committed suicide. All of this strains Garrigan's nerves, yet he does not make any solid plans to leave the country.

Stone asks Garrigan to kill Amin, citing reports of Amin's atrocities. More British citizens are expelled. Amin calls Garrigan in for a talk and puts him in prison for a day. While in prison, Garrigan sees torture and atrocities, one involving a friend and fellow physician from Mbarara. Garrigan plans to leave Uganda but still does not.

It is now 1976 and a group of hijackers with the Palestinian Liberation Organization have commandeered a plane to Entebbe Airport near Kampala. Amin negotiates with the hijackers to have the non-Jews released, but it is eventually left to the Israeli government to storm the airport and rescue the Jews and Israeli citizens. Garrigan is called to the airport to treat some of the passengers. Later that day, Garrigan receives a phone call from Sara, who is now a colonel in the Israeli army, and he realizes that she was not only a doctor while in Mbarara but also an Israeli spy. Amin asks Garrigan to deliver a box to a small plane taking off from Entebbe. Later, Garrigan hears that the plane exploded in flight.

Garrigan begins making plans to escape Uganda by driving across the border into Tanzania, which is now at war with Uganda. He decides that he must try to find Gugu in Mbarara and take him away. On his way out, Garrigan loses his van, is bitten by a mamba snake and cared for by locals, and discovers that Gugu has become a murderer for Amin's regime. He passes out during an attack on Mbarara and awakens to find himself with the Tanzanian Defense Forces. He stays with them during their advance toward Kampala, serving as a medic for the soldiers.

Garrigan finds Amin hiding in Kampala, speaking to the severed head of the Archbishop of Uganda. Amin asks Garrigan to help him escape and Garrigan agrees, but Amin never shows up at the appointed meeting place. Giving up on Amin, Garrigan steals a boat and rows across the lake to Kenya.

Once in Kenya, Garrigan is treated like a war criminal, but the British Embassy is able to get him on a plane to London. Stone meets him as he dis-

embarks from the plane. Stone, who Garrigan now realizes is an intelligence operative who has helped arrange for his release from Kenya, tells Garrigan that, because he gave up his British citizenship in Uganda at Amin's request, he cannot simply return to England. "There is the question, in any case, of whether you are now a fit person to be admitted to Great Britain at all," says Stone. Garrigan must sign an agreement stating that he acted on his own in Uganda.

Because Stone wants Garrigan to state publicly that his actions in Uganda were his alone and not directed by the British government, he places the doctor in the care of a public relations expert who arranges for a few well-orchestrated press conferences. As soon as possible, Garrigan leaves London for a small cottage in Scotland he has inherited. Here he begins writing the memoir that is *The Last King of Scotland*. The book closes with Garrigan receiving a phone call from Amin, now living in Saudi Arabia. Amin asks if he should intervene on behalf of the Americans to help them rescue hostages taken by the Iranian government. Garrigan does not answer but puts the receiver down and goes outside to do some gardening.

Characters

His Excellency Idi Amin

Idi Amin is the president of Uganda, having seized power from President Apollo Obote in early 1971. He is an actual historical character, but Foden has given him fictional qualities in the novel.

Garrigan treats Amin for an injury sustained in an automobile accident, and the president is so impressed that he demands that Garrigan be his personal physician in the capital city of Kampala. At first, Amin has little use for Garrigan and his skills, but soon he calls Garrigan in for a number of minor medical concerns. When Amin is in severe gastric pain, he calls for Garrigan, who proceeds to burp him "like with babies." From this point, a bond develops between the two men.

Amin suffers from delusions of grandeur, believing that everything he says and thinks is of monumental importance; his full title is President for Life Field Marshall Al Hadj Doctor Idi Amin Dada, VC, DSO, Lord of All the Beasts of the Earth and Fishes of the Sea, King of the Scots and Conqueror of the British Empire in Africa in General and Uganda in Particular. He sends telegrams of advice to world leaders and makes statements that sound both crazy and frightening—especially when they come from a ruler with absolute power. Foden gives an immediate sense of Amin's personality at the book's start as he describes some strange moments at a state dinner. During a monologue about wigs, Amin states, "I do not want Ugandans to wear the hair of dead imperialists or of Africans killed by imperialists." Amin later launches into an even more uncomfortable topic, noting, "I have eaten human meat. It is very salty."

Amin's rule eventually deteriorates. Near the story's end, most nations have placed an embargo on trade with Uganda, and the country is suffering from extreme poverty and disease. When Tanzanian troops enter the capital city, Garrigan finds Amin hiding in the basement headquarters of his secret jail and torture facilities, begging for help to escape. Garrigan hears from Amin for the last time when Amin calls him from Saudi Arabia, where he has found refuge, asking whether he should help the United States negotiate a deal with Iran for the release of American hostages.

Kay Amin

Kay Amin, another character based on a real person, is Idi Amin's second wife. (He was a polygamist who ultimately had five wives.) She is the daughter of a clergyman and was once a university student. She becomes Peter Mbalu-Mukasa's lover. When Kay becomes pregnant, Peter asks Garrigan to help him perform an abortion, but he refuses, afraid of what Amin might do. The next week, Garrigan hears from colleagues that Peter failed to do the abortion properly and that Kay bled to death. Peter commits suicide the next day with an overdose of sleeping pills. Despite rumors to the contrary, Garrigan insists that Amin had nothing to do with Kay's death or Peter's suicide; yet when Garrigan sees Kay's body at the morgue, it has been dismembered.

Bonney

See Boniface Malumba

Doctor Garrigan

See Nicholas Garrigan

George Garrigan

George Garrigan is Nicholas Garrigan's father. He is a Presbyterian minister and a rather solemn man. When Garrigan left for Uganda, his father was displeased that his son was not planning to stay in Scotland and set up a general medical practice, further straining the already tense relationship between the two men. George Garrigan dies during Nicholas's second year in Uganda, but his son decides not to fly to Scotland for the funeral.

Jeanie Garrigan

Jeanie Garrigan is Nicholas Garrigan's mother. Garrigan claims that he has inherited his mother's capacity for hard work and "worry." According to her son, she dies from "pure grief" soon after the death of her husband. He does not leave Uganda to attend her funeral in Scotland.

Moira Garrigan

Moira Garrigan is Nicholas Garrigan's sister. While he is serving as Amin's physician, she asks her brother, "How did you let yourself get so close to such a man?" Garrigan mails to Moira the tapes and journals he has made of his experiences, and she is able to send them on to the cottage where Garrigan writes his memoirs.

Nicholas Garrigan

Nicholas Garrigan is the novel's narrator, a young Scottish physician who goes to Uganda working for the Ministry of Health through the British Overseas Development Agency. After serving at a clinic in a small provincial town for nearly two years, Garrigan is called to treat the country's leader, Idi Amin, who has suffered a sprained wrist in an automobile accident. Amin is so impressed by Garrigan that he demands that the doctor move to Kampala to become his personal physician.

Garrigan finds Amin both charming and repugnant. The major struggle in the novel is within Garrigan, between the part of him that is aware of Amin's brutality and the part of him that is "more fascinated than frightened." He must either leave Uganda or take action against the atrocities. Even before Garrigan meets Amin on the road outside Mbarara, he is curious about the man. After he hears Amin refer to himself as "the last rightful King of Scotland," Garrigan begins to feel a special connection with the ruler, as if "it had some special relevance for me. As if I were his subject." Garrigan develops a particular affection for the leader, despite Amin's reputation for ruthless murders and bizarre statements and behaviors.

Garrigan is not a typical hero; in fact, he bears many of the qualities of an antihero. He has little courage and spends much time worrying about his own personal safety. He fails at many of his relationships, and both of his love interests eventually reject him. Ties to his family and friends back in

Scotland are almost nonexistent, and when the going gets tough, he usually runs away. For example, he leaves for Kampala and Amin once the rural clinic in Mbarara falls on hard times. When Amin's brutality and insanity become obvious, Garrigan resolves to "build a castle" within himself. After arriving in England, having escaped Uganda and possible prosecution for his actions as part of Amin's staff, Garrigan seeks refuge on an isolated Scottish island where he writes his memoirs and lives the remainder of his life.

Ed Howarth

Ed Howarth is the public relations manager Stone assigns to Garrigan upon his return to London. Howarth arranges a few press conferences for Garrigan and coaches him on what he should say.

Colonel Armstrong Kuchasa

Colonel Kuchasa is an officer with the Tanzanian forces that move on Kampala at the end of the book. He rescues Garrigan from a battle in Mbarara and lets him stay in an armored personnel vehicle during their march from Mbarara to Kampala.

Major Mabuse

Major Mabuse was simply a taxi driver before Amin's coup, but in Amin's regime he is a feared military leader. He is reported to have been involved in killing two young American tourists who got in his way.

Boniface Malumba

Garrigan meets Boniface Malumba, a young Ugandan student of food science from Mbarara, while on the bus from Kampala to Mbarara. Malumba is friendly and gives Garrigan advice about living in Uganda. He also invites Garrigan to his family's house for lunch, where Garrigan meets the entire family and spends a pleasant afternoon. Malumba is killed in the fighting that breaks out between pro-Obote forces and Amin's army.

Gugu Malumba

Gugu is Boniface Malumba's fun-loving younger brother. He is the only member of his family to survive the fighting between pro-Obote forces and Amin's army that spreads to Mbarara. Sara and Garrigan take him in at the clinic after the attack, but he is so traumatized that he will not speak. A distant relative arrives one day to take him away. The next time Garrigan sees Gugu, he is one of Amin's murderers in the Mbarara region. Gugu dies during a battle with the Tanzanian forces.

Peter Mbalu-Mukasa

Peter Mbalu-Mukasa is one of the African doctors at Mulago Hospital and a colleague of Garrigan's. Mbalu-Mukasa becomes Kay Amin's lover and one night begs Garrigan to help him perform an abortion on her. Garrigan is too frightened that Amin will discover his role in their illicit affair and refuses to help. Garrigan later hears from his colleagues that Kay has bled to death and that Mbalu-Mukasa has committed suicide, but there are rumors that Amin had them both murdered.

Doctor Alan Merrit

Garrigan works for Alan Merrit at the Mbarara clinic. Merrit is about fifty years old and has what Garrigan calls "a bizarre white streak down the middle of his brown hair." He is married to Joyce Merrit, and they have lived and worked in Uganda for more than twenty years. Joyce calls him by his nickname, Spiny. Merrit is displeased when Garrigan decides to leave Mbarara and become Amin's physician. The Merrits are eventually expelled from Uganda along with other British citizens.

Joyce Merrit

Joyce Merrit is Alan Merrit's wife. She is very hospitable to Garrigan when he shows up at the clinic, providing him with meals and a place to stay until he is settled in his own bungalow.

President Obote

Idi Amin seizes power from Ugandan President Obote on the day Garrigan arrives in Uganda. Apollo Obote was the actual president of Uganda until 1971, when Amin overthrew this government.

Marina Perkins

Marina Perkins is the wife of the British ambassador to Uganda. According to Garrigan, Marina is a moderately attractive woman, although he describes her mouth as being like "a little fig." She accompanies Garrigan on a boat trip and picnic, where Garrigan makes an unsuccessful attempt to seduce her. She becomes angry and doesn't want to have anything to do with Garrigan after this incident. Later, Garrigan sees her sitting with Freddy Swanepoel's hand on her knee. She is eventually expelled from Uganda, along with her husband and other British officials.

Ambassador Robert Perkins

Ambassador Perkins is the British ambassador to Uganda and is married to Marina Perkins. Garrigan is not impressed with the overweight ambassador and refers to him as a "sponge" and the "standard Foreign Office issue: plastered-down hair, a large body shifting in its bristly suit."

Ivor Seabrook

Ivor Seabrook is an "old Englishman" and physician working at the Mbarara clinic. When Garrigan first meets Seabrook, he notices that he has the look of a "long-term tropical alcoholic."

Spiny

See Doctor Alan Merrit

Nigel Stone

Nigel Stone works at the British Embassy in Kampala and asks Garrigan to "keep a weather eye out for anything untoward" at the Mbarara clinic. When Garrigan returns to Kampala as Amin's doctor, Stone asks him to give Amin a drug to moderate his behavior. A while later, after the full extent of Amin's massacres is apparent, Stone asks Garrigan to kill Amin and promises him that the British government will put a large amount of money in his account and "look after" him.

Stone is also the official who arranges to have Garrigan freed from a Kenyan jail on charges of conspiring with Amin, and he meets Garrigan at the airport when he returns to London. Stone also forces Garrigan to sign a statement swearing that all of his actions in Uganda were done of his own accord, not at the direction of the British government.

Freddy Swanepoel

Freddy Swanepoel is a South African pilot based in Nairobi who works for Rafiki Aviation. He describes his job as transporting "things for the Kenyan and Ugandan governments. And other bits and pieces." Garrigan first meets him at the hotel bar when he arrives and notes that everything about Swanepoel is "chunky and muscular, even his face."

Later, Garrigan sees Swanepoel and Marina Perkins having a tryst at a restaurant. Swanepoel dies when Garrigan unknowingly delivers a package containing a bomb from Amin to Swanepoel, just as Swanepoel is about to take off from Entebbe. The plane explodes and both Swanepoel and his passenger die.

Jonas Wasswa

As Idi Amin's minister of health, Jonas Wasswa appoints Garrigan to his position as Amin's personal physician. Amin eventually has Wasswa killed.

William Waziri

Garrigan becomes good friends with William Waziri, a Ugandan doctor trained in the United States who works at the Mbarara clinic. Waziri speaks to Garrigan about local lore and history while they make their regular trips to the countryside to conduct vaccination clinics. At about the time that fighting between pro-Obote forces and Amin's army increases near Mbarara, Waziri takes a vacation but never returns. Later, when Garrigan is dragged down into Amin's secret jail and torture chambers, he sees that Waziri is one of the victims and witnesses his death.

Major Archibald Drummond Weir

Major Weir is a British intelligence officer, originally from Scotland, stationed in Kampala. Garrigan finds him disturbing and frightening. He has built what Stone calls "a magnificent flying machine," a small, radio-controlled contraption that he flies on the grounds of the British Embassy. Weir returns to London under mysterious circumstances, which leads Garrigan to believe that he was recalled for "being too friendly with Amin"; Stone, however, asserts that Weir was "too talkative." When Garrigan returns to his island in Scotland, he finds a newspaper article about Weir, stating that he is a "nationalist extremist" and the "most successful bomber in Scottish history."

Sara Zach

Garrigan falls in love with Israeli physician Sara Zach almost as soon as they become acquainted at the Mbarara clinic. She behaves in a very efficient and standoffish manner, and it takes a while before she and Garrigan become lovers. While she is working at the clinic, Garrigan notices that there are a few things about her that don't quite make sense for a doctor: she takes notes at Amin's rally in Mbarara; her shortwave radio not only receives but is able to transmit information; and she spends an inordinate amount of time with a local Israeli road-building crew. She brushes off Garrigan's attempts to find out more about her activities. After their love affair ends suddenly, Sara disappears from the clinic.

Garrigan does not hear from her for years until he receives a phone call at his house in Kampala. A hijacked plane is sitting on the runway at Entebbe, and she calls—identifying herself as a colonel in the Israeli armed forces—to ask Garrigan if he will try to convince Amin to free the hostages. Garrigan refuses but realizes then that she was probably a spy for the Israelis while working at the Mbarara clinic.

Themes

Questions about Ethical Behavior

Throughout the book, Garrigan struggles with the question of whether his behavior is ethical. The first instance of this is when he travels to Mbarara on a crowded bus, and Ugandan soldiers pull the bus over to collect money from the passengers. Everyone provides money to the soldiers except for one man who claims to be a Kenyan diplomat. The soldiers retaliate by hitting him with the end of a rifle, which rips open a huge gash in his face. Garrigan keeps quiet until the soldiers leave and then moves to give the Kenyan first aid. The Kenyan reacts angrily, demanding to know, "What good are you to me now?" Furthermore, he says that the soldiers would have left the bus alone if Garrigan, a white person, had come forward. According to the Kenyan, Garrigan had power that he did not use at the appropriate time.

This scene is a precursor for what is to come in Garrigan's life. During the entire time he works for Amin, he knows about the horrible and unspeakable violence his boss directs, yet he does nothing. When the British Embassy asks him first to modify Amin's behavior and later to kill Amin with drugs, Garrigan shrugs his shoulders. His only reaction is to imagine how exciting it would be to do these things because they are so much like actions found in a James Bond story. Even after rejecting the request to kill Amin based on his position as a doctor, Garrigan thinks, "It would be rather grand to rid the world of a dictator." On the other hand, Garrigan admits that he actually likes Amin. "I could kill Amin and get away with it," he says. "But there was, I conceded it to myself again, something in me that actually *liked* the man, monster though he was." In another incident, Sara calls Garrigan and begs him to get involved in the hijacking incident by urging Amin to release the hostages. Garrigan responds instead "I can't get involved in all that . . . I'm not made for this kind of thing."

Loneliness and Friendship

Garrigan is a lonely man with few close ties to other people. Garrigan admits that the death of his pet donkey was the most significant event in his childhood and that the family home was emotionally stifling. When he hears that his father has died, he chooses not to travel to Scotland for the funeral or to be with his mother and sister. A short time later, when his mother dies, he makes the same decision to remain in Uganda.

Once in Uganda, Garrigan fits in well at the Mbarara clinic, but he seems to focus more on the flora and fauna than on the people he works with. Long-term relationships do not seem to be his forte, and many of the people he gets along with at Mbarara either meet with bad ends or are not who he imagined them to be. His relationship with Sara is long in its development but is over rapidly and without much discussion. She suddenly decides that she is no longer his lover and eventually leaves without a word being said. A few years later, she turns up as an Israeli spy, making Garrigan realize that he did not know her as well as he had thought. Boniface, whom Garrigan meets on the bus into Mbarara, dies with his family during a rebel attack on the town. Boniface's brother, Gugu, becomes a maniacal killer in Amin's troops. When friends come to Garrigan for help, he rarely extends his hand, usually because he is afraid of the consequences. While living in Kampala as Amin's physician, he associates with a few people but has no deep friendships. The one time he reaches out to someone it is to the British ambassador's wife, who becomes angry at his assumption that she is interested in him.

Amin represents the closest relationship Garrigan has. As the book moves along, he spends more and more time with the ruler and shares conversations with him that are much more intimate than those he has with anyone else. Garrigan seems to relish taking care of and protecting the despot; he feels warmth in response to Amin's childlike behavior and the "nurserylike atmosphere" of his quarters. In the beginning of their relationship, "I even felt a sneaking sense of affection towards him," Garrigan remembers. He admits later that his life is focused on Amin, even though the closer he gets to the ruler the fewer illusions he has. "Still I stayed, more fascinated than frightened," recalls Garrigan.

Relationship of African Nations to the Western World

The relationship between African nations and the West is a complicated one in the novel and in history. In the novel, Africans seem to hold both

Topics for Further Study

- Based on what you learn about Garrigan in the novel, do you think he is a good doctor? Explain your answer.

- One of the turning points in the novel occurs in 1976, when members of the Palestinian Liberation Organization hijack an airplane and divert it to Entebbe Airport near Kampala, Uganda. Research what actually happened and write a news story as if you are a journalist covering the event a few days after the Israelis stormed the plane.

- Many historians, scientists, and others have argued that Idi Amin's violent and bizarre behavior can be attributed to mental degradation from an advanced case of syphilis. In the novel, Garrigan rejects this theory. Investigate what has been written about Idi Amin while he was president of Uganda, and, using the information you uncover, make your own argument about why he acted as he did.

- Garrigan mentions a number of times that he hears news stories about the Scottish independence movement on the radio. Investigate this effort by Scots to make their country independent of Great Britain. Create a time line, beginning in the 1600s and continuing through today, that shows the important dates and events of this movement.

- HIV/AIDS cases in Africa have recently received a lot of attention in the press and from political and medical leaders worldwide. Research the current status of HIV/AIDS in Uganda. Have rates for these diseases increased or decreased over the past decade? What is the government doing to combat HIV infection? How does Uganda compare with other African countries in this regard?

disdain and respect for Westerners. For example, Amin's fascination with Scotland and his corresponding affection toward the Scot Garrigan come from his exposure to the nation and its people while training as a soldier. Amin believes that, in their struggle for independence from England, the Scots have decided that he is their liberating king, much as he sees himself as the liberator of Uganda and all of Africa.

The impact that Western colonization has had on the continent is apparent in the book and evokes anger and contempt from many of the African characters. The Kenyan on the bus is angry when Garrigan fails to use his supposed power as a white man to stop the thieving soldiers. Waziri laughs when Garrigan says that he wants to see "the real Africa" and remembers with some derision that in the recent past all whites who came to Africa were considered "miracle workers."

Style

The Antihero

Garrigan is the protagonist of Foden's novel but not its hero. This antihero has none of the personal qualities that define a traditional hero in literature: courage, physical strength, exceptional intellect, emotional stamina, and the ability to recognize and fight against evil. Garrigan, as the novel's antihero, feels helpless against what he perceives as great odds. He runs from possible pain, is fearful of death, and does not help those in need—except when the need can be met by his role as a medical doctor. Garrigan relishes his role as the underdog; when he arrives in Kampala for the first time, he is frightened and searches for someone to tell him what to do next. When he does take a stand, it is usually without many repercussions, such as when he and Sara temporarily bring Gugu into their home. Garrigan admits later that the arrangement was a sham and that he and Sara were "using Gugu to live out some kind of fantasy family life" as a hedge against the craziness happening around them.

Foreshadowing

Foden has written this book as if the writer is actually the protagonist Nicholas Garrigan pulling together his memoirs of when he was Idi Amin's physician. The narrative is in the first person, and Garrigan often interjects what he is thinking as he writes the memoir from his cottage in Scotland. Because of this, Foden (through Garrigan's character) often inserts a present-day comment that provides a hint about what is to come in the narrative.

For example, while Garrigan and Sara are watching one of Amin's political rallies, he notices that she is taking notes. When he asks her about it, she gives him a vague answer, and he remarks as an aside, "How could I have been so thickheaded, I wonder now," indicating that something *was* amiss with Sara, though at the time he does not share with the reader what that something could be. Garrigan later notices a shortwave radio in Sara's room, similar to the ones everyone else owns at the medical compound except that hers can also transmit. In this way, Foden offers small pieces of a mystery that is not completely solved until later. Later in the story, Sara calls Garrigan. It is apparent from her conversation that she was not only a physician but also a spy.

In another instance, Garrigan lets slip at the story's start that his adventure to Uganda does not turn out as he might have imagined. In describing what he expected his work to entail in Uganda, Garrigan gloomily says "had I known, on arrival, the breadth of activity that his later should involve, I would have gotten straight back on the plane."

Use of Historical Characters and Events

Some critics have referred to *The Last King of Scotland* as a *roman à clef*, a work in which historical figures appear as fictional characters. While Garrigan and others in the novel are purely fictional characters, Foden has woven them into events and characters that are very much a part of history.

In addition to Idi Amin, Foden includes other historical figures such as Margaret Thatcher, an English political leader; Queen Elizabeth of England; the Iranian religious leader Ayatollah Khomeini; U.S. president Richard Nixon; and hijacking victim Dora Bloch. Foden uses most of these figures simply to add texture and a sense of realism to his novel; Amin is the primary historical figure for whom he has created day-to-day actions and a developed personality.

Foden also includes actual historical events in the novel, such as Idi Amin's overthrow of President Apollo Obote in 1971, the hijacking and subsequent raid of an airplane from Tel Aviv, the struggle for Scottish independence, and the overthrow of Amin by Tanzanian armed forces. Like the historical figures, actual events give the book a realistic atmosphere. The feeling of realism is further enhanced by Foden's use of fictional journal entries and news clippings.

Historical Context

The Rule of Idi Amin

Idi Amin was the ruler of Uganda in East Africa from 1971 to 1979. He had a reputation as an unpredictable and violent man, and his policies led directly to the brutal murder of hundreds of thousands of his countrymen.

The facts of Amin's early years are disputed, but during the 1950s he was the heavyweight boxing champion of Uganda, and in the 1960s he rose rapidly through the ranks of the Ugandan army. As a reward for his help during a critical battle, President Apollo Obote named Amin the commander of the country's armed forces. Their relationship deteriorated, and in 1971 Amin overthrew Obote in an armed coup. Garrigan arrives in Kampala, the nation's capital, on the day of the coup.

In his first year as president, Amin ordered the massacre of troops he suspected of being loyal to Obote. In 1972, Britain and Israel rejected Amin's demands for large increases in military aid; Amin sought and received assistance from Libya and Soviet Russia. He became the first black African leader to denounce Israel in favor of the Palestinian cause. In addition, Amin made a number of anti-Semitic remarks and publicly praised Adolf Hitler for killing Jews. This is about the time in the novel when Sara and her Israeli colleagues, some British diplomats, and all Indians and Asians are expelled from Uganda. Because Indians and Asians owned and ran most of the businesses in Uganda, the country's economy collapsed.

After a failed 1972 coup attempt by Tanzanian-supported Obote forces, Amin became even more repressive and brutal. Amin's regime is reported to have murdered anywhere between three hundred thousand and five hundred thousand civilians before he was ousted in 1979 by Tanzanian troops who, after recapturing land that Amin had invaded in 1978, continued marching to the capital, Kampala. Amin fled first to Libya but eventually accepted asylum in Saudi Arabia.

The Israeli Raid on Entebbe

In 1976, a group of Palestinian and West German terrorists (the latter group also known as the Baader Meinhof Gang) hijacked an Air France airplane filled with more than one hundred Israelis and forced it to land at Entebbe Airport near Kampala. In the novel, Garrigan assists with medical care for the hostages.

Compare
&
Contrast

- **1970s:** Idi Amin asks Garrigan to investigate a fatal "new disease" among his soldiers. Although Garrigan finds nothing out of the ordinary, he wonders later, with the advent of HIV/AIDS, whether he was treating some of the earliest cases.

  Today: The HIV/AIDS infection rate for adults in Uganda is 8.3 percent, and about 820,000 people are suspected to be living with HIV/AIDS.

- **1970s:** Idi Amin seizes power from President Apollo Obote in 1971 and promulgates a reign of terror for the next eight years.

  Today: After seizing power in 1986, President Yoweri Museveni is elected Ugandan chief of state in the March 2001 popular elections.

- **1970s:** Idi Amin expels from Uganda all Indians and Asians, who own and run a majority of the businesses in the country. As a result, Uganda's economy collapses and shortages of basic goods are widespread.

  Today: In the last decade, the Ugandan economy has performed solidly, thanks to continued investment in the rehabilitation of the country's infrastructure, reduced inflation, and the return of many previously exiled Indian-Ugandan business people. Unfortunately, Ugandan involvement with the ongoing war in the Democratic Republic of the Congo could cause many of these economic advances to slip.

Some believe that Idi Amin, Uganda's president at that time, was involved in supporting the terrorists and allowed them to land the plane and use Entebbe as a base for their operations. His dislike for Israel was well known, and he may have been seeking a way to embarrass his adversary. A successful Israeli commando raid freed nearly all of the hostages; as revenge, Amin had hostage Dora Bloch murdered.

Scottish Independence Movement of the 1970s

Scotland has been an administrative division of Great Britain since the early 1700s. Scottish nationalism once again became a significant political issue in the twentieth century, especially in the 1960s and 1970s. Oil was discovered during this period in the North Sea, giving Scots more confidence in their ability to maintain a strong economy independent of Britain. Calls for independence were heard in the mid-1970s general elections, and in 1974 the Scottish Nationalist Party won eleven of Scotland's seventy-two seats in Parliament.

In the novel, Idi Amin claims to be the "last rightful king of Scotland" and says that he is "the first man to ask the British government to end their oppression of Scotland." He sees himself as the liberator of Scotland, just as he feels that he has liberated Uganda from British rule. Amin's obsession with all things Scottish can be traced to his training with Scottish soldiers. In the novel, Garrigan also mentions that "an eccentric Scottish officer" during Amin's years as a young soldier dressed some of the members of the King's African Rifles corps in khaki kilts.

Critical Overview

Foden's award-winning first novel received high praise from critics for its fascinating topic as well as for the deft manner in which its author handled the story's ethical issues and the sometimes gruesome details surrounding the violent rule of Uganda's Idi Amin. Peter Wolfe, writing in the *St. Louis Post Dispatch*, calls the novel "stunning" and "surehanded," and according to Margaret Flanagan in *Booklist*, the novel is "packed with moral ambiguity [and] the dynamic narrative provides a vivid portrait of one of the most surrealistic despots in modern African history."

Idi Amin

Chris King, writing in *Newsday*, is not as enamored of Foden's narrative. King complains that, while many episodes including Amin are "hilarious," they eventually become predictable. Foden's use of childhood flashbacks "is a dubious narrative decision that weakens the satire," according to King. King compares the book to the novel *Forrest Gump*, in which "a fool has been superimposed unconvincingly over some very important history, trivializing everything he touches." What works in Winston Groom's novel does not work in Foden's novel, writes King, because Gump understood his limitations while Garrigan is simply "awash in existential self-pity."

Many reviewers have found Garrigan's character unlikable and confusing. In his review in The *Australian*, Tom Gilling calls Garrigan "a difficult figure to sympathize with or care about," one having "little sense of personality." Michael Upchurch, however, appreciates Garrigan's character and notes in the *New York Times Book Review* that "therein lies the admirable risk" Foden has taken in the novel. Merle Rubin in *The Christian Science Monitor* suggests that Foden has created in Garrigan a character whose weaknesses hit a little too close to home for some readers—"a well-meaning individual who becomes an accomplice to evil."

Because the novel includes historical figures as characters, many critics have focused on Foden's accuracy and on his use of history in a book that is not presented as a factual account. In a review in *History Today*, Richard Rathbone praises Foden for his careful research that makes the book "terrifying real." Rathbone views the book as not only an entertaining read but also "a brilliant analysis of the essence of a brutal dictator." Upchurch admires how the novel's fictional and historical aspects blend smoothly even though the novel "occasionally carries the whiff of the library stacks" and heavily reflects the journalistic background of its author. However, Christopher Hess argues in the *Austin Chronicle* that, by the second half of the novel, the plot is forced into "easy devices and contrived twists" by the excessive use of historical fact.

Considering the book as a fictional memoir, David Haynes, writing in the *Minneapolis Star Tribune*, lauds the use of realistic news clippings and journal entries that help Foden's audience "believe that what we are reading really happened." However convincing much of Foden's novel may be, though, Haynes is less enthusiastic about whether Garrigan's character is truly a man who would not leave Uganda when the going got tough. For the novel to work completely, Haynes argues, Foden must create a believable scenario in which Garrigan's utter naïveté leads him to remain in Uganda, but he does not succeed in this. "Foden can't quite create a convincing balance between Garrigan's guilelessness and the character's well-informed, historically accurate telling of the story," he asserts.

Many critics have praised Foden's novel for its similarities to the works of other Western authors famous for writing about Africa. Wolfe sees the influence of Graham Greene in the novel, as it is filled with corrupt leaders and spies and takes place in the third world. A number of reviewers have compared the novel with those of Joseph Conrad. *Kirkus Reviews* finds "Conradian tones" in the novel and Hess calls Garrigan's experiences in the novel "Conradesque."

Reviews such as one that appeared in *Publishers Weekly* have noted the satirical qualities of the novel. Walter Abish, writing for the *Los Angeles Times*, associates Foden's writing style with the satirical and farcical style of Evelyn Waugh's novels. "The introspective Garrigan experiences a failure of nerve that Waugh used with great relish," he notes. Gilling also sees similarities between Waugh and Foden but believes that Foden "has a more solemn purpose" in his work.

Criticism

Susan Sanderson

Sanderson holds a Master of Fine Arts degree in fiction writing and is an independent writer who has lived in Africa. In this essay, Sanderson examines Nicholas Garrigan's attempts to cut himself off from the events and people around him in The Last King of Scotland.

In Giles Foden's novel *The Last King of Scotland*, Nicholas Garrigan is a man feverishly contradicting British poet John Donne's often quoted line, "no man is an island entire of itself." Garrigan is an isolated man with few close friends and little contact with his family. Many of his attempts to reach out to another person are either ill-timed or ill-advised, especially his relationship with Idi Amin, the ruthless but childlike dictator of Uganda. Death is all around Garrigan, yet he refuses to believe this, building a wall between himself and reality.

While Garrigan does not openly say that he seeks to be as untouched as an island, Foden indirectly alludes to Donne's famous "island" metaphor by having Garrigan's father use another famous line from the same paragraph in Donne as a joke. "Ask not for whom the Bell's tolls, it tolls for you," jokes Garrigan's father, referring to a popular brand of whiskey. Given the events of the novel, the full quote from Donne is particularly applicable to Garrigan's circumstances:

> No man is an island entire of itself; every man is a piece of the continent, a part of the main. Any man's death diminishes me because I am involved in mankind; and therefore never send to know for whom the bell tolls; it tolls for thee.

Garrigan is a man who has sought to cut himself off and not be "a part of the main." While serving as Amin's personal physician, he is aware of the atrocities Amin perpetrates. His response after a particularly horrific period is to "build a castle" within himself and make himself "impregnable." This is why he cannot ever "*be useful*," as he so desperately desires; to be useful one must typically live among those one wishes to help.

Through his actions, Garrigan tries to ignore the truth in Donne's statement that "any man's death diminishes me because I am involved in mankind." No matter how hard he struggles against attachment, Garrigan is not completely disassociated from the deaths Amin causes. Each one of those deaths *does* diminish him in some way, which is why, by the end of the novel, Garrigan is a physical, psychological, and spiritual wreck.

Garrigan's past and present tell the story of a man desperate to avoid meaningful connections. His childhood was spent as the son of a solemn and emotionally dead Presbyterian minister and his wife. In addition to his father being disappointed that he would not practice general medicine in Scotland, Garrigan remembers his father condemning him to a life filled with predestined misery. "You are as set for damnation as a rat in trap," says his father. Religion covered the family like "fine soot," remembers Garrigan, giving his childhood a dark and dusty image. The warmest relationship the young Garrigan seems to have developed was with his pet donkey, Fred, who eventually died from eating too many grass cuttings.

As an adult, Garrigan has not come to terms with his parents and their treatment of him. He is working at the Ugandan rural clinic when he learns of his father's death. His mother's death soon follows, but he does not fly to Scotland to be with his family on either occasion. Looking back on this, Garrigan suspects that something in him "had begun to close down."

This is not to say that Garrigan has no feelings and does not make any connections with the people around him, but simply that, when he does connect with another person, it is temporary and not as deep as he had thought. Most of the people he gets to know well either leave suddenly or die. For example, he falls in love with Sara Zach, the Israeli physician at the clinic, but is clueless about her true purpose for being in Uganda. Sara's actions are not typically those of a doctor: she takes notes during one of Amin's rallies in Mbarara; her shortwave radio not only receives broadcasts but can also transmit messages; and she spends an inordinate amount of time with an Israeli road-building crew.

One day Sara is gone, her bungalow bearing signs of hurried packing. The next time Garrigan hears from her is three years later, when she is a colonel with Israel's armed forces. A hijacked plane is sitting on the runway at Entebbe, and she calls to ask Garrigan if he will try to persuade Amin to help free the hostages. Garrigan refuses but realizes that she was probably a spy for the Israelis while working at the clinic. He realizes that he never did know her as well as he had previously thought.

For him to remain an untouched island, Garrigan must move through the novel like the proverbial monkey who can hear no evil. Early in the novel, his ears become so clogged that he has trouble hearing and is convinced that he has an infection in need of antibiotics. Sara correctly diagnoses the problem as a blockage and cleans out Garrigan's ears. In this case, she literally opens her lover's ears; later, she attempts to open his ears figuratively when she tells him "things will go badly here" and pleads with him to leave Uganda. He dismisses her concerns and ignores all of the signs around him that Amin's despotic rule will lead to certain death. Amin expels Indians, Asians, and Israelis from the country, and he makes anti-Semitic comments, yet Garrigan remains oblivious. In retrospect, he realizes that the phrase "*I should have known*" sums up his life.

Garrigan's other primary relationship in the novel is with Idi Amin. His affinity for Amin at first appears to be a genuine antidote to what has been missing from his previous relationships. Their conversations at first seem genuine, but upon further examination it is apparent that the Scottish physician is only fooling himself. Garrigan's relationship with Amin depends upon his ability to deny the havoc Amin creates all around him.

> His response after a particularly horrific period is to 'build a castle' within himself and make himself 'impregnable.'"

Garrigan is gradually drawn into Amin's world, but the connection he makes with Amin is that of an observer who gets trapped, not that of a friend. When new to Uganda, Garrigan hears Amin announce that he is "the last rightful King of Scotland" and thinks this may have some "special relevance" for himself, "as if I were his subject," he remembers. After Garrigan successfully treats Amin for gastrointestinal distress, the two go out on the town as if they were old college chums. By the time most of the world's nations have condemned Amin for his brutality and bizarre behavior, Garrigan is deeply involved with him. Even while agreeing with the West German Chancellor that a particular Amin statement is "an expression of mental derangement," Garrigan pursues his fascination with the Ugandan ruler. "My life had already fallen into a pattern that concentrated on Amin. The closer I got to him, the fewer my illusions about him—and still I stayed, more fascinated than frightened," recalls Garrigan.

To continue living in Uganda under Amin's rule, Garrigan creates a fantasy world for himself—something with which he has experience. For example, while working at the rural clinic, he and Sara take in a friend's younger brother, Gugu, who is orphaned as a result of the fighting surrounding the town. Meanwhile, Garrigan is oblivious to the war raging around him and to the fact that the clinic and his relationship with Sara are "going downhill." Looking back on this period in his life, Garrigan admits that he "had been using Gugu to live out some kind of fantasy family life." His association with Amin soon becomes a similar fantasy, and Garrigan is able to convince himself when he hears of the atrocities that they are exaggerated. Only when he begins to consider seriously the possibility of killing Amin, as requested by a British official, does Garrigan make the decision to leave Uganda. What finally provokes him to wake up and leave is the realization "that [he] had become

> **When Garrigan describes other people in the first person, he is seeing them through his own filter of the world. . . ."**

enough like Amin to contemplate killing him for the sheer pleasure of it."

When Garrigan finally escapes Uganda and arrives in London, it is not to his sister or close friends that he returns. An uncle has bequeathed to Garrigan a small cottage on a tiny island in an isolated corner of Scotland, and that is where he finds shelter from the storms of the previous eight years. By literally moving to an island, Garrigan believes that he has, at last, placed himself apart from humanity. Foden, though, has other plans for the Scottish doctor. Just as Garrigan finishes writing his memoir of horror, he receives a phone call from Amin, ensconced in Saudi Arabia but still able to contact his former personal physician. Garrigan, despite his best efforts, discovers that he still "is a piece of the continent, a part of the main," as Donne writes, very much connected to the hundreds of thousands who have died in Uganda.

Source: Susan Sanderson, Critical Essay on *The Last King of Scotland*, in *Novels for Students*, The Gale Group, 2002.

Douglas Dupler

Dupler has published numerous essays and has taught college English. In this essay, Dupler looks at how the concept of identity plays a central role in a novel with a postcolonial setting.

Postcolonial studies has arisen as a literary field as scholars think about the changes occurring in the cultures and individuals that have become free of British colonial rule. Postcolonial studies concerns itself with the analysis of the nationalism and politics that brought about colonial rule and then dismantled it. The field also considers differences between people that led to concepts like nationalism; how these differences are created and sustained by cultures and individuals; and how they become conflicts. In the postcolonial world, first and third world

cultures often collide, and in these conditions, racial and gender differences are often magnified as well. The concept of *identity* is a major consideration in postcolonial studies because the ways in which people identify themselves and their world also determine what differences they might have with others. There is personal identity, which is the way individuals see themselves, and cultural identity, which are ideas of identity given to individuals by their societies. Identity is central to Giles Foden's novel, *The Last King of Scotland*. This novel is positioned as a postcolonial novel, being set amidst the chaos of political change in the ex-British African country, Uganda, showing the collision of politics, cultures, and individuals. In the midst of this postcolonial setting, the complex issue of identity, both personal and cultural, underlies and influences the characters and their stories.

Nationalism is a form of cultural identity and can impose identities upon individuals. The concept of nationalism is a major influence for the characters in *The Last King of Scotland*. Early in the story, Nicholas Garrigan, the main character, notices a sign that says, in large print, "YOUR COUNTRY IS YOUR FAMILY," foreshadowing the intricate manner in which all the characters relate with the cultures they are from. Garrigan identifies strongly with his own country of Scotland; his first-person narrative makes it clear throughout that he is Scottish and that being such implies certain traits and behaviors. Early on, he tells the reader that he is in "an inappropriately northern place to embark upon this northern tale," making clear that although he is writing of Africa, he is located, literally and figuratively, in Scotland. Garrigan also remarks that he was "brought up according to the strictest precepts," or, in other words, his culture told him specific ways to act and perceive. In tough times, Garrigan tells himself that he must "cultivate the discipline of his native land," appealing to his national identity when his personal one is uncertain.

Nationalism as identity can be subtle in its effects. Among people from the United Kingdom, Garrigan makes it clear that he is Scottish and quite different from the English. At one point, Garrigan notes that he is "missing Britain," but quickly corrects himself by adding, "Or Scotland. Home." From a native Ugandan's standpoint, this correction would seem meaningless; there would be little difference between an English person and a Scottish one. Garrigan shows this also, when many of the Africans he meets consider him English, until he informs them otherwise.

Garrigan identifies other people he meets in the story by immediately pointing out their national identities, whether it is the South African Freddy Swanepoel, the Israeli Sara Zach, the many native Africans he meets, or his fellow British working in Uganda. And like Garrigan, other characters also identify with nationalistic markers. In their first major conversation, Sara Zach identifies Garrigan as Scottish, telling him, "I never met a Scot before." Garrigan replies that he is a "typical example" of a Scottish person, choosing cultural identity over an individual one. However, when pressed to explain himself, Garrigan has trouble defining what a typical Scottish person would be like, showing confusion about his own self-concept. His best reply is that being Scottish means that he likes football, rugby, and drinking. Sara Zach thinks this idea is absurd, and then resorts to her own nationalistic idea that Israeli men would identify themselves very differently. Nationalism permeates even the small moments between characters of the book; the other doctors with whom Garrigan works view him as a "Scottish doctor," a seemingly insignificant but telling perception.

Garrigan's personal identity is a complex one. While he frequently mentions his personal connection to Scotland, he can't help but think of his father, who dies while Garrigan is in Africa. He describes his father as a strict Presbyterian minister who had a particular view of the world and of Garrigan. One of Garrigan's earliest memories is of his father telling him that he is "set for damnation," and Garrigan has gone against his father's advice by moving to Africa. Garrigan has memories of times when he did not receive enough attention from his father, and also thinks of his father in close moments with Idi Amin, such as when Amin is sick in bed and during Amin's wedding. When Garrigan is very ill with a fever and having a crisis, he dreamily recalls his last conversation with his father, who told him to "minimize the harm" he could do in the world. Garrigan pleads out loud to his father to understand him, verbalizing his feelings that he has been disapproved of by a father who is no longer there. Garrigan has internalized his father's disapproving view of him, and this faulty self-concept affects him deeply, robbing him of the integrity needed to stand up to the corruption of the dictator Amin.

Garrigan hardly mentions his mother at all, except to note that she "died of grief" when his father passed away. Not only Garrigan's mother, but all the important women to Garrigan in the novel are vague to him and to the reader. Garrigan seems

What Do I Read Next?

- First published in 1902, Joseph Conrad's *Heart of Darkness* was the model for Francis Ford Coppola's movie *Apocalypse Now*. In *Heart of Darkness*, an ivory company assigns Marlow the task of finding a stranded riverboat in the Belgian Congo and bringing back the company's top representative, whose behavior is becoming erratic. Marlow witnesses horrors and brutalities he could never have imagined.

- Foden's second novel is *Ladysmith* (2000). It tells the story of the South African town of Ladysmith, its residents, and how they survive a four-month siege by Boer forces. The novel is based partly on the letters of Foden's great-grandfather, a British soldier in South Africa at the end of the nineteenth century.

- Critics have compared *The Last King of Scotland* to the writings of British author Graham Greene. In 1961, Greene published *A Burnt-Out Case*, the tale of a spiritually dead man who reconnects with himself by living at a leper colony in the Belgian Congo.

- Foden's writing style has also been compared to that of Evelyn Waugh, an author known for his satirical wit. In his 1938 novel *Scoop*, Waugh tells the humorous story of journalist William Boot's trip to a fictional African country to cover a nonexistent revolution. Boot has no experience as a war correspondent but manages to get a story.

incapable of understanding women in the story beyond superficial description. Garrigan has a relationship with Sara Zach that is filled with empty conversation, and he knows her so little that only after she is gone does he realize that she was a spy. Garrigan also attempts to get to know Marina Perkins, the ambassador's wife, but completely misreads her and alienates her with a try at seduction. Later in the story, he is surprised to find out that she is having an affair, which upsets him greatly.

Women preparing food in Kampala, Uganda, where the novel is set

There are revealing differences in how Garrigan presents European and African characters in the story. The European characters tend to be shadowy, strange, and untrustworthy. The English are either spies attempting to manipulate the government of Uganda behind the scenes, such as Nigel Stone and Major Weir, or depressed bureaucrats stuck between the two worlds of England and Africa, like Doctor Merrit and his wife. Sara Zach is an Israeli spy who deceived Garrigan. Freddy Swanepoel, a white South African, is a shady character with underworld connections. Marina Perkins is unpredictable and carrying out a clandestine affair. There is another white character who is briefly but strongly introduced in the book, Anglo-Steve (or, English Steve). This man has gone all the way into Africa, disappearing to live in the bush and believed to be crazy. When Garrigan identifies himself as sharing European heritage, but views all other Europeans as strange, misplaced characters, he undermines his image of himself. This can also be seen the other way around: Garrigan, having a shaky image of himself, projects questionable images of the people he most closely associates with. Hence the problems in completely understanding identity. Garrigan seems to understand this complexity of identity when he states early on, "Can you tell the truth when you are talking to yourself?"

Just as there is a trend in the way Garrigan identifies European characters, he also shows patterns when describing African characters. Early in the story, on his trip to Mbarara through the countryside of Uganda, his bus ride is interrupted by soldiers who harass the passengers. Garrigan backs down to a soldier's demands for money, while a Kenyan man stands up to them and pays the price by getting hurt. Garrigan describes this African man as brave and "dignified," and feels "ashamed" and "embarrassment" when thinking of himself in comparison. This scene shows many of the feelings that Garrigan has for Africans throughout the book. They are either faceless soldiers performing inhuman violence that fills him with fear, or strong and dignified people that make him feel inferior.

Nowhere is this paradoxical view of Africans more apparent than in the way Garrigan views Idi Amin. Amin fills him with fear, but also attracts him with many qualities Garrigan admires. In the beginning of the story, Garrigan finds that he "couldn't say no" to Amin's personality, which is "punish or reward." Time and again in the story, Garrigan is witness to Amin's violence as well as to his brilliance in manipulating people and events.

Garrigan's relationship with Amin is complicated by the fact that it is a reversal of the long-ingrained identities created by colonialism. In the past, the differences between Europeans and Africans were also the differences between the powerful and the subordinated. Amin is a masterful manipulator of people because he understands these subtle identity problems and plays upon them. In calling himself the "last king of Scotland," he deftly places himself between Garrigan and England, and also makes himself both a sympathizer and superior to Garrigan.

When analyzing identity issues, the very way in which this story is told presents complexities. When Garrigan describes other people in the first person, he is seeing them through his own filter of the world; thus his descriptions of them may say just as much about Garrigan and his culture as they do about the other people and their cultures. The field of postcolonial studies has addressed this complex issue of identity in narrative. Postcolonial studies has asserted that the way identities are formed, both personal and national, helped shape and propel colonialism. Colonialism spread because of the way in which a dominating culture identifies with the culture being dominated. Dominant cultures create attractive images of the other culture. The subordinate culture becomes a figment of the dominant culture's imagination, and individuals of the other race and culture have certain useful identities impressed upon them. These are never real, but these images create certain behaviors. For example, part of the allure for the British people who colonized Africa was the idea that in Africa they could recover a forgotten or better part of themselves. Tired, depressed bureaucrats in worn-out cities could imagine the other culture as a place of fertility and strength, of endless opportunity, of vitality that they themselves had used up. This image of Africa differed greatly from the real thing, but it was the image that took them there, that propelled the spread of colonialism.

This imagining of the African culture shows up in Garrigan. He recalls dream images he had as a child of a place with "a sensuous geography of temples and jungles." Garrigan wonders about what had led to all his problems in Africa, his "malignant destiny," and then mentions the "special vision of myself that took me there in the first place." Reality for Garrigan eventually differs from his imagination. When Garrigan is confronted by the harsh situation of warfare, he thinks of the English actor Michael Caine in a movie about Africa— another deeply ingrained image that is confronted by the real image. Garrigan says that the "old vision of Africa I'd had, the same that led me there and doomed me: it returns like a specter," or an unreal image that haunts him. Garrigan also acknowledges that his problem is that "the world doesn't deliver what I seek." Even some of the Africans in the book understand the identity that has been put upon them by Europeans. Waziri, a Ugandan, asks Garrigan if he wants to see "the real Africa," with a "slight mocking tone in his voice." This real vision of Africa turns out to be a superstitious dance that is put on "for the tourists."

Garrigan also identifies with the colonial myth of the tired, effete European going to a land of vitality and strength. On his first day in Africa, when Garrigan sees soldiers, he states, "I was conscious of my nakedness, of my pale, presbyter's face . . . my narrow chest . . . and my long, thin legs." This is in stark contrast to the way Garrigan describes his own symbol of Africa, Amin, who has "a quality of naked, visceral attraction." Garrigan is fascinated by Amin's "physically dominating" presence which "radiated a barely restrained energy." Beside Amin, Garrigan becomes weak and filled with "hopeless perplexity." In a revealing summary of his first meeting with the dictator, Garrigan invests a sentence with double meaning when he writes, "I had no way of getting back myself." He is talking about going home, but also speaking of losing himself and his own identity when confronted by the powerful vision of Amin. Garrigan describes Amin as appearing like "a being out of a Greek myth." This is interesting because myths are stories that cultures tell to define themselves and their place in the world, or stories told to define identity. For Garrigan, Amin represents an identity that renders him powerless because it plays upon the deepest stories he knows. Other Europeans share this mythology of Africa. Swanepoel says to Garrigan, "we all come back here," because Africa is the "[c]radle of the human race!" By including Garrigan as "we," he is identifying with him as a person sharing European heritage, as well as sharing the common myth of Africa as a place of primal vitality that contains something that must be recovered.

Garrigan's identity problems take their toll. Because Garrigan doesn't understand the complexities of identity as well as Amin and is confused about his own personal and cultural identity, he becomes susceptible to this dictator and eventually under his control. In the end, he is forced to look back upon his life in Africa from a vantage point of exile on an island in Scotland. His disapproving and confused self-identity have come true; his identity problems created problems with his integrity that consume him, and he is forced to rewrite his story to come to terms with his new identity.

Source: Douglas Dupler, Critical Essay on *The Last King of Scotland*, in *Novels for Students*, The Gale Group, 2002.

Sources

Abish, Walter, "Guess Who's Coming to Dinner?," in *Los Angeles Times*, January 10, 1999, p. 8.

Flanagan, Margaret, "The Last King of Scotland," in *Booklist*, Vol. 95, No. 8, p. 726.

Gilling, Tom, "Buffoon Defies Reality," in *Australian*, July 24, 1998, p. 11.

Haynes, David, "Quirkily Written First Novel Traces the Rise and Fall of Idi Amin as Uganda's Dictator," in *Minneapolis Star Tribune*, January 24, 1999, p. 16F.

Hess, Christopher, "The Last King of Scotland: A Novel," in *Austin Chronicle*, March 29, 1999.

"An Interview with Giles Foden," in *Boldtype*, http://www.randomhouse.com/boldtype/1298/foden/interview.html (last accessed February, 2002).

King, Chris, "Into Africa," in *Newsday*, November 8, 1998, p. B12.

Rathbone, Richard, "The Last King of Scotland," in *History Today*, Vol. 48, No. 7, July 1998, p. 60–62.

Review of *The Last King of Scotland*, in *Kirkus Reviews*, September 1999.

Review of *The Last King of Scotland*, in *Publishers Weekly*, October 19, 1998.

Rubin, Merle, "Charisma Overwhelms a Good Man's Revulsion," in *Christian Science Monitor*, Vol. 91, No. 16, p. 20.

Upchurch, Michael, "President for Life," in *New York Times Book Review*, November 15, 1998.

Wolfe, Peter, "Novelist Refuses to Sell Idi Amin Short," in *St. Louis Post-Dispatch*, November 22, 1998, p. D5.

Further Reading

Hanson, Thor, *The Impenetrable Forest*, iUniverse.com, 2000.
  In this photograph-filled book, Hanson tells how he lived in Uganda's Impenetrable Forest, working with local guides and trackers to develop a tourism program in the new national park.

Isegawa, Moses, *Abyssinian Chronicles*, Knopf, 2000.
  In this Ugandan epic set during the 1960s and 1970s, Isegawa tells the story of an extended family and a divided country. Mugezi, the book's narrator, remembers how he survived life in Idi Amin's Uganda.

Maier, Karl, *Into the House of the Ancestors: Inside the New Africa*, John Wiley and Sons, 1997.
  Maier draws on his ten years traveling throughout Africa to bring the news of Africans reviving and expanding upon their cultures' rich traditions. The book is based on hundreds of interviews and combines history with contemporary reporting.

Mutibwa, Phares, *Uganda since Independence: A Story of Unfulfilled Hopes*, Africa World Press, Inc., 1992.
  Mutibwa has written an analysis of the country under President Yoweri Museveni—calmer than the preceding twenty years but not without its problems.

Ofcansky, Thomas, *Uganda: Tarnished Pearl of Africa*, Westview Press, 1996.
  In this book, Ofcansky, an analyst for the United States Department of Defense, first gives a brief history of Uganda before its 1962 independence from Britain. He concentrates on the period between 1962 and 1994, examining Uganda's politics, culture, economy, and foreign policy.

Looking Backward: 2000–1887

Looking Backward: 2000–1887, published in the United States in 1888, created an international sensation associated with very few other books in history. The author, Edward Bellamy, although a prolific writer of short stories, essays, and novels, is remembered almost solely for this utopian novel. The premise of the story is that Julian West, a privileged citizen of 1887 Boston, awakes from a 113-year trance-induced sleep to discover that the majority of the world enjoys peace, prosperity, and equality.

Bellamy, a sensitive man keenly aware of the injustices and inequities of nineteenth-century culture, uses *Looking Backward* to espouse his views on social and economic reform. There is the barest of plots, little character development, and virtually no action. The book consists almost entirely of conversations between West and his hosts that reveal how the "perfect" society works. Despite the literary flaws, the strength of Bellamy's ideas attracted a worldwide audience. Not only his nationalized system of labor and commerce, but also his technological predictions and his attempt to treat women equally stirred great debate. Within a few years after its publication, there were over 160 "Bellamy Clubs" around the United States promoting the Nationalism that Bellamy proposed.

Aligned with the Populist party, the Nationalist movement affected legislation and labor relations until its demise during the Spanish-American War. By 1900, the book had been translated into more than twenty languages and had sold more

Edward Bellamy

1888

Edward Bellamy

copies than any other American book except *Uncle Tom's Cabin*. It was the second book to sell over a million copies. Dozens of other utopian novels followed in its wake, but social commentators continue to rank *Looking Backward* as second only to Karl Marx's *Das Kapital* in world influence.

Author Biography

Born on March 26, 1850, in Chicopee Falls, Massachusetts, Edward Bellamy was the third son of a Baptist minister and a Calvinist mother. He came from a long line of New England families going back two centuries. His outspoken father, Reverend Rufus King Bellamy, and his well-educated mother, Maria Putnam, taught him the morality, work ethic, and social justice that marked his works. Although Bellamy would espouse no religious beliefs in later life, he maintained the tenets of optimism, humanitarianism, and sense of commitment that he learned in childhood.

Bellamy's birthplace was a mill town where he observed the disparity between the harshness of life for the laborers and the decadence of the wealthy. By age ten, he had started writing essays on social reform. At the age of seventeen, after fail-

ing to pass the physical examination for entrance into West Point, Bellamy took up studies at Union College in Schenectady, New York. He also studied in Germany for a year and observed the desperation of urban life throughout his European travels. He passed the bar exam with distinction in 1871. However, Bellamy was so disillusioned when his first and only case required him to evict a widow, that he immediately abandoned the law to become a newspaper editor.

Bellamy married Emma Sanderson in 1882, and they had two children: a son, Paul, in 1884 and a daughter, Marion, in 1886. Forced by ill health to give up his editorial career, Bellamy devoted himself to writing. By 1888, he had published 30 short stories in prominent magazines and four novels. His sensitive awareness of the social problems of his times, including strikes, destitute tenement life, and exploitative greed, drove him to write *Looking Backward* in an effort to bring about reforms. This book, though not a skilled literary work, gained international fame and influence. "Bellamy Clubs" sprang up across the country as people engaged in debate over social issues. While the accompanying political movement did not last much beyond 1895, many attitudes and laws were changed forever in American life.

From that point on, Bellamy was primarily occupied by lecture tours and other speaking engagements. In 1891, he founded a Boston newspaper, the *New Nation* to be his mouthpiece, but increasing illness forced him to suspend publication before long. However, in response to criticism of *Looking Backward*, Bellamy published a sequel entitled *Equality* in 1897. This novel, with even less plot and more theory than its predecessor, was not well received and had little impact. By the end of his career, Bellamy had written over 500 articles and was recognized for his psychological and speculative short stories and novels. He died of complications of tuberculosis and digestive disorders on May 22, 1898.

Plot Summary

Chapters One–Two

The first two chapters of *Looking Backward* are used to introduce the main character and narrator, Julian West. Although he addresses the audience in the year 2000, he reveals that he was born in 1857. He follows that announcement with an explanation of the culture of the late nineteenth century, using an analogy in which he compares the social structure to that of a coach being pulled by the masses while certain people sit on top. He admits that, as a member of the privileged class of Boston society, he was one of those riding instead of pulling the coach. His story begins in 1887 when he is thirty years old and planning to marry a wealthy woman named Edith Bartlett. Their wedding is delayed because multiple labor strikes impede construction of their new house. A chronic insomniac distressed by these circumstances, West calls upon a mesmerist to induce sleep with a trance. Doctor Pillsbury instructs his servant to visit West's underground bed chamber, built to keep out disturbing noises, and wake him the next morning.

Media Adaptations

- *Looking Backward* has been recorded in unabridged form by Blackstone Audiobooks. It is available for both rental and purchase at http://www.blackstoneaudio.com

Chapters Three–Seven

West awakens 113 years later. His chamber is discovered by Dr. Leete and his daughter, Edith, while inspecting a construction site in their back yard. It seems that his house burned down, killing his servant, and leaving others to assume that he perished in the fire. West finds it hard to believe that it is the year 2000 until he goes up to the house-top and sees familiar landmarks in a Boston that has changed very much. Dr. Leete explains that there is no longer any private commerce, for all people work in the Industrial Army commanded by the government. The nation is the sole capitalist and there are no more states, political parties, or politicians. Leete claims that there is no motive to be corrupt and no profit or misuse of power possible. All citizens work three years in manual labor, then choose a career.

Chapters Eight–Twelve

On the second day, West awakens early, confused and distressed. He takes a walk through Boston and fears losing his mind. But Edith comforts and calms him. He begins asking questions again, based on the changes he saw in the streets. He learns that no money is used, for there is an entirely different system for the distribution of goods. Instead, people use credit cards for transactions, and each citizen is given the same amount of credit to spend. Edith takes him shopping at the neighborhood store, where all goods are samples and the same as that in every other ward. Orders are placed and the actual item is immediately sent to the buyer's house. Upon their return, Edith introduces him to their piped-in music. The conversation with Dr. Leete turns to matters of inheritance, housekeeping done by the public, and the practice of

medicine. Then the system of apprenticeships, grades, and ranks in the Industrial Army are explained, as well as the care of those who, because of infirmity, cannot work.

Chapters Thirteen–Fifteen

Each day, West is introduced to new facets of contemporary culture. On the morning of the third day, he awakens to a musical alarm clock and has a strange dream about the Alhambra. His first conversation is about the trade system with other countries. Edith then takes him to their library where he reads Dickens. That evening, he takes his first trip to the community dining hall, using covered sidewalks in the rain. He discovers that, while home life is simple, public buildings are magnificent. Following dinner, the conversation is an explanation of the publishing system, the creation of periodicals by subscription, and the election of editors.

Chapters Sixteen–Eighteen

West pays a visit on the fourth day to the central warehouse with Dr. Leete. He is told that he will be given a position as a lecturer on the nineteenth century at the university. The conversation turns to the system of government and the election of the president and other officials. He also learns about the pursuits of retirement after the age of forty-five, and the fact that there are no professional sports.

Chapters Nineteen–Twenty

On a morning walk on the fifth day, West notices that the state prison is gone. This discovery leads to a conversation that explains the legal system of the year 2000. There are no jails because the criminally inclined are treated in hospitals. There also is no lying, no lawyers or judges, no states, and no legislators. That afternoon, West visits his old chamber with Edith and tells her something about his former life.

Chapters Twenty-one–Twenty-three

For his tour on the sixth day, Dr. Leete takes West to the city's schools and colleges, and they discuss the free educational system available to citizens until they reach the age of twenty-one. West notices how healthy everyone appears in this improved world. The after-dinner conversation covers the state of business and the national wealth. That evening, West tries to no avail to extract from Edith a secret he knows she is keeping from him.

Chapters Twenty-four–Twenty-seven

After sharing papers from his own time with Dr. Leete, West learns that the labor parties gave way to a benevolent national party that supervises all activities. He then asks about the place of women in society and learns that they are also in the Industrial Army. However, they have segregated jobs and have no chance for the highest positions of leadership. Nonetheless, they are given the same credits as men, so they are in no way dependent upon a husband for support. Consequently, marriages are all "love matches," with the women being most attracted to the men with the highest work ethic and social conscience. The seventh day being a Sunday, West inquires about church services and learns that one can listen to a sermon broadcast to the homes. A lengthy sermon follows that praises the changes of the twentieth century and declares that society is on the verge of heaven itself. That afternoon, West confesses his love for Edith and is gratified to find that she returns his affections. He then learns that she is the great-granddaughter of his fiancée in 1887.

Chapter Twenty-eight

West awakens the next day to find himself back in his bedchamber in 1887. Stunned by the change, he wanders around the streets of Boston and is appalled by what he sees. Eventually, he makes his way to his fiancée's house, where he interrupts an elaborate dinner. When he tries to explain his revulsion to the 1887 state of affairs, the guests are angered and start to throw him out. At that point, he really wakes up to find himself back in the year 2000. The novel ends with an expression of his tremendous gratitude for his good fortune at being in the "golden century."

Characters

Edith Bartlett

Julian West's fiancée in the nineteenth century. She is from a wealthy family and becomes the great-grandmother of Edith Leete.

Mr. Barton

A "telephone" preacher, his lengthy sermon is the author's way of including a discourse on morality.

Doctor Leete

Julian West wakes up from his 113-year trance in the home of Doctor Leete and his family. Doctor Leete then becomes West's main source of information about society in the year 2000. This information is conveyed almost exclusively in long conversations. Conveniently, Dr. Leete is retired, so he has plenty of time to spend with West, and, as a physician, is critical to the plot in that he is able to bring West out of his trance. Critics wonder that Dr. Leete has such a thorough knowledge of all aspects of the workings of his culture.

Edith Leete

The daughter of Doctor Leete, Edith is named after her great-grandmother, Edith Bartlett, and has a great affinity for this ancestor. She keeps this information a secret from West because she wants to win his affection on her own and not as a replication of the nineteenth-century Edith. Nonetheless, she believes that she may be a reincarnation of her great-grandmother so that the first Edith can fulfill her commitment to West. Edith Leete instantly falls in love with West and is often his companion and guide.

Mrs. Leete

The wife of Doctor Leete and the mother of Edith, Mrs. Leete makes only a few brief appearances in the novel. Her major role is to tell West about the connection to Edith Bartlett.

Doctor Pillsbury

A mesmerist and "Professor of Animal Magnetism." Because Pillsbury leaves Boston permanently for New Orleans on the night he places West into a sleep-inducing trance, he is not available to tell anyone about West's subterranean chamber when West's house burns down. Consequently, West is assumed dead and not found for 113 years.

Sawyer

Described by West as his "faithful servant," Sawyer was taught how to awaken West from Dr. Pillsbury's trances. It is assumed that Sawyer perished in the fire that destroyed West's house. Since only Sawyer and Pillsbury knew about West's basement bedroom, and Pillsbury had left town, there was no one to tell rescuers where to find West.

Julian West

The narrator of the novel, Julian West is a thirty-year-old man of means in 1887 Boston. He has no family but is engaged to an upper-class woman named Edith Bartlett. Their marriage awaits the completion of their new house. A severe insomniac, West sleeps in an underground bedroom to keep out noise and often solicits the assistance of a mesmerist, Dr. Pillsbury, to put him to sleep. Only Pillsbury and West's servant, Sawyer, know of the existence of this chamber. By coincidence, Pillsbury leaves town the night he puts West into a deep trance, which is the same night that West's house burns down and Sawyer dies in the fire. Consequently, West remains in his trance for 113 years until he is discovered by the Leete family. Thus begins his new life in Boston in the year 2000. His description of what he sees and learns in the first week is the story of the novel. He finds himself in a socialist utopia that seemingly has solved all the problems of the world he knew in 1887. He also falls in love with Edith Leete, who turns out to be the great-granddaughter of his previous fiancée, Edith Bartlett.

Themes

Alienation

Julian West experiences time travel, not space travel, so he does not awaken to a world of aliens. Nonetheless, he finds himself in a different world, for the Boston of 2000 is as foreign to him as another planet might have been. Nationalism has transformed America into a culture foreign to that which West knew in his own time. He feels alienated as all strangers do and asks Edith, "Has it never occurred to you that my position is so much more utterly alone than any human being's ever was before that a new word is really needed to describe it?" He then calls himself a "strange uncanny being, a stranded creature of an unknown sea." But in his dream that takes him back to the nineteenth century, he realizes that he has become estranged

Topics for Further Study

- Although the dream structure was only an intermittent part of the novel, the reader is momentarily led to believe that what is happening in the year 2000 is a dream. What other novels or films use the dream structure throughout (Examples: *The Wizard of Oz* and *The Family Man*)?

- Make a list of the developments, both technological and social, that Bellamy predicts. Note those that have come to pass in some form or another. Why did his other predictions fail to come true?

- Compare Bellamy's proposed economic and governmental system to that of communism. What are the similarities? What are the differences?

- How would you rewrite this story to make it a better and more interesting novel? What elements of composition (dialogue, action, characters, scenes, etc.) would you change or add to make this more a work of literature than a social commentary?

- Research the labor situation of the late 1800s and compare it to that of today. What improvements have been made? Name some laws that have been passed to protect the workers.

from that time, too. Knowing that Edith's love will cure his loneliness, he then gratefully embraces his new life in the better world of 2000.

Commerce

Related to the discussion of industry, Bellamy details the exchange of goods and services. He describes the local stores in each ward, the district warehouse, the delivery system and so on. Bellamy's theory was that if business were nationalized, the lack of competition would eliminate greed and the procurement of goods would be much simpler and more convenient.

Gender Roles

When Bellamy advocated equality for all citizens in *Looking Backward*, he included women. At a time when Susan B. Anthony and Elizabeth Cady Stanton were publishing *The Revolution*, the rights of women was certainly a topic that would concern a man like Bellamy. However, his forward thinking was cemented in nineteenth-century attitudes, and his attempt to be fair remains severely chauvinistic. Nonetheless, for a book written in 1888 to give women occupations outside the home and equal wages is truly striking.

Human Rights

Bellamy promotes the cause of human rights throughout his book. He summarizes his philosophy when Dr. Leete tells Julian West,

> The title of every man, woman, and child to the means of existence rests on no basis less plain, broad, and simple than the fact that they are fellows of one race—members of one human family.

It is accepted in Bellamy's 2000 that if you are a human being, regardless of nationality, race, disability, or gender, then you are entitled to full citizen benefits, an education, and freedom from want.

Industry and Labor

The first inquiry that Julian West makes about the new century in which he finds himself is "What solution, if any, have you found for the labor question? It was the Sphinx's riddle of the nineteenth century." The Industrial Revolution brought great wealth to a few tycoons and misery to many laborers. A utopian novel not only pictures how things could be, but also, by contrast, points out how bad things actually are. Bellamy's intent in *Looking Backward* was not just to dream of a better future but to cause his contemporaries to think about solutions for the problems of the times. Consequently, most of the book is devoted to discussions of the industrial "evolution," the Industrial army, the assignment of labor, and the equal distribution of wealth.

Innovation

Since Bellamy used a futuristic novel to promote his nationalistic ideals, he needed to make predictions about the year 2000 other than the social and economic state of affairs that were his primary concern. After all, nationalism would not appear successful if there were not also technological advances and other innovations resulting from the creative freedom his utopia allowed. Although Bellamy did not approach the accuracy or imagination of Aldous Huxley or Jules Verne, he made some amazing predictions, including credit cards, skyscrapers, piped-in music, speaker phones, and mass broadcasts.

Love

While *Looking Backward* is undeniably a treatise on social reform, Bellamy makes his long lecture palatable to the reader by weaving in a love story. On one level, the book is a romantic novel about a young man who loses love when he is strangely transferred from one century to another, only to find love again in the person of his sweetheart's namesake and great-granddaughter. Besides romantic love, this book espouses the theme of love for humankind. Bellamy believed that people are capable of sincerely caring about each other's welfare, and so, in his utopia, people willingly sacrifice personal gain for the benefit of all.

Morality

Among the many superior facets of Bellamy's fictional twentieth century is the morality of its citizens. In addition to being from a long line of New England preachers, Bellamy was extraordinarily sensitive to social justice issues. Naturally, then, his utopia is a culture of honesty and compassion. All citizens are equal, the disabled and the criminal are treated with dignity and understanding, and there is no greed or envy. Bellamy's idealistic book advocates that humans are basically good and decent and will subjugate individual desires for the common good.

Perfection

What distinguishes utopias from other imaginary places in literature is the supposed state of perfection achieved by government and society. Bellamy tries to sell his plan for perfection by repeatedly using phrases such as "perfect organization," "the system is certainly perfect," "a paradise of order, equity, and felicity," "heaven's vault," and "golden century." Furthermore, the question and answer dialogue device Bellamy uses allows West to present problems from the nineteenth century and always have them answered by the Leetes with the "simple" solutions that the superior twentieth century society has devised.

Relational Time

Julian West is not a time traveler in the sense of using a time machine or manipulating temporal physics to transport himself from age to age. Nor does he continue to age as he sleeps, as Rip Van

Winkle did. He stays thirty years old during his 113-year trance. Bellamy wanted to write a book that described wonderful possibilities for the future, and West's trance was the means Bellamy devised to move him from 1887 to 2000. For its time, *Looking Backward* was a futuristic novel. Now that time has passed 2000, it is a study in the relationship of time, civilization, and social/technological evolution.

Social Classes

In the first chapter of *Looking Backward*, Bellamy provides the parable of the coach as a means of describing the differences among the social classes of his time. Thus the heart of Bellamy's concern for society is established and carried throughout the book as he explains how a nationalized system of commerce and a moral concern for each other could eliminate class divisions. He reiterates the abuses of the class system at the end of the book when he dreams of returning to the nineteenth century and once again observes the disparity of life between the squalor of poverty and the excesses of wealth.

Socialism/Communism

Bellamy was very careful not to use the word "socialism" when espousing his philosophy of government. Nonetheless, the "Nationalist" movement he started with *Looking Backward* was very closely related to both socialism and communism because it gave the state control over commerce, espoused economic and social equality for all citizens, and featured centralized government.

Style

Allegory

One of the most famous elements of *Looking Backward* is the coach allegory in the first chapter. In an allegory, the writer tells a story, or parable, in which the people, things, or events described have a different meaning; that is, they are symbolic of the lesson or explanation the writer is giving. Bellamy compares the society of the nineteenth century to the image of a "prodigious coach" to which the masses are harnessed and driven by hunger, while the elite sit on top trying not to fall off and lose status.

Diction

Bellamy's diction—that is to say, his manner of writing and of the speech of his characters—is nineteenth-century prim and effusive. His book on the year 2000 might still be read as widely as George Orwell's *1984* if its language were easier for a modern audience to read. Other notable writers of Bellamy's time largely used ordinary language, but perhaps Bellamy's proper New England upbringing was too deeply imbedded in his manner of speaking for him to make the transition. It is ironic that a writer who wanted to save the masses could not write in the language they used.

Didacticism

Bellamy's style is didactic, in that *Looking Backward* was intended to be morally instructive. Although the reforms that led to his utopian society were in government and industry, it is obvious that Bellamy believed that the elimination of poverty and greed would result in a completely moral and humanitarian society. Dr. Leete tells Julian West, "The only coin current is the image of God, and that is good for all we have." In effect, then, Bellamy was telling people that they needed to live a morally sensitive life such as the one he described, and that his proposed reforms were a means to achieve this heaven on earth.

Genre

Looking Backward is a utopian novel. The first and perhaps greatest example of utopian literature is Plato's *Republic*. The term *utopian*, however, originated in 1516 with Sir Thomas More's book *Utopia*, which is about an imaginary place with an ideal political state and way of life. Since then, all such books have been called "utopian," and most use the structure of an adventurous traveler finding some remote country. The fact that there have been many different versions of utopia illustrates that one person's concept of paradise is not necessarily synonymous with that of another person. Further examples include: *New Atlantis*, Francis Bacon, 1627; *News from Nowhere*, William Morris, 1891; and *Lost Horizon*, James Hilton, 1934.

Point of View

Bellamy uses a first person point of view in *Looking Backward* so that the narration will seem more like a real story being told by someone who lived through the experience. Since Bellamy was espousing his own views on socio-economic issues, it was probably also easier for him to use "I" because the message of the story was coming from him, not the character.

Setting

Bellamy sets *Looking Backward* in Boston, but a Boston one would find hard to recognize because it is the city as Bellamy imagined it in the year 2000. Therefore, although the reader is given a recognizable name and a few familiar landmarks, the setting is a city of Bellamy's own creation. It includes magnificent public buildings, covered sidewalks during inclement weather, virtually no crime, and no chimneys. Material prosperity was evident because Bellamy needed to show the success that nationalism would bring.

Historical Context

Looking Backward was written in the late 1800s about the late 1800s. America had just been through two very difficult decades: the 1860s brought the War Between the States and Reconstruction; the 1870s saw an agricultural depression, a labor panic in 1873, and a major railroad strike in 1877. The power of corporate trusts and political machines seemed uncontrollable. Banks and railroads exploited western lands and the people who lived there. Coal smoke choked the air and gave miners black lung disease. Anarchists blew up buildings and threatened political stability. The Labor Movement and the Women's Movement gained momentum as labor problems continued to boil and female suffrage became a major issue. Militant political groups such as the Grangers and the Populists came into being.

The demand for labor brought many new immigrants to America and many farm families to the cities. The conditions of the urban tenements were horrific. People lived amid filth, noise, and danger. Several families might live in one small apartment with inadequate sanitation. Disease was rampant. With no laws to protect them, women and children, as well as men, worked very long hours under unsafe conditions. Children were sometimes beaten. Eventually, the poor rebelled. For example, in 1886, a rally for an eight-hour workday turned into the bloody Haymarket Riot in Chicago. Boston, the setting of the story, was virtually paralyzed by strikes by the mid-1880s. Bellamy brings this factor into play in the story when he mentions that West's marriage is delayed by the strikes that prevent workers from finishing his new house.

It was a time of social upheaval as the Industrial Revolution led to enormous wealth for a few while grossly exploiting the labor force. Working class violence and Gilded Age opulence greatly disturbed the middle class. Americans wanted a better world, and they were in love with utopian stories that gave them hope for a peaceful and prosperous future. Consequently, an eager audience rushed to read Bellamy's book denouncing capitalism and describing a system that he claimed would lead to equality and contentment.

The impact of *Looking Backward* has never been matched by another American publication. Like *Uncle Tom's Cabin*, it touched upon the issues that most deeply disturbed the American public. As a result, Bellamy Clubs organized around the country to discuss the potential of Nationalism. Political party platforms adopted some of Bellamy's ideas and translated them into legislation that still affects America today. The book was published in millions of copies and translated into all major languages. After Marx's *Das Kapital*, it became the most influential book on socialist systems in the world.

Bellamy's influence on American and world culture has been enormous. A list of those who have acknowledged a debt to Bellamy includes many notables: educator John Dewey, labor leader Eugene V. Debs, politician Clement Atlee, and writers Jack London, Carl Sandburg, Upton Sinclair, Erich Fromm, H. G. Wells, Leo Tolstoy, and Maxim Gorki. Bellamy's first biographer was Arthur E. Morgan, an engineer who became chairman of the Tennessee Valley Authority under Franklin Roosevelt and later president of Antioch University. Morgan asserted that the creators of the New Deal in the 1940s were also influenced by ideas proposed in *Looking Backward*.

The popularity of *Looking Backward* led to a multitude of other utopian novels. Both notable writers such as William Dean Howells (*A Traveler from Altruria*) and previously unknown writers had their own ideas about what would constitute a utopian society. Dystopian novels also abounded as people began to suspect that the future could be worse instead of better. Even though several of these works are now much better known than *Looking Backward*, the phenomenal impact of this work on American thought is still given respectful credit.

Compare & Contrast

- **Late 1800s:** Booming industrialization demands a large, cheap workforce. The numbers of women and children laborers increases dramatically, but living conditions for poor families often remain squalid. Demands for better pay and working conditions lead to strikes and violence. Between 1881 and 1905 there are approximately 37,000 strikes across the country.

  Today: Labor unions and laws protect worker interests. Children are prohibited from working until a certain age, and all workplaces have regulations about safety, hours, and wages.

- **Late 1800s:** Monopolies and trusts control most of the industrial power in the country, and enormous wealth is concentrated in the hands of a few such as Rockefeller (oil), Vanderbilt (railroads), Morgan (banks), Carnegie (steel), and Duke (tobacco).

  Today: Antitrust laws prevent the use of unfair competition by conglomerates to drive small businesses out of the market. The most notable recent antitrust case involved Microsoft.

- **Late 1800s:** Many new inventions appear, including the typewriter, the telephone, electric street lamps, electric streetcars, the first electric generating plant, the gasoline motor, and the transatlantic cable.

  Today: Patents continue to be issued at an astronomical rate. Computers, word processors, solar and nuclear energy, automobiles, airplanes, and cell phones have evolved from the industrial age, as well as thousands of new technologies that Bellamy could not have imagined.

- **Late 1800s:** The Gilded Age is in its prime. Besides ruthless graft in business and government, the age is distinguished by the conspicuous consumption of America's wealthiest families. Notably, massive "summer cottages" are built in Newport, Rhode Island, at the cost of millions each.

  Today: Very few of the Newport mansions are still used as homes. The most extravagant are now historical museums that bring a large tourist industry to the seaside town, including the Duke estate and the various Vanderbilt mansions. The fortunes connected with these families are either dissipated or in foundations.

- **Late 1800s:** The women's suffrage movement is active across the country. The National Woman Suffrage Association is founded in 1869, the same year the Wyoming Territory granted women the right to vote. In 1878, a constitutional amendment for female suffrage is introduced in Congress but is not passed until 1920, the same year that the League of Women Voters is organized.

  Today: Women not only vote but also hold public office and are members of virtually every occupation. Nonetheless, salaries for women lag behind those of men, despite Bellamy's dream that by 2000 women would receive equal compensation. Women are still greatly outnumbered by men in government and corporate positions of power.

- **1887:** Edward Bellamy introduces the idea of the credit card to pay for goods and services in his book *Looking Backward*.

  Today: The first comprehensive credit card was introduced in 1950 by Diners Club. Credit cards are now readily available and can be used for almost any kind of transaction.

- **Late 1800s:** Edward Bellamy proposes universal education to the age of twenty-one in his book *Looking Backward*, but in 1890 only four percent of young people ages fourteen to seventeen, mostly male, are enrolled in school.

  Today: All children must attend school until approximately the age of sixteen (varies by state). More women than men attend college.

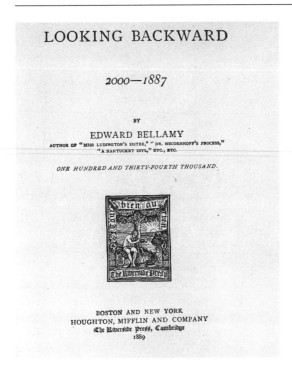

LOOKING BACKWARD

2000—1887

BY

EDWARD BELLAMY

AUTHOR OF "MISS LUDINGTON'S SISTER," "DR. HEIDENHOFF'S PROCESS,"
"A NANTUCKET IDYL," ETC., ETC.

ONE HUNDRED AND THIRTY-FOURTH THOUSAND.

BOSTON AND NEW YORK
HOUGHTON, MIFFLIN AND COMPANY
The Riverside Press, Cambridge
1889

Title page from an 1889 edition of the work

Critical Overview

While *Looking Backward* may have sold millions of copies and had worldwide influence, its enthusiastic reception in 1888 was based on the ideas for social and economic reform Bellamy proposed, not the book's literary merit. As a treatise on social reform, the book is generally admired. However, negative criticism abounds concerning Bellamy's omissions and misinterpretations.

Gail Collins points out in her 1991 article for *The Nation* that, although Bellamy believed technology would make life easier in the year 2000, he fails to show anything but a few innovative gadgets, and the rest is much the same as it was in 1887. "We learn that factories are no longer dirty but we never see them in action. . . . The industrial army does the washing and the cooking, not washer-dryers and microwave ovens," says Collins. Collins also notices that, "Throughout the book, West manages to tour the city . . . without ever speaking to anyone except the Leetes, or encountering any blacks, Catholics or other descendants of the working class."

From the beginning, critics have also found Bellamy too idealistic about human nature. An 1889 article by Nicholas Gilman in the *Quarterly Jour-*

nal of Economics thought Bellamy's futuristic society impossible to achieve as long as human nature remains the same. It is naïve to think that people will respond en masse to logic and reason or to an altruistic desire to share. While good may be able to overcome evil, greed and the desire to feel superior will live on. In addition, Bellamy underestimates the importance of incentives if he thinks that simple honors or increases in rank will motivate workers to improve their efforts. Furthermore, as Linda Simon asks in a 1999 profile on Bellamy for *World and I*, "If life became too easy, if one's needs were met by a paternalistic government, what would motivate men and women to achieve greatness?"

Martin Gardner says in an article for the *New Criterion* that, "though admirable in its indictment of unfettered capitalism and in its enthusiasm for building a better world, it projected a cure as bad as, if not worse than, the disease." Many critics agree. While Bellamy's ideas are intriguing and have had sufficient merit to affect the development of socialism, the bottom line is that his system is not voluntary. Everyone attends school until a certain age. Everyone must enter and leave the Industrial Army at a certain age on a certain day, and so on. There is apparently little room for diversity, a limited choice of music and goods, no variety of restaurants, and no change of atmosphere.

Another area that is stifling is the choices given to women. Bellamy's segregation of the sexes is the most controversial topic of his novel. It offends modern readers and was a source of consternation to feminists of his time. Still, his contemporaries hailed the relative freedom and equality that he foresaw for women as a definite improvement over the conditions of the times. They felt that they could work with the idea of economic equality and go from there.

In a 2000 article for *Harper's Magazine*, Russell Jacoby finds a multitude of faults in Bellamy's utopian novel: monopolies have merely been replaced by one "gargantuan state trust"; the idea of being mustered into the Industrial Army is not appealing, nor is the argument supporting it persuasive; the idea of marrying for love alone is fine, but not if it is celebrated as a step toward sexual selection to improve the species. Nonetheless, Jacoby forgives Bellamy because he is, like all of us, "a creature of his time, and his willingness to imagine a future radically different from his present did not absolve him of some typical nineteenth-century prejudices. The willingness is what makes him different from us."

Articles and books about *Looking Backward* have been produced in every decade since its publication. A number came out in the year 2000 to compare Bellamy's projections with the actuality of the landmark year. William Dean Howells panned the novel in 1888 in *Harper's*, then wrote his own utopian novel. Howells disliked the book because he thought socialism dangerous. William Morris wrote in *Commonweal* in 1889 that the book was dangerous because it might turn people away from socialism if they disliked Bellamy's personal version of it. These differences of opinion are typical of critics, especially concerning a work as controversial as *Looking Backward*.

Criticism

Lois Kerschen

Kerschen is a writer and public school district administrator. In this essay, Kerschen concentrates on Bellamy's references to women in his novel and how his attempt to liberate women failed to understand the full extent to which women can participate in the world.

Of the twenty-eight chapters that comprise Edward Bellamy's *Looking Backward*, only one is devoted to the discussion of the role of women in the society of the year 2000, and that is not until the twenty-fifth chapter. This lack of attention to women is somewhat understandable, as the book was mainly intended to promote Bellamy's ideas on economic reforms. Nonetheless, the lack of inclusion of women in a more substantial manner and the paternalistic elements that Bellamy maintains in his new society indicate that he was limited in his ability to think beyond the tenets established by his breeding, social status, and gender.

Looking Backward is about rebuilding the structure of government and industry in a centralized, nationalized form such that all people would share equally in the nation's wealth. Bellamy believed that if privation could be eliminated, then the innate good nature of people would lead them to pursue endeavors that would benefit society as a whole instead of constantly pursuing money for personal survival. The connection to women's rights is that, once the motivation for greed and competition no longer existed, a more generous society would be inclined to treat each citizen equally, even women.

> There are many different ways to find fulfillment in life, and all people would have to have the freedom to choose their own path if there is ever to be a Utopia."

Bellamy supported women's suffrage, but he contended that, without economic equality, the vote would not have sufficient impact to give women full citizenship. According to Daphne Patai in her introduction to the book *Looking Backward 1988–1888*, Bellamy repeatedly emphasized in his writings that economic equality was an

indispensable prerequisite for any pursuit of justice and political equality. For all his lack of attention to the myriad ways in which women's subordinate status vis-à-vis men is articulated, Bellamy noted that this status rested first and foremost on an economic dependence that must be abolished.

An important benefit that results from economic independence is the freedom to marry for love instead of wealth and social position. Dr. Leete guesses correctly that the dependence of women "must always have remained humiliating" and resulted, in effect, in women having "to sell themselves to men to get their living." He questions why it did not occur to the people of West's time "that it was robbery as well as cruelty when men seized for themselves the whole product of the world and left women to beg and wheedle for their share."

In addition to being cognizant of the social pressures on upper-class women, Bellamy was aware of the misery suffered by working-class women in the nineteenth century. Thus, his intent was to eradicate all poverty, exorbitant wealth, and class distinctions. Bellamy felt that the new social order must arise from the middle class to combat the excesses of the very wealthy and, in turn, to take care of the poor who did not have the education or the means to effect their own liberation. The feminist movement in Bellamy's time was comprised mostly of literate, middle-class women, so Bellamy wanted to recruit these other social re-

What Do I Read Next?

- *A Connecticut Yankee in King Arthur's Court* (1889) is Mark Twain's time-travel novel. After being knocked unconscious in nineteenth-century Connecticut, Hank Morgan wakes up in the Camelot of King Arthur and the Knights of the Round Table. What ensues is both an enjoyable comedy and a disturbing satire about human society.

- *The Time Machine*, by H. G. Wells, is the ultimate time travel story. First published in 1895, it is still a popular publication. Wells paints a dark picture of the future of civilization as he transports his Time Traveler to the year 802,701 when there are only two races of human-like people left in a world of horror. The traveler's quest is to find his stolen time machine so that he can escape.

- *Equality* is Edward Bellamy's sequel to *Looking Backward*. Published in 1897, this novel clarifies some of the theories that Bellamy proposed in the first work. However, the large buildings and mass services of the city are replaced by technologically connected small villages where the advantages of community are enhanced by more space and a closeness to nature.

- Edith Wharton's *The House of Mirth* (1905) provides an excellent picture of society in the Gilded Age. This novel illustrates many of the class status problems outlined in *Looking Backward*, most specifically those of women who are forced to marry for social and economic security instead of love.

- The rise of realism in American literature in the late nineteenth century resulted in Hamlin Garland's *Main-Travelled Roads*, a collection of short stories about Midwest farm families published in 1891. In these stories is a heartrending description of the desperation of the hardworking rural laborers alluded to in *Looking Backward*.

- In 1932, Aldous Huxley published his predictions about the future of humanity in *Brave New World*. A dark portrayal of the effects of science on human nature, this dystopian novel is eerily accurate to a much greater extent than the few technological predictions that Edward Bellamy made.

- George Orwell's *Animal Farm* (1946) uses animal characters to portray the tragedy of the human condition. Based on the Russian Revolution, this book is a satire on the utopian hopes of the people and the corruption of their communist leaders.

- An example of the dystopian novel is *1984*, published by George Orwell in 1949. A utopian novel such as *Looking Backward* promotes the belief that humans will rise to the greater good and achieve peace and prosperity. But Orwell's vision of the future was one of perpetual warfare and totalitarian control over the actions and thoughts of the people.

- Published in 1982, Arthur Lipow's *Authoritarian Socialism in America: Edward Bellamy and the Nationalist Movement* traces the Nationalist movement from its background in post–Civil War reform movements to the democratic changes made in the 1890s. Lipow reminds readers that Bellamy, like Thomas Jefferson, felt that reform would come from the educated, not the working classes.

---

formers to his cause with *Looking Backward*. With that in mind, Sylvia Strauss concludes in her article "Gender, Class and Race in Utopia" that Bellamy cast his socialist program in the form of a conventional romance, to "further attract female readers who, more than men, were drawn to the novel as a source of entertainment and enlightenment."

Nonetheless, a chauvinistic attitude is evident from the tone of the first mention of Mrs. Leete and Edith. The description is entirely about their attractive appearance and seems more generated by desire than detail. From that point on, Mrs. Leete is almost invisible, and Edith has a place only as the romantic interest. Almost all of the conversations discussing modern society take place with the other male, Dr. Leete. The only thing Edith gets to explain about their way of life is, stereotypically, shopping. Edith is described as an "indefatigable shopper" who prefers to spend her money on pretty clothes, and there is an assumption, on her part as well as his, that women, past and present, did the shopping.

Oddly enough, the clothes that she wears seem to be of the same style as that of the women of the late nineteenth century. Bellamy tells the reader in a note in chapter four that "the differences between the style of dress and furniture of the two epochs are not more marked than I have known fashion to make in the time of one generation." Why such little change after several generations? Bellamy knew that the feminists of his time wanted to change styles to allow for more comfortable activity. Some were already advocating, and wearing, pants and shorter skirts. Perhaps Bellamy did not want to expend the energy to think of a new style of dress for the year 2000 when his intent was to discuss government and economics. Perhaps he wanted his nineteenth century audience to be able to identify with the characters in his book. Either way, he merely avoided the issue by claiming that styles had not changed.

Another practice that seems not to have changed since the nineteenth century is that of men convening in a room separate from their women to smoke cigars and discuss weighty issues. One has to wonder why the women did not have sufficient intellectual curiosity to ask dozens of questions of a man who came from another century. Early in the novel, "Dr. Leete, as well as the ladies, seemed greatly interested in my account of the circumstances under which I had gone to sleep in the underground chamber. All had suggestions to offer to account for my having been forgotten there." Beyond the initial excitement of the mystery, however, the women in this novel are dismissed as having interest only in being good hostesses or in a romantic relationship.

Throughout the story, the ladies always retire earlier in the evening than the men. Not only did this traditional practice allow the men to stay up drinking and smoking without interference from the women folk, but it also stemmed from the belief that women, as more delicate creatures, needed more rest than the sturdy men. Consequently, when Dr. Leete explains the differences between the occupations of men and women, he says

> Women being inferior in strength to men ... the heavier sorts of work are everywhere reserved for men, the light occupations for women. . . . Moreover, the hours of women's work are considerably shorter than those of men, more frequent vacations are granted, and the most careful provision is made for rest when needed.

The continued existence of male dominance is revealed by Dr. Leete's explanation that women are "permitted" to work by the men of their day only because it has been found that a "healthful and inspiriting occupation" is "well for body and mind."

When Julian West inquires about housekeeping, the traditional occupation of women, he exhibits further sexist expectations, in that he turns from Dr. Leete to direct his question to Mrs. Leete. She replies that there is "none to do." Laundry, cooking, and sewing are all done by public workers. Mrs. Leete adds, "We choose houses no larger than we need, and furnish them so as to involve the minimum of trouble to keep them in order." Keeping the houses in order sounds like housekeeping. Bellamy does not appear to consider dusting, making beds, mopping floors, washing dishes or the myriad of other tasks that comprise housekeeping. But what would a man of Bellamy's time and social station know about such things? He's never done any housework. To him housekeeping is "woman's work" and a world with "none to do" must be "a paradise for womankind!"

After all, two of the feminist writers of Bellamy's time, Abby Morton Diaz and Marie Howland, had established freedom from housework as a goal of women's liberation in their books *The Schoolmaster's Trunk* and *Papa's Own Girl*, both published in 1874. Patai concludes that their influence caused Bellamy to incorporate their ideas into *Looking Backward* , believing that they articulated the dreams of all women.

> But Bellamy did not give women much scope for the leisure time they had and which both Diaz and Howland provided for in their respective books. Dr. Leete, Bellamy's surrogate in the novel, does not have a high regard for women's intellect, capacity to govern, or ability to pull their weight equally with men in the labor force.

West assumes then that, if women do not have housework to do, they must have nothing else to do. He says, "I suppose that women nowadays, having been relieved of the burden of housework, have no employment other than the cultivation of their charms and graces." Dr. Leete replies, "So far as we men are concerned, we should consider that they amply paid their way … if they confined themselves to that occupation." Neither has any inkling that he is being insulting to women.

In fact, Bellamy departed radically from the others in the suffragist movement, for he believed strongly that the two genders have different talents. Dr. Leete, speaking for Bellamy, tells West that, "The lack of some such recognition of the distinct individuality of the sexes was one of the innumerable defects of your society." Child care is still the sole responsibility of women in the year 2000. Women in the industrial army are segregated into certain types of work, not only because of supposed physical limitations but also because of assumed differing inclinations. Furthermore, top leadership positions are available to men alone.

Through Dr. Leete, Bellamy advocates "giving full play to the differences of sex rather than in seeking to obliterate them." To avoid women seeking careers that would put them in an "unnatural rivalry with men," Bellamy created a society in which women have "a world of their own." Sadly, the declaration that "they are very happy with it" comes from Dr. Leete and not from one of the women whose testimony would have carried more credibility and less paternalism. To further confuse the situation, neither Edith nor Mrs. Leete ever seems to go to work or do anything more laborious than flower arranging or shopping.

It is to Bellamy's credit, however, that women are included in the industrial army at all, and that they do not leave upon marriage. The latter factor indicates that Bellamy understood that marriage is no more an occupation for women than it is for men. Nonetheless, what positions of leadership women do have in his 2000 society are reserved for wives and mothers "as they alone fully represent their sex." To state that a woman is somehow incomplete if she is not married or a mother is as insulting as implying that grace and charm are all a woman needs to succeed. There are many different ways to find fulfillment in life, and all people would have to have the freedom to choose their own path if there is ever to be a Utopia.

Since the beginning of time, there has been a belief among most cultures that it is a law of nature that women are responsible for maintaining morality. As a man, and one with strong moral convictions, Bellamy accepted the primordial notion that the favors of a woman are a reward for a man's good behavior. Therefore, he incorporates into his utopian society a sexual system of motivation for the laborers. "Our women sit aloft as judges of the race and reserve themselves to reward the winners." "Radiant faces" are averted to laggards. Celibates are "almost invariably men who have failed to acquit themselves creditably in the work of life." By this means of sexual selection, as in the animal kingdom, only the hardest working and those with the most admirable attributes become husbands and fathers. Thus, with "a sense of religious consecration," women serve as the "wardens of the world to come."

There are multiple flaws in *Looking Backward*. It is not great literature. It is, however, one of the most influential books in the world, which just goes to show the power of a good idea. Although Bellamy did not really understand women and failed to give them true equality in his book, he did give them an economic equality that has not been achieved to this day. He also caused the people of the late nineteenth century to give new consideration to the role of women in society.

Source: Lois Kerschen, Critical Essay on *Looking Backward: 2000–1887*, in *Novels for Students*, The Gale Group, 2002.

Wilfred M. McClay

In the following essay, McClay discusses the setting of Bellamy's utopian Boston, with an emphasis on martial and economic themes.

Given the connection Bellamy made between martial valor and solidarity, it is of considerable importance that the story of *Looking Backward* opens in Boston on Decoration Day, the holiday honoring the memory of Northerners who fell in the Civil War. Julian West, the protagonist-narrator, has paid his respects at the Mount Auburn grave of his fiancée's brother, who had been killed in the war, and has returned to dine that evening with his fiancée, Edith, and her upper-crust family, the Bartletts. We soon discern that Julian is a deeply troubled man. Some of his plaints stem from the disordered state of the times, which were marked by increasing class division, accelerating social tension, and labor agitation and strikes. Not that the well-insulated Mr. West Feels any sympathy for the insurgent laboring classes; indeed, at the height of his exasperation, he wishes (as Caligula wished of the Romans) that "they had but one neck that he might cut it off." He especially resents the strike-related work stoppages that have repeatedly delayed completion of his new house and have thereby postponed his marriage to the lovely Miss Edith Bartlett.

But there are clearly deeper sources for Julian's trepidation. He has been fighting a battle with chronic insomnia, regularly finding it impossible to sleep for two or more consecutive nights. To combat this problem, he built a secret sleeping chamber beneath his old house, a subterranean refuge into which "no murmur from the upper world ever penetrated," and which, because of its inaccessibility and secrecy, was also an ideal place for him to protect his valuables from theft or fire. But even with the help of this bunker-like enclosure, wherein he found himself enveloped by "the silence of the tomb," secure in the knowledge that his hoarded wealth was safe nearby, he still often found himself unable to sleep and frequently had to call on the services of a mesmerist to lull him into slumber. Julian's unease, then, stems not from a disordered world but from a disordered soul. His dark, private sleeping chamber is a figuration of the deathly grotto of the purely individual life, which cuts itself off from the "upper" world in frantic pursuit of personal peace and worldly ease.

As night falls on Decoration Day in 1887, the agitated Julian finds he must once again go to his mesmerist for relief. But after he finally drifts off to sleep, a fire apparently sweeps through his house and consumes its contents—including, it was believed, Julian himself, in fact, however, Julian survives the inferno and continues to sleep undisturbed until the year 2000. At that time he is finally discovered and is taken into the household of a Dr. Leete, who proceeds to revive him, and then introduces him to the spectacle of a drastically transformed and perfected Boston. Thereafter the book alternates between long, highly didactic discussions between Julian and the Leetes about the operating principles of this radiant new world and the melodramatic episodes in the subplot of Julian's psychological development. The latter revolves around Julian's anguish over his now-riven identity and his growing romantic attraction to Dr. Leete's daughter, who is, like his nineteenth-century fiancée, named Edith.

From the beginning, the descriptions of utopian Boston offered by the Leete family touch characteristic Bellamy themes. He never missed an opportunity to contrast the sordid spectacle of nineteenth-century selfishness and wastefulness with the lustrous twentieth-century ideals of solidarity and efficiency. That contrast is prepared by Bellamy's justly celebrated comparison of nineteenth-century American society to a "prodigious coach" in which men and women scrambled and clawed at

> "To readers in the late twentieth century Bellamy (and his readers) may seem laughably naive for having failed to ponder the enormous abuses to which *Looking Backward*'s prescriptions could lead."

one another for the sake of a few privileged seats on top, where they could be pulled along in airy comfort by the tightly harnessed "masses of humanity," men and women reduced to beasts of burden. Dr. Leete's discourses develop that theme: the need to overcome competitive individualism through a spirit of cooperation and combination. When the disbelieving Julian is allowed to view the new city of Boston from Dr. Leete's rooftop, he finds himself especially astonished by the orderliness and opulence of the city's streets and buildings. Yes, responded Dr. Leete, he had heard of the squalor of nineteenth-century cities, a result of that era's "excessive individualism," which had prevented the sustenance of any meaningful "public spirit."

The utopia of *Looking Backward* did not set out to overthrow industrialism to humanize and purify it. Consider, for example, the labor problem that so bedeviled the world Julian had left behind. The great labor disturbances of the nineteenth century, Dr. Leete patiently explained, had merely been inevitable outgrowths of the increasing concentration of capital under a more and more consolidated industrial system. Although that system had resulted in enormous social inequities and degradation of labor, it was also productive of staggering economic efficiencies—efficiencies that made thinkable, for the first time in human history, the universal dispersion of a high level of material wealth. Thus, such a system was not to be abandoned.

The key to managing this problem lay in the very process of economic consolidation that "had been so desperately and vainly resisted" by those who yearned for preindustrial simplicity. Consolidation was not the enemy; it was, in fact, "a process which only needed to complete its logical evolution to open a golden future to humanity." In other words, the nineteenth century's enormous pains and dislocations should be attributed, not to the forces of consolidation, but to an *unfinished* consolidation.

By the early twentieth century, however, "the evolution was completed by the final consolidation of the entire capital of the nation," whereby the governance of the nation's industry and commerce was turned over to a single syndicate representing the people and therefore devoted to pursuit of "the common interests for the common profit." Indeed, the nations itself had become "the one great business corporation … the one capitalist … the sole employer … the final monopoly." Perhaps most remarkable of all, this colossal transformation had occurred without pressure of violence or coercion; indeed, it had been proposed by the great corporations themselves and was readily accepted by a people who had gradually become convinced of the virtues of large-scale enterprises. The epoch of industrial consolidation, the era of trusts, found its consummation in the establishment of "The Great Trust."

In this new order, the diffuse energies of solitary selves found a home where they fused with the new social order, coalescing from an aggregation of ordinary men, singly so feeble, into a single magnificent body, a coursing river of blue. And Bellamy could not adequately describe this new order without returning, again and again, to military imagery. Once the nation had come to assume proprietorship of all industrial enterprises, a citizen's service in "the industrial army" became a universal obligation, precisely analogous to the obligation of universal military service. The industrial army follows a military organizational chart, divided into ten great departments; the chief of each division is comparable to a commander of an army corps, or a lieutenant general, with generals of separate guilds reporting to him. These ten officers form his council for the general in chief, who is the president of the United States. The president is chiefly responsible for administrative oversight of the industrial army and the Great Trust; his political duties (as well as those of the Congress) have dwindled down to few or none.

This military style of administrative bureaucracy had evidently yielded economic advances unimaginable even under the highly productive regime of nineteenth-century capitalism. Bellamy

did not hesitate to define those benefits in the language and imagery of warfare. "The effectiveness of the working force of a nation, under the myriad-headed leadership of private capital," explained Dr. Leete, "as compared with that which it attains under a single head, may be likened to the military efficiency of a mob, or a horde of barbarians with a thousand petty chiefs, as compared with that of a disciplined army under one general—such a fighting machine, for example, as the German army in the time of Von Moltke." Of course, the mere achievement of such efficiencies, however remarkable, would not have been enough to satisfy Bellamy's deeper moral concerns, But these concerns, too, were answered by the reconceptualization of the nation as an army. The martial virtues of unselfish valor could now be expressed in the ordinary labors of the ordinary civilian. "Now that industry," Dr. Leete tells Julian West, "is no longer self-service, but service of the nation," it follows that "patriotism, passion for humanity, impel the worker as in your day they did the soldier. The army of industry is an army, not alone by virtue of its perfect organization, but by reason also of the ardor of self-devotion which animates its members."

How appropriate, then, that the social-reform ideology and movement to which *Looking Backward* gave rise adopted the name of Nationalism—even if Bellamy used that term to evade the opprobrium, as well as the unwanted emphasis upon class division and class conflict, attached to the word *socialism*. But Nationalism was more than just a prudent name; it was also an honestly descriptive one. It acknowledged the degree to which the national principle, victorious over all other contenders in the clash of the Civil War, served as the animating principle for Bellamy's social vision. The purpose of the "national party," explained Dr. Leete, "was to realize the idea of the nation with a grandeur and completeness never before conceived"; it was not to be merely "an association of men for certain merely political functions," but it was to be "a family, a vital union, a common life, a mighty heaven-touching tree whose leaves are its people, fed from its veins, and feeding it in turn." The national party sought "to raise patriotism from an instinct to a rational devotion," by making their country into "a fatherland, a father who kept the people alive and was not merely an idol for which they were expected to die."

With the book's concluding chapter, the plot suddenly takes a new turn, as Julian finds himself suddenly transported back to the nineteenth century. It appears, for the moment, that his entire experience of utopian Boston has been nothing more than a dream. Now he finds himself cursed by his glimpse of glory, for he must see the social iniquities and horrors of his native century through eyes informed by a vision of twentieth-century perfection.

Julian's journey backward thus becomes a journey through hell, in which the disparities of wealth, the shameless cynicism of advertising, the programmatic wastefulness of a capitalist economy, the disarray of industry and labor, the "debauching influence" of money and banks, and the "drawn and anxious" faces of the people in the streets overwhelm him with horror and pity. He wanders the streets of the city in a dazed, aimless, disoriented state. The only moment of comfort comes, characteristically, when he happens upon a military parade marching down Tremont Street. He responds to the sight with intense relief: "Here at last were order and reason, an exhibition of what intelligent cooperation can accomplish" through "perfect concert of action" and "organization under one control." Stumbling upon this small-scale Grand Review reminded him of his own glimpse of the New Jerusalem.

Finally Julian somehow turns up at his fiancée's house on Commonwealth Avenue and is invited to join the family and its guests for dinner. Like a sonata, Julian's tale has returned to the place where it began; but the recapitulation has shifted into an agitated minor key. After his experience in the street, he finds himself nauseated by the splendor of the Bartletts' table and by the jolly spirits of the complacent diners. Like a biblical prophet who cannot contain his disgust, he explodes into a condemnation of them for their indifference to the suffering all around them: "Do you not know that close to your doors a great multitude of men and women, flesh of your flesh, live lives that are one agony from birth to death?"

But the stunned company, far from being moved to self-examination by this reproach, becomes impatient and then angry with Julian. Finally Mr. Bartlett has him thrown out of the house. At that climactic moment, Julian awakens and discovers he has been saved: to his great joy, he finds that he is still in Dr. Leete's house. His harrowing return to the nineteenth century had been the dream; the splendor of the twentieth century was the reality. As the book concludes, a tearful Julian kneels before his beloved Edith Leete and confesses to her

his unworthiness "to breathe the air of this golden century."

Bellamy's persistent religious sensibilities were especially evident in these final pages. The scene at the Bartletts resounded with biblical overtones, not the least among them being the language and symbolism of crucifixion. ("I have been in Golgotha," raves the half-mad Julian at his dinner hosts; "I have seen Humanity hanging on a cross!") But the crucifixion becomes his own, a symbolic death suffered when Mr. Bartlett casts him out of the house; being thus ostracized and forsaken becomes the price of his intercession. But blessed are those persecuted for righteousness' sake, for theirs is the kingdom of heaven; and Julian's passion is followed by resurrection, in the form of his awakening to the "real" world of the year 2000. His social death fulfills the dictum that one must die to world and self before entering into new life.

This logic also recalled the religion of solidarity, which proclaimed that the infinitude of the "upper world" inhabited by the "second soul" was more real than the finite realm occupied by the ego-personality. Such, too, was the superordinate reality possessed by Bellamy's cherished vision of the New Jerusalem, a consolidated social order in *this* world to which the troubled and inadequate ego could turn and yield itself wholly. Yet that last analogizing step, from "upper world" to perfected social world, was a giant one, challenging the essential meaning of the dictum about dying to the world. It was essentially the same step that would be taken by the proponents of the Social Gospel, reform-minded liberal Protestant ministers such as Washington Gladden and Walter Rauschenbusch, who argued that the redemptive mission of the Incarnation had come properly to rest in the social and economic reorganization of this world, the making of an earthly paradise.

To any apprehension that so monolithically centralized a state might be a formula for tyranny, *Looking Backward* seemed almost incredibly oblivious. At times, Bellamy's innocence seems so extreme that the modern reader can read them only with a grim smile. To readers in the late twentieth century who know the harm that such fantasies can produce in the hands of an aggrandizing state, Bellamy (and his readers) may seem laughably naive for having failed to ponder the enormous abuses to which *Looking Backward*'s prescriptions could lead.

There are two points to be made in this connection, however. First, there is the obvious fact that Bellamy's era's concerns are not ours; the passage of time has dramatically changed our aims and our fears, and it will do so again. Second, and more relevant to the present day, is the fact that the discontents of Bellamy, and perhaps those of his readers, were ultimately far more spiritual than political in character. Bellamy was not merely seeking social and economic justice in proposing the wholesale reconstitution of the social order. He was seeking answers to problems of ultimate meaning in individual lives, answers that would rescue the Julian Wests of the world from their grottoes of sleepless misery. *Looking Backward* was so wildly popular partly because it was able to trade so effectively upon the fading cultural capital of American Protestantism, even as it was transforming that capital into something new and worldly.

Such a transformation, however, may do justice to neither religion nor politics. In appealing to the idea of the nation as a great community, a great trust, or a great family, Bellamy touched a profound emotional chord in his readers, who longed to see their society transformed into a vessel of connectedness and love. Few of us are immune to such longings, and there is much to cherish in them. But there is also much to distrust. It is surely significant that Bellamy found military images, especially the idea of compulsory national service, to be more compelling figures of solidarity and sacrifice than those of family or community, which compete with the unitary state. It is perhaps a coincidence, but an irresistibly meaningful one, that Bellamy's perfect solidaritists came from the planet Mars. Bellamy's redirection of a self-sacrificial imperative toward the reform of the social order ran the risk of corrupting both religion and politics by effacing the line between them.

The desire to find meaning in life by sanctifying one's social world and the objects of one's labors should not be scorned. But it runs two risks. First, the risk of making us the self-conscious creators, rather than the discoverers, of what is sacred—a typically modern exercise in narcissism and futility. Second, the risk that, in seeking too ardently for a politics of meaning, it may lose sight of the meaning of politics. Even the founder of Bellamy's religious tradition insisted upon rendering unto Caesar what is Caesar's. There is more than one lesson in that.

Source: Wilfred M. McClay, "Edward Bellamy and the Politics of Meaning," in *American Scholar*, Spring 1995, pp. 268–71.

Merritt Abrash

In the following essay, Abrash looks into the public acceptance of Bellamy's Looking Backwards.

A certain nineteenth-century writer, also active in journalism, created an extraordinary utopian vision in which all productive facilities were owned by society. Unlike the great majority of earlier utopian proposals, this one was specifically applicable to full-blown industrial technology and organization which, under centralized rational direction for use rather than profit, was presumed capable of providing all the world's people with the material necessities of a good life. This writer also envisioned an egalitarian incomes policy and the elimination of social classes. His vision spread rapidly and became part of western civilization's heritage of powerful ideas.

The summary thus far clearly fits Edward Bellamy—and just as clearly fits Karl Marx. But when we move ahead to the reception of their doctrines, a sharp divergence appears. Marx was fiercely attacked, harried out of one country after another, and his name became among respectable people a byword for social and economic iniquity. Bellamy, on the other hand, became an honored citizen, and his formula for utopia was accepted even by its opponents as within the bounds of legitimate American political discourse.

What accounts for so dramatic a contrast in American reaction to visions sharing similarly radical institutional features? To the individualistic American mind, in fact, Bellamy's regimented industrial army should have seemed more outrageous than the Marxist withering away of the state. But *Looking Backward* found advocates in factories, farms, colleges, and New England drawing rooms alike. Why should it have commanded respectful attention from such disparate elements of a citizenry notoriously resistant, then as now, to economic or political programs straying very far from the middle of the road?

Obviously Bellamy succeeded in domesticating Marxist ends and means so that they seemed compatible with American ideals and traditions—no mean feat. Even more remarkable is that he apparently accomplished this more or less incidentally. He did not set out to tame Marxist theory as a whole, or to take the sting out of particular fear-inducing elements, for the good reason that he was not a student of Marxism. Surprisingly enough, he had probably not even read Marx at the time he wrote *Looking Backward.*

Although there is no sure proof of this proposition, we have Bellamy's own word for it that "I have never been in any sense a student of socialistic literature, or have known more of the various socialist schemes than any newspaper reader might." This disclaimer receives support (although at a much earlier date) from a line in his review of Nordhoff's *The Communistic Societies of the United States*: "The words socialist and communist fall unpleasantly on American ears, being generally taken as implying atheistic and superstitious beliefs and practices and abnormal sex relations" (Edith Leete's hyper-Victorianism arouses readers' concerns about *any*, sex relations in Boston 2000, without worrying about abnormal ones.) Nothing in Bellamy's writings up to *Looking Backward* indicates awareness of the subtlety, scope, and intellectual rigor of Marx's scientific socialism.

The long chapter on *Looking Backward* in Krishan Kumar's recent survey of utopias concludes that Bellamy had not studied Marx before writing the book, but did so afterwards. That may be the most plausible scenario. It means, however, that Bellamy, through coincidence or intuition, succeeded in defusing every incendiary feature (in American eyes) of Marxism without any clear idea of what Marxism was. If Bellamy had been an expert on Marx, and had deliberately set out to restate each threatening element of Marxism in a form acceptable to American sensibilities, there is scarcely anything, as will be explained below, that he would have written differently in *Looking Backward.*

It should be noted first, however, that deliberation does seem likely in the extraordinary care taken not to portray any mass or collective aspects of Boston 2000. Readers get so absorbed in the utopian substance of what Julian West is *told* that they fail to notice that direct depiction of the society in action is virtually absent. The astonishing fact is that, insofar as *Looking Backward* tells a story, there are no people in Boston other than the Leetes; the only exceptions are a sales clerk and a waiter, neither of whom has any lines of dialogue or is otherwise individuated. The Leetes seem to have no relatives and no friends. No one ever visits them, even though they have the hottest attraction in town on their premises. When they walk to the dining house—or when Edith and Julian go to the ward store—they do not run into acquaintances. The entire novel takes place, after Julian finds himself in the year 2000, in a city which is, for all novelistic purposes, unpopulated except for the three Leetes.

> **Marx was fiercely attacked, harried out of one country after another, and his name became among respectable people a byword for social and economic iniquity. Bellamy, on the other hand, became an honored citizen."**

Bellamy goes to great lengths to maintain this isolation. Julian is taken to a school and a warehouse, but about the former he cautions, "I shall not describe in detail what I saw in the schools that day," and comments only upon physical culture instruction. The visit to the warehouse receives a single paragraph in which Julian provides an analogy in lieu of description. Typically, the reader gets more information on the subject (not much in any case) from what the Leetes tell him elsewhere than from what he observes on the spot.

Furthermore, the telephone transmission system of which Bellamy makes so much has undermined two important nineteenth-century forms of public social interaction: apparently no one goes to concerts and few to church (the hugely popular Mr. Barton, be it noted, preaches *only* by telephone). "At home we have comfort, but the splendor of our life is, on its social side, that which we share with our fellows," says Doctor Leete, but nothing in the novel illustrates this.

It is, in fact, the comfort of home which establishes the tone of the new society for Julian. And a thoroughly bourgeois home it is: father works, mother runs the household with the aid of public facilities and (if necessary) hired help, and daughter shops. Levelling of society? Common ownership? Dictatorship of the proletariat? Free love? Few of the proletarian attributes of Marx's communism—whether ascribed by boosters or detractors—find lodgement in these benign pages. Not only do the working classes not rule in *Looking Backward*, they are shunted even further out of the sight of Bellamy's contemporary middle-class reader than their real-life counterparts of 1888. It is significant that the nearest Julian gets to proletarians is at the warehouse, where the work consists of order filling and distribution rather than production. Of labor or laborers in factories, there is not even a pretence of first-hand description anywhere in the book.

The only scenes with great numbers of people in the novel—in fact, virtually the only ones with more than five—are in the Boston of Julian's nightmare. Here Bellamy vividly portrays "throngs" and "swarms"—what an ingenious reversal, that it is *communism* which will obviate mass action and provide the individual with the physical and social space needed for the good life! This is characteristic of the way in which *Looking Backward* soothes a whole range of fears that assailed most Americans (and to a large extent still do) at the mere mention of Marxism.

For example, the fundamental assumption of unresolvable class conflict is sidestepped by the happy assurance that you can "make ten times more profit out of your fellow men by uniting with them than by contending with them." This, Doctor Leete explains, failed to be perceived by a nineteenth century blinkered by individualism. Once the principle of maximum efficiency through cooperation is recognized, desire for gain becomes a reason for consensus, not conflict, and the industrial army's hierarchical organization is deprived of class attributes.

The expropriation of capital, which sent chills down the spines even of many Americans who had little to be expropriated, was rendered benign by two facts: the big capitalists, in the form of corporations, voluntarily accepted the new arrangements, and the arrangements themselves could be expressed in the familiar image of corporation and stockholders, made reassuringly analogous to nation and citizens. After all, captains of industry and industrial army generals share similar executive characteristics, and it is a fair guess that the latter were initially drawn from the former.

The fear of stagnation resulting from the elimination of monetary incentives is combatted with a variety of alternative inducements. Public esteem, wider career choice, prestigious awards, and, most effective of all, the fact that "our women sit aloft as judges of the race and reserve themselves to reward the winners," encourage excellence in the industrial army. Actually, in this regard Bellamy shrewdly appealed to better instincts than Marx,

maintaining that human beings are as capable of responding to considerations of honor and pride as to those of material benefit or historical inevitability.

One of Bellamy's most successful modifications of what was popularly assumed to be Marxist doctrine was in the matter of uniformity. Satires on Marxism (and, in fact, on *Looking Backward* as well) make much of a dull sameness descending upon society as a consequence of a single noncompetitive supplier filling the needs of a population lacking differentials in income, education, and basic outlook. Bellamy, however, neatly end runs this by allowing each person to apportion income as he or she chooses, so that equal incomes need not mean uniform patterns of consumption. Furthermore, new products and activities can be introduced by means of clusters of individuals pooling their incomes for whatever joint purpose they please, even to the extent of starting a newspaper or a religious congregation of any persuasion. *Looking Backward* makes much of the variety of fulfillments among its citizens, as well it might; this was one of Bellamy's most brilliant strokes in making Americans feel comfortable with goals passionately condemned when championed by Marxists.

Even the regimentation inseparable from the industrial army is lightened by the delightful prospect of complete release at age forty-five from the necessity of making a living. If Bellamy and Marx had run against each other for public office, Karl would have had a lot of trouble topping that one. ("To each according to his needs" is pretty dry compared with—to invent a Bellamyite slogan—"Fully alive after forty-five!")

But of course Marxism was disreputable less because of its visionary institutional features and social policies than because of its insistence upon materialism, determinism, and political revolution. Materialism gets its comeuppance in Mr. Barton's sermon, which ends in an evocation of something rather like the culminating starchild in Arthur Clarke's *2001*. "For twofold is the return of man to God 'who is our home', the return of the individual by way of death, and the return of the race by the fulfillment of the evolution, when the divine secret hidden in the germ shall be perfectly unfolded. The long and weary winter of the race has ended. Its summer has begun. Humanity has burst the chrysalis. The heavens are before it." When Friedrich Engels wrote in 1877 of the Marxist utopia: "It is the ascent of man from the kingdom of necessity to the kingdom of freedom", he coined a neat secular slogan, but not one to soothe the fears of upright citizens who equate materialism with atheism.

Determinism is undercut by Doctor Leete's pronouncement that the system under which humanity lives in 2000 is "entirely voluntary, the logical outcome of the operation of human nature under rational conditions." A "logical outcome" might be considered determinism of a sort, but the role of reason is more decisive than in the case of historical inevitability. Bellamy presents the breakthrough into utopia as the result of intelligent human choice made under the guidance of a benevolent yet practical ethic—all more temperate and flattering than the rigid impersonality implied by historical determinism.

Those attributes of choice and reason also exorcise, in Doctor Leete's narration, the most immediate bugbear of nineteenth-century Americans in regard to Marxism: the necessary overthrow of the government. Bellamy dismisses the whole issue of revolutionary violence with breathtaking offhandedness. No sooner does Julian West conjure up the specter of the "great bloodshed and terrible convulsions" that must have occurred during the massive transition to the world of 2000, than Doctor Leete, no doubt casually tapping the ash off his cigar, assures him that there was "absolutely no violence." Everyone—masses and corporations alike—understood that the time had come for the great change; "there was no more possibility of opposing it by force than by argument." The rest of his little speech—the only time the actual changeover to utopia is referred to—is replete with phrases describing scales dropping from eyes: "they came to realize," "were now forced to recognize," "had come to be recognized as an axiom." The new dispensation, one gathers, was not only not resisted, but was welcomed on all sides as, if anything, overdue. No threat to law and order in *this* revolution!

Thus were put into acceptable American terms all the major aspects of Marxism likely to arouse unreasoning hostility—"artfully" put, one would say, except that the weight of evidence is that Bellamy was not even aware he was doing it. Then what accounts for the extraordinary aptness of his treatment of the radical themes he shared with Marx? The answer surely lies in the fact that the two men were working within profoundly different traditions, German philosophical systematizing in the case of Marx, American pragmatism in that of Bellamy.

Marx presented his utopian future as the capstone of an ineluctable historical progression fueled by complex interactions between mind and matter. Bellamy's utopia is simply the outcome of a rational society's elimination of malfunctions through the logical application of existing organizational techniques, subject to an ethical code that already commanded a consensus. Marxism was, as far as its possibilities of acceptance in America went, mired in abstruse theory promising universal upheaval in practice; *Looking Backward*, in contrast, is blissfully free of theoretical framing, its communism could be assimilated to American ideals and traditions because it was presented as a platform of pragmatic reform to be acted upon by enlightened consensus. The crowning touch in its appeal, it may be speculated, lay in the fact that it sounded as if it would "work"—not "had to" or "ought to," but *would*. With that, Bellamy's inadvertent Americanization of Marxism was complete.

Source: Merritt Abrash, "*Looking Backward*: Marxism Americanized," in *Extrapolation*, Vol. 30, No. 3, Fall 1989, pp. 237–42.

Sources

Collins, Gail, "Tomorrow Never Knows," in *Nation*, Vol. 252, No. 2, January 1991, p. 60.

Gardner, Martin, "Looking Backward at Edward Bellamy's Utopia," in *New Criterion*, Vol. 1, Issue 1, Sept. 2000, p. 24.

Jacoby, Russell, "*Looking Backward: From 2000–1887*," in *Harper's Magazine*, Vol. 301, Issue 1807, December 2000, pp. 79–80.

Patai, Daphne, "Introduction—The Doubled Vision of Edward Bellamy," in *Looking Backward, 1988–1888: Essays on Edward Bellamy*, University of Massachusetts Press, 1989, p. 14.

Peyser, Tom, "Looking Back at *Looking Backward*," in *Reason*, Vol. 32, Issue 4, Aug. 2000, p. 34.

Simon, Linda, "Looking Forward," in *World and I*, Vol. 14, Issue 6, June 1999, p. 291.

Strauss, Sylvia, "Gender, Class, and Race in Utopia," in *Looking Backward, 1988–1888: Essays on Edward Bellamy*, edited by Daphne Patai, University of Massachusetts Press, 1989, pp. 71, 74.

Further Reading

Bowman, Sylvia E., *Edward Bellamy*, Twayne Publishers, 1986.

Considered one of the best of the Bellamy biographies, this analytical study covers his life, his philosophies on reform, and the impact of his works.

Halewood, W. H., "Catching Up with Edward Bellamy," in *University of Toronto Quarterly*, Vol. 63, No. 3, Spring 1994, pp. 451–61.

Halewood examines the elements of *Looking Backward* that have caused it to become a relatively unknown work today despite its enormous original impact.

Patai, Daphne, ed., *Looking Backward, 1988–1888: Essays on Edward Bellamy*, University of Massachusetts Press, 1989.

This collection of eight essays from critics who were contemporaries of Bellamy to modern critics provides an insightful variety of views about Bellamy and his works.

Trahair, Richard, "Looking Backward: 2000–1887, 2nd ed.," in *Utopian Studies*, Vol. 8, No. 2, Spring 1997, pp. 118–20.

This book review of a new edition of Bellamy's primary work by Bedford Books is a quick but excellent overview of the novel and its influence.

Weinberg, Robert L., "*Looking Backward, Going Forward*," in *Nation*, Vol. 272, Issue 5, Feb. 2001, pp. 32–35.

This short but good review of Bellamy's book includes speculation about what Bellamy might think of the actual year 2000.

Losing Battles

Eudora Welty
1970

In her autobiography, Eudora Welty called *Losing Battles* the most difficult piece of writing she ever produced. She first envisioned what became her longest novel as a short story. When the novel was published in 1970, Welty was a long-established, highly respected writer who had not published a novel in fifteen years. *Losing Battles* is a departure from most of her other work both in its setting (the hill country of northeastern Mississippi) and its form (dramatic, rather than narrative). Most scholars and critics consider the book the pinnacle of her comedic writing, and it was an immediate success with critics and readers alike.

Losing Battles takes place at a large family reunion in the little town of Banner. The occasion is the ninetieth birthday of the matriarch, Granny Vaughn, but the most eagerly awaited guest is Granny's great-grandson, Jack, who escapes from prison one day before he is scheduled to be released so that he can attend the reunion. The Renfros and Beechams are a gang of eccentrics and storytellers, and the bits of family history they tell one another at the reunion—a litany of losing battles—make up the heart of the novel.

Author Biography

Eudora Alice Welty was born in Jackson, Mississippi, on April 13, 1909, to Chestina and Christian Welty. With her two younger brothers, she was

Eudora Welty

reared in Jackson, although neither of her parents was from the Deep South. Her father came from Ohio, and her mother was from West Virginia. Both were teachers by trade until the family moved to Mississippi, where Christian entered the insurance business. Welty remembered having a very happy childhood in which she was surrounded by books and loved listening to her parents read to each other in the evenings. She also recalled how much she loved listening to the ladies in town trade stories, and her habit of noting their speech patterns and colloquialisms served her well when she began writing about the South.

After completing her public education in Jackson, Welty attended Mississippi State College for Women from 1925 to 1927, finishing a bachelor of arts degree in 1929 at the University of Wisconsin. At the encouragement of her father (who wanted her to have a reliable trade), she studied advertising at Columbia University from 1930 to 1931. When her father died suddenly, however, she returned home to Jackson permanently. She worked various jobs with newspapers and a radio station before going to work for the Works Progress Administration, a government program established during the depression that assigned people to work on public projects for much-needed income. Welty also took up photography, snapping pictures of all

kinds of people (mostly African Americans) in her native Mississippi. Her first published story, "Death of a Traveling Salesman," appeared in 1936, after which Welty's stories were accepted by top publications such as *Atlantic* and *Southern Review*.

During Welty's early writing career, her work was often narrowly defined as regionalist or feminist writing. Still, she was admired by other writers, and her first collection of short stories, *A Curtain of Green*, left critics eagerly anticipating Welty's future work. Over the next thirty years, Welty had over fifteen books published, including short fiction, novels, and nonfiction. In her autobiography, *One Writer's Beginnings*, Welty wrote that *Losing Battles* was the most difficult to write of all her books; she told a *New York Times* reporter that she spent six to eight years working on it.

In the 1970s and 1980s, there was renewed interest in Welty's work, partially because of the rise in feminist criticism. (Welty preferred to distance herself from feminism.) Readers and critics continue to be drawn to her writing for her unique style, her handling of daily life, and her depictions of everyday heroism. Her work was recognized with prestigious awards such as a Guggenheim Fellowship in 1942; the O. Henry Award in 1942, 1943, and 1968; the National Institute of Arts and Letters literary grant in 1944; the Gold Medal for fiction in 1972; and a Pulitzer Prize in 1973 for *The Optimist's Daughter*.

Welty died of complications of pneumonia on July 23, 2001, in her hometown. She was ninety-two.

Plot Summary

Part One

As *Losing Battles* opens, it is August in the hill country of northeast Mississippi. The time is the 1930s. A rooster crows, and night slowly recedes to reveal an old farmhouse.

The family awakens and prepares for a large family reunion that will honor the ninetieth birthday of the matriarch, Granny Vaughn, who lives in the house with her granddaughter, Miss Beulah; Beulah's husband, Ralph Renfro; their daughters, Ella Fay, Etoyle, and Elvie; their son, Vaughn; Gloria, who is the wife of their elder son, Jack; and Jack and Gloria's baby, Lady May. They all are excited about the reunion, and especially about the fact that Jack will be coming.

First to arrive are Uncle Curtis and his wife, Aunt Beck, with their sons and grandchildren. They bring peaches, chicken pie, and gifts. Next come Uncle Dolphus and Aunt Birdie with their children, grandchildren, and gifts. Uncle Percy and Aunt Nanny, whose two children have died in infancy, arrive with gifts. All talk excitedly about seeing Jack.

Uncle Noah Webster arrives with his new wife, Aunt Cleo. Gloria appears, and most of the guests compliment her beauty. Mr. Renfro's "old maid sister," Lexie, arrives.

Uncle Percy begins to tell the story of how Jack ended up in prison: One morning, Ella Fay went into Curly Stovall's store to buy some candy. Curly teases her about the fact that her family owes him money but is too poor to pay, and to prove him wrong, Ella Fay produces a gold ring she has taken from the family Bible to show off at school. (The ring belonged to her grandmother, who had drowned long ago.) Curly grabs the ring and refuses to return it. When Jack hears of this, he goes to the store, fights with Curly, and takes Curly's safe, into which Curly had put the ring. The safe comes open while Jack carries it home, and all the contents—including the ring but very little money—are lost. Curly presses charges against Jack for aggravated assault, and Jack is sentenced to the state penitentiary. Jack's best friend, Aycock Comfort, who came to Jack's aid during the fight, is also jailed.

The story of Jack's courtship of Gloria is also told. Jack was taken to the penitentiary immediately after his wedding.

During the telling of the story, Jack and Gloria's fourteen-month-old daughter, Lady May, makes her appearance.

Jack arrives and is greeted with joy. He meets his daughter for the first time. Soon after, Uncle Homer and Auntie Fay arrive, and Homer tells Jack that the car Jack just lifted out of a ditch belongs to Judge Moody, the same judge who sentenced him to prison. Homer heard about this at the icehouse, where he stopped to buy ice for the reunion. Apparently the man who caused the judge to veer into a ditch recognized both Judge Moody and Jack, and has spread the word. Everyone, including Jack, is outraged that Jack has unknowingly helped the judge, whom they despise, and Jack vows to find the man and put his car back into a ditch. Although everyone is enthusiastic about the idea, Gloria in-

sists that only she and Lady May will accompany Jack on his errand.

Part Two

On their way to find Judge Moody in his car, Jack and Gloria run into Brother Bethune, the Baptist preacher who will officiate at the reunion. Brother Bethune tells Jack that he saw Judge Moody recently and knows that the judge will be coming by them soon. Jack and Gloria wait for their opportunity to force the judge's car into a ditch. They are at the top of Lovers' Leap, a high hill with a sharp drop-off known as Banner Top. The road on which the judge will be driving is below them.

At the last minute, the plan goes awry. Gloria slips at the top of the hill and falls all the way down. Jack, holding the baby, tries to help her and also falls. They land on opposite sides of the road; the baby gets away from them and into the road just as the judge's car is bearing down. Gloria throws herself on the baby at the last second, and the judge is forced to drive his car, a Buick, up Banner Top. It stops just short of going over the edge.

The judge and his wife jump out of the car, and Aycock Comfort, who has come along, jumps into the backseat for fun. Jack discovers that the car, still running, is balanced precariously on a wooden sign stuck into the ground. If Aycock moves, it will plummet off the cliff.

Jack is now eager to help the judge, for he has saved Gloria and Lady May. All efforts to find a way to get the Buick down safely fail, however, and passersby are unable or unwilling to help. (Uncle Homer passes by, having left the reunion to campaign for justice of the peace.) One of the passing vehicles is a busload of teachers who are bound for the home of Miss Julia Mortimer, a retired teacher who has died that morning. Gloria is very upset to hear this, as Miss Mortimer was her benefactor. Gloria is an orphan, and Miss Mortimer took her in and helped her get an education.

Part Three

Jack, Gloria, and Lady May return to the reunion, leaving Aycock in the car. Judge and Mrs. Moody go along, as they have nowhere else to go. Brother Bethune has arrived, as has Uncle Nathan. Jack assures the family that Judge Moody has saved Gloria and Lady May and should be treated kindly.

Amid various family stories, the judge is made aware of who Jack is. At first, he does not remember Jack, but when given enough details of the trial, the judge remembers. Jack also tells everyone that he escaped from prison one day before his scheduled release to make the reunion and that he rode most of the way holding onto the spare tire on the back of the judge's car. Mrs. Moody has to point out to her husband that it was Jack who helped them out of a ditch earlier that day.

Brother Bethune recounts some family history, says grace, and everyone eats dinner. Granny opens her presents.

Among the stories told is how Ellen and Euclid Beecham, the parents of Miss Beulah and her brothers, drowned when their children were young. Their deaths appear to be suicide, but the family members prefer to leave this ambiguous.

Part Four

Willy Trimble, a neighbor, arrives with more details about the death of Miss Julia Mortimer. Willy found her fallen down in the road that morning and took her home, where she died. This leads the family members to reminisce about Miss Mortimer, though unkindly. They all resent her efforts to teach them. Most spiteful of all is Miss Lexie, who had been living with Miss Mortimer and taking care of her.

Willy also brings a book he found on Miss Mortimer's bed. The judge discovers that she has written her will in the book and that it demands that all her former students attend her burial. The family is outraged by this.

Gloria reveals that Miss Mortimer warned her that if she married Jack their child would be handicapped. This implies that the teacher had reason to believe that Gloria and Jack were related. The aunts begin to ponder who could have been Gloria's parents. They soon conclude, based on bits of hearsay and circumstantial evidence, that Sam Dale Beecham, the beloved youngest brother of Miss Beulah, who died during World War I, was Gloria's father. They are thrilled about this, as it makes Gloria truly one of the family—by blood as well as by marriage.

They all return to talking unflatteringly about Miss Mortimer; they are angry that she warned Gloria against marrying Jack. Miss Lexie talks at length about her senility. The judge then reveals that he came to Banner today because he had received a letter from Miss Mortimer, his old friend, asking him to come. He reads the letter, hoping that the family will see in it what a noble spirit the teacher had, but they do not.

Part Five

The talk returns to Gloria's parentage, and the judge points out that they have no real proof that Sam Dale was her father. He also points out that, if he was, Jack and Gloria are cousins, and their marriage is illegal in Mississippi. This causes much distress.

Uncle Homer returns to the reunion. He has been at Miss Mortimer's wake and reports that there are many, many people there, some from quite far away. It is clear that not everyone shares the family's low opinion of her.

Uncle Nathan reveals a story about his past that only Granny and Miss Beulah have known. Years ago, he killed a man named Dearman. This is why Nathan is constantly on the move and allows himself no comfort; he is doing penance for his crime. It is implied that Nathan killed Dearman because Dearman had impregnated Sam Dale's girlfriend. This means that Dearman, not Sam Dale, was Gloria's father, and therefore Jack and Gloria are not cousins.

Everyone except Uncle Nathan, Miss Lexie, and the Moodys leaves the reunion to go home. The rest go to bed.

Part Six

The next morning, in the rain and with much trouble, Jack and the judge finally get the judge's car off Banner Top. Aycock jumps out of the car just before it plunges over the edge.

Much to Jack's consternation, Ella Fay reveals that she and Curly—the very man who caused Jack to be sent to jail—are going to marry.

Everyone attends Miss Mortimer's burial at Banner Cemetery.

Jack and Gloria walk home from the cemetery. Jack is happy to be home with his family and ready to face the challenge of trying to support them on the farm.

Characters

Aunt Beck Beecham

Aunt Beck is married to Uncle Curtis Beecham. She is the nicest and most soft-spoken of all the aunts. She often interjects kind and reassuring comments when the other aunts are teasing or challenging someone.

Aunt Birdie Beecham

Aunt Birdie is married to Uncle Dolphus Beecham.

Aunt Cleo Beecham

Aunt Cleo is the newest member of the clan, having recently married Uncle Noah Webster Beecham. She is hearing many of the family's stories for the first time. She is confident, friendly, good-natured like her husband, and openly curious. She asks questions that keep the others' stories going.

Uncle Curtis Beecham

Curtis and the other Beecham uncles are Granny Vaughn's grandsons and Miss Beulah's brothers. Curtis is married to Aunt Beck.

Uncle Dolphus Beecham

Uncle Dolphus, another of Granny's grandsons, is married to Aunt Birdie.

Aunt Nanny Beecham

Aunt Nanny is married to Uncle Percy Beecham. When she arrives at the reunion, Welty writes that she "hauled herself up the steps as though she had been harnessed into her print dress along with six or seven watermelons."

Uncle Nathan Beecham

Uncle Nathan, the eldest grandson of Granny Vaughn, is the only bachelor and an oddball even among his colorful relatives. He is a self-styled itinerant evangelist who paints crude signs with religious messages and sticks them in the ground as he travels. He plants a sign on Banner Top, the local Lovers' Leap, just before Judge Moody's car roars up the hill, and the car ends up balanced on the sign just short of plummeting off the cliff.

Unlike the rest of the Beechams, Nathan talks very little, and he never eats at the reunion. Near the end of the novel, it is revealed that Nathan, many years before, killed a man to avenge a wrong done to his brother, Sam Dale, and then allowed authorities to hang another man for the crime. His solitary, nomadic lifestyle is his way of doing penance.

Uncle Noah Webster Beecham

Uncle Noah Webster, another of Granny's grandsons, has recently married Aunt Cleo. He is jovial and affectionate.

Uncle Percy Beecham

Uncle Percy, another of Granny's grandsons, is married to Aunt Nanny. Percy has a "weak and ragged" voice, a definite disadvantage in a family of storytellers. He tells his share of tales, however.

Sam Dale Beecham

Sam Dale is long deceased at the time of the story. He was the youngest of Granny's grandsons and died as a soldier during World War I, though not in combat. He appears in the family stories the others tell at the reunion.

Brother Bethune

Brother Bethune is an elderly Baptist preacher who comes to the reunion to fill the role that had previously been filled by Grandpa Vaughn, who has died since the last reunion. He recounts the family history and says the blessing before the meal. Brother Bethune is forgetful and senile, and the aunts do not hesitate to say aloud that he can't fill Grandpa Vaughn's shoes.

Auntie Fay Champion

Auntie Fay, Ralph Renfro's sister, is married to Homer Champion.

Homer Champion

Homer is married to Auntie Fay. At the time of the reunion, he is campaigning against Curly Stovall for justice of the peace. Like Curly, he will do anything to get votes. He spends the day out campaigning—primarily at Miss Julia Mortimer's wake—rather than with his family at the reunion. Because he puts his own political success above family loyalty, the family does not like him.

Aycock Comfort

Aycock Comfort is Jack's close friend. On the day that Jack fought with Curly Stovall and stole his safe, Aycock involved himself in his friend's dispute enough to be sentenced to prison along with Jack. On the day of the reunion, Aycock escapes along with Jack. After Mrs. Moody's car has climbed Banner Top, Aycock jumps into the back seat for fun before the seriousness of the situation is discovered. When the others realize that the car is delicately balanced on one of Nathan's signs, Aycock has to spend the night in the car to maintain the balance and keep the car from plummeting.

Mrs. Maud Eva Moody

Mrs. Moody is Judge Moody's wife. She is riding with him when he is forced to drive their car—

actually, it is her car—up Banner Top to avoid hitting Gloria and Lady May.

Judge Oscar Moody

Judge Moody is the judge who sentenced Jack to prison after his trial in connection with fighting with Curly Stovall and stealing his safe. As a result, the entire extended family despises the judge.

Judge Moody drives from the county seat, Ludlow, to Banner on the day of the reunion while Jack and Aycock manage to stow away on the back of his car undetected. When the judge runs his car into a ditch, Jack helps him get it out, without realizing who he is. When Jack discovers the judge's identity, he vows to track down the judge and put his car back into a ditch. The plan goes awry, however; the car the judge is driving ends up stuck at the crest of Banner Top, and the judge and his wife end up at the reunion.

Miss Julia Mortimer

Miss Julia was the local teacher in Banner for many years and taught most of the family members at the reunion. She retired some years before the reunion takes place, and Miss Lexie Renfro has been living with her and taking care of her. She dies on the morning of the reunion, and everyone attends her burial the next day.

Miss Beulah Renfro

Miss Beulah is Granny's granddaughter and the sister of Nathan, Curtis, Dolphus, Percy, Noah Webster, and the deceased Sam Dale. She is married to Ralph Renfro and is the mother of Jack, Ella Fay, Etoyle, Elvie, and Vaughn.

Miss Beulah and her family live with Granny on her farm. Miss Beulah loves her brood, especially Jack. She is rather shrill, rude, and cranky, especially on the subject of anyone who, in her eyes, has mistreated a member of her family. During the reunion, she, as hostess, continually bustles in and out of the kitchen and around the tables.

Ella Fay Renfro

Ella Fay is the eldest daughter of Miss Beulah and Ralph Renfro. She is sixteen at the time of the reunion and is described as "the only plump one" of the girls. Her tussle with Curly Stovall over a family heirloom leads to the fight that lands her older brother, Jack, in jail. Jack is dismayed at the end of the novel to find out that Ella Fay and Curly plan to marry.

Elvie Renfro

Elvie is the youngest daughter of Miss Beulah and Ralph Renfro. She is seven at the time of the reunion and something of a firecracker. When everyone is trying to figure out how to get Mrs. Moody's car off Banner Top, she runs home, jump-starts the old school bus that sits in the family's yard, and drives it to the site.

Etoyle Renfro

Etoyle is the middle daughter of Miss Beulah and Ralph. She is nine at the time of the reunion. A fun-loving tomboy, Etoyle often watches scenes unfold from a perch in a tree.

Gloria Renfro

Gloria is Jack's wife and Lady May's mother. An orphan, Gloria came to Banner as a novice schoolteacher about two years before the reunion. The families of the town drew straws to see which one would board Gloria, and the Renfros drew the short straw. Jack fell in love with Gloria and courted her, and the two were married the day Jack went off to prison.

Gloria is a quiet, private person, which makes her both an enigma and an aggravation to the Beecham-Renfro clan. For her part, she longs for the day when she and Jack can have their own home, away from his family, whom she sees as his biggest problem in life. She tells Jack, "Oh, if we just had a little house to ourselves, no bigger than our reach.... And nobody would ever find us! But everybody finds us."

Jack Renfro

Jack, nineteen, is the eldest son of Miss Beulah and Ralph Renfro, and he is the golden boy of the family. On the day of the reunion, it is his arrival that everyone eagerly awaits. The family hasn't seen Jack since he was put in prison—unjustly, in the opinion of all—a year and a half before.

Jack is a good-natured, compassionate, hardworking but mischievous young man who loves his family and his wife. He was sent to prison for fighting with Curly Stovall and stealing his safe after Curly took a family heirloom (their mother's wedding ring) from his sister Ella Fay. Jack only wanted to get back the ring, and Curly knew this but pressed charges anyway.

Jack is guided by his own sense of what is right, and by the needs and wishes of his family, rather than by the law. He is honest to a fault; when Judge Moody asks him in court if he did all he is accused of doing, Jack answers, "Yes sir, and a little bit more."

Because Jack's father, Ralph Renfro, is handicapped from an injury, the family depends on Jack to make the farm productive. The time he spends in prison causes them real hardship, and when he returns, all are counting on him to bring better times.

Lady May Renfro

Lady May is Gloria and Jack's daughter. She is fourteen months old at the time of the reunion. Because Jack has been in prison for a year and a half and her parents married the day he went into prison, it is clear that she was conceived out of wedlock.

Miss Lexie Renfro

Miss Lexie is Ralph Renfro's unmarried sister. She has been living with and caring for the retired schoolteacher Miss Julia Mortimer, who dies on the day of the reunion.

Mr. Ralph Renfro

Ralph is married to Miss Beulah. He is partially disabled as a result of a dynamite accident that occurred just before his marriage. Mr. Renfro is the town's "demolition expert," but, based on events and comments in the novel, he seems to not be very good at this job.

Vaughn Renfro

Vaughn is the twelve-year-old son of Miss Beulah and Ralph Renfro. During the time that Jack spent in prison, Vaughn had to do the work of a man to help keep the farm going.

Curly Stovall

Curly Stovall is the villain of the novel, though not a completely despicable one. He owns the store in Banner, and it is his tussle with Ella Fay that leads Jack to fight with him and steal his safe, which in turn lands Jack in prison.

At the time of the reunion, Curly is the justice of the peace. Homer Champion is campaigning against him, and the election is to take place two days after the reunion, the day after Miss Julia Mortimer's burial.

Miss Ora Stovall

Miss Ora is Curly Stovall's sister and lives with him behind the store.

Willy Trimble

Willy is a neighbor of Miss Beulah and Jack Renfro. He is helpful and well-meaning but something of a pest. Miss Beulah predicts that Willy will find an excuse to show up at the reunion, and when he does, she is rude to him but allows him to stay. It is Willy who finds Miss Julia Mortimer as she is dying.

Granny Vaughn

Granny is the matriarch of the clan, and the reunion is held to celebrate her ninetieth birthday. She dozes much of the time and talks little, and when she does speak up, her words are usually tart. When Brother Bethune's recounting of the family history is dragging on too long, and the preacher muses that perhaps Grandpa Vaughn is in heaven wondering why Granny doesn't come to join him, Granny says, "Suppose you try taking a seat. Go over there in the corner."

Themes

Family

The theme of family as both a positive and a negative force pervades *Losing Battles* from beginning to end. As the sun rises on the opening pages, four generations of a family wake up in the farmhouse they share. The family reunion that is about to begin will bring dozens more members of the extended family onto the stage. The story will show the family as a support system and a refuge but one with a dark side.

Although the occasion for the reunion is Granny Vaughn's ninetieth birthday, the center of attention is Jack, her eldest great-grandson, who is returning home for the reunion after spending a year and a half in prison. Welty uses Jack, more than any other character, to portray the positive elements of the family. Family is the hub around which Jack's life revolves. His decisions, actions, and feelings all are determined by his relationship to his family. Through other characters' descriptions of him, it is clear that Jack is loyal to his family and that, until he went to prison, he worked hard to help support them. He went to prison for trying to get back a family heirloom that had been forcibly taken from his sister. His only real objection to being imprisoned was that it deprived him of his family and them of his labor, which was much needed on the farm.

Topics for Further Study

- A primary theme of the novel is the struggle between individual identity and family identity. Which do you think is more important: a strong sense of self and independence, or strong family ties and togetherness? Is it possible to have both? Use examples from your life and the lives of people you know to support your answer.

- Which character in the novel do you most identify with? Why?

- Do research to learn about life in northeast Mississippi today. How has life changed since the time portrayed in the novel? How has it remained the same? Make a Venn diagram or a chart to show the differences and similarities. Consider such things as education, occupations, standard of living, family size, availability of health care, etc.

- Choose one passage in the novel that you think is especially amusing. Analyze the passage to see what makes it funny. Notice things such as the author's choice of language, pacing, etc. Try your hand at comedic writing by writing either an additional humorous scene for the novel or an amusing story based on something that happened in your own family.

- Given what you know about the family and the setting of the novel, and about the decades after the 1930s, write a short biography for Lady May. Consider how much education she received, whether she traveled, whether she married, and so on.

Jack's wife, Gloria, is an orphan who has no family of her own. Her dream is for she and Jack and their baby to have their own home, away from Jack's family. She feels that his family is Jack's biggest burden and tells him that she can never love them. Although Jack loves Gloria dearly, he always argues with her—sweetly but firmly—when the subject is his family. He cannot imagine choosing to live away from them and cannot see them as anything but a positive force in his life.

In return, the family gives Jack unconditional acceptance and support. When he appears in court, the whole family is there with him, and when he is sent to prison, as far as they are concerned, it is the law and the judge that are wrong, not Jack. In a sense, Jack *was* wronged, not so much by the judge but by another outsider, Curly Stovall, who has also incurred the family's collective wrath. Yet the family's support for its members is sometimes taken to such an extreme that it becomes destructive, replacing truth with wishful thinking and even outright lies.

Near the end of the story, the ever-curious Aunt Cleo demands to know the secret behind Nathan's odd behavior. Before anyone else can speak and possibly tell the truth, Miss Beulah answers:

> "Sister Cleo, I don't know what in the world ever guides your tongue into asking the questions it does!" Miss Beulah cried. "By now you ought to know this is a strict, law-abiding, God-fearing, close-knit family, and everybody in it has always struggled the best he knew how and we've all just tried to last as long as we can by sticking together."

Having already heard that Jack has just escaped from the penitentiary to attend the reunion, Aunt Cleo knows, as does everyone else, that Miss Beulah has embedded at least one lie in her defense of Nathan; the family is not exactly law-abiding. And the listeners at the reunion, along with readers, have a strong sense that Miss Beulah is telling an even bigger fib. When Jack presses Nathan to finally share whatever it is he has kept bottled up for years, Nathan confesses that he killed a man to avenge his deceased younger brother Sam Dale and then allowed authorities to hang a black man for the crime. At that, Miss Beulah asks Nathan, "Now what did you want to tell that for? . . . We could've got through one more reunion without that, couldn't we? Without you punishing yourself?"

Miss Beulah is so protective of her family, so committed to a view of events that holds them all blameless, that she desires to push murder—a double murder, really, since an innocent man was executed—under the rug. Therein lies the dark side of family ties. She refuses to acknowledge any truth that is unkind to her family, and so truth becomes subjective and twisted. There are other instances, too, in which various family members choose a comfortable lie over an inconvenient truth.

Throughout the story, Welty weighs the positive aspects of family against the negative. In the end, the good outweighs the bad. The story ends with Jack, Gloria, and their baby walking home to the old farmhouse that has been home to generations of his family. Jack will do his best to fulfill his family's expectations that he can make the farm productive and profitable again, lifting them all out of poverty. He begins to sing the old hymn "Bringing in the Sheaves," and, Welty writes, "All Banner could hear him and know who he was."

Style

Simile

Losing Battles is filled with similes, all of them fresh and inventive, some wildly unexpected. The following all appear on a single page:

> The dust Uncle Homer had made still rolled the length of the home road, like a full red cotton shirt-sleeve.

> The farm was as parched now as an old clay bell of wasp nest packed up against the barn rafters.

> Heat, like the oldest hand, seized Jack and Gloria by the scruff of the neck and kept hold.

> They marched through the cornfield, all husks, robbed of color by drought as if by moonlight.

> This frequency is not uncommon.

Welty's similes give the narrative a rich texture by piling image upon image. The images are unified in that all portray the sights, sounds, smells, tastes, and sensations of life in the rural South at a particular time. This heaping-up of images has the effect of immersing readers in the time, place, and life of the story.

Dialogue

Virtually all of *Losing Battles* is written in dialogue; the third-person narrator appears only infrequently to set a scene or manage a transition. The technique is appropriate, because nearly everyone in the entire extended family at the reunion is a storyteller and a nonstop talker. The constant, overlapping chatter gives the impression that no thoughts are kept private or left unexpressed; whatever comes into these characters' minds is immediately put into words and sent out to all within earshot. With one exception, the narrator never takes readers inside the mind of a character.

The few characters who do not talk constantly are singled out for their silence, and it is clear that their restraint marks them as black sheep and outsiders. The oddball itinerant and self-styled evangelist Nathan comes to the reunion each year, stands like a sentinel behind Granny's chair, and neither eats nor joins in the storytelling. The other quiet one is Gloria, the outsider who is a foil in every way for the clannish, verbose Renfros and Beechams. They remark on her insistence on keeping her thoughts to herself as they might remark on the customs of headhunters; it is beyond them. Miss Beulah declares, with all the charity she can muster, that Gloria has

> a sweet voice when she deigns to use it, she's so spotless the sight of her hurts your eyes, she's so neat that once you've hidden her Bible, stolen her baby, put away her curl papers, and wished her writing tablet out of sight, you wouldn't find a trace of her in the company room, and she can be pretty. But you can't read her.

Among the Renfros and Beechams, there is no such thing as enough good qualities to make up for keeping quiet.

Southern Gothic Literature

Some of Welty's writing is associated with the southern gothic style, and there are elements of this style in *Losing Battles*. Southern gothic writing features settings located in the American South, grotesque characters who are outcast, and bizarre events. Although the overall tone of *Losing Battles* is light and comedic, there are moments when the gothic element prevails. One such moment is when the clan is around the table and Mr. Renfro offers Uncle Nathan the "heart" of a watermelon—the sweetest, choicest portion. When Nathan raises his hand to refuse the watermelon, the following dialogue ensues:

> "Hey!" Aunt Cleo cried. "Ain't that a play hand?"

> Uncle Nathan's still uplifted right hand was lineless and smooth, pink as talcum. It had no articulation but looked caught forever in a pose of picking up a sugar lump out of the bowl. On its fourth, most elevated finger was a seal ring.

> "How far up does it go?" asked Aunt Cleo.

> "It's just exactly as far as what you see that ain't real," said Miss Beulah. "That hand come as a present from all his brothers, and his sister supplied him the ring for it. Both of 'em takes off together. Satisfied?"

> "For now," Aunt Cleo said, as they all went back to their seats.

The choice of words ("play hand," "pink as talcum"), the ring, Aunt Cleo's undisguised curiosity, and the fact that the hand belongs to Nathan, who

Compare & Contrast

- **1930s:** The United States is in a severe economic depression triggered by a stock market crash. Poverty and unemployment are widespread; hunger is common.

  1970s: The United States is in a recession triggered by an oil shortage. The Organization of Petroleum Exporting Countries (OPEC) raises prices and cuts production to punish the United States and Europe for their support of Israel. Economic growth slows, and inflation and unemployment are high.

  Today: The U.S. economy faces uncertainty. The longest period of prosperity in the nation's history appears to be over as economic growth slows, the stock market is rocked by instability, and the country becomes involved in war overseas.

- **1930s:** At a time when people have little or no money, and before the age of electronic entertainment, storytelling is a widely practiced and much appreciated art. When people have leisure time, they are likely to gather and listen to family members recall family stories and old tales, as the Renfros and Beechams do in *Losing Battles*.

  1970s: Television is in virtually every American home, and going out to the movies is a popular form of entertainment. Instead of telling stories, Americans are more likely to watch them on a screen.

  Today: In addition to television and movies, entertainment is now available via the Internet; home movies on video, DVD, and satellite; videogames; and more. Increasingly, people spend their leisure time alone, focusing on their preferred form of entertainment.

- **1930s:** The fictional Granny Vaughn, who was born in the 1840s and is celebrating her ninetieth birthday, has lived half a century beyond her life expectancy at birth, which was forty years. Her great-granddaughter Lady May, now a toddler, has a life expectancy of about sixty-five years.

  1970s: A woman born in the United States during the 1970s has a life expectancy of about seventy-seven years.

  Today: A woman born in the United States today has a life expectancy of about eighty years.

is odd enough without it, all combine to make the scene grotesque.

Historical Context

The Great Depression

Within two years of the 1929 stock market crash, economic depression was worldwide. In the United States, the drop in the gross national product (the amount of goods and services produced in a year) by 1933 sent that index lower than it had been in twenty years. Because of widespread poverty, the country's production capacity far outstripped the ability of consumers to buy. Factories closed, and young men wandered the country searching for work. Unemployment soared from a pre-crash rate of just over 3 percent to more than 25 percent in 1933. Farmers began dumping or holding back their products to protest the low prices they were receiving, which was not enough to cover the cost of growing the food.

The results for poor and middle-class Americans were disastrous. Many families lived in small shantytowns called Hoovervilles (after Herbert Hoover, the president at the time of the crash) on the outskirts of cities. In the South, 20 percent of all farms were foreclosed between 1930 and 1935, and their owners were evicted. Americans in all regions were hungry.

Losing Battles contains many indirect references to the depression and its effects on Boone County, Mississippi. When the family is discussing a man named Ears Broadwee who is out of work, Aunt Nanny says, "He may have to go to the CC Camp if something more to his liking don't come along." She is referring to the Civilian Conservation Corps, established by Congress in 1933 as part of President Franklin D. Roosevelt's New Deal plan for restoring the economy. Young, single men joined the corps, where they lived in camps and worked for the federal government. The work involved improving national parks and other natural resources; for example, CCC workers built trails and tourist facilities in the parks. In 1935, half a million men lived and worked in 2,600 camps; most sent their paychecks home to relatives that desperately needed them.

It is also mentioned at the reunion that the federal government recently sent "wormy apples" to Mississippi, part of a food assistance program. And several references are made to the fact that Gloria is nursing Lady May past the age when a little girl would normally be eating solid food. Gloria says that she does this because food is scarce.

Life in the Rural South

Welty's fictional farmers of Banner, Mississippi, are dealing not only with the depression but also with drought and poor soil, and these conditions were all too common in the 1930s. Topsoil had been worn out by overfarming and by farmers' failure to rotate crops. Yields were down, and farmers had to work harder for what they were able to wrench from the land.

The reason that Jack and his family are so outraged by Judge Moody's sentencing Jack to prison is that he is needed on the farm to feed his large family. Jack's father, Mr. Renfro, is partially disabled from an old injury, so Jack's strength is essential to keeping the farm running. Judge Moody and others acknowledge that being needed at home is an excuse that often gets prisoners released.

Jack and his siblings miss a lot of school because they are needed to work at home, and this, too, is historically correct. During the depression, education became a luxury that many could not afford. Schools closed throughout the South because there was no money to pay teachers. Those schools that stayed open often had few pupils and short school years.

Critical Overview

Losing Battles appeared in 1970 to virtually unanimous praise from critics and is still praised today. *New York Times* critic James Boatwright called the novel "a major work of the imagination and a gift to cause general rejoicing." He continued:

> *Losing Battles* is conclusive evidence of what many have long believed: that Eudora Welty possesses the surest comic sense of any American writer alive. It is a comedy . . . that presents character without fake compassion or amused condescension, a comedy that releases, illuminates, renews our own seeing, that moves in full knowledge of loss, bondage, panic, and death.

Paul Bailey, in *Times Literary Supplement*, wrote that in this "exceptionally beautiful novel" Welty had outshone some of her foremost peers:

> The prevailing tone is one of glorious ordinariness, but one that never sinks into the terminally cute— pace *Our Town* and the jottings of Brautigan, Saroyan, and Vonnegut. The humanity that is everywhere demonstrated in *Losing Battles* does not cuddle itself. . . . It simply and necessarily informs what is probably the quietest masterpiece to be written in America since the death of Willa Cather.

Similarly, Sara McAlpin, in *The Southern Review*, commended the author's subtle, complex characters, declaring that the family in the novel "is both nurturing and stifling, affirming and negating, supportive and destructive." This balanced portrayal, McAlpin wrote, "enriches rather than diminishes Welty's final presentation of family" and "underscores Welty's extraordinary sensitivity to the complexities of ordinary human beings, as well as her profound respect for the value of each individual person."

Discussing several works of Welty's fiction, C. Vann Woodward wrote in the *New York Times Book Review*:

> Miss Welty seems at her best with sprawling families assembled for rituals, ceremonies, or reunions. For example, the riotous romp and clatter of the Renfros and Beechams and the Banner community through *Losing Battles*.

Criticism

Candyce Norvell

Norvell is an independent educational writer who specializes in English and literature. She holds degrees in linguistics and journalism. In this essay,

> It is the indomitable spirit of Jack and his family that make this novel a comedy, not their ability to rise above circumstances. . . . Somehow, the Beechams and the Renfros lose all the battles but still manage to win the war."

Norvell discusses the significance of the title of Losing Battles.

The sprawling Beecham-Renfro clan that populates *Losing Battles* certainly has its endearing qualities. Granny and her grandchildren, in-laws, great-grandchildren, etc., are amusing, and they are survivors. They are loyal to one another, and they take care of their own. The best of the brood, young Jack Renfro, is as loving and lovable a character as readers will find in any work of fiction. Yet there is something about them that a reader could almost miss amid all their hilarity and weirdness: all of them, even Jack, are losers. The book is so funny and the characters are so buoyant that it is easy to forget the title and to fail to notice that virtually all the family's battles are losing battles. In most cases, they manage to lose in more ways than one.

A good example is the battle between Jack and Curly that ends with Jack in prison and with multiple losses for his family. First, Jack fails to recover the ring, a family heirloom, that Curly has grabbed from Ella Fay. Curly's safe comes open as Jack is carrying it home, and the ring falls out. Curly's possessions and the little bit of money that was in the safe are recovered, but the ring is never found. Second, Jack goes to prison for assaulting Curly. Not only is he separated from his wife on their wedding day but there are dire consequences for his family, who need him to work the farm. When Jack returns from prison, his old horse Dan and a wrecked truck he had been putting back together have both been lost to Jack's adversary Curly. Curly is the storekeeper, and things Jack loved have been traded for things the family needed.

Even so, Jack has not finished losing this battle. At the end of the story, Ella Fay, the sister who allowed Curly to grab the ring, reveals that she is going to marry Curly. Jack will have to accept into his family the man who sent him to prison and took his prized possessions from his destitute family. The tussle for which Jack came flying to defend his family's honor, for which he was sent to prison, and for which family treasures were lost (driving his family further into poverty), turns out to have been a mere flirtation. Curly Stovall is going to end up not only with Jack's horse and his truck but with his sister, to boot.

Thanks to Curly, Jack and the family meet their next adversary, Judge Moody. When the judge sentences Jack to prison for assaulting Curly, the family makes him their personal enemy and blames him for all they suffer in Jack's absence. They call him names and long for revenge, but their efforts will be defeated.

First, Jack unknowingly helps the judge by lifting his car out of a ditch. Next, Jack's plan to put the car back into a ditch goes awry. Jack's wife and child end up in harm's way; the judge manages to swerve and avoid hitting them, making the judge a hero. Now Jack very much wants to help the judge get his car off the precipice of Banner Top. But all his efforts to help the judge are as fruitless as were his efforts to harm him. Everyone who comes along is either unable or unwilling to help. Jack tries to use his family's mule and the old school bus that sits in their yard, but his resources are not up to the task.

Again, Jack has begun a battle that will only lead to a series of losses and humiliations. After spending a good part of the day of his family reunion trying to get the judge's Buick down from its perch, Jack has no choice but to invite the judge and his wife back to the reunion. He brings the enemy into camp, heralding the judge as a hero. Jack and the others try to save face by explaining that they are welcoming the judge without forgiving him, but the judge refuses to be convinced that he needs forgiving.

Jack's humiliation is made complete when the reunion ends and Judge and Mrs. Moody are led to Jack's bed—one in which Jack hasn't slept for a year and a half, thanks to the judge—and Jack and Gloria must sleep on the porch floor. Chalk up another loss for Jack and the Renfros.

In a different way, the family also loses a lifelong battle with Miss Julia Mortimer, quite possibly the most serious loss of all. They talk at the reunion about how they hated her for trying to teach them when they didn't care to learn. They consider books worthless, reading a waste of time, and any suggestion that they should improve themselves an insult. Miss Julia was not like them, so they despise her and are not capable of seeing anything good in her. They have never wanted anything but to escape her, and yet, here, too, they have failed. Miss Julia has the bad timing to die on the day of their reunion, so that they must be reminded of her. Miss Lexie, who has been her live-in caretaker, relates at length how, as Miss Julia fell further and further into senility, Lexie tried her utmost to keep her from communicating with the outside world. Lexie took the old woman's pencil away and refused to mail her letters or to give her mail that came for her. Once again, this is a losing battle. The old teacher managed to get two letters off to her old friend Judge Moody and to scrawl her will into a book with a pin when she had nothing else to write with. As Judge Moody tries to make the family see that the nobility of the human spirit has triumphed, if only in a small way.

In addition, in her will Miss Julia has managed to make one final imposition on her ungrateful former students. She commands that they all be present at her burial. Despite the fact that they despise her, the Beechams and Renfros are aware enough of her authority—and naïve enough—that they sit around questioning whether they still have to obey the teacher even when she is dead. The judge makes clear that, by his authority, if not by hers, they are to accommodate her last wish. Not only do they have to attend the burial, they confront the evidence that Miss Julia was not the monster they all made her out to be. There are many prominent people at the graveside service, including some who have driven all the way from other states. There are doctors and lawyers, and there is even a telegram from a governor. Miss Julia has some success stories; it's just that the Beechams and Renfros are not among them. In the battle between ignorance and knowledge, the Beechams and Renfros chose the side of ignorance and never realized that, in doing so, they were destined to lose.

The novel ends with Jack walking home from the burial, where he faces his next battle: the struggle to make the farm profitable in spite of economic depression and drought. The reader is quite sure by this time that it will be another losing battle, but Jack clearly has thoughts of a different kind. He sings the old hymn "Bringing in the Sheaves," seemingly confident of a bountiful harvest. It is the indomitable spirit of Jack and his

> *Something of the Mississippi hill country at a particular moment on a particular summer morning has been grasped, snatched from the dream of time passing, and framed. . . ."*

family that make this novel a comedy, not their ability to rise above circumstances; their willingness to get beaten and keep fighting, not their ability to win. Somehow, the Beechams and the Renfros lose all the battles but still manage to win the war—or at least survive it.

Source: Candyce Norvell, Critical Essay on *Losing Battles*, in *Novels for Students*, The Gale Group, 2002.

Richard Gray

In the following essay, Gray examines how Welty has used William Faulkner's style of repetition and interweaving lives within Losing Battles, *and discusses how her characters use talking and storytelling to remain connected to each other and to reality.*

"Maybe nothing ever happens once and is finished," observes Quentin Compson famously in *Absalom, Absalom!*

> *Maybe happen is never once but like ripples maybe on water after the pebble sinks, the ripples moving on spreading, the pool attached by a narrow umbilical water-cord to the next pool which the first pool feeds has fed, did feed, let this second pool contain a different temperature of water, a different molecularity of having seen, felt, remembered, reflect in a different tone the infinite unchanging sky, it doesn't matter: that pebble's watery echo whose fall it did not even see moves across its surface too at the original ripple-space, to the old ineradicable rhythm.*

It may seem perverse to begin talking about *Losing Battles* by quoting *Absalom, Absalom!* After all, *Absalom, Absalom!* is arguably William Faulkner's most Gothic novel, where the abiding Southern presence seems to be Edgar Allan Poe. It is melodramatic, even tragic, whereas *Losing Battles* is comic; it deals with the ghost-haunted gentry, while *Losing Battles* invites us into the lives of hill people fallen upon hard times. Faulkner's narrative weaves backwards and forwards over centuries, between Virginia, Haiti, Mississippi, New Orleans, and Harvard. Welty's, on the other hand, focuses on just a day and a half during the Depression and a family reunion; while not quite observing a classical unity of time and place, it seems to be quietly edging in that direction. Quite apart from the Faulknerian resonance of the title, however (which reminds us that Welty shares with her fellow Mississippian a quite un-American interest in the romance of failure and a typically Southern sense of the reality of defeat), there is in *Losing Battles* a deeply Faulknerian sense of the way many lives are woven into one life: repetition and revision are seen here as the norms of consciousness and narrative—so that *maybe nothing ever happens once and is finished*. "I wanted," Welty has said, when talking about how she came to write this novel, "to get a year in which I could show people at the rock bottom of their lives." But the year and more specifically the day that supplies the centerpiece of the story become a tapestry into which Welty can then weave the story of other days in other years. The family reunion, the ninetieth birthday of the oldest member of the clan, "Granny" Elvira Jordan Vaughn, becomes *attached by a narrow umbilical water-cord* to pools of memory, the *old ineradicable rhythm* of life as it has been lived by the Renfros and the Beechams for four generations along with the lives of various neighbors. "I wanted," Welty has also said in connection with this book, "to see if I could do something that was new for me: translating every thought and feeling into speech. . . . I felt that I'd been writing too much by way of description, of introspection on the part of my characters." That suggests exactly how Welty weaves the connections between past and present here, connecting one pool, one moment in space and time to another, just as Faulkner does, through the human voice debating, recollecting, revising, reinventing, each character constructing his or her own version of place and past. With sympathy and humor, *Losing Battles* describes people waging a disgracefully unequal struggle against circumstances but remaining hopeful despite everything—remaining so, above all, because they use old tales and talking as a stay against confusion, a kind of temporary defense.

"We need to talk, to tell," said Faulkner of Southerners once, "since oratory is our heritage." He might have been referring to the characters in *Losing Battles*. "Can't conversation ever cease?" asks one character, an outsider, towards the end of the novel, and any reader can easily see what he means. The Beechams and the Renfros, who make up the majority at this family reunion, never seem to stop talking. There are tall tales, family legends, personal memories, folk humor, religious myth, stories of magic and mystery, and everyone seems to possess his or her own storytelling technique. People comment on one another's storytelling abilities: when Uncle Percy Beecham, for example, begins to imitate the characters he is describing, his sister-in-law Birdie Beecham comments appreciatively, "he gets 'em all down pat . . . I wish I was married to him. . . . He'd keep me entertained." The dead, along with the living, are praised for their verbal gifts. Grandpa Vaughn, for instance, is chiefly remembered for his eloquence as a preacher, which his replacement as the local Baptist leader, the unfortunate Brother Bethune, can never match. "The prayer he made alone was the fullest you ever heard," recalls one of his grandsons, Uncle Noah. "The advice he handed down *by itself* was a mile long!" Sometimes, advice is offered to a novice speaker while he or she is speaking. "What's Normal?" asks Lexie Renfro when Jack Renfro's wife Gloria refers to her time at Normal School. "Don't skip it! Tell it!" Lexie receives advice in turn when she is about to embark on one of her more heartless tales about her experiences as a nurse: "Let's not be served with any of your stories today, Lexie," Beulah Renfro warns her. Always accompanying the main text, the talk requiring the reunion's attention, there is a subtext of comment, criticism, and anecdote, like that background of anonymous voices, inherited folk speech and wisdom, that gives resonance to traditional ballads and epic. There is the constant sense, in fact, that each tale or conversation, however trivial, belongs to a larger body of speech, a continuum of storytelling; stories knit into one another, one anecdote recalls another in the series, and tales are told which we learn have been told many times before: "I wish I'd had a penny for every time I've listened to this one," murmurs Ralph Renfro as his wife Beulah begins to recall the story of her parents' mysterious drowning. Weaving backwards and forwards in time, repeating and embroidering, the family reunion fashions a rich tapestry of folk-speech: a web of words that constitute their identity, their moment in space and time.

The figure of weaving is chosen advisedly here, not least because the dearest gift that "Granny" Elvira Jordan Vaughn receives on her birthday is a quilt:

"Believe I'll like the next present better. I know what *this* is." Granny told them, as she took the box covered in yellowing holly paper. . . . She took out the new piece-quilt. A hum of pleasure rose from every man's and woman's throat.

When the mire of the roads had permitted, the aunts and girl cousins had visited two and three together and pieced it on winter afternoons. It was in the pattern of "The Delectable Mountains" and measured eight feet square. . . .

It is not difficult to catch the connection between the literal and metaphorical webs that compel our attention in *Losing Battles*. Both are expressions of communality, representing the strenuous effort to weave a pattern out of—and, in the end, against—the difficulties, discontinuities and downright mess that constitute the basic fabric of these lives. Despite the "mire," the women of the family have struggled to make something that gives them a sense of identity, personal and communal: a feeling of being connected with their neighbors, their family, and their ancestors—other women who have woven something substantial in which to live and, eventually, to die (" 'She'll be buried under that,' said Aunt Beck softly. 'I'm going to be buried under "Seek No Further," ' said Granny, 'I've got more than one quilt to my name that'll bear close inspection.' ") And despite the mess, the battles constantly lost that define their material existences, both women and men also fight to weave an identity out of their words, to use language, not only to give themselves a local habitation and a name, but to make them feel a part of that habitation—its present, its past, and its possible futures. It is entirely appropriate that, immediately following the presentation of the quilt to Granny, all the voices at the reunion rise "as one" in song:

Gathering home! Gathering home!
Never to sorrow more, never to roam!
Gathering home! Gathering home!
God's children are gathering home.

In form and message, the song alerts us to that need for "home," for being and being a part of something that finds its expression in family gatherings, folk-art, and folk-speech. It is also entirely appropriate that the narrative should add this comment—this bass-note, as it were—to that song:

As they sang, the tree over them, Billy Vaughn's Switch, with its ever-spinning leaves all light-points at this hour, looked bright as a river, and the tables might have been a little train of barges it was carrying with it, moving slowly downstream. Brother Bethune's gun, still resting against the trunk, was travelling too, and nothing at all was unmovable, or

What Do I Read Next?

- *Eudora Welty* (1986), by noted literary scholars Harold Bloom and William Golding, provides biographical and critical overviews to aid the student of Welty's novels and short stories.

- Fellow Mississippian William Faulkner's 1930 *As I Lay Dying* is the story of a poor southern family on a journey to bury their mother. While this book touches on some of the same issues as *Losing Battles* (such as death and family relationships), Faulkner's treatment of these themes is dramatically different from Welty's.

- Flannery O'Connor's *The Complete Stories* (1996) provides a comprehensive look at the short stories of another important female writer from the South. O'Connor, like Welty, also wrote novels but is more strongly associated with short fiction.

- The *Collected Stories of Eudora Welty* (1982) includes all forty-one of Welty's published short stories. Welty is recognized primarily for her short fiction, and this collection is an ideal introduction to her work.

- Welty's autobiographical *One Writer's Beginnings* (1984) is a rare glimpse into the author's life experiences. Her writing style is the same blend of humor, observation, and sensitivity that readers enjoy in her fiction.

empowered to hold the scene still fixed or stake the reunion there.

"Nothing at all was unmovable": the metamorphoses of nature continue, despite our elaborate patternings, our attempts to tame and subdue things. The song, or speech, takes place within a world of flux and constant transformation; it can only give the temporary sense—or, rather, illusion—of stability and control.

There is another reason why the figure of the web seems so appropriate here when talking about the evident need of the characters in *Losing Bat-*

tles to talk and to tell. Faulkner once suggested that *The Brothers Karamazov* would have been a much shorter and much better book if Dostoevsky had "let the characters tell their own stories instead of filling page after page with exposition." He was joking, of course, in his own typically deadpan way, but the joke contained a serious point. Like Lexie Renfro, Faulkner believed that people need to "Tell it!"; that all people, not just Southerners, need to speak themselves into being. And, unlike Lexie, Faulkner clearly felt that this was not just a moral imperative but an existential one—not just something that human beings should do, in other words, but had to do if they were fully to function as human. The key text here is, again, *Absalom, Absalom!*, and the key passage is one embroidering an image with which any reader of *Losing Battles* would be broadly familiar:

> you are born at the same time with a lot of other people, all mixed up with them . . . all trying to make a rug on the same loom, only each one wants to weave his own pattern into the rug and it can't matter, you know that, or the Ones that set up the loom would have arranged things a little better, and yet it must matter because you keep on trying or having to keep on trying.

The sense of struggle is foregrounded more here than it is in Welty's use of the practice and figure of quilting. Even here, though, we should remember the mire through which the women struggle to make the quilt—and, of course, the darker shadows cast upon that practice by all those circumstances to which Welty's chosen title for the book alerts us. Battle is never very far from either Welty's or Faulkner's mind when they talk about talking. In both *Absalom, Absalom!* and *Losing Battles*, human experience is seen as a kind of feverish debate in which each participant, eagerly or otherwise, struggles to make himself heard, fights to weave his own pattern into the complex web of voices that constitute his life. Both books allow or rather compel the characters to tell their own stories—not for economy's sake of course, so as to save "page after page of exposition," but so as to make the simple, fundamental point that this is how we make our lives.

Voices, talking: the entire process of a life assumes for Welty, as if does for Faulkner, the character of a seamless pattern of dialogue. The individual human being—be he or she a Quentin Compson or a "Granny" Vaughn—is seen entering a web of relations that constitute human history. To this extent, both writers produce works that are genuinely dialogic, works in which, as Mikhail Bakhtin

suggested, "a character's word about himself and his world is just as fully weighted as the author's word usually is." "Language, discourse," Bakhtin insisted, ". . . is almost the totality of human life." This could almost stand as an epigraph for either *Absalom, Absalom!* or *Losing Battles*. So, for that matter, could this longer observation of Bakhtin's, which returns us to a familiar image and an abiding obsession:

> The living utterance, having taken its meaning and shape at a particular historical moment in a socially specific environment, cannot fail to brush up against thousands of living dialogic threads . . . it cannot fail to become an active participant in social dialogue.

Welty would almost certainly resist the terms Bakhtin uses here. She belongs, after all, to "a verbal community"—to use Bakhtin's phrase—that was and is quite different from the one Bakhtin himself knew. However, that should not blind us to the fact that for both of them, as Faulkner, communication implies community. What Welty's characters do is what Bakhtin argues the human subject *must* do and therefore the fictional character should do: engage in "the *social* dynamics of speech," as *part of* and yet also *apart* from a common verbal culture. As social beings and yet autonomous individuals, Welty's people participate in what Bakhtin would have called a "great dialogue" or "open dialogue," in which "the object is precisely the passing of a theme through many and various voices." It is, of course, the passing that matters, the process of dialogue. For Welty, as for Bakhtin, language, speech, is an open system, a "mobile medium" (as Bakhtin puts it) that resists closure. "Each individual utterance," Bakhtin observed, "is a link in the chain of speech communication." By its very nature, that chain is of indefinite length or duration; it can have no beginning or end. The possibility of a final, finalizing discourse is consequently excluded, along with the claims of an authoritative one. Each talker is involved for a while in what Bakhtin calls "a continuous and open-ended . . . dialogue" that went on long before they began talking and will continue long after. We are reminded of the potentially unending nature of the human debate, the web of words we weave, when, towards the end of *Losing Battles*, Uncle Noah Webster says this to Gloria, his niece:

> Gloria, this has been a story on us that never will be allowed to be forgotten. Long after you're an old lady without much further stretch to go, sitting back in the same rocking-chair Granny's got her little self in now, you'll be hearing it told to Lady May [Gloria's baby daughter] and all her hovering brood. . . . I call this a reunion to remember . . . !

Even the reunion that supplies the setting for most of the novel is to be given substance and weight, it seems, a sense of authenticity, by the feeling that it will one day be the subject of, rather than the occasion for, talk. What happens here and now will become part of a story by being woven into the fabric of speech.

Part of this story that Uncle Noah refers to is the suspicion, entertained at least for a while, that Gloria may in fact be a Beecham, entitled by blood rather than marriage to be a part of the reunion. Clearly, the possibility of incest that this raises is of little interest to the family. What excites them is the bright hope that they can press this apparent outsider into the group, and so close the magic circle around themselves even tighter. "Say Beecham! . . ." the women chant at Gloria, "Can't you say Beecham? What's wrong with being Beecham?" This is a Southern family romance with a vengeance, in which, as in so many romances from the region, the family tries to enforce relationship, to press the unwilling into membership. For a moment, we are invited to consider a darker side to the reunion, the more coercive element implicit in the talk. After all, the way the family bears down on Gloria is almost like a rape:

> . . . the aunts came circling in to Gloria . . .—all the aunts and some of the girl cousins . . .

> . . . a trap of arms came down over Gloria's head and brought her to the ground. Behind her came a crack like a firecracker—they had split open a melon.

> She struggled wildly at first as she tried to push away the red hulk shoved down into her face, as big as a man's clayed shoe, swarming with seeds, warm with rain-thin juice.

> They were all laughing. "Say Beecham!" they ordered her, close to her ear. They rolled her by the shoulders, pinned her flat, then buried her face under the flesh of the melon with its blood heat, its smell of evening flowers. Ribbons of juice crawled on her neck and circled it, as hands robbed of sex spread her jaws open.

Not a corncob, on this occasion, but a melon. But it serves a similar purpose to that of the notorious instrument of violence in Faulkner's *Sanctuary*. It enables those "robbed of sex" to force themselves and their will, for a while, upon an unwilling victim; it becomes part of a strategy of violence, to make "one of them" become "one of us." The other part of that strategy is, of course, the chant that accompanies and reinforces the action, turning a violent series of impulses into an equally violent ritual. The chant—"Say Beecham!" "Can't you say Beecham?"—reminds us that what these women

are trying to do is drown Gloria's voice and being in their own. "I don't want to be a Beecham!" Gloria cries, just before she is forced to the ground. But the aunts and cousins want her to change her speech: to "say" the name that articulates a new identity. "I achieve consciousness," Bakhtin argued, "I am conscious of myself and become myself only while revealing myself for another, through another, and with the help of another. . . . To be means to be for another, and through the other, for oneself." However, neither Welty nor her characters need any help—from Bakhtin or anyone else—to realize that, in human terms, to say is to be, that it is through speech that people enter into consciousness of self and community and so into the possibility of deliberate, moral action. The women who try to force Gloria to "Say Beecham!" understand, only too well, how words enable identity. Through their incantation, they register their own innate sense of the power, and the human inevitability, of language; they also offer us a measure of just how much that power can be used for good or ill.

"A reunion," Welty once said in an interview,

> is everybody remembering together—remembering and relating when their people were born and what happened in their lives, what that made happen to their children, and how it was they died. There's someone to remember a man's whole life, every bit of the way along. I think that's a marvellous thing.

That also explains very clearly why the Beechams and Renfros need to talk, and the way talk enables them to escape from their loneliness into a sense of being and belonging. To put it simply, they feel they are there because they say they are and other people say so too. Yet all the while they are saying so, there are warnings about the other side of things. Quite apart from those elements and moments in the narrative (like the attack on Gloria) that recollect the darker possibilities of language, there are reminders all the time of the mystery of personality, the secret phases of experience, the accidents in life—all those things that no dictionary, no web of words can ever quite accommodate. Gloria Renfro is important here, too, because, despite all the pressure that is put upon her, she continues to insist that she is different—not a Beecham or a Renfro but an orphan, alone and apart. "I'm here to be nobody but myself," she declares at one point, and elsewhere, "I'm one to myself, and nobody's kin, and my own boss, and nobody knows the one I am or where I came from." Sometimes she comes close to feeling defeated. "Oh, if we just had a little house to ourselves. . . .

And nobody could ever find us," she exclaims to her husband, and then adds hopelessly, "But everybody finds us. Living or dead." At the end of the book, however, she has not given up. She is still insisting on her separateness, her's and other people's essential privacy ("people," she declares, "don't want to be read like books")—still standing out against the family and what she, at least, sees as the imprisoning web of its stories.

And then there is Judge Oscar Moody, a rather different matter from Gloria, but still a reminder that the story told at the family reunion is a partial one. He is a comic ghost at the feast, brought there by chance, cut off by education and social position from the easy-going manners of his hosts, and slightly embarrassed by the recollection that it was he who put Jack Renfro in jail. The event that brings him and his wife to the reunion is a car accident. Swerving to avoid Gloria and her baby, the Judge drives his Buick off the road, and it ends up balanced uncertainly on the edge of a precipice called Banner Top. There it provides a grotesque reminder of the way things happen to spoil even our best-laid plans; the accident, in short, calls our attention to the accidental. It seems elephantine, or at least less than sensitive to Welty's light touch, to add that it also offers a comic emblem of the precarious nature of things, the abyss that hovers beneath us and our chattering. Still, the emblem is there, however delicately or allusively it may be sketched in; and it is highlighted by such nice touches as the hickory sign on which the Buick rests as it sticks out over Banner Top, which asks the question, "Where Will YOU Spend Eternity?" The question is never answered, of course, just as the plaintive demands made by the Judge's wife to be returned immediately to "civilization" never meet with a satisfactory response. But the reader is reminded by such things that there are other dimensions of experience, different vocabularies standing on the edge of this particular verbal world. The sign warns us that any sign merely marks out a boundary.

As far as warnings of this kind are concerned, however, one character stands head and shoulders above the rest: Miss Julia Mortimer. During the course of the reunion, the news is brought that Julia Mortimer has died. Many of those present were taught by her, and they remember her, not necessarily with affection, as a magisterial presence. Now they rehearse her story, trying to recollect what sort of impression she made on them. This impression is summed up, really, by their response to her own words in a letter that Judge Moody, another of her ex-pupils, reads out to them. The letter, written by Julia Mortimer not long before her death, is a sort of apologia, an explanation or defense of the aims that sustained her throughout her career. "All my life," she confesses defiantly, "I've fought a hard war with ignorance. Except in those cases that you can count off on your fingers, I lost every battle." The reaction of the Beechams and Renfros, as they listen, is notable for three things above all: uneasiness, incomprehension, and amusement. "Don't read it to us!" several of them cry before the Judge begins, then, when he has begun, "I can't understand it when he reads it to us. Can't he just tell it?" "I don't know what those long words are talking about," complains one hearer, Aunt Birdie Beecham, while another one, Beulah Renfro, appears to speak for most of the Judge's audience when she concludes, "Now I know she's crazy. We're getting it right out of her own mouth, by listening long enough." Julia Mortimer, it is clear, spoke in another idiom, a language foreign to most of those assembled at the reunion. She believed in enlightenment, progress, making something of oneself. "She had designs on everybody," Uncle Percy Beecham recollects, "she wanted a doctor and a lawyer and all else we might have to holler for some day." She also believed in travelling beyond the horizons of one's local community and culture; for instance, she told one Beecham, Uncle Nathan, to see the world. "He took her exactly at her word," comments Beulah Renfro, Nathan's sister. "He's seen the world. And I'm not so sure it was good for him." All her life, in fact, she was committed to a vocabulary and vision that demoted the Beechams, the Renfros, and all that their reunion represents to the level of the provincial, the backward, and the ignorant ("you need to give a little mind to the family you're getting tangled up with," she apparently told Gloria just before her marriage). The Beechams and Renfros, in turn, hardly began to understand her when she was alive, nor do they want to now that she is dead. As they see it, she was domineering, eccentric, or, more simply, crazy. Welty's point is not, of course, that either side is right in this debate, although by setting her book well back from the time of writing it, she may have been working from the assumption that the forces of progress represented by Miss Julia have been losing less of this particular battle recently than those embodied in the family reunion. What she is doing, rather, is giving a further edge, another accent to the talk of the family reunion—throwing the "remembering and relating" of these hill folk into sharper relief by reminding us of other forms of intelligence, other ways of turning the world into words that for good *and* ill it happens to leave out.

There is also the simple, brute fact of Julia Mortimer's dying. Lexie Renfro was Miss Julia's nurse, and the news of her death prompts Lexie to recall what she was like during the final stages of her life. "All her callers fell off, little at a time, then thick and fast," Lexie remembers. They were put off by her abrasive manner, her unwillingness to suffer fools gladly; and Miss Julia was left waiting, sitting in her front yard, for people who never came. "I used to say," Lexie declares, "'Miss Julia, you come on back inside the house. You hear? People . . . aren't coming visiting. Nobody's coming.'" But evidently Miss Julia took no notice. So for her own good, Lexie insists, with that bland authoritarianism characteristic of so many nurses, she tied her charge to the bed: "I didn't want to, but anybody you'd ask would tell you the same: you may have to." Miss Julia was reduced to writing letters, incessantly and feverishly. With her tongue hanging out, Lexie recalls with amazement, "Like words, just words, was getting to be something good enough to eat." Lexie mailed them, she admits, because she "couldn't think . . . what else to do with 'em;" and it is, of course, one of those letters that Judge Moody reads out to the bewilderment of the family. Eventually, though, even this resource was taken away from her; Miss Julia's pencil was snatched from her hands by her ever-solicitous keeper ("I could pull harder than she could," says Lexie triumphantly), and she was then reduced to the mere gesture of writing—shaping words with her finger on the bedsheet or her palm. Then Lexie left her—"I had the reunion to come to, didn't I?" she asks her audience plaintively— and it was while she was by herself that Julia Mortimer died, virtually imprisoned, it seems, denied books or writing material, without close friends, visitors, or even sympathy.

The final picture Julia Mortimer presents is a pathetic one, certainly, but pathos is not Welty's primary aim. What she is alerting us to here is something else: a series of subtle variations on the theme of old tales and talking and the need to tell that all her characters share. Miss Julia, the former schoolteacher, betrays the same compulsion as the men and women whom she once taught—to communicate and so substantiate, to create a feeling of being someone somewhere rather than just anyone anywhere through the use of language. In her case, the language is more a written than a spoken one; but that perhaps is less significant than the fact that, for her, the compulsion becomes exactly and sim-

ply that—a compulsion. She continues to write herself into life even when the instruments of writing are denied her. Her hands trace out an identity— or, to be more accurate, the need for an identity— far more starkly and finally than even the voices of the Beechams and Renfros ever can. Nobody receives the message, nothing is even written, but Miss Julia still continues to resist death through her compulsive and constant gesture. Faulkner once claimed that everything ever written ultimately carries one message, "*I was here.*" And Miss Julia seems to be repeating that message, with a change of tense, as she runs her fingers over her palm or the bedsheet. Not quite "*I was here*," more "*I am here*"; as long as she writes, she senses, she still is. If Miss Julia's writing herself—that is, her writing from, about, and finally *of* herself—is a shadowy transcription of the speaking themselves, talking themselves into being, favored by her former pupils, then the isolation from which she writes, during her final days, acts in turn as a *memento mori*—a haunting reminder of the vacuum over which any bridge of words is built. The letters, visible and invisible, are another sign like that one on Banner Top, "Where Will YOU Spend Eternity?" They offer the chilling message that, whatever communication and community we may enjoy during our lives—and, in particular, on occasions like a reunion—we must all eventually die alone.

Of course, Julia Mortimer is not the only person writing herself into life; Eudora Welty is doing the same, or something similar. Behind the tellers of the tales in *Losing Battles* lies the teller of the tale *Losing Battles*; the web of words is one that also speaks the message for Welty, "*I was here.*" It is a web of words that begins to establish itself as just that—a web of words, an elaborate verbal construct—right from these opening sentences on the first page:

> When the rooster crowed, the moon had still not left the world but was going down on flushed cheek, one day short of full. A long thin cloud crossed it slowly, drawing itself out like a name being called. The air changed, as if a mile or so away a wooden door had swung open, and a smell, more of warmth than wet, from a river at low stage, moved upward into the clay hills that stood in darkness.

> Then a house appeared on its ridge, like an old man's silver watch pulled once more out of its pocket. A dog leaped up from where he'd lain like a stone and began barking for today as if he meant never to stop.

A portrait like this is a triumph of specificity and containment. Welty presents us here with a shifting, evanescent place which nevertheless seems to have been caught for a while and composed. We are in that allusive, metamorphic and yet somehow briefly harmonized environment where, after the gift of the quilt to "Granny" Vaughn, the members of the family reunion sing their song. Something of the Mississippi hill country at a particular moment on a particular summer morning has been grasped, snatched from the dream of time passing, and framed; and in catching it, Welty matches up to her own description of the ideal photographer or story-writer who knows, she says, just "when to click the shutter," the precise instant at which people or things "reveal themselves." Yet for all that, something has been squeezed out and remains elusive, some quality of the moment remains uncaught and seems to slip through the artist's fingers, eluding every one of her traps and snares. The way this is intimated to the reader is subtle but inescapable. The prose never stops emphasizing its own fragility and artfulness. It is compulsively metaphorical, insistently figurative and even sportive, as though the author were trying to point out that this is, after all, an artifact, a pattern made out of words. Within the space of three sentences, for instance, a cloud is compared to a name; the air is said to change "as if … a wooden door had swung open"; and a house suddenly appears in the dawn light like a watch pulled out of a pocket (and not just *any* watch or *any* pocket: here as elsewhere, the figurative reference assumes a dramatic life of its own). The very insistence of this, the constant use of "like" or "as if," little touches such as the metaphor of naming or the dog apparently believing he is barking/voicing the day into life—all help to remind us that the writer's language, like every other means used to alleviate our separateness, is an imprecise and not entirely trustworthy medium. Even when fought with this weapon, it seems, all battles must be losing battles, although they are never irretrievably lost.

For Faulkner, writing was a quest for failure; for Welty, evidently, it is a losing battle—but a battle that must constantly be fought. And, for both writers, there is clearly a link between their own art and the broader human project that their characters dramatize—of trying to spin a sense of reality out of language. "The mystery lies," Welty has said, "in the use of language to express human life." All her work is concerned with that mystery: the aboriginal impulse that, as she sees it, we all share to render life comprehensible through the use of the spoken and written word. It is, perhaps, wrong to place too much emphasis ultimately on the role the

Southern love of talk has played in her life. It is important, certainly, for Welty just as it was for Faulkner; but it is important in that it allows her, just as it did her fellow Mississippian, to learn very early about the power and possibilities of speech—and then quickly led her from this to understanding the vital part that language plays in *all* our lives, regardless of whether we are Southern or not. Quite simply, she came to know through the Southern "need to talk" that we all need to talk in order fully to live. It is hardly an accident, after all, that two of the three sections of Welty's book about her beginnings as a writer place the major emphasis on voice: "Listening" and "Finding a Voice." Nor is it by chance that one crucial moment in what Welty calls her "sensory education" is described in this way:

> At around six, perhaps, I was standing by myself in our front yard waiting for supper, just at that hour in a late summer day when the sun is already below the horizon and the risen full moon in the visible sky stops being chalky and begins to take on light. There comes a moment, and I saw it then, when the moon goes from flat to round. For the first time it met my eyes as a globe. The word "moon" came into my mouth as though fed to me out of a silver spoon. Held in my mouth the moon became a word. It had the roundness of a Concord grape Grandpa took off his vine and gave me to suck out of its skin and swallow whole, in Ohio.

The beauty of a passage like this, like the intricate beauty—on a larger canvas—of her novels, is that Welty manages to convince the reader that words are simultaneously everything *and* nothing. They are everything because they constitute all the world we make for ourselves. Issuing out of our fundamental, definitively human rage for order—not only to see, but to know—they are as vital to us as breath. They register for us the irresistible otherness of things in terms that are, at their best, vivid and sensory. Another American writer, William Carlos Williams, suggested that a thing known passes from the outer world to the inner, from the air around us into the muscles within us. And the word "moon" seems to achieve the same vital transit. As Welty recalls it, "moon" is not just an abstract, arbitrary sign, it has the "roundness" of a sensory object—it generates the sense that contact between the namer and the named has taken place. This is a gift, offered with "a silver spoon," that we are all offered, although very few of us can take as much advantage of that gift as Welty does. And it can fill us with a sense of presence, as it does the six-year-old girl recalled here. We, like her, can feel that we know and can participate in the world through the word. It is everything, then. It is, however, also quite literally nothing. The word "moon," despite the way it assumes shape and fullness in the mouth, is "no thing"; it is, at best, a powerful, sense-laden sign for the mysterious, distant object that shimmers in the evening sky. Caught in this moment, in effect, as it is caught at length in a novel like *Losing Battles*, is the sense that the world must remain irreducibly other, set apart from all our attempts at naming. Just below the web of words that we are continually spinning in order to tell ourselves that we live is the "something" that must always remain ungrasped and unknown, the "something" that is intimated, for example, in a shifting, metamorphic natural scene, the loneliness of an outsider, or in rumors of the abyss and death. *Losing Battles* is a comic novel, certainly, and as definitively Southern in its own way as *Absalom, Absalom!* But its comedy offers a serious revelation of the human impulse that, above all, makes us human; and its Southerness enables a clearer general understanding, a vivid and universally valid declaration, of the extraordinary ways of words. At least one question is answered, then, by the time the novel draws to a conclusion. "Can't conversation ever cease?" The answer is "no," not while there are people like the Beechams and Renfros around—which means, finally, any people at all.

Source: Richard Gray, "Needing to Talk: Language and Being in *Losing Battles*," in *Southern Literary Journal*, Vol. 29, No. 2, Spring 1997, pp. 72–86.

Eve Kornfeld

In the following essay, Kornfeld discusses the reconstruction of American law within the stories of Welty's Losing Battles.

I

In the 1960s, in my home town of Jackson, the civil rights leader Medgar Evers was murdered one night in darkness, and I wrote a story that same night about the murderer (his identity then unknown) called 'Where Is the Voice Coming From?' But all that absorbed me, though it started as outrage, was the necessity I felt for entering into the mind and inside the skin of a character who could hardly have been more alien or repugnant to me. Trying for my utmost, I wrote it in the first person. I was wholly vaunting the prerogative of the short-story writer. It is always vaunting, of course, to imagine yourself inside another person, but it is what a story writer does in every piece of work; it is his first step, and his last too, I suppose.

(Eudora Welty, *One Writer's Beginnings*)

> A central place in the family's tales of their losing battles is reserved for their contacts with the law."

In recent years, legal scholars have started to examine the complex interconnections between the politics of narrative and the social construction of American law. Informed both by critical legal studies and poststructuralist perspectives, these theorists view American legal history as a series of contests of power, unequally joined. American law depends upon the telling of stories, but not all stories are heard. Mindful of the centrality of narrative to the construction of legal meaning and social power, these scholars (many of whom are women or men of color) seek empowerment for traditional outsiders through the construction of alternative legal narratives. They argue that the compelling force of narrative itself might create a new sense of empathy with the powerless in America, and fuel the reconstruction of American law across class, race and gender boundaries. They hope that many Americans will join Eudora Welty in her attempt to enter "into the mind and inside the skin" of people traditionally alien and even repugnant to them. This paper will explore this nascent analysis of legal narrative and the construction of power, as well as the imaginative combination of some of its central concepts and the reconstruction of American law envisioned in Welty's own tales of the Depression years in rural Mississippi, *Losing Battles*.

II

The new approach to American law is rooted in a poststructuralist analysis of knowledge and power, and a recognition of the complex ways in which reality and subjectivity are socially constructed though largely unrecognized discursive practices. Those social arrangements which seem natural, essential, inevitable and immutable are merely representations, created and sustained by patterns of human perception, language and narrative. Language actively inscribes rather than transparently describes the world. To tell one's stories to an audience, then, is to operate within a discourse that shapes social reality; one either consciously or unconsciously perpetuates or challenges prevailing relationships of power. No one who talks or writes can choose not to participate in this process, whether the manifest topic is war, economics, medicine, gender or race relations, or law.

This central insight involves a fundamental deconstruction of the objectivist theory of truth, which has supported American law as well as most other Western intellectual systems for centuries. As Kim Lane Scheppele explains, objectivist theory "holds that there is a single neutral description of each event which has a privileged position over all other accounts. This single, neutral description is privileged because it is objective, and it is objective because it is not skewed by any particular point of view." The law's quest for truth, therefore, leads to earnest attempts "to locate this privileged description, the one that enables the audience to tell what *really* happened as opposed to what those involved *thought* happened. . . . Truth, in this view, is what remains when all the bias, all the partiality, all the 'point-of-viewness' is taken out and one is left with an objective account free of the special claims of those who stand to gain."

The very serious flaw in this objectivist theory of truth and justice is that there simply are no neutral, objective observers. As psychologists have demonstrated repeatedly over the past few decades, all observers bring to a situation a set of expectations, values and beliefs that determine what they will be able to see and hear. Two individuals listening to the same story will hear different things, by emphasizing those aspects that accord with their learned interpretations and experiences and ignoring those aspects that are dissonant with their views of the world. While this is true of any two individuals, it is still more evident among individuals from different social groups. People with widely varying social experiences and situations tend to see the same event in distinctly and systematically different ways. Hence there is no possible escape in life or in law from selective perception, or from subjective judgments based on prior experiences, values and beliefs.

For these reasons, battles of simple description—or the legal construction of facts—can be just as important and ferocious as battles of complex legal interpretation. Legal stories "may diverge, then, not because one is true and another is false, but rather because they are both self-believed descriptions coming from different points of view informed by different background assumptions about how to make sense of events." Legal judgments, based entirely upon competing stories about events that judges and juries never witness, validate some stories as truth and reject others as false. The social danger in this apparently neutral procedure is that, historically, the legal construction of facts and judgments "has a distinctive selectivity, one that tends to adopt the stories of those who are white and privileged and male and lawyers, while casting aside the stories and experiences of people of color, of the poor, of women, of those who cannot describe their experiences in the language of the law." The only way to create the sense of objective neutrality is systematically to exclude the stories and judgments of those situated differently in the social world. But this is illusory truth and justice indeed.

If some of this traditional exclusion of social outsiders from American law is attributable to naive theories of objective truth or unconscious legal habits, there can be no doubt that it also reinforces and sustains the power of the dominant group in American society. The narratives that we allow ourselves to hear act to construct American law and society. Thus the privileging of the hegemonic legal narratives of white males is doubly invidious: not only does it render invisible, silent and powerless once again those whose voices have never been heard in American law, but it construes their silence as consent. The abstract language and apparently objective narratives of "neutral law"—including the search for "original intent"—mask continued and continuous contests of social power.

No theorist unmasks these legal contests of power more effectively than the African-American scholar Patricia Williams. As she convincingly argues, "Blacks and women are the objects of a constitutional omission which has been incorporated into a theory of neutrality. It is thus that omission is really a form of expression, as oxymoronic as that sounds: racial omission is a literal part of original intent; it is the fixed, reiterated prophecy of the Founding Fathers." Given this historical context, "the limitation of original intent as a standard of constitutional review is problematic. . . . Neutrality is from this perspective a suppression, an institutionalization of *psychic* taboos as much as segregation was the institutionalization of *physical* boundaries." Moreover, under the new laws of equal opportunity, the social text remains remarkably unchanged: "The rules may be color-blind but people are not." Therefore, the retreat to arguments of original intent and the insistence on formal "neutrality" in American legal discourse ignore historical context and social text alike, and simply perpetuate the injustices of centuries of American law and society.

To counter this long tradition of social exclusion through legal abstraction, Williams tells her own stories of painful discrimination, in her own powerful voice. Indeed, it might be argued that the stunning force of Williams's stories, told in the first person, contributes significantly to the effectiveness of her critique of formal equal opportunity and, more broadly, of legal abstraction and neutrality. Other legal scholars (especially women and men of color) have also begun to construct alternative legal narratives, in the hope of empowering traditional outsiders to American law. Mari Matsuda, Milner Ball, Richard Delgado, Derrick Bell and others "show in the telling of alternative stories how selective narratives come to have the power of truth, though there may be other versions that lead to other conclusions, other ways of seeing." Their alternative narratives, too, constitute interrogations of objectivist theories of truth and justice.

Exposing the politics of narrative and the contests of power underneath "neutral law" is but the first step in the long process of the reconstruction of American law. To this fundamental critique must be added new visions of truth and justice. Counterhegemonic legal storytelling offers such visions, in direct juxtaposition with the privileged story of traditional American legal values. Thus Mari Matsuda, in proposing legal sanctions for racist speech, moves between two stories: "The first is the victim's story of the effects of racist hate messages. The second is the first amendment's story of free speech. The intent is to respect and value both stories. This bipolar discourse uses as method what many outsider intellectuals do in silence: it mediates between different ways of knowing in order to determine what is true and what is just." Matsuda's counterpoint allows us to hear lost voices and to see long-hidden visions of truth and justice in America.

Similarly, Milner Ball approaches the American story of origins itself with a dual consciousness of its regenerative and exclusive power. The story of liberty and equality has been successfully expanded and claimed by some traditional outsiders of late, but certainly not by all: "While the struggle to gain equality for black people may be a prime instance of the transformative effect of the story, the continuing practice of violence against Indian tribes is a critical instance of its destructive effect. The story is a good one, but bound up with and in-

separable from its goodness and success, it has also served aggression and exclusivity." Ball's desire both to affirm and disaffirm the American story of origins leads him to supplement it with other constitutive narratives and their alternative visions of truth and justice.

Recognizing the limitations of narrative power ("It may transform, but it cannot transfigure"), Ball nonetheless adds devastating Amerindian perspectives on the American story of origins in the hope of creating a dialogic polyphony that might itself be transformative of American law. Separated from the false constraints of "original intent", then, the American story of origins itself might be made truer and more just: "That the American story of origins is still being written is one of the reasons that its effects, content, and telling are not finally settled. Its substance and meaning are still contested. The story of the circumstances attending the foundation conserves but also transforms and is transformed, as polyphonic narrative should in a democratic society." In this sense, telling alternative stories is a performative act, and the contest of power in which it knowingly engages may begin to reconstruct American law.

The construction of alternative legal narratives thus presents a searing critique of the assumptions of "neutral law," and proposes other possible visions of truth and justice. This theoretical bent is accompanied, however, by strongly instrumental, local efforts to reconstruct American law. Indeed, Ball's recovery of the "story of the circumstances attending the foundation," like Williams' recounting of personal stories of unequal opportunity, seeks to provide the necessary context for immediate, fairer judgments for Amerindians and other people of color. Close attention to historical context and particular, personal experience characterize what Matsuda calls "outsider jurisprudence." Its proponents' methodology is "grounded in the particulars of their social reality and experience. This method is consciously both historical and revisionist, attempting to know history from the bottom." Their quest to know history from the bottom up has led these legal scholars to the sources of the new social history, including private journals, oral histories, and "stories from their own experiences of life in a hierarchically arranged world."

"Outsider jurisprudence" often employs its knowledge of historical context and personal life experiences pragmatically and locally. Existing always on the boundaries between the courts and the streets, the new jurisprudence of women and men of color "accepts the standard teaching of street wisdom: law is essentially political. It accepts as well the pragmatic use of law as a tool of social change, and the aspirational core of law as the human dream of peaceable existence. If these views seem contradictory, that is consistent with another component of jurisprudence of color: it is jurisprudence recognizing, struggling within, and utilizing contradiction, dualism, and ambiguity." Thus Matsuda, Derrick Bell and others focus realistically on the "need to attack the effects of racism and patriarchy in order to attack the deep, hidden, tangled roots," and seek concrete "legal tools that have progressive effect," such as affirmative action, desegregation, reparations, and the criminalization of racist speech. In Matsuda's judgment, "stories are a means of obtaining the knowledge we need to create just legal structure."

If counterhegemonic narratives provide the local knowledge that outsiders need to reconstruct American law, they may also have a larger and more direct impact on that reconstruction. Well-constructed alternative narratives may also compel insiders to listen to outsiders for the first time. As Richard Delgado argues, the insinuative, non-coercive structure and tone of stories "invite the reader to suspend judgment, listen for their point or message, and then decide what measure of truth they contain." Thus effective "counterstories" can subtly subvert the dominant group's own stories with their comfortable assumptions about natural superiority and deserved power. Apparently innocent, alternative narratives can shatter the insiders' complacency and disturb their tranquil sleep: "They can show that what we believe is ridiculous, self-serving, or cruel. They can show us the way out of the trap of unjustified exclusion. They can help us understand when it is time to reallocate power. They are the other half—the destructive half—of the creative dialectic."

The alternative narrative's potential subversion of the "comfortable dominant complacency that is the principal anchor dragging down any incentive for reform" is particularly important in America, of course, because insiders continue to hold the reins of power; any legal or social reform must include them and induce them to undertake "a type of willing death." Outsiders simply cannot afford to talk only to themselves. Thus the seductive power of narrative might play a crucial, positive role in the process of legal reconstruction, by "overcoming otherness" and "forming a new collectivity based on the shared story." A powerful method of both destruction and creation. "legal storytelling is an engine built to hurl rocks over walls of social complacency that obscure the view out from the citadel. But the rocks all have messages tied to them that the defenders cannot help but read. The messages say, let us knock down the walls, and use the blocks to pave a road we can all walk together."

To succeed fully in reconstructing American law, then, "outsider jurisprudence" must tap and cultivate an appreciation of context and a toleration of difference among dominant social groups long used to regarding abstract, "neutral" language and principles as the highest form of justice. Above all, the legal reformers' venture depends upon the ability and willingness of dominant Americans to develop and exercise a new sense of empathy with the powerless. As Lynne Henderson explains, empathy involves three basic phenomena: "(1) feeling the emotion of another; (2) understanding the experience or situation of another, both affectively and cognitively, often achieved by imagining oneself to be in the position of the other; and (3) action brought about by experiencing the distress of another (hence the confusion of empathy with sympathy and compassion). The first two forms are ways of knowing, the third form a catalyst for action."

Traditional legal discourse systematically "disallows the language of emotion and experience" and thus insists upon "an impoverished view of reason and understanding—one that focuses on cognition in its most reductionist sense." This traditional demand for rationality, order and control deprives American law of a rich source of knowledge and a possible impetus to reform. Empathic understanding might enlarge the visual field and reveal hidden moral and social problems: "The stories or narratives of the law can be heard differently, and more meanings will be available to legal discourse through explicit attempts to understand the situation and experience of others. This can lead to revolutions in habitual legal thinking and transformation of legal problems." The long-term result could be "normatively better legal outcomes."

Unfortunately, empathy (especially for those differently situated in the social world) does not come naturally to everyone. Empathy must be deliberately developed. Arguably, the best possible method of tapping and building empathy is to engage in counterhegemonic legal storytelling itself, placing narratives rich in emotional experience within legal frameworks. Effective empathic narrative "includes descriptions of concrete human situations and their meanings to the persons affected in the context of their lives. It is contextual, descriptive, and affective narrative, although it need not be 'emotional' in the pejorative sense of overwrought. It is, instead, the telling of the stories of persons and human meanings, not abstractions; it is a phenomenological argument."

Precisely because they focus upon context, personal experience and human feeling, then, alternative legal narratives seem to enjoy the best chance of developing the empathy in the dominant social group upon which all serious legal reform depends. Those who tell and those who listen to these stories may succeed most in "making the jump" that Eudora Welty describes "into the mind, heart, and skin" of another human being, whether "a man or a woman, old or young, with skin black or white." Counterhegemonic legal narratives may thus be critical in creating the dialectic of empathic understanding and social change envisioned by "outsider jurisprudence." In the end, the reconstruction of American law may depend as much on giving full, rich voice to those long silenced in American courts and society, as on a sophisticated theoretical analysis of the politics of narrative.

III

There can be little doubt that Eudora Welty is one of the consummate storytellers of twentieth-century America. Born to a region, period and family rich in traditional oral culture, Welty early acquired an enduring delight in narratives of all kinds, oral and written. Since her mother and her mother's female friends were the principal oral storytellers of her youth, Welty's own developing narrative perspective was distinctly feminine and, in a strongly patriarchal Southern culture, at least gently interrogatory of the established systems of power. At the same time, Welty's love of narrative and extraordinary empathy with all of her characters infuse her fictional explorations of Southern families and communities with a special caring quality. As the literary critic Carol Manning notes, "Welty characterizes concretely the day-to-day lives and special events of some quite ordinary people. And she makes us care for them. Portraying them in depth, she attaches them firmly to time and place, reveals their pasts, leads us to wonder about their futures, and shows us the social and cultural milieus which have formed them." Attention to context, the personal experiences of ordinary people, and empathic understanding mark Welty's mature narratives.

Eudora Welty's many stories and novels simultaneously celebrate and reproduce the tradition of oral storytelling, and literally give voice to the perspectives of a great variety of characters. Her portraits of a tremendously diverse oral culture stand out even among Southern writers. In Manning's judgment, "Not only are Welty's characters perhaps the most loquacious in Southern fiction, but they also tell more tales, and a greater range of tales, than do other characters." Unlike other Southern authors who draw upon the oral tradition, Welty incorporates many tales of the recent as well as the distant past into her repertory, and includes many more storytellers than "the conventional narrators of such tales in Southern literature—blacks, fathers, elderly aunts, grandparents, and a few other adults." Most distinctively, Welty "puts the tale, whatever its subject and whoever its speaker, in the natural, conversational language of its speaker or speakers. The chatter of her characters, contributing greatly to the noisy, bustling tone of her works, is a major distinction between her treatment of the oral tradition and its portrayal by many other writers."

Most significantly for our purpose, Welty seems to recognize the complex politics of narrative itself, as she subtly portrays her characters shaping the recent and distant past through their oft-told stories. "Whether their tales result from boredom, from a long habit of talking, from nostalgia for the past, from a desire to entertain, from an attempt to honor and please others, or from a combination of these, the family and community do not recount events as they actually occurred but instead reshape the reality behind the tales to accord with their needs and values." Competing or self-contradictory narratives themselves frequently lead us to this realization. This sophisticated demonstration of the (often unconscious) construction of social reality through narrative lends Welty's literature an unusual richness; at once ironically critical and undeniably fond of human creativity, Welty embraces multiplicity. Women and men, young and old, poor and rich, black and white, illiterate and literate, are all permitted to tell their own stories, with their own emphases, concerns, rhythms and intonations, in Welty's mature fiction.

Nowhere does this complex, multivocal narrative style have a more potent counterhegemonic effect than in Welty's novel of 1970, *Losing Battles.* Set in the clay hills of northeast Mississippi in the 1930s, this long comic novel chronicles a series of losing battles waged by an extended rural family; not least of these losing battles is the neverending one against poverty itself. But we are not simply told the Vaughn-Beecham-Renfro clan's history. Even more fully than in her other novels, in *Losing Battles* Welty abandons the device of the omniscient narrator and allows the family to reveal themselves and their struggles through their many overlapping and partially contradictory stories, told at a reunion celebrating the ninetieth birthday of Granny Vaughn. As Welty explained in an interview, "I needed that region, that kind of country family, because I wanted that chorus of voices, everybody talking and carrying on at once. I wanted to try something completely vocal and dramatized. Those people are natural talkers and storytellers, in a remote place where there was time for that." The result is a thoroughly democratic novel in which dialogue occupies roughly ninety percent of 436 pages, and "the interplay of the characters, what each person says and how others react to his or her words, is the chief means of characterization." Children and adults, women and men, adored and disliked members of the family all participate in the process of creating the family's history, through their competing and sometimes cacophonous narratives.

A central place in the family's tales of their losing battles is reserved for their contacts with the law. Literary scholars have neglected this aspect of the novel, but there can be no doubt about its importance. Despite Miss Beulah Renfro's protestation that hers was a "strict, law-abiding, God-fearing close-knit family" as the novel and reunion begin, the family awaits the return of her son and their hero, Jack, from an eighteen-month incarceration in the state penitentiary. As part of a long-standing feud between the Vaughn-Beecham-Renfro and the neighboring Stovall families, Jack and Curly Stovall had done battle verbally and physically two years before. When Curly took Jack's dead grandmother's gold wedding ring (the family's sole remaining treasure) from Jack's little sister in payment of the family's debts at his (formally their) store, Jack beat Curly up country-style, covered him with fertilizer, stuffed him into a coffin in the store, and then carried off on his back the heavy safe in which the ring had been stowed. On Jack's trek across country to the Renfro farm, the safe popped open and the ring was lost. This mock-heroic epic struggle ended in an equally strange legal battle, as Curly pressed charges and then posted bail for Jack. But the good-humored fun ended with the trial itself.

As the family relates the story in the first hundred pages of the novel, the trial was one of the family's major losing battles. Strictly applying the abstract rules of law, the courtroom judge completely missed the long-standing and good-natured elements of the feud. In the courthouse in the town of Ludlow (a foreign place to the family), Judge Moody effectively silenced Jack, unable to hear his inarticulate, abbreviated defense and demanding instead a story that Jack could not tell. As Beulah notes, "we knew full well he wasn't going to stand up in front of the public and tell 'em any of our business." Jack was unable to explain that he had defended his family's honor and diminishing property against the rival clan that had (legally) stolen from and indebted them for generations; he did claim, in a very few words but with total confidence, that he had to be acquitted, because his family needed him so badly to work their heavily-mortgaged farm. But Judge Moody summarily dismissed this contextual defense. In the eyes of context-blind American justice, Jack had committed robbery and aggravated battery upon a governmental official (Curly was town marshal, after all). Jack was packed off to prison for two years, the judge proclaimed, as "a lesson to the rest" to cease "taking things in [their] own hands" and to respect the law and those who own property and have been "raised to office." But as Jack's mother confesses, a far different lesson passed from insider to outsiders in this blatant contest of legal and social power: "'Of course that judge never got it through his head what it was all about!' yelled Miss Beulah. 'Born and bred in Ludlow, most likely in the very shadow of the courthouse! A man never spent a day of his life in Banner, never heard of a one of us!'"

At the seriocomic heart of the novel, the clan captures the judge and compels him to listen to the repressed narratives of the legal outsiders, and hence to reconsider his initial judgment. In a series of comic misadventures, Jack escapes from prison a day before his parole in order not to disappoint his family at their reunion. Hitching a ride on the back of the fancy car of the hopelessly-lost and unrecognized Judge Moody, Jack first rescues the car from a ditch, and then learns of the judge's identity and determines to force the car back into a ditch, only to watch the judge swerve to avoid Jack's wife and baby and end up with his car teetering precariously on a peak overlooking a ravine. Filled with gratitude, Jack insists that the judge and his wife take refuge in the only possible place, the family reunion.

Here the serious side of the drama unfolds. Forced to sit in a child's school desk chair—the only remaining seat at the bustling reunion—and really to hear for the first time the outsiders' stories of poverty, illness and endurance, the judge is rendered silent. In his learner's chair rather than on his bench, Judge Moody develops a new sense of empathy with the family's long train of losing battles. His empathic understanding is reinforced as the judge personally witnesses Curly Stovall's crass commercial meanness (Curly, who has appropriated Jack's truck and horse in his absence, bickers over the price of rescuing the Moodys' car, and blithely leaves them stranded while he attends to his re-election campaign), as well as Jack's deep sense of honor and family loyalty (now transferred in part to the judge for saving Jack's wife and baby). Judge Moody's comprehension of the complex nature of Jack's "crime" also deepens, as he watches the genial greeting and ritualized rough play of the two rivals. Following Jack's heroic, if somewhat ill-conceived rescue of the damaged car, Judge Moody implicitly reverses his original misconceived judgment. He certainly does not send Jack back to prison for escaping early or renewing his "assault" on Curly in a new fight over the truck, as he certainly would have done eighteen months before. Rather, the former adversaries in legal conception solemnly, if wordlessly, proclaim their new understanding: "Judge Moody put out his rope-burned hand, Jack put up his bloody one, and they shook."

Before the daring and hilarious rescue of the car, and while still in the learner's seat, Judge Moody is called upon to render a second judgment. The issue is the identity of Jack's wife, Gloria, an orphan of unknown parentage. Here the Vaughn-Beecham-Renfro clan acts as the prosecutor and insider, attempting to encircle, own and overwhelm the silent outsider, Gloria. Affronted by Gloria's "proud" insistence on her own, mysterious identity and her reluctance to participate in the noisy reunion, the family attempts to claim her as the illegitimate daughter of Jack's long-dead uncle, Sam Dale Beecham. In a powerful scene reminiscent in some ways of a gang rape, the women of the family force the resisting Gloria to the ground and stuff watermelon "as big as a man's clayed shoe" down her throat, as they try to force the recalcitrant outsider to acquiesce in their interpretation of her identity. "'Say Beecham!' they ordered her, close to her ear. They rolled her by the shoulders, pinned her flat, then buried her face under the flesh of the melon with its blood heat, its smell of evening flowers. Ribbons of juice crawled on her neck and circled it, as hands robbed of sex spread her jaws open. . . . 'Come on, sisters, help feed her! Let's

cram it down her little red lane. Let's make her say Beecham! *We* did!' came the women's voices."

Gloria valiantly and wisely refuses to accede to this eradication of her difference. Indeed, the stakes are high not only emotionally, but also legally: the family's interpretation would make Gloria Jack's first cousin; by Mississippi law, their marriage could be annulled, their baby daughter declared illegitimate, and Jack returned to prison for breaking yet another legal prohibition. Hence the importance of Judge Moody, silent witness and now judge of the legal issue. Before his eye-opening experiences at the reunion, Judge Moody would probably have enforced the technical letter of the law; indeed, he has ventured into the rural wilderness specifically to investigate this claim. But now he sees and worries about the context: "'It's that baby. I think we'll have to close one eye over that everlasting baby,' Judge Moody said in the same heavy voice."

Given this new empathy and concern about relationships, the judge hears different parts of the proffered evidence and constructs a different, more generous legal narrative. Stressing a portion of ninety-year-old Granny Vaughn's convoluted oral testimony (suggesting that Sam Dale Beecham was accidentally emasculated in infancy and couldn't have fathered Gloria) over another, Judge Moody sets aside the only written evidence (a letter from Sam Dale claiming Gloria's supposed mother as his wife and her baby as his own). The evidence on either side is ambiguous in the extreme, but the judge's empathy for the outsider in this case clearly affects his judgment. From his learner's seat, Judge Moody uncharacteristically rules that there "was no prior knowledge between the partners" and, therefore, no crime committed: "You end up doing yourself the thing you hate most, the thing you've deplored the loudest and longest. . . . Here I am, taking the law into my own hands."

Even this unwonted action fails to exhaust Judge Moody's new empathy with outsiders, or his unexplained legal decisions at the reunion. The most serious and painful case is reserved for last. This is the case of the consummate outsider, Uncle Nathan Beecham, the truly silent evangelical itinerant who litters the country with apocalyptic signs. From the most deeply buried family story we learn that many years before, Nathan had murdered the greedy lumber speculator who had first appropriated, stripped and exhausted much of the family's land; Nathan had then stood by silent and watched as an innocent black man was hung for the murder. Struck mute by his own guilt and the law's inability to protect the powerless, Nathan had cut off his right hand and exiled himself from his home and family. He appears at the reunion as a stranger. Remarkably, as long-silent Nathan's story is finally and fully heard, Welty realizes at last her goal of "entering into the mind and inside the skin" of a murderer. Moved to empathic understanding of the complicated context of the crime and the prolonged suffering of the criminal, Judge Moody again reaches an uncharacteristic and extraordinary decision. Once more, he takes the law into his own hands and implicitly pardons Nathan by taking no further action. Thus the judge reaffirms his growing conviction that not all legal narratives could be heard in American courts.

Finally, the novel invites us to ponder the impact of his new empathic understanding of outsiders on Judge Moody himself. Initially the main effect is disorientation, as the judge feels himself "lost" without his abstract conceptual moorings. As he wanders literally and figuratively through "a maze" of alien dirt roads and attitudes, Judge Moody loses his customary sense of reality; in the midst of the reunion, he confides to his wife, "Nothing wrong. Only I don't care quite the same about living as I did this morning." And yet, as he is compelled to occupy the learner's chair and listen to alternative conceptions of truth and justice, the judge's sense of reality broadens and deepens. He sees as never before the importance and complexity of human relationships and responsibility, and confronts his own weakness in avoiding the calls for help of a sick and aged friend. Bending the abstract rules of law and acknowledging the importance of context and human experience seem to permit even the quintessential representative of American law to grow and mature.

In joining hands with the outsiders and singing "Blest Be the Tie" to complete the reunion, Judge Moody also embraces Beulah's alternative vision of justice and truth, "we're all part of it together, or ought to be!" Traditional adversaries are reconciled, in large measure, as an insider develops a new empathic understanding of counterhegemonic legal narratives, and the outsiders "forgive" him his former lack of understanding. Stories may be all this poor family have left, but stories have power; as Jack concludes of an old family foe, "I reckon I even love her . . . I heard her story." The novel closes upon "the faces of losers and winners, the forgotten and the remembered, still there together and looking like members of the same family." Thus begins the slow, painful reconstruction of

American law through the power of narrative, as imaginatively envisioned by Eudora Welty.

Reflecting in 1971 upon her own long career, Welty confided that the "form of human vision" she had most valued was that "charged with sympathy." She revealed that her central aesthetic and philosophical goal had been formed as she photographed poor, rural, black and white Mississippians for the Works Progress Administration during the Depression: "But away off one day in Tishomingo County, I knew this, anyway: that my wish, indeed my continuing passion, would be not to point the finger in judgment but to part a curtain, that invisible shadow that falls between people, the veil of indifference to each other's presence, each other's wonder, each other's human plight." Resembling "outsider jurisprudence" in inspiration and content, then, Eudora Welty's vision of personal and social transformation rests upon the dual power of polyphonic narrative and empathy. Its richness reveals the promise of a reconstruction of law for all Americans.

Source: Eve Kornfeld, "Reconstructing American Law: The Politics of Narrative and Eudora Welty's Empathic Vision," in *Journal of American Studies*, Vol. 26, No. 1, April 1992, pp. 23–39.

Sources

Bailey, Paul, "Gloriously Ordinary," in *Times Literary Supplement*, June 4, 1982, p. 608.

Boatwright, James, "I Call This a Reunion to Remember, All!," in *New York Times*, April 12, 1970.

McAlpin, Sara, "Family in Eudora Welty's Fiction," in *Southern Review*, Vol. 18, No. 3, Summer 1982, pp. 480–94.

Woodward, C. Vann, "Southerner with Her Own Accent," in *New York Times Book Review*, February 19, 1984, p. 7.

Further Reading

Bloom, Harold, *Eudora Welty: Comprehensive Research and Study Guide*, Chelsea House, 1999.
   Bloom offers a thorough reference to Welty's short stories, for which she is best known. Ideally suited for the reader new to Welty's work, this book explains themes, techniques, and contexts for Welty's short fiction.

Champion, Laurie, ed., *The Critical Response to Eudora Welty's Fiction*, Greenwood Publishing Group, 1994.
   This volume offers the collected criticism of Welty's writing from the 1940s to the early 1990s. The criticism included is drawn from journals (literary and

general interest) and contains critical treatments of Welty's fiction by scholars of American and Southern literature.

Price, Reynolds, ed., *Eudora Welty Photographs*, University Press of Mississippi, 1993.

Using Welty's early photographs, Price shows Welty's personal view of the South. The book includes an introductory interview conducted by Price with Welty concerning her photographs.

Weston, Ruth D., *Gothic Traditions and Narrative Techniques in the Fiction of Eudora Welty*, Louisiana State University Press, 1994.

Weston reviews Welty's work in terms of the gothic tradition to show how she uses gothic themes and narrative techniques within the southern literary framework.

Main Street

Sinclair Lewis
1920

Main Street, originally published in 1920, is the story of a sophisticated young woman who moves to a small town in the American Midwest in 1912 and struggles against the small-minded culture of the citizens who live there. The town, Gopher Prairie, is closely patterned on Sauk Centre, Minnesota, which is where Sinclair Lewis grew up, although the book makes clear that it could be any of thousands of towns across the heartland. Carol Kennicott (née Milford), the protagonist of this novel, is a fascinating study in complexity: she loves her husband enough to live in Gopher Prairie with him, yet nearly enters several affairs in her longing for freedom; she hates the town for its gossip and its simplicity but wants nothing more than to make it better. The book touches on eternal American issues, such as women's rights, business among friends, and the spirit of anti-intellectualism that has always been at the center of small-town America, where sensitivity is often equated with self-absorption.

Main Street was an immediate, phenomenal success when it was published in 1920, making it the book of the century up to that point. It was the first in a string of novels written by Sinclair Lewis in the 1920s, including *Babbitt*, *Arrowsmith*, and *Elmer Gantry*, that established him as one of the preeminent authors of American literature. In these works, Lewis presents a response to a form of simplistic enthusiasm that tends to run through American culture, examining institutional religion, art, business, patriotism, and medicine with a skeptical

eye. In 1930, he became the first American author to be awarded the Nobel Prize for literature.

Author Biography

Harry Sinclair Lewis was born in 1885 in Sauk Centre, Minnesota, a small town on the Central Plains that provided the inspiration for *Main Street*'s Gopher Prairie. His father was a physician and, like Will Kennicott in the novel, was excessively concerned with appearances and proud of the rugged simplicity of his neighbors. Growing up, Lewis knew that he was considered odd by his fellow townspeople and that their narrow judgments did not prevail throughout the world at large. He attended Sauk Centre High School and in 1903 went to Yale, where he developed his writing, eventually becoming editor of the *Yale Literary Magazine* and publishing in the local New Haven newspaper. During extended breaks from college, he traveled the country, at one time working as a janitor in the New Jersey commune that was started by novelist Upton Sinclair.

Lewis graduated Yale with a bachelor's degree in 1908. He married Grace Livingston Hegger in 1914, and they had one son. The couple traveled while he worked various temporary jobs in the publishing industry and wrote a string of novels that were meant to be commercially successful, though not necessarily artistic.

Lewis's career changed in 1920, with the publication of *Main Street*. Not only was it his first book to gain widespread critical praise, but it was a phenomenal financial success as well, selling 295,000 copies in its first year. The book established him as a literary figure of the first magnitude, a position that he held for the rest of the decade but that slipped away from him thereafter. During the twenties, Lewis produced satirical novels that mirrored the hypocrisy of American life and are still recognized as standards of American literature. *Babbitt* (1922) showed a shallow-minded but enthusiastic salesman; *Arrowsmith* (1925) examined doctors and the medical community; and *Elmer Gantry* (1927) presented a revivalist preacher and con man. *Dodsworth* (1929) is a serious examination of the strains that success puts on marriage. (Lewis divorced his first wife in 1928 and married pioneering newspaperwoman Dorothy Thompson.)

His work received high praise, although it did not always please Lewis. He rejected the 1925 Pulitzer Prize for *Arrowsmith* because he objected

Sinclair Lewis

to the award's stated goal of recognizing the book that "best presents the wholesome atmosphere of American life, and the highest standards of American manners and manhood." He did, however, accept the Nobel Prize for literature in 1930, the first American novelist ever awarded that recognition.

For the next twenty-one years, Lewis was a senior statesman of American literature, but he never produced any work that equaled the novels of the twenties. He wrote nine more novels, but only two—*It Can't Happen Here* and *Kingsblood Royal*—are worth the attention of modern readers. Personal hardships also clouded his later years, particularly his divorce from Dorothy Thompson in 1942 and the death of Wells, his son from his first marriage, in France during World War II.

Lewis died in Rome in 1951.

Plot Summary

Part I

Main Street concerns the struggle faced by a free-minded woman, Carol Kennicott, who has been raised to be artistic and inquisitive but is confined to life in a small town on the Minnesota plains. The book opens with Carol in college in

Media Adaptations

- *Sinclair Lewis: Main Street Revisited* is a 1998 videocassette from Thomas S. Klise Company. It includes photos of Lewis and his boyhood home and examines his most popular books, *Main Street* and *Babbitt*, looking at how the author's background formed both.

- *Sinclair Lewis: The Man from Main Street* is a 1986 videocassette produced by WBGU of Bowling Green, Ohio, and distributed by Ohio Humanities Resource Center.

- Books on Tape, Inc., produced an audiocassette version of *Main Street* (slightly edited) in 1987. It is packaged in two parts, each part includes seven cassettes.

- An unabridged version of *Main Street*, read by Barbara Caruso, is available from Audio Books, Inc., and can be downloaded from Amazon.com's audio division, Audible.com.

- A 1980 radio drama based on the novel *Main Street* was produced by Jabberwocky studios and made available on cassette.

- Encyclopedia Britannica Educational Corporation and Lewis biographer Mark Schorer collaborated on a 1975 videocassette called *Sinclair Lewis*, part of the series *The American Experience in Literature*.

- In 1975, Minnesota Public Radio released a cassette version of a program by Roland Paul Dille, entitled *Sinclair Lewis*. It examines Lewis's writings on small towns, American culture, and American ethics. Dille was a professor of English and the president of Moorehead University.

Minneapolis, full of lofty aspirations that even her classmates find intimidating. After receiving her degree, she lives in Chicago for a year before taking a job in the public library in St. Paul. After three years, she meets Dr. Will Kennicott at a party at a friend's house.

As Dr. Kennicott courts her, he talks with pride about the town he lives in, Gopher Prairie, telling her about the colorful characters who live there and their simple, earnest, moral values. Arriving in town as Kennicott's bride, Carol is disappointed to find the citizens crass and humorless and the town ugly and unimaginative. She pushes her insecurity aside, hoping to fill the role of a dutiful wife. With Kennicott's urging, she makes plans to bring culture to the town.

Many of the citizens treat Carol with suspicion, but being married to a physician gains her entry into upper-class society. The other wives are shocked when she brings up subjects such as sex and labor unions. At parties, the doctor's friends are accustomed to telling the same jokes and performing the same "stunts," such as comic songs or ethnic stories. When it comes Carol's turn to throw a party, she decides on an exotic Chinese theme. Later, she hears that people thought she was showing off and being extravagant with her husband's money.

Carol attends the Jolly Seventeen, a bridge club, but is made to feel uncomfortable by sarcastic remarks. The women's study club, the Thanatopsis Club, invites her to be a member, but she is shocked to find that the meeting she attends about "English poetry" intends to cover *all* English poetry in one afternoon, indicating that the town women's interest in art is superficial at best. Her idea to revitalize city hall and turn it into a meeting center for the whole town becomes lost as various locals promote their own plans, the end result being nothing is done.

Carol does find some members of the town who think as she does. Going for a walk on a winter afternoon, she runs into Miles Bjornstam, a carpenter and handyman. He invites her into his shack and talks with her about his socialist ideas, recognizing in her a true spark of independence that everyone else in town appears to be missing. The town schoolteacher, Vida Sherwin, is a member in good standing with the women's clubs, but she can also appreciate the plans that Carol has for the place, counseling her toward patience and making her feel in her loneliness that she is not unreasonable, just a little impetuous.

Carol finds a lawyer, Guy Pollock, to be some sort of a kindred spirit. Pollock is an outcast like her, a reader and a gentle spirit. She makes up an excuse to visit him at his office one afternoon, and throughout their conversation there is an excitement and awkwardness that makes her come away suspecting that she may be falling in love with him. In the argument that ensues between Carol and her husband, she sees the world through his perspective, and she realizes that it is Will she loves. When she runs into Guy after that, in public places, they are uncomfortable together, and nothing more is made of the affair that nearly started between them.

Part II

As life goes on in Gopher Prairie, Carol still finds herself dissatisfied. She is disappointed when she sees the angry Red Swede, Miles Bjornstam, soften his defiant stance as he falls in love with Carol's maid Bea and marries her, buying his own dairy farm and becoming a part of capitalist society. She organizes a small theater company with the help of Guy and Vida, but the citizens who expressed interest in participating only show up sporadically and want to put on a melodrama called *The Girl From Kankakee*, which Carol realizes, soon after the raising of the curtain, is "a bad play abominably acted."

Soon after that, Carol has a baby, Hugh. The narrative explains that Vida Sherwin came close to having an affair with Will Kennicott in 1911, a year before he met Carol, and that now, in 1914, Vida's jealousy of the Kennicott baby drives her to pursue and marry a shop clerk. After that, relations between Carol and Vida are strained, as Vida becomes even more solidly planted in Gopher Prairie society and her old disappointment over losing Kennicott eats away at her.

Maud Dyer, the wife of Kennicott's friend Dave Dyer, comes to visit Kennicott at his office. She talks about how mean and frugal her husband is and how lonely she has become, and then she invites Kennicott to come to see her at home that night, when Dave is out at work. He struggles against the impulse and then gives in to it, starting an affair.

Carol and her baby spend time with her former maid, now Bea Bjornstam, who also has a baby boy. The local women find this relationship improper, because of their class differences. When Bea and the baby become ill with typhoid fever, they cannot get a nurse to stay with them, so Carol becomes her former maid's nurse. The baby dies, and then Bea dies. Miles Bjornstam leaves town, cursing the callous heartlessness of Gopher Prairie.

A new young man, Erik Valborg, arrives in town. He is a tailor's apprentice, but he wears colorful, stylish clothes and reads and writes poetry. The locals give him the insulting name of "Eliza-

beth" and play tricks on him. When Carol meets him, though, she finds him sensitive and intelligent, even though some of his theories about art are vague. He wants to design women's clothes, and Carol encourages him to follow his dream. Their infatuation with each other comes to a head one night when Erik convinces her to go for a walk in the woods with him. While they are walking, Will Kennicott drives up and, without a word of jealousy, insists on driving them home. At home, he describes what life would be like for Carol to be married to a young assistant tailor who might never be worth anything as an artist. The next day, Erik leaves town on a train, as Miles did.

Part III

Carol takes Hugh and goes to live in Washington D. C. for a few years. She gets a job in the government and shares an apartment with some single girls. While there, she is able to lead the urbane lifestyle that she always imagined: going to concerts, museums, and lectures. She is able to freely talk about progressive social movements, such as suffrage for women.

Kennicott does not try to restrict her freedom. He writes sometimes but does not come to see her until she has been in Washington more than a year. Then he is uncertain about whether they are still married. Carol slowly warms to him, however, and they take a trip together to South Carolina.

A discussion about her situation with "a generalissima of suffrage" convinces Carol to return to Gopher Prairie. When she does so, she is five months pregnant with her second baby, a daughter. Back in Gopher Prairie, she is less defensive of the small-mindedness and more willing to suffer the unthinking insults of ignorant citizens. She takes small positions with the women's group and allows the publicity-seeking mayor to take over and corrupt her idea for a Community Day celebration, all the while planning a better life for her children.

Characters

Bea Bjornstam

See Bea Sorenson

Miles Bjornstam

Bjornstam is a socialist, an opponent of those who make money off the labor of others. Friends and enemies refer to him as "The Red Swede." Carol is attracted to him as a friend because he is one of the few people in Gopher Prairie who is not afraid to speak openly against the stringent social order. He works odd jobs and travels when he wants, until he marries Carol's maid, Bea. He then starts a dairy but does not get along with his customers or neighbors. When Bea is dying, he chases away a group of women who come visiting, calling them hypocrites. After the deaths of his wife and son, Bjornstam leaves for Alaska, cursing Gopher Prairie. Cruel, untrue rumors are spread about him.

James Blausser

Blausser is a land speculator who comes to Gopher Prairie and starts a campaign to increase civic pride in order to attract people to the town. He is an exciting speaker—Lewis describes him as "a born leader, divinely intended to be a congressman but deflected to the more lucrative honors of real estate." His "booster" campaign is so superficial in its unreal praise of the town that it disgusts Carol, especially when her husband compares it to her own desire to make the town better.

Cyrus Bogart

Cyrus, who goes by Cy, is a teenager who lives with his widowed mother near the Kennicott house. As a teenager, he commits small pranks on his neighbors, the Kennicotts, throwing tomatoes at their house and putting frightening pictures in the windows. Once, going into her garage, Carol overhears Cy talking to another boy, mocking the way she goes about her chores, as he has observed while peeping in her windows. Later, he goes out with Fern Mullins, the schoolteacher who is boarding at his house, and tries to get her drunk. When she won't cooperate, he gets drunk himself and tries to rape her; he later spreads rumors that cost Fern her job.

Mrs. Bogart

Mrs. Bogart is the old woman who runs the boardinghouse across the alley from the Kennicott's house. She is opinionated, nosy, and hypocritical. She often drops in to gossip, and her gossip is often laced with thinly veiled innuendoes about Carol's behavior, insinuating that Carol is less moral than community standards require. In fact, Mrs. Bogart's son Cyrus is a bully and a hooligan. When Cy tries to rape Fern Mullins, Mrs. Bogart accuses Fern of corrupting him and chases her out into the street, shouting at her, ruining the woman's good name and job because she cannot see her son as the street punk that the rest of the town recognizes him to be.

Percy Bresnahan

The millionaire president of the Velvet Motor Company in Boston, Bresnahan is a native of Gopher Prairie. He is a legendary figure that the inhabitants of the town speak of with pride. When he comes to the town, he is friendly with everyone, but in secret he makes a pass at Carol, who is both repulsed by him and intrigued by his urbanity. When she later lives in Washington, she sees Bresnahan in a restaurant flirting with two girls, and the person she is with says he is well known around town as a slow-witted bore.

Cy

See Cyrus Bogart

Maud Dyer

Maud is the wife of Will Kennicott's friend Dave Dyer, who owns the drug store. She goes to see the doctor at his office one afternoon, complaining about the way her husband takes her for granted and is stingy with money. She convinces Kennicott to come to her house while her husband is at work and have an affair with her.

Elizabeth

See Erik Valborg

Carol Kennicott

Carol is the heroine of this novel. She is the daughter of a judge who encouraged his children to be curious and to read. The book opens when Carol is a student at Blodgett College in Minneapolis, where she forms a number of enthusiasms, including sociology. After graduating, she lives for a year in Chicago and then returns to work in the St. Paul Library until friends introduce her to Will Kennicott, who convinces her to marry him and live with him in Gopher Prairie. She finds the town dismal and unimaginative but sets about trying to change it. She suggests improvements to buildings on Main Street but is told that they would cost too much; she throws a Chinese themes party, but her guests just seem bewildered by the strangeness of it all; she tries to organize a theater company, but the locals are not interested in putting on a good show, and the newspaper heaps insincere praise on a mediocre production. She soon finds out that the neighbors mock her strange ways. Her husband has the same mind-set as the neighbors and carefully chides her for wanting to be different. After meeting Guy Pollock, the lawyer, she sees him as a rare individualist and finds herself falling in love with him only later to decide that his contrariness is just as much a part of Gopher Prairie as others' conformity. She later finds herself falling for Erik Valborg, a younger man who looks up to her for advice on how to leave his tailoring job and become an artist. Kennicott finds them together and makes Carol see that an affair with Valborg would be disastrous and unsatisfying, although the town gossips talk about their relationship for years afterward.

Carol takes her son with her and leaves Gopher Prairie to live in Washington, D.C. There she secures a job with the government and lives with other independent women, soaking up the big-city culture and political freedom. When Kennicott comes to see her, he does not ask her to come home but instead is as nice to her as he can be, to help her make up her mind. In the end, Carol returns to Gopher Prairie pregnant with Will Kennicott's daughter. She has a new worldliness that makes her immune to the sly gossip of her peers or to the social stagnation that bogs down all of her new ideas about social improvement.

Doctor Will Kennicott

Will Kennicott is a country doctor who is proud of his little town but who is also in love with his wife who cannot get along with the town or its citizens. He is an unimaginative man of precise habits, who goes through a nightly ritual of checking the furnace before going to bed and whose idea of conversation at a party is to talk over the performance of his automobile. He convinces Carol to come with him to Gopher Prairie by showing her pictures of the town and the farm country surrounding it, hoping that she will fall as powerfully in love with country living as he is. During their marriage, he is sometimes amused and sometimes confused by the schemes that she comes up with to transform the town. Carol embarrasses him, but at the same time he believes that she is right for the town.

Dr. Kennicott is respected in Gopher Prairie, and he is dedicated and efficient as a surgeon. In one scene, Carol assists him as he amputates a farmer's arm on the man's kitchen table, and Will only tells her later that the anesthetic they used could easily have been ignited by the kerosene lamp they used and blown them all up. He is also dedicated to his marriage, and at a crucial point he takes Carol away from town to travel for several months on the West Coast. When Carol decides that she needs to move to Washington by herself, he respects her decision and does not even try to contact her for more than a year. When he goes out East to see her, he is shy and unassuming, disappointed when she tells him to stay at a hotel rather than stay with her. She becomes interested in him all over again and goes traveling with him, eventually becoming pregnant with his daughter. He says that he will not ask her to return to Gopher Prairie but that he will welcome her if she does return.

Carol Milford

See Carol Kennicott

Adolph Morgenroth

Morgenroth is a local farmer. Will Kennicott amputates Morgenroth's arm on the kitchen table of his farm, with Carol assisting for the first time.

Fern Mullins

Fern is a twenty-two-year-old woman who has just finished college and who is soon to start teaching in the high school. Carol is attracted to her because they have similar artistic interests. They plan to start a little theater together. Fern goes to a party with Cyrus Bogart, a twenty year old who is still in high school. He gets very drunk, and while she is trying to take him home in a borrowed carriage, he tries to rape her. The next morning, the widow Bogart, who runs the rooming house she lives in, throws Fern out for corrupting her son and convinces the members of the school board not to hire her. Fern goes back to Minneapolis, but her parents will not believe that she was innocent when the people of Gopher Prairie turned against her, and they throw her out; in addition, she finds herself blacklisted from teaching jobs because of the rumors of immorality.

Guy Pollock

Guy is the first person in Gopher Prairie with whom Carol feels an intellectual bond. He is a lawyer, somewhere around thirty-eight, she thinks. (He is actually forty-seven.) Guy is sensitive and intelligent and well read. Within a year of her marriage, she considers whether she is falling in love with Guy. One evening, when she stops in at his office, their conversation leads to the town's moral standards, and Guy tells Carol that even her husband is involved with the competitive game-playing. When she expresses her discouragement, Guy says he believes that she wants what he wants: "to go back to an age of tranquility and charming manners. You want to enthrone good taste again." His assessment of her is wrong enough to make her realize that she is not in love with him, that she only hoped to be, and that they are too different.

Raymie

See Raymond Wutherspoon

The Red Swede

See Miles Bjornstam

Vida Sherwin

Vida is the town schoolteacher. When Carol first arrives in Gopher Prairie, Vida is one of the few townspeople to make her feel comfortable. She is educated in the arts, and she is friendly to Carol, offering advice on how to deal with the established social groups. It is not until more than halfway through the novel that Lewis reveals the reason Vida feels so bound to Carol: she herself had an affair with Will Kennicott a year before he married Carol, an affair that was cut short because she panicked, afraid of sexuality. She marries Raymie but is distant and resentful toward Carol afterward.

Aunt Bessie Smail

Bessie Smail is Will Kennicott's aggressive, elderly aunt, who has lived on a farm all her life and who has little social sense. She blurts out opinions and criticisms of Carol in her presence, unaware that she is being offensive. Aunt Bessie and her husband, Uncle Whit, buy a store and move to Gopher Prairie, where they fit in comfortably with the other ill-bred citizens, making Carol feel even more trapped by public scrutiny.

Uncle Whittier Smail

Kennicott's uncle ran a creamery in North Dakota and sold it for a profit. After visiting the Kennicott's and making rude remarks about Carol, the Smails find a grocery store for sale in Gopher Prairie and buy it.

Stewart Snyder

Stewart is a classmate of Carol's in college. He hints that he is interested in her, that she would make a good wife for a lawyer, and that in fact he intends to become a lawyer, but she is too interested in artistic pursuits to notice his attention.

Bea Sorenson

Bea is the first maid that Carol hires in Gopher Prairie. The other wives disapprove of the good wage that Carol pays Bea and the way she treats her like a friend. Their friendship strengthens when Bea quits being a maid to marry Miles Bjornstam.

When Bea is dying of typhoid and cannot hire a maid, Carol stays with her day and night.

Mrs. Swiftwaite

Mrs. Swiftwaite is a dressmaker who acquires a reputation for promiscuity almost immediately after she comes to town. Men gather at her house and drink, joking about what a fun woman she is. Carol is offended that Mrs. Bogart would suggest that Will might be seduced by Mrs. Swiftwaite, even while he is carrying on an affair with Mrs. Dyer.

Erik Valborg

Erik is a sensitive young man in his mid-twenties, the son of a gruff farmer. Erik comes into Carol's life when she has been married a few years and has a son. Erik has effeminate ways, dressing colorfully and talking flamboyantly. (At one point, Carol notes that he overuses the word "glorious.") Erik works at the tailor shop, but what he really wants to do is design women's clothes. The locals pick on him and tag him with the unflattering nickname Elizabeth. Having heard him mocked, Carol is fascinated with him when she finally meets him, and, after hearing him talk about art, she realizes that he is just like her and wonders if she is falling in love with him. Once when they take a walk in the woods at night, Will Kennicott approaches them in his car and insists on driving them home. Erik leaves town soon after professing his love for Carol in a letter. For years, she hears townspeople gossiping about her and Erik. While in Washington, Carol sees Erik acting in a movie under the name "Erik Valour," and she reflects on how ridiculous her fascination with him was.

Mrs. Westlake

Mrs. Westlake is the wife of the older doctor in town. Will tells Carol never to talk to her because she is such a ruthless gossip, but Mrs. Westlake befriends Carol at a time when the town makes her feel particularly lonely and vulnerable, and so Carol ends up talking with her about things that she and Will do and things that they like. Later, it turns out that Mrs. Westlake has spread Carol's secrets all over town.

Raymond Wutherspoon

Raymond "Raymie" Wutherspoon is a shop clerk with little ambition. When he marries Vida Sherwin, she pushes him to demand a higher position at the Bon Ton shop where he works, and so his employers make him a one-sixth partner. He returns from the First World War with the respected rank of major, but the town's respect for him quickly wears off as he resumes his position at the store.

Vida Wutherspoon

See Vida Sherwin

Themes

Prairie Life

To some extent, the attitudes that prevail in the book's fictional setting, Gopher Prairie, are a result of the town's geological circumstances. As Lewis makes clear, the towns scattered across the North American Great Plains plateau were set off in virtual isolation from the rest of the world before the twentieth century. At the time when the novel takes place, from 1912 to 1920, automobiles were unreliable, with thin, smooth tires that offered little traction in wet or snowy conditions and simple engines that gave out frequently even under normal conditions, jammed by common problems, such as "carbon buildup," that are not serious today. Telephone service was secure within a town, but the wires that stretched along country roads were weak and vulnerable to the elements, and long distance service was very costly. Living in isolation most of the time, with travel especially hampered during the winter, the citizens of prairie towns fed off each other's ideas, prejudices, and wisdom, without the benefit of fresh ideas from the other towns in their own state, much less from the great metropolitan centers or from other countries.

Identity

Most of Carol Milford Kennicott's struggles stem from her attempts to find a convincing and satisfactory identity for herself. It is clear that she thinks of herself as some sort of artist and that she is knowledgeable in various aspects of sciences, but she has a difficult time blending all of her theories together with her environment to provide an identity that she can be proud of. In college, she takes a particular interest in sociology, but she never pursues it formally as a profession. Dining at a boarding house, she is pressed to name her particular artistic interest, and, suffering under the pressure of the traveling salesmen's mockery, she blurts out, "archeology," a subject that had been on her mind at the time but certainly not a subject that identifies her interests throughout the novel. She tries to start a little theater company, but none of her fel-

Topics for Further Study

- In the last chapters of the novel, Carol lives in Washington among suffragists. Research the women's suffrage movement between 1915 and 1920 and relate the movement's political goals to the lives that Lewis describes.

- Just how isolated was Gopher Prairie? Find out the distance from Minneapolis to Sauk Centre, the town that Gopher Prairie is based on, and then research how long it would take a train to travel that distance in the first decades of the twentieth century.

- Research women's fashions from the time when this novel takes place, finding examples of clothes that would have been common and ones that would have been considered artistic and ornate, such as Erik Valborg might have designed.

- What was the gas that was used against American troops in World War I? What effect would it have had on someone like Raymie Wutherspoon, who still suffered from it when he came home from the war?

- For travelling around the countryside, Dr. Will Kennicott alternates between using his Ford motor car and a horse-drawn carriage. Examine the mileage per hour and limitations of both.

- Do you think that the story would have ended this way today, with divorce as common as it is? Why or why not?

- Speak to a member of a local literary club, and find out what he or she thinks of the Thanatopsis Society's attempt to cover English literature in one afternoon. What would be a more realistic time frame?

- The "Watch Gopher Prairie Grow" campaign that is initiated late in the novel seems to bring little result. Find out what slogan your town or city is using to boost civic pride, and report on its success.

low citizens takes his or her task very seriously, and so Carol gives up on it, discouraged. She attends the literature discussion group but finds it shallow. She encourages Erik Valborg to be a poet, even though she knows that he is not very good.

The one identity that Carol is unwilling to consider is the one that she fits into, judging from external standards: the identity of a Gopher Prairie society matron. She sees the other women in her social class as either lacking or suppressing the intelligence, curiosity, and personality that she believes a person should have.

Part of Carol's dilemma about recognizing her own identity stems from the fact that the housewife identity that she works so hard to resist is closely bound to the "wife" identity that comes naturally to her. Even though Carol often views Will Kennicott as a dull and weak-willed man, there are times, such as when she assists him in surgery at Adolph Morgenroth's farm, when she greatly admires him. Her true identity is that of caregiver: she shows it in nursing Bea, in her desperate attempt to save Fern Mullins, in her desire to lead and teach Erik Valborg, and by the certainty she shows as a protector of her children. Living in other circumstances, where a family woman's identity would not presume mind-numbing conformity, Carol might have come to know herself much sooner than she does in this novel.

Status Quo

Status quo is a Latin term referring to the existing state of affairs. In *Main Street*, the status quo of Gopher Prairie is that men and women attend social gatherings with others of their class, tell the same jokes and stories that they always tell one another, and make the same empty, inoffensive observations. It is a situation with which all are content. Seeing this idea of "normality" as an outsider and knowing that the world holds much, much more, Carol sets out to challenge the status quo.

Changing the status quo can seldom come quickly because social patterns do not become the status quo quickly. People find comfort in the familiar, and so they are resistant to change. In the case of a town like Gopher Prairie, the resistance is even stronger when the citizens believe that the people trying to cause change are outsiders. With Carol, as with Erik Valborg, the citizens of Gopher Prairie prove to be bemused at attempts to change tradition because they feel no real threat to the status quo can come from art. They do, however, fear sexual corruption of their youth and the organiza-

tion of the farmers whose work they exploit. Fern Mullins is run out of town because some people fear that she might make young people aware of sexuality while they are still in high school, changing the existing order. The organizer from the National Nonpartisan Defense League is thrown out of town before he has a chance to speak because people fear what he has to say and how his words will work to change the social order. They run him out on a rail, using the weak excuse that he would have supported America's enemy, Germany, if he had been allowed to talk. As Kennicott explains it, "Whenever it comes right down to a question of defending America and our constitutional rights, it's justifiable to set aside ordinary procedures." In other words, he supports violating the law in a case in which someone might be a threat to the status quo.

Sex and Sexuality

For its time, *Main Street* offered readers a fairly open discussion of sexuality. Although sexual activity is never overtly referred to, there are quite a few places where the idea of it is unavoidable. At one level, there are the instances in which sexuality is implied by referring to milder forms of it, such as when, at the end of Chapter 3, Carol and Will's courtship fades away from a discussion about having babies with a dreamy mix of romance and touching: "As his arms moved toward her," Lewis writes, "she answered all her doubts with, 'Sweet, so sweet.'" A parallel case is the romance that Will had with Vida Sherwin a year earlier. The novel describes it as a "love-affair," and Vida treats it with the seriousness that would be used for a sexual relationship in modern writing, although the narrative mentions nothing more explicit than hand-holding and hugging.

The affair between Will and Maud Dyer is never described in detail, but it is safe to assume that it reaches a physical level, because Will tries to confess it to Carol when he goes to Washington: "I haven't always been absolutely, uh, absolutely, proper." The relationship between Carol and Erik is preempted by Will's sudden appearance, but it is likely that, leaving the prying eyes of the city and going into the woods at night, with the guilt that she felt about it before and after the fact, they were headed for a sexual liaison.

Style

Point of View

Most of *Main Street* is told from a third person, limited omniscient point of view. It is third person because the narrative voice is not that of one of the characters who appears in the book: the speaker never refers to himself or herself as "I" but, instead, always relates the actions of the characters in terms of what "he" or "she" did or said. It is an omniscient voice because it has access to human thoughts and is not just limited to describing objective reality as it could be observed by anyone. It is considered limited, however, in that for most of the novel, the narrative can only relate ideas and incidents that have been experienced by Carol: the range of information that the narration can tell readers is limited to things that Carol would know about. Usually, the narrative voice does not relate any information that is beyond Carol's experience.

There are exceptions to the norm, however. In some cases, the narrative voice shifts point of view and relates ideas that are in the heads of other characters, which no one else, including Carol, could directly experience. For instance, chapter 25 starts with Will Kennicott's thoughts. "Carrie's all right. She's finicky, but she'll get over it. But I wish she'd hurry up about it!" It is only after a few sentences that the source of these ideas is identified: "Dr. Will Kennicott was brooding in his office." Later in that same chapter, there is another point of view shift, as the narrative focuses on the way Hugh sees the world and eventually begins talking for him: "In his office Father had tools fascinating in their shininess and curious shapes, but they were sharp." These are obviously Hugh's thoughts because they refer to Will as "Father," although the narrative voice uses words, such as "fascinating," that would not be used by a three-year-old to describe what he sees.

Foil

A foil is a character whose function in a novel is to help readers understand the character of another by holding the opposite values. In this book, Aunt Bessie Smail functions as a foil for Carol because she sees the world from an entirely different perspective. Aunt Bessie supports old-fashioned values, conventional morality, subservience of women to their husbands, and anti-Semitism; she is opposed to farmers' cooperatives, divorce, and liquor. Bessie and her husband, Whittier, whose views are practically the same as hers, take a condescending view toward anyone who sees the world

differently from the way they see it: "They were like the Sunday-afternoon mob staring at monkeys at the Zoo, poking fingers and making faces and giggling at the resentment of the more dignified race." Carol disagrees with the ideas of many in Gopher Prairie, but the attitude of the Smails, and the clear disdain that Sinclair Lewis has toward them, marks them as counterexamples. They exist in the book to show the opposite of the values that Lewis wants to promote.

Another example of a foil is Mrs. Bogart. Lewis makes no secret of the fact that she does not have the values that this book holds to be worthwhile, even from the very first time she is introduced:

> Mrs. Bogart was not the acid type of Good Influence. She was the soft, damp, fat, sighing, indigestive, clinging, melancholy, depressingly hopeful kind. There are in every large chicken-yard a number of old and indignant hens who resemble Mrs. Bogart, and when they are served at Sunday dinner, as fricasseed chicken with thick dumplings, they keep up the resemblance.

Mrs. Bogart and Aunt Bessie are not foils for Carol only because they have different values from hers; the point of the book is that most of the people with whom she associates have different values. They are her foils because they are so closely involved with her. Carol can choose to stay away from the Thanatopsis Club or the Jolly Seventeen, but Mrs. Bogart is a neighbor, and a prying, curious one at that. Aunt Bessie is brought into the story relatively late in the book to further interrupt Carol's privacy: as a relative of Will Kennicott's, Carol has to be involved with her whether she likes it or not.

Historical Context

The Rise of the Middle Class

The American middle class, a category that most citizens fall into today, developed during the period marked by the end of the Civil War in 1865 and the start of World War I in 1914. During that time, the development of industry and the westward expansion across the North American continent provided opportunities for wealth on scales previously unheard of. Key industries, such as steel, petroleum, banking, and railroads, were controlled by a few individuals who established monopolies, fixing prices and making deals with their suppliers to run competitors out of business. There were

Compare & Contrast

- **1920:** The year that *Main Street* is published, the Nineteenth Amendment to the Constitution grants the vote to women.

  Today: Voting rights are strictly enforced. Women are considered a powerful political bloc that politicians try to gain support from.

- **1920s:** The first commercial radio broadcast signal is sent out of KDKA in East Pittsburgh, using a technology that will eventually allow people from coast to coast to share a common experience simultaneously.

  Today: Many low-wattage local radio stations are available across the world via the Internet.

- **1920s:** A town like Gopher Prairie could hire an advertising consultant to design a brochure that exaggerates the town's features, hoping to lure prospective businesses.

  Today: Small towns are even more likely to hire media consultants to help polish their images.

- **1920:** The national prohibition against alcohol, mentioned in the novel's final pages, goes into effect on January 16, in accordance with the Eighteenth Amendment to the U.S. Constitution. Prohibition lasts thirteen years.

  Today: Many draw parallels between the government's inability to keep liquor out of the hands of the populace during Prohibition and the current influx of illegal drugs.

- **1920s:** The United States has twenty million telephones, twice as many as it had two years earlier. A long-distance phone call from New York to Chicago takes twenty-three minutes to be channelled through.

  Today: Phone calls travel near the speed of light through fast fiber optic lines.

- **1920s:** For the first time, the census reports America's urban population to be larger than the rural population, 54 million to 51.1 million.

  Today: The urban population has more than tripled the 1920 census figure at 187 million, while the rural population has barely grown, at 61.7 million.

---

different levels of income, but most citizens were closer to poverty than wealth. This situation became nearly intolerable during the depression that hit the country in 1893 and lasted for four years. Much of the country suffered economic hardship: more than 15,000 business firms failed, and at least seventy-four railroads, which had constituted the nation's growth industry, filed for government protection. Without the social "safety nets" such as unemployment insurance and Medicaid, which are now available to help people with low income, there was much suffering and death.

One result of the 1893 depression was that the wealthy captains of industry came to be seen as villains who were bleeding the country dry. Such famous figures as John D. Rockefeller of Standard Oil, Andrew Carnegie of United States Steel, and railroad magnate J. Pierpont Morgan were dubbed "robber barons," enemies of the working people. Politicians found it in their interest to enforce laws, such as the previously ignored Sherman Antitrust Act of 1890, which served to limit the unbridled acquisition of those already holding most of the wealth.

Just as the political conditions became favorable to a more equal distribution of wealth, manufacturers were mass-producing consumer products that the growing middle class could spend their incomes on. Vacuum cleaners, telephones, and phonographs were the must-have items at the turn of the century. Catalog outlets, such as Sears, Roebuck and Company and Montgomery Ward, made the same merchandise available to every home in the land. Those who were at the bottom of the social ladder were pushed upward by poor immigrants entering the country in one of the greatest expansions the country has ever known: in the first decade of the twentieth century, nine million immigrants arrived. The influx of cheap immigrant labor gave people more time for leisure activities such as reading, and mass-market magazines, such as *McCall's* and *Cosmopolitan*, gave advertisers the opportunity to show off new styles and inventions. As the middle class spent more, more middle-class jobs in manufacturing and distribution developed.

Progressivism

As already mentioned, the early decades of the century were a time when citizens favored increased power for the government. This new attitude of governmental involvement manifested itself in many different forms. The most mainstream of them was the enforcement of antitrust laws: Theodore Roosevelt won the 1901 election by campaigning as a "trust-buster," and after eight years in office, William Howard Taft succeeded him by promoting similar policies. Politicians who worked at changing the political structure, giving the government more power and more involvement in the lives of the citizenry, were called "progressives."

But the Progressive Movement of the early twentieth century was not limited to mainstream politics. In fact, so many small movements are today lumped into the category of "progressive" that the word has lost much of its value as a description. In short, movements intended to change society for the betterment of the downtrodden and struggling have all, at one time or other, been called progressive. This would include the temperance movement against alcohol, the Socialist movement (of which Lewis was a member), farmers' alliances, industrial labor unions, opposition to child labor, support for mothers with dependent children, and the struggle against racism.

The Women's Movement

Many of the influential social movements in the beginning of the twentieth century were spearheaded by women. Prohibition of alcohol, for example, was an idea that had supporters since the founding of the country, but it was not until the Women's Christian Temperance Union was formed in 1873 that it gathered enough support to be passed as a law in 1920. Women were also instrumental in passing new laws to prohibit child labor. At the turn of the century, a movement toward settlement houses, for helping poor immigrants who would otherwise starve, spread across the country. These social establishments, including the most famous one, Jane Adam's Hull House in Chicago, were usually started and run by women, and their existence indicated a milestone for women who were able and willing to work and who could effect change in their communities.

The most obvious period during which women changed the political landscape was the epoch of the Suffrage Movement, which is mentioned favorably in the final chapters of the novel. It is one of the country's oldest political movements, dating back before the Civil War. Throughout the latter eighteenth century, the movement was active and vocal, splitting into two parties, the National Suffrage Association of Susan B. Anthony and Elizabeth Cady Stanton and the American Woman Suffrage Union of Harriet Ward Beecher. These two groups, representing different degrees of militant thought, joined together as one in 1890 and began the arduous task of changing state laws in order to get women's right to vote put on ballots, in the process of passing a Constitutional amendment. The result did not come until 1920, when, after a surge of feminist activity in the previous decade, the Nineteenth Amendment provided women with the right to vote.

Critical Overview

In 1930, Sinclair Lewis became the first American to receive the Nobel Prize for literature, beating out such notable literary figures as Ernest Hemingway, William Faulkner, F. Scott Fitzgerald, and Langston Hughes, who were all published authors at the time. Within a few years, critics began to speculate that Lewis's great decade, which spanned from the publication of *Main Street* in 1920 until the time he received the Nobel, was at an end. He wrote until his death in 1951, but, with few exceptions, he never received the critical praise that he had in the twenties. Lewis's career is generally viewed in three parts, made up of his early novels, the novels of the 1920s (which are, in general, the only ones that any but a literary scholar would read today), and those that came after 1930.

Before *Main Street* was published, critics scarcely paid any attention to Lewis's work. Of the six novels that he published between 1914 and 1919, only one, *The Job*, gave much consideration to the social setting that surrounded it. Of the others, as Sheldon Norman Grebstein wrote in 1962:

> These books do contain flashes of satire, considerable authenticity of fact and detail, some realistic

Sinclair Lewis's boyhood home in Sauk Centre, Minnesota, a model for Gopher Prairie

characters and situations, and even statements of indignation at social injustice—factors which all reveal Lewis's capacity for seriousness; but in the main they are the work of Lewis the romancer, cheerful, buoyant, reassuring.

Main Street marked the emergence of Lewis as a novelist, both in critical and in economic terms. Readers swarmed to it, and within months it became the best-selling novel of the twentieth century up to that point. Critics saw its flaws but also recognized that they were far outpaced by the significant advancement it represented in the country's quest to come to know itself. Still, the book's huge success and unorthodox method of storytelling made them hold back with some reservation about what they thought. With the publication of *Babbitt* two years later, a pattern began to form, confirming that *Main Street* was not just a fluke. As H. L. Mencken explained after reading *Babbitt*:

> The theory lately held in Greenwich Village that the merit and success of *Main Street* constituted a sort of double-headed accident ... blows up with a frightful roar toward the middle of *Babbitt*. The plain truth is, indeed, that *Babbitt* is at least twice as good a novel as *Main Street* was—that it avoids all the most obvious faults of that celebrated work, and shows a number of virtues that are quite new.

In short, critics found that Lewis had more than just one great book in him.

As his career marched forward, *Arrowsmith* in 1925 and *Elmer Gantry* in 1927 continued to impress, although the decade did include some lesser efforts, such as *Mantrap* in 1926 and *The Man Who Knew Coolidge* in 1928. *Dodsworth*, published in 1929, has a mixed reputation: some critics categorize it as one of Lewis's great novels, whereas others consider it to be the first step in his decline.

It was not long after the Nobel Prize that critics began to suspect that Lewis's greatest days might already be over. A 1933 biographical sketch of the novelist by Carl Van Doren notes that many doubted his ability even then. "His decade, they have pointed out, is dead," Van Doren wrote. "The ten years which began with *Main Street* in 1920 ended in 1930 with the award of the Nobel Prize. Historians have filed him away with the classics, arguing about the shelf on which he belonged." Even though Van Doren's point was that such critics were shortsighted, the critics that he was trying to refute proved to be eerily prophetic. Lewis spent the rest of his career, like the time before the twenties, writing books that had occasional flashes of inspiration lost amid hundreds of pages of mediocre work.

By the 1940s, critics took for granted that Sinclair Lewis would always come out with new novels, finding little to get excited about with each one. When Edmund Wilson reviewed Lewis's novel *Cass Timberlane* in 1945, he acknowledged the author's persistence in a review entitled "Salute to an Old Landmark." "We have had Lewis around for so long," Wilson wrote, "so consistently being himself, that he has become a familiar object, like Henry Ford or the Statue of Liberty, about which, if one has been living in America, one does not think very much." Wilson noted that Lewis's style had improved since the time he read one of his novels, but he also pointed out that he, like most others, did not take the time to read Lewis's books when they came out: "I had not read him for years, and had heard little about him except routine complaints that he was repeating himself and going to pot." Four years later, John Woodburn summed up Lewis's career in an article for the *New Republic* titled "Lament for a Novelist" with the observation that the author's storytelling ability had swung wildly, from one extreme to the other, until it stopped swinging and stayed down, with one bad book after another:

There was at least a pendulum movement and an element of surprise: if *Arrowsmith* was followed by *Mantrap*, *Dodsworth* came along to redeem *The Man Who Knew Coolidge*. Somewhere about 1934 or 1935, depending on how you felt about *It Can't Happen Here*, the pendulum got stuck on the down stroke. The last six novels ... have been monotonously bad, a soggy mishmash of sentimentality and half-digested social consciousness, through which one looks in vain for the robust rancor, the boisterous humor and the broad but often lethal satire that won Lewis the 1930 Nobel Prize.

Critical assessment has stayed fairly stable since Lewis's death. The novels before 1920 are considered interesting for biographical purposes, to show the novelist in development. The main novels between 1920 and 1930 are considered classics of American literature. Only *It Can't Happen Here* and *Kingsblood Royal* are considered worth reading of his post-1920 work. *Main Street* is still considered his best novel.

Criticism

David Kelly

Kelly is an adjunct professor of English at College of Lake County and Oakton Community College in Illinois. In the following essay, Kelly examines why Lewis's use of repetition instead of traditional plot development has led some critics to label his novel an achievement in sociology but not fiction.

There can be little dispute of the fact that Sinclair Lewis's book *Main Street* has had a profound and lasting influence on what people think of when they think of the American small town. Since its publication, it has no longer been possible to think of the pleasures of the little community—the sense of oneness and the admirable determination that makes independence possible—without also thinking of its dark, smothering aspects at the same time. The book sold over a million copies in its time and keeps selling at a steady pace today, as readers examine truths about this culture that have stayed the same throughout nearly a century. This, despite the fact that urban sprawl, population boom, multiculturalism, and a shifting economy have nearly erased the industrial class that was on the rise when Lewis wrote. In spite of the book's obvious power, however, there are still literary purists who resist calling Sinclair Lewis a great novelist, categorizing him instead as a sociologist who could recognize trends in the culture and make up characters to rep-

> "Carol's artistic endeavors may seem to go over and over the same material, but in fact they represent a downward spiral, making true artistry in that town seem impossible."

resent various types but lacked the imagination to spin all of the different types into one complete story.

Criticism like this occurs as a result of the weaknesses in *Main Street*. Its characters seldom achieve any more depth of personality than the figures in advertising who exist to represent certain character types, and the book flings them into and out of situations so carelessly that readers are constantly reminded of the author's controlling hand. There is hardly any plot, just one instance in Carol Kennicott's life followed by another. All of these distinct elements are fine for unmasking hypocrisy and other hidden social trends, as a sociologist would do, but they do not make for great fiction. According to this school of thought, Lewis cannot be considered an unimportant writer, but he can't be considered a talented novelist either.

This roundabout way of accepting Lewis's impact while denying his skill in his chosen profession presumes that the more interwoven the plot of a novel is, the more successful it is. In fact, *Main Street* is successful precisely because it allows the story line to meander around, spinning its wheels in the mud of Gopher Prairie just as Carol Milford Kennicott spins her wheels, only occasionally catching on to the illusion that she is actually going somewhere. An intricate plot, with each scene leading to the next, advancing the story, and building to a climax that seems to be necessarily the only place this story could have gone, would not serve the point that Lewis was trying to make.

Instead of a "woven" plot, *Main Street* relies upon recurrences and similarities. Events do not cause each other so much as they echo one another. People in Carol's life resemble others, and things happen that seem just like things that have already been told about. This often is a sign of a weak novelist, who cannot keep inventing new possibilities and is forced to recycle ideas that have already been explored. In this case, though, the pattern of repetition creates its own narrative form, and it is one that serves to make readers understand what it is like to be Carol. If the novel is about her search for identity, then it is only fitting that she and the readers should have to see things and then see other things that look like the first things before any sense of understanding is earned.

The most obvious case of events in Carol's life in Gopher Prairie repeating each other concerns her romantic intrigues with Guy Pollock and Erik Valborg. The similarities of the two cases are inescapable, which makes the differences that much more telling. They are both artistic outcasts, both cases in which her need for intellectual companionship nearly draws her over a line into infidelity. In many ways, her tension over Erik is a simple repeat of the internal struggle that she underwent several years and hundreds of pages earlier when, walking home after a heartfelt moment with Guy, she asked herself, "Am I to be trusted?" Not much seems to have been changed from one case to the next, until the reader adds an awareness of the relative circumstances. Guy is older and makes Carol feel young; Erik is younger and makes her feel old. Guy is a loner who shuts himself up in his office, hoping to be ignored by the town; Erik is an extrovert who draws attention to himself because he is able to laugh at negative public opinion. The trajectory from the first case to the second defines Carol's growth, her movement from uncertainty to defiance, even as the other events in her life seem to be dragging her down into defeat. The relationship between these two would not be so telling about who Carol is if they were not so eerily similar, even though, in making them so, Lewis supports some critics in their thesis that the main character fails to grow.

But, even though these opportunities for infidelity are the most attention-grabbing in Carol's story, they are not necessarily the most significant elements in the character profile laid out for readers in *Main Street*. There are other cases in which this style of repetition is just as obvious. Throughout the book, ideas, motifs, and characterizations come back in familiar forms, again and again, building to an overall impression of the inescapable sameness that engulfs Carol's life once she moves to Gopher Prairie.

Her character grows in ways that she is not even aware of, affected by the patterns of the world around her. The book traces Carol's hunt for identity, but only a few of the significant moments Lewis describes are part of an *active* search. The others are reminders. Beside her romantic affairs, there are at least four other identities that she tries on, and each identity takes on a life beyond the one that she thought she was adopting. She tries her hand at being a pillar of the community, an arbiter of artistic sensibilities, and a modern woman. If Lewis had allowed the failures of all of these endeavors to fall on Carol's head, he would have ended up with a much more hopeless story than he intended. It makes sense to blend her failures with the failures of others and to let readers draw their own connections.

When she first arrives in Gopher Prairie, for instance, Carol tries to petition the town leaders to build an important and ambitious civic center, but she meets with disappointment and frustration. The point is made strongly enough, but then it is made again when Vida Sherwin shames her into leading a Campfire Girl troop and yet again when she arranges the fund for a visiting nurse for the poor families on the outskirts of town. After involving herself and extracting herself from countless town projects, the last example from this line comes at the end of the book when the "Community Day" of her dreams is intercepted by a local political hack, who corrupts her concept for his own glory. Carol's attempts to change the social life of Gopher Prairie meet with more and more success as she becomes less and less involved in them, a point that exists more in the circumstances around her than in her psyche. To follow a traditional plot thread of one defeat leading to the next attempt would miss this point.

Carol tries to make her mark on the town's artistic sensibilities. She attends a meeting of the "women's study group," the Thanatopsis Society, only to find that the Gopher Prairie women think they can adequately explore all of English poetry in one afternoon. Her shaky social standing prevents her from pointing out the flaw in this thinking. She takes the lead in forming a "Little Theater" group, hoping to be more influential, but the same forces that suppress her in the Thanatopsis Society drag the theater group down to mediocrity. Both examples are needed to show how strongly the town is resistant to change. Late in the story, the theater group that mirrored the Thanatopsis society is itself mirrored in a new theater group that is planned by Carol and her friends Fern Mullins and Erik Valborg. The inability to even get this new idea past the talking stage, due to the personal calamities that befall the participants, makes the earlier watered-down version look desirable. Carol's artistic endeavors may seem to go over and over the same material, but in fact they represent a downward spiral, making true artistry in that town seem impossible.

One more noteworthy identity that Carol tries to adopt is that of an independent, modern woman. This is almost impossible in Gopher Prairie, where people only know her as the wife Will Kennicott brought to town. At a party soon after her arrival, Carol tries to shake off the stereotypical "wife" personality by talking openly and frankly about forbidden subjects such as labor unions, experimental education, and daring her husband to strip to his underwear and jump into a cold lake on their honeymoon. Her attempt to shake up the social order is only moderately successful: she does not liberate her neighbors' minds, but she does make them look at her as someone who is different from them. Her youthful unwillingness to conform later shows up in Fern Mullins, who comes to town and ignores the standards of behavior expected of a school-teacher. Unlike Carol's case, in which nonconformity led to discomfort among her neighbors, Fern's openness about moderate drinking and being in the presence of men leads to her losing her career before she has started her first job, and being run out of town. Again, this familiar occurrence, mirroring Carol's bid for freedom, has yet another echo later in the book when a speaker from the National Non-partisan League is run out of town on a rail.

Main Street is filled with dozens of other instances that are replayed by ghostly shadows of themselves. Jim Blausser, the real-estate developer and feel-good guru, has a function in the book almost identical to that performed by Percy Bresnahan. Aunt Bessie Smail is almost indistinguishable from Mrs. Bogart in her opinions. The trip to Red Squaw Lake, with the women left behind to cook while the men fish, is the basis for the hunting trip in the last chapter that has Carol shooting with the men. The trip to California, which Kennicott takes to soothe Carol's frustration, is later copied by the short trip to South Carolina during which she presumably becomes pregnant. The two children of Carol and Will Kennicott provide a clear opportunity to view different attitudes, because they are from different times in the marriage and of different genders.

The novel does not follow any direct path in tracking Carol's growth but instead offers a series of instances and examples. Readers and critics

> Quixotism induces an ambivalent and confusing response, for it embodies both foolishness and idealism."

might find this to indicate a weakness on the part of Sinclair Lewis, and they would probably be right: his other novels are also episodic. But the author's presumed weakness does not negate the fact that this technique works in this book. Life in Gopher Prairie is bleak and hopeless for Carol, and readers come to feel this best when they discover the enigmatic ways in which things relate to each other.

Source: David Kelly, Critical Essay on *Main Street*, in *Novels for Students*, The Gale Group, 2002.

Martin Light

In the following essay, Light examines the quixotic overtones in Lewis's Main Street.

Sinclair Lewis's attitude toward the activity of writing can be seen in his letters to his publisher reporting his progress with *Main Street*. The letters overflow with excitement, even though the making of an important novel was for him then, as always, a job as wearing as the most strenuous manual labor. "Whether it's good or not," he wrote, "of course I can't tell, but there is this fact usually indicative of some excellence: I'm enormously enjoying writing it . . . indeed I'm not thinking of much else." He *was* thinking of other matters, however; as a former writer of commercial fiction and as a former employee of a publisher's promotion department, he could not help but concern himself with sales. He gave some thought to marketing his short stories and to advertising his recent novel *Free Air*. He was involved in all the activities of his profession.

He sensed, according to these letters, what *Main Street* might mean to him: "... all my thoughts and planning are centered in *Main Street*—which may, perhaps, be the real beginning of my career as a writer." And later: "I believe that it will be the real beginning of my writing. No book and no number of short stories I've ever done have ever meant a quarter of what this does to me." In the spring of

1920 he wrote that the pace was exhausting, but his excitement was unabated: "Yesterday . . . was the first day I'd taken off in eleven days; even last Sunday I worked till 5:30 P.M. I'm revising with the most minute care and, I fancy, with success."

Then at the end of July he completed the book. He had managed to finish it, Lewis said, "only by working eight hours a day, seven days in most weeks, though a normal number of daily hours of creative writing is supposed to be about four. . . .[sic] I never worked so hard, and never shall work so hard, again . . . unless Comes the Revolution and I am driven from writing to real work, like bricklaying or soldiering or being a nurse-maid." He thus concludes with characteristic irony, belittling enough and repeated often enough so that one may wonder what his reservations about writing were. He spoke of writing as "sweaty and nerve-jangling," and said that pure research in a laboratory would have pleased him more. To some extent such yearning is one of Lewis's poses. Yet a study of his books does show that he chose research in the laboratory as a metaphor for the life best lived, though he also commended the careers of the physician, the inn-keeper, and the architect. For instance, "I never quite get over the feeling," Lewis told an interviewer in 1947, "that writing isn't much of a profession, compared with being a doctor, that it's not quite manly to be sitting there on the seat of your pants all the time." Professor Perry Miller remembered a conversation following an outburst of temper when Lewis discovered that his brother Claude would not attend one of the novelist's lectures during their tour of Europe. Miller writes that Lewis cried out: "It's been that way from the beginning. . . . I wanted to write, and I've worked like hell at it, and the whole of Sauk Centre and my family and America have never understood that it is work, that I haven't just been playing around, that this is every bit as serious a proposition as Claude's hospital. When you said that Claude did not want to hear my lecture . . . you set up all the resentments I have had ever since I can remember." Even after he returned to Sauk Centre in 1916 as a successful young author of two novels and a number of stories that had appeared in the *Saturday Evening Post*, the townspeople let him know they considered writing as only "nearly" as choice a trade as medicine, law, the ministry, or even manufacturing. Against these feelings, which he would have throughout his life, Lewis set to work—to hard work—composing *Main Street*.

In his studies of the influence of Cervantes on European and American literature, Professor Harry Levin mentions the resemblance Carol Kennicott bears to Emma Bovary, who is the archetype of the "female quixote." But neither Carol nor *Main Street* has been analyzed thoroughly as an expression of quixotism, though such an analysis can uncover sources of the novel's vitality and appeal. An approach through quixotism can bring us to a better understanding of Carol's ambitions, illusions, conflicts, persistence, and defeat. When seen as the story of a woman with a mind shaped by romantic notions, who challenges the community with her impractical idealism and suffers rebuffs and self-doubt, *Main Street* appears to have more purpose, unity, and psychological interest than many readers have been willing to concede to it.

The quixote's career begins in the library. Of Emma Bovary, Professor Levin writes: "From the drab milieu she has known as a farmer's daughter, her extracurricular reading conjures up the allurements of escape: steeds and guitars, balconies and fountains, medieval and Oriental vistas." We may say much the same thing about Carol, for she can conjure up a bower of roses, a château, a Chinese entertainment, an exotic Frenchman, a poet-lover. She brings to Gopher Prairie a romantic model of what a village should be and a fantasy of her role in life. However, as she settles into her plain and frigid Gopher Prairie home, so different from the one she has imagined, she cries, "How these stories lie!"

The opening chapters of *Main Street* give only fragmentary information about Carol's childhood, but they suggest an environment that encouraged romanticizing. She recalls that her father was "the tenderest man in the world." He created "Christmas fantasies" from "the sacred old rag doll at the tops of the tree," and he would transform the terrors of the night into a "hearth-mythology" of "beneficent and bright-eyed creatures." There were the "tam htab, who is woolly and blue and lives in the bathroom" and "the ferruginous oil stove, who purrs and knows stories." Her father let her read anything she wished, and she is said to have "absorbed" Balzac, Rabelais, Thoreau, and Max Müller at an early age. But what Carol saw in Thoreau, one suspects, was woodsy escapism and inaction, for at one point she recalls, "I used to sit there on the cliffs above Mankato for hours at a time, my chin in my hand, looking way down the valley, wanting to write poems."

At college she announces that she hopes to "conquer the world." Vaporous images from her further reading point to the reformist mission that she must undertake. "She wanted, just now, to have a cell in a settlement-house, like a nun without the bother of a black robe"; from the cell she will improve "a horde of grateful poor." The icon of her dormitory room is "a miniature of the Dancing Bacchante." Having glanced at a book on town improvement, she plans to convert a village to the greens and garden-walls of France. Or she wishes to "turn a prairie town into Georgian houses and Japanese bungalows." She declares, "I don't understand myself but I want—everything in the world! Maybe I can't sing or write, but I know I can be an influence in library work. Just suppose I encouraged some boy and he became a great artist!"

Meanwhile she is learning to transmute reality. For instance, as she climbs along the banks of the Mississippi, she sees the river as her fanciful mind dictates. She listens to the fables of the river "about the wide land of yellow waters and bleached buffalo bones to the West; the Southern levees and singing darkies and palm trees toward which it was forever mysteriously gliding; and she heard again the startled bells and thick pulling of high-stacked river steamers wrecked on sand-reefs sixty years ago. Along the decks she saw missionaries, gamblers in tall pot hats, and Dakota chiefs with scarlet blankets." She has created a tableau peopled with figures of her own imagining—dreams, Lewis says later, "governed by the fiction she had read, drawn from the pictures she had envied." To give another illustration of her fancy, at the commencement exercises at Blodgett College "she saw the palms as a jungle, the pink-shaded electric globes as an opaline haze, and the eyeglassed faculty as Olympians."

During a year in Chicago after graduation, these impulses are strengthened. Carol spends an evening at a bohemian studio party, where she hears talk of "Freud, Romain Rolland, syndicalism, the Confédération Générale du Travail, feminism vs. haremism, Chinese lyrics, nationalization of mines, Christian Science, and fishing in Ontario." Significantly, her first job is at the library in St. Paul where, while she works, she reads "scores of books." The subject list is especially suited to the development of her fancy: "volumes of anthropology …, Parisian imagistes, Hindu recipes for curry, voyages to the Solomon Isles, theosophy with modern American improvements." At dances, "in dread of life's slipping past, she turned into a bacchanal." Her sense of mission returns; she will transform and redesign a prairie town.

At this point, Dr. Will Kennicott enters her life. He woos her by exploiting her desire to find a pur-

pose for herself, declaring that his village needs her. Dr. Kennicott provides a notable occasion for us to apprehend the way in which the vision of the quixote converts reality to illusion. As we noted earlier, he shows Carol some photographs, and, though they are streaked and vague, she perceives them as (in her need for adventure) she must. She sees his amateurish snapshots of lakes as "etchings" that delineate "snow in crevices of a boggy bank, the mound of a muskrat house, reeds in thin black lines." Intuiting Carol's nature, Kennicott uses one picture especially well. It shows a forest clearing and a log cabin. In front of the cabin is "a sagging woman with tight-drawn hair, and a baby bedraggled, smeary, glorious-eyed." Kennicott tempts Carol by saying, "Look at that scared baby! Needs some woman with hands like yours. Waiting for you!" Carol succumbs. Such photographs will return later in the novel, when Kennicott is courting Carol again after her flight from Gopher Prairie. At the middle when she visits the home of this baby in the snapshot, she would tell him of Prince Charming, but he doesn't understand.

After Carol and the doctor marry, they ride the train into Gopher Prairie, the town she will "conquer" and reform. She has her first view of the reality she must work with. When she sees their house and her room, the shock is great. She blames her reading. "She glanced at the houses; tried not to see what she saw; gave way in: 'Why do these stories lie so? They always make the bride's homecoming a bower of roses. Complete trust in the noble spouse. Lies about marriage. . . . And this town— O my God! I can't go through with it. This junkheap!'" She has read "too many books." She goes to the bedroom window "with a purely literary thought of village charm—hollyhocks and lanes and apple-cheeked cottagers." What she sees is "the side of the Seventh-Day Adventist Church—a plain clapboard wall of a sour liver color." *This* was "the terraced garden below her boudoir"—"How these stories lie!" Muttering, "I'm mildly insane," she goes out to see the village, the "empire" she is going to "conquer." She takes that memorable promenade which we have already noted. She finds a Main Street characterized by the reek of blood from the meat market, by yellow buildings, by a cat sleeping on the lettuce in the grocery window. But Carol is not broken by that view of the village. For a long time she survives and returns to the fray. Her resiliency originates in her transmuting imagination; she is like Don Quixote with bandaged head taking to the road once more. Her enthusiasm, at least at first and in one so young ("plastic" and "innocent," as Lewis says) is even engaging.

Her adventures test not only Carol's notions but also the beliefs and actions of society. In the face of the challenge that she brings, members of the community reveal themselves as corrupt and hypocritical—or at least foolish in their own way. For instance, when Carol attends her first party in Gopher Prairie, she carries to it the image of herself as "a smart young married woman in a drawing room, fencing with clever men." She expects good talk, and she believes that she can enter into conversation as an equal to the men. But they have been arguing all evening about the kind of dog an old-timer had owned years ago. When Carol confronts them with a question about labor relations, she draws from them remarks that are the hallmark of Lewis's satire. Jackson Elder asserts that he is for freedom and constitutional rights: "If any man don't like my shop, he can get up and git. Same way, if I don't like him, he gits. And that's all there is to it." He mumbles on about such "poppycock" as profit-sharing, welfare work, insurance, old-age pensions. It "enfeebles a workman's independence—and wastes a lot of honest profit."

By such a pattern of challenge and reaction throughout the novel, each satiric monologue achieves its organic place. At every thrust from Carol, a villager exposes his own foolishness or hypocrisy about education, economics, politics, religion. Each encounter provides Lewis with the opportunity to exhibit his virtuosity in creating the grotesque rantings of gossips, churchwomen, preachers, journalists, and boosters. Carol induces the community to expose itself. Her own response to these encounters remains unchanging, nonetheless. Even as she drags herself homeward from them, past a "hulking house," "a streaky yellow pool," a "morass," she tells herself that "her beautiful town" still exists—in her mind. She believes in the village she has imagined. What she is now seeking is a person to share it with.

Several secondary figures in *Main Street* reinforce Carol's quixotism. Guy Pollock, whom Lewis declared to have been the protagonist of the book in its earliest conception (though no draft of that version exists and Lewis's biographer doubts whether such a version ever got on paper)—Pollock too is maddened by reading. He "hints his love" for Sir Thomas Browne, Thoreau, Agnes Reppelier, Arthur Symons, Claude Washburne, and Charles Flandrau, authors who can nourish the fancy. Carol visits Pollock at his rooms, where he reveals the content of his imagination. Here, he says, are his "office, town-house, and château in Picardy. But you can't see the château and townhouse (next to the Duke of Sutherland's)." Of course Carol *can* see them, quite as well as he can. Carol and Pollock discuss the possibility of reforming the town, but Pollock is by now incapable of rebellion. Like Prufrock, he wishes only to be an attendant, "the confidant of the old French plays, the tiring-maid with the mirror and the loyal ears." Carol wonders whether Pollock might be her Prince Charming, but she later realizes that he was only a frame on which she hung "shining garments."

Toward her husband, Carol feels a genuinely painful conflict. Kennicott is a capable doctor, but his very competence is paradoxically a problem for Carol, who finds that capable people are often shallow and bigoted. At their best, without what Lewis would two years later call "babbittry," these figures are heroes, "doers," for whom "all this romance stuff is simply moonshine." Kennicott shows admirable courage and ability as a physician and surgeon in several crises. But even at such moments Carol must recreate him in romanticized and literary terms: she "saw the drama of his riding by night to the frightened household on the distant farm; pictured children standing at a window, waiting for him. He suddenly had in her eyes the heroism of a wireless operator on a ship in a collision; of an explorer, fever-clawed, deserted by his bearers, but going on—." She tells Pollock that he and she are "a pair of hypercritical loafers, . . . while [Will] quietly goes and does things." She restates the dichotomy: to deal with the farmers Kennicott "speaks a vulgar, common, incorrect German of life and death and birth and the soil," while she reads "the French and German of sentimental lovers and Christmas garlands." Such a division lies at the heart of the book, though Will calls Carol neurotic, and she labels him stupid. But Carol, the doctor, and the novel itself are considerably more complex than this formulation suggests, and Carol knows it upon reflection. This complexity is creditable in ways that have been forgotten by Lewis's detractors. Carol knows that Kennicott is not simply a quiet doer. He is noisy, opinionated, narrow, prejudiced, quarrelsome, and unfaithful, and the novel takes pains to display him as such. Carol's neurosis, meanwhile, is compounded of idealism, enthusiasm, doubt, disillusionment, and alienation.

In the midst of her despair, Carol inquires into books once more in an effort to understand herself and her village. Formerly, in reading popular stories and plays, Carol had found only two traditions about the American town. The first tradition, she reports, "is that the American village remains the one sure abode of friendship, honesty, and clean sweet marriageable girls ... The other tradition is that the significant features of all villages are whiskers, iron dogs upon lawns, gold bricks, checkers, jars of gilded cat-tails, and shrewd comic old men who are known as 'hicks' and who ejaculate 'Waal I swan.'" Her experience of Gopher Prairie, however, tells her that the town thinks "in cheap motor cars, telephones, ready-made clothes, silos, alfalfa, kodaks, phonographs, leather-upholstered Morris chairs, bridge-prizes, oil-stocks, motion-pictures, land-deals, unread sets of Mark Twain, and a chaste version of national politics." With this small town, Carol—along with hundreds of thousands of young people like her—is not content. She believes that she has derived insight and other "convictions" from her recent reading. She has "driven" her way through books of a somewhat different kind from those she read as a girl. These books were written by the "young American sociologists, young English realists, Russian horrorists; Anatole France, Rolland, Nexo, Wells, Shaw, Key, Edgar Lee Masters, Theodore Dreiser, Sherwood Anderson, Henry Mencken, and all the other subversive philosophers and artists whom women were consulting everywhere."

One night she talks to her friend Vida Sherwin about the dullness, the rigidity, and the sterility of the village. Vida, a "realist," suggests measured steps toward reform. But Carol, for all her new reading and thought, replies that she wants "startling, exotic things": "Strindberg plays, and classic dancers—exquisite legs beneath tulle—and (I can see him so clearly!) a thick, black-bearded, cynical Frenchman who would sit about and drink and sing opera and tell bawdy stories and laugh at our proprieties and quote Rabelais and not be ashamed to kiss my hand!" This is a moment of considerable psychological importance. Whatever the booklist of "American sociologists, French realists, Russian horrorists" may have brought her, Carol's quixotic nature defeats her efforts at new understanding. Her transforming imagination turns Gopher Prairie back into fantasy land.

Romantic love, the motif that particularly directs the yearnings of the female quixote, enters *Main Street* about three-fourths of the way towards its end. When Erik Valborg appears in Gopher Prairie, he is less a substantial character than a projection of what Carol fancies him to be. Much of the confusion surrounding her platonic escapade with Erik occurs because she waivers between at

A suffragist protesting in New York City in 1912. The Suffragist Movement was in full swing when the novel was published in 1920, with women gaining the right to vote that year

least two images of him. At times she recognizes that he is a commonplace, uneducated, shallow young man; at other times she believes him to be a poet—a Keats or Shelley or (as Lewis plays with Carol's values) an Arthur Upson. Carol is insistent: "He's Keats—sensitive to silken things.... Keats, here! A bewildered spirit fallen on Main Street. And Main Street laughs." Thinking of him later, however, she asks herself, "Was he anything but a small-town youth bred on an illiberal farm and in cheap tailor shops?" Valborg himself, like Pollock, brings to his relationship with Carol his own quixotism. It is reported that he reads a great deal, but his taste tends toward "Suppressed Desires" and "The Black Mask." He recalls that, when he lived in Minneapolis, he used to "tramp clear around Lake Harriet, or hike out to the Gates house and imagine it was a château in Italy and I lived in it. I was a marquis and collected tapestries—that was after I was wounded in Padua."

Valborg continues to stimulate and confuse Carol's romantic imagination. While she is doing household tasks, she pictures "herself and a young artist—an Apollo nameless and evasive—building a house in the Berkshires or in Virginia; exuberantly buying a chair with his first check; reading poetry together." She wishes him to be a "playmate," not a lover. She is always dissatisfied, however. In moments of self-awareness, she calls her love affair "pitiful and tawdry. . . . A self-deceived little woman whispering in corners with a pretentious little man." Then she makes a sudden quixotic shift: "No, he is not. He is fine. Aspiring." She is in a turmoil of distraction. She wishes Erik were "a fighter, an artist with bearded surly lips." But "they're only in books." Her mind is spinning, but not toward suicide, like Emma's; Carol knows all too well that the tragedy of her life is "that I shall never know tragedy, never find anything but blustery complications that turn out to be a farce." One moment she is convinced she loves Erik; the next she cannot love him because his wrists are too large, his nose is too snub. She knows that the poem he writes her ("Little and tender and merry and wise/ With eyes that meet my eyes") is bad. After Carol and Erik have wandered, talked, and daydreamed for some time, Kennicott confronts her. He is certain he knows what has poisoned her mind: "these fool stories about wives that don't know when they're well off." Her affair ends when Will chases Erik out of town.

About forty pages remain in the novel. Now the problem is whether Carol will retain her illusions or face whatever reality Gopher Prairie presents. She might somehow find a balance of dream and fact that would result in growth. In fact, Levin suggests that the quixotic experience need not end negatively, for it can lead to maturity. But when Carol breaks from Gopher Prairie and settles in Washington, she seems not much different from the person she was before, though she believes herself to be changing. For instance, the "Washington" she finds (or, one suspects, creates) is a city of "leafy parks, spacious avenues, twisty alleys," of "negro shanties turned into studios, with orange curtains and pots of mignonette," of marble houses and butlers and limousines, and "men who looked like fictional explorers and aviators." After a year, her husband comes to woo her back. His gesture is exactly the one he had made when he first courted her about ten years earlier, and her response is just what we expect and fear. "He tossed over to her thirty prints of Gopher Prairie and the country about. . . . She remembered that he had lured her with photographs in courtship days; she made a note of his sameness, his satisfaction with the tactics which had proved good before; but she forgot it in the familiar places." She has built no defense against this well-intuited appeal to her illusions, though she thinks that she has developed what she calls "personal solidarity." Back in Gopher Prairie she wears her eyeglasses on the street (perhaps because she wishes to see more clearly now). The townsmen say of her that "she knows a good deal about books—or fiction anyway," and of her affair with Valborg that it was "just talking books and all that junk." She believes that, though she may not have "fought the good fight," she has kept faith with her ideals.

By seeing Carol Kennicott as a quixote, we come to realize that Lewis could criticize both his heroine and the village. He tried, in his flamboyant, crude, and often careless way, to anatomize a woman torn among illusions and realities. For Carol, Lewis drew upon an archetype, so that Carol touched familiar responses in readers in America, where quixotism has long existed but has not been fully recognized as an important aspect of the national character. In the sub-literature and popular culture of the late nineteenth and early twentieth centuries, romance flourished. We have already noted the cults associated with the Orient, the medieval, the adventurous, the Kiplingesque, poesy, and vagabondia. These formed a state of mind which attracted and repelled several generations of writers. Mark Twain, who understood much of what made and moved America, portrayed quixotism in *Tom Sawyer*, *Huck Finn*, *Life on the Mississippi*, and *A Connecticut Yankee*. A towering figure like Mark Twain gathers ideas from the past and opens up potentialities for future writers. His indications of the presence of quixotism in American life are significant; Lewis also sensed such a presence and the conflict that attends it.

Quixotism induces an ambivalent and confusing response, for it embodies both foolishness and idealism. The story of Carol Kennicott is a record of resultant ambiguities. Recognizing that the book is uneven and in some ways inconclusive, we can speculate that the quixotic elements in Lewis's nature disallowed the kind of transcendence that Cervantes and Flaubert achieved. Lewis came to *Main Street* after writing five apprentice novels, among them *The Trail of the Hawk* and *Free Air*, in which young Americans travel the roads in pursuit of adventure and golden ladies. Perhaps he called *Main Street* "the real beginning" of his career because he believed that he was freeing himself from the shackles of romance by satirizing a literary idea of the village that maddens its readers and that had misled him for too long. Carol was his vehicle and victim. Now he was joining a realistic movement that was already well under way without him.

What Do I Read Next?

- The novel that Sinclair Lewis wrote after *Main Street* was *Babbitt*. Published in 1922, it is about a middle-aged salesman and his uncomfortable search for meaning in an increasingly impersonal world. A Bantam Books edition, published in 1998, is currently available, with an introduction by John Wickersham.

- In chapter 14 of *Main Street*, Lewis says, "Her preparations for stalking out of the Doll's House were not yet visible." The reference is to Henrik Ibsen's 1879 play, *A Doll's House*, about a strong-willed wife who defies social custom when she finds that she can no longer be kept by a husband who loves her but does not respect her intelligence. Dover Press published a thrift edition of this play in 1992.

- French writer Gustav Flaubert's Emma Bovary is often referred to as clearly being a model for Carol Kennicott—they both are women who find their spirits suppressed by their roles as wives of small-town doctors. The 1857 novel *Madame Bovary* is available in a Bantam Classics edition, published in 1982.

- A generation before Lewis made his reputation for taking a naturalist approach to the American small town, Theodore Dreiser gained fame for applying the same techniques to urban life. His novel *Sister Carrie* (1900) shows a young country girl who is ruined by the stifling coldness of the city, driven to a life of degradation and prostitution. Signet has a 2000 reissue edition with an introduction by Richard Lingeman.

- In 1899, novelist Kate Chopin attracted a storm of controversy with her novel *The Awakening*, about a married woman's growing awareness of her own intelligence and sensitivity. It is currently available from Avon in a 1994 edition.

- Willa Cather was a writer whose best works documented life on the prairie at the beginning of the twentieth century. Her novel *My Antonia* is about a Bohemian peasant girl who grows up on a Nebraska farm, in circumstances similar to those Lewis describes. It was first published in 1918 and is currently available in a 1995 edition from Houghton Mifflin.

- One of Lewis's contemporaries was Sherwood Anderson, whose collection of short stories, *Winesburg, Ohio*, is a master work of American fiction. First published in 1919, it looks at the stifling effects of small-town life through the eyes of teenage boy, who recognizes his hometown as a place of "grotesques." Bantam published a new edition in 1995.

At any rate, I think that we are better informed about *Main Street*—and better able to assess it—if we see it as an account of a quixotic figure—idealistic, disillusioned, of limited vision, yet a challenge to the community. Amidst the comedy, she is, if not tragic, at least worthy of our concern, because her idealism drives her into further suffering. She has been shown that her vision is faulty, weakly inspired, and mistaken, but she continues to see as her aspirations demand. She is more honest and more deceived than anyone around her, and thereby both more trapped and more alive.

Yet Carol continues to seem bewildered in a postscript to the novel, when, later, in an article called "Main Street's Been Paved" written for the *Nation* magazine during the presidential election of 1924, Lewis glanced again at his characters and the condition of their lives. His attitude toward Will Kennicott remained ambivalent. At first, he indicated high praise for the doctor, such praise as he consistently expressed toward the practical "doers" in America: ". . . for him I held, and hold, a Little Brother awe. He is merely a country practitioner, not vastly better than the average; yet he is one of these assured, deep-chested, easy men who are always to be found when you want them, and who are rather amused by persons like myself that go sniffing about, wondering what it all means." This statement seems an echo of Sauk Centre's disapproval of young Harry's "readin' and readin'" in contrast to its admiration for the practical physicians of the Lewis family. It reflects the doubts implanted by the provincial attitude that thought and writing—that art itself—are of no value. Who of the village inquisitors could understand that preparation for the writing career required dreaming and reading and scribbling, and that money and recognition would be slow to appear? One thinks of Lewis's return to Sauk Centre at about thirty-two as an established writer, of his pride in telling the townspeople that he was paid fifteen hundred dollars for a magazine serial which he turned out in two weeks' time; they were awed but not convinced.

Unfortunately, his heroine in *Main Street* falls into the category of small town failures (along with the other impractical dissenters of Gopher Prairie—Miles Bjornstam, Fern Mullins, and Guy Pollock). In "Main Street's Been Paved" Lewis shows us a very beaten "Carol." I have argued that at the end of the novel itself her change or growth was unconvincing. If one considers the *Nation* essay, one doubts even more all Lewis's pretense about her important Washington experience and her personal solidarity. She is hardly recognizable; she appears tired and timid and dumpy; she intends to vote, not for liberal and humanitarian LaFollette, but for Coolidge. Guy Pollock reports that "the doctor has convinced her that to be denunciatory or even very enthusiastic isn't quite respectable." Apparently there was some miscalculation of Carol's "solidarity." But we are not to be left with a simple approval of Kennicott; Lewis, in spite of his awe, is nevertheless aware of Kennicott as a symbol of something dangerous. Lewis lets Guy Pollock, the village lawyer, have the last word. Pollock says, "We've been bullied too long by the Doc Kennicotts and by the beautiful big balloon tires that roll over the new pavement on Main Street—and over our souls." Lewis seems to have shifted to Pollock as spokesman, while meting out to Carol, who will vote for Coolidge, a kind of punishment for the inadequacy of the fanciful notions she, after all, was given by him.

Does *Main Street* pose a choice between Carol's way and Will's way? If he must choose between Carol's qualities as expressed in the novel itself (sensitivity, humanitarianism, curiosity, thoughtfulness, and desire for change and improvement—mixed, however, with impracticality, pretentiousness, artiness, and foolish dreaming) and Will's qualities (practicality, courage, and bluntness—mixed, similarly, with insensitivity, dullness, and scorn for art), which way would Lewis choose? Some critics feel an uncertainty in the novel because of the equivocation between these qualities. Others may feel that the strength of the novel lies in such complexities. Of herself and her husband, Carol theorizes: "There are two races of people, only two, and they live side by side. His calls mine 'neurotic'; mine calls his 'stupid.' We'll never understand each other, never." The tension of the book may be that there is an impossible choice between sensitivity/foolishness and practicality/dullness. But Lewis does shift back and forth in attitude—now praising, now mocking, now admiring, now satirizing. The people of the empire of the Middle West have posed a difficult problem. Lewis continued to ponder the question in subsequent novels until he achieved a resolution in *Dodsworth*. It is sufficient for the moment, though, that in *Main Street* he had taken auspicious steps forward in his attempt to define man, woman, and marriage, and in his continuing search to understand America. Here he had vividly portrayed the provincial locale, commenting upon it in satire which helped open the American mind to new perceptions. He had aroused sleeping consciences to an awareness of hypocrisies and social injustices. He had touched some deeper notes in his portrayal of the heroine—through her loneliness, her misdirected aspirations, and her difficult struggle to find an identity.

Source: Martin Light, "Chapter 6: *Main Street*," in *The Quixotic Vision of Sinclair Lewis*, Purdue University Press, 1975, pp. 60–72.

Sources

Grebstein, Sheldon Norman, *Sinclair Lewis*, Twayne Publishers, 1962, p. 38.

Mencken, H. L., "Portrait of an American Citizen," in *Sinclair Lewis: A Collection of Critical Essays*, Prentice-Hall, 1962, pp. 20–26.

Van Doren, Carl, *Sinclair Lewis: A Biographical Sketch*, Kennikat Press, 1933, p. I.

Wilson, Edmund, "Salute to an Old Landmark: Sinclair Lewis," in *New Yorker*, October 13, 1944, pp. 101–102, 104.

Woodburn, John, "Lament for a Novelist," in *New Republic*, May 16, 1949, pp. 16–17.

Further Reading

Bucco, Martin, *"Main Street": The Revolt of Carol Kennicott*, Twayne, 1993.

One of the few book-length examinations of this novel, this study looks at its subject from a number of different angles. Most of the book is comprised of essays proposing different theoretical viewpoints.

Davies, Richard O., *Main Street Blues: The Decline of Small-Town America*, Ohio State University Press, 1998.

Davis only uses Lewis's novel as an inspiration and focuses most of his study on his own home town of Camden, Ohio. Still, the points that he makes about small towns in the twentieth century bring the novel's concerns into the present.

Light, Martin, *The Quixotic Vision of Sinclair Lewis*, Purdue University Press, 1975.

This overview of Lewis's entire career looks at his struggle against prevailing ideas. The main theme of the book, comparing Lewis and his characters to Cervantes' Don Quixote, is well presented.

Lingeman, Richard, *Sinclair Lewis: America's Angry Man*, Random House, 2002.

This is the most recent biography of Lewis from an author whose previous works have included a biography of Theodore Dreiser and *Small Town America: A Narrative History, 1620–Present*.

Parrington, Vernon, *Sinclair Lewis: Our Own Diogenes*, Haskell House Publishers, 1974.

Parrington's view of Lewis is entirely reverent and perhaps a little too tame to really capture the author's fervor.

Schorer, Mark, *Sinclair Lewis: An American Life*, McGraw-Hill, 1961.

Schorer is one of the preeminent scholars on Lewis, and his book about him has stood as the authoritative biography for forty years.

The Mayor of Casterbridge

Thomas Hardy

1886

The Mayor of Casterbridge, originally entitled *The Life and Death of the Mayor of Casterbridge: A Story of a Man of Character*, was first published serially in a London periodical in 1886. The first publication in book form was later that year. Thomas Hardy was an established author at the time and had published nine previous novels (a first, unpublished novel has been lost), but *The Mayor of Casterbridge* is considered his first masterpiece; some regard it as his greatest tragic novel.

The Mayor of Casterbridge is, from beginning to end, the story of Michael Henchard, a skilled farm laborer who, in a drunken rage, sells his young wife, along with their infant child, to a passing sailor. Most of the novel takes place eighteen to twenty years after this event. When the sailor is reported lost at sea, the cast-off wife and now-grown daughter set out to find Michael, who has become an affluent businessman and the mayor of Casterbridge. Michael's success is temporary, though, as circumstances and his own weaknesses of character combine to bring about his downfall in spite of his attempts to right the wrong he committed years before.

Author Biography

Thomas Hardy was born June 2, 1840, in a village near Dorchester in the southwestern region of England that would become the setting for his novels.

His father, Thomas, was a builder and mason; his mother, Jemima Hand, was a cook.

After attending schools in his village, Bockhampton, and in Dorchester, Hardy was apprenticed at age sixteen to his father's employer, an architect. While learning architecture, Hardy studied the classics with a university-educated tutor named Horace Moule. In 1862, Hardy moved to London, where he worked as an assistant architect, read widely, and began writing. Poems that he submitted to periodicals were rejected, but an article, "How I Built Myself a House," was published.

Hardy's work took him back to Dorchester and then to Weymouth, where he met Emma Lavinia Gifford, whom he married in 1874. Hardy also began writing novels at this time, and it was Emma who encouraged him to leave architecture and write full time. His first published novel, *Desperate Remedies*, came out in 1871 and was quickly followed by two others. (His first, unpublished novel has been lost.) But it was *Far from the Madding Crowd*, published in 1874, that ensured his reputation. By the late 1870s, he was an established member of England's literary elite.

The Mayor of Casterbridge, published in 1886, was considered pivotal in Hardy's career, as its male main character was more fully developed than those in previous novels. *The Mayor of Casterbridge* also represented a new achievement in the novel form by successfully blending a psychological portrait of one man with a depiction of the social realities of a particular time and place. Other major works of this period were a collection of short stories, *Wessex Tales* (1888), and the dark and controversial *Tess of the D'Urbervilles* (1891). Reaction to *Jude the Obscure* (1896) was so harsh that Hardy gave up writing novels. He published his first volume of poetry, *Wessex Poems*, in 1898 and continued to write poetry throughout his remaining years.

In 1912, just after Hardy had completed a final revision of his novels, his wife died. He married Florence Emily Dugdale, who had been his secretary, in 1914. Hardy worked on his autobiography, *The Early Life of Thomas Hardy*, which was ostensibly written by his second wife, and burned his private papers. The autobiography, as well as the last volume of Hardy's poetry, *Winter Words*, was published posthumously in 1928.

Hardy was honored during his lifetime with the British government's Order of Merit (1910) and with honorary doctorate of literature degrees from Cambridge University in 1913 and from Oxford

Thomas Hardy

University in 1920. He died January 11, 1928, in Dorchester after a brief illness. His ashes are interred in Poets' Corner, Westminster Abbey in London, though his heart is buried in the grave of his first wife.

Plot Summary

Chapters 1–2

As the novel opens, Michael Henchard and his wife, Susan, are walking toward a village in Wessex in southwestern England. Susan is carrying their infant daughter, Elizabeth-Jane. It is a late summer afternoon in the mid-1800s. Michael, a skilled farm laborer, is looking for work. Hardy describes the man and woman as being distant from each other and in low spirits. Hardy makes clear that Susan is naïve and malleable.

They enter a shop that sells furmity, a grain-based dish, and order their dinner. Michael quickly discerns that the proprietor, whom Hardy calls "the furmity woman," will spike his furmity with rum for an added payment. He gets drunk and tells those around him that he has ruined his chances for success by marrying too young and would sell his wife if he could. Michael refuses to drop this idea, and finally a sailor offers to meet the five-guinea price that Michael has set. To the shock of the crowd, the sale is made, and Susan and the baby leave with the sailor.

Michael sleeps off the rum in the furmity shop and wakes up to realize what he has done. Feeling remorse, he does two things: he goes to a church and makes a vow that he will not drink hard liquor for twenty-one years (one year for each year he has lived), and he determines to search for Susan and get her back. He searches for months but does not find Susan and the sailor.

Chapters 3–4

About eighteen years have passed. Susan and the sailor, Newson, lived for about twelve years in Canada and then returned to England. Susan's daughter, Elizabeth-Jane, knows nothing about Michael Henchard or Susan's "sale" to Newson; she believes that her mother and Newson are married and that she is Newson's daughter.

Some time ago, Susan had confided in a friend about her past and that she was not legally married to Newson. The friend made Susan understand that she was not bound to Newson in any way; that is, that her "sale" was illegal and did not obligate her to Newson or make their arrangement legal. Susan was upset by this new perspective on her situation and told Newson that she didn't know if she could continue living with him. On his next trip to sea, Newson was reported lost and presumed dead.

Susan and Elizabeth-Jane then set out to find Michael Henchard. Susan hopes that Michael will be able and willing to provide some help for Elizabeth-Jane—financial help or some sort of start in life—as Newson has left her very little. They return to the village where Michael sold Susan and find the furmity woman. The furmity woman tells Susan that Michael returned about a year after the sale of his wife. He instructed the furmity woman that if a woman ever asked for him, she should give the information that Michael had gone to Casterbridge. The next morning, Susan and Elizabeth-Jane leave for Casterbridge.

Chapters 5–8

As Susan and Elizabeth-Jane arrive in Casterbridge, a crowd is gathered in front of a hotel where a fancy dinner is being held. The windows have been opened so that the commoners on the street can hear what is being said at the dinner. Susan and Elizabeth-Jane learn that Michael Henchard is the mayor of the town and is seated at the head of the table. He is also said to be a widower. Elizabeth-Jane, who has been told that they are going to see a distant relative by marriage, is delighted to find that he is so successful. Susan is surprised that the drunken, impetuous young man she knew has become so successful, and she dreads meeting him.

During the dinner, Henchard, a grain merchant, is challenged by some in the crowd who accuse him of having sold wheat that had gone bad. Henchard responds that he did not know the wheat was bad and wishes there was some way to make bad wheat into good wheat, but as there is not, so nothing can be done.

A young Scotsman sends a note in to Henchard, who reads it and leaves the dinner to find the writer of the note. It happens that the young man, Donald Farfrae, is staying in the room next to Susan and Elizabeth-Jane's at the Three Mariners inn. Thus, the two women overhear Farfrae's conversation with Henchard when the mayor arrives. Farfrae's note has told Henchard that Farfrae knows a way to make the bad wheat usable, and Farfrae shares the method with Henchard. Henchard tries to persuade Farfrae to come to work for him, but Farfrae says that he is bound for America.

Susan overhears Henchard say that he does not drink alcohol because of something shameful that he did when he was young. This gives Susan hope that Henchard might be willing to help Elizabeth-Jane.

Later in the evening, Farfrae enthralls the crowd at the inn's bar with his singing. Elizabeth-Jane, who witnesses this because she is helping to pay for her room by serving in the bar, develops an attraction to Farfrae.

Chapters 9–12

The next morning, Susan sends Elizabeth-Jane to Henchard's house with a note asking him to meet her. When Elizabeth-Jane arrives, she is shocked to see Farfrae working in Henchard's office. Farfrae and Henchard had met again early that morning, and Farfrae agreed to work for Henchard after all.

While Elizabeth-Jane is waiting for Henchard, a man named Jopp appears. Henchard had promised this man the job he has now given to Farfrae, but he sends Jopp away without apology.

Michael reads Susan's note and asks Elizabeth-Jane some questions. He then writes a response to Susan, setting a meeting, and encloses five guineas—the exact amount for which he sold her.

The implication is that he is agreeing to take her back, although she has not asked this.

Michael and Susan meet secretly outside the town. Michael proposes to Susan that he will court her as if he has never met her before and marry her. Susan agrees. He offers to begin supporting Susan and Elizabeth-Jane immediately and asks Susan's forgiveness.

Henchard returns home and tells Farfrae, whom he likes and trusts, the whole story of his past, which he has until now kept secret. Henchard tells Farfrae that there is one thing that stands in the way of his now making things right with Susan: There is a woman in another town whom Henchard has offered to marry, thinking that Susan was probably dead. Henchard had an affair with this other woman, by which she was disgraced, and he offered to marry her to repair her reputation. He now asks Farfrae to write to the woman and explain why Henchard cannot marry her after all, and Farfrae agrees.

Chapters 13–16

Henchard provides a house and servant for Susan and Elizabeth-Jane and begins courting Susan. They are married in November of the same year. The townspeople wonder why Henchard has married beneath him. Henchard moves his wife and "stepdaughter" into his house and treats them kindly.

Farfrae improves Henchard's business, and Henchard learns that the townspeople now have more respect and affection for Farfrae than for himself. Henchard humiliates a habitually tardy employee by making him go to work without his britches, but Farfrae reverses Henchard and lets the man go home and finish dressing. This causes Henchard and Farfrae to argue.

On a holiday, Henchard and Farfrae plan competing celebrations for the townspeople. Henchard's festivities are rained out, while Farfrae's dance (under a tent) is a huge success. At Farfrae's dance, Henchard angrily declares that Farfrae's term as his manager is almost over, and Farfrae agrees. In a scene that recalls the morning after Henchard sold Susan, Henchard later regrets what he said and realizes that Farfrae really plans to leave his employ.

Chapters 17–20

Farfrae hints to Elizabeth-Jane that he would marry her if he had more money. He then goes into business for himself but makes a point not to com-

Media Adaptations

- Unabridged audio versions of *The Mayor of Casterbridge* have been published by Books on Tape, Inc. (1983), Chivers Audio Books (1991), John Curley and Associates (1991, with Tony Britton as reader), and the Audio Partners Publishing Corporation (1998, with John Rowe as reader).

- *The Mayor of Casterbridge* was made into a seven-part television miniseries in the United Kingdom in 1978. It was directed by David Giles III and written by Dennis Potter. Alan Bates starred as Henchard, Jack Galloway as Farfrae, Janet Maw as Elizabeth-Jane, and Anne Stallybrass as Susan.

- A 2001 made-for-television movie of *The Mayor of Casterbridge* was directed by David Thacker and written by Ted Whitehead. Ciarán Hinds starred as Henchard, James Purefoy as Farfrae, Jodhi May as Elizabeth-Jane, and Juliet Aubrey as Susan.

pete with Henchard. Henchard, however, treats Farfrae as an enemy and forbids Elizabeth-Jane to see him.

Susan becomes ill. Before she dies, she writes a letter addressed to Henchard, which he is not to open until Elizabeth-Jane's wedding day.

Soon after Susan's death, Henchard reveals to Elizabeth-Jane that he is her father. In looking for proof of his original marriage to Susan (he needs this to prove that he is her father and have her name legally changed to his), he finds the letter that Susan has left and reads it. It reveals that Elizabeth-Jane is not Henchard's daughter; that child died a few months after Henchard sold Susan, and the Elizabeth-Jane he knows is Newson's daughter. Henchard is distraught and decides not to tell Elizabeth-Jane. His behavior toward her changes, though; he criticizes her and increasingly avoids her. She feels unhappy and bereft.

Visiting her mother's grave, Elizabeth-Jane encounters a woman she has never seen before and tells the woman her life story. The woman says that she is moving to Casterbridge and invites Elizabeth-Jane to live with her as her companion. Elizabeth-Jane agrees.

Chapters 21–26

Elizabeth-Jane asks Henchard's permission to take the companion position she has been offered, and Henchard is relieved to see her go. He is surprised, though, when he hears that a Miss Templeman will employ her. This is the woman with whom Henchard once had an affair, the woman he was about to marry before Susan arrived in Casterbridge. She has changed her name to escape the past scandal of her affair with Henchard. Henchard, now free of Susan, has heard that Miss Templeman, also called Lucetta, has just come into a large inheritance, and he wants to marry her.

Elizabeth-Jane moves into Miss Templeman's house. Farfrae goes to see Elizabeth-Jane but is attracted to Miss Templeman, and the attraction is mutual. Henchard asks Miss Templeman to marry him, but she delays her answer. Henchard later discovers that Farfrae is his rival in love as well as in business. Elizabeth-Jane feels rejected by both Farfrae and Henchard.

Henchard now hires Jopp, the man whose job was taken by Farfrae early in the novel, and instructs him to use every legal means of ruining Farfrae's business. Henchard then foolishly speculates on rising grain prices, and when the harvest is good and prices fall, he must take out huge loans to keep his business going. Blaming Jopp for this, Henchard fires him, and he vows to get revenge.

Chapters 27–30

Henchard forces Lucetta to agree to marry him by threatening to reveal their past affair if she will not.

Henchard, though no longer mayor, is still a local judge. He is called to hear the case of an old woman accused of public obscenity. This turns out to be the furmity woman who witnessed Henchard's sale of his wife. The woman exposes Henchard in court, and he admits the deed. Lucetta, who had thought Henchard's wife was dead, hears of this and leaves town for a few days.

It is revealed that Lucetta married Farfrae during her absence, feeling released from her promise to marry Henchard by the news about his having sold his wife. When Henchard learns of the mar-riage, he again threatens to expose Lucetta's scandalous past. Farfrae moves into Lucetta's house, and Elizabeth-Jane, because she has feelings for Farfrae, moves out.

Chapters 31–37

Because of the revelation about his past and coincidental business losses, Henchard is ruined. He declares bankruptcy and moves to a cottage owned by Jopp. Farfrae buys Henchard's business, house, and furniture. Henchard asks Farfrae to give him work as a laborer, and Farfrae agrees. Henchard hates Farfrae, though, who now owns all that was once his and is married to his former lover. The twenty-one years of Henchard's oath have passed, and he is drinking again. He begins to utter threats against Farfrae.

The current mayor dies, and the town council elects Farfrae to replace him.

Henchard has some letters that Lucetta wrote him years ago, during their affair. He knows that these letters, if made public, would ruin both Lucetta and Farfrae, but he has too much feeling for Lucetta to do the deed. However, he stupidly assigns the vengeful Jopp to return the letters to Lucetta. Jopp reads the letters aloud at a tavern, and the crowd plans a "skimmity-ride," in which effigies of Henchard and Lucetta will be paraded through the town to publicize their past affair.

Chapters 38–41

Henchard challenges the smaller, frailer Farfrae to a wrestling match to the death, but, when he is in a position to kill Farfrae, Henchard lets him go.

The skimmity-ride takes place. Lucetta is so horrified by it that she has a seizure and dies.

Newson appears at Henchard's cottage. He says that his being lost at sea was a ruse to let Susan out of their relationship. Newson has acquired wealth and now wants to share his money and his remaining years with his daughter. Henchard tells Newson that Elizabeth-Jane is dead. Newson accepts this and leaves town.

Henchard and Elizabeth-Jane renew their affection for each other, and she decides to take care of him.

Chapters 42–45

About a year later, Henchard and Elizabeth-Jane are running a small shop and making a living. Farfrae and Elizabeth-Jane begin spending time to-gether.

Henchard sees Newson outside of town and re-alizes that Newson somehow knows that Elizabeth-Jane is alive and has returned for her. Unable to bear the loss of his "daughter," Henchard leaves Casterbridge. When Elizabeth-Jane meets Newson and learns that he is her father, she turns against Henchard.

Farfrae and Elizabeth-Jane are married. Hen-chard thinks that perhaps he was wrong in assum-ing that Newson was in Casterbridge to see Eliza-beth-Jane, and, full of hope, he returns to Casterbridge on the evening of the wedding. He sees Newson dancing with Elizabeth-Jane and knows he has lost her. She sees him and is cold to him, and he apologizes and leaves for good.

A month later, Elizabeth Jane feels remorse for her treatment of Henchard, and she and Farfrae set out to find him. Several miles from Casterbridge a man at a humble cottage tells them that Henchard lived there but died less than an hour previously. He has left a will requesting that Elizabeth-Jane not be informed of his death and that no funeral be held for him. Elizabeth-Jane, touched by his acceptance of his fate, abides by his wishes.

Characters

Donald Farfrae

A young Scot who arrives in Casterbridge at about the same time as Susan and Elizabeth-Jane, Donald Farfrae becomes Michael Henchard's busi-ness manager. He quickly becomes Henchard's only trusted friend and, later, his adversary in both business and love.

Hardy draws Farfrae as Henchard's counter-part in every way. He is physically small, polite and charming, careful and controlled, forward thinking, and methodical. Whereas Henchard pro-pels his fate through moments of rash behavior, Farfrae is cool and calculating in all he does. Al-though his personality is friendly and engaging, Farfrae maintains a certain detachment from peo-ple and events, always considering the possible consequences of his decisions and actions before he makes them. As a result, his path through life is as smooth as Henchard's is rough.

Farfrae initiates a relationship with Henchard by providing information that is a great help to Henchard in solving a business problem and by re-fusing Henchard's offer of payment for the infor-mation. Henchard is so grateful and impressed that he talks Farfrae into abandoning his plans to go to

America and convinces him to take a job as Hen-chard's business manager.

Because Farfrae is more organized and me-thodical than Henchard, the business prospers un-der his management. Farfrae is ambitious enough to eventually go into business for himself, though, and this enrages Henchard even though Farfrae, in his typically principled way, tries to minimize com-petition between the two firms.

Farfrae courts Elizabeth-Jane and even hints that he would marry her if he were in a financial position to do so, but when he meets the newly wealthy Miss Templeman—Henchard's former lover whom he, too, is again courting—he turns his affections to her and marries her.

Farfrae's careful approach to life wins him all that was once Henchard's: at Henchard's bank-ruptcy sale, Farfrae buys his business, home, and furniture. He marries Henchard's former lover and, after she dies, marries Elizabeth-Jane. Farfrae even becomes the highly respected and well-liked mayor of Casterbridge.

For Farfrae, though, the competition between Henchard and himself is never personal or mean-spirited. When the destitute Henchard asks Farfrae for a job, Farfrae hires him and makes sure that he himself never gives Henchard orders. Farfrae also offers to give Henchard any furniture or personal belongings that he would like to have back from the bankruptcy sale.

The Furmity Woman

The furmity woman runs the shop in which Michael, at the beginning of the novel, gets drunk and sells Susan. She appears again eighteen years later, when Susan and Elizabeth-Jane return to the village where the sale occurred to try to find Hen-chard. The furmity woman is still there and re-members that Henchard returned a year after the sale. She tells Susan that Henchard told her that he was moving to Casterbridge and that if a woman ever came asking for him, the furmity woman should pass on this information.

The furmity woman makes a final appearance in Casterbridge to seal Henchard's fate. Henchard is a judge, and the furmity woman, when brought before him on a public obscenity charge, recog-nizes him and tells the court about this shameful past.

Elizabeth-Jane Henchard

As the novel opens, Susan is carrying an in-fant daughter named Elizabeth-Jane. She takes the baby with her when she goes off with Newson, and when readers see Susan eighteen years later, again with her daughter, Hardy gives the impression that this is the same infant grown up. Only later do readers learn that Henchard's daughter died a few months after he sold Susan and that this girl is Newson's daughter.

As Susan and the eighteen-year-old Elizabeth-Jane set about finding Henchard, Elizabeth-Jane knows nothing about her mother's marriage to Henchard. She thinks that her mother and Newson were legally married and that now Susan is in search of a distant relative by marriage who may be of some help to them.

Early in the novel, both Elizabeth-Jane's natural beauty and her innate intelligence have been compromised by her poverty. She has no education and no prospects in life. This is why Susan is willing to risk the possibility of being rejected and humiliated again by Henchard; she sees him as her daughter's only hope for a better life.

Once Henchard begins providing for her, Elizabeth-Jane blossoms both physically and socially. She becomes the town beauty and is admired by young men, including Farfrae, with whom Elizabeth-Jane has been quite taken since their first meeting.

Hardy draws Elizabeth-Jane as a healthy mixture of levelheadedness and deep feeling. When Henchard's money allows her nice clothes, she enjoys them but doesn't overspend or flaunt her position. She also takes advantage of her newfound leisure by reading and studying to improve herself; she has always been embarrassed by her lack of education. When Farfrae abandons her for Miss Templeman, Elizabeth-Jane simply withdraws quietly although she loves him.

Unable to hold a grudge or remain bitter, Elizabeth-Jane finally marries Farfrae after Miss Templeman dies. And although she lashes out at Henchard when she finds out that he has lied to keep her from Newson, she soon forgives him and goes to find him. She is touched by Henchard's will and honors his wishes.

Michael Henchard

Michael Henchard is the towering but tragic hero of *The Mayor of Casterbridge*; the novel is his story. He is physically large and powerful. His character is a strange mixture of the light and the dark. Henchard is true to his word. Until he hires Farfrae, he runs his business with few written records, and the townspeople know that they can trust him to keep the contracts he makes orally. Yet he sometimes says things that are rash and even cruel and then follows through on them just as if they were contracts made in good faith. Such an outburst causes him to sell his wife at the beginning of the novel. Henchard has the willpower and determination to keep an oath for twenty-one years, yet he seems to rarely think ahead, and, in a single moment of ire, he can do a deed that ruins years of effort. He is so honest that when the furmity woman exposes his past, he readily admits that she is telling the truth, and when he declares bankruptcy, he willingly turns over everything but the clothes on his back to his creditors. Yet when Newson comes looking for Elizabeth-Jane, Henchard tells him she is dead.

Henchard begins the novel a young man who is poor but who at least possesses a skill, the vigor of youth, and a wife and child. Yet he is convinced that his early marriage has ruined his chances in life. After shamefully ridding himself of the wife and child, he forswears the alcohol that undoubtedly fueled the deed and almost completely forswears the company of women, channeling all his energies into his business. And so, at first, the punishments that he imposes on himself for selling Susan lead to his success.

But fate and Henchard's own abiding guilt conspire to destroy him. Fate places Donald Farfrae in his path, and Henchard chooses first to bring the man into his business and then to make him an adversary—the thoughtful, self-possessed adversary who will end up with impetuous Henchard's public office and stature, his wealth, his business, his home, his furniture, his lover, and, finally, his stepdaughter. To help cruel fate along, Henchard indulges in one self-destructive act after another. When he would like to ruin Farfrae's business, he instead speculates foolishly and ruins his own. When he wishes to return some highly inflammatory letters to a former lover, he entrusts the delivery to a man who openly hates him. When Elizabeth-Jane is all he has left in the world, he tells lies that are sure to estrange her from him.

Henchard ends up much poorer than he began, having lost, for a second and final time, his wife and her child and having lost the strength and potential of youth. At the end of the novel, he walks away from Casterbridge utterly alone and soon dies in the hut that has been his final home. He dies before he can know that Elizabeth-Jane has softened toward him, and his will makes clear that he would have wanted it so. His final wish is, in effect, to be obliterated for his sins, which a lifetime of penance was insufficient to obliterate in his own mind. His will asks that Elizabeth-Jane not be informed of his death, that no ceremony mark his passing, that no flowers mark his grave, and "that no man remember me."

Susan Henchard

Susan Henchard is Michael's wife as the novel opens. Hardy portrays her as being naïve and resigned to an existence over which she is powerless. The small efforts she makes to control her fate are useless; she steers Henchard away from what is clearly a saloon to a place that appears not to serve alcohol only to find that the proprietor in fact sells rum on the sly.

When Michael sells her to a sailor, Susan assumes that the transaction is valid and that she must stay with him. She lives peaceably with him for many years and bears him a daughter before a friend finally makes her realize that she is not bound by Henchard's act.

After the sailor is presumed dead at sea, Susan sets out to find Henchard, hoping to benefit her daughter. It never seems to occur to her that he might have an obligation to Susan herself. Once she finds out that Henchard is mayor of the town and well off, far from desiring to take advantage of him or ruin him, she wishes she could leave Casterbridge without meeting him. For the sake of her daughter, she goes through with her plan to approach him.

Even the townspeople of Casterbridge see that Susan has no sense of self; they call her a "ghost." Soon after she has seen Elizabeth-Jane on her way to being established in the way Susan had hoped for, Susan dies.

Jopp

Jopp is a lowlife villain who is driven by dark emotions. The day that Henchard hires Farfrae to be his business manager, Jopp shows up in the office having been previously offered the job that Farfrae now has. Informed that the position is no longer available, Jopp goes away steaming and bent on revenge.

Further events fuel this desire. Among other things, Henchard does finally hire Jopp but then fires him unreasonably when Henchard's own business decisions prove disastrous. Henchard foolishly gives Jopp his chance for revenge when he asks Jopp to deliver to Miss Templeman a package of scandalous letters. Jopp reads the letters aloud to a tavern crowd, which then plans the "skimmity-ride" (a parading of effigies through the town to call attention to adultery) that ends in Miss Templeman's death and Henchard's further humiliation.

Newson

Newson is the sailor who buys Susan at the beginning of the novel. He shows that he does have some scruples when he says that he will take Susan only if she is willing to go with him. His relationship with Susan and with Elizabeth-Jane is portrayed as kind and cordial. When Susan comes to understand that their relationship is not legitimate, Newson does her a kindness by having himself reported lost at sea, allowing her to leave his house without guilt and with a small amount of money.

Newson's basic decency is seen later in his desire to share his wealth with Elizabeth-Jane, in his acceptance of Henchard's word that she has died, and in his lack of bitterness when he discovers that Henchard has lied to him. At the end of the novel, Newson lives within sight of the sea but also near his daughter.

Lucetta Templeman

Lucetta Templeman is a superficial, unthinking woman who, like Henchard, suffers several reversals of fortune and ends badly. Henchard has an affair with her before Susan arrives in Casterbridge, and this affair ruins Lucetta's reputation. To try to repair the damage, Henchard, thinking that Susan is probably dead, offers to marry Lucetta. Before the marriage takes place, though, Susan returns, and Henchard must call off the wedding.

After Susan dies, Lucetta inherits wealth, and Henchard renews his interest in her. Lucetta is more interested in Farfrae, though, and marries him. When Lucetta's old letters to Henchard become public, the scandal of their affair returns to haunt them both, and Lucetta is so distraught by this that she suffers a seizure and dies. Farfrae soon realizes that Lucetta was not a good match for him and that, had she lived, their marriage would not have been happy.

Themes

Blind Fate

The idea of a blind, arbitrary fate is a central theme in Hardy's fiction. Although this fate is blind, it is not neutral but almost always cruel. It

Topics for Further Study

- Hardy originally subtitled *The Mayor of Casterbridge* "A Story of a Man of Character." What is meant by the phrase "a man of character?" Do you think it was an appropriate subtitle for the novel? Explain your answer.

- Compare and contrast Michael Henchard and Donald Farfrae. What traits do they have in common, and what differences are there between the two men?

- Name a single character trait that you think is the cause of Michael's downfall and explain why you think that trait, above all others, is Michael's tragic weakness.

- In *The Mayor of Casterbridge*, Susan allows herself to be "sold" and willingly goes with the man who has "bought" her. What else might Susan have done? What alternatives did she have? Do some research about rural life in England at the time, and list only alternatives that were realistically available to a woman such as Susan. Then explain which alternative you think is the best choice for Susan—one of those you have listed or the action she takes in the novel—and why.

- Hardy set all of his novels in the Wessex region of England where he was born. In *The Mayor of Casterbridge* and other novels, he used real places—towns, roads, bodies of water, and even shops and hotels. He used the real names of some of these places and gave fictional names to others. Imagine that you are going to write a novel set in the region where you live. Draw a map of the region, showing the towns, roads, and other places that will appear in your novel. For each place, decide whether you will use its real name or make up a name and write the names on your map. Finally, write a one-page description of the region shown in your map. Make your description as detailed as possible to give readers a feel for the place; describe the landscape, people, animals, weather, sounds, smells, and so on.

is a force that brings suffering and feels no pity or remorse.

In *The Mayor of Casterbridge*, blind fate manifests as a series of ruinous coincidences and unforeseeable circumstances. Such coincidences and circumstances seem to conspire against Michael Henchard from the opening scenes. There are two shops offering food at the fair; one clearly advertises that it sells liquor, but the other seems not to do so. Susan, knowing Michael's weakness for alcohol, steers him to what seems to be the "safer" of the two establishments. But, as fate would have it, the proprietor there sells rum on the sly, and Michael is soon drunk and loudly insisting on his desire to sell his wife.

Next, along comes a coincidence in the person of a man who has both the money and the inclination to accept the offer that Henchard has been unwilling to let drop in spite of attempts by his wife and others to silence him. The man happens to be a sailor who takes Susan to Canada, far beyond Michael's reach as he searches for her.

And so the tide of fate that will carry Michael inexorably to his tragic end gathers strength. It is not swayed by Henchard's repentance, by his shame, by his vow not to drink, or by his lifelong efforts to right his wrong. It is as if a curse has been uttered and cannot be withdrawn.

Relationship between Character and Fate

In *The Mayor of Casterbridge*, more than in some of Hardy's other fiction, the theme of blind fate is interwoven with a second theme that might at first seem contradictory: the theme of personal character as the molder of fate. Every coincidence or unforeseen circumstance is paired with a choice. Henchard could have refused the furmity woman's rum, but did not. He could have refused Newson's offer to buy Susan, which would have required the courage and strength of character to admit that the offer was a drunken mistake.

Circumstance and character hold a conversation throughout this novel. Each circumstance is a question that Henchard must answer, and each answer both illustrates what kind of man Henchard is and determines what kind of man he will become. In the beginning, Henchard has much control over his fate; more than once, he is presented with the opportunity to prevent the curse from being uttered. But once he has sold Susan, his choices have much less power. A line has been crossed, a process has been set in motion, a deed has been done that all of Michael's future efforts will be inadequate to erase. Although he makes many moral choices from that moment on—to forswear alcohol and to "remarry" Susan, for example—Michael has lost control of his fate.

As these two themes of blind fate and personal character weave through the novel, Hardy leaves readers to interpret just how the two relate. Judging by Michael Henchard's end, though, Hardy's message seems to be that each choice a person makes limits future choices and that a single bad choice can put a person forever at the mercy of blind, uncaring fate. Michael Henchard can be compared to a seaman in a storm who, in a moment of carelessness, loses his grip on his ship's wheel and is never able to regain control of his course.

Style

Victorian Literature

It was during the Victorian period (1837–1901) that the novel became the dominant literary form, and Hardy is considered one of the major novelists of the era, along with Charles Dickens, William Makepeace Thackeray, Rudyard Kipling, Charlotte Brontë, Emily Brontë, and many others. It was common for novels to be published serially, in magazines or in stand-alone sections. *The Mayor of Casterbridge* was first published serially, in twenty installments, in an English periodical called *The Graphic* in 1886. It was published simultaneously in the United States in *Harper's Weekly.* Hardy's original manuscript, with some sections missing, is at the Dorset County Museum in Dorchester.

The Mayor of Casterbridge was published in book form as soon as the serial publication was complete. Many novels of this period differ slightly in their serial and book forms (authors were aware of the serial format as they wrote and structured their stories to keep readers interested from one week to the next), but this book differs substantially from the serial novel. In the serial form, for example, Henchard marries Lucetta. Hardy's biography (supposedly written by his second wife but actually written almost entirely by Hardy himself) reveals that he felt this novel had been badly damaged by the demands of serial publication and that his revisions for the book publication were not adequate to repair the story. The text of the novel that is available to today's readers is the final revision

that Hardy did for the 1912 Wessex Edition of his novels.

Victorian novels often deal with social issues. While social issues play a role in *The Mayor of Casterbridge*, the novel was a departure from the norm because it focused consistently on a single character, Michael Henchard. Because of this limited focus, the novel is shorter and has a smaller cast of characters than many novels of the time.

Wessex Setting

Like all of Hardy's fiction, *The Mayor of Casterbridge* is set in southwestern England in the region once known as Wessex. The area was invaded, settled, and named by the Saxons, who ruled it as a kingdom, in ancient times. It extended from the English Channel north to the Thames River and from Windsor Forest in the east to the Cornish coast in the west.

While most novelists set their stories in real places, Hardy is distinctive for two reasons. First, although the author traveled widely, in the writing of his novels and stories, he never strayed beyond the boundaries of his native region. In his 1912 general preface to his final, revised version of his novels, Hardy explained, "there was quite enough human nature in Wessex for one man's literary purposes." He further explained, somewhat unnecessarily, that his characters "were meant to be typically and essentially those of any and every place . . . beings in whose hearts and minds that which is apparently local should be really universal."

Second, Hardy, unlike other authors, rarely invented features to add to the real landscape of Wessex. He describes the towns and farms, the roads and hotels, and the smallest details as they really were. When Hardy describes a house, it is likely that readers in his time knew exactly which house he had borrowed for his tale.

In some cases, Hardy used real place names; in others, he gave fictional names to real places. While Stonehenge and Southhampton appear under their actual names, Casterbridge is, in reality, Hardy's hometown of Dorchester. In his 1912 preface, Hardy points out that his general rule was to use the real names of the major towns and places that mark the general boundaries of Wessex and to use fictional, disguised, or ancient names for most other places.

Even Hardy's characters are based on real people more than most fictional characters are. Most are composites of people he knew or knew of and his own embellishments. He borrowed bits of characters and story lines from the folklore and ballads of Wessex. The fact that he lived a long life in Wessex and had access to church records in his early work as an architect and church restorer gave him an intimate knowledge of local life and its too-frequent tragedies.

Gothic Elements

Gothic fiction was popular between about 1760 and 1820. Gothic authors used threatening environments (the foreboding hilltop castle on a stormy night); brooding, malevolent characters; dark secrets; and the supernatural and occult to instill a sense of horror in their readers. Gothic fiction has influenced much of the fiction written in the past two hundred and fifty years, and Gothic elements were prominent in the novels of the Victorian age. In the novels of Charles Dickens, Sir Walter Scott, Charlotte Brontë, and others, these elements made the dark side of human nature palpable to readers.

Gothic elements appear throughout *The Mayor of Casterbridge*. One striking example is the meeting between Henchard and Susan at the old Roman amphitheater called the Ring. The Ring is outside the town, and Henchard and Susan meet there at dusk. Before Hardy narrates their meeting, he spins a long, ghostly description of the place that infuses it with a history of gloom and gore. Readers are reminded of the bloody Roman sports for which the place was built. They are told that the Ring was long the home of Casterbridge's gallows and treated to a lurid description of a murderess being "half-strangled and then burnt there in the presence of ten thousand spectators." Even now, Hardy assures readers, the Ring is the setting for violent crimes, and some old people have had visions of the amphitheater filled with cheering Roman soldiers and have actually heard their bloodthirsty roaring. By the time Hardy finally brings Henchard and Susan to the scene, he has made readers feel that there truly is something dark about their purpose here, though on the surface their meeting is cordial.

Coincidence

Coincidence, too, was a common plot device in Hardy's time and one of which he makes frequent use in *The Mayor of Casterbridge*. For example, the furmity woman happens to stumble into Casterbridge, of all towns, and at just the right time and in just the right circumstance to do Henchard great harm. The weather happens to change just when Henchard is vulnerable to ruin because of his risky attempt to destroy Farfrae.

There are two ways of looking at Hardy's coincidences. Some readers and critics say that they make the story unrealistic and therefore less effective than it would otherwise be. Others point out that coincidences are not, in and of themselves, unrealistic, as life has its fair share of them. The question, this latter group would say, is whether the coincidences themselves are realistic or not. In the case of *The Mayor of Casterbridge*, the answer seems to be at least a qualified "yes." The furmity woman has been cast as a merchant who travels around the region, so it is not incredible that she would show up in Casterbridge. Anyone who has ever farmed can testify that there is nothing more unpredictable, more uncontrollable, and, seemingly, more contrary to the wishes of farmers than the weather.

Hardy employs coincidence to help him—and his readers—explore the nature of fate. He leaves open the question of whether coincidences are merely chance suggesting that fate is blind or whether what appear to be coincidences are actually directed by some supernatural hand that guides men and women to the fates they "deserve."

Historical Context

Victorian England

The Victorian age began in 1837, when eighteen-year-old Queen Victoria ascended to the British throne, and ended with her death in 1901. Victoria and her husband, Albert, set the tone of English life and culture for most of a century. It was a time of social and moral conservatism; the "family values" of the time were similar to those touted in late-twentieth-century America. Pragmatism was valued above romance, duty above pleasure.

Beneath the veneer of gentility and commitment to duty and family, the Victorian age, like every era, had its dark side. Prostitution flourished, and lurid crime stories—both true and fictional—were popular. Hordes of small children living by their wits on the streets of London and other cities were a testament to the limits of the commitment to family. The wife-selling incident that is at the center of *The Mayor of Casterbridge* is a fictional instance of a type of transaction that did, indeed, occur in rural England in the nineteenth century.

The early Victorian period was a time of social reforms. Laws were passed governing working

Compare & Contrast

- **Late Nineteenth Century:** The price of English grain is falling due to competition from overseas farmers. Better transportation and refrigeration mean that foreign farmers can ship grain to England and undercut local farmers. Large estates in the grain-growing regions of England, such as Hardy's Wessex, face falling profits and in some cases are broken up into smaller holdings. Unemployment is high among farm workers. Dairy and fruit farmers prosper, however, as they do not face foreign competition.

  Today: England imports most of its food, including grain. England's crop income is only about one-third of that from livestock and dairy products, but southern England is still an important farming region. Farms are much smaller than they were in Hardy's time, averaging less than two hundred fifty acres, and are much more mechanized. Major crops are wheat, potatoes, barley, sugar beets, and oats.

- **Late Nineteenth Century:** The Third Reform Bill of 1884 extends the vote to male farm workers in England; previously, only men of the upper social classes were allowed to vote. In addition, laws are changed to make it possible for upper-class women to retain their property when they marry, to vote in local elections, and to attend universities. Working-class women such as Susan in *The Mayor of Casterbridge* still have virtually no rights under the law.

  Today: All men and women in England have the right to vote in all elections, and well over one hundred women serve in Parliament. Women also have property rights and access to higher education that equal those of men.

- **Late Nineteenth Century:** Queen Victoria, namesake of the Victorian age, celebrates her golden jubilee—fifty years of rule—in 1887 and her diamond jubilee in 1897.

  Today: Queen Elizabeth II takes the throne in 1952 and will celebrate her golden jubilee in 2002.

---

conditions of women and children (they could not work in underground mines, for example), and attempts were made to improve conditions in prisons and insane asylums. Efforts to broaden access to education (England had no public schools at the time) stalled because of controversy over the Church of England's role in expanded education. Writers such as William Makepeace Thackeray and Charles Dickens took up the cause of reform, using their writing to point out the need for prison reforms and education and the evils of industrialization and the class system.

In the middle of the nineteenth century, England was experiencing unprecedented political, industrial, and economic power, fueled by the Industrial Revolution and by wealth from the colonies. All forms of transportation boomed; railroad ridership increased sevenfold, and the shipbuilding industry grew. Living standards of the working class and middle class were buoyed, and

trade unions were formed to promote the interests of skilled workers.

By the late 1800s, Queen Victoria had ruled for fifty years. The British had consolidated their rule of India, and the empire was expanding, especially in Asia and Africa. Domestically, however, the economy was faltering. The United States and Britain took over as the world's leading producers of manufactured goods, and British farmers suffered from foreign competition. Economic hardships sparked immigration to the British colonies and to the United States. More than two hundred thousand Britons left home each year during the 1880s—as Newson did and as Farfrae intended to do in *The Mayor of Casterbridge*.

Life in Nineteenth-Century Wessex

According to Hardy (and scholars agree), a history book could hardly give a more accurate picture of life in nineteenth-century Wessex than does

Fictional map of the Southeast England region of Wessex, the setting for the novel

Hardy's fiction. In his general preface to the final Wessex Edition of his novels, in 1912, Hardy wrote:

> At the dates represented in the various narrations, things were like that in Wessex: the inhabitants lived in certain ways, engaged in certain occupations, kept alive certain customs, just as they are shown doing in these pages.... I have instituted inquiries to correct tricks of memory and striven against temptations to exaggerate in order to preserve for my own satisfaction a fairly true record of a vanishing life.

Critical Overview

On January 2, 1886, the day on which the first installment of *The Mayor of Casterbridge* was published, Hardy wrote in his diary, "I fear it will not be so good as I meant." Although Hardy's fiction up to this point had received mixed reviews, critics generally disagreed with the author about the quality of this book and gave it high marks. Hardy's autobiography says of the novel, "others thought better of it than he did himself" and mentions that the author Robert Louis Stevenson liked the book and even asked Hardy for permission to adapt it as a play (which Stevenson never did). H. M. Alden's review in *Harper's New Monthly Magazine* in 1886

began, "In *The Mayor of Casterbridge*, Mr. Hardy seems to have started with the intention of merely adventurous fiction and to have found himself in possession of something so much more important." Alden continued, "Mr. Hardy has never achieved anything more skillful or valuable . . . we are not sure that he has not placed himself abreast of Tolstoy and the greatest of the continental realists."

Through the decades, the consensus has remained that *The Mayor of Casterbridge* is one of the greatest novels of a great writer. Hardy's characterization—especially of Michael Henchard—has most often been singled out for praise. Martin Seymour-Smith wrote in the introduction to a 1978 edition of *The Mayor of Casterbridge* that Hardy "penetrates very deeply into character. He can show us how a man's 'being attracts his life.'" This unwavering focus on the character of one powerful man as he "attracts his life" is what set *The Mayor of Casterbridge* apart from other novels of its time. In his widely read 1949 book, *Thomas Hardy: The Novels and Stories*, Hardy scholar Albert J. Guerard wrote:

> Henchard . . . stands at the very summit of his creator's achievement; his only tragic hero and one of the greatest tragic heroes in all fiction. He takes his place at once with certain towering and possessed figures of Melville, Hawthorne, and Dostoevsky.

But critics and scholars point out, too, that Hardy wrote novels for a popular audience (because he wrote to earn a living), and he was even more consistently successful with the public than he was with critics. When *The Mayor of Casterbridge* was published, it was as much talked about by readers as it was by critics. Such popularity could only be gained by telling a good story and by exhibiting an understanding of and compassion for human beings. Guerard concluded of Hardy:

> His final and unmistakable appeal therefore rests ... on the popular storytelling of a singularly uninhibited imagination ... and, above all, on an incorrigible sympathy for all who are lonely and all who long for happiness.

> " Hardy writes of Henchard, 'He cursed himself like a less scrupulous Job.' . . . Here, Henchard is compared . . . with perhaps the greatest icon of suffering ever written and read about."

Criticism

Candyce Norvell

Norvell is an independent educational writer who specializes in English and literature. She holds degrees in linguistics and journalism. In this essay, Norvell discusses two techniques that Hardy uses in his novel to make his main character both realistic and symbolic.

Critics through the decades have agreed that Michael Henchard is one of the towering figures of literature. Henchard is powerful because he is both an individual and an icon. He seems to readers to be a real person—a person who evokes sympathy and compassion because he has the same kinds of weaknesses that readers themselves have and experiences the same kinds of loneliness, guilt, fear, and defeat. At the same time, Henchard seems larger than life—like a symbol, rather than a mere example, of humanity.

Hardy uses many techniques to give Henchard these dual aspects. This essay explores two of these techniques: Hardy's grounding Henchard in a real-life setting to make him human, and Hardy's associating Henchard with other larger-than-life characters to make him iconic.

Hardy's perennial Wessex setting and his exact historical details help to make Henchard seem like a real person who lived and suffered just as Hardy's story has it. After all, if the place is real and the way of life is real and all the sights, sounds, smells, and tastes described are really part of history, then any character who is set down in the midst of it all will seem not like a character at all but just as much a part of history as the scene itself. Hardy's specific details and historical accuracy earn him so much credibility that it is easy for readers to believe that his narrator is relating a story from memory, not from imagination, that is, that Michael Henchard's life is history, not story.

When Michael and Susan enter a shop to have dinner, Hardy tells readers that they eat furmity and then describes the archaic dish, even listing the ingredients. The author takes pains to be specific and authentic. He could have written that Michael and Susan ate potato soup and saved himself the trouble of explaining an unfamiliar meal. But Hardy is telling about a real time and place, and he feels bound to tell what people actually ate there. By doing so he makes the reader's suspension of disbelief automatic and complete. The story that contains such minute and peculiar detail must certainly be a true story, and the people in it must, therefore, be real people.

Making Henchard real and human is important because Hardy wants readers to identify with him and care about him—to be affected by his suffering and his story. But it is also important to make Henchard symbolic so that readers understand that this story is not *just* the story of one man's life; it is also about how life works for all human beings. Hardy must draw Henchard in such a way that his story is understood to be a timeless tale that has played out—the same in essence and different only in the details—countless times in countless settings and with countless players. This Hardy does through references to other such players. These references serve to associate Henchard with his fellow tragic figures, from the biblical Saul to the Greek Achilles to Napoleon and by that association to make him timeless and enduring, as they are.

What Do I Read Next?

- Hardy's *Far from the Madding Crowd* was published serially in 1874 and is ranked as a Victorian classic. It is the story of a woman farmer and her three suitors. Author Virginia Woolf commented that this book "must hold its place among the great English novels." It has the distinction of being Hardy's only novel to offer readers a happy ending.

- Hardy's *Tess of the D'Urbervilles* was published in 1891 and has always been one of his most popular novels. It tells the tragic story of Tess, a young farm worker on the estate of the wealthy D'Urbervilles. Working to support her drunken father and the rest of her family, she is raped and impregnated by a son of her employer. When her baby dies, she moves away and is courted by a hardworking young man. But tragedy continues to follow her.

- *Selected Poetry: Thomas Hardy* (1996), edited by Samuel Hynes as part of the World's Classics series from Oxford University Press, is a good introduction to Hardy's poetry. The collection spans Hardy's writing career and includes poems that influenced later poets, including Ezra Pound and W. H. Auden.

- *Wuthering Heights*, by Emily Brontë, was published in 1847 and is also considered one of the classics of Victorian literature. The novel is a story of romance and revenge. Like Henchard in *The Mayor of Casterbridge*, the main character of this novel undergoes more than one reversal of fortune.

- *Little Dorrit*, by Charles Dickens, was first published serially in 1857. Another Victorian classic, Dickens's book tells the story of Amy Dorrit, born in the debtors' prison where her father lives. Major themes are social class, financial reversals, and romance.

- *Vanity Fair*, by William Makepeace Thackeray, was published serially in 1847–1848 in London. Like *The Mayor of Casterbridge*, *Vanity Fair* focuses on the personal characters of its major players and on how their integrity (or, in most cases, the lack of it) affects their lives and fates. Its central figure, Becky Sharp, is one of the most infamous characters in all of literature.

- *The Cambridge Companion to Thomas Hardy* (1999), edited by Dale Kramer, is a collection of essays that provides a comprehensive overview of Hardy's life and work, including how the philosophy, science, and religion of his time influenced his work.

Hardy writes, when Farfrae leaves Henchard's employ and opens his own business, "Henchard was stung into bitterness: like Bellerophon, he wandered away from the crowd. Bellerophon is a character in the Greek epic *The Iliad* who is deserted by the gods and who in turn deserts human society and wanders alone.

When Henchard learns that Elizabeth-Jane is not his daughter, Hardy writes, "Like Prester John's, his table had been spread, and infernal harpies had snatched up the food." Prester John is a character in *Orlando Furioso*, a well-known Renaissance poem by Ludovico Ariosto. Prester John is a wealthy king who nevertheless starves because harpies (monsters with women's heads and birds' bodies who snatch things away from their rightful owners) snatch the food from his table.

When Henchard's decline is well underway, Hardy compares him to Napoleon, writing, "That dinner at the King's Arms with his friends had been Henchard's Austerlitz: he had had his successes since, but his courses had not been upward." Napoleon won the Battle of Austerlitz, and it was both the pinnacle of his career and the beginning of his destruction. Similarly, the dinner at the King's Arms was the high point of Henchard's success but also, unbeknownst to him at the time, the beginning of his downfall. On that day Susan Henchard arrived in Casterbridge, and it was her arrival that set in motion his ruin.

A final example: When Farfrae understandably distrusts Henchard's motives and refuses to return to Casterbridge with him, Hardy writes of Henchard, "He cursed himself like a less scrupulous Job." There is probably no more well-known sufferer than the biblical Job. Here, Henchard is compared—and, with the qualifier "less scrupulous," compared unfavorably—with perhaps the greatest icon of suffering ever written and read about.

Hardy has planted Henchard's feet firmly in the dust of Wessex and thus made him real, individual, and touchingly human. But he has also drawn Henchard's shadow so that it extends beyond Wessex and the nineteenth century to distant places and times. He has made Henchard both small enough to be pitiable and large enough to be unforgettable. In that feat, Hardy created what Albert J. Guerard, in *Thomas Hardy: The Novels and Stories* , called "one of the greatest tragic heroes in all fiction."

Source: Candyce Norvell, Critical Essay on *The Mayor of Casterbridge*, in *Novels for Students*, The Gale Group, 2002.

Sources

Alden, H. M., Review of *The Mayor of Casterbridge*, in *Harper's New Monthly Magazine*, November 1886, pp. 961–62.

Guerard, Albert J., *Thomas Hardy: The Novels and Stories*, Harvard University Press, 1949.

Seymour-Smith, Martin, Introduction, in *The Mayor of Casterbridge*, Penguin Books, 1978, p. 21.

Further Reading

Armstrong, Tim, *Haunted Hardy: Poetry, History, Memory*, St. Martin's Press, 2000.

This volume focuses on Hardy's poetry and its frequent references to death and ghosts—particularly ghosts of lost children.

Bettey, J. H., *Rural Life in Wessex, 1500–1900*, Sutton Publishing, 1989.

This nonfiction look at rural Wessex before and during Hardy's time offers an in-depth view of the part of England in which Hardy set much of his work.

Mallett, Phillip, ed., *The Achievement of Thomas Hardy*, Palgrave, 2000.

These essays explore Hardy's fiction and poetry, covering elements such as the nature of storytelling and the relationship between poems and songs.

Mitchell, Sally, *Daily Life in Victorian England*, Greenwood Publishing Group, 1996.

This comprehensive look at both city and country life in Victorian England covers social classes, morals, economics and finance, laws, and more. It includes excerpts from primary source documents and illustrations.

Turner, Paul D. L., *The Life of Thomas Hardy: A Critical Biography*, edited by Claude Rawson, Blackwell Publications, 1998.

Each of this book's thirty-two chapters explores the biographical and literary context of one of Hardy's works. One interesting aspect of Hardy's life covered here is his self-education in Greek and Latin and the later influences of Greek tragedy, Latin poetry, and Shakespeare on his work.

Rumble Fish

S. E. Hinton
1975

S. E. Hinton's third novel, *Rumble Fish* (1975), is similar to her first two novels, *The Outsiders* and *That Was Then, This Is Now*, in that it stars a troubled teenager from a precarious background and is told from a young man's point of view. However, it's different from the two previous books because they both featured teenagers who were more intelligent and sensitive than their peers and who were wiser by the end of the book. In contrast, in *Rumble Fish* Rusty-James is a victim of circumstance in a story that does not provide much hope for his future.

Like Hinton's other books, this novel helped to shape the young adult genre, moving it toward realism and away from the wholesome, overly nice story lines that had prevailed before Hinton began writing her gritty tales. Hinton's style has been widely imitated by other writers since her debut in 1967.

The book was an ALA Best Book for Young Adults in 1975, was listed as one of the Best Books of the Year by *School Library Journal* in 1975, and won a Land of Enchantment Book Award from the New Mexico Library Association in 1982. In 1988, Hinton was awarded the Margaret A. Edwards Award for her body of work.

Author Biography

Susan Eloise Hinton was born in 1950 (some sources say 1948) in Tulsa, Oklahoma. Her first

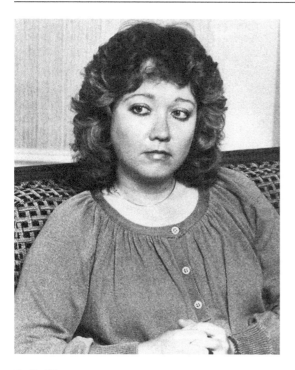

S. E. Hinton

book, *The Outsiders*, was published when she was seventeen. A tomboy, Hinton wrote the book because the teen books then available were too wholesome and sweet for her tastes. The novel deals with rivalry between students of different social classes, poverty, alcoholism, drug abuse, and teenage angst. Because the main character was male, her editors urged her to conceal her own gender by using her initials instead of her full name.

Hinton began writing the book during her sophomore year. She didn't think of publishing it until the mother of one of her schoolmates, who was a professional children's writer, took a look at it and told Hinton to send it to her agent. Hinton did, and the novel was accepted for publication on the night of her high school graduation.

Publication of the book brought intense attention to Hinton, who was busy studying education at the University of Tulsa, marrying her husband, David Inhofe, and having a family. Four years later, she published another book, *That Was Then, This Is Now*, another story of troubled youth. *Rumble Fish* came out in 1975, and *Tex* was published in 1979. Her fifth young adult book, *Taming the Star Runner*, was published in 1988. She has also written two books for younger readers.

Despite her relatively small number of titles, Hinton's work has had a major impact on literature for children, helping to shape the direction of young adult literature by moving it toward less idealized, more realistic portrayals of the lives of teenagers. Certainly, she has struck a nerve among young readers, who respond to her depictions of their peers and their emotional pain.

In 1988, Hinton was honored with the Margaret A. Edwards Award for career achievement. Over ten million copies of her books are in print, and films have been made of four of her novels.

Plot Summary

Chapter One

The novel opens five or six years after the main action, as Rusty-James runs into his old friend Steve, whom he hasn't seen in all that time. They are on the beach, far from the original action. Rusty-James has been "bumming around," not working since getting out of the reformatory after serving five years, and Steve is on vacation from college, where he's studying to become a high school teacher. Steve invites Rusty-James to dinner, an invitation he has no intention of accepting. Steve is too much of a reminder of some bad times.

Chapter Two

This chapter begins six years earlier, when the boys were around thirteen and fourteen. Rusty-James is in Benny's, a local hangout, when a kid named Midget informs him that Biff Wilcox is out to kill him because of something Rusty-James said to Biff's girlfriend. Rusty-James arranges to meet Biff in the vacant lot behind a pet store, and both plan to bring friends. Although gang wars are supposedly a thing of the past—a ban enforced by Rusty-James's older brother, the Motorcycle Boy— the Motorcycle Boy has disappeared and Rusty-James says he's going to fight if he has to and he's not going to get caught without any backup.

Chapter Three

Rusty-James goes to see his girlfriend, Patty. She's mad at him because she heard that he went up to the lake with Smokey and his cousin and some girls, but he tells her nothing happened, and they settle down to make out. She's nervous about his upcoming fight with Biff Wilcox and reminds him that he promised to quit fighting. However, she can't say much because she once went after another

Media Adaptations

- *Rumble Fish* was made into a film in 1983 by Francis Ford Coppola, with Matt Dillon as Rusty-James and Micky Rourke as the Motorcycle Boy; the film also starred Dennis Hopper, Tom Waits, and Nicolas Cage. Hinton also makes a brief appearance. She and Coppola collaborated to write the screenplay.

- The novel was adapted as a record and cassette by Viking in 1977.

- Another recording was produced by Recorded Books LLC in 1985.

girl with a broken bottle because the girl was flirting with Rusty-James.

He leaves her and goes back to Benny's, where a lot of kids are waiting for him. Steve is not there. He goes to the empty lot with Smokey and another friend, B. J. Biff and five other guys are there, and Biff is high on something, making him look and act crazy. Biff also has a knife, and Rusty-James is armed only with a bike chain. They fight, and Rusty-James wins. In the middle of the fight, the Motorcycle Boy shows up, saying, "I thought we'd stopped this cowboys and Indians crap." Rusty-James is distracted by this, and Biff grabs the knife off the ground and slices Rusty-James down his side. Steve shows up and tells Rusty-James he should go to the hospital, but Rusty-James refuses.

The Motorcycle Boy says he's been in California but says little about the trip. They go home, and Motorcycle Boy pours wine over the knife cut to sterilize it.

Chapter Four

The next day, Rusty-James goes to school despite his wound. He misses math, plays poker during lunch, and stands out of gym, where the coach offers him five dollars to beat up another kid who's been giving the coach trouble. After school, Rusty-James goes to Benny's, where all the kids are im-

pressed with his knife cut. Steve comes in and says his mother is sick in the hospital. Rusty-James leaves and steals some hubcaps, and when the owner and some friends chase him, he jumps from one roof to the next, urging Steve to do the same. Steve does, almost falling two stories down, and it turns out that the pursuers have given up and the leap wasn't necessary. Rusty-James passes out from his wound, the running, and lack of food, frightening Steve, who begins crying.

Chapter Five

They both go home. Rusty-James runs into Cassandra, who has a crush on the Motorcycle Boy. She is college educated and from a wealthy family, but she has moved to their part of town and has become a drug addict. Rusty-James finds the Motorcycle Boy at home, takes care of his wound, and their father comes home, less drunk than usual. He is a mild man, who reads a lot when he isn't drinking, but he's completely detached from his sons' lives. Rusty-James doesn't hate him but doesn't like him either. Smokey comes by around midnight with his cousin, and they go to the lake and hang out with some girls and drink. When he gets home, his father mentions that a policeman is out to get him, the Motorcycle Boy, or both of them. The next day, Rusty-James skips school and sleeps until noon.

Chapter Six

That afternoon, Rusty-James gets expelled from school for skipping class, fighting, swearing, arguing with teachers, and so forth. The guidance counselor, Mr. Harrigan, tells Rusty-James that he will be transferred to Cleveland High, where all the "bad" kids are sent. Rusty-James doesn't want to go there because Biff Wilcox and his group run that school. The alternative is the Youth Detention Center. Rusty-James knows that a lot of paperwork must be done before anyone can come after him, so he decides to take his chances in the meantime. He goes to Patty's, but she's mad at him because she's heard that he was up at the lake with some girls, and she dumps him. He's upset but can't cry. He finds the Motorcycle Boy, and they arrange to go to the other side of the river that night. The Motorcycle Boy shows Rusty-James a magazine that has the Motorcycle Boy's picture in it, taken when he was in California.

Chapter Seven

They go across the bridge that night, to a honky-tonk area. Steve comes along and, surprisingly, takes a drink when Rusty-James offers it. They go to a porn movie but leave when a pervert in the men's bathroom accosts Steve. The Motorcycle Boy tells Rusty-James that he saw their mother when he was out in California and also tells Rusty-James that when Rusty-James was two, he was left alone in the house for three days when his mother left and his father went on a drinking binge. Rusty-James is nonplussed by this, not really grasping its connection to his present fear of being alone. Rusty-James and Steve wander around, making a little trouble, and end up at a party where they drink some more.

Chapter Eight

Later they end up in a bar, where they drink some more. When they leave, two guys mug them, but the Motorcycle Boy shows up just in time. Rusty-James has a head injury, and Steve is scared to death.

Chapter Nine

The next day, Rusty-James's head hurts so much that he decides to visit a free clinic, but when the doctor says he has to be admitted to the hospital, he flees to Steve's house, where Steve has been beaten up by his father for staying out drinking all night. Rusty-James tells Steve they should both follow the Motorcycle Boy around for a while, but they can't think of a good reason. Clearly, Rusty-James is afraid of being abandoned if the Motorcycle Boy disappears again. Steve refuses, angering Rusty-James, who grabs him. Rusty-James is startled to realize that now, like the Motorcycle Boy's, his hearing is gone. Steve says, "I've tried to help you, but I've got to think about myself some." He also says, "You better let go of Motorcycle Boy. If you're around him very long you won't believe in anything." This is the last time Rusty-James sees Steve for many years.

Chapter Ten

Rusty-James spends the rest of the day in Benny's, waiting for the Motorcycle Boy to show up. Patty comes in, ignores him, and sits with Smokey. Rusty-James and Smokey go outside, and Smokey confesses that he set things up so that Patty would think Rusty-James was cheating on her with the girls up at the lake. Smokey also says, "If there were gangs around here, I'd be president, not you." Surprisingly, Rusty-James doesn't bother to fight back against either of these insults. He quietly agrees to let Smokey have Patty and the leadership of the group. If he wants to "keep his rep," he would

have to fight Smokey, and he's in no shape to do that now, either physically or emotionally.

B. J. tells Rusty-James that the Motorcycle Boy is in the pet store looking at fish. Rusty-James finds him there. The fish are Siamese fighting fish, brilliantly colored; they are "rumble fish" that would kill each other if they were put in the same tank. "If you leaned a mirror against the bowl they'd kill themselves fighting their own reflection," the Motorcycle Boy says. They leave, and the store owner closes up.

Chapter Eleven

That night, the Motorcycle Boy and Rusty-James go back to the pet store and steal the fish, which the Motorcycle Boy wants to release in the river. The Motorcycle Boy lets out all the animals in the store and heads to the river with the fish. The cop who's been trying to get him and Rusty-James, Officer Patterson, shoots the Motorcycle Boy without warning, and he dies, as do the fish, who are too far from the river when the Motorcycle Boy falls and drops their bowl. Rusty-James is arrested and notices that, like the Motorcycle Boy, he is now also color-blind. The red flashing light on top of the police car is gray. He slams his fists through the window of the police car and slashes his wrists on the shards.

Chapter Twelve

With this chapter, the action moves forward five or six years to the time when the book started. Steve tells Rusty-James that he made up his mind to get out of their bad neighborhood, and he did, never looking back. He tells Rusty-James, "If you want to go somewhere in life you just have to work till you make it." Rusty-James replies, "Yeah. It'll be nice when I can think of someplace to go." They are on totally different wavelengths, and even though Steve invites Rusty-James for dinner, Rusty-James knows he won't go, because Steve is too much of a reminder of the past. "I figured if I didn't see him, I'd start forgetting again. But it's been taking me a lot longer than I thought it would," he says.

Characters

Smokey Bennet

Smokey, named for the unusual color of his eyes, is one of Rusty-James's friends and a member of the group, but he is nervous about gang violence. When Rusty-James says of the "old days" when he was eleven, "A gang really meant somethin' back then," Smokey says, "Meant gettin' sent to the hospital once a week." Smokey is not a loyal friend; he sets things up to make it look like Rusty-James is cheating on his girlfriend Patty so she'll dump Rusty-James and Smokey can go out with her. He also tells Rusty-James that if the gangs were still around, he would be president, not Rusty-James.

B. J.

B. J. is a friend of Rusty-James's, one of the group. He is fat but tough. As Rusty-James says, "Tough fat guys ain't as rare as you think."

Cassandra

Cassandra was a student teacher at the high school the year before, and the Motorcycle Boy was in one of her classes. She fell in love with him, and although she has a college education and comes from a good family, she moved into an apartment in Rusty-James's part of town and now follows the Motorcycle Boy around. She doesn't wear makeup, often goes barefoot, and has a lot of cats. Rusty-James views her as phony because she tries to talk like the Motorcycle Boy, saying "meaningful" things. She is a drug addict, whose habit the Motorcycle Boy detests.

Mr. Harrigan

Mr. Harrigan is the guidance counselor at Rusty-James's school. Rusty-James says, "There was something about Mr. Harrigan that made my mind go kind of blank, even when he was swatting me with a board."

Weston McCauley

McCauley is a former friend of the Motorcycle Boy and used to be second lieutenant in the Packers, the local gang. He's a heroin addict now.

Midget

Midget is a tall, skinny kid who notifies Rusty-James that Biff Wilcox is out to get him.

Motorcycle Boy

The Motorcycle Boy, whose real name the reader never learns, is Rusty-James's older brother and hero. He got his name because he loves motorcycles and steals them and rides them. He is not interested in owning one, though. He is color-blind and sometimes deaf as a result of motorcycle accidents, and although he is a charismatic, natural leader, he's also odd—not quite connected to the rest of humanity. Rusty-James says, "He had strange eyes—they made me think of a two-way mirror. Like you could feel somebody on the other side watching you, but the only reflection you saw was your own." He has been expelled from school for scoring "perfect tests"; it's clear that the authorities assumed he was cheating but not clear whether he actually was. It seems that he might be much smarter than the school gives him credit for because he reads a great deal. He has always seemed older than his real age, and he tells Rusty-James, "I stopped bein' a little kid when I was five." When he was fourteen, storekeepers stopped asking for his ID, so he could buy liquor. At the same age, he was the leader of the gang, the Packers, and older kids asked for his advice. Later, he decided that gang violence was stupid and boring and put a stop to it. He detests drug addicts, and rumor has it that he once killed a junkie. He tells Rusty-James that if he ever uses drugs, he'll break Rusty-James's arm, and Rusty-James believes him.

Roy Patterson

Roy Patterson is a police officer who has a grudge against Rusty-James and the Motorcycle Boy and is constantly on the lookout for a way to "get" them. In the end, he kills the Motorcycle Boy without warning when the Motorcycle Boy is stealing fish from a pet store.

Patty

Patty is Rusty-James's girlfriend. Her mother is a nurse who works nights, and Patty has to stay home and take care of her little brothers. She has bleached blond hair and is tough. She once went after another girl with a broken bottle because the girl was flirting with Rusty-James.

Don Price

Price is a smart-alecky kid who's been giving Coach Ryan trouble. Ryan offers Rusty-James five dollars to beat him up.

Rusty-James

Rusty-James, whose legal name is Russel-James, is fourteen during the main action of the book but talks and acts like someone much older and tougher. He confesses that he's not very bright and that he has a temper. He steals, curses, smokes, drinks, and gets into fights about once a week, although he hasn't lost one in two years. He idolizes his older brother, Motorcycle Boy, and wants to be just like him because Motorcycle Boy is "the coolest person in the whole world." He doesn't think much about the future, or the past, preferring to live in the present. His friend Steve is important to him because Steve is perhaps the only stable person he has ever known. Rusty-James was left alone in his parents' house for three days when he was two years old because his mother left the family, taking the Motorcycle Boy, and his father disappeared on a three-day drinking binge. Perhaps because of this, Rusty-James hates to be alone and dreads the day the Motorcycle Boy will leave home for good.

Rusty-James's Father

Rusty-James's father, whom his sons call "the old man," is an alcoholic. He has been to law school and has a large vocabulary and an educated way of speaking. He is "a middle-sized, middle-aged guy, kind of blond and balding on top, and has light-blue eyes. He was the kind of person nobody ever noticed. He had a lot of friends, though, mostly bartenders." He is completely detached from his sons and views them the way an anthropologist would view an unfamiliar tribe. "What strange lives you two lead," he says mildly when he learns that Rusty-James has been cut in a knife fight.

He began drinking when Rusty-James's mother left: he went on a three-day binge, and it was, according to him, the first time he was ever drunk. He says of his marriage and his downfall from lawyer to skid-row drunk, "Our marriage was a classic example of a preacher marrying an atheist, thinking to make a convert, and instead ending up doubting his own faith." This implies that his wife was some sort of criminal. He says, "She married me for fun, and when it stopped being fun she left."

Rusty-James's Mother

Rusty-James's mother left the family when Rusty-James was two and the Motorcycle Boy was six. At first, she took the Motorcycle Boy with her, but then she abandoned him, and eventually he was taken back to his father and Rusty-James. She now lives out in California and apparently is still unstable, moving from relationship to relationship. When the Motorcycle Boy finds her, she's living with a movie producer but is thinking of "moving in with an artist who lived in a tree house up in the mountains."

Coach Ryan

Ryan is the gym teacher at Rusty-James's school. Rusty-James dislikes him because he thinks the coach is a phony. The coach uses teen slang and tries too hard to be friends with Rusty-James, which makes Rusty-James suspicious. Rusty-James says, "I hoped to hell when I was grown I'd have better things to do than hang around some tough punk, hoping his rep would rub off on me."

Steve

Steve is Rusty-James's best friend and, like Rusty-James, is fourteen. He looks like he's twelve and acts forty. According to Rusty-James, "he could say stuff that I wouldn't let anybody else get away with." He comes from a good family and is scared of violence. He is shy with girls, doesn't smoke, and doesn't drink until later in the novel. He has "dark-blond hair and dark-brown eyes and a face like a real sincere rabbit." He is, according to Rusty-James, smarter than Rusty-James. Rusty-James protects him from other people who want to beat him up and listens to his many worries. In exchange, Steve does Rusty-James's math homework and lets Rusty-James copy his history homework so Rusty-James won't flunk. However, this is not the only reason Rusty-James is close to him. Rusty-James says, "Maybe it was because I had known him longer than I'd known anybody I wasn't related to." Steve's parents, on the other hand, don't even know that he knows Rusty-James.

Biff Wilcox

Biff is a member of another group, formerly allies of Rusty-James's group, now enemies. Rusty-James notes that if the old gang wars were still going on, Biff would be leader of his gang, the Devilhawks. He is tougher and more dangerous than most kids.

Themes

Poverty

Although Steve and Rusty-James agree that their neighborhood is not "the slums," they note that it's "crummy." They live in a poor area. Steve's family is better off because his father apparently has a job, but Rusty-James and the Motorcycle Boy have to scavenge, steal, and hope their father won't drink up all of his welfare check before they get a piece of it. When Rusty-James is hungry, he finds some sardines, crackers, and milk in the kitchen, remarking, "I ain't picky. I like about anything." The reader gets the sense that there was

Topics for Further Study

- Some critics of the novel have said that Hinton's portrayal of teenagers is not realistic because the young people in her book are tougher than any real people would be. Do you agree? Why or why not?

- Recent statistics show that gang violence is a problem throughout the United States. Do some research to find out what makes young people more likely to join gangs. What does research tell us that young people are looking for when they join gangs?

- The Motorcycle Boy is color-blind and sometimes deaf because of all his motorcycle accidents. Find out about color blindness. What is it, who has it, and how do they get it? Is it common for people to have color blindness as a result of accidents?

- Hinton has admitted that her portrayal of girls in the book is somewhat out of date. Do you agree with this? Provide specific examples to support your answer.

---

not much else in the house, other than his father's bottles of "sneaky pete."

Alienation and Abandonment

"For a tough kid I had a bad habit of getting attached to people," Rusty-James says in the beginning of the book, and as the story progresses, the reader finds out why. Abandoned by his mother as a toddler, left alone by his father for three days while his father went on a drunken binge, he learned early to fear solitude and at the same time to be wary of other people. His biggest fear, throughout the book, is that the Motorcycle Boy will leave for good.

The only time in the book when Rusty-James says he feels truly alive is when he, Steve, and the Motorcycle Boy cross the river and find themselves among crowds of people, cruising cars and listening to music. Rusty-James says, "I couldn't explain how I feel. Jivey, juiced up, just alive. The lights, I mean, and all the people." In contrast, nothing else in the book causes him to vary from his heavy emotional tone. Going to the lake with friends or making out with his girlfriend don't provide the pleasure that it seems they should; these are all just things to do to fill in time.

One of the most interesting aspects of Rusty-James's alienation and emotional homelessness is that no one in their apartment has his own room or even his own bed. The apartment has a cot and a mattress, and Rusty-James, the Motorcycle Boy, and his father sleep on either of them. "It didn't matter which," Rusty-James says. The reader is given the sense that they don't need three places to sleep because it's very rare that all three of them are home at the same time. There's no comfort in their house, very little food, and no stable routine. Their father is not interested in their lives, except for feeling mild curiosity about their exploits, and is completely emotionally detached from them, never providing meals, guidance, or a stable presence. As a parent, he's a total failure, so that, although he's physically present, he has emotionally abandoned both his sons.

Although Rusty-James's father has done this, Rusty-James still loves him, "sort of." He decides that he loves Patty, the Motorcycle Boy, and Steve, "sort of." In the end, his father proves worthless, Patty leaves him, the Motorcycle Boy is killed, and Steve decides that he's had enough of the rough and dangerous life and chooses to turn away from Rusty-James. Rusty-James is left utterly alone, just as he was as a young boy.

Death in Life

Everyone in the book, with the exception of Steve, is dead on the inside—trapped, stagnant, going nowhere. The Motorcycle Boy is doomed, "born in the wrong era, on the wrong side of the river, with the ability to do anything and finding nothing he wants to do," according to his father. In addition, he's now partially deaf and color-blind as a result of all his fighting and motorcycle crashes, disabilities that further cut him off from others and limit his potential. He is not interested in overcoming these problems. He almost seems to enjoy the splendid isolation they give him.

Rusty-James is trapped by his blind admiration for the Motorcycle Boy and never gives a thought to his future or to his past, and his awareness of the present is like an animal's, not involving any reflection or thought. He comments that he has never been good at school, and, indeed, his consciousness seems, at times, almost like that of a zombie. When the Motorcycle Boy tells him that he is afraid to be alone because he was frightened by being abandoned as a little child, Rusty-James looks at him stupidly. He says, "What he was saying didn't make any sense to me. Trying to understand it was like trying to see through fog." He seems to spend most of his time in this fog, just getting through the days, never really thinking too deeply about anything.

Their father is also emotionally detached and dead, interested in his next drink, but not particularly in his children. He occasionally shows flashes of understanding, as when he describes the Motorcycle Boy's character, but usually regards his sons with utter detachment; for example, when Rusty-James is wounded in the knife fight, he only remarks mildly, "What strange lives you two lead." Instead of remarking on the wound or encouraging Rusty-James to seek medical care for it, he gives Rusty-James ten dollars and then asks the Motorcycle Boy if he had a nice trip to California. This makes it clear that no matter what happens, the boys are basically on their own. Their father is unable, or unwilling, to help them or provide any guidance.

Usually a symbol of life and movement, the river in *Rumble Fish* is the opposite, as stagnant and doomed as the characters. Early in the book, Rusty-James throws his cigarette butt into the water, remarking that it's so full of trash that it will make no difference. Later, he comments on the horrible smell that emanates from the river, a result of pollution. The fact that the Motorcycle Boy decides to release the fighting fish into this river is ironic—they will likely die as soon as they hit the filthy water. It's a grand gesture but a senseless one, and like the fish, these boys will never escape the evils of their environment.

Style

First-Person Narrative

The book is written in first person from Rusty-James's point of view, which allows the reader to see events only as Rusty-James sees them, leading to some interesting questions about Rusty-James's perception and how much of it is accurate. In particular, it's not clear whether his suspicions of some adults are correct or not. For example, he is cynical about Cassandra and her motives and doesn't trust her because she gave up her rich family to come and live in his bad neighborhood and follow his brother around. He is also suspicious of Coach Ryan because Ryan is friendly with him. Although it's clear that both Coach Ryan and Cassandra have problems and motives of their own, readers may wonder whether they're as bad, or as selfish or phony, as Rusty-James thinks they are.

In addition, the one-sided presentation of events from Rusty-James's perspective is poignant because readers may see the gaps and flaws in his reasoning when he does not. He wants more than anything to be like his brother, but from the reader's point of view, this ambition is questionable: his brother has accomplished nothing, is going nowhere, and has lost both his color vision and his hearing through his own lack of good judgment. And although the Motorcycle Boy is apparently a natural leader, it's clear that he will never really use this gift for anything constructive because he is so emotionally damaged. This sad fact is lost on Rusty-James. Although in many other ways he seems much older than his fourteen years, in his unswerving admiration of his brother, he seems much younger.

Use of Slang

The book is written in a tough, breezy style, as Rusty-James would speak but without any curse words. It seems unbelievable that the characters in the book would not curse, but obviously Hinton could not depict their talk realistically and have the book published for a young-adult audience. Instead, she implies cursing, as when Rusty-James says, "I said something to her I wouldn't normally say to a chick, but she really got on my nerves. She didn't flinch."

In addition, with rare exceptions, Hinton avoids using any slang that would make the book unnecessarily dated. Although it was written in 1975, most of the dialogue could appear in a book now and pass unnoticed. The few exceptions are largely street names for drugs—bennies, sneaky pete, horse—which typically undergo rapid evolution.

Historical Context

Rumble Fish was published in 1975, but Hinton wrote it during the early 1970s. At the time, the Vietnam War was still raging, and the war polarized the American population between those who supported it and those who vehemently protested

Compare & Contrast

- **1970s:** Most members of gangs are between the ages of twelve and twenty-one, and it's rare for females to be involved in gang violence.

  Today: Gang members may be as young as nine or as old as thirty, and although males still outnumber females by fifteen to one, the number of young women in gangs is increasing.

- **1970s:** Weapons used in gang violence are relatively simple, such as knives and chains, and opposing gang members meet face-to-face to fight.

  Today: Gang members may use AK-47s or Uzis, and drive-by shootings have replaced vacant-lot rumbles.

- **1970s:** Fifteen percent of whites and twenty-six percent of African Americans drop out of high school.

  Today: Four percent of whites and seven percent of African Americans drop out of high school. Reasons given include "didn't like it," failing, job-related problems, and pregnancy.

- **1970s:** Fewer than half the states in the United States and about one hundred counties in those states report gang violence.

  Today: Every state, as well as the District of Columbia, and twelve hundred counties report gang violence.

---

against it. The U.S. government finally withdrew its last troops from combat in 1973, but the war left lasting scars on the psyches of everyone, from the soldiers involved to those who had never left home. In all, 3 million soldiers participated in the war; 58,000 were killed, 1,000 were missing and never found, and 304,000 were wounded.

The growing use of drugs by young people, which became popular in the 1960s, continued in the 1970s, affecting people of every social class. In 1975, First Lady Betty Ford commented in an interview that she thought her own children had smoked marijuana.

The Civil Rights and feminist movements were still fighting for equal rights for minorities and women. Although many women supported the feminist movement, its effects were slow to trickle throughout American culture so that, like the girls in *Rumble Fish*, many women still felt that their status was derived from that of the man they were with. And although great strides had been made toward ensuring equal rights to people of all races, racial tensions still divided society, as shown by Rusty-James's unease at realizing that he and Steve are the only white boys in a black bar.

In world politics, the United States and the Soviet Union were superpower nations, each with influence or control over a large portion of the world. The two nations regarded each other with unease, suspicion, and a constant wariness, a situation known as the "Cold War." Conflict between communism and American democracy weighed on people's minds, along with the constant awareness that any open war between the two powers might end in nuclear annihilation. This tension was eased slightly in 1975 by the symbolic linking of the Soviet Soyuz and the American Apollo spacecraft while in orbit.

Economically, the United States experienced a serious recession from about 1973 to 1975, largely caused by rising oil prices. This recession was the most serious contraction of industrial production since the Great Depression and had widespread effects on employment and attitudes throughout the country.

Culturally, the options for entertainment and connection to other people were much less diverse than they are today. Most cities had only a handful of television stations, unlike the dozens or hundreds of cable channels available to many people today. Videogames, video players, personal computers, e-mail, and the Internet were unknown; even hand-held calculators were an expensive novelty.

Matt Dillon (center) as Rusty-James and Mickey Rourke (right) as the Motorcycle Boy in the 1983 film version of the novel

Critical Overview

In *School Library Journal*, Jane Abramson commented that the book was "stylistically superb" and that it "packs a punch that will leave readers of any age reeling." A *Publishers Weekly* reviewer wrote, "Ms. Hinton is a brilliant novelist," and Margery Fisher, in *Growing Point*, noted, "Once more in the American urban scene is a book as uncompromising in its view of life as it is disciplined." She also wrote, "Of the three striking books by this young author, *Rumble Fish* seems the most carefully structured and the most probing." Jay Daly wrote in *Presenting S. E. Hinton*, "In the end we respond to *Rumble Fish* in a much deeper way than we do to [her previous book] *That Was Then, This Is Now*. It's an emotional, almost a physical response, as opposed to the more rational, intellectual reaction that the other book prompted." He also commented that the book "works as a novel. . . . And there is a name usually given to this kind of success. It is called art."

However, not all critics agreed that the book was superb. In the *Nation*, Michael Malone remarked that he found it difficult to believe that Hinton's novels, including *Rumble Fish*, are realistic portraits of average American teenagers. He commented that the books' popularity is largely due to their action-packed narratives, simplistic plot structures, intense emotional tone, and well-defined principles. He noted that adults are rarely present and that girls also play only vague cameo roles: "In this world the stories, like the streets, belong almost exclusively to tribes of adolescent males."

In her defense, Hinton commented in an interview in *Seventeen*:

> I started writing before the women's movement was in full swing, and at the time, people wouldn't have believed that girls would do the things that I was writing about. I also felt more comfortable with the male point of view—I had grown up around boys.

Malone commented that he was mystified by others' claims that *Rumble Fish* and Hinton's other books are realistic and that, in his opinion, because of their lack of reality, "despite their modern, colloquial tone, [Hinton's books] are fairy tale adventures" and the gang fights in them are "as exotic as jousts in *Ivanhoe* or pirate wars in *Treasure Island*."

To bolster his case that the novels are mythic, he noted that the settings are vague; the action could take place anywhere. In addition, the novels' setting in time is also hard to pin down.

Malone also described Hinton's prose style as being at times "fervid, mawkish and ornate" and said that the morals in her fictional universe are "as black-and-white as an old cowboy film."

In the *Times Literary Supplement*, Jane Powell commented that the book is disappointing because of Rusty-James's victimization and his evidently doomed fate. As she notes, by the end of the book, "There can't even be a glimmer of hope for the future."

Hinton revealed in the production notes to the film version of the book that the book was difficult to write because of the contrast between Rusty-James, who is a simple character, and the Motorcycle Boy, who "is the most complex character I've ever created. . . . It's about over-identifying with something which you can never understand, which is what Rusty-James is doing. The Motorcycle Boy can't identify with anything."

Criticism

Kelly Winters

Winters is a freelance writer. In this essay, Winters considers Hinton's depiction of girls, boys, young adults, and adults in her novel.

Hinton has often been criticized for the emphasis on male toughness and machismo in her books. In *Rumble Fish*, the portrayal of Patty and other girls is simplistic; the reader never really gets a sense of Patty as a living, breathing person, and she seems mainly interested in her appearance and in going out with the toughest boy. Hinton once explained that she grew up before the feminist movement, that the girls she knew in high school were more concerned with their hair and makeup than anything else, and that girls derived their status not from who they were but from who their boyfriends were. This is borne out by the action in the book. When the balance of power shifts so that Smokey is top dog in the group, Patty coolly shifts her affections to him without a backward glance.

This makes her seem shallow, which she is, but so is Rusty-James's affection for her; at one point, kissing the top of her head, he notes that she has dark roots in her hair. He comments, "I like blond girls. I don't care how they got that way." The reader senses that it's not so much her personality—of which she doesn't have much—that attracts him but simply that she's female, blond, and likes him. At one point, he includes her in a list of people he loves, but he's unmoved by her defection to Smokey at the end of the book, even though this was prompted by Smokey's deception.

Other than Patty, girls are rarely mentioned in the book. Although he's incredulous that Steve, at fourteen, would be shy about girls, for Rusty-James, they're still barely a blip on his mental radar screen. Girls are just there, like furniture. When he goes to the lake, he names the boys he goes with but says, "There were some girls and we built a fire and went swimming." The text implies that he kissed or made out with the girls but that it didn't mean anything to him; whatever happened, he's already forgotten it; it was just something he did, and the girls didn't even have names or personalities.

In addition, the degree of male toughness or machismo in the book seems exaggerated, leading to unrealistic behavior. Rusty-James is just fourteen, and he's been deeply wounded emotionally throughout his life, but he's as tough as a hardened Marine when it comes to physical suffering. After sustaining a knife slash deep enough to expose his ribs, he just grits his teeth when his brother pours alcohol over the wound and goes to school the next day. He doesn't even bandage it, even though the wound is obviously deep enough to require stitches and the pain would inhibit most people from moving around at all. All he says is, "I wasn't feeling too hot and I was bleeding off and on, but I usually go to school if I can." It seems unbelievable that he wouldn't simply stay home, especially since his father doesn't care and he is not close to any of his teachers. After school, he goes out and shoots a game of pool, seemingly oblivious to his wound, and runs for blocks and leaps from one roof to another after stealing some hubcaps. During the chase he becomes aware of the pain: "My side was killing me." And later, after the rooftop leap, he finally passes out. What's surprising is that he didn't pass out sooner and that he didn't remark on the pain while bending over to shoot pool.

The next day he washes out the wound again, noting, "It hurt real steady, not bad, but steady like a toothache." That night he goes swimming up at the lake and only later wonders if the lake water might have infected the wound. It seems unlikely that the wound wouldn't have hurt when the water touched it or when he swam, possibly reopening it. Throughout the book, his awareness of the wound comes and goes, but it never affects him the way one would assume it would affect any normal person.

The main characters in the book are all teenagers—the Motorcycle Boy is nineteen, Biff Wilcox is sixteen, and Rusty-James and Steve are fourteen. However, they are as burned-out and jaded as any war-ravaged adults. Rusty-James says casually, "I get annoyed when people want to kill me for some stupid little reason. Something big, and I don't mind it so much." This implies that others have wanted to kill him, and for various reasons; death threats mean nothing to him now. When threatened, he reacts without thinking about much other than how many supporters his enemy has brought with him.

Similarly, Rusty-James is jaded about sex and women. He treats Patty like an object, and when he goes to an X-rated movie with the Motorcycle Boy and Steve, he spends much of his time watching the other people in the theater, the Motorcycle Boy, and Steve, who is amazed at what's on the screen. He's seen so much of it before that the film seems unremarkable to him; he tells Steve, "I seen better."

> " Rusty-James is just fourteen, and he's been deeply wounded emotionally throughout his life, but he's as tough as a hardened Marine when it comes to physical suffering."

Because his father is a drunk, Rusty-James is familiar with the effects of alcohol, and he has friends who use hard drugs like heroin; he stops over at a friend's house but leaves when he finds the friend is shooting up. "He was there, with some other people, but they were all spacey and nervous and dopey, doing horse." This is apparently a normal occurrence in his neighborhood; he reports it in the same tone anyone else would use to say, "They were home, but they were busy cleaning, so I left."

At times, Rusty-James gives the reader the sense that he wishes he could be a kid and that he resents the adults who have left him to grow up so fast. He claims to love his father although he doesn't like him, but in a telling incident, he shoves an old drunk man off the sidewalk because the old man is in his way. Although the old man is not his father, he could easily be; the reader senses that the anger he feels at the old man for blocking his way is really aimed at his father, for blocking his growth in life. As he points out, his father has never "done" anything to him, like beat him or abuse him; his father has simply done nothing: he drinks and reads and ignores his sons. What Rusty-James doesn't really understand, however, is that "doing nothing" is as harmful to children as physical abuse, and he has every right to be angry at his father.

Coach Ryan, who is friendly to Rusty-James, turns out to be unethical when he offers Rusty-James five dollars to beat up another boy. Rusty-James has never trusted him, because he thinks Ryan is impressed by Rusty-James's toughness and wants to gain from his reputation; he thinks Ryan wants to be friends with him in the same way that some one might like to own a mean and vicious dog because it will enhance his own status.

Mr. Harrigan, the guidance counselor, does not offer guidance at all but seems more like a warden. He doesn't make any effort to find out why Rusty-James acts the way he does but punishes him and eventually gives him an ultimatum: Rusty-James is going to be transferred to a school where they know how to deal with "his kind." Rusty-James says of Harrigan, "My mind went kind of blank. There was something about Mr. Harrigan that made my mind go kind of blank, even when he was swatting me with a board, like he had two or three times before."

Harrigan asks a typically adult question: "Don't you think it's time you gave some serious thought to your life?" Rusty-James thinks, "Well, I had to worry about money, and whether or not the old man would drink up his check before I got part of it, and whether or not the Motorcycle Boy would pick up and leave for good, and I had a cop itching to blow my brains out." These are all serious worries, and, ironically, Rusty-James's focus on them is what prevents him from thinking about his life the way society would want him to; he can't care about school or the normal youthful things because he's had these problems thrust upon him by irresponsible adults. Obviously, Harrigan is just spouting the adult authority figure "party line" instead of really trying to get to the bottom of the problem.

Cassandra is closer in age to Rusty-James than any other adults, but, like them, she's abdicated any real adult responsibility by following the Motorcycle Boy around and becoming a drug addict. She's a substitute teacher, but her behavior suggests that if and when she becomes a full-time teacher, she'll be just like Harrigan and Ryan, so steeped in her own problems that she's unable to help her young students toward learning, emotional health, and true maturity.

Source: Kelly Winters, Critical Essay on *Rumble Fish*, in *Novels for Students*, The Gale Group, 2002.

Jay Daly

In the following excerpt, Daly explores the structure and themes Hinton employs to develop the characters and their relationships to each other in Rumble Fish.

Structure and Technique

As she did in *The Outsiders*, Hinton employs a frame to the story, the main body of which is a series of events that occurred five years earlier. The story is framed by the first and last chapters, which describe the surprise meeting of Rusty-James, the book's narrator, and Steve Hays, who had been his best friend during the time the story describes. The story is, in effect, a piece of Rusty-James's memory, and memory, the ability to remember things (or, conversely, to forget them) is a concern that appears throughout the narrative.

There is not much cause and effect in this story. In *The Outsiders* there is a random element to the act of violence that triggers the story—the stabbing in the park—but once that has occurred the rest of the story proceeds with absolute fidelity to the motivations of its characters. Once Johnny stabs Bob, everyone behaves exactly as they would be expected to behave, and the story gathers momentum toward its proper conclusion. In *Rumble Fish* there is no such turning point, no crucial act or omission (unless it is the simple returning to town of the Motorcycle Boy) after which the action of the story becomes inevitable. Instead it is all random, and it is all inevitable. Like a Greek tragedy dressed in modern black leather and denim, *Rumble Fish* is the story of human subservience to fate, to a destiny over which, finally, there can be no control.

We receive all our information in the story through the consciousness of Rusty-James. As with Ponyboy in *The Outsiders* and Bryon in *That Was Then, This Is Now*, this is the narrator's story, filtered through the narrator's point of view. Once again, this technique of first-person narrative permits an immediate involvement on the part of the reader. With Rusty-James we are struck from the beginning by his basic honesty and ingenuousness. "I ain't never been a particularly smart person," he tells us. "But I get along all right." Despite his submission to the macho world in which he lives ("I get mad quick, and I get over it quick"), his voice is a voice whose candor we trust. If we know at times that he is fooling himself we never feel that he is trying to fool us; this adds poignancy to some of his comments about himself, where the war between his outer toughness and his inner sensitivity seems to be proceeding without his notice. "For a tough kid," he says, "I had a bad habit of getting attached to people." In the early stages of the book, in fact, his teenage braggadocio is both entertaining and revealing:

I get annoyed when people want to kill me for some stupid little reason. Something big, and I don't mind it so much.

I'm always in dumb classes. In grade school they start separating dumb people from smart people and it only takes you a couple of years to figure out which one you are.

We can't help but feel that, with an attitude like this, he is not quite so dumb and uncomplicated as he makes himself out to be. As a result we warm up to him further.

In addition to this quality of immediacy, there are two other attributes of the first-person narrative that are of particular importance in *Rumble Fish*. The first is that it must often operate by suggestion. It must somehow transfer to the reader an awareness that is not yet present in the mind of the narrator. Rusty-James's relationship with his girlfriend Patty is a useful example of this. She treats him like a yo-yo, leading him on and then suddenly breaking up with him. Despite this treatment, he continues to believe that they share what he has been told is love. "I wondered if I loved anybody," he asks himself, and answers, "Patty, for sure." But in the very same paragraph we read: "Then I thought of people I could really count on, and couldn't come up with anybody."

In similar fashion, his preoccupation with appearance, with his looking like the Motorcycle Boy, or like his mother, and with sight, vision, builds up throughout the book until it pays catastrophic dividends at the end. We can feel it coming, because of the accumulation of evidence that has made us sensitive to it, but Rusty-James, whose "loyalty is his only vice," doesn't see it coming until it runs him down.

It is interesting to note that, since this story is so obviously a memory, recalled in its entirety in later times, there should be in the voice of the narrator some indication that he is speaking from an older, wiser vantage. It is common to stick phrases like "if I knew then what I know now," or "I couldn't have been more wrong," at strategic spots, usually near the end of chapters, to push the story along. Hinton in fact uses this device in *The Outsiders*; at the end of chapter 3 Ponyboy thinks: "Things gotta get better, I figured. They couldn't get worse. I was wrong."

In *Rumble Fish* there is a curious absence of this older-but-wiser voice. The reader accepts this inconsistency without complaint, in part because of the natural complicity of the reader and the author on behalf of the story, but there is more to it. There is a clear sense from the beginning chapter that Rusty-James is still not in complete possession of "the truth" of his story, that he has instead been running away from it. We get the sense that he is confronting this story for the first time, that it is as new to him as it is to us. The immediacy of the first-person narrative allows us to share along with him the pain and perplexity of his discovery.

> Like Mr. Kurtz in Conrad's *Heart of Darkness*, the Motorcycle Boy has seen too deeply into the secrets of things, into a reality that is gray and desperate."

The third quality of first-person narration that is important here is its ability to capture in the emotion of the narrator the mood of the times. The sense of confusion, of helplessness in the narrator renders the novel's theme of blind fate and destiny far more effectively than description ever could. As Rusty-James proceeds through the book his voice changes subtly. His apparent arrogance at the beginning ("Pain don't scare me much" ...) becomes eroded, and the uncertainty of the murky world he sees around him begins to break through his rather fragile self-confidence. "All my life, all I had to worry about was real things, things you could touch, or punch, or run away from. I had been scared before, but it was always something real to be scared of—not having any money, or some big kid looking to beat you up, or wondering if the Motorcycle Boy was gone for good. I didn't like this being scared of something and not knowing exactly what it was. I couldn't fight it if I didn't know what it was."

At last he discovers that "nothing was like I thought it was ... everything was changed," but in this he is not entirely correct. In fact nothing has changed, everything is exactly as it was; the only change is his awareness of it, an awareness that had crept into the reader's imagination much earlier, as the tone of the novel shifted ever so gradually from teenage braggadocio to human helplessness.

Because *Rumble Fish* is such an elusive, dreamy book, progress in the story is made by an accretion of awarenesses, a repetition of imagery. It is not so much a question of events turning uncontrollable as it is a growing awareness that events have always been out of the characters' control. The references to time and memory (as instigators of the characters' present lives), to the fleeting color and dreary monotone of life, to insanity and vision, to Greek tragedy and the idea of destiny, all of these gather strength as the novel progresses until the resolution of the story is quite beyond the ability of the characters to change it.

Like the colorful Siamese fighting fish, the Motorcycle Boy, and, to an extent we don't at first realize, his brother, Rusty-James, are trapped by a kind of biological necessity. Victims of their own destiny, of circumstances over which they had no say, their options for the future are very much the classical hero's options. They can, like the Motorcycle Boy, make the Promethean choice—to steal the fire, set free the fish—and suffer the inevitable Promethean punishment of the gods. Or, like Rusty-James, they can try to endure, but this latter choice—to live on in a world stripped of meaning, a world uncolored by hope—is in many ways the more difficult of the two. "I figured if I didn't see [Steve], I'd start forgetting again," Rusty-James says. "But it's been taking me longer than I thought it would."

It may take him the rest of his life.

Imagery and Metaphor

The most striking and persistent image of the book is certainly that of color and monotone, and of vision in general (with all that the word implies). Part of the reason that the movie version offended those of more delicate sensibility was that it took this central metaphor of the book and turned it into a much more visual presence in the film. The film is shot in black-and-white, mimicking the color-blind world of the Motorcycle Boy, with only the fish, bright red and blue, colored individually onto the screen. The result was either blatant exhibitionism (for those who hated the film) or movie magic (for those who loved it).

The contrast between color and monotone is much more subtly handled in the book. The Motorcycle Boy, that model of perfection in the world of *Rumble Fish*, is color-blind. His color blindness is not just a problem with red and green; it is total. The world to him looks like "Black-and-white TV, I guess… That's it." Hinton's decision to bestow upon this larger-than-life figure the curious imperfection of color blindness is, I think, inspired, and it reflects the enchantment of this particular book, as well as the levels of meaning with which it operates in the reader.

Our first reaction to the color blindness is that it sets the Motorcycle Boy apart from the ordinary. It is, after all, a relatively uncommon condition.

Furthermore, it is a condition with hereditary connotations, the kind of malady, like hemophilia, that besets royal houses, a condition of imperfection that at the same time suggests a privileged blood line. And of course the question of heredity, of propinquity, is a recurring obsession with this family, and with Rusty-James in particular. He is forever wondering who looks like whom in the family, and who has inherited what from each of his parents. It is of extreme importance to him that he find a permanent spot in the hopelessly dispersed and unresponsive family lineage represented by his absent mother and his functionally absent father.

Rusty-James yearns most of all for a merging with his brother, but the color blindness is a clear and constant reminder of how dissimilar they are. Rusty-James loves color. He loves the colored lights of the city because for him they represent life in all its vibrant potential. He's proud of the uncommon color of his hair, "an odd shade of dark red, like black-cherry pop." In one of his better lines, early in the book, he says, "I like blond girls. I don't care how they get that way."

Color is an important symbol of life for Rusty-James but he would give it up in a minute (just as he would kill to have someone finally say that he resembles his brother) for the more profound message of color blindness. The color blindness of the Motorcycle Boy is a sign that he is one of the Elect, the special ones, and Rusty-James mistakes this sign of exceptionality for the designation he truly seeks, that of belonging. Rusty-James will grasp at straws, and it is only at the end of the book, when in an earth-shattering moment he is allowed to participate in his brother's tragic imperfection, that the bleak reality of the Motorcycle Boy's vision becomes apparent to him.

All of this would have justified Hinton's use of the motif of color blindness and assured it a central place in the novel. The weight of the metaphor goes deeper, though, and it finally defines the world of *Rumble Fish* as surely as it marks the character of the Motorcycle Boy.

"Sometimes," the Motorcycle Boy says, "it seems to me that I can remember colors, 'way back when I was a little kid. That was a long time ago." This wistful comment suggests that the Motorcycle Boy's color blindness is not a congenital condition at all. It suggests instead that this vision of his is something he's attained, a product of his life. Whether his attainment of this vision is to be considered a gift or a deprivation is not clear. What is clear is that, in *Rumble Fish* at least, the world of light and color that Rusty-James so admires is exposed as an illusion, a child's vision, and the monotone world of the Motorcycle Boy is the reality.

The Motorcycle Boy is the classical hero turned upside down. He's the "perfect knight," the "pagan prince," who sees into the heart of things, "the laughter shining dark out of his eyes." "[The Motorcycle Boy] saw things other people couldn't see, and laughed when nothing was funny. He had strange eyes—they made me think of a two way mirror. Like you could feel somebody on the other side watching you, but the only reflection you saw was your own."

Like Mr. Kurtz in Conrad's *Heart of Darkness*, the Motorcycle Boy has seen too deeply into the secrets of things, into a reality that is gray and desperate. He has seen too much to be able to live a normal life in the world of colored lights and party sounds. In fact, like the tragic hero of that earlier book, he has seen too much to be able to live at all.

The book itself gradually takes on his vision. Things become murky, and motivations blurred. It culminates in Rusty-James's finally getting what he has so devoutly wished for, a merging of his identity with that of his idolized brother, in the penultimate scene by the river. This scene is rendered in such a way that one can only see it as a case of the curtain being suddenly torn open, revealing the brutal reality behind it. "The next thing I knew I was thrown up against a police car and frisked. I stared straight ahead at the flashing light. There was something really wrong with it. I was scared to think about what was wrong with it, but I knew, anyway. It was gray. . . . Everything was black and white and gray. It was as quiet as a graveyard . . . I was in a glass bubble and everyone else was outside it and I'd be alone like that for the rest of my life."

Hinton's deft handling of imagery and symbol does not confine itself to color and vision. The river, which divides the main part of the city from the boys' neighborhood, becomes a powerful symbol of their life, their world. The Motorcycle Boy stares into the river, as if looking for messages. Rusty-James thinks that the river stinks; he'd just as soon get away from it. The contrast to the river is, of course, the ocean, which the Motorcycle Boy had the chance to see (and didn't) in California and which entrances Rusty-James. "No kidding," he says of the Motorcycle Boy's trip to California. "The ocean and everything" "Kid," the Motorcycle Boy responds, cryptically, "I never got past

What Do I Read Next?

- Hinton's *The Outsiders* (1967) tells the story of the rivalry between two gangs.

- In *That Was Then, This Is Now* (1971), Hinton depicts two foster brothers who drift apart as one becomes involved with drugs and crime and the other focuses on school.

- Hinton's *Tex* (1979) describes two boys who can't rely on their unstable father and turn to each other for support.

- Robert Cormier's *The Chocolate War* (1974) is a story of a boy who resists both a gang and the authority figures at his school.

- Paul Zindel's *The Pigman* (1975) depicts two young people, alienated from their families, who turn to an old man for support and become involved in a tragedy.

the river." It is significant that when the Motorcycle Boy decides to liberate the rumble fish from their glass bowls (recalling the glass bubble in which he lives) he wants to see "if they'd act that way (destroy one another) in the river." His dramatic attempt to release the Siamese fighting fish is an effort not to save them, or even to free them, really; it is merely the preparation for the real test, the trial by combat. The Motorcycle Boy is not much interested in their salvation; he is more interested in measuring how their colorful belligerence, their legendary powers of self-destruction perform in the real world, in his monotone world of the river. Ironically, neither he nor the fish are permitted to complete this test. Rusty-James is there to watch. "I was at a dead run at the first shot, and almost to the river by the second. So I was there when they turned him over, and he was smiling, and the little rumble fish were flipping and dying around him, still too far from the river." This is an impressive image, reminiscent of the Viking funeral in *Beau Geste* (the name in French means beautiful, but empty, act), the larger-than-life hero and his totem dying together on the banks of that dark river.

The totemic relationship between the Motorcycle Boy and the rumble fish brings us to one last observation on the sustained imagery of the novel. There is in *Rumble Fish* a continued effort to imply animal surrogates for nearly all the main characters. Hinton had done this in other novels (Mark the lion, notably, in *That Was Then, This Is Now*), but there is in no other Hinton book the relentless identification of people with specific animals. Early on, Rusty-James notes that "the animals reminded me of people. Steve looked like a rabbit. He had … a face like a real sincere rabbit." This is a descriptive image, used once, but Hinton does not seem to want us to forget this identification. On the roof after the hubcap escapade Steve looks like a rabbit again, and, later, after his mother has gone into the hospital, he "looked like a sincere rabbit about to take on a pack of wolves."

The other characters have their own animal descriptors. The Motorcycle Boy "looked like a panther or something." When Steve shows his displeasure at something the Motorcycle Boy says, he looks like "a rabbit scowling at a panther." The picture of the Motorcycle Boy in the magazine "made him look like a wild animal out of the woods."

The Motorcycle Boy is, fittingly, associated with the panther, exotic and sleek, while Rusty-James is compared most often with a more familiar and domestic creature: a dog. He feels "the hairs of my neck starting to bristle, like a dog's." After he's nearly killed by muggers he makes "a grunt that sounded like a kicked dog." This identification is part of his self-image, and it is revealing to note that, among all the animals he could have chosen, he chooses the common, loyal, unremarkable dog. Even sadder is the animal the Motorcycle Boy assigns to him, the chameleon, which changes its very appearance to suit its environment and thus belongs everywhere, and nowhere.

Besides being graphic and descriptive (who can help picturing Steve as the sincere rabbit or the Motorcycle Boy as the sleek panther?), the association with animals reemphasizes the primacy of fate and destiny in the lives of the characters. What choice does an animal have in being what it is? Hinton's continued introduction of animal references also prefigures the final scene, where the Motorcycle Boy frees all the animals and casts his lot with the rumble fish.

At first glance the rumble fish seem to come out of nowhere. Their existence isn't even mentioned until the very end of the book. How is it that they are suddenly thrust into a position of such crucial importance, prominent enough to give the book its title?

The answer is that their role has been suggested all along, their existence predicted as surely as if Cassandra, the Motorcycle Boy's girlfriend (who is associated with cats, the animal symbol of prophecy), had gone into a white-eyed trance and begun raving about them. It wouldn't have mattered anyway, if she had. In Greek mythology Cassandra is given the gift of prophecy and then punished by Apollo, who ensures that nothing she says, no disaster she correctly predicts, will be believed by anyone who hears her. In *Rumble Fish*, where destiny is forever unalterable, the mythical punishment remains in effect.

Destiny and Biological Necessity

There are characters in all the Hinton novels who appear to be victims of a destiny they are not able to escape. This destiny may be the product of an accident of birth or a quirk of society (or a combination of both) but whatever the cause, it is usually final, and often fatal. Dallas Winston in *The Outsiders* is doomed from the first time we meet him; he can't escape his fate because it is a part of himself. Neither, apparently, can Mark in *That Was Then, This Is Now*, although his case is a little less satisfactory. In her fourth book, *Tex*, the entire cast of characters lines up behind placards reading "Those Who Go and Those Who Stay"; once it's decided which they are (a gypsy fortune-teller may make the decision) their fate is sealed. "Will and fate," Travis asks himself in *Taming the Star Runner*, "Which one had the biggest say in your life?"

A similar situation exists in *Rumble Fish*. Rusty-James, whom Steve compares to "a ball in a pinball machine," has given up on his ability to make decisions about his life before the story even begins. Biff Wilcox wants to kill him; Patty wants to break up with him; nothing he can do about it. That's just the way things are. It is instructive to remember just how trivial the so-called causes of these two major rifts are. In the first case he is almost killed as a result of "something [he] said to Anita at school." Who's Anita, anyway? In the second case he loses Patty, someone he professes to love, over an incident at the lake that is of such importance that it occupies one full sentence in the book. Why doesn't he fight back? Why doesn't he even try to make his case with Patty?

He doesn't try because he has come to believe that it won't do any good. Things are what they are, and nothing he can do will change that.

Rusty-James does have aspirations, of course, but they involve magical transformations rather than effort on his part. It is his hope that he will someday be like the Motorcycle Boy, and he bases this hope on heredity. Biology is destiny for Rusty-James, or at least he hopes it is.

"We look just like each other," I said.

"Who?"

"Me an' the Motorcycle Boy."

"Naw."

"Yeah, we do."

The Motorcycle Boy was the coolest person in the whole world. Even if he hadn't been my brother he would have been the coolest person in the whole world.

And I was going to be just like him.

The irony, unfortunately, is that he succeeds. Biology becomes destiny, although it is necessarily an imperfect copy. Steve makes the connection in the two frame chapters at the beginning and end of the book:

"Rusty-James … you gave me a real scare when I first saw you. I thought I'd flipped out. You know who I thought you were for a second? … You know who you look just like?

"I never thought you would, but you do. You don't sound like him, though. Your voice is completely different. It's a good thing you never went back. You'd probably give half the people in the neighborhood a heart attack."

Belonging and Being Alone

Rusty-James, the tough kid with the bad habit of getting attached to people, is one of Hinton's most ingenuous, most likable creations. He is indeed as loyal as a pet dog, and equally incapable of guile. He can't even play poker because (though he doesn't agree) his friends can read his every emotion in his face. It is therefore all the more tragic when he is transfigured (in an operation only partly successful, like a botched job done by a mad scientist in a horror movie) into the cold, featureless persona of the Motorcycle Boy. All he ever wanted was to belong. Somewhere. Anywhere.

His need for other people, his yearning to belong somewhere, permeates the consciousness of the book. Hinton's characters have always had a bad start at belonging—most of them have dead, absent, or ineffectual parents—but for none of them is the need for a place in life, amongst other people, as strong as it is for Rusty-James. For Rusty-James it is almost a matter of life and death.

I can't stand being by myself. That is the only thing I am honest-to-God scared of.

"I don't like bein' by myself. I mean, man, I can't stand it. Makes me feel tight, like I'm being choked all over."

There is an ostensible explanation for this fear. It is given by the Motorcycle Boy, in his sometimes exasperating, emotionless monotone. "When you were two years old, and I was six, Mother decided to leave. She took me with her. The old man went on a three-day drunk when he found out. He's told me that was the first time he ever got drunk. I imagined he liked it. Anyway, he left you alone in the house for those three days. We didn't live where we do now. It was a very large house. . . . I suppose you developed your fear of being alone then."

A two-year-old left in the house alone for three days could develop a great many things, including death. The Motorcycle Boy's explanation is a little too pat, a little too convenient. It was a mistake on Hinton's part to imagine that we needed this kind of traumatic antecedent for the pervasive yearning to belong that exists in Rusty-James's character. The fact of his mother's abandonment of them would have been quite enough; Rusty-James succeeds on his own, in the strength and pure longing of his voice, to convince us of the impact this abandonment has had on him.

The reverse of belonging is, naturally, being alone, and there is no one more alone than the Motorcycle Boy, living in a glass bubble which Rusty-James inherits at the end of the book. At the risk of being redundant, we must once again mention the irony: Rusty-James, whose very nature is built around the need for people (he makes lists of people he likes, when he's alone, because "it makes me feel good to think of people I like—not so alone") is led by his reverence for the Motorcycle Boy to the precise condition that terrifies him. He is truly and finally alone.

The Perfect Knight and the Misfit

Which brings us to the Motorcycle Boy. The firstborn son of a morganatic marriage between a mysterious, absent, movie-actress mother and a cerebral, formal, lawyer-turned-drunkard father, the Motorcycle Boy comes stocked with all manner of mythic associations. His name, "like a title or something," his ability to crack Biff Wilcox's wrist "like a matchstick," his inherited imperfection, his profound and eerie effect on everyone he encounters, everything about the Motorcycle Boy is of unearthly stature. When the Motorcycle Boy is expelled from school, Rusty-James wants to know why.

"How come you got expelled?" I asked.

"Perfect tests."

You could always feel the laughter around him, just under the surface, but this time it came to the top and he grinned. It was a flash, like lightning, far off.

"I handed in perfect semester tests."

Everything about the Motorcycle Boy is preternatural, even his laughter, especially his laughter. "As far as I could tell," Rusty-James says, "he never paid any attention to anything except to laugh at it."

"That cat is a prince, man," says the black pool player during his match with the Motorcycle Boy. "He is royalty in exile." This summation is echoed by the boys' father, in his "perfect knight" speech, recalling the archetypal perfect knight, Sir Galahad, from the Holy Grail legend. Galahad is also gifted with uncommon vision, with the ability to see into the secrets of things, "those things that the heart of mortal man cannot conceive nor tongue relate." Like the Motorcycle Boy, the character of Sir Galahad is often perceived to be "a cardboard saint, [whose] austere virtue excludes humanity." Galahad succeeds in his quest for the Holy Grail—only a perfect knight can accomplish this—but the Motorcycle Boy's quest is directionless, his goal unidentified, and whether his smile at the end is an indication of the success or the failure of his private quest is open to debate.

The implications, for both the Motorcycle Boy and Rusty-James, of their father's "perfect knight" speech are worth considering. "Russell-James," the father says, "every now and then a person comes along who has a different view of the world than does the usual person.... [The Motorcycle Boy] is merely miscast in a play. He would have made a perfect knight, in a different century, or a very good pagan prince in a time of heroes. He was born in the wrong era, on the wrong side of the river, with the ability to do anything and finding nothing he wants to do."

After this speech Rusty-James says, in his wide-eyed, great-hearted innocence, once again, "I think I'm gonna look just like him when I get older. Whaddya think?" His father is shocked by this pronouncement, and looks at him as if seeing him for the first time. What he sees startles him, and then reduces him to pity. "You poor child," he says. "You poor baby."

The flip side of the perfect knight is the misfit. The father's "perfect knight" speech could just as easily be called his "misfit" speech, and it applies to Rusty-James as well. He, too, is miscast in the play, born in the wrong era. He, too, is out of touch with the times, though his options are fewer and his "time of heroes" is more recent. With typical misunderstanding, Rusty-James locates this heroic time with the era of the gangs, just recently passed, which he imagines would have provided him with meaning, belonging. He even romanticizes that time out of its own chronology; for him the heroic era was "a long time ago, when there were gangs."

His misapprehension of the reality of the gang era doesn't make him any less the misfit in the present time. The lot of the misfit is never a pleasant one. In Flannery O'Connor's short story "A Good Man Is Hard to Find" there is a chilling, murderous character known only as The Misfit. There is nothing particularly heroic about The Misfit; the only startling thing about him is the utter amorality and the cold expressionlessness with which he goes about the business of murdering, one by one, the members of a family whose car has broken down. At the end of the story The Misfit engages the grandmother of the family in an extended, almost overrational explanation of why he lives as he does in a world where the possibility of redemption, of meaning, is so uncertain. The grandmother, who is doddering in and out of reality, mistakes him in a visionary moment for one of her children and she reaches out to touch him. He recoils in horror and kills her. The last words of the story, spoken in a final attempt at self-justification, by The Misfit, are "It's no real pleasure in life."

The Motorcycle Boy couldn't have said it any better.

The Problem of the Motorcycle Boy

Steve says of the Motorcycle Boy, "[H]e is the only person I have ever met who is like somebody out of a book. To look like that, and be good at everything, and all that." Thus does one of the book's characters state the main problem about the Motorcycle Boy: People in books should not themselves appear to come out of books; that's too much of a jump for any character to make, and the Motorcycle Boy, who doesn't make the river at the book's end, doesn't make the jump into fully realized existence either. He's just too distant, too idealized, too detached, and finally, too inhuman to be taken seriously as a character. Robert Berkvist, in his otherwise not very probing review of *Rumble Fish* in the *New York Times Book Review*, makes the entirely accurate observation that the Motorcycle Boy "clanks through the story like a symbol never quite made flesh."

If Hinton thought to introduce some humanity into the character by means of the color blindness (and it is not my belief that she did), the result is quite the opposite. His color blindness, along with his occasional deafness and his general other-worldliness, only serve to set him off further from the rest of humanity. His detachment is so total that he ignores the person closest to him, the person who truly cares about him, his brother, Rusty-James.

Numerous times in the novel Rusty-James makes statements like "one of the few times he ever paid any attention to me," "he never paid much attention to me," "in case the Motorcycle Boy forgot I was with him," and "the Motorcycle Boy was watching me, amused but not interested." The key is that given the depth of feeling the reader has built up around the character of Rusty-James, we should hate this Motorcycle Boy character for the way he treats his hero-struck younger brother. In fact, though, we don't feel much about the Motorcycle Boy, pro or con. We don't feel much because he's not real; it would be like trying to raise an emotion about a lounge chair or a suitcase.

There is the matter of his speech, for one thing. How are we to deal with a character who talks like this? "It's a bit of a burden to be Robin Hood, Jesse James and the Pied Piper. I'd just as soon stay a neighborhood novelty, if it's all the same to you. It's not that I couldn't handle a larger scale, I just plain don't want to."

Hinton tries to have Rusty-James explain this away by saying, "Sometimes, usually on the streets, he talked normal. Then sometimes he'd go on like he was reading out of a book, using words and sentences nobody ever used when they were just talking." This just doesn't wash; it's too unreal. The only useful purpose to this kind of speech is that it makes the heredity case once again; it links the Motorcycle Boy with his father, who talks the same way. Compare the father's quizzical "What strange lives you two lead" with the Motorcycle Boy's "What a funny situation ... I wonder what I'm doing here," after Rusty-James is injured in the mugging scene. (A few pages earlier, when Rusty-James thought he was dying, he thinks, "I pictured

my father at my funeral saying, 'What a strange way to die.'" Rusty-James has a talent for capturing the essence of character.)

In Hinton's defense, the problem she bit off when she chose to create the Motorcycle Boy is a problem that not many authors have solved well. The problem of the Motorcycle Boy is the problem of trying to create a larger-than-life character—the saint, the seer, the mystic—and at the same time animating that character with the common spark of humanity we all recognize. (She makes a better choice in *Taming the Star Runner* by placing the symbolic weight on the horse, a character she doesn't have to worry about making human.) Not many writers are able to pull this off. In recent American writing an example of one who tried mightily (and ultimately failed) is J. D. Salinger, with his character Seymour Glass (another idolized older brother). Seymour Glass, who appears in a number of Salinger's books, finally becomes such a prisoner of his spiritual detachment and doomed purity that the reader can't wait for him to do himself in and get it over with. Like Sir Galahad (or David Bowie's Major Tom), Seymour ascends so far into the stratosphere that it becomes clear that he is never coming back down.

Ordinarily this should prove fatal to a novel, a major character who fails to break through two dimensions into at least the suggestion of a rounded existence, but not so in *Rumble Fish*. *Rumble Fish* succeeds in spite of the Motorcycle Boy because *Rumble Fish* is not the Motorcycle Boy's story at all (despite Hinton's comment that "the Motorcycle Boy haunted me" and that he was the reason she forced herself to come back to the book, after it had been put aside for so long). It's Rusty-James's story, actually, and from the point of view of the reader's allegiance it is the Motorcycle Boy who plays squire to Rusty-James's knight, and not the other way around.

We can forgive the clanking of the Motorcycle Boy because our attention is focused on Rusty-James. The spark of humanity that is missing in the Motorcycle Boy is a roaring fire in Rusty-James, and it is our concern with this conflagration that gives the book its impact. We imagine that the main thrust of the story is about the Motorcycle Boy, but in this we are fooled (intellectually, not emotionally) by a sleight of hand. As we have seen, upon closer inspection, all the themes of the book, even those having to do with perfection and perfect knighthood, are concerns of the character of Rusty-James as well as the Motorcycle Boy. If we sometimes cringe at the behavior of the Motorcycle Boy, we never look away, because in fact it is never the Motorcycle Boy we are truly looking at. What we are looking at is a distorted mirror, "a distorted glass" reflection of Rusty-James.

In the end we respond to *Rumble Fish* in a much deeper way than we do to *That Was Then, This Is Now*. It's an emotional, almost a physical response, as opposed to the more rational, intellectual reaction that the other book prompted. Whatever its defects, whatever its ambitions only partly achieved, *Rumble Fish* works as a novel. In its appeal to the mythic element in life, in its living, breathing creation of the pilgrim character of Rusty-James, the book works. And there is a name usually given to this kind of success: It is called art.

Source: Jay Daly, "*Rumble Fish*," in *Presenting S. E. Hinton*, Twayne, 1987, pp. 68–84.

Sources

Abramson, Jane, Review of *Rumble Fish*, in *School Library Journal*, October 1975, p. 106.

Chaston, Joel D., "Hinton, S(usan) E(loise)," in *St. James Guide to Young Adult Writers*, 2d ed., edited by Tom Pendergast and Sara Pendergast, St. James Press, 1999, pp. 376–78.

Daly, Jay, *Presenting S. E. Hinton*, Twayne, 1987.

Fisher, Margery, Review of *Rumble Fish*, in *Growing Point*, May 1976, p. 289.

Hinton, S. E., *Rumble Fish Production Notes*, No Weather Films, 1993.

Hinton, S. E., and Lisa Ehrlich, "Advice from a Penwoman," in *Seventeen*, November 1981, p. 32.

Malone, Michael, "Tough Puppies," in *Nation*, March 8, 1986, pp. 276–80.

Powell, Jane, "Urban Guerrillas," in *Times Literary Supplement*, October 30, 1970, p. 125.

Review of *Rumble Fish*, in *Publishers Weekly*, July 28, 1975, p. 122.

Further Reading

Corliss, Richard, "*Rumble Fish*," Film review, in *Time*, October 24, 1983, p. 90.
    Corliss reviews the Francis Ford Coppola film version of the novel.

de Montreville, Doris, and Elizabeth J. Crawford, eds., *Fourth Book of Junior Authors*, H. W. Wilson, 1978.
    This reference work examines Hinton's life and early work.

Lyons, Gene, "On Tulsa's Mean Streets," in *Newsweek*, October 11, 1982, p. 105.
    Lyons takes a look at the city where Hinton grew up and how it appears in her fiction.

Silvey, Anita, Review of *Rumble Fish*, in *Horn Book*, November–December 1975, p. 601.
    Silvey provides a review and discussion of Hinton's book.

Stanek, Lou Willett, *A Teacher's Guide to the Paperback Editions of the Novels of S. E. Hinton*, Dell, 1980.
    This guide examines Hinton's novels from a teacher's perspective.

Sutherland, Zena, "The Teen-Speaks," in *Saturday Review*, January 27, 1968, p. 34.
    Sutherland examines Hinton's depiction of teenagers in this article.

Shizuko's Daughter

Kyoko Mori

1993

The plot of Kyoko Mori's first novel, *Shizuko's Daughter*, published in New York in 1993, follows a story line very similar to the author's own life. The female protagonist of the story experiences very difficult and often traumatic experiences as she is growing up, such as the suicidal death of her mother and the harsh treatment she receives from her father and stepmother. The novel explores the challenging reality of a young, pubescent girl who is living in Japan and who rebels against the strict discipline imposed upon her by her father and the Japanese culture. For many reasons, she is often alone throughout the story. One cause of her loneliness is that she does not relate to others who accept their status in life without questioning it.

The idea of the novel began as a short story that Mori wrote during the summer while she was in graduate school. In an article titled "Staying True to the Story," for *The Writer*, Mori states that this short story was "the first story in which I was able to write about what I knew but didn't understand." She explains that at first she used to write about things that she understood "all too well." This, however, bored her. "There was no mystery in it for me, let alone for my readers," she writes. So she began by thinking about her grandmother's life, about her relationship with her grandmother, about what her mother's life might have been like, and finally about what her own life would have been like if she'd done things just a little differently. It was from these considerations that *Shizuko's Daughter* was born.

Kyoko Mori

Stating her philosophy about writing in "Staying True to the Story," Mori comments, "each character comes to us already half-formed, in the midst of his or her conflict. Our job as writers is to define and develop that conflict, to follow and ponder the story that unfolds." This philosophy is very clearly followed in this, her first novel.

Author Biography

Kyoko Mori was born in Kobe, Japan, in 1957. When she was twelve years old, much like the young girl in *Shizuko's Daughter*, Mori's mother, Takako, committed suicide. Also like her fictional female character, Mori's childhood was traumatized by the harsh and sometimes physical disciplines that her father, Hiroshi, imposed on her, as well as by the unloving attitude of her stepmother, Michiko. There were, in other words, many similarities between Mori's childhood and the story of the young girl in Mori's novel.

Shortly before her death, Mori's mother decided that sending her daughter to the traditional Japanese public high school with its rigorous examination process would drain her daughter of her

creative energies. So she helped Mori apply to Kobe Jogakum, a school in Japan that had been founded by two American women in 1890, and that focused its curriculum on the arts and language. When Mori graduated, she taught English for a while. Then, at the age of nineteen, in 1976, she moved to the United States, by herself, to attend Rockford College, a liberal arts college in Illinois. In 1979, Mori earned her bachelor's degree there.

During graduate school at the University of Wisconsin in Madison, Mori met her future husband. She eventually earned a doctorate in creative writing and found a teaching job in Green Bay, Wisconsin, at St. Norbert College, where she taught writing. The couple stayed together through most of their twenties and into their thirties, but then, as Mori states in her memoir, *Polite Lies: On Being a Woman Caught Between Cultures* (1997), "I decided to be divorced because I began to sit alone in the kitchen late at night, as sad and silent as my mother had been." Despite the divorce, Mori writes that she had a good relationship with her husband. She states in her book *The Dream of Water* (1995), her first memoir, that her husband completely understood her chosen path of writer, in which her work shaped her life. "I think of myself primarily as a writer, not as a wife," she writes. And her husband accepted this, but there still remained inside of her something that made her unhappy about her marriage. Unhappiness is a theme that drives much of her writing. She strives to unravel the causes of this sadness by working through them creatively in her novels and memoirs.

After her divorce, Mori eventually moved away from Green Bay, having found a job at Harvard University. Currently, she is a Briggs-Copeland lecturer at Harvard, where she teaches creative writing. She lives in Cambridge, Massachusetts. Mori's other publications include *Fallout Poems* (1994), another young adult novel called *One Bird* (1995), and her novel *Stone Field, True Arrow* (2000).

Plot Summary

Chapter 1: Housebound

The first chapter of Mori's *Shizuko's Daughter* begins with Shizuko, the protagonist's mother, dreaming about the small village in which she grew up. The phone awakens her. It is her daughter, Yuki, who tells her mother that her piano teacher will be late for Yuki's lesson, thus causing Yuki to return home later than anticipated. Shizuko assures Yuki that this will not cause any difficulties. Although the tone of her mother's voice concerns Yuki, she decides to wait for Miss Uozumi rather than forego the lesson.

Meanwhile, Shizuko begins her process of readying herself for her suicide. She sits down and writes two notes. She asks for her husband's forgiveness, blaming only herself for the unhappiness that has led her to this act. In her note to Yuki, she writes that Yuki must always remember that she loves her. Then she adds, "When you grow up to be a strong woman, you will know that this was for the best."

She goes to the kitchen, closes the door, and lays the two notes on the table. After turning on the gas on the stove, she sits down on the floor. She thinks about a comment that she wrote in the note to her husband: "I am almost happy at this last hour," she had written. Then she had added, "and I wish you to be." When she thinks over this last sentiment, she changes her mind about it and reaches up to the table, finds the note to her husband, and tears it into very small pieces.

Chapter 2: The Wake

Yuki and her aunt Aya are packing all of Shizuko's clothes and jewelry. Aya comments, "Nobody would think you were only twelve," making reference to Yuki's composed reactions to her mother's death. Already, Yuki is tired of such remarks. Yuki reflects on how she came home from her lesson the day before to find her mother on the kitchen floor. Looking back, she wonders if her mother was still alive when she first found her. She tries to remember whether her mother was breathing. When Yuki telephoned her father, he told her not to call an ambulance because it would cause too much commotion in the neighborhood.

Yuki goes downstairs to the living room, and when her aunt sees her, she suggests that the dress that Yuki is wearing is of an inappropriate color. Aya takes Yuki upstairs to find a dress in a darker or more muted tone. The only appropriate dress that Aya finds is an old choir uniform. Yuki's mother had made all of Yuki's other clothes, using brightly patterned materials. When her aunt leaves the room, Yuki begins to put on the choir outfit. As she does this, she hears voices wailing downstairs. She drops the dress to the floor and goes into her clothes closet with all the vivid colors, sits down on the floor, and shuts the door.

Chapter 3: Tiptoes

One year later, Yuki is sent up to a hotel dressing room where her father's future bride is preparing herself for her wedding. Yuki's future stepmother, Hanae, states that there should be no hard feelings between her and Yuki. She says, "You'll probably hear people say all kinds of bad things about me because I was married to your father so soon after your mother's tragic death." She then suggests that Yuki shouldn't believe any gossip concerning a supposed affair that she and Yuki's father had been carrying on.

Yuki is very uncomfortable in the room and tells Hanae that the smell of makeup is making her sick. Then she runs out of the room. Yuki finds her Aunt Aya and begs her to repeat the story about how her grandmother had arranged a wedding for Yuki's mother and how Yuki's mother had refused to take part in an arranged marriage. Her aunt repeats the details of how Shizuko had moved to Kobe to find a job. That was how she'd met Yuki's father.

Later, during the wedding ceremony, as a ceramic bowl of sake is passed around the room, Yuki purposefully drops it when it is given to her. The breakage, in Yuki's mind, mimics the earlier breaking of a rice bowl at her mother's funeral, an act performed so her mother's ghost would not haunt the house. Yuki breaks the sake bowl so her father will not forget her mother.

Chapter 4: Irises

Yuki, who had been living with her Aunt Aya until her father's marriage, experiences another dramatic turn in her life. She moves in with her father and stepmother, but they close themselves off to her. She goes into the kitchen and notices that all her mother's ceramic pieces are gone, except for one tea service. She remembers her mother taking her to street fairs to watch potters create their wares. The recent move into her father's house reminds Yuki of another transition, when she and her mother had packed up all the household goods to move to a new house closer to the mountains. She compares the warm feelings that she and her mother shared in that move to the coldness that she feels now in this house, now that her father's new bride has moved in.

Yuki looks out at the garden and remembers how her mother had dug up many of the plants from the old residential yard and replanted them here in the home where Yuki now lives with her stepmother. Although her stepmother has changed many things, she has not yet converted the garden.

Chapter 5: Pink Trumpets

Yuki runs track for her school team. She is one of the star athletes. Neither her father nor her stepmother ever attends Yuki's events, and she is painfully aware that the other students and their parents feel sorry for her.

While waiting for her event, Yuki watches Sachiko Murai, a record-breaking hurdler. Yuki wants to meet the young girl and is glad when Sachiko easily wins her race. After Yuki's event, she and Sachiko bump into one another and plan to meet later.

Chapter 6: Sundays

Sachiko and Yuki meet on Sundays until the end of summer, when Sachiko confesses that she is no longer going to be running cross-country. Yuki wants to maintain the friendship but suspects that Sachiko's mother no longer wants Sachiko to be Yuki's friend.

Chapter 7: Yellow Mittens and Early Violets

Yuki is allowed to visit her grandparents on the third anniversary of her mother's death, but she is uncomfortable there. Just before she leaves, her grandfather collapses, which startles Yuki, and she finally opens up emotionally to her grandmother.

Chapter 8: Grievances

Hanae (Yuki's stepmother) is cleaning the house and thinking about how dirty Yuki is. She decides to get rid of all Yuki's old clothes and is descending the stairs when Yuki comes home and confronts her. Hanae pushes Yuki back, and Yuki falls down several steps, hurting her ankle. A few minutes later, Hanae accuses Yuki of trying to hurt her. When Yuki goes to her room, Hanae takes the clothes outside so the garbagemen can collect them. She then walks into the kitchen, takes down Yuki's mother's ceramic tea set, and smashes it.

Chapter 9: Homemaking

Yuki is in a homemaking class at school. She does not get along well with her teacher, so when the teacher needs a volunteer to go out into the woods to gather some colorful items for the table arrangement, Yuki asks to go, but the teacher tries to deny her. Eventually, Yuki's classmates convince the teacher that Yuki is the best choice since she is so artistic.

Chapter 10: The Golden Carp

Yuki's aunt Aya is getting married to an old friend of Yuki's mother, Mr. Kimura. Yuki remembers the first time she met Mr. Kimura, who apparently had a crush on Yuki's mother at one time. Her mother might have considered leaving Yuki's father for Mr. Kimura but knew if she left, she would have lost Yuki. Later, after Yuki's mother's death, Mr. Kimura comes by to offer his condolences. It is then that he meets Yuki's aunt. After that, Aya credits Yuki for introducing them to one another.

Chapter 11: Winter Sky

Chapter 11 covers the wedding ceremony of Aya and Mr. Kimura. At dinner, Yuki tells her mother's family that she has decided to go to a college that focuses on the arts. Mr. Kimura assures her that he is certain she could gain entrance into the more prestigious national university, but Yuki says, "That isn't for me. My teachers agreed. I wouldn't fit in at a national university. I don't want to fit in." She then further explains that she also wants to go to this particular school because it is located a great distance away from her father and stepmother.

Yuki becomes angry and walks outside. She is confused about all of her emotions. Mr. Kimura joins her, and they discuss relationships. Mr. Kimura has been divorced. Yuki's Aunt Aya is widowed. Yuki asks if it is worth falling in love. Mr. Kimura's comment is that "it may not turn out right" but, in some ways, that "means more because the odds are against us."

Chapter 12: Gladioli

Yuki is at home and sneaks up into the attic in the middle of the night to look through all the boxes to chose something special to take with her to school. She senses that she may never return home. She is about to leave Kobe for college. In the end, she decides that none of the items in the boxes are better than the memories she already carries with her. So she leaves everything behind.

Chapter 13: Silent Spring

Yuki's father comes home one night to find all the boxes that had been in the attic now piled up on the front porch. Hanae asks Yuki's father to burn them all. Hideki takes the boxes to the back yard and must open them up and take out the items a handful at a time to get them to burn. The boxes are filled with Yuki's and Shizuko's clothing, as well as mementos that Shizuko had saved over the years. In the process of going through the boxes, Hideki runs across his dead wife's sketchbook. He looks through it and decides to keep it.

Chapter 14: After the Rain

Chapter 14 takes place at Yuki's grand-mother's place. Masa thinks about Yuki's recent visits from her break at college. She has asked Yuki to live with her. While Masa is working in the gar-den, Takeo, Yuki's grandfather, suffers what ap-pears to be a heart attack and dies.

Chapter 15: The Effects of Light

Isamu is a photographer and a new school friend of Yuki's. Yuki thinks about whether she wants to become involved with Isamu. When she returns from work, she finds two things waiting for her: a note saying that Isamu has called and her mother's sketchbook, which her father has mailed to her. Yuki, after looking through the sketches, de-cides that her mother must want her to move be-yond her unhappiness. So she calls Isamu, thus sig-nifying that she is ready to become emotionally involved with him.

Chapter 16: Epilogue

Almost a year later, Masa is at home, baby-sitting her grandson, Tadashi, who keeps himself entertained by cutting off the heads of flowers and trapping small tree frogs in a jar. Masa is tired of death, and when the young child takes a nap, she frees the tiny frogs. When the boy wakes up, Masa finds him playing at the old wooden slide that her husband had made when her children were small.

Characters

Aunt Aya

Aya is Yuki's aunt and Yuki's mother's sister. It is Aya who comes to Yuki's aid as soon as she hears about Yuki's mother's suicide. She helps Yuki prepare herself for the changes that are about to come upon her. It is also Aya who takes Yuki and raises her during the year between Yuki's mother's death and her father's remarriage. Aya be-comes a cross between a big sister and a mother figure for Yuki. Aya ends up marrying a former friend of Yuki's mother.

Mr. Kimura

Mr. Kimura is an old schoolmate of Yuki's mother, Shizuko. He appears in a flashback when Yuki recalls seeing her mother express happiness in his presence. At one point in Shizuko's life, it is insinuated, Shizuko may have considered divorc-ing her husband for Mr. Kimura. However, ac-cording to Japanese tradition, Yuki's father could have contested, thus prohibiting Shizuko custody of Yuki had Shizuko gone through with the divorce.

Mr. Kimura appears later in the story when he comes to the house to offer his condolences to Yuki upon her mother's death. It is at that time that he meets Aya, Yuki's aunt. The two form a relation-ship and eventually announce their plans to marry.

Yuki is allowed to attend the wedding, and it is Mr. Kimura who comes to Yuki after she be-comes angry at the wedding dinner table. Mr. Kimura is a sensitive man, and he is able to talk intelligently to Yuki. He confesses to Yuki that he too once thought that sharing love with someone else might not be worth all the pain and confusion. However, he tells her that he finally came to the conclusion that it is better to experience love and its pain than not to experience love at all and that it is worth all the risks involved.

Masa

Masa is Yuki's maternal grandmother. Al-though there are times when she becomes very angry with her grandmother, Yuki loves Masa very much. Although her father prohibits Yuki from vis-iting her grandmother very often, Yuki has a lot of memories of spending summers with her mother at Masa's house. It is not too difficult for Yuki to maintain a close relationship with Masa despite how infrequently they are allowed to spend time together.

Masa is very disturbed by her daughter's death. She says that it is very unfair for a daughter to die before her parents. Masa is a traditional Japanese person. She is intelligent and rather open-minded. However, she does not always understand Yuki's emotional outbursts or the way Yuki always seems to get into trouble, such as when she was a child and climbed up a tall tree and got stuck there, or like the time she ran through a glass door in her at-tempts to catch an insect. Although Yuki is often angry with Masa, Masa is very forgiving.

When Yuki goes away to college, it is to Masa's home that she returns when she needs to make contact with her familial roots. At one point, Masa gives Yuki all her old kimonos so that Yuki can cut the material and make other types of gar-ments. It is through Masa that Yuki introduces her boyfriend to the family.

Mrs. Murai

Mrs. Murai is Sachiko's mother. Sachiko is a running mate of Yuki's. Mrs. Murai is skeptical of Yuki when she finds out that Yuki's mother died under suspicious circumstances. It is suggested that Mrs. Murai tells Sachiko to end her relationship with Yuki.

Sachiko Murai

Sachiko is one year older than Yuki and attends a different school, but the two girls meet at a sporting event and become friends. They get together every Sunday to run. Sachiko teases Yuki for being so innocent about boys. She also encourages Yuki's confidence in herself. At the end of the summer, Sachiko makes excuses to end her friendship with Yuki.

Isamu Nagano

Isamu is the first boyfriend that Yuki has. Isamu meets Yuki in college. He is a photographer and teaches Yuki how to capture light on film. Isamu is very sensitive and his affections are apparent. He appears at the end of the story and represents Yuki's opening her emotions and trusting someone.

Hanae Okuda

Hanae is Yuki's stepmother. Hanae had a long affair with Yuki's father while he was still married to Shizuko. She is a small-minded person without much education. She is very petty, dictatorial, sneaky, and jealous. She brings havoc into Yuki's life.

Hanae has no need of Yuki and rarely speaks to her unless it is to scold her. She has no interest in what Yuki is doing at school. Hanae is only interested in what the neighbors think, so she keeps her house spotless, lies to cover social errors, and berates Yuki's blunt honesty.

Hanae is told by her doctors that she will never have a child. She is too old, they say, and Hanae blames Yuki's father for making her wait so long before he would consent to get her pregnant. Hanae does not understand Yuki or Yuki's mother; neither does she comprehend the close relationship between the mother and the daughter. In an attempt to destroy Yuki's memories of her mother, Hanae tries to rid the house of everything that Shizuko ever bought or made. Hanae is not even happy with Yuki's father. She is constantly arguing with him about how careless he is with Yuki in disciplining her.

Hideki Okuda

Hideki is Yuki's father. It is hard to understand Hideki. He rarely shows his emotions, except when he is angry with Yuki, which is often. Other than when he is angry, he usually remains silent. Hideki refuses to allow Yuki to visit her mother's relatives. He never goes to any of Yuki's school events. Although he knows that Yuki is struggling to pay for her college, he never offers to help her. At one time, Hideki appears to have been in love with Shizuko. There is a slight glimpse into his emotions for his first wife when he finds her sketchbook, which Hanae has asked him to burn. Eventually, Hideki sends the sketchbook to Yuki, but he does not include a note explaining his actions.

Shizuko Okuda

Shizuko is Yuki's mother. Although she commits suicide in the first chapter, her presence is felt throughout the novel. Shizuko was an artist. She loved colors and emotions. She loved flowers and things that were different. She encouraged Yuki to be different but often worried about her at school because she was so different.

It is suggested that Shizuko suffered from depression. There are several possibilities for what might have caused this. She was very different from the traditional Japanese woman of her time. She liked to wear vivid colors, whereas her peers wore muted tones. She refused an arranged marriage that her mother had set up with a wealthy family. She moved away from her family and found a job and a man that she thought she could love. She was enthralled with the unusual and shopped at art fairs rather than at department stores. These characteristics set her apart, making her an outsider in her culture, much as Yuki becomes.

Shizuko also knew that her husband was having an affair. She suffered in silence, staying with the marriage even though her husband was seldom home, because she did not want to take the chance that she might lose her child in a custody battle. Shizuko thought it was better, in the end, that she take her own life, thus ridding Yuki of her mother's depressive moods.

Yuki Okuda

Yuki is the protagonist of the story. She is twelve years old when the story opens and she finds her mother dead on the kitchen floor. Yuki is a very bright and very open young woman. She has trouble dealing with the hypocrisy that she sees around her. Yuki, like her mother, is an artist with a flare for the unusual. This places her outside of her traditional culture, which includes most of her peers.

Yuki suffers through most of her pubescent years because of her mother's death. She does not have anyone who encourages or counsels her. She has no one to turn to when she tries to sort out her emotions. Her father does not support her in any way except that he provides her with a roof over her head and food in the refrigerator.

Most of the time, Yuki suppresses her emotions. However, because she holds in the way she feels, she also has emotional outbursts. She lashes out at everyone around her, including her grandparents whom she loves. She tries to form friendships with her peers, but she is lacking social skills. Her blunt honesty often gets her in trouble.

Yuki is a gifted child in many different ways. She is intelligent and does well at school. Her artistic skills are well known. She is also a talented athlete. Instead of succumbing to the difficulties that face her, Yuki takes the talents and gifts that she has and finds a way out of her predicaments. She fights for her rights and finds a way to attend the college she chooses. By the end of the story, she takes the final step in facing her emotions when she decides to take a chance on learning to love Isamu.

Tadashi

Tadashi is the grandson of Masa and Takeo and a cousin of Yuki's. He appears in the epilogue and represents the continuity of life.

Takeo

Takeo is Yuki's maternal grandfather. He and Masa are husband and wife. Takeo's strongest moment in the story is when he tries to get Yuki to eat while she is visiting his house. When Takeo comes from the garden with a basket full of strawberries, he falls and hurts himself. This makes Yuki aware of how much she cares for her grandfather. Soon after this incident, Takeo dies.

Miss Uozumi

Miss Uozumi is Yuki's piano teacher. Although she never appears in the story, it is because of her tardiness on the day of Yuki's mother's suicide that Yuki does not come home until her mother is dead. Throughout the story, Yuki thinks about what might have happened had Miss Uozumi held the piano lesson on time.

Themes

Death

Either actual death or reference to death is a recurring theme in this story. The novel begins with the suicide of Shizuko, Yuki's mother; this suicide flavors the rest of the story, hanging over all of the events of Yuki's life. Because of her mother's death, Yuki is pushed deeper and deeper into herself. Her mother, who was an artist, encouraged Yuki to think independently. This attitude, however, did not provide Yuki with the skills to deal with the Japanese culture, which disapproved of the concept of the individual. Thus, upon her mother's death, a great support for Yuki's personality also died.

Toward the end of the story, Yuki's grandfather dies. It is at her maternal grandparents' home that Yuki receives the most positive sense of family life. So the death of her grandfather represents yet one more instance where she loses love in her life.

Tradition versus Nonconformity

The timing of this novel corresponds to the budding of women's lib in Japan. The liberation movement in Japan, especially in comparison to the revolution in the United States, is subtle, thus making Yuki's actions and thoughts appear radical.

The traditional role of the woman is very clearly defined in Japan. From the type of clothes she wears and the kind of makeup she applies to her face to the courses she studies if she should decide to go to college, all are dictated to her through a long tradition of social rules. Despite her intelligence, skills, or natural talents, she is expected to marry by a certain age, to give up her profession, and to focus all her efforts on the welfare of her husband and her children. She is also expected to maintain social grace, which often means that she does not express her true feelings.

In *Shizuko's Daughter*, Yuki breaks almost every traditional social rule. She does not understand accepting things just because that is what every other woman has done for thousands of years. She wears brightly colored clothes of original patterns that her artistic mother makes for her. She insists on her right to observe her inclination toward vegetarianism. When she is angry, she speaks her mind. If someone lies to her, she makes him or her aware that she knows the truth is not being told. At the wedding of her father and stepmother, Yuki, during the ceremony of communal sharing of the sake, drops the bowl on purpose to make her feelings toward her father's marriage known. In other

Topics for Further Study

- Shizuko, the mother in Mori's *Shizuko's Daughter*, suffered from depression. Write a research paper on the topic of depression. What are some contemporary causes of depression, and what are the medical and therapeutic treatments for this disease? Also look into the social implications of depression. Are there any taboos on the discussion of this disease? What are the personal ramifications of depression in terms of its affect on family members?

- Suicide is a topic that has been covered in many different literary works. Find at least two poems or one other novel or short story that deals with this topic and compare them to *Shizuko's Daughter*. Suggestions include some of Sylvia Plath's poems, Susanna Kaysen's book, *Girl Interrupted*, and William Styron's memoir, *Darkness Visible*.

- Research the traditional role of Japanese women. Has that role changed since World War II? How has Western culture affected Japanese women? How do the lives of women living in the United States compare with the lives of Japanese women?

- Read Kyoko Mori's memoir *The Dream of Water*, which offers more insight into the background from which her novel was written. Then write a poem to Mori, expressing your feelings about one of the main topics that has ruled her life; it could be based on her mother's suicide, her father's or her stepmother's mistreatment of her, or the alienation that Mori has felt as an outsider from her traditional and inherited culture.

words, Yuki fights for her independence, her sense of the individual, something that goes against the grain of Japanese traditions.

Loss

Through death, Yuki loses her mother. But it is more than just her mother that is lost; Yuki also loses her emotional support, her childhood, her op-

timism, and possibly her closest friend. When her father remarries, Yuki must give up her summers with her maternal relatives. Eventually, her stepmother throws away all of Yuki's clothes, including the ones that Shizuko made for her. Yuki's stepmother replaces everything in the house that represents Shizuko, from the handcrafted dinner plates and bowls to the boxes in which Shizuko saved little mementos from Yuki's childhood.

Yuki acknowledges her tremendous loss upon her mother's death when she shuts herself into her clothes closet. This event symbolizes her eventual closure to the world. With her mother alive, she was encouraged to be different. Having lost her mother, she has also lost her source of confidence. She knows that she is alone. In the dark closet, even though Yuki reaches up to touch the bright clothes, she can no longer see the colors.

With the loss of her mother's love, Yuki also loses her sense of humor. In its place are anger, frustration, and bitterness. While children her age giggle at frivolous things, Yuki lives in a solitary world that is cold and painful. She must learn to take care of herself. Inside her head she must recreate her mother's voice, encouraging her to go on. These tactics are precarious, at best, and often Yuki's anger boils over the top as she lashes out, unable to keep her feelings inside of her. She has lost her buffer. She has no place to go and no person to turn to for help in understanding her emotions.

Style

Setting

Shizuko's Daughter is set in Kobe, a large city on Japan's main island, Honshu. Kobe, a major industrial and cultural center of Japan, is situated on a narrow strip of land that sits between the Inland Sea and a range of mountains. In the course of the story, two other cities are mentioned, Himeji, a much smaller city also located on the main island, and Nagasaki, located on the southernmost island of Kyushu.

Kobe is where most of the story occurs. It is where Yuki, the protagonist, spends most of her time. It is where she lives until she goes away to college. Himeji exists in a more rural environment, and it is Yuki's mother's hometown. It is to Himeji that Yuki goes when she visits her maternal grandparents. Nagasaki is where Yuki goes when she leaves home to attend college. Nagasaki is located on a different island than Kobe, thus giving Yuki a sense of detachment or release from her father and stepmother who still live in Kobe.

As the story is set in Japan, the story reflects the traditional customs of that culture. To understand the emphasis on particular colors in reference to clothes, the reader has to grasp the concept of conformity that is of great importance in Japan. Fitting in without making a spectacle of oneself is very important in the Japanese culture. Yuki's clothes are clearly not clothes that fit in. The role of women in Japanese marriage must also be understood. First there is the accepted practice in Japan of husbands having extramarital affairs. Then there is (more so during the 1970s setting of this story than in more recent times) the social stigma that makes divorce an almost impossible choice. Adding to this is the power that a husband has to claim his offspring should his wife insist on leaving him. Yuki's father also has the right to insist that Yuki not visit her maternal relatives after Shizuko's suicide. This decision is observed by the rest of the family as a normal, accepted practice.

Point of View

Shizuko's Daughter is told through a third person narrator, as if someone were watching what was happening and then relating it to the reading audience. This third person narrator switches point of view from chapter to chapter, sometimes telling the story through the thoughts and vision of Shizuko (Yuki's mother), as in the first chapter, sometimes making observations through Masa (Yuki's grandmother), as in the last chapter. However, most of the story is told by the third person narrator observing life, as well as the internal dialogue, as Yuki expresses it.

Flashback

Most of the chapters in this book begin with the present tense, with the narrator discussing what is happening at that particular moment. It is through the present event that the narrator then remembers something from the past. In this way, the author is able to fill in the details that lead up to the present moment. For instance, since Yuki's mother dies in the first chapter, the narrator, through flashback scenes, relates to the reader the possible reasons for her depression and subsequent suicide. Allowing the audience to view past events helps readers understand Yuki's emotional outbursts, facilitating empathy for the protagonist.

Journal Entries

Although this story is not written in a first person point of view, the use of dates as part of the title of each chapter gives the feeling that this story is written as if it were a journal. Despite the fact that the third person narrator switches from one character to another in various chapters, the specific dates carry over, thus providing a sense that there is some omniscient narrator who is recording the events in a special, universal journal. In this way, the story reads as if it were fact, an actual occurrence.

Historical Context

Japanese Women—Education and Employment

With the booming economy that Japan experienced in the 1960s and 1970s, the role of women saw, in Japanese terms, dramatic changes. Women, who traditionally were married young and stayed home to rear the children, were now finding jobs as the demand for goods and materials soared. Women were beginning to postpone marriage and to take their college education more seriously. There was also a budding awareness of women's rights.

The major role for women in Japan has been, and still remains, that of wife and mother. However, during the United Nations Decade for Women (1975–1985), three legal changes occurred in Japan. First, Japanese women were allowed to pass their nationality to their children (previously this had been a privilege given only to men); second, widows could inherit a larger share of their deceased husband's property; and finally, Japan adopted an Equal Employment Opportunity law.

Before the Equal Employment Opportunity law was passed, most companies would not even consider hiring women who had a degree from a four-year university. It was understood that these women, by the time they reached the age of twenty-five, would be married. Once married, the women would retire from the workforce to stay home, give birth, and raise the children. So it was considered a better economic practice to hire women with only a high school or junior college education. Although the law was passed, Japan's workforce continues to be predominantly male, according to Jane Condon in her article "The Quiet Revolution: Changing Roles of Women," with the largest group of working women still remaining what is called "office ladies" or "office flowers," women who mostly run errands and answer phones.

Japanese Women—Marriage and Children

In Japan there is a saying, writes Condon, "Women are like a Christmas cake—no good after the twenty-fifth." This refers to the belief that all women should be married before they reach the age of twenty-five. If they aren't, pressure is applied by family, friends, and even fellow employees or supervisors. Although the social customs of arranged marriages are not as strict as they once were (only in 1947 did women and men win the right to marriage by mutual consent), a modern version of matchmaking still occurs in what is estimated as one-fourth of all marriages.

Whether Japanese women work or not, the responsibility of raising the children solely rests on the woman's shoulders. In the end, when the children finally leave home, how they function in society is seen as either a credit or a failure on the part of the mother. If a child does well in school and is accepted into the better colleges, it is because the mother has trained the child properly.

Although divorce rates are rising in Japan, there continue to be social pressures on the couple to stay together for the sake of their children. Divorce, especially for the Japanese woman, is considered a social stigma. Because of the fact that few companies rehire women who once quit their jobs to be married and have children and that alimony support is nominal, the economic ramifications of divorce are severe for women.

Japanese Women—Suicide and Depression

Suicide in Japan has a long tradition. The ceremonial *hara-kiri* was performed historically when someone committed what they thought was an unforgivable social error. In other situations, Japanese warriors committed suicide that symbolized loyalty or sacrifice. However, in modern times, much like in other countries around the world, suicide is most often committed due to severe depression.

During the 1950s, Japan ranked within the top five countries with the highest suicide rates in the world. Although this ranking has dropped over the years, the number of women committing suicide has risen. The number one reason for female suicide is depression. In Japan, despite its modern fa-cade, there remain social taboos on seeking help from mental health professionals. To go to a psychiatrist is to admit that one is crazy.

Japanese women often receive mixed messages from their society. The traditional rules dictate that a woman marry, stay home, and raise children, whereas the modern, technological world encourages a woman to be bold and go out into the world and work hard in college so she can partake in the business world. However, if a woman decides to pursue a profession and delay her marriage, she is ostracized. If, on the other hand, she pursues a college education but retires from the business world when she marries, she feels that she has wasted all her efforts. Managing a house and rearing children, with modern devices available to help her, do not consume as much of her time and effort as they might have for her grandmother. Since business does not look favorably upon women who want to return to work after their children are in school, the only outlet women find are school-related events such as membership in the local PTA or taking on a somewhat unfulfilling part-time job. If a woman should pursue this route, she must not only work outside of her home, but she must also continue full responsibility of the home and the children, as the husband is not required to share in domestic chores.

Added to these pressures are social traditions that demand that a woman "look the other way" in relation to her husband's extramarital affairs. In addition, men who want to climb the economic ladder are required not only to work long hours but also to socialize after work, often drinking until late and returning home exhausted. These factors create pressures in a marriage, leaving many women either feeling unfulfilled or overwhelmed with domestic detail. Without an outlet, these conditions can lead to depression and eventually suicide.

Critical Overview

Mori's writing has captured the attention of literary reviewers. She has also gained their respect as a writer. Praise comes from a wide range of sources, such as John Philbrook, writing in the *School Library Journal*, who describes Mori's writing as "beautiful and sensitive prose [that] evokes a world of pungent memories and harsh realities." *Kirkus Reviews* claims that *Shizuko's Daughter* is a "beautifully written book about a bitterly painful coming of age" and concludes that her book marks a

A street in Kobe, Japan, where the novel is set

"splendid debut." Following in this same line of praise, the *Horn Book Magazine*'s Nancy Vasilakis describes Mori's first published book as a "skillfully structured novel." Vasilakis then goes on to state, "Mori paints beautiful pictures with words, creating visual images that can be as haunting and elliptical as poetry." Rounding out this criticism of Mori's first published writing is a *Publisher's Weekly* review that declares Mori's book to be a "quietly moving novel" that depicts "keen imagery," as Mori pays attention to details that "produce an emotionally and culturally rich tale tracing the evolution of despair into hope."

Mori has published several books since *Shizuko's Daughter*, and the reviews continue to come out in her favor. Hazel Rochman, writing in *Booklist*, states that in Mori's second young adult novel, *One Bird*, "Mori writes with subtlety and drama." Mori's memoir, *The Dream of Water*, published in 1994, is "beautifully written,"according to a *Publishers Weekly* reviewer. Mori's second book of memories, *Polite Lies: On Being a Woman Caught Between Cultures*, is reviewed in *Booklist* where it states that Mori "sensitively examines" the cultural differences between Japan and the United States through the use of "exquisite language." Kay Meredith Dusheck, writing in the *Library Journal*, states that Mori's second memoir shows "the in-

sight evident" in her previous works and describes this book as a "strong collection [that] binds one woman's old country with her new one."

As Mori continues to publish, the reviews about her books continue to assure her that she is doing a great job. Although she is sometimes criticized for ruminating over the same themes in most of her works—those of separation, loneliness, and loss—her ability to write gracefully and simply is never in question.

Criticism

Joyce Hart

Hart has degrees in English literature and creative writing and is a published writer of literary themes. In this essay, Hart ponders the symbolic significance of the last chapter, or epilogue, of Mori's novel.

Only two sections out of the sixteen that make up Kyoko Mori's novel *Shizuko's Daughter* are written without the appearance of the protagonist, Yuki: the first chapter, during which Yuki's mother commits suicide, and the last, referred to as the epilogue. Although it is quite evident why Mori might

> The abrupt transition of the epilogue may be unsettling, leaving the reader wondering why the protagonist has disappeared. However, upon closer reading, the symbolism becomes evident, allowing the reader to conclude that the story has come to a perfect ending."

have chosen not to include Yuki in the chapter about her mother's final moments, it is curious that she decided, after devoting all the other chapters to her protagonist, not to include Yuki in the epilogue. Instead, the focus in the last chapter is on the character Masa, Yuki's grandmother. It is through Masa's vision and reflection that the novel ends. The abrupt transition of the epilogue may be unsettling, leaving the reader wondering why the protagonist has disappeared. However, upon closer reading, the symbolism becomes evident, allowing the reader to conclude that the story has come to a perfect ending.

The epilogue begins on the morning of Yuki's grandmother's seventy-fifth birthday. Masa is Yuki's maternal grandmother, the adult who, more clearly than any other character, represents a loving parental figure for Yuki. Upon awaking on her birthday, Masa's vision first takes in the family altar. This altar is a shrine to all her ancestors and relatives who have died before her. Besides having lost her husband, Masa has also lost some of her children, among them Yuki's mother. The narrator describes Masa's thoughts as she looks at the altar and remembers other mornings when she ritualistically placed offerings on the altar. When she married her husband, the ancestors to whom she made offerings were like "a large white cloud," Masa remembers. In other words, when she was young, the word *ancestors* was more or less an abstract concept that covered intangible feelings. However, now that she is seventy-five, having lived a long life, faces and memories are attached to that word.

In particular, she thinks specifically about her husband, Takeo, and her daughter, Shizuko.

By creating this scene, Mori has brought her story full circle. Having begun with the death of Shizuko and then having made Masa, at the end, reflect on the death of her daughter brings the reader back to the beginning of the story. Mori doesn't stop there, however. She not only takes the reader back to the opening events, but she also encourages the reader to reflect on the entire passage of the story from beginning to end. By having Masa think about the two major deaths in Mori's tale, the suicide of Yuki's mother and the death of Yuki's grandfather (which occurs near the end of the novel), the reader travels, via Masa's thoughts, from the events of the opening pages of this book through all but the final passages. In this way, in just the first two paragraphs of the epilogue, Mori has created a short but concise summary of her story. She does not, however, conclude her story there.

There is something else going on in the epilogue. The tone of this segment, although it resounds with the idea of death, reflects something more uplifting, more positive. Throughout the preceding chapters of the novel, the overall tenor is that of sadness, loneliness, frustration, and anger. However, here, in the epilogue, a sense of rebirth and hope exists.

In the first sentences of this final section, Mori has Masa wake up to music and "painted images of Buddha in his various manifestations." Both music and the Buddha can be said to represent the full spectrum of emotions behind the variety of challenges that life presents. Music is played at weddings as well as at funerals, for instance. In addition, as if to emphasize that there are several ways to look at the circumstances of life, Mori refers not just to a single version of the Buddha but rather to all his various expressions; thus, the mood of this novel has changed, the focus has altered, and it is hinted that rather than looking at life through a haze of gloom, this chapter is going to take on some other aspect. Just as Masa has "taken to sleeping in the family room" since her husband died so that she can "forget momentarily" that he no longer is there with her, Mori, too, changes her point of reference.

Continuing with this theme of change, Mori has Masa rise from her bed, and, as the grandmother folds her futon, she gazes at its quilted cover. The quilt has been made from many different kimonos that her children wore when they were children, when they were teenagers, and when they were young adults. This leads Masa to remember other kimonos, too. The last time Yuki visited her, Masa had given her granddaughter some of her old kimonos, which Yuki then took back to school with her and transformed into vests. Taking these old materials (as well as the memories surrounding them) and turning them into something else more useful symbolizes the changes that Mori is attempting to relate. Mori also has Yuki send a photograph to Masa, showing off the new vests she has made. "I wanted to wear the same things you did," Yuki writes to her grandmother, "only in a different way."

Masa next prepares herself for the arrival of her grandson Tadashi. Upon mentioning the child's name, Mori makes a connection between Tadashi and Yuki, by having Masa remember, "Yuki was the only person he seemed to like from the first time he saw her." Tadashi is a sullen child. His moods, much like Yuki's throughout the previous chapters, are heavy and mournful. He is also prone to fighting children his age, and that is why his grandmother must watch him while his mother goes to work. At first, when Tadashi arrives, the mood of death prevails.

While Masa works in the garden, Tadashi catches tiny frogs and places them inside a tightly sealed jar where they wait for their imminent suffocation. Masa tries to distract him from his endeavors when she suggests that he help her clear the garden by pretending the weeds are enemy soldiers whom Tadashi must decapitate. This mood shifts when Tadashi takes a nap and "his mouth, so often distorted sullenly while he was awake, relaxed in his sleep and his face was flushed from the morning in the sun." At this point, Masa looks over at the jar full of frogs. She feels sorry for them and, tired of the thought of death, she opens the lid and, while Tadashi sleeps, releases the frogs.

From this point, the epilogue turns to symbols of birth. First, Masa sees a cicada, which has just risen from the earth. Having cast away its larval shell, it is drying its new form on the screen of one of Masa's windows. Later, when Masa lies down for a nap, she thinks about another of her birthdays, when Shizuko was still alive. Her daughter had brought her flowers and a new kimono made of silk that Shizuko had wrapped around her mother in soft layers "like a cocoon." These images of rebirth and transformation stand in stark contrast to the earlier images of death and sadness. They are positive and hopeful symbols that lead to the final scene.

Masa awakens from her nap to the noise of Tadashi running up the steps of an old wooden slide that Masa's husband made many years previously for her own small children. Tadashi had been afraid of the slide, concerned that it might give him splinters and then worried that he was too big for the slide and might break it. Before taking his nap, Masa encouraged Tadashi to try out the slide, which he did once before going into the house. As the story ends, however, Tadashi is filled with enthusiasm, running and sliding down the slide "in an almost frenzied circle of movement." Watching him, Masa sees all her children running and sliding, "laughing and chattering." The epilogue ends with Masa laughing and crying "copious tears, until her chest and shoulders ached from joy."

It is through this scene that Mori ends her story. Here is a child (who could represent Yuki, in particular, or the future, in general), who has overcome his fear and, at least momentarily, his anger and sorrow. The circle of children, like the circle from birth to death, the circle from the beginning of the story to its culmination, is capable of causing a full range of emotions. Sometimes those emotions become so entangled that it is hard to sort them out, to separate them. Often they are so closely related that they all come out at the same time in the form of tears. In the epilogue, Mori appears to be telling her readers (and maybe even reminding herself) that even though life may contain many difficult challenges, people should not give up hope. It is possible that she could not convey this message to Yuki whom she may have believed still had to learn this lesson. Masa, on the other hand, who has lived through many more experiences and who is preparing for her own death, has the wisdom that is required to transform even death into something as positive as peace. It is on that note that the novel ends, presenting a conclusion that rises above depressing emotions and offering an absolute contrast to the opening tragic scene, thus giving the overall effect of a perfectly balanced rhythm.

Source: Joyce Hart, Critical Essay on *Shizuko's Daughter*, in *Novels for Students*, The Gale Group, 2002.

Douglas Dupler

Dupler has published numerous essays and has taught college English. In this essay, Dupler shows how symbolism is related to memory and time in a novel.

For as long as novels have been written, novelists have grappled with the issue of how to

> In this novel, objects in nature serve to symbolize past events and provide a backdrop for the emotions of the characters."

portray the passage of time in their stories. In the nineteenth century, novelists frequently used the epic form of the novel, creating sweeping stories that take place over long expanses of time with actions occurring mainly in chronological order. This form was used by authors such as Charles Dickens, Leo Tolstoy, Jane Austen, and countless others. Novelists have also experimented with other ways of dealing with time in novels. In the early twentieth century, James Joyce wrote a long, complex story that takes place in only one day, in the landmark modern novel, *Ulysses*. Joyce told his story with the realization that people, at any moment, have access to vast portions of time through the process of memory and recollection. Kyoko Mori's novel, *Shizuko's Daughter*, has aspects of both of these ways of dealing with time in storytelling. This novel proceeds chronologically from beginning to end, showing various points in the six years that pass in the lives of the main characters. Within this linear passage of time, the characters are also able to move around in time, as they remember past events.

Shizuko's Daughter begins with its most affecting event: Shizuko, an unhappy wife and mother, commits suicide. The first chapter begins with a date, "March 1969," as do the remainder of the chapters, which proceed chronologically and inform the reader of the passage of time. The novel is told from a third-person point of view, which allows insights into the thoughts and memories of the characters. The structure of the novel relies on narrative flashbacks to inform the reader of the depth of experience and emotions of the main characters. These flashbacks are triggered by objects that symbolize events of the past.

As Shizuko acts out her tragedy in the first scene, many of the important symbols of the following story are introduced. First, there is nature, which serves as a backdrop and an influence for the characters and their emotions. Dreamily, Shizuko thinks of "white cherry blossom petals that were blowing about in the wind." She remembers the "rainy morning" of her mother-in-law's death, while the smell of gas "reminded her of the tiny yellow flowering weeds that had grown near her parents' house." In this first scene, there are also several references to clothing, such as Yuki's "pink spring dress," and the pieces of cloth from Yuki's new skirt, which remind her of "butterfly wings." Near her end, Shizuko imagines Yuki in this new skirt, which would flutter in the wind "like the sail of a new ship." Throughout the remainder of the novel, these particular symbols—nature, flowers, and clothing—appear again and again, serving as markers that connect the present moment of the characters to this major emotional event of the past.

One day after her mother's death, clothing begins to symbolize the drastic change that has just occurred in Yuki's life. Her Aunt Aya begins folding her mother's clothes, which "hung limp," representing death. Yuki has also seen the clothing for the new dress her mother had been making, which leads her to question why the suicide happened. Things no longer fit correctly in Yuki's world, down to the fact that she cannot pick the correct clothes for the funeral. As her aunt goes through her clothes to find an appropriate dress, Yuki feels "utterly humiliated." Yuki understands that her life has irrevocably changed when she cannot bring herself to zip up her new dress, and she finally collapses in her closet of clothes. A year later, at her father's wedding, Yuki is still plagued by this ill-fitting event: the dress she wears makes her itch. Throughout the rest of the story, clothing remains a central symbol connecting the present to the past, and Yuki saves the clothing her mother had made for her until the very end. Yuki accesses the clothing when she needs to sort through her memories.

In this novel, objects in nature serve to symbolize past events and provide a backdrop for the emotions of the characters. In recalling an important conversation with her mother before her suicide, Yuki thinks of the rain, which "was coming down with enough force to shatter the fragile cups of flowers." These memories have shattered the innocence of Yuki. Flowers play a particularly symbolic role in the novel. During her father's wedding, Yuki can "almost smell the wisteria blossoms," which makes her remember her mother and question her father. She wants to ask him: "Can't you remember . . . the scent of flowers and

What Do I Read Next?

- Mori has written two memoirs. The first one, published in 1995, is *The Dream of Water*. This memoir covers Mori's trip back to Japan, thirteen years after moving to the United States. As Mori travels back to her homeland, she also travels back through her memories, many of the same memories that triggered her writing the novel *Shizuko's Daughter*. Although the novel and memoir differ slightly from one another, the reader is given a fuller and even more dramatic glimpse into the psychological challenges that Mori has faced in coming to grips with her mother's suicide, her father's callous response to her, and her stepmother's immature attempts to keep Mori disconnected from her maternal relatives.

- Mori's second memoir, *Polite Lies: On Being a Woman Caught between Cultures* (1997), includes twelve essays that deal with Mori's observations of the role of women as seen through her experiences with her native Japanese culture and her adopted American culture. She writes about the effects of language and social customs, the role of women in the family, how women relate to their bodies, and how women in both cultures deal with their drive to improve their status through education and professional experience.

- Another novel written by Mori is called *One Bird* (1995). It tells the story of a teenage girl whose mother decides to divorce her father and return to her family's village. According to Japanese tradition, this estranges the mother from her daughter, as her husband forbids any contact between the two. The story is written as if Mori is thinking through the possibilities of what might have happened if her own mother had not committed suicide but had only physically removed herself from her husband. In other words, this novel is a different take on the circumstances of her first book, *Shizuko's Daughter*.

- *Walk Two Moons* (1994), by Sharon Creech, is a Newberry Medal winner and tells the story of a teenage girl's attempts to find her mother who has suddenly disappeared. As the young protagonist travels to Idaho with her grandparents, she exposes her hidden emotions about the loss of her mother by telling a story of a friend who has gone through similar experiences. Although the topic of the story is sad, the grandparents offer a loving and humorous touch. This is a story about loss and the rites of passage into adulthood.

- A collection of poems compiled from across many different cultures of the world and focused on the theme of loneliness, *Pierced by a Ray of Sun: Poems about the Times We Feel Alone* (1995) is a great companion to anyone who has ever felt as if he or she were the only person alive. This collection contains beautifully crafted poems from masters such as May Sarton, Emily Dickinson, Adrienne Rich, Carl Sandburg, and Rainer Maria Rilke. The variety of poetic voices offers inspiration and hope during times of despair and sadness.

- Joy Kogawa's *Obasan* (1982) tells the story of a young woman living in Canada whose mother returns to Japan to visit her family right before the attack on Pearl Harbor. Because of this incident, the mother is trapped in Japan and cannot return to her family. The young girl, along with the remaining members of her family, is then forced to move to a relocation camp until the end of the war. The story is told in reflection and covers her feelings of loss and the mistreatment of Japanese people during World War II.

- If you have ever considered writing your own memoir, a good place to start might be to read Denis Ledoux's *Turning Memories into Memoirs: A Handbook for Writing Lifestories*. Ledoux doesn't do all the work for the writer, but his book is capable of heading any potential memoir author in the right direction. He offers insight and inspiration for writers attempting to overcome the fears and challenges of delving into old memories to create a good book.

A Japanese woman in traditional clothing—a tradition Yuki rebels against

green leaves" that reminds her so much of her mother. In another scene, Yuki recalls working with flowers alongside her mother. Her mother had said, "I always wondered if the dead people can really smell those flowers," which made Yuki feel "a chill down her back," so flowers, for Yuki, are associated with fear and death. The symbolism of the flowers has many layers. The chrysanthemums smell like funerals. The violas are hardy plants that "bloom and multiply on their own," just as Shizuko claims Yuki would do if she were no longer alive. Yuki associates irises with guilt, because she had thought of irises when her mother asked her if Yuki could survive without her. Whenever Yuki is plagued by the thought of not having said redeeming words to her mother, she thinks of irises: "When the irises faded, they shriveled into themselves like punctured balloons and dried up." When Yuki understands the difficulty of living with grief, she takes strength in the flowers, remembering that: "Her mother was right about the flowers. They were hardy."

The use of flowers as symbolism continues throughout the novel. When Yuki meets Sachiko and her mother during a track meet, flowers serve as pointers to memories of her own mother. Yuki suddenly remembers that "her mother had shown

her how to pick an azalea blossom." Yuki's memories are still overwhelming at this point in the story; on the flowers "there were spots of intense sweetness" and Yuki wishes she could "suffocate with their sweetness." Flowers also symbolize changes to the characters in the story, or reflect upon their mental states. When Yuki senses her friendship with Sachiko is fading, she notices that "petals had begun to curl at the edges. Soon, the frost would break them into a pile of broken stems."

Symbolism also plays a part in describing the subtle transitions that characters undergo in the novel. In her school, Yuki is afraid of dissecting frogs in science class, thinking, "it's wrong to cut open something," and claiming she already knows what she'll "find inside." On a symbolic level, this is another way for her to say that she has been avoiding going inside herself. It is at this point in the story that Yuki begins her own healing work of coming to terms with her hidden memories and with her mother's death. She has decided to begin sketching pictures of the clothes that her mother had made for her. She goes at this sketching project with energy because "she didn't want to forget anything." Moments later, Yuki confronts another fear, by stealing the jar of dead frogs from the science room, which have a smell that "reminded her of standing outside the crematorium while her mother's body was burned." Releasing the dead frogs from the jar is the same as releasing her own bottled-up memories; she is forced to confront the things that have been closed off for so long. It is interesting that one of the scenes near the end of the book also uses this same symbol of frogs, only the frogs in the jar are alive, having been found by Masa's grandchild, showing the change from despair to hope that has taken place.

Symbols are also important to other characters remembering their pasts throughout the novel. Yuki's stepmother, Hanae, "couldn't stay in the attic for more than five minutes" without being overwhelmed by unpleasant memories of her secret affair with Yuki's father. Hanae is so plagued by memories that she compulsively cleans and dusts the house, keeping it clear of objects that might trigger recollection. Beneath her compulsion lies the sad thoughts that she cannot have a child, as well as jealousy and anger toward Yuki and her father. Hanae finally breaks down and destroys a set of pottery that Yuki's father had saved for Yuki, one of the last heirlooms left from Yuki's mother. However, it is more than just pottery, on the symbolic level: "broken pieces filled the sink while Hanae counted her grievances against the living and the dead." Yuki's father has "never told Yuki that he was saving the tea set for her." When these characters repress their memories, the symbols for them become intolerable. Hanae also violates Yuki's memory of Shizuko by destroying the clothing that her mother had made for her. These memory cues are so powerful for the characters that they cause violence, such as when Hanae pushes Yuki down the stairs when taking away Yuki's old clothes.

Throughout the novel, Yuki's father, Hideki, is portrayed as distant, silent, and uncaring. One of the only times that he shows feelings for Yuki is near the end of the story, after Yuki has moved out, when he is reluctant to destroy Yuki's belongings. Hideki finally carries out Hanae's request to destroy the boxes; while handling these mementos, he is flooded with memories: of childhood, of Yuki, and of his former wife. He is destroying these items, ultimately, because he is plagued by a "useless sense of guilt." Hideki finds a book of Shizuko's sketches and secretly looks through it. Dried flowers are pressed between the pages and are all that is left of a relationship that was once sweet and filled with living flowers. Reminiscing, Hideki "was staring at the brittle flowers, the memory escaping him and leaving him with nothing but faded ink smudges." The last image of Hideki in the book is one of pain and despair; he can no longer avoid the many symbols that force him to confront his memories and his past.

Just as nature contains symbols that remind the characters of the painful events of the past, nature also displays promising symbolism. Near the end of the novel, Masa thinks to herself that it is "a wonder that the flowers came back every year." This sentence has a dual meaning. The flowers still remind her of Shizuko, as she recalls the lavender that "bloomed profusely" the year after her daughter's death. Memories of this event come back every year. At the same time, these flowers represent renewal, healing, and the indomitable living force of nature. Takeo reaffirms this metaphor, because when "he looked at the irises now, he knew again that Yuki was going to be all right." Despite the tragic event, he realizes that "Yuki had not changed all that much," just like the perennials that appear the same each year. After Yuki hears of Takeo's death, "flowers floated into Yuki's memory," and she, as well, is confronted by symbols of recollection. Nature helps Yuki understand her own healing process, and her own relationship with time, as when she reflects on the persimmon fruit that her grandfather had given her. At first, the "fruit was bitter when it came off the tree," but

"Yuki and her mother would eat them through the winter, reminders of their summer in the country." Nature turns in cycles, and the bitterness of the past can have a purpose and can be transformed.

Yuki's identification with symbols and their relationship with memory has a major effect on her life: she decides to be an artist, a person who works with symbols, emotions, and memories. She is eager to go away to school, "then it would be as though the last six years had never happened." However, as she is packing up her things, Yuki comes to understand that she cannot simply forget the past six years, because her memories are still attached to the objects around her. Yuki has a flashback to a presentation she gave at school on a painting by Monet. Looking at the painting, or the symbols of an artist's memory, Yuki realizes that whatever "was important about the painting could not be put into speech." This realization comes at the same time Yuki decides to leave all her mother's things behind. At last, Yuki comes to terms with the memories that these physical objects symbolize. She no longer has to either avoid or sanctify the objects, because "[t]hese things were not necessary for her to go on remembering." Then she realizes that she and her mother "are moving on," leaving behind "nothing but empty spaces" that are "turning green," or regenerating and renewing once again, just like nature.

In the end, Yuki is living independently at college and getting on with her life. Her interest in photography shows the new relationship she has with objects and memories. Before, she was committed to sketching the symbols that reminded her of her mother, which indicated her need to control the symbols that had such a power over her memory. Her new interest in photography shows a change; she can now confront the present in its clearest terms, and she is committed to facing the world as it is, no longer filtering it through her own perceptions, but "taking pictures of the surrounding light."

Source: Douglas Dupler, Critical Essay on *Shizuko's Daughter*, in *Novels for Students*, The Gale Group, 2002.

Sources

Condon, Jane, "The Quiet Revolution: Changing Roles of Women," in *Video Letter from Japan II: A Young Family*, The Asia Society, 1990, pp. 18–24.

Dusheck, Kay Meredith, Review of *Polite Lies: On Being a Woman Caught between Cultures*, in *Library Journal*, Vol. 122, No. 17, October 15, 1997, p. 79.

Mori, Kyoko, *The Dream of Water*, Ballantine Books, 1995.

———, *Polite Lies*, Ballantine Publishing Group, 1997.

———, "Staying True to the Story," in *The Writer*, Vol. 114, March 2001, p. 26.

Pearl, Nancy, Review of *Polite Lies: On Being a Woman Caught between Cultures*, in *Booklist*, Vol. 94, No. 7, December 1, 1997, pp. 590–91.

Philbrook, John, Review of *Shizuko's Daughter*, in *School Library Journal*, Vol. 39, No. 6, June 1993, p. 132.

Review of *The Dream of Water: A Memoir*, in *Publishers Weekly*, Vol. 241, No. 45, November 7, 1994, p. 54.

Review of *Shizuko's Daughter*, in *Kirkus Reviews*, February 1, 1993.

Review of *Shizuko's Daughter*, in *Publishers Weekly*, Vol. 240, No. 4, January 25, 1993, p. 87.

Rochman, Hazel, Review of *One Bird*, in *Booklist*, Vol. 92, No. 4, October 15, 1995, pp. 396–97.

Vasilakis, Nancy, Review of *Shizuko's Daughter*, in *Horn Book Magazine*, Vol. 69, No. 5, September–October 1993, pp. 603–04.

Further Reading

Fine, Carla, *No Time to Say Goodbye: Surviving the Suicide of a Loved One*, Main Street Books, 1999.

> Fine personally experienced the suicide of someone she loved, and this book reflects the battle that ensued as she tried to cope with her emotions. Using not only her personal experience, but also advice from professionals in the field of mental health, Fine writes about the full range of emotions, including guilt, anger, and confusion, that confronts a person who is forced to experience the death of someone close to him or her, in particular, death by suicide with the complications caused by social taboos on the subject.

Leonard, Linda Schierse, *The Wounded Woman: Healing the Father-Daughter Relationship*, Shambhala Press, 1999.

> As a Jungian analyst, Leonard examines the relationship between daughter and father as a key to self-understanding. Using examples from her own life and those of her clients, Leonard exposes the problems and conflicts that can arise from the bond created in this relationship.

Lippit, Norika Mizuta, ed., *Japanese Women Writers: Twentieth Century Short Fiction (Asia and the Pacific)*, M. E. Sharpe, 1991.

> This is a collection of fourteen short fictional works, translated by the editors, that reveal the range and degree of women writers' participation in modern life and in the historical development of modern Japanese literature. The book is a good overview of the various topics and styles of modern Japanese women writers.

Morley, Patricia A., *The Mountain Is Moving: Japanese Women's Lives*, New York University Press, 1999.

> Morley wraps together current fiction, government data, and interviews of women living in Japan to examine the most relevant issues facing women in that culture. She asks Japanese women to answer tough questions as they reflect on the advantages as well as on the ancient cultural taboos that guide their lives. This is an excellent introduction into what it means to grow up female in Japan.

Shoeless Joe

W. P. Kinsella
1982

Canadian writer W. P. Kinsella's first novel, *Shoeless Joe*, published in Boston in 1982, is an ingenious baseball story that smoothly weaves together fact and fantasy. The narrator, Ray Kinsella, is a baseball fanatic and dreamer who owns a farm in Iowa. One day he hears a mysterious voice saying, "If you build it, he will come." Ray believes this is an instruction to build a baseball field at his farm and that the "he" is his father's hero, Shoeless Joe Jackson, one of the greatest baseball players of all time. Jackson was banned from baseball for life following the Black Sox Scandal of 1919, in which he and seven other players accepted bribes to throw the World Series. From this premise, Kinsella spins his tale full of magic and nostalgia. Shoeless Joe shows up, and Ray continues to pursue his dream, even traveling cross-country to kidnap the reclusive writer J. D. Salinger, who joins Ray in his quest to restore the broken dreams of the past.

Set in idyllic rural Iowa and told in lyrical, poetic, sometimes sentimental prose, *Shoeless Joe* is a story of the power of the imagination and the triumph of love. It is about dreams and hope and trust and the fulfillment of long-buried desires. The dominant note throughout is the characters' consuming love of baseball, which is presented almost as a religion, and is contrasted, favorably, with the spiritual dryness of conventional Christianity.

Shoeless Joe was made into the popular movie *Field of Dreams* in 1989, and for a while the words "If you build it, he will come" became almost as well-known in American popular culture as the

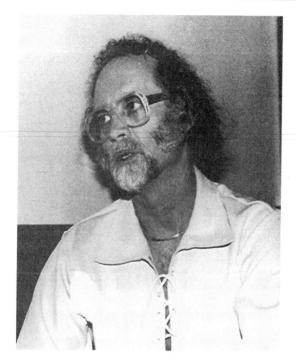

W. P. Kinsella

famous phrase "Say it ain't so, Joe," allegedly spoken by a young fan to Shoeless Joe during the Black Sox Scandal.

Author Biography

William Patrick Kinsella was born on May 25, 1935, on a farm in Edmonton, in northern Alberta, Canada, the son of John Matthew and Olive Mary (Elliott) Kinsella. Kinsella did not attend school until fifth grade, but he caught up quickly and graduated from high school in 1953. After graduation, he worked at a variety of jobs in Edmonton. He was a government clerk, an insurance investigator, and then owner of a restaurant. He did not attend college until he was in his late thirties, receiving a Bachelor of Arts degree from the University of Victoria, British Columbia, in 1974. He then received a Master of Fine Arts degree from the University of Iowa in 1978 and taught English for five years at the University of Calgary, Alberta, from 1978 to 1983.

Kinsella always thought of himself as a writer and published his first story when he was seventeen. His first story collection was *Dance Me Outside* (1977), about the Native North Americans of

the Ermineskin Reservation in Alberta, Canada. *Born Indian* (1981) and *Mocassin Telegraph* (1983) were similar collections. Kinsella's novel *Shoeless Joe* (1982) was his first popular success, and it was made into the movie *Field of Dreams*, starring Kevin Costner, in 1989.

Since 1983, Kinsella has been a full-time writer and has carved a niche for himself as a writer of baseball fiction. In addition to *Shoeless Joe*, he has written several more novels, including *The Iowa Baseball Confederacy* (1986), *Box Socials* (1991), and *The Winter Helen Dropped By* (1995). Story collections focusing on baseball include *Shoeless Joe Jackson Comes to Iowa* (1980), the title story that formed the basis of the novel *Shoeless Joe*, and *The Further Adventures of Slugger McBatt* (1988), which was reissued as *Go the Distance* (1995). Kinsella's most recent publications are *Magic Time* (1998), a novel about a college all-star who revives his baseball career by moving to Iowa, and *Japanese Baseball* (2000), a new collection of baseball stories.

Kinsella was awarded a Houghton Mifflin Literary Fellowship in 1982; he has also received a fiction award from the Canadian Authors Association (1982), a Vancouver writing award (1987), and the Stephen Leacock medal (1987). He was decorated with the Order of Canada in 1994, and in 1987 he was named Author of the Year by the Canadian Library Association.

Kinsella married Mildred Irene Clay in 1965, and they had three children before divorcing in 1978. In 1978, Kinsella married Ann Ilene Knight. They were divorced in 1997. Kinsella married for the third time, in 1999, to Barbara L. Turner.

Plot Summary

Chapter 1: Shoeless Joe Jackson Comes to Iowa

Shoeless Joe begins with the narrator, Ray Kinsella, a young farmer in Iowa, describing how one day when sitting on the verandah of his home, he heard the voice of a ballpark announcer saying, "If you build it, he will come." Ray, who is a highly imaginative man and great lover of baseball, takes this as an instruction to build a baseball field in one of the cornfields at his farm. At first, he builds only a left field. Ray believes that the "he" that the voice refers to is Shoeless Joe Jackson, who gained notoriety for his part in a bribery scandal that marred the 1919 World Series.

One night, baseball players appear on the field, including Shoeless Joe in left field, and Ray settles down to watch him play. In Ray's eyes, the scene is as complete as at any major-league park he has visited. But he notices that Shoeless Joe is the only player who appears to have any substance; the others are shadowy, ghost-like. Ray talks to Shoeless Joe, who tells him about his love of baseball, and Ray promises that he will finish the whole field.

Chapter 2: They Tore Down the Polo Grounds in 1964

Ray finishes building the entire field; it takes him three baseball seasons. One by one, the so-called Unlucky Eight, the Black Sox baseball players who were banned for life in 1920, appear. Now only the right fielder and the catcher are still shadowy. Ray's daughter Karin also has the ability to see the games that take place. Next, Ray hears the baseball announcer say, mysteriously, "Ease his pain." Ray intuitively understands this to be a message about the reclusive writer J. D. Salinger. On the basis of a newspaper article he once read, Ray believes that Salinger is a baseball fan but that he has not seen a game live for over twenty-five years. Ray decides to visit Salinger in New Hampshire and take him to a baseball game at Fenway Park in Boston. Another link that connects Ray to Salinger is the fact that in one of his short stories, Salinger created a character named Ray Kinsella. There is also a character named Richard Kinsella in Salinger's book, *The Catcher in the Rye*, and Ray has a twin brother by that name.

On his long drive, Ray stops to attend ball games in Chicago, Cleveland, Pittsburgh, and Yankee Stadium in New York. When he reaches New Hampshire, he waylays Salinger outside his home and, in a mock-kidnapping, persuades the surprised writer to accompany him to Fenway Park. Ray tells his story, and they talk about writing. At the Boston Red Sox game, Ray tries to get Salinger to talk about his pain, but Salinger says he has none. During the game, Ray receives yet another mysterious message, this time from the scoreboard. It concerns a baseball player named Moonlight Graham who played once for the New York Giants in 1905. Ray knows that he has another assignment to fulfill, and he receives a message telling him to "Go the distance." Salinger also hears this, and he and Ray agree to travel to the small town of Chisholm, Minnesota, to discover what they can about Archie "Moonlight" Graham.

Chapter 3: The Life and Times of Moonlight Graham

As they make the long drive to Minnesota, where Graham died in 1965, Salinger tells Ray that he also received a message saying, "Fulfill the dream." They visit the Baseball Hall of Fame in Cooperstown, New York, and get information about Graham's one and only major-league game. When they arrive in Chisholm, they discover from a newspaper obituary that Graham had been the town's doctor for many years and was deeply loved in his community.

At night Ray goes walking, and through some magical transformation, he encounters Doc Graham as a seventy-five-year-old man. The year is 1955. They go to Graham's office at the school, where Graham explains how he got the nickname Moonlight. As they talk about his career, he says that if he had one wish, it would be to hold a bat in a major-league game, something that he never did in his career.

Next morning, Salinger and Ray decide to go back to Iowa so that Salinger can see the baseball field. On their way out of Chisholm, they pick up a young man in a baseball uniform who is looking for a place to play. The young man says his name is Archie Graham.

Chapter 4: The Oldest Living Chicago Cub

The three of them head for Iowa, stopping off in Minneapolis to explore a baseball field at night. Going on to Iowa City, Ray stops at the Bishop Cridge Friendship Center, where his friend, ninety-one-year-old Eddie Scissons, the oldest living Chicago Cub, lives. Ray invites Eddie to his farm because he wants to show him the baseball field. Ray has also received another obscure message about sharing and betrayal that he assumes is about Eddie.

When they reach the farm, Ray finds his twin brother Richard there, whom he has not seen for over twenty years. Richard works with a carnival that has stopped in Iowa City. Ray takes his other friends for a tour of the baseball field and knows he will only be able to answer their questions when the magic unfolds once more. In the meantime, his financial situation is increasingly desperate. His brother-in-law, Mark, is trying to buy the farm, and Mark announces that he has the legal right to foreclose on the farm if Ray does not get up to date on the mortgage payments. Mark and his business partner, Bluestein, are buying up farms in the area

Media Adaptations

- *Shoeless Joe* was made into the movie *Field of Dreams*, directed by Phil Alden Robinson and starring Kevin Costner, in 1989.

and using computer farming to modernize them, a concept that Ray dislikes.

When the magic happens again, there is a new player on the field—the catcher for the White Sox. His name is Johnny Kinsella, Ray's father, but Ray cannot bring himself to face him. On the field, Moonlight Graham gets his wish.

An exasperated Mark tells Ray that Eddie has been lying about his past, that he'd never played for the Chicago Cubs. But Ray has known this for a long time anyway. Not long after this, Eddie gets his wish when, as Kid Scissons, he pitches for the Chicago Cubs on Ray's magical field. But Eddie does not perform well. He urges Ray to speak to his father. Shortly after, Eddie dies. He is buried at the baseball field in his Chicago Cubs uniform.

Mark and Bluestein arrive and claim they have legal temporary custody of the farm. Ray orders them off the property at gunpoint, but the confrontation ends when Karin, Ray's young daughter, takes a fall. She is unconscious and has difficulty breathing, until young Moonlight Graham magically metamorphoses into the older Doc Graham and saves her life.

Salinger envisions a way that Ray can pay off his debts and keep the farm: the baseball field will become a magnet for tourists. Just as he says this, the first cars full of visitors begin to arrive. And that night, Ray plucks up courage to speak to his father. Richard, who up to this point has been unable to see what the others see, speaks to him as well.

Chapter 5: The Rapture of J. D. Salinger

When Ray learns that the players have invited Salinger out after the game, he is jealous until he

realizes that, as a result of this, Salinger may well get his deepest wish, which is to play baseball at the Polo Grounds, the home ballpark of the New York Giants that was torn down in 1964.

Characters

Abner Bluestein

Abner Bluestein is the hard-nosed business partner of Mark, Ray Kinsella's brother-in-law, who wants to evict Ray from his farm.

Archie Graham

Archie Graham, also known as Moonlight Graham, is based on a real person who played once for the New York Giants in 1905. He appears in the novel in two forms. First, he is an old man, Doc Graham, a doctor in the small Minnesota town of Chisholm. Ray meets him in a magical episode of time travel that takes him back to the year 1955 when Graham is seventy-five years old. Doc Graham has some eccentric habits, such as chewing paper and spitting it out, but he is a good-hearted man who is loved and respected in his community, where he takes care of all who seek his assistance. He tells Ray that he got his nickname one night when, after a minor league game, he went outside the motel for a walk, dressed in his baseball uniform. A teammate spotted him, and he was Moonlight Graham ever after. Graham also appears in the novel as a young man dressed in a baseball uniform who travels from Minnesota to Iowa with Salinger and Ray in search of a game to play. He ends up playing on Ray's fantasy field and thus gets the chance to bat in the major leagues.

Gypsy

Gypsy is the girlfriend of Richard Kinsella. She works in the change booth at the carnival. She is tough but also kind and wise, and she has an open heart that enables her to perceive all the baseball games taking place in Ray's magic field.

Shoeless Joe Jackson

Shoeless Joe Jackson was one of the greatest baseball players of all time. His career with the Chicago White Sox ended in 1920 when he admitted to being involved in a plot to throw the 1919 World Series. He was banned from the game for life. In the novel, Ray believes that although Shoeless Joe may have accepted money from gamblers, he did not deliberately throw the series but was the victim of greedy baseball owners. Shoeless Joe is one of Ray's heroes, and he is the first baseball player to appear on Ray's baseball field. Shoeless Joe is presented not only as a legendary baseball player but also as a man who loved the game and who would have played just for food money. He tells Ray that being banned for life was the equivalent of having part of himself amputated.

Annie Kinsella

Annie Kinsella is Ray Kinsella's red-haired, twenty-four-year-old wife. She is pretty, full of life and good humor, and very loving. She always supports her husband and encourages him to fulfill his dreams, never once reproaching him for being impractical, even as their debts mount.

Johnny Kinsella

Johnny Kinsella is Ray's father. He served in World War I and was gassed at Passchendaele, after which he settled in Chicago and became a White Sox fan. He also played semi-pro baseball in Florida and California before marrying and settling in Montana. At the time of the story, he has been dead for twenty years. He and his son Ray appear to have been close, and he instilled his love of baseball into Ray. Shoeless Joe was his hero. Johnny Kinsella appears in the novel as a young man, playing catcher in games at Ray's baseball park. At first, Ray does not know how to approach him, but later he does so, and he realizes that he can talk with his father about many things.

Karin Kinsella

Karin Kinsella is Ray's five-year-old daughter. Like her father, she is gifted with imagination and has no trouble seeing the baseball games that take place in the cornfield at the farm.

Ray Kinsella

Ray Kinsella is the narrator of the story. He was raised in Montana, and his father passed on to him a love of baseball. Ray later moved to Iowa to study, and he fell in love with the state and decided to stay. He married Annie, the daughter of his landlady. Unable to find congenial work, Ray took a job as a life insurance salesman, which he hated. Then, Annie suggested that they rent and later buy a farm. Although he has little expertise in farming and machinery of any kind baffles him, Ray takes great pride in the farm. However, times are such that it is very hard for a small farmer to flourish, and he falls badly into debt. Impractical in matters of money, he makes almost no effort to right his finances. His wife's family dislikes him, and he has equally negative feelings about them. Ray also dislikes organized religion, big business, and people in authority who do not use their authority well.

Whatever his shortcomings in practical life, Ray is gifted with imagination, an open heart, and the ability to conceive a great dream and work at it until it comes true. When he hears the mysterious voice saying, "If you build it, he will come," he immediately understands what it means and sets about building the baseball field. He is also motivated by a desire to rekindle the enthusiasm for baseball of his favorite writer, J. D. Salinger, and to heal Salinger's pain. Ray drives a thousand miles cross-country to make this happen. In the end, Ray is vindicated. His dreams come true because of the depths of his own belief in them. He also becomes the agent whereby the dreams of others can be fulfilled, but in this he realizes that he is only playing his part in some larger plan, the origins of which he does not speculate about. Ultimately, what is most important to Ray is not baseball but love of family and friends.

Richard Kinsella

Richard Kinsella is Ray's twin brother. He and Ray have not seen each other since the morning of their sixteenth birthday. On that day, Richard quarreled with their father and walked out of the house. No one in the family has seen or heard of him since, until one day he shows up at Ray's farm. It transpires that he works with a traveling carnival that has stopped in Iowa City. Richard is at first unable to see what happens in the baseball cornfield, but he asks Ray to teach him how to do it. Eventually, Richard is able to perceive and speak to their father.

Mark

Mark is a professor at the University of Iowa in Iowa City, and Ray's brother-in-law. His area of expertise is the corn weevil. He is also a businessman and, with his partner, Bluestein, owns apartment blocks and several thousand acres of farmland. Practical and with an interest in the latest technology, Mark is the opposite of Ray, the dreamer. Mark wants to buy Ray's farm so he can modernize it, and he pursues his goal ruthlessly, only to be foiled at the end by Salinger's creative ideas for how Ray can pay off his debts.

Moonlight

See Archie Graham

J. D. Salinger

J. D. Salinger is the real-life reclusive author of *The Catcher in the Rye*. In the novel, Salinger is presented as a kind man with a sense of humor, although since he no longer writes and publishes, he is also denying himself his greatest talent. When he is way-laid by Ray at his home, he agrees to accompany him to the Red Sox game in Boston. Then he joins Ray in his research into Moonlight Graham's life in Minnesota and also goes to Iowa to see for himself the baseball field where Shoeless Joe and the other famous players perform. As a writer with a developed imagination, Salinger is well able to perceive everything that takes place on Ray's baseball park. When he receives an invitation to accompany the players beyond the baseball park into a world beyond ordinary reality, Salinger promises Ray that he will resume his writing career.

Eddie Scissons

Eddie Scissons is a very old man whom Ray befriends several years before the story begins. Ray rents and later buys Eddie's farm. Eddie lives at the Bishop Cridge Friendship Center in Iowa City and claims to be the oldest living Chicago Cub. He has many stories to tell about baseball and claims to have followed the Cubs for eighty years. They have been his whole life, and he wants to be buried in his Chicago Cubs uniform. It transpires, however, that Eddie has been lying. He never played for the Cubs. The best he could manage was to play part-time, for one year, for a Class D team in Montana. Eddie eventually gets his wish when, as Kid Scissons, he pitches for the Chicago Cubs on Ray's baseball park. But he performs poorly and is devastated by the experience. Although he gets what he wants, it does not make him happy. However, when Eddie dies, his wish to be buried in his Cubs uniform is honored.

Themes

Religion

Shoeless Joe has countless references and allusions to religious beliefs and practices. Kinsella presents a strong contrast between traditional Christianity and what he regards as a truer, more life-promoting form of religion, mediated by the game of baseball. Traditional religion is presented in an entirely negative light. It is epitomized in Ray's perceptions of his wife's family. Annie's mother is self-righteous and judgmental, and she makes a point of bringing her religion into any conversation. Mark, Ray's ruthless brother-in-law, is also a fundamentalist Christian, who dislikes atheists and Catholics. Mark has three brothers, named Matthew, Luke, and John. Together with Mark, these are the names of the evangelists who wrote the four gospels, which underlines Ray's quarrel with Christianity. Other examples of people who adhere to traditional Christianity are Eddie Scissons's three daughters, who are presented as dour, unimaginative, and joyless.

In contrast, baseball is presented as a kind of quasi-religion. "We're not just ordinary people, we're a congregation," says Ray of the baseball fans. A ballpark at night "is more like a church than a church." Ray imagines fans waiting for a game to start, sitting "in silence, in awe, in wonder, in anticipation, in joy"—rather like worshipers in a cathedral. The element of joy is what is conspicuously lacking in Ray's perceptions of the way Christianity is normally lived.

Baseball provides the experience of calmness and stability for which people often look to religion. Baseball is soothing because "it is stable and permanent." As he looks around Boston's Fenway Park, Ray remarks that "the year might be 1900 or 1920 or 1979, for all the field itself has changed. Here the sense of urgency that governs most lives is pushed to one side." Baseball also offers the possibility, like religion, of miraculous events that can transcend or reverse time. In a baseball game, Ray says, anything can happen: "Tides can reverse; oceans can open." And of course, this is exactly what happens in Ray's magical baseball park. Through Ray's dedicated love of baseball, the dead can live again—another promise that traditional Christianity makes to its followers.

Imagination, Dreams, and Reality

Shoeless Joe is a wish-fulfillment, fantasy novel in which the dead come back to life, dreams come true, and old wounds are healed. It asserts the primacy of imagination over the demands of practical life. For example, Ray makes no attempt to get out of his mounting pile of debt. To all outside observers (except for his loyal wife, Annie), he is heading for disaster and his only practical option is to sell the farm. But Ray is one of the least practical characters imaginable. He insists on following his dreams and making them into reality. To accomplish this, he must be alert to the prompting of his intuition and his heart. He must do apparently crazy things, like driving cross-country to take a reclusive writer to a baseball game. He must never lose sight of his goal, he must ignore advice by well-meaning people, and he must trust in his vision. He must also work hard at the physical task of turning his cornfield into a baseball park. He seeds, waters, sands, and rakes the field. This is clearly a metaphor for watering his own imagination, allowing the hidden desires and hopes to push up to the surface. In digging deep into his own consciousness, Ray accesses the things that need healing, both in himself and in others. He taps into the universal level of life, where everything is connected. From there he can become the instrument by which the "cosmic jigsaw puzzle," in which everything has its proper time and place, can move to completion. As long as Ray sticks to his task, providence will take care of the rest. It is significant that, in the end, there proves to be no dichotomy between the imaginative and the practical life. By following his imagination, Ray also creates the means to pay off his debts—through the throng of tourists that come to see the magical ballpark—and to continue to live at the farm.

Father and Son

The relationship between father and son is at the heart of the novel. Ray's father passed on his love of baseball to his son, and his hero was Shoeless Joe, whom he believed to have been innocent of the charges that led to his lifetime ban from baseball. This is why Shoeless Joe is the first player to appear on Ray's baseball field. It is not only a chance for him to right the wrong that was done to him, but it also makes it possible for Ray to appease the spirit of his father, who has been dead for twenty years. When Ray first sees and talks to Shoeless Joe, his thoughts quickly turn to his father, and he wants him to play catcher with the resurrected White Sox. When this dream comes true and he sees his father as a twenty-five-year-old man, he does not know how to approach him, but, after making the first move and speaking to his father as a friend, he thinks of all the things he will want to talk about: "I'll guide the conversation . . . and we'll hardly realize that we're talking of love, and family, and life, and beauty, and friendship, and sharing." What Kinsella suggests here is simple: those to whom we are closest can remain so, even after death, if our hearts and minds remain open; the barriers between the living and the dead are not as insurmountable as they might seem. Ray's twin brother, Richard, is the immediate beneficiary of Ray's discovery. Unlike Ray, Richard quarreled with their father. Richard had not reconciled with his father by the time of his father's death—but Ray teaches the initially un-

Topics for Further Study

- Why is Karin usually the first person to see the baseball games on Ray's field?

- Is *Shoeless Joe* just a harmless fantasy, or does it have relevance for day-to-day life? What guidance for how life should be lived does Ray provide?

- Research the Black Sox Scandal of 1919. What is the evidence for and against the guilt of Shoeless Joe? Were the owners really to blame because they underpaid their players?

- Should Shoeless Joe be inducted into the Baseball Hall of Fame, even if he was guilty? What might be the arguments for and against this proposition?

- Kinsella has commented that today's major league baseball players and owners are greedy and have no regard for the baseball fan. He thinks that admission prices are too high and many fans may prefer to watch minor league games in which players still play for the love of the game. Do you agree with Kinsella's opinion? What arguments could be made for or against his views?

- Watch the movie *Field of Dreams*, and write an essay explaining how the movie differs from the novel. Do you think the film is an effective adaptation? What does the movie lose or gain by substituting the fictional black writer Terrence Mann for J. D. Salinger?

comprehending Richard to see his father on the ballpark, so Richard can also be a part of the restored wholeness of the family.

Style

Similes and Metaphors

Kinsella's use of simile and metaphor, in which something is compared to something else generally unlike it in a way that brings out the resemblance between the two, is the most noticeable aspect of his style. The similes and metaphors come thick and fast. The first seven pages alone include the following examples: the wind "is as soft as a day-old chick"; speakers at baseball stadiums are "like ancient sailors' hats"; small items accumulate at one end of the sloping verandah "like a herd of cattle clustered with their backs to a storm"; Annie falls into Ray's arms "like a cat that you suddenly find sound asleep in your lap"; black clouds lumber off "like ghosts of buffalo." Later examples include extended metaphors, such as this one describing the rumors that circulate about J. D. Salinger. They are "like mosquitoes from a swamp and buzz angrily and irritatingly in the air." Kinsella cannot resist immediately following this with yet another simile, in which Ray, whose favorite author is Salinger, says he collected those rumors "as a child might collect matchbooks and stash them in an unruly clamor in a dresser drawer already full of pens, tape, marbles, paper clips, and old playing cards."

Style

Kinsella writes in a lyrical, poetic style. This is particularly noticeable when he evokes the landscape of Iowa when the magic of the baseball field is in the air. Just before Shoeless Joe appears for the first time, for example, Ray senses that the magic is approaching, "hovering somewhere out in the night like a zeppelin, silky and silent, floating like the moon until the time is right." After Ray's first talk with Shoeless Joe, "A breath of clover travels on the summer wind. Behind me, just yards away, brook water plashes softly in the darkness, a frog shrills, fireflies dazzle the night like red pepper. A petal falls."

These and other descriptions of the Iowa landscape add to the feeling of enchantment that Kinsella wishes to create. He appeals directly to the senses, exactly as Ray instructs Salinger to do: "Open up your senses, smell the life all around you, touch it, taste it, hear it." This is the key to seeing the way Ray sees, and Kinsella gives his reader all the help he can. Consider for example the appeal to sight and smell in the following description: "Moonlight butters the whole Iowa night. Clover and corn smells are as thick as syrup." The image of moonlight buttering the night is particularly striking and effective.

The evocative lyricism extends to the descriptions of the baseball players and their games. This, for example, is the young Archie Graham in action:

He cranks up his arm, rears back, and throws, and the ball . . . travels in a white arc, seeming to leave behind a line like a streak of forgotten rainbow as it drops over the fence, silent as a star falling into a distant ocean.

When Eddie tells Ray that his uncle had a gift for "describing the beauty and mystery of baseball," his words could equally be applied to Kinsella the author.

The descriptions of Ray's wife Annie and his relationship with her have a similar kind of sensual radiance. It is as if everything within the scope of Ray's deep imaginative response to life appears in the light of this soft, romantic glow.

Symbolism

When Ray visits the carnival in Iowa City to meet Gypsy, she shows him part of the show. In a trailer, there are about a dozen glass containers. Each contains a faded black and white photograph of a deformed fetus. Kinsella attaches some importance to this, since just before the incident, Ray's daughter Karin repeats several times the sales patter she has heard from Richard: "the world's strangest babies are here." The reader is meant to take notice.

The grim image of twelve dead fetuses symbolizes the stifled, aborted dreams that Ray has brought back to life in his enchanted baseball park. The twelve are the eight banned White Sox players, including Shoeless Joe Jackson, as well as Moonlight Graham, Eddie Scissons, Johnny Kinsella (Ray's father) and J. D. Salinger.

The image recalls an incident in Ray's childhood when he shot a sparrow. To discourage him from such activities, his mother told him to bring the bird to life again. Obviously, he was unable to do that, but Ray has since learned that there are some things that can be brought back to life—forgotten hopes and frustrated desires. The sparrow incident is linked to the image of the dead fetuses when Ray calls his mother, reminds her of the dead sparrow, and tells her she must come and see "what I've brought to life." He means the baseball field, but the following day he visits the carnival and sees the glass cases. Kinsella leaves the reader to make the symbolic connection.

Historical Context

Shoeless Joe Jackson

Shoeless Joe Jackson was born in rural poverty in Greenville, South Carolina, in 1888. When he

Compare & Contrast

- **1920s:** After the Black Sox Scandal of 1919, baseball is at a low point in its history. Baseball owners are worried that spectators will stay away, thinking the game is corrupt. To punish the players and reassure the public, eight players, including Shoeless Joe Jackson, are banned from baseball for life in 1920.

  1980s: Baseball player Pete Rose, the all-time leader in hits, is banned for life in 1989 by baseball commissioner Bart Giamatti for betting on baseball. Also, Giamatti refuses to consider a request to reopen the Jackson case.

  Today: Controversy still exists over whether Shoeless Joe Jackson should be inducted into the Baseball Hall of Fame. In 1999, Republican representative Jim DeMint of South Carolina introduces a resolution calling for Jackson to be "appropriately honored" for his achievements.

- **1920s:** Baseball players earn low salaries. The average annual salary in the major leagues is about $5,000 to $6,000. There is no players' union, and players do not have agents, so they are in a weak bargaining position.

  1980s: Salaries for major league baseball players rise steadily. In 1981, the average salary is $185,651. By 1989, this has risen to $512,084. In November 1989, Kirby Puckett becomes the first $3-million-a-year player. Within a month, three other players, Rickey Henderson, Mark Langston, and Mark Davis, all top the $3-million mark.

Today: In 2001, nineteen major league baseball players have contracts with average annual values of $12.5 million or more. Many baseball fans believe salaries are too high and are not in the best interests of the game. A Gallup poll in April 2001 reports that 79 percent of fans think that major league baseball owners should be allowed to put a cap on the total amount of money available for players' salaries.

- **1920s:** Although African Americans are not allowed to play major league baseball, there are many black professional teams. The Negro National League is founded in 1920.

  1940s: Baseball takes the first steps to racial integration. In 1945, the Dodgers sign Jackie Robinson, who in 1947 becomes the first African American to play in the major leagues.

  1980s: Los Angeles Dodger vice president Al Campanis is fired after saying on ABC's *Nightline* that African Americans do not have the abilities to succeed in baseball management. The statement brings attention to the lack of African Americans in leadership positions in baseball and other professional sports. A drive to increase minority hiring begins, and, within two years, an African American, Bill White, is appointed National League president.

  Today: Although heavily represented in sports such as professional baseball, football, and basketball, African Americans remain underrepresented in leadership positions.

---

was only six, he worked seventy-hour weeks at the local cotton mill with his father. There was no opportunity for formal educational, and Jackson grew up illiterate. He joined the mill's baseball team at the age of fifteen and within five years was playing in the local minor league team, where he earned his nickname by playing in stocking feet.

In 1908, Jackson joined the major league Philadelphia Athletics, and, in 1910, he was traded

to the Cleveland Indians. Five years later, he was traded to the Chicago White Sox.

The White Sox were owned by the miserly Charles Comiskey, who refused even to pay for the team's laundry, which earned them the nickname, Black Sox. The players were inadequately paid. The highest annual salary Jackson ever earned with the Black Sox was $6,000. Comiskey also favored contracts that placed all power in the hands of the

Burt Lancaster (left) as Archie "Moonlight" Graham and Kevin Costner as Ray Kinsella in Field of Dreams, *the 1989 film based on the novel*

owner rather than the player. In the novel, Ray laments the Ten Day Clause, "which voided contracts, could end any player's career without compensation, pension, or even a ticket home."

Although all the details are still not known, the conspiracy was initiated by first baseman Chick Gandil, who recruited the other players. Gamblers offered each of the eight players $20,000 to lose the 1919 World Series. At the time, the White Sox were a formidable team and were expected to beat the Cincinnati Reds—but they lost the series. Jackson received $5,000 but later tried to give it back.

It is by no means certain that he helped to throw the series. He did, however, bat .375 to lead all players; he collected twelve hits and made no errors in the field. These statistics have led many fans to argue (including Ray's father in the novel) that he did not participate in the conspiracy.

A year later, after an investigation initiated by sportswriters, Jackson and two of the other players confessed to a grand jury. A famous story is told of a young boy pleading with his idol as he left a Chicago courthouse, "Say it ain't so, Joe." Jackson reportedly replied, "I'm afraid it is, kid."

Baseball Commissioner Kenesaw Mountain Landis banned all eight players from baseball for life. In 1921, a jury acquitted all eight players, but this was because evidence, including the players' signed confessions, had been stolen and was unavailable.

Jackson returned to Greenville, where he and his wife ran a successful dry-cleaning business. Jackson played semi-pro baseball in the South Georgia League until the age of forty-five. There are legends, disputed by some baseball historians, that he sometimes played elsewhere under a false name. The novel begins with Ray recalling how his father had claimed to have seen Shoeless Joe, "playing in a tenth-rate commercial league in a textile town in Carolina, wearing shoes and an assumed name."

Jackson remains to this day one of the great baseball players of all time. His lifetime batting average (.356) is the third best in major league history. Ty Cobb called him the "best natural hitter he ever saw."

Jackson died of a heart attack in 1951 at the age of sixty-three.

Critical Overview

Shoeless Joe was well received by reviewers. Barry Schweld, in *Library Journal*, called it a "triumph of imagination . . . the tone is gentle and sweet." Schweld compared the novel to the work of Bernard Malamud, Robert Coover and others, concluding that like those writers, Kinsella had spun a "wonderful myth out of the ritual of baseball." *Publisher's Weekly* declared it to be "the most imaginative and original baseball novel since 'The Natural,'" and concluded, "fanciful, if somewhat lightweight, the novel attests to the timeless game and the power of love." Maggie Lewis in *Christian Science Monitor* joined the chorus of praise, commenting that "Kinsella does wonders in this book: The visual fantasies are so rich that whether you believe them or not, you can't help imagining them."

William Plummer in *Newsweek* was a little more tough-minded. He called *Shoeless Joe* a "wonderfully hokey first novel," adding that the subplots "are a hasty pudding" and the Salinger of the novel was not "smart or quirky enough" to have created the character Holden Caulfield in *The Catcher in the Rye*. However, Plummer concluded that "such complaints seem mean-spirited, tin-

eared, in the face of the novel's lovely minor music."

Shoeless Joe has gained lasting popularity with the reading public, owing in part to the success of the movie *Field of Dreams* (1989). Literary critics have given it less attention, although several scholarly articles have explored such topics as Kinsella's baseball metaphors, his presentation of different attitudes to religion, and his social conservatism. There is a general consensus that the book is Kinsella's finest achievement in the realm of baseball fiction, a subgenre to which he has devoted much of his writing career.

Criticism

Bryan Aubrey

Aubrey holds a Ph.D. in English and has published many articles on twentieth-century literature. In this essay, Aubrey discusses the parallels between Ray Kinsella's vision in Kinsella's novel and some elements of traditional Christianity. He also points out the social and political implications of Ray's nostalgic dream.

"Is this heaven?" asks Shoeless Joe early on in the novel. "No, it's Iowa," replies Ray. In reality, however, Ray's magical baseball field has many of the characteristics of the Christian heaven, and Ray himself resembles an apostle of Christ, proclaiming the "good news" of salvation to all who believe. Seen in this light, *Shoeless Joe* appears to resemble an extended religious parable that creates, out of the rituals and artifacts of baseball, the trappings of a new religion, with much of its creed borrowed from the traditional elements of Christianity. While it is tempting to see the novel in this way, Kinsella is careful to repudiate the idea that baseball can be worshiped as a religion. He does this by contrasting Eddie Scissons and Moonlight Graham, highlighting the different role that baseball plays in each of their lives. Also, close analysis of Ray's heavenly Iowan field suggests that its saving values of love and hope rest on political and social underpinnings that may bring their universality into question.

The parallels between Ray's enterprise and that of an evangelist inspired by Old and New Testaments are unmistakable. Ray is a Moses bringing his people to the promised land, flowing with milk and honey. The promised land happens to be Iowa, lyrical descriptions of which occur on and off

> "Should we, then, worship baseball, the most perfect of games, embodiment of beauty and granter of our desires, a stable point of reference in a changing world? The perhaps surprising answer Kinsella gives is no."

throughout the story. And in Ray's magical, blessed baseball field, he offers healing sanctuary first for Shoeless Joe, an outcast and a sinner, just as Jesus made a point of eating with tax collectors (the outcasts of his day) and sinners. Ray also brings to enlightenment his long-lost brother, Richard, who resembles the prodigal son in the story told in Luke's gospel (Luke 15: 11–32). And like any good evangelist, Ray goes out in search of the lost sheep, as in the story told in Matthew, chapter 15, about the man who leaves his ninety-nine sheep to search for the one sheep that is lost, and rejoices greatly when he finds it. The lost sheep in *Shoeless Joe* takes the form of J. D. Salinger. When Ray finds him, Salinger epitomizes the error made by the third servant in the parable of the talents related in the gospel of Matthew, chapter 25. This is the servant who was given one talent (a unit of currency) by his master and buried it in the ground rather than doing as the other servants did—using what they had been given and so multiplying it. Kinsella's Salinger is a brilliant writer, blessed with the ability to touch people deeply with his words, but he has chosen not to share his gift with others. In the language of the New Testament, he is hiding his light under a bushel instead of letting it shine out. Ray, the baseball evangelist, must try to awaken him from his spiritual torpor.

Ray succeeds even better than he must have expected, for not only does Salinger, at the end of the novel, promise to let his light shine (that is, to write again), he is also the one who is permitted to experience the rapture. This is a reference to the Christian belief, based on a passage in Paul's first letter to the Thessalonians (4:17), that when Christ returns, believers will be caught up in the air to meet him. The equivalent in the novel is the invitation the baseball players extend to Salinger to join them after the game. They permit him to enter whatever spiritual world they inhabit when they are not hitting and fielding baseballs. This is a world the nature of which Ray can only guess at, but there are strong hints that Salinger will there have all his buried hopes and desires met.

In short, then, Ray's baseball field is the medium through which the ideal, transfigured, paradise state emerges and is made known. It is a condition, a state of consciousness, in which instead of being recalcitrant to human desire, life takes on the very shape of the fulfilled wish. It is similar to the description given in the Book of Revelations about the new Jerusalem that is made manifest after the return of Christ: "God will wipe away every tear from their eyes, and death shall be no more, neither shall there be mourning nor crying nor pain any more, for the former things have passed away" (21:4). As Annie says in the novel, "It's so perfect here."

Should we, then, worship baseball, the most perfect of games, embodiment of beauty and granter of our desires, a stable point of reference in a changing world? The perhaps surprising answer Kinsella gives is no. He is careful to point out that this quasi-religious world, just like its Christian counterpart, has its devil. And that this devil is ready to tempt the baseball lover, promising everything but leading him astray. The devil comes in the unlikely form of Eddie Scissons. When the reader first meets Eddie, he carries a white cane, on the top of which is a brass serpent's head. This is obviously meant to be a symbol. The serpent is, of course, the Biblical symbol of the devil. It was the devil in the form of the serpent that first tempted Eve, and in the New Testament, the devil is described as a liar and the father of all lies. In the novel, it transpires that Eddie has been lying for over forty years about his life, claiming to have played for the Chicago Cubs when he did not. The lie has become so pervasive it has taken over his entire life. He lives in a fantasy, a make-believe world that has no relation to real life. He has made a false god out of baseball, and this becomes abundantly clear when he stands on the bleachers and gives his long, high-flown sermon on baseball as the word of salvation. His speech is accompanied by Ray's impressions that are clearly meant to be negative: Eddie's voice "is filled with evangelical fervor"; a moment later he "shakes his head like a fundamentalist who can quote chapter and verse for every occasion." Eddie is a man who has taken his enthusiasm too far, and his life becomes a lie.

It might appear, of course, that Ray himself is sometimes in danger of doing the same. But although he is a baseball fanatic, he is aware of the dangers of not keeping his feet on the ground. When Salinger muses about whether there is a baseball devil, because Ray seems so possessed by the game, Ray replies with impeccable common sense, "Anything taken too seriously becomes a devil."

The more apt contrast with Eddie, however, is not Ray but Moonlight Graham, the man who made one brief appearance with the New York Giants in 1905 and then spent most of the rest of his life as a doctor in the small town of Chisholm, Montana. Although he loved baseball, he always kept a sense of what was really important in life. He tells Ray:

> If I'd got to be a doctor for five minutes, now *that* would have been a tragedy. You have to keep things in perspective. I mean, I love the game, but it's only that, a game.

Far more important for Doc Graham was finding a place in a community where he belonged, where he could express love and show his caring nature. For over forty years, Doc Graham was the good doctor who always had time for his patients. The baseball wish he expresses to Ray—to hold a bat in a major league game—is very much a secondary consideration for him. This is shown, as Charles Beach points out in his article, "Joyful vs. Joyless Religion in W. P. Kinsella's *Shoeless Joe*," in the incident where Karin almost chokes to death. Moonlight Graham leaves the baseball field where he is playing and magically metamorphoses into Doc Graham, in which guise he can save the little girl's life. Ray believes that Doc can never go back to being Moonlight Graham again. But it does not matter because the doctor has his priorities right.

But does Ray have *his* priorities right in all respects? What are the social and political implications of the kind of "heaven" he envisions in the Iowa heartland? Bryan K. Garman, in his essay, "Myth Building and Cultural Politics in W. P. Kinsella's *Shoeless Joe*," argues that the social environment out of which Ray's paradisiacal world springs is a very conservative one. It reflects an America not transfigured but frozen at a particular point in time.

The conservatism of Ray's worldview is clear from the nostalgia that pervades the novel. *Shoeless Joe* can be seen as one long hymn to the past. Ray is always looking back to a golden time. He hates the changes that he observes in Iowa City, for example, where the proliferation of fast-food franchises, motel chains, and muffler shops destroy bit by bit the city's traditional ambience. Ray also dislikes technology and the changes it brings to farming, including his own farm:

> Now a new breed of land baron is buying out the farmers one by one, and I suppose corn farms like mine soon will be operated by computer. Instead of a farmhouse and family, there will be a small metallic box studded with red, green, and blue lights, which will tell a foreman which quadrant needs water and in which area the cutworms are hatching.

Perhaps most important, as Garman points out, Ray's persistent nostalgia showers adulation on the game of baseball during a period when African Americans were not allowed to play in the major leagues. (They were not admitted until 1947.) This is also a period in history when a woman's place was firmly in the home. In the novel, this preference for a conservative attitude regarding gender roles shows up in the treatment of Annie. She occupies a subordinate place in Ray's world, offering him constant support, allowing him to do whatever he wants while her main task is taking care of domestic chores. She has no thought of a career of her own. Similarly, when Salinger climbs aboard the same backward-looking train, he also envisions the future of Ray's baseball field in nostalgic terms that idealize a particular period of history. Salinger's vision includes not only the quaint "squarish cars parked around a frame schoolhouse" but also domestic arrangements in which women labor hard and long at food-preparing chores: "women shelling peas in linoleum-floored kitchens, cradling the unshelled pods in brindled aprons, tearing open corn husks and waiting for the thrill of the cool sweet scent."

Many people today, feminists and others, might feel that such times were less than ideal, hardly deserving of the sentimental, rosy glow with which Kinsella imbues them. Although reading the novel for its political and social implications may upset the finely developed and charming fantasy— after all, who cannot love a story in which wishes come true and life is one long baseball game?—it also brings to light some underlying assumptions that must play a part in any critical evaluation. What is heaven for some may not be so heavenly for others.

Source: Bryan Aubrey, Critical Essay on *Shoeless Joe*, in *Novels for Students*, The Gale Group, 2002.

> " In much the same way that Reagan's masculinity and appeal to nostalgia absolved the sins of America's recent past, Ray's field wipes away the transgressions of baseball's history and returns the game to its fabled innocence."

Bryan K. Garman

In the following essay, Garman looks at the mythic structure of Kinsella's Shoeless Joe.

The mythic vision of America and its national pastime which W. P. Kinsella constructed in *Shoeless Joe* ([1982] 1991) has extended into millions of American imaginations, both in the form of the novel and its film adaptation, *Field of Dreams* (1989). Kinsella built the myth, and people came to live it. Perhaps literary critic Neil Randall best articulates the popular response to *Shoeless Joe* when he calls it a "moral book" which "makes us come away in the end feeling 'pretty damn good about being alive for the rest of the day.'" But when we read beyond what Randall calls "fantasy and the humor of fellow-feeling," and explore the context of the novel's morality, an unsettling portrait of America emerges. In this essay, I will argue that Kinsella engenders a culturally conservative world, which reflects the historical circumstances of the 1980s and reproduces the ideology of Ronald Reagan's presidency. By discussing the text within the framework of Reagan's America and the social history of baseball, this paper shows that Kinsella's nostalgic world is characterized by a mythic history of consensus, a fraternal and patriarchal order, and discrimination based on race and gender.

The most insightful and important scholarly articles written about Kinsella's vision of America have addressed the film, *Field of Dreams*, rather than the novel. Like *Shoeless Joe*, the film absolves the legendary Chicago White Sox leftfielder Shoeless Joe Jackson of his involvement in the so-called Black Sox scandal of 1919. Reviewer Harlan Jacobson astutely observes that the film "wishes aloud that America could return to the innocent days of white baseball. When there were no stains on the American honour, no scandals, no dirty tricks, no surprises. When everything was pure and clean and simple, and, well, white. When the Sox stayed white." The critic is so appalled by this longing for the past that he claims the film "takes on shades of the Weimer Republic ... *Field of Dreams* weeps for what is not now and never was. It remembers America before it lost control." As a corollary to Jacobson's argument, Pauline Kael suggests that the film reconciles the counterculture of the 1960s with the conformists of the 1980s, and argues that the movie is "close to saying: Don't challenge your parents' values, because if you do you'll be sorry. It's saying: 'Play Ball' with the American political system.["] Finally, Frank Ardolino, who discusses the theme of innocence in *Field of Dreams* and in two other baseball movies (*Bull Durham* and *Eight Men Out*) which were released in the late 1980s, concludes, "The wide-shouldered 1950s figure of Ronald Reagan dominates these films for better or worse."

Reagan's shoulders carried the complacency and stability of the Eisenhower era to the White House, where conservative pundits used it to shore up the mythic consensus of history which undergirded his presidency. Warren Susman argues that history "comes into existence" when "the social order itself must be rationalized." The act of writing history, he tells us, "brings order out of the disarray" of circumstances and is "often used as the basis for a political philosophy that while explaining the past offers also a way to change the future. History thus operates ideologically." Perhaps no one understood this concept as well as those who choreographed the Reagan presidency. The master of the image and communication, Reagan narrated a history that projected American tradition and myth into the present and future. His mythic vision sought to redeem a powerful American patriarchy, which had been emasculated by recent events: the embarrassment of Vietnam, the challenge of the counterculture and the civil rights movement, the shame of Watergate, the frustration of the Iranian hostage crisis, and the failed attempt to end it. While Jimmy Carter asked Americans to sacrifice and settle for second best, Reagan vowed to put America first. To overcome what he perceived as aberrations in the country's history, Reagan rearmed and remasculinized America, reintroduced a fervent patriotism, and, perhaps most importantly, recaptured a mythic American past. Biographer Garry Wills assesses the Reagan mystique:

> We want to 'retain' what we never had—a mythical frontier life, an America where merit and hard work were the only paths to success, where the government did not interfere with the workings of the market's invisible hand: the past, that is, as Reagan thinks he lived it, where performing and earning merged, and the part to be performed was always that of the meritocrat . . . . For others, Reagan offers not only a path of entry into such an America, a relic of its reality, but a guarantee of its continued existence into our time. In several senses, he gives us the past as present . . . .

With the world as he knew it threatened by feminism, the Soviet Union, and the rapid development of technology, Reagan invoked and evoked America's Golden Age and became a stalwart for the status quo.

The television advertising campaign which the Reagan-Bush ticket unleashed during the 1984 presidential election brilliantly illustrates the Reagan administration's reliance on a mythic past. In the advertisement entitled "America is Back," an orchestra's euphony and images of domestic tranquility appeal to our sentiments, while we hear the narrator's serene and confident voice-over:

> In a town not too far from where you live, a young family has just moved into a new home. Three years ago even the smallest house seemed completely out of reach.
>
> Right down the street one of the neighbor's just bought himself a new truck—with all the options.
>
> The factory down by the river is working again—not long ago people were saying it would probably be closed forever.
>
> Just about every place you look, things are looking up.
>
> Life is better. America is back. And people have a sense of pride they never thought they'd feel again. So it's not surprising just about everyone in town is thinking the same thing.
>
> Now that our country is turning around, why would we ever turn back?

While this narration evokes the nostalgic neighbourhood of 1950s Main Street America, the video provides the appropriate images: an elderly man with a straw hat sits on his porch and peers over his newspaper to watch the new family move in next door; a little girl excitedly runs to her father's new truck; the night watchman greets his coworkers as they return to the factory; a barber sweeps the sidewalk in front of his shop; an elderly couple walks down the street eating ice cream; and, finally, there is a parade which features the high school band, a teen queen waving to the crowd, a shining red fire engine, and well-groomed children brandishing American flags.

Through these nostalgic images, the Reagan camp attempted to establish a tranquil consensus which was devoid of internal conflict. In this made-for-television community, black and white Americans live and work together and women work in the home. Reagan was able to convince America that we were part of an idealistic, conflict-free past which, although it never existed, was being relived in the present. Wills writes of Reagan, "He renews our past by resuming it. His approach is not discursive, setting up sequences of time or thought, but associative; not a tracking shot, but montage. We make the connections. It is our movie." The montage presented in "America is Back" was so intoxicating that many of us who suspected that Reagan's performance was merely the extension of his acting career still felt compelled to embrace his popular ideology. In short, we saw Reagan rehearse the myth so often that we began to believe it. Similarly, *Shoeless Joe*'s Eddie Scissons convinced himself that he played for the Chicago Cubs. After Ray's brother-in-law, Mark, reveals that the "oldest living Chicago Cub" never played in the big leagues, the aging Eddie admits, "If I can't have what I want most in life, then I'll pretend I had it in the past, and talk about it and live it and relive it until it is real and solid and I can hold it to my heart like a precious child. Once I've experienced it so completely, no one can ever take it away from me." Throughout his presidency, Reagan and many of his constituents seemed to operate under the same principle.

Kinsella explains that *Shoeless Joe* is "about a perfect world. It's about a man who has a perfect wife, a perfect daughter and wants to keep it that way" (Knight 1989 . . .). We might see pictures of Carter and Mondale hanging in the office of the *Free Press* when Ray and J. D. Salinger visit Doc Graham's hometown of Chisholm, Minnesota, but Kinsella's definition of perfect is more in line with Carter's successor's. To create his perfect world, Ray must, like Reagan, travel into the American past and revive its myths. As he returns to Iowa City with the "kidnapped" Salinger and the young Archie "Doc" Graham (whose dream to bat in the major leagues will be fulfilled on Ray's field), Ray laments the commodification of the Iowa landscape and the loss of the nostalgic small town. The "shady streets, very old white frame houses, porch swings, lilacs, one-pump gas stations, and good neighbors" have been replaced by "fast-food franchises that spring up everywhere like evil mushrooms, by concrete-and-glass buildings, muffler shops, and Howard Johnson motels. Each of these destroys a little more history. Iowa City is a town of grandfathers fighting a losing battle against time."

Longing for the retention of a world which is lifted "right out of a Norman Rockwell painting," Ray joins the good fight and tries to preserve it. He and Annie are cultural throwbacks, "meat and potato people" who both come from humble backgrounds and try to make their living from the land. In effect, they are archaeologists who actually live the type of life which they are trying to resurrect. In recovering antique glassware and crockery which is buried in their backyard, they rediscover and preserve the artifacts of the halcyon days when milk was delivered to houses in glass bottles. While their farmhouse becomes the museum for these antiques of material culture, Ray's baseball field preserves the mythic values of the period in which his house was built.

In much the same way that Reagan's masculinity and appeal to nostalgia absolved the sins of America's recent past, Ray's field wipes away the transgressions of baseball's history and returns the game to its fabled innocence. This purification ceremony occurs when Ray resurrects Shoeless Joe Jackson, the leftfielder of the 1919 Chicago White Sox, who was one of eight White Sox players implicated in the Black Sox scandal. Labouring under stingy owner Charles Comiskey, the eight Black Sox accepted bribes to throw the 1919 World Series, and were subsequently banned from baseball for life by the game's first commissioner, Kennesaw Mountain Landis. That Jackson, the most capable player in the group, took the money is certain; that he threw the series is not. As Ray explains, his impressive statistics suggest that there was no compromise in his play. Still, the Black Sox placed an indelible blemish on baseball's character and represented a nadir in American sports culture. "Say it ain't so, Joe," the apocryphal words uttered by a young fan who waited for his heroes outside of the court proceedings, recorded the disappointment and disillusion of an entire generation. America's national pastime, often thought to be the purest of its sports, had lost its innocence.

The ball park announcer's voice in *Shoeless Joe* implicitly charges Ray, as Jacobson suggests, to make the Black Sox white again, a task he accomplishes, in part, through his sympathetic representation of Jackson. Speaking as if he were trying to convince himself of the truth of his words, Ray calls

the ballplayer a "symbol of tyranny of the powerful over the powerless" who fell victim to "the circumstances": "The players were paid peasant salaries while the owners became rich." An illiterate South Carolina farm boy, Jackson, who was duped by more experienced men, epitomizes the innocence of the past. Baseball, not money, was his concern. "I loved the game," he tells Ray. "I'd have played for food money. I'd have played free and worked for food. It was the game, the parks, the smells, the sounds. . . . It makes me tingle all over like a kid on his way to his first doubleheader." If, as Eddie Scissons preaches in his baseball revival meeting, the word "baseball" has the ability "to raise the dead," it also has the capacity to forgive the sins of the past. Upon his second coming into Kinsella's nostalgic world, Jackson "dip[s] [himself] in magic waters" and is forgiven by the "great god baseball." When the fallen hero implicitly confesses his sin, the magic waters baptize him in the name of baseball, wash away the wrongdoings of the Black Sox, and return them to the innocence of childhood. Ray's idyllic field suspends the Black Sox's life sentence and exonerates them from their crime.

While the "magic waters" of baseball allow Shoeless Joe to begin his career anew, the sport's regenerative properties also have a soothing effect on Salinger and Richard, Ray's twin brother. When Salinger disappears with the players into the mysterious corn field, there is hope that he will regain the creativity and passion that he had as a younger writer. Apparently, Ray has eased the author's personal pain, but because he identifies Salinger so closely with Holden Caulfield, he feels compelled to heal the general adolescent rage that the protagonist of *The Catcher in the Rye* embodies. Calling Salinger's book "the definitive novel of a young man's growing pains," Ray says, "Growing up is a ritual. . . . Everything is experienced for the first time. But baseball can soothe even those pains, for it is stable and permanent, steady as a grandfather dozing in a wicker chair on a verandah." Like the grandfather figure Reagan, who at age sixty-nine was the oldest man elected to his first term of the presidency, Ray wants a stable world that will erase the anger and rebellion of the 1960s counterculture, and stall America in the perpetual innocence and consensus of the Eisenhower era. Ray accomplishes this feat by reuniting his family. Twenty years after Richard left home in a fit of adolescent rage, he unexpectedly appears at Ray's farm. His return enables him to resume his relationship with his father, whom Ray has resurrected as a catcher on the field of dreams. In the process, we see the family, a standard icon in Reagan's mythology, reconstituted, and patriarchy restored. Richard's regrettable adolescent tantrum has ended, and he returns to the innocence and simplicity of childhood where patriarchal authority will remain unquestioned.

It is appropriate that Kinsella organizes his ceremony of forgiveness around baseball, for the sport has long been associated with the themes of regeneration and innocence. In mid-nineteenth century America, when baseball became popular, it furnished a pastoral retreat for urban middle-class men. Afternoons in the park removed these respectable merchants, proprietors, and clerks from the filth and unpleasantries of the city, and delivered them to the landscape of the American farm. The combination of vigorous exercise and the calmer environs of the park provided these men a powerful form of recreation, a pastime which was readily transferred to the modern professional game. Even today the most aesthetically pleasing of the major league ball parks, particularly those that have maintained natural grass playing fields, serve as respites from the homogeneous urban concrete and the city's morally complex and hectic pace. But the cyclical structure of the professional baseball season also offers both players and fans the annual opportunity for re-creation. While for many the end of winter is signalled by the arrival of the first spring flowers, baseball fans mark the changing seasons with the annual convocation of Florida's Grapefruit League. Wizened veterans rehabilitate from nagging injuries and stage comebacks, while hopeful young rookies nervously struggle to fill a void that a recently retired superstar has left behind him. Each team approaches the upcoming season with optimism, hoping to atone for the sins and failures of the previous campaign. The fans are all too willing to forgive, and they too internalize the promise of the new year. They watch their favourite teams and players stagger through the young season of April and May, see the pennant races take shape by the mid-summer All-Star break, and watch them race to their conclusion just after the dog days of August. October brings a cool conclusion to the season's nine-month gestation and crowns a new World Series champion. Three long months later, fans are again willing to forgive the failures of their heroes, and the cycle begins anew when they enthusiastically embrace the hope of yet another baseball season. Because these cyclical traditions are reinforced by their ties to the natural growing season, they constitute a powerful regenerative ritual which is not present in any other major sport.

What Do I Read Next?

- Like *Shoeless Joe*, Kinsella's second novel, *The Iowa Baseball Confederacy* (1986) has mystical overtones of magic and religion as revealed in the rituals of baseball. A man who tries to prove there was a minor league in Iowa in the early 1900s is whisked back in time to witness and participate in it.

- *Say It Ain't So, Joe!: The True Story of Shoeless Joe Jackson* (2nd ed., 1999), by Donald Gropman, is a readable, well-researched biography of Shoeless Joe Jackson. The author argues that Jackson had no involvement in the Black Sox scandal of 1919.

- *The Boys of Summer* (1972), by Roger Kahn, is a classic piece of baseball writing. Kahn grew up as a fan of the Brooklyn Dodgers, and, as a young journalist, he traveled with the team in 1952 and 1953. His memoir includes poignant accounts of the lives of the players after their playing days were over.

- *Eight Men Out: The Black Sox and the 1919 World Series* (1962), by Eliot Asinof, is the most comprehensive investigation of the famous scandal. It makes for a vivid and exciting read.

- *The Legend of Bagger Vance*, by Steven Pressfield, does for golf what *Shoeless Joe* did for baseball. It's a novel about golf that also presents golf as a metaphor for life, for which it draws on the religious philosophy of the classic Indian text, the *Bhagavad Gita*.

- Some critics regard *The Natural*, by Bernard Malamud (1952), as the greatest baseball novel ever written. The main character, Roy Hobbs, is a composite of Joe Jackson, Babe Ruth, and Eddie Waitkus; his bat, Wonderboy, is a refashioning of Jackson's famous bat, called Black Betsy.

While Kinsella is aware that baseball subjects its faithful to a cyclical rebirth pattern, he also understands that each trip to the ball park revives even the cynic "who gave up the sports page for the Dow Jones Average when he was twenty-one." In his monologue near the end of the novel, Salinger indicates that baseball has a purifying and rejuvenating effect on all who watch it. He explains that Ray's magical baseball field is so powerful that pilgrims will come to it as "innocent as children" and "find they have reserved seats somewhere in the grandstand or along one of the baselines—wherever they sat when they were children and cheered their heroes." Kinsella carefully reconstructs the childhood of the white middle-aged man who, as a young boy, chose his heroes from American war generals, Saturday afternoon Westerns, and baseball players whose daily progress he followed on the radio or in the morning newspaper's box scores. Most young baseball fans share their earliest experience of the sport with their fathers, and attendance at any game during adulthood invariably summons associations which cause the fan to remember the simplicity and dependence of his or her childhood. The older fans who come to Ray's field of dreams will immerse themselves in nostalgia and remember afternoon games, radio broadcasts, Ted Williams, and perhaps even such attitudes as anticommunism and an unquestioned American patriotism. For nine innings, the fans are reborn as innocent as children and the memories they recall of their childhood enable them to rehearse a mythic consensus.

The structure of the game itself ensures that this rebirth occurs within a specific conservative cultural framework. In the more than 125-year-old history of professional baseball, the rules of the game have changed very little: the pitcher's mound has been moved a bit further away from home plate; owners insist that games be played at night; the American League employs the designated hitter rule; and salaries, of course, have increased exponentially. These alterations have had little effect on how the game is played, however. The hit-and-run play, for example, looks and works the same whether the manager who called it was the venerable Philadelphia Athletics' Connie Mack or the new Colorado Rockies' Don Baylor. Major League Baseball executives have developed the concepts of stability and permanency by marketing their products with nostalgic references to the game's past. Most professional teams hold annual old-timer's games and many have abandoned modern-style uniforms for more nostalgic ones. Moreover, professional baseball employs vital statistical categories which ensure that the old timers will not be forgotten. Certain numbers and names are held out

as virtually unattainable standards against which all men who play the game are judged. When a player establishes himself as the all-time leader in a particular statistical category, many years typically pass before he is displaced. Babe Ruth (who played from 1914 to 1935) held the mark for career home runs at 715 until Hank Aaron (1954–76) eclipsed the total nearly forty years after Ruth retired. Ty Cobb's (1905–28) 4,191 hits eventually gave way to Pete Rose's 4,204 (1963–85), and Walter "Big Train" Johnson's (1907–27) 416 career pitching victories will probably never be challenged. Such statistics provide the game with a stronger sense of stability than other professional sports.

Throughout the history of professional baseball, playoff formats have been altered, teams have moved from city to city, stadiums have become more standardized, and the management in the front offices has changed dramatically. But, while the business of baseball is different than it was when it first began, and the America which exists outside of the ball park has undergone tremendous transformations in the past 125 years, the game that is played between the foul lines has remained relatively stable. Drawing on baseball's regeneration myth and stable, self-contained history, Kinsella uses the voice of J. D. Salinger to associate many of the same values with baseball that Reagan associated with America:

> I don't have to tell you that the one constant through all the years has been baseball. America has been erased like a blackboard, only to be rebuilt and then erased again. But baseball has marked the time while America has rolled by like a procession of steamrollers. It is the same game that Moonlight Graham played in 1905. It is a living part of our history, like calico dresses, stone crockery, and threshing crews eating at outdoor tables. It continually reminds us of what once was, like an Indian-head penny in a handful of new coins.

Kinsella erases the sins of the past by imbuing the game with the innocence of childhood and evoking memories of a younger and simpler America. In short, baseball stabilizes Kinsella's world in the same way Reagan stabilized America. Depressions, wars, and civil unrest have altered the American landscape, but in Kinsella's narrative baseball provides a version of Reagan's orthodox past. In a dynamic world of Star Wars, Middle East terrorists, and American feminists, it satisfies the "certain compulsion ... for orderliness" which Ray and so many Americans have. Watching the Red Sox in Fenway Park, Ray concludes that baseball "is the most perfect of games, solid, true, pure and precious as diamonds. If only life were so simple. I have often thought, "*If only there was a framework to life, rules to live by.*" *Shoeless Joe* touches our emotions because it celebrates the traditional values of an irrecoverable age that Ronald Reagan seemed to make tangible. As James Earl Jones says, as Terrence Mann, in *Field of Dreams*, baseball offers the promise that "what once was good can be again." There is more to Kinsella's myopic vision, however, than goodness.

While baseball re-creates itself in the image of its old heroes to function as a living part of American history, Reagan's nostalgia refashioned America in the same manner. Although his renowned advertising strategists claimed that it was morning again in America, we were not awakening to a new morning. Rather, Reagan's day dawned in a mythic society which, like Kinsella's, espoused a conservative morality. As Garry Wills writes, Reagan "not only represents the past, but resurrects it as a promise of the future." The president appealed to "traditional" small-town values and religious mores and presented them as a way to rejuvenate America, a political philosophy that won considerable praise from Rev. Jerry Falwell's Moral Majority and other fundamentalist groups. In Kinsella's novel, Ray tells us that he detests Christian fundamentalism in all forms, but his actions suggest that he too follows fundamentalist doctrines. "The kind of people I absolutely cannot tolerate," he tells us, "are those, like Annie's mother, who never let you forget they are religious. It seems to me that a truly religious person would let his life be example enough ..." But if Ray condemns dogmatic Christianity, his fanatical adherence to the mythic history of baseball ensures that he will hold an ideological position which resembles the fundamentalist's. In *Shoeless Joe*, baseball functions as old-time religion, and Ray is the preacher who seeks to convert the infidels. The great god baseball welcomes the troubled (Salinger), the sinner (Shoeless Joe), the outcast (Eddie Scissons), the forsaken (Moonlight Graham) and the prodigal son (Richard) back into the fold, and restores or reconfirms the conservative values which they held before they strayed from the flock. These values—which place emphasis on order, the male-dominated family, and moral and racial purity—have their origins in the Victorian culture in which baseball was founded.

When Salinger articulates the vision that will save Ray's farm, he tells Ray that when the people come to his field, "It will be almost a fraternity, like one of those tiny, exclusive French restaurants that have no sign." Baseball's mythic history has traditionally claimed that the sport is the most innocent and democratic of games, but Salinger's statement is informed by the historical context in which the game was born. Historian Warren Goldstein notes that as early as 1860, the democratic myth was expressed in the *Beadle's Dime Base-Ball Player*:

> Employers willingly and cheerfully gave their employees time to play base ball.... All classes of society, the mechanic, the merchant, the professional classes, the school children, the collegiates, the aged and the young ... the affluent member of society, all joined in the sport .... Everything seemed to indicate that an American national out door pastime, fraught with influences the most beneficial and desirable, had been established, and so indeed it had.

This myth, which is perpetuated by Kinsella, holds, in part, that baseball was an egalitarian sport until owners such as Comiskey corrupted it. Goldstein points out, however, that capitalists have had financial interests in the game since at least 1867, when the Cincinnati Red Legs were incorporated. Moreover, because baseball clubs were originally founded as social fraternities, their function was always more than purely athletic. These organizations, which usually maintained a clubhouse, held annual galas, and oftentimes conducted elaborate picnics and dinners after games, provided a homosocial space for aspiring men of the "respectable" classes. Goldstein estimates that between the years 1855 and 1870, baseball fraternities had the following demographic composition: twenty percent were "high white collar" workers, a third were skilled craftsmen, with the remaining forty-four to forty-eight percent described as "low white collar or proprietors." Sufficient funds were always required to maintain these organizations, and certainly many business and professional contacts were made within the circles of the baseball fraternity. It would seem, then, that the "good old days"—the days in which baseball was not a business—did not exist for long.

Kinsella's misrepresentations, however, do not stop here. Indeed, as Goldstein explains, baseball germinated in a specific social-historical milieu, and consequently contained class, race, and gender biases which Kinsella fails to acknowledge. Specifically, when baseball fraternities became popular in the 1850s, the Know-Nothing party manifested itself as a sign of anti-immigration sentiment which was permeating the country. Carl Degler explains that the party's primary goal "was the elimination of the foreigner as a political force." To that end, the Know-Nothings sought to prohibit immigrants from holding public office and to increase "the waiting period for naturalization from five to twenty-one years." Although the Know-Nothings failed to implement their platform, they had considerable representation in American political offices from 1855 to 1861. Degler points out that even Senator Henry Wilson of Massachusetts, the headstrong reformer, associated himself with the party.

The existence of the Know-Nothings expressed the profound desire of many middle-class, native-born Americans to create a purely self-contained and homogeneous nation that was free of the cacophony and pluralism of immigrant cultures. In many respects, the brotherhood of baseball was an extension of this nativist impulse, for it took steps that would distinguish itself from the vast new immigrant populations which entered America between 1830 and 1860. Goldstein suggests that after mid-century the game was "straddling a cultural boundary" between the middle and working classes, but avers that those who did identify with the game sought to differentiate themselves from the rough culture of the "poor and unskilled and 'unrespectable'" population which was increasingly comprised of immigrants. Baseball fraternities consequently presented their sport as the "manly" game and contrasted it to such "boyish" working-class pursuits as boxing. Baseball players were expected to act like gentlemen on the field rather than unrefined pugilists. Within the framework of the language that the baseball fraternities used to establish their manhood, there existed the connotations of class distinctions. Goldstein writes:

> The fact that the same rancor was directed at the lower classes suggests that the question of 'maturity' or 'manly' behavior had a class content as well. It further suggests that the language of age and class could be used (at least from the top down) interchangeably, perhaps especially when the scorn originated with a combination of middle-class professionals and 'respectable' skilled craftsmen, and was aimed downward at the unskilled workers, laborers, and street arabs who did not belong to their clubs and did not aspire to the self-controlled respectability of their betters.

While such classism differs significantly from nineteenth-century racism, these class prejudices inform the history of racial discrimination which has plagued organized baseball. If white immigrants had little of the "self-controlled respectability of their betters," the African-American slave was thought to have even less. Nativists and the baseball fraternity strived to attain white middle-class purity, and if the slave economy alone did not prohibit blacks from participating in the baseball fraternity, theories of racial purity and miscegenation did.

Don Murray argues that readers "are drawn toward Kinsella's world because of its goodness and gentleness" and suggests that "despite the racial context of his work, only a minority of his readers (perhaps *they* are the perceptive ones?) see him as a racist." In reading *Shoeless Joe*, we are compelled to ask what Kinsella's treatment of race suggests about race relations in American culture and organized baseball. What does it mean for the author to assert that *Shoeless Joe* is about a "perfect world" and then situate this utopia in a region which has a very small minority population? Moreover, why does Kinsella locate his perfect world in a time when African Americans were not permitted to play major-league baseball?

The history of African Americans and other minorities in baseball does not penetrate Kinsella's narrative. In fact, his text does much to perpetuate the fraternity of racial purity by not only making the Black Sox white again, but by deracinating baseball and America. To be sure, Kinsella's representations of race are unflattering at best, and Ray has little respect for people of colour. One of the first items he notices on Joe Jackson's uniform is "an American flag with forty-eight stars," a signifier of a self-contained America which had not yet admitted the Asian populations of Alaska and Hawaii to its citizenship. Like Ronald Reagan and the nativists, Ray wants to put America first and keep it pure. As he tells Mark, "You owe the land something. . . . It's not just a product. Not plastic and foam and bright paint imported from Taiwan or Korea, meant to be used once and discarded." While Ray describes the products of Asian labour as disposable, he sees the occupation of the American farmer and the cultural product of baseball as permanent symbols of a far superior national culture. Asian cultures may have appropriated baseball, but Ray would never concede American ownership of it. In his narrowly defined view, baseball is America, and because the World Series is played solely by North American teams, America is the world. Indeed, few players of Asian descent have broken the professional ranks, and until the recent purchase of the Seattle Mariners by a group of Japanese investors in June of 1992, the organizations resisted the presence of foreign owners altogether.

Perhaps Kinsella commits his most insidious (mis)reading of the past by failing to mention baseball's most reprehensible sin: until 1947, African

Americans were not permitted to play in the major leagues. While Ray's fantasy recalls many of the great players of baseball history, the only black players he mentions are Willie Mays, Reggie Jackson, and a few Minnesota Twins players from the late 1970s. The introduction of Reggie Jackson into text occurs under notable circumstances, for, in Annie's view, Joe Jackson supplants the New York Yankees' outfielder from his position. When Ray informs his wife that Shoeless Joe has arrived on the Kinsella farm, she asks, "Is he the Jackson on TV? The one you yell, 'Drop it, Jackson' at?" Reggie Jackson typically played rightfield for the Yankees, but in Annie's mind the unassuming, hard-working, and white Joe Jackson replaces the always flamboyant Reggie, and thereby restores white integrity, manhood, and self-control to the game. In Kinsella's world, it is this latter characteristic that is particularly lacking in the African-American community. As Ray walks through a Chicago ghetto near Old Comiskey Park, he feels so threatened by the African Americans he sees in this deprived environment that he "picture[s] young black men in felt fedoras going on a lavish spending spree with [his] very white Iowa credit cards." This passage is indicative of two points. First, the representation of African Americans as thieves who have little self-restraint and wear felt fedoras confirms the most virulent racial stereotypes, and thereby objectifies the black population. Ray is so blinded by the mythic history of baseball, however, that he fails to recognize his thoughts as being racist. Second, the passage illustrates the systematic discrimination in which baseball clubs have engaged against poor African Americans. Professional teams frequently erect their stadiums in black, poverty-stricken neighbourhoods, and, in the process, deprive local inhabitants of housing and inconvenience them with the large crowds that attend the games. Many major-league clubs have placed their stadiums in such areas, actions which indicate that they look upon these neighbourhoods as expendable.

Although economic statistics from the 1980s would prove otherwise, Reagan's selective reading of America and its history of race relations promotes a myth of consensus where blacks and whites live together in equality. Kinsella's representations of blacks and his desire to return baseball to an era which existed before Jackie Robinson broke the colour barrier, however, suggest that he prefers to isolate his "perfect world" from African Americans altogether. As an individual, W. P. Kinsella may or may not be a racist; we simply cannot draw any

conclusions from reading one of his works of fiction. We can, however, clearly conclude that the world he envisions, the culture in which it is embedded, and the baseball fraternity all have racist underpinnings.

While Kinsella's representations of race subjugate blacks to whites, his representations of women place them under the control of men. Salinger explains that when crowds of people come to Ray's farm to see Shoeless Joe play again, the experience will conjure memories of "women shelling peas in linoleum floored kitchens, cradling the unshelled pods in brindled aprons, tearing open corn husks and waiting for the thrill of the cool sweet scent." These unmistakably domestic images recall the drudgery of preparing all food by hand (there are no frozen vegetables, instant cake mixes, or microwaves in this kitchen), and relegate the woman to monotonous and often unrewarding household chores. Moreover, the images associate the woman with the role of reproduction: she carries the pea pods to term in her apron and gives birth to the vegetables by removing their shells. In Kinsella's world, the ideal woman keeps bare feet on the linoleum floor, happily bears the labour of motherhood, and performs the domestic obligations that will sustain the man in his pursuits. Goldstein suggests that women played a similar supportive domestic role in the establishment of the baseball fraternity. He writes, "Baseball clubs and promoters wanted women at games as evidence of the game's popularity. Many spectators would be drawn by the legitimacy that only women could confer to the game. Most important, however, women were supposed to help men control themselves on the ball field . . . women personified the standards of behavior that could, theoretically, keep men's behavior within certain boundaries." In short, these Victorian women "were to domesticate" the ball field, and without their supporting and submissive role, the fraternity of baseball, and middle-class patriarchal life as a whole, would not have developed as we know it.

Like her Victorian counterpart, Annie assumes a submissive role in the novel and embodies the middle-class domestic ideal. While Ray travels across the country to fulfil his outlandish dreams, Annie, a woman who is much younger than her husband, never questions him, remains at home to care for their daughter, and contends with their financial difficulties. She is the team player who executes countless sacrifices for the well-being of her family. While her other friends "were going to be nurses, teachers, pilots, or movie stars," Annie

Joseph "Shoeless Joe" Jackson

chose Ray "for her occupation," a task which requires her to support, comfort, and believe in him at all costs. Regardless of what Ray does, "she will be waiting for [him]" when he returns; as she says, "Whatever happens, I'm with you, Champ."

Annie's faith does not go unappreciated, however. After making love with his wife, Ray thinks, "I wish I had some kind of fame to dedicate to her . . . I see myself making my acceptance speech, thanking party faithful, then calling Annie forward to share the applause, the adoration." He implies that behind every man there is a good woman who can not earn her own applause, but who must bask in the glory and honour of her husband's fame. In Kinsella's perfect world, good women remain confined to the home where both their domestic and child-bearing labour can be concealed, devalued, and controlled. Such an arrangement prevents and discourages them from participating in the fraternity of baseball. If, when watching the game, Annie is "bored or too hot or too cold she can go back to the house" and resume her domestic duties. Fortunately for Ray, her "sense of baseball history is not highly developed"; she "is a spectator, not a fan. Like a reader who reads a whole book without caring who wrote it, she watches, enjoys, forgets, and doesn't read the box scores and standings

in the morning paper." If Annie belonged to the fraternity, Ray's world would not be possible. In the home, she stays away from his fraternal business and allows men to labour in the world outside to produce a masculine definition of perfection. Because she dutifully encourages her husband to follow his dream, she is appropriately rewarded when thousands of fans visit the field and help alleviate the family's financial worries. The "separate spheres" ideology which characterized Victorian America, and was reclaimed as one of the chief components of Reagan's America, is alive and well in Kinsella's narrative.

When Ray and Salinger "go the distance" to investigate Doc Graham's idyllic life in Chisholm, they excavate the doctor's obituary, which states that the era of the paternalistic country doctor "was historic. There will never be another quite like it." But when Doc Graham finally gets a chance to bat in the major leagues, Ray's ball field brings the era of this 1950s small town back to life. This resurrection simultaneously fills the reader with hope for the future and nostalgia for the past. Salinger might write again. Shoeless Joe might play left field again. With hard work the family farmer, always the true meritocrat, can stand up to the "new breed of land baron" who proposes to operate farms by computer. Dreams can come true. And people will come.

In the emotionally touching scene where Ray walks across the outfield lawn with his brother and father, he tells us, "I'll guide the conversations, like taking a car around a long, gentle curve in the road, and we'll hardly realize we're talking of love, and family, and life, and beauty, and friendship, and sharing . . ." Reagan's popularity and the success of his advertising campaign suggest that many Americans wanted someone to lead them through this familiar sentimental landscape. His television commercial entitled "Spring '84" did just that. Accompanied by similar music and the same voice that we hear on the "America is Back" commercial, this advertisement opens with an old pick-up truck pulling away from a white farmhouse. The shot of the house is beautifully framed, highlighting the buttercup covered fields which surround it. "This is America, spring of '84," says the voice which then introduces various representations of Reagan's America to us: two young girls in Easter bonnets, an elderly couple watching young children play, a clown standing in front of a busy carousel, an interracial basketball game, an astronaut drifting in space. As we watch these images flash before us, we hear the following text:

Just four years ago people were saying its [America's] problems were too big and too difficult to be handled by any one president. Yet what do we see now? Jobs are coming back. Housing is coming back. And for the first time in a long time, hope for the future is coming back.

As the commercial ends, the final frame shows the old pick-up truck carrying the farmer home at sundown after a hard day's work in his fields. Similarly, *Shoeless Joe*, Ronald Reagan, and baseball bring us home to America's Golden Age. They take us back to a mythic time when things were less complex, when leaders seemed to be in control, and a powerful patriarchy seemed a bit more certain about where America was headed and what dreams needed to be fulfilled. If you build the myth, people will indeed come. On reading Kinsella's novel, watching a Reagan political commercial, or attending a baseball game, many Americans have declared, "This must be heaven." These mundane pastimes make us feel good, whether we want them to or not. And good feelings sell books, win elections, and call millions each year to the field of dreams.

Source: Bryan K. Garman, "Myth Building and Cultural Politics in W. P. Kinsella's *Shoeless Joe*," in *Canadian Review of American Studies*, Vol. 24, No. 1, Winter 1994, pp. 41–59.

Neil Randall

In the following essay, Randall explores the 'fellow-feeling' of Kinsella's Shoeless Joe.

In his essay on Jean Paul Friedrich Richter, Thomas Carlyle writes of a humor that manifests itself in smile rather than laughter. "Richter is a man of mirth," says Carlyle, whose humor is "capricious . . . quaint . . . [and] heartfelt." The three adjectives represent for Carlyle the essence of what he terms "true humor" because they suggest Richter's enormous respect for humanity. "True humor," he goes on to say, "springs not more from the head than from the heart; it is not contempt, its essence is love; it issues not in laughter, but in still smiles, which lie far deeper." These smiles are not Hobbesian smirks of superiority but genuine signs of compassion for, sympathy toward, and empathy with the object of the humor. Carlyle further provides a direct link between humor and both pathos and nobility; the link is the smile of the caring man. For Carlyle, this smile is one of "fellow-feeling":

> It has sometimes been made a wonder that things so discordant should go together; that men of humour are often likewise men of sensibility. But the won-

> "Perhaps the most notable quality of *Shoeless Joe* is its continual attempt at joyfulness."

der should rather be to see them divided; to find true genial humour dwelling in a mind that was coarse or callous. The essence of humour is sensibility; warm, tender fellow-feeling with all forms of existence.

The humor of fellow-feeling denies humor that negates or denies life. Black humor, of course, with its laughter at the fallen, is anti-Carlylean, but in some senses so is Mikhail Bakhtin's carnival humor, not because it is life-denying (it expressly is not) but because its dependence on the "lower body stratum" and indecent language renders it, in Carlyle's terms, "coarse or callous." True humor, for Carlyle, is affirmative without being coarse, a celebration of life without the outrageousness of Bakhtinian festivity. The problem with such humor, of course, is that it is apt to become, well, mushy. Out of context, the phrase "warm, tender fellow-feeling with all forms of existence" gives an image of a flower-child communing with nature on a soft-focus day in 1967, hardly the stuff of an inspiring novel. But the humor of fellow-feeling in fiction, I think, despite its inherent nostalgic dangers, is more complex than this. It demands that we grow to love the characters, and it forces us to examine why we do so. If done well, and this is the hard part, Carlylean humor asks of us a willing suspension of distrust and cynicism.

One of the twentieth century's most renowned practitioners of Carlylean fellow-feeling is J. R. R. Tolkien. *The Lord of the Rings* demands that we suspend cynicism, asks us to smile benignly on its hobbits, and insists that we love its characters. If we do so, we are rewarded with beauty and terror, joy and sorrow, and a true sense of the sublime. If we do not, the book is meaningless. Edmund Wilson, among others, found Tolkien's demands impossible, even as W. H. Auden accepted and praised them. But Tolkien knew precisely what he was asking. His famous essay "On Fairy Stories" presents his theories of fantasy, one of them being the insistence on the "consolation of the happy ending." Among the important elements of this consolation is the experience, in the reader, of the fantastic "turn":

It is the mark of a good fairy-story, of the higher or more complete kind, that however wild its elements, however fantastic or terrible the adventures, it can give to child or man that hears it, when the "turn" comes, a catch of the breath, a beat and lifting of the heart, near to (or indeed accompanied by) tears, as keen as that given by any literary art.... In such stories when the "turn" comes we get a piercing glimpse of joy, and heart's desire, that for a moment passes outside the frame, rends indeed the very web of story, and lets a gleam come through.

The "piercing glimpse of joy," Tolkien goes on to say, is "a sudden glimpse of the underlying reality or truth." The Tolkienesque turn, to be sure, takes us beyond Carlyle's "warm, tender fellow-feeling," but the two ideas are clearly related. The goals for both men, one through humor and the other through fantasy, are truth, goodness, and, we can presume, beauty.

Toward the end of W. P. Kinsella's *Shoeless Joe*, Moonlight Graham walks off the playing field of Ray Kinsella's magical ballpark to treat Ray's daughter, Karin. Ray describes the scene as follows:

Then I feel compelled to look at the baseball field. In order to do that, I stand up and walk a few steps up the bleacher. What I see is Moonlight Graham loping in from right field, lithe, dark, athletic: the same handsome young man who played that one inning of baseball in 1905. But as he moves closer, his features begin to change, his step slows. He seems to become smaller. His baseball uniform fades away and is replaced by a black overcoat. His baseball cap is gone, supplanted by a thatch of white hair. As I watch, his glove miraculously turns into a black bag. The man who without a backward glance walks around the corner of the fence—a place where none of the other players will venture—is not Moonlight Graham, the baseball player of long ago, but the Doc Graham I spoke with on the moonlit night in Chisholm, Minnesota, when I flew softly across the dimensions of time....

I wonder how much he has sacrificed to save Karin's life. It seems to me that he will never be able to walk back onto the ballfield as Moonlight Graham. He has violated some cosmic rule that I vaguely know exists, and do not even attempt to understand.

To understand how such an incident triggers a humor of fellow-feeling, and I argue that it does, it will help to examine the stylistics, the "turns," and the necessity for belief in Tolkienesque fantasy. *Shoeless Joe* merges Carlyle's humor with Tolkien's fantastic, and the resulting demands on the reader are many.

In fantasy, Tolkien writes in "On Fairy Stories," "new form is made ... Man becomes a sub-creator." Furthermore, for the subcreation, the Sec-

ondary World, to be successful, requires the reader's belief. Tolkien distinguishes between the need for "belief" and the more commonly used Coleridgean "willing suspension of disbelief," suggesting that the latter is necessary only if the former fails:

"willing suspension of disbelief" ... does not seem to me a good description of what happens. What really happens is that the story-maker proves a successful "sub-creator." He makes a Secondary World which your mind can enter. Inside it, what he relates is "true": it accords with the laws of that world. You therefore believe it, while you are, as it were, inside. The moment disbelief arises, the spell is broken; the magic, or rather art, has failed. You are then out in the Primary World again, looking at the little abortive Secondary World from outside. If you are obliged, by kindliness or circumstance, to stay, then disbelief must be suspended (or stifled), otherwise listening and looking would become intolerable. But this suspension of disbelief is a substitute for the genuine thing, a subterfuge we use when condescending to games of make-believe, or when trying (more or less willingly) to find what virtue we can in the work of art that has for us failed.

We do not suspend disbelief, then, until belief itself has been lost, and then we never recapture the initial belief. For enchantment to work, for the Secondary World to be accepted, we must believe in it in a primary way.

The demands placed on the reader of *Shoeless Joe*, then, are great. The book asks of us the highest degree of belief: we must accept a magical ballpark within the Primary World of modern Iowa. Tolkien himself, in his creative works, never makes such enormous demands; he never brings the Primary World into his texts. Even fantasies that do contain both Primary and Secondary Worlds—Michael Ende's *The Neverending Story*, Guy Gavriel Kay's The *Fionavar Tapestry*, Stephen Donaldson's *The Chronicles of Thomas Covenant*—rarely have both worlds operating at the same time. *Shoeless Joe*'s Secondary World *seems* to be confined to the magical ballpark (a technique similar to the closed-off world of Peter S. Beagle's *A Fine and Private Place*), but in fact it is not. J. D. Salinger, another of Ray's creations, hears the Voice while watching a baseball game in Fenway Park, and Moonlight Graham appears during Ray's visit to Chisholm. The Secondary World, in fact, seems to follow Ray around, another feature that tests our belief.

Shoeless Joe's success at drawing our belief (and most of the reviews suggest that it has been successful) is the result, I think, of the book's use of Carlylean fellow-feeling. Ray must appear to us as a character with whom we can sympathize, with whom we can share the bizarre journey he makes across the continent to kidnap Salinger and the unreal circumstances under which Shoeless Joe Jackson comes to life. If we are to be drawn into the world without the willing suspension of disbelief, we must never lose sympathy with Ray's quest. To retain that sympathy, Ray must prove himself worthy; he must invoke our fellow-feeling. He must, in short, enchant us.

Linguistically, says Tolkien, the adjective has, in its ability to transform nouns, the power of enchantment:

> The human mind, endowed with powers of generalization and abstraction, sees not only *green-grass*, discriminating it from other things . . . but sees that it is *green* as well as being *grass*. But how powerful, how stimulating to the very faculty that produced it, was the invention of the adjective: no spell or incantation in Faerie is more potent. . . . When we can take green from grass, blue from heaven, and red from blood, we have already an enchanter's power.

One short passage from the first part of *Shoeless Joe* will suffice to demonstrate the Tolkienesque stylistics in Kinsella's descriptions. This kind of passage can be found almost by opening the book at random:

> I carried out a hose, and, making the spray so fine it was scarcely more than fog, I sprayed the soft, shaggy spring grass all that chilled night. My hands ached and my face became wet and cold, but, as I watched, the spray froze on the grass, enclosing each blade in a gossamer-crystal coating of ice. A covering that served like a coat of armor to dispel the real frost that was set like a weasel upon killing in the night. I seemed to stand taller than ever before as the sun rose, turning the ice to eye-dazzling droplets, each a prism, making the field an orgy of rainbows.

The adjectives "soft," "shaggy," and "spring," which precede "grass," alter the meaning of "grass," making us see not only that it is grass, but also that it is spring, shaggy, and soft. "Spring" imbues the grass with youth and hope, "shaggy" with both the domesticity of a living-room carpet and the playful innocence of the family sheep-dog, and "soft" with a pleasurable tactility and a dreamlike quality. The spray does not simply cover the grass with ice; it works magic by "enclosing each blade in a gossamer-crystal coating of ice." All elements of this non-finite clause are important to the creation of magical effect: "enclosing" suggests a loving, godlike attention to "each blade," and the metaphoric noun-modifier "gossamer-crystal" emphasizes both the fineness of the strand and the glasslike beauty of the coating. These modifiers, in

turn, render the harsh monosyllable "ice" beautiful rather than deadly, a notion confirmed by the subsequent simile of the armor. Finally, the ice is magically transformed through metaphor not once but twice, into " eye-dazzling droplets" (itself an adjectively oriented phrase) and then into a prism. As a prism, the ice further transforms, making the field "an orgy of rainbows," and rainbows themselves are signs of magical legend. The act of watering the grass is now an act of enchantment.

Baseball itself, Ray tells us, enchants. It is both timeless, with largely unchanging rules and a wholly unhurried atmosphere, and perfect, "solid, true, pure and precious as diamonds." Furthermore, like all enchantments, it can transform:

> Within the baselines anything can happen. Tides can reverse; oceans can open. That's why they say, "The game is never over until the last man is out." Colors can change, lives can alter, anything is possible in this gentle, flawless, loving game.

With its transformative abilities and its qualities of gentleness, flawlessness, and lovingness, baseball brings together Tolkienesque fantasy and Carlylean humor. Baseball becomes, of course, a metaphor for what Ray espouses as important writing, the gentle, flawless, loving kind practiced by Salinger in *The Catcher in the Rye*, a metaphor realized only at the novel's end when Salinger accompanies the ghostly players through the fence, promising Ray that he will fulfill his duty as writer. With that promise, baseball and writing become one.

"The consolation of fairy-stories," writes Tolkien, is "the joy of the happy ending":

> this joy . . . is not essentially "escapist" or "fugitive." In its fairy-tale—or other-world— setting, it is a sudden and miraculous grace; never to be counted on to recur. It does not deny the existence of *dyscatastrophe*, of sorrow and failure; the possibility of these is necessary to the joy of deliverance; it denies (in the face of much evidence, if you will) universal final defeat and in so far is *evangelium*, giving a fleeting glimpse of Joy, Joy beyond the walls of the world, poignant as grief.

Perhaps the most notable quality of *Shoeless Joe* is its continual attempt at joyfulness. Ray Kinsella, the narrator and main character, is above all a happy man, one who understands the possibility of joy as it comes through the magic of creation and the fulfillment of dreams. To Salinger he says, "I'm one of the few happy men in the United States," and the novel certainly bears this out. But for Tolkien joy does not imply only happiness; in fact, he states that the "joy of deliverance" is possible only through "dyscatastrophe," through sorrow and failure. What separates the joy of true fantasy from the sentimentality of simple nostalgia is precisely this dyscatastrophe. What dyscatastrophe means is that true joy is achieved only with the recognition of immense loss.

The moments of joy mixed with loss Tolkien calls "turns." For Tolkien, the turn gives us—along with "a catch of the breath, a beat and lifting of the heart," and "a piercing glimpse of joy"—not only "a 'consolation' for the sorrow of this world but a satisfaction, and an answer to that question, 'Is it true?'." There are at least four major turns in *Shoeless Joe*: Kid Scisson's failure on the diamond; Ray's questioning of the phantom ballplayers; Salinger's departure at the novel's end; and Moonlight Graham's sacrifice. Each provides a moment that is true in Ray's world as he has defined it, and each brings the emotional reactions and the glimpse of joy that Tolkien demands.

Eddie Scissons, the fraudulent "oldest living Chicago Cub," receives, through the magic of Ray's ballpark, a chance to fulfill his desire to pitch for the Cubs. Ray's magic has already granted Moonlight Graham his dearest wish—to play in the majors—and we expect that Scissons will be similarly successful. But, unlike Graham, Scissons simply is not good enough for the majors; his chance on the mound fails, and he is humiliated. "[W]hen most people reach out for their heart's desire," Ray tells us, "it appears not as a horse but as a tiger, and they are rewarded with snarls, frustration, and disillusionment." Scissons' failure is a turn precisely because it *is* a failure, and we have not seen Ray's magic fail before. That failure confirms the "truth" of Ray's Secondary World because in its allowance for failure it ceases to be a Never-Never Land and becomes a valid Secondary World.

The novel's second turn similarly destroys the seemingly pure felicity of Ray's magic. When Ray asks of the ballplayers, "What do you become when you walk through that door in center field?," he is asking the question that has, throughout the novel, concerned us as well. But in asking it he is attempting what seems an impossible task: to bridge the gap that must exist between the subcreator and his creation. Of all the characters in the book, Ray alone is unable to discover precisely what his magic does. This gap seems confirmed by the placement of the question: immediately after the players have asked Ray if they can help work the farm to make it profitable, a similar attempt to cross the gap between Primary and Secondary Worlds. Like Ray,

we have feared throughout that attempting such a crossing will destroy the magic completely, and now our fears are confirmed:

> "But can you do that," I say. "I've never seen any of you anywhere except on the field. What do you become when you walk through that door in center field?"
>
> The silence that follows is long and ominous. I feel like I have just stomped across an innocent children's game, or broken a doll.
>
> "We sleep," says Chick Gandil finally.
>
> "And wait," says Happy Felsch.
>
> "And dream," says Joe Jackson. "Oh, how we dream. . . . " He stops, the look of awe and rapture on his face enough of an explanation.
>
> The magic has been broken.

As in the Eddie Scissons case, the magic cannot process an impossible wish, one at odds with the truth of Ray's Secondary World. The turn here is first that the question has been asked and second that the answer has broken the magic. We fear it has been irretrievably lost.

J. D. Salinger, at the end of the novel, provides another turn by leaving with the players through the gate in center field. He thus becomes the only character to leave the Primary World and enter the Secondary. We are initially startled at this crossing, especially after the destruction of magic at Ray's attempt to bridge the worlds, but Salinger's "rapture," as the title of the last section calls it, becomes possible when we realize that he is as much Ray's creation as are the players and is thus not subject to the same law as Ray. Salinger's explanation of why the players chose him, and not Ray, further clarifies the incident and establishes the turn:

> "I thought of turning them down," says Salinger. "I really did. Telling them it was you who created them—you who deserves to be first. But then I thought, they must know; there must be a reason for them to choose me, just as there was a reason for them to choose you, and Iowa, and this farm. . . .
>
> "If you can package up your jealousy for a few minutes, you'll see that I'm right. I'm unattached. My family is grown up. And," he says, smiling sardonically at me, "if I have the courage to do this, then you'll have to stop badgering me about the other business [publishing new fiction]. I mean, publishing is such a pale horse compared to this. But what a story it will make"—and his voice rises— "a man being able to touch the perfect dream. I'll write of it. I promise."

Salinger can enter the Secondary World because he has understood his moral duty as a writer.

This is, of course, the end of Ray's quest—to find Salinger and "ease his pain." We catch our breath at the mere possibility of Salinger's entering the Secondary World, and we feel the joy of the quest's fulfillment. But it is a joy mixed with loss: like Ray, we have come to know Salinger, and with his passing something of happiness also passes.

The final turn I shall discuss is Moonlight Graham's sacrifice (quoted above). As a Tolkienesque turn it is perhaps the most climactic scene in the book: Graham is the only character to make the transition from the Secondary to the Primary World, and the nobility of his action is wondrous. Of all the scenes in the novel, this is, I think, the most likely to elicit the tears that accompany a turn, first for Graham's nobility and second for his subsequent show of humility. "Well, now," he says immediately after making the transformation from Moonlight Graham to Doc Graham, "it's lucky I happened on the scene, Ray Kinsella. That little girl wouldn't have lasted much longer." Graham here is no longer the Moonlight Graham we have come to know but is rather the Doc Graham we met on Ray's journey through time in Chisholm, Minnesota, and this consistency furthers the internal truth of Ray's Secondary World. Once again the turn mixes a "piercing glimpse of joy" (at Graham's nobility) with a profound sense of loss (at what Graham has given up).

Graham's sacrifice reflects as well the novel's theme of moral duty. Moonlight Graham must face his duty as a doctor to save a life, thereby sacrificing his dream of baseball. J. D. Salinger must realize his duty as a writer, thereby sacrificing his solitude. And Ray Kinsella must affirm his duties as husband/father and as enchanter, thereby sacrificing his desire to enter his own Secondary World and keep it for himself. In essence, each of these duties demands the sharing of one's gifts: Graham his medical skill, Salinger his writing, Ray his magic, and all their ability to impart joy.

On seeing the magical baseball game for the first time, Salinger insists that Ray share it:

"This is too wonderful to keep to ourselves. You have to share."

"With whom?" [Ray asks.] "How many? How do we select? And first, how do we make people believe?"

. . .

"You're difficult to convince."

"The pot calling the kettle names. But don't you see, we have little to do with this. We aren't the ones who decide who can see and who can't. Wouldn't I let my own twin brother see my miracle if I could? But more

important than that, the way you feel now is the way people feel who react to your work. If I share, then so must you."

Moral fiction is one of *Shoeless Joe*'s primary concerns, going so far as to speak internally of it. Ray frequently attempts to convince Salinger to publish, but Salinger refuses on the grounds that readers will not allow it. "It's a sad time when the world won't listen to stories about good men," he says. "It's one of the reasons I don't publish anymore."

Source: Neil Randall, "*Shoeless Joe*: Fantasy and the Humor of Fellow-Feeling," in *Modern Fiction Studies Special Issue: Modern Sports Fiction*, Vol. 33, No. 1, Spring 1987, pp. 173–80.

Sources

Beach, Charles Franklyn, "Joyful vs. Joyless Religion in W. P. Kinsella's *Shoeless Joe*," in *Aethlon: The Journal of Sport Literature*, Vol. 16, No. 1, Fall 1998, pp. 85–94.

Garman, Bryan K., "Myth Building and Cultural Politics in W. P. Kinsella's *Shoeless Joe*," in *Canadian Review of American Studies/Revue Canadienne d'Etudes Americaines*, Vol. 24, No. 1, Winter 1994, pp. 41–62.

Lewis, Maggie, Review, in *Christian Science Monitor*, July 9, 1982, p. 14.

Merlock, Ray, "Shoeless Joe: From Pickens County to the Field of Dreams," in *South Carolina Review*, Vol. 22, No. 2, Spring 1990, pp. 68–76.

Plummer, William, "In Another League," in *Newsweek*, August 23, 1982, p. 64.

Review, in *Publishers Weekly*, February 26, 1982, p. 141.

Schweld, Barry, Review, in *Library Journal*, April 1, 1982, p. 745.

Further Reading

Joffe, Linda S., "Praise Baseball. Amen: Religious Metaphors in *Shoeless Joe* and *Field of Dreams*," in *Aethlon: The Journal of Sport Literature*, Vol. 9, No. 2, Spring 1992, pp. 153–63.

    Joffe discusses some of the allusions to Christianity in the novel and also the differences between the novel and the movie.

Kirtz, Mary K., "Canadian Book, American Film: Shoeless Joe Transfigured on a Field of Dreams," in *Literature/Film Quarterly*, Vol. 23, No. 1, 1995, pp. 26–31.

    Kirtz argues that the film *Field of Dreams* eliminates the feminine "moral presence" in the novel and presents the story as a "man's story" with a patriarchal political message.

Lord, Timothy C., "Hegel, Marx, and *Shoeless Joe*: Religious Ideology in Kinsella's Baseball Fantasy," in *Aethlon: The Journal of Sport Literature*, Vol. 10, No. 1, Fall 1992, pp. 43–51.

> Lord shows how baseball serves as a metaphor for religion. He also demonstrates that the way in which Ray handles the threat to his farm shows his philosophical assumptions about spiritual and material reality.

Pellow, C. Kenneth, "Shoeless Joe in Film and Fiction," in *Aethlon: The Journal of Sport Literature*, Vol. 9, No. 1, Fall 1991, pp. 17–23.

> Pellow argues that the film *Field of Dreams* is not a satisfactory version of the novel. It strips the novel of its poetry and distorts its political and social themes.

Glossary of Literary Terms

A

Abstract: As an adjective applied to writing or literary works, abstract refers to words or phrases that name things not knowable through the five senses.

Aestheticism: A literary and artistic movement of the nineteenth century. Followers of the movement believed that art should not be mixed with social, political, or moral teaching. The statement "art for art's sake" is a good summary of aestheticism. The movement had its roots in France, but it gained widespread importance in England in the last half of the nineteenth century, where it helped change the Victorian practice of including moral lessons in literature.

Allegory: A narrative technique in which characters representing things or abstract ideas are used to convey a message or teach a lesson. Allegory is typically used to teach moral, ethical, or religious lessons but is sometimes used for satiric or political purposes.

Allusion: A reference to a familiar literary or historical person or event, used to make an idea more easily understood.

Analogy: A comparison of two things made to explain something unfamiliar through its similarities to something familiar, or to prove one point based on the acceptedness of another. Similes and metaphors are types of analogies.

Antagonist: The major character in a narrative or drama who works against the hero or protagonist.

Anthropomorphism: The presentation of animals or objects in human shape or with human characteristics. The term is derived from the Greek word for "human form."

Antihero: A central character in a work of literature who lacks traditional heroic qualities such as courage, physical prowess, and fortitude. Antiheroes typically distrust conventional values and are unable to commit themselves to any ideals. They generally feel helpless in a world over which they have no control. Antiheroes usually accept, and often celebrate, their positions as social outcasts.

Apprenticeship Novel: See *Bildungsroman*

Archetype: The word archetype is commonly used to describe an original pattern or model from which all other things of the same kind are made. This term was introduced to literary criticism from the psychology of Carl Jung. It expresses Jung's theory that behind every person's "unconscious," or repressed memories of the past, lies the "collective unconscious" of the human race: memories of the countless typical experiences of our ancestors. These memories are said to prompt illogical associations that trigger powerful emotions in the reader. Often, the emotional process is primitive, even primordial. Archetypes are the literary images that grow out of the "collective unconscious." They appear in literature as incidents and plots that repeat basic patterns of life. They may also appear as stereotyped characters.

Avant-garde: French term meaning "vanguard." It is used in literary criticism to describe new writing that rejects traditional approaches to literature in favor of innovations in style or content.

B

Beat Movement: A period featuring a group of American poets and novelists of the 1950s and 1960s—including Jack Kerouac, Allen Ginsberg, Gregory Corso, William S. Burroughs, and Lawrence Ferlinghetti—who rejected established social and literary values. Using such techniques as stream of consciousness writing and jazz-influenced free verse and focusing on unusual or abnormal states of mind—generated by religious ecstasy or the use of drugs—the Beat writers aimed to create works that were unconventional in both form and subject matter.

Bildungsroman: A German word meaning "novel of development." The *bildungsroman* is a study of the maturation of a youthful character, typically brought about through a series of social or sexual encounters that lead to self-awareness. *Bildungsroman* is used interchangeably with *erziehungsroman*, a novel of initiation and education. When a *bildungsroman* is concerned with the development of an artist (as in James Joyce's *A Portrait of the Artist as a Young Man*), it is often termed a *kunstlerroman*. Also known as Apprenticeship Novel, Coming of Age Novel, *Erziehungsroman,* or *Kunstlerroman*.

Black Aesthetic Movement: A period of artistic and literary development among African Americans in the 1960s and early 1970s. This was the first major African-American artistic movement since the Harlem Renaissance and was closely paralleled by the civil rights and black power movements. The black aesthetic writers attempted to produce works of art that would be meaningful to the black masses. Key figures in black aesthetics included one of its founders, poet and playwright Amiri Baraka, formerly known as LeRoi Jones; poet and essayist Haki R. Madhubuti, formerly Don L. Lee; poet and playwright Sonia Sanchez; and dramatist Ed Bullins. Also known as Black Arts Movement.

Black Humor: Writing that places grotesque elements side by side with humorous ones in an attempt to shock the reader, forcing him or her to laugh at the horrifying reality of a disordered world. Also known as Black Comedy.

Burlesque: Any literary work that uses exaggeration to make its subject appear ridiculous, either by treating a trivial subject with profound seriousness or by treating a dignified subject frivolously. The word "burlesque" may also be used as an adjective, as in "burlesque show," to mean "striptease act."

C

Character: Broadly speaking, a person in a literary work. The actions of characters are what constitute the plot of a story, novel, or poem. There are numerous types of characters, ranging from simple, stereotypical figures to intricate, multifaceted ones. In the techniques of anthropomorphism and personification, animals—and even places or things—can assume aspects of character. "Characterization" is the process by which an author creates vivid, believable characters in a work of art. This may be done in a variety of ways, including (1) direct description of the character by the narrator; (2) the direct presentation of the speech, thoughts, or actions of the character; and (3) the responses of other characters to the character. The term "character" also refers to a form originated by the ancient Greek writer Theophrastus that later became popular in the seventeenth and eighteenth centuries. It is a short essay or sketch of a person who prominently displays a specific attribute or quality, such as miserliness or ambition.

Climax: The turning point in a narrative, the moment when the conflict is at its most intense. Typically, the structure of stories, novels, and plays is one of rising action, in which tension builds to the climax, followed by falling action, in which tension lessens as the story moves to its conclusion.

Colloquialism: A word, phrase, or form of pronunciation that is acceptable in casual conversation but not in formal, written communication. It is considered more acceptable than slang.

Coming of Age Novel: See *Bildungsroman*

Concrete: Concrete is the opposite of abstract, and refers to a thing that actually exists or a description that allows the reader to experience an object or concept with the senses.

Connotation: The impression that a word gives beyond its defined meaning. Connotations may be universally understood or may be significant only to a certain group.

Convention: Any widely accepted literary device, style, or form.

D

Denotation: The definition of a word, apart from the impressions or feelings it creates (connotations) in the reader.

Denouement: A French word meaning "the un-knotting." In literary criticism, it denotes the resolution of conflict in fiction or drama. The *denouement* follows the climax and provides an outcome to the primary plot situation as well as an explanation of secondary plot complications. The *denouement* often involves a character's recognition of his or her state of mind or moral condition. Also known as Falling Action.

Description: Descriptive writing is intended to allow a reader to picture the scene or setting in which the action of a story takes place. The form this description takes often evokes an intended emotional response—a dark, spooky graveyard will evoke fear, and a peaceful, sunny meadow will evoke calmness.

Dialogue: In its widest sense, dialogue is simply conversation between people in a literary work; in its most restricted sense, it refers specifically to the speech of characters in a drama. As a specific literary genre, a "dialogue" is a composition in which characters debate an issue or idea.

Diction: The selection and arrangement of words in a literary work. Either or both may vary depending on the desired effect. There are four general types of diction: "formal," used in scholarly or lofty writing; "informal," used in relaxed but educated conversation; "colloquial," used in everyday speech; and "slang," containing newly coined words and other terms not accepted in formal usage.

Didactic: A term used to describe works of literature that aim to teach some moral, religious, political, or practical lesson. Although didactic elements are often found in artistically pleasing works, the term "didactic" usually refers to literature in which the message is more important than the form. The term may also be used to criticize a work that the critic finds "overly didactic," that is, heavy-handed in its delivery of a lesson.

Doppelganger: A literary technique by which a character is duplicated (usually in the form of an alter ego, though sometimes as a ghostly counterpart) or divided into two distinct, usually opposite personalities. The use of this character device is widespread in nineteenth- and twentieth-century literature, and indicates a growing awareness among authors that the "self" is really a composite of many "selves." Also known as The Double.

Double Entendre: A corruption of a French phrase meaning "double meaning." The term is used to indicate a word or phrase that is deliberately ambiguous, especially when one of the meanings is risqué or improper.

Dramatic Irony: Occurs when the audience of a play or the reader of a work of literature knows something that a character in the work itself does not know. The irony is in the contrast between the intended meaning of the statements or actions of a character and the additional information understood by the audience.

Dystopia: An imaginary place in a work of fiction where the characters lead dehumanized, fearful lives.

E

Edwardian: Describes cultural conventions identified with the period of the reign of Edward VII of England (1901-1910). Writers of the Edwardian Age typically displayed a strong reaction against the propriety and conservatism of the Victorian Age. Their work often exhibits distrust of authority in religion, politics, and art and expresses strong doubts about the soundness of conventional values.

Empathy: A sense of shared experience, including emotional and physical feelings, with someone or something other than oneself. Empathy is often used to describe the response of a reader to a literary character.

Enlightenment, The: An eighteenth-century philosophical movement. It began in France but had a wide impact throughout Europe and America. Thinkers of the Enlightenment valued reason and believed that both the individual and society could achieve a state of perfection. Corresponding to this essentially humanist vision was a resistance to religious authority.

Epigram: A saying that makes the speaker's point quickly and concisely. Often used to preface a novel.

Epilogue: A concluding statement or section of a literary work. In dramas, particularly those of the seventeenth and eighteenth centuries, the epilogue is a closing speech, often in verse, delivered by an actor at the end of a play and spoken directly to the audience.

Epiphany: A sudden revelation of truth inspired by a seemingly trivial incident.

Episode: An incident that forms part of a story and is significantly related to it. Episodes may be either self-contained narratives or events that depend on a larger context for their sense and importance.

Epistolary Novel: A novel in the form of letters. The form was particularly popular in the eighteenth century.

Epithet: A word or phrase, often disparaging or abusive, that expresses a character trait of someone or something.

Existentialism: A predominantly twentieth-century philosophy concerned with the nature and perception of human existence. There are two major strains of existentialist thought: atheistic and Christian. Followers of atheistic existentialism believe that the individual is alone in a godless universe and that the basic human condition is one of suffering and loneliness. Nevertheless, because there are no fixed values, individuals can create their own characters—indeed, they can shape themselves—through the exercise of free will. The atheistic strain culminates in and is popularly associated with the works of Jean-Paul Sartre. The Christian existentialists, on the other hand, believe that only in God may people find freedom from life's anguish. The two strains hold certain beliefs in common: that existence cannot be fully understood or described through empirical effort; that anguish is a universal element of life; that individuals must bear responsibility for their actions; and that there is no common standard of behavior or perception for religious and ethical matters.

Expatriates: See *Expatriatism*

Expatriatism: The practice of leaving one's country to live for an extended period in another country.

Exposition: Writing intended to explain the nature of an idea, thing, or theme. Expository writing is often combined with description, narration, or argument. In dramatic writing, the exposition is the introductory material which presents the characters, setting, and tone of the play.

Expressionism: An indistinct literary term, originally used to describe an early twentieth-century school of German painting. The term applies to almost any mode of unconventional, highly subjective writing that distorts reality in some way.

F

Fable: A prose or verse narrative intended to convey a moral. Animals or inanimate objects with human characteristics often serve as characters in fables.

Falling Action: See *Denouement*

Fantasy: A literary form related to mythology and folklore. Fantasy literature is typically set in non-existent realms and features supernatural beings.

Farce: A type of comedy characterized by broad humor, outlandish incidents, and often vulgar subject matter.

Femme fatale: A French phrase with the literal translation "fatal woman." A *femme fatale* is a sensuous, alluring woman who often leads men into danger or trouble.

Fiction: Any story that is the product of imagination rather than a documentation of fact. Characters and events in such narratives may be based in real life but their ultimate form and configuration is a creation of the author.

Figurative Language: A technique in writing in which the author temporarily interrupts the order, construction, or meaning of the writing for a particular effect. This interruption takes the form of one or more figures of speech such as hyperbole, irony, or simile. Figurative language is the opposite of literal language, in which every word is truthful, accurate, and free of exaggeration or embellishment.

Figures of Speech: Writing that differs from customary conventions for construction, meaning, order, or significance for the purpose of a special meaning or effect. There are two major types of figures of speech: rhetorical figures, which do not make changes in the meaning of the words, and tropes, which do.

Fin de siecle: A French term meaning "end of the century." The term is used to denote the last decade of the nineteenth century, a transition period when writers and other artists abandoned old conventions and looked for new techniques and objectives.

First Person: See *Point of View*

Flashback: A device used in literature to present action that occurred before the beginning of the story. Flashbacks are often introduced as the dreams or recollections of one or more characters.

Foil: A character in a work of literature whose physical or psychological qualities contrast strongly with, and therefore highlight, the corresponding qualities of another character.

Folklore: Traditions and myths preserved in a culture or group of people. Typically, these are passed on by word of mouth in various forms—such as legends, songs, and proverbs—or preserved in customs and ceremonies. This term was first used by W. J. Thoms in 1846.

Folktale: A story originating in oral tradition. Folktales fall into a variety of categories, including legends, ghost stories, fairy tales, fables, and anecdotes based on historical figures and events.

Foreshadowing: A device used in literature to create expectation or to set up an explanation of later developments.

Form: The pattern or construction of a work which identifies its genre and distinguishes it from other genres.

G

Genre: A category of literary work. In critical theory, genre may refer to both the content of a given work—tragedy, comedy, pastoral—and to its form, such as poetry, novel, or drama.

Gilded Age: A period in American history during the 1870s characterized by political corruption and materialism. A number of important novels of social and political criticism were written during this time.

Gothicism: In literary criticism, works characterized by a taste for the medieval or morbidly attractive. A gothic novel prominently features elements of horror, the supernatural, gloom, and violence: clanking chains, terror, charnel houses, ghosts, medieval castles, and mysteriously slamming doors. The term "gothic novel" is also applied to novels that lack elements of the traditional Gothic setting but that create a similar atmosphere of terror or dread.

Grotesque: In literary criticism, the subject matter of a work or a style of expression characterized by exaggeration, deformity, freakishness, and disorder. The grotesque often includes an element of comic absurdity.

H

Harlem Renaissance: The Harlem Renaissance of the 1920s is generally considered the first significant movement of black writers and artists in the United States. During this period, new and established black writers published more fiction and poetry than ever before, the first influential black literary journals were established, and black authors and artists received their first widespread recognition and serious critical appraisal. Among the major writers associated with this period are Claude McKay, Jean Toomer, Countee Cullen, Langston Hughes, Arna Bontemps, Nella Larsen, and Zora Neale Hurston. Also known as Negro Renaissance and New Negro Movement.

Hero/Heroine: The principal sympathetic character (male or female) in a literary work. Heroes and heroines typically exhibit admirable traits: idealism, courage, and integrity, for example.

Holocaust Literature: Literature influenced by or written about the Holocaust of World War II. Such literature includes true stories of survival in concentration camps, escape, and life after the war, as well as fictional works and poetry.

Humanism: A philosophy that places faith in the dignity of humankind and rejects the medieval perception of the individual as a weak, fallen creature. "Humanists" typically believe in the perfectibility of human nature and view reason and education as the means to that end.

Hyperbole: In literary criticism, deliberate exaggeration used to achieve an effect.

I

Idiom: A word construction or verbal expression closely associated with a given language.

Image: A concrete representation of an object or sensory experience. Typically, such a representation helps evoke the feelings associated with the object or experience itself. Images are either "literal" or "figurative." Literal images are especially concrete and involve little or no extension of the obvious meaning of the words used to express them. Figurative images do not follow the literal meaning of the words exactly. Images in literature are usually visual, but the term "image" can also refer to the representation of any sensory experience.

Imagery: The array of images in a literary work. Also, figurative language.

In medias res: A Latin term meaning "in the middle of things." It refers to the technique of beginning a story at its midpoint and then using various flashback devices to reveal previous action.

Interior Monologue: A narrative technique in which characters' thoughts are revealed in a way that appears to be uncontrolled by the author. The interior monologue typically aims to reveal the inner self of a character. It portrays emotional experiences as they occur at both a conscious and unconscious level. Images are often used to represent sensations or emotions.

Irony: In literary criticism, the effect of language in which the intended meaning is the opposite of what is stated.

J

Jargon: Language that is used or understood only by a select group of people. Jargon may refer to terminology used in a certain profession, such as computer jargon, or it may refer to any nonsensical language that is not understood by most people.

L

Leitmotiv: See *Motif*

Literal Language: An author uses literal language when he or she writes without exaggerating or embellishing the subject matter and without any tools of figurative language.

Lost Generation: A term first used by Gertrude Stein to describe the post-World War I generation of American writers: men and women haunted by a sense of betrayal and emptiness brought about by the destructiveness of the war.

M

Mannerism: Exaggerated, artificial adherence to a literary manner or style. Also, a popular style of the visual arts of late sixteenth-century Europe that was marked by elongation of the human form and by intentional spatial distortion. Literary works that are self-consciously high-toned and artistic are often said to be "mannered."

Metaphor: A figure of speech that expresses an idea through the image of another object. Metaphors suggest the essence of the first object by identifying it with certain qualities of the second object.

Modernism: Modern literary practices. Also, the principles of a literary school that lasted from roughly the beginning of the twentieth century until the end of World War II. Modernism is defined by its rejection of the literary conventions of the nineteenth century and by its opposition to conventional morality, taste, traditions, and economic values.

Mood: The prevailing emotions of a work or of the author in his or her creation of the work. The mood of a work is not always what might be expected based on its subject matter.

Motif: A theme, character type, image, metaphor, or other verbal element that recurs throughout a single work of literature or occurs in a number of different works over a period of time. Also known as *Motiv* or *Leitmotiv.*

Myth: An anonymous tale emerging from the traditional beliefs of a culture or social unit. Myths use supernatural explanations for natural phenomena. They may also explain cosmic issues like creation and death. Collections of myths, known as mythologies, are common to all cultures and nations, but the best-known myths belong to the Norse, Roman, and Greek mythologies.

N

Narration: The telling of a series of events, real or invented. A narration may be either a simple narrative, in which the events are recounted chronologically, or a narrative with a plot, in which the account is given in a style reflecting the author's artistic concept of the story. Narration is sometimes used as a synonym for "storyline."

Narrative: A verse or prose accounting of an event or sequence of events, real or invented. The term is also used as an adjective in the sense "method of narration." For example, in literary criticism, the expression "narrative technique" usually refers to the way the author structures and presents his or her story.

Narrator: The teller of a story. The narrator may be the author or a character in the story through whom the author speaks.

Naturalism: A literary movement of the late nineteenth and early twentieth centuries. The movement's major theorist, French novelist Emile Zola, envisioned a type of fiction that would examine human life with the objectivity of scientific inquiry. The Naturalists typically viewed human beings as either the products of "biological determinism," ruled by hereditary instincts and engaged in an endless struggle for survival, or as the products of "socioeconomic determinism," ruled by social and economic forces beyond their control. In their works, the Naturalists generally ignored the highest levels of society and focused on degradation: poverty, alcoholism, prostitution, insanity, and disease.

Noble Savage: The idea that primitive man is noble and good but becomes evil and corrupted as he becomes civilized. The concept of the noble savage originated in the Renaissance period but is more closely identified with such later writers as

Jean-Jacques Rousseau and Aphra Behn. See also Primitivism.

Novel of Ideas: A novel in which the examination of intellectual issues and concepts takes precedence over characterization or a traditional storyline.

Novel of Manners: A novel that examines the customs and mores of a cultural group.

Novel: A long fictional narrative written in prose, which developed from the novella and other early forms of narrative. A novel is usually organized under a plot or theme with a focus on character development and action.

Novella: An Italian term meaning "story." This term has been especially used to describe fourteenth-century Italian tales, but it also refers to modern short novels.

O

Objective Correlative: An outward set of objects, a situation, or a chain of events corresponding to an inward experience and evoking this experience in the reader. The term frequently appears in modern criticism in discussions of authors' intended effects on the emotional responses of readers.

Objectivity: A quality in writing characterized by the absence of the author's opinion or feeling about the subject matter. Objectivity is an important factor in criticism.

Oedipus Complex: A son's amorous obsession with his mother. The phrase is derived from the story of the ancient Theban hero Oedipus, who unknowingly killed his father and married his mother.

Omniscience: See *Point of View*

Onomatopoeia: The use of words whose sounds express or suggest their meaning. In its simplest sense, onomatopoeia may be represented by words that mimic the sounds they denote such as "hiss" or "meow." At a more subtle level, the pattern and rhythm of sounds and rhymes of a line or poem may be onomatopoeic.

Oxymoron: A phrase combining two contradictory terms. Oxymorons may be intentional or unintentional.

P

Parable: A story intended to teach a moral lesson or answer an ethical question.

Paradox: A statement that appears illogical or contradictory at first, but may actually point to an underlying truth.

Parallelism: A method of comparison of two ideas in which each is developed in the same grammatical structure.

Parody: In literary criticism, this term refers to an imitation of a serious literary work or the signature style of a particular author in a ridiculous manner. A typical parody adopts the style of the original and applies it to an inappropriate subject for humorous effect. Parody is a form of satire and could be considered the literary equivalent of a caricature or cartoon.

Pastoral: A term derived from the Latin word "pastor," meaning shepherd. A pastoral is a literary composition on a rural theme. The conventions of the pastoral were originated by the third-century Greek poet Theocritus, who wrote about the experiences, love affairs, and pastimes of Sicilian shepherds. In a pastoral, characters and language of a courtly nature are often placed in a simple setting. The term pastoral is also used to classify dramas, elegies, and lyrics that exhibit the use of country settings and shepherd characters.

Pen Name: See *Pseudonym*

Persona: A Latin term meaning "mask." *Personae* are the characters in a fictional work of literature. The *persona* generally functions as a mask through which the author tells a story in a voice other than his or her own. A *persona* is usually either a character in a story who acts as a narrator or an "implied author," a voice created by the author to act as the narrator for himself or herself.

Personification: A figure of speech that gives human qualities to abstract ideas, animals, and inanimate objects. Also known as *Prosopopoeia*.

Picaresque Novel: Episodic fiction depicting the adventures of a roguish central character ("picaro" is Spanish for "rogue"). The picaresque hero is commonly a low-born but clever individual who wanders into and out of various affairs of love, danger, and farcical intrigue. These involvements may take place at all social levels and typically present a humorous and wide-ranging satire of a given society.

Plagiarism: Claiming another person's written material as one's own. Plagiarism can take the form of direct, word-for-word copying or the theft of the substance or idea of the work.

Plot: In literary criticism, this term refers to the pattern of events in a narrative or drama. In its simplest sense, the plot guides the author in composing the work and helps the reader follow the work. Typically, plots exhibit causality and unity and have a beginning, a middle, and an end. Sometimes, however, a plot may consist of a series of disconnected events, in which case it is known as an "episodic plot."

Poetic Justice: An outcome in a literary work, not necessarily a poem, in which the good are rewarded and the evil are punished, especially in ways that particularly fit their virtues or crimes.

Poetic License: Distortions of fact and literary convention made by a writer—not always a poet—for the sake of the effect gained. Poetic license is closely related to the concept of "artistic freedom."

Poetics: This term has two closely related meanings. It denotes (1) an aesthetic theory in literary criticism about the essence of poetry or (2) rules prescribing the proper methods, content, style, or diction of poetry. The term poetics may also refer to theories about literature in general, not just poetry.

Point of View: The narrative perspective from which a literary work is presented to the reader. There are four traditional points of view. The "third person omniscient" gives the reader a "godlike" perspective, unrestricted by time or place, from which to see actions and look into the minds of characters. This allows the author to comment openly on characters and events in the work. The "third person" point of view presents the events of the story from outside of any single character's perception, much like the omniscient point of view, but the reader must understand the action as it takes place and without any special insight into characters' minds or motivations. The "first person" or "personal" point of view relates events as they are perceived by a single character. The main character "tells" the story and may offer opinions about the action and characters which differ from those of the author. Much less common than omniscient, third person, and first person is the "second person" point of view, wherein the author tells the story as if it is happening to the reader.

Polemic: A work in which the author takes a stand on a controversial subject, such as abortion or religion. Such works are often extremely argumentative or provocative.

Pornography: Writing intended to provoke feelings of lust in the reader. Such works are often condemned by critics and teachers, but those which can be shown to have literary value are viewed less harshly.

Post-Aesthetic Movement: An artistic response made by African Americans to the black aesthetic

movement of the 1960s and early '70s. Writers since that time have adopted a somewhat different tone in their work, with less emphasis placed on the disparity between black and white in the United States. In the words of post-aesthetic authors such as Toni Morrison, John Edgar Wideman, and Kristin Hunter, African Americans are portrayed as looking inward for answers to their own questions, rather than always looking to the outside world.

Postmodernism: Writing from the 1960s forward characterized by experimentation and continuing to apply some of the fundamentals of modernism, which included existentialism and alienation. Postmodernists have gone a step further in the rejection of tradition begun with the modernists by also rejecting traditional forms, preferring the anti-novel over the novel and the antihero over the hero.

Primitivism: The belief that primitive peoples were nobler and less flawed than civilized peoples because they had not been subjected to the tainting influence of society. See also Noble Savage.

Prologue: An introductory section of a literary work. It often contains information establishing the situation of the characters or presents information about the setting, time period, or action. In drama, the prologue is spoken by a chorus or by one of the principal characters.

Prose: A literary medium that attempts to mirror the language of everyday speech. It is distinguished from poetry by its use of unmetered, unrhymed language consisting of logically related sentences. Prose is usually grouped into paragraphs that form a cohesive whole such as an essay or a novel.

Prosopopoeia: See *Personification*

Protagonist: The central character of a story who serves as a focus for its themes and incidents and as the principal rationale for its development. The protagonist is sometimes referred to in discussions of modern literature as the hero or antihero.

Protest Fiction: Protest fiction has as its primary purpose the protesting of some social injustice, such as racism or discrimination.

Proverb: A brief, sage saying that expresses a truth about life in a striking manner.

Pseudonym: A name assumed by a writer, most often intended to prevent his or her identification as the author of a work. Two or more authors may work together under one pseudonym, or an author may use a different name for each genre he or she publishes in. Some publishing companies maintain "house pseudonyms," under which any number of authors may write installations in a series. Some authors also choose a pseudonym over their real names the way an actor may use a stage name.

Pun: A play on words that have similar sounds but different meanings.

R

Realism: A nineteenth-century European literary movement that sought to portray familiar characters, situations, and settings in a realistic manner. This was done primarily by using an objective narrative point of view and through the buildup of accurate detail. The standard for success of any realistic work depends on how faithfully it transfers common experience into fictional forms. The realistic method may be altered or extended, as in stream of consciousness writing, to record highly subjective experience.

Repartee: Conversation featuring snappy retorts and witticisms.

Resolution: The portion of a story following the climax, in which the conflict is resolved. See also *Denouement.*

Rhetoric: In literary criticism, this term denotes the art of ethical persuasion. In its strictest sense, rhetoric adheres to various principles developed since classical times for arranging facts and ideas in a clear, persuasive, appealing manner. The term is also used to refer to effective prose in general and theories of or methods for composing effective prose.

Rhetorical Question: A question intended to provoke thought, but not an expressed answer, in the reader. It is most commonly used in oratory and other persuasive genres.

Rising Action: The part of a drama where the plot becomes increasingly complicated. Rising action leads up to the climax, or turning point, of a drama.

Roman a clef: A French phrase meaning "novel with a key." It refers to a narrative in which real persons are portrayed under fictitious names.

Romance: A broad term, usually denoting a narrative with exotic, exaggerated, often idealized characters, scenes, and themes.

Romanticism: This term has two widely accepted meanings. In historical criticism, it refers to a European intellectual and artistic movement of the late eighteenth and early nineteenth centuries that sought greater freedom of personal expression than that allowed by the strict rules of literary form and logic of the eighteenth-century neoclassicists. The Romantics preferred emotional and imaginative ex-pression to rational analysis. They considered the individual to be at the center of all experience and so placed him or her at the center of their art. The Romantics believed that the creative imagination reveals nobler truths—unique feelings and attitudes—than those that could be discovered by logic or by scientific examination. Both the natural world and the state of childhood were important sources for revelations of "eternal truths." "Romanticism" is also used as a general term to refer to a type of sensibility found in all periods of literary history and usually considered to be in opposition to the principles of classicism. In this sense, Romanticism signifies any work or philosophy in which the exotic or dreamlike figure strongly, or that is devoted to individualistic expression, self-analysis, or a pursuit of a higher realm of knowledge than can be discovered by human reason.

Romantics: See *Romanticism*

S

Satire: A work that uses ridicule, humor, and wit to criticize and provoke change in human nature and institutions. There are two major types of satire: "formal" or "direct" satire speaks directly to the reader or to a character in the work; "indirect" satire relies upon the ridiculous behavior of its characters to make its point. Formal satire is further divided into two manners: the "Horatian," which ridicules gently, and the "Juvenalian," which derides its subjects harshly and bitterly.

Science Fiction: A type of narrative about or based upon real or imagined scientific theories and technology. Science fiction is often peopled with alien creatures and set on other planets or in different dimensions.

Second Person: See *Point of View*

Setting: The time, place, and culture in which the action of a narrative takes place. The elements of setting may include geographic location, characters' physical and mental environments, prevailing cultural attitudes, or the historical time in which the action takes place.

Simile: A comparison, usually using "like" or "as", of two essentially dissimilar things, as in "coffee as cold as ice" or "He sounded like a broken record."

Slang: A type of informal verbal communication that is generally unacceptable for formal writing. Slang words and phrases are often colorful exaggerations used to emphasize the speaker's point; they may also be shortened versions of an often-used word or phrase.

Slave Narrative: Autobiographical accounts of American slave life as told by escaped slaves. These works first appeared during the abolition movement of the 1830s through the 1850s.

Socialist Realism: The Socialist Realism school of literary theory was proposed by Maxim Gorky and established as a dogma by the first Soviet Congress of Writers. It demanded adherence to a communist worldview in works of literature. Its doctrines required an objective viewpoint comprehensible to the working classes and themes of social struggle featuring strong proletarian heroes. Also known as Social Realism.

Stereotype: A stereotype was originally the name for a duplication made during the printing process; this led to its modern definition as a person or thing that is (or is assumed to be) the same as all others of its type.

Stream of Consciousness: A narrative technique for rendering the inward experience of a character. This technique is designed to give the impression of an ever-changing series of thoughts, emotions, images, and memories in the spontaneous and seemingly illogical order that they occur in life.

Structure: The form taken by a piece of literature. The structure may be made obvious for ease of understanding, as in nonfiction works, or may be obscured for artistic purposes, as in some poetry or seemingly "unstructured" prose.

Sturm und Drang: A German term meaning "storm and stress." It refers to a German literary movement of the 1770s and 1780s that reacted against the order and rationalism of the enlightenment, focusing instead on the intense experience of extraordinary individuals.

Style: A writer's distinctive manner of arranging words to suit his or her ideas and purpose in writing. The unique imprint of the author's personality upon his or her writing, style is the product of an author's way of arranging ideas and his or her use of diction, different sentence structures, rhythm, figures of speech, rhetorical principles, and other elements of composition.

Subjectivity: Writing that expresses the author's personal feelings about his subject, and which may or may not include factual information about the subject.

Subplot: A secondary story in a narrative. A subplot may serve as a motivating or complicating force for the main plot of the work, or it may provide emphasis for, or relief from, the main plot.

Surrealism: A term introduced to criticism by Guillaume Apollinaire and later adopted by Andre Breton. It refers to a French literary and artistic movement founded in the 1920s. The Surrealists sought to express unconscious thoughts and feelings in their works. The best-known technique used for achieving this aim was automatic writing—transcriptions of spontaneous outpourings from the unconscious. The Surrealists proposed to unify the contrary levels of conscious and unconscious, dream and reality, objectivity and subjectivity into a new level of "super-realism."

Suspense: A literary device in which the author maintains the audience's attention through the buildup of events, the outcome of which will soon be revealed.

Symbol: Something that suggests or stands for something else without losing its original identity. In literature, symbols combine their literal meaning with the suggestion of an abstract concept. Literary symbols are of two types: those that carry complex associations of meaning no matter what their contexts, and those that derive their suggestive meaning from their functions in specific literary works.

Symbolism: This term has two widely accepted meanings. In historical criticism, it denotes an early modernist literary movement initiated in France during the nineteenth century that reacted against the prevailing standards of realism. Writers in this movement aimed to evoke, indirectly and symbolically, an order of being beyond the material world of the five senses. Poetic expression of personal emotion figured strongly in the movement, typically by means of a private set of symbols uniquely identifiable with the individual poet. The principal aim of the Symbolists was to express in words the highly complex feelings that grew out of everyday contact with the world. In a broader sense, the term "symbolism" refers to the use of one object to represent another.

T

Tall Tale: A humorous tale told in a straightforward, credible tone but relating absolutely impossible events or feats of the characters. Such tales were commonly told of frontier adventures during the settlement of the west in the United States.

Theme: The main point of a work of literature. The term is used interchangeably with thesis.

Thesis: A thesis is both an essay and the point argued in the essay. Thesis novels and thesis plays share the quality of containing a thesis which is supported through the action of the story.

Third Person: See *Point of View*

Tone: The author's attitude toward his or her audience may be deduced from the tone of the work. A formal tone may create distance or convey politeness, while an informal tone may encourage a friendly, intimate, or intrusive feeling in the reader. The author's attitude toward his or her subject matter may also be deduced from the tone of the words he or she uses in discussing it.

Transcendentalism: An American philosophical and religious movement, based in New England from around 1835 until the Civil War. Transcendentalism was a form of American romanticism that had its roots abroad in the works of Thomas Carlyle, Samuel Coleridge, and Johann Wolfgang von Goethe. The Transcendentalists stressed the importance of intuition and subjective experience in communication with God. They rejected religious dogma and texts in favor of mysticism and scientific naturalism. They pursued truths that lie beyond the "colorless" realms perceived by reason and the senses and were active social reformers in public education, women's rights, and the abolition of slavery.

U

Urban Realism: A branch of realist writing that attempts to accurately reflect the often harsh facts of modern urban existence.

Utopia: A fictional perfect place, such as "paradise" or "heaven."

V

Verisimilitude: Literally, the appearance of truth. In literary criticism, the term refers to aspects of a work of literature that seem true to the reader.

Victorian: Refers broadly to the reign of Queen Victoria of England (1837-1901) and to anything with qualities typical of that era. For example, the qualities of smug narrowmindedness, bourgeois materialism, faith in social progress, and priggish morality are often considered Victorian. This stereotype is contradicted by such dramatic intellectual developments as the theories of Charles Darwin, Karl Marx, and Sigmund Freud (which stirred strong debates in England) and the critical attitudes of serious Victorian writers like Charles Dickens and George Eliot. In literature, the Victorian Period was the great age of the English novel, and the latter part of the era saw the rise of movements such as decadence and symbolism. Also known as Victorian Age and Victorian Period.

W

Weltanschauung: A German term referring to a person's worldview or philosophy.

Weltschmerz: A German term meaning "world pain." It describes a sense of anguish about the nature of existence, usually associated with a melancholy, pessimistic attitude.

Z

Zeitgeist: A German term meaning "spirit of the time." It refers to the moral and intellectual trends of a given era.

Cumulative
Author/Title Index

Cumulative Author/Title Index

Cumulative Nationality/Ethnicity Index

African American

Algerian

American

Asian American

Yoshimoto, Banana
Kitchen: V7

Jewish

Bellow, Saul
Herzog: V14
Seize the Day: V4
Kafka, Frank
The Trial: V7
Malamud, Bernard
The Fixer: V9
The Natural: V4
Wiesel, Eliezer
Night: V4

Mexican

Esquivel, Laura
Like Water for Chocolate: V5
Fuentes, Carlos
The Old Gringo: V8

Native American

Dorris, Michael
A Yellow Raft in Blue Water: V3
Erdrich, Louise
Love Medicine: V5
Marmon Silko, Leslie
Ceremony: V4
Momaday, N. Scott
House Made of Dawn: V10

Nigerian

Achebe, Chinua
Things Fall Apart: V3
Emecheta, Buchi
The Bride Price: V12
The Wrestling Match: V14

Norwegian

Rölvaag, O. E.
Giants in the Earth: V5

Polish

Kosinski, Jerzy
The Painted Bird: V12

Romanian

Wiesel, Eliezer
Night: V4

Russian

Bulgakov, Mikhail
The Master and Margarita: V8
Dostoyevsky, Fyodor
The Brothers Karamazon: V8
Crime and Punishment: V3
Nabokov, Vladimir
Lolita: V9

Rand, Ayn
Atlas Shrugged: V10
Solzhenitsyn, Aleksandr
*One Day in the Life of Ivan
Denisovich:* V6
Tolstoy, Leo
War and Peace: V10

South African

Gordimer, Nadine
July's People: V4
Paton, Alan
Cry, the Beloved Country: V3
Too Late the Phalarope: V12

Spanish

Saavedra, Miguel de Cervantes
Don Quixote: V8

Swiss

Hesse, Hermann
Demian: V15

West Indian

Kincaid, Jamaica
Annie John: V3

Subject/Theme Index

M